Oxford Readings in

The series provides students and scholars with a representative selection of the best and most influential articles on a particular author, work, or subject. No single school or style of approach is privileged: the aim is to offer a broad overview of scholarship, to cover a wide variety of topics, and to illustrate a diversity of critical methods. The collections are particularly valuable for their inclusion of many important essays which are normally difficult to obtain and for the first-ever translations of some of the pieces. Many articles are thoroughly revised and updated by their authors or are provided with addenda taking account of recent work. Each volume includes an authoritative and wide-ranging introduction by the editor surveying the scholarly tradition and considering alternative approaches. This pulls the individual articles together, setting all the pieces included in their historical and cultural contexts and exploring significant connections between them from the perspective of contemporary scholarship. All foreign languages (including Greek and Latin) are translated to make the texts easily accessible to those without detailed linguistic knowledge.

Oxford Readings in Classical Studies

All available in paperback

Oxford Readings in Classical Studies

Euripides

Edited by
JUDITH MOSSMAN

OXFORD
UNIVERSITY PRESS

OXFORD

UNIVERSITY PRESS

Great Clarendon Street, Oxford OX2 6DP

Oxford University Press is a department of the University of Oxford.
It furthers the University's objective of excellence in research, scholarship,
and education by publishing worldwide in

Oxford New York

Auckland Bangkok Buenos Aires Cape Town Chennai
Dar es Salaam Delhi Hong Kong Istanbul Karachi Kolkata
Kuala Lumpur Madrid Melbourne Mexico City Mumbai Nairobi
São Paulo Shanghai Taipei Tokyo Toronto

Oxford is a registered trade mark of Oxford University Press
in the UK and in certain other countries

Published in the United States
by Oxford University Press Inc., New York

© Oxford University Press 2003

British Library Cataloguing in Publication Data

Data available

Library of Congress Cataloging in Publication Data

Euripides / edited by Judith Mossman.
p. cm. — (Oxford readings in classical studies)
Includes bibliographical references.
1. Euripides—Criticism and interpretation. 2. Mythology, Greek, in literature. 3. Tragedy.
I. Mossman, Judith. II. Series.
PA3978 .E884 2002   882′.01—dc21   2002192560

ISBN 0-19-872185-4
ISBN 0-19-872184-6 (pbk.)

1 3 5 7 9 10 8 6 4 2

Typeset by Newgen Imaging Systems (P) Ltd, Chennai, India
Printed in Great Britain
on acid-free paper by
Biddles Ltd., Guildford & King's Lynn

PREFACE

> *Winnie-the-Pooh* is, as practically everyone knows, one of the
> greatest books ever written, but it is also one of the most
> controversial. Nobody can quite agree as to what it really
> means! . . . Like other casebooks, such as those on Harper's
> Ferry, Edith Wharton, and the personality adjustment difficul-
> ties of Poe and Ezra Pound, this one is frankly designed to keep
> you in confusion. Try as you may, you will find it impossible to
> decide which of the critics represented has 'the word' about
> Pooh . . .

So begins the Preface of Frederick C. Crews's *The Pooh Perplex*, a
splendid parody of various types of literary criticism and of the humble,
but useful, genre of the student casebook. Like many parodies, it
encapsulates some important truths about its models. All casebooks
aim to present the reader with a variety of different approaches to
one subject or author, and that inevitably, and rightly, results in a
multifaceted product which by definition does not give you 'the
word' about the subject—indeed, why write about any subject so
easy of resolution? This casebook is no exception. Indeed, because the
author with which these essays are concerned is particularly enigmatic, difficult, and diverse, it may be more 'confusing' than most
such collections. That has certainly complicated the choice of
material, since the fact that Euripides' surviving output is so much
greater and more diverse than Aeschylus' or Sophocles' means that it
was impossible simply to include an essay on each play. Euripides has
also provoked more controversy over the centuries than either of the
other great dramatists, and that means that any collection which
aims to include pieces representative of scholarly views of the last
thirty or forty years is bound to include essays which contradict one
another (and none of them necessarily represents the point of view of
the editor). The Publisher's policy for this series is to avoid including
excerpts from books or very recent pieces, and this has been adhered
to, though many of the authors have been kind enough to make
some revisions to their contributions. It is still, inevitably, the case

that some very distinguished work has not been able to be included, if only for reasons of space, and that is a matter for regret.

Two of the essays have been specially translated for this collection, and I wish to thank my collaborators (who did most of the work) most warmly for the professionalism with which they tackled a difficult and sometimes wearisome task.

Finally, I wish to record my personal and professional debt to three great Euripideans who sadly died while this volume was in preparation: Desmond Conacher, Kevin Lee, and Charles Segal. All were fine scholars and singularly kind and charming people, who will be greatly missed by all who knew them.

CONTENTS

Introduction: Euripides in the Twenty-First Century

CARTHAGE. Give her to me! Will somewan go and get somewan. You've killed her, ya've killed her.

HESTER. Yees all thought I was just goin' to walk away and lave her at yeer mercy. I almost did. But she's mine and I wouldn't have her waste her life dreamin' about me and yees thwartin' her with black stories against me.

CARTHAGE. You're a savage!

HESTER. Ya won't forget me now, Carthage, and when all of this is over or half remembered and ya think ya've almost forgotten me again, take a walk along the Bog of Cats and wait for a purlin' wind through your hair or a soft breath be your ear or a rustle behind ya. That'll be me and Josie ghostin' ya.

Marina Carr's *By the Bog of Cats*, a reworking of Euripides' *Medea* set in rural Ireland, was first performed in 1998.[1] Many details are different (two sons become one daughter, Josie, for example, and Hester Swane, the vengeful rejected tragic mother, dies at the end of the play), but there remain the same central issues of love, revenge, and alienation (importantly, Hester Swane is a 'tinker', rejected and despised by the local settled community), and even some elements of the structure of Euripides' play, in the series of confrontations between Hester and her tormentors. The excerpt quoted above, which comes just before Hester does her death-dance with the Ghost Fancier, a mysterious supernatural figure, has obvious similarities to Medea's taunts to Jason. There is no chariot of the Sun, no Athens, but for Hester there is escape in death. The play powerfully affected the Abbey theatre audience, especially the moment of the infanticide, and touched many contemporary nerves, racism and child abuse in particular being urgent concerns in Ireland as elsewhere. Carr's

---

[1] Carr 1998.

decision to use Euripides as an inspiration was central to the play, and very far from unique in the context of Irish contemporary drama.[2]

It is indeed possible that academic and popular interest in Euripides in the late twentieth and early twenty-first centuries is at its strongest across the world since the sixteenth. The prevalence of productions and adaptations of Euripides attests to popular interest (and the study of these performances is in itself now a vigorous and important branch of Euripidean scholarship);[3] new texts,[4] new commentaries,[5] new translations,[6] new studies[7] abound. Plays once neglected have been reassessed and are now being studied more intensively.[8] Directions in Euripidean scholarship are of course part of the trend in tragedy scholarship as a whole, but it is no longer the case that critics turn to Euripides last.[9]

[2] See e.g. Macintosh 1994, McDonald 1997, and Burian in Easterling 1997, 228–83.

[3] The keynote speech at a recent major conference on Euripides in Banff, Canada, delivered by Helene Foley, was on the performance and adaptation of Euripides in the 20th cent. The perceived importance of the reception of Greek tragedy in general is attested by the space devoted to it in the new *Cambridge Companion to Greek Tragedy* (Easterling 1997): four chapters, one-third of the book (with another chapter on the original audience). The bibliography is growing: see e.g. McDonald 1992 and 1997. Euripides and the cinema is also much studied: see e.g. McDonald 1983, Mackinnon 1986. Of course, the essays in this volume are all in themselves exercises in reception, as was the act of selecting them; one in particular (Heath) shows what constructive use can be made of the history of a text's reception.

[4] Diggle 1984, 1981, 1994; see also the Teubner series of texts of individual plays (e.g. van Looy 1992) with very useful bibliographies, and the new Loebs (Kovacs 1994, 1995, 1998, 1999). While we wait for Kannicht's definitive edition of the fragments, we at least have Austin 1968, the exceptionally useful Collard, Cropp, and Lee 1995, and now Diggle 1998 to rely on. On the methodology of textual criticism of Euripides see Goldhill 1986*b* and (partly in response) Kovacs 1987*b*.

[5] The Aris and Phillips series has performed a tremendous service; see also e.g. Wilkins 1993, Mastronarde 1994, Gregory 1999.

[6] James Morwood's versions continue to appear in the Oxford World's Classics series (Morwood 1998, 1999, 2001); Euripides is also duly represented in the Greek Tragedy in New Translations series (General editors William Arrowsmith and Herbert Golder/Peter Burian and Alan Shapiro, published by Oxford: e.g. Reckford and Lembke 1991) and the Cambridge Translations from Greek Drama series (Series Editors John Harrison and Judith Affleck, published by Cambridge: e.g. Franklin 2000, Harrison 2000).

[7] Including studies of single plays which also offer insights into Euripides' other work: e.g. Goff 1990; Croally 1994; Mossman 1995; Allan 2000.

[8] e.g. *And.*, *Hcld.*, *Hec.*, *Pho.*, *Or.*

[9] Taplin's statement, 'Now I will not disguise the fact that I find Euripides the least great of the three great tragedians' (1978, 28) is perhaps unlikely to be couched in quite that way today. One very important recent book on Greek tragedy (McClure 1999) omits discussion of Sophocles, not Euripides.

Others have very usefully discussed the history of Euripidean scholarship from the beginnings to the 1980s and beyond;[10] here all space will permit is some discussion of where Euripidean criticism appears to be heading now, and some brief contextualization of the essays in this collection.

What sort of classic essays will be contained in the next *Oxford Readings in Classical Studies: Euripides* published *c.*2020 (assuming we are all still here)? Very probably, as I have already implied, there will be more essays on reception than there are in this volume. I would hope that the next few years might also yield some good work on Euripides and his use of language.[11] Euripides' manipulation of genre and his relationship to other ancient authors continues to fascinate, and is likely to go on doing so, and perhaps work on the nature of other ancient genres such as history and biography, Hellenistic and Roman poetry, and the novel, could profitably be applied to tragedy; and the discussion of Euripidean stagecraft remains generally a lively area despite its problems.[12] Debate here has already largely turned from discussion of *Realien* to the manipulation of audience expectation, and this trend is likely to continue in the absence of new archaeological evidence. The great 'issues' which dominate the discussion of Euripides, as they dominate his works, seem set to continue to do so: women, barbarians, social status, war, politics. Just how avant-garde Euripides' plays were with regard to all of these is hardly a question which has been answered, or is likely to be. And Euripides' portrayal of the gods, myth, cult, and the supernatural remains as controversial a subject as ever. It seems probable, then, that although the balance between these topics might alter in any future collection, they would all be represented,

[10] See e.g. Michelini 1987, Heath in this volume, and Goldhill in Easterling 1997, 324–47.

[11] In some recent work on tragedy language has been studied more perhaps as a series of key words and concepts than as the basic medium of tragic emotion—as ancillary, rather than as essential. More work is now being attempted on aspects of tragic language: see now McClure 1999, Mossman 2001, Lloyd 1999, and, most imaginatively, Silk in Silk 1996, 458–96. On Sophocles' language see now Budelmann 2000.

[12] Despite valuable insights in, for example, Hourmouziades 1965 and Halleran 1985, there is still no work on Euripidean stagecraft as comprehensive or as thoughtful as Taplin 1977 on Aeschylus. For a rigorous critique of performance criticism and very useful bibliography, see Goldhill 1993; see also Wiles 1997. Work on the original circumstances of performance and on ancient reperformance of Greek tragedy, including Euripides, consistently illuminates more aspects of Athenian society than theatre alone: see e.g. Goldhill 1987 and Wilson 2000.

though perhaps by studies which made use of new approaches: different types of historicism, perhaps, or even applying narratological concepts to drama (see n. 56 below).

   The old debates continue to resurface, and there is every reason to suppose that, in changing guises, they will go on doing so in the future, partly, perhaps, because they are the descendants of the debates Euripides wanted his audience to have. Questions of the magnitude of those posed by these texts were not meant to be solved, but must be confronted again and again by those who watch and read these uncomfortable plays.[13] That said, it can still be instructive to look back at the efforts of earlier critics to tackle the dilemmas in Euripides. The issue of what was new or distinctive about Euripides is one which concerns many of the essays in this volume, which is interesting in itself: it is not a question nearly so often asked about Aeschylus or Sophocles, even though most, perhaps all, of Sophocles' extant plays are contemporary with Euripides'. Would it be asked if we did not know that Euripides was the youngest of the three tragedians? Surely the answer is yes. It might be differently phrased, but the texts themselves do seem to embody a desire for difference, an urge to be distinctive.[14]

   The first essay, Karl Reinhardt's famous 'The Intellectual Crisis in Euripides', well illustrates the desire to seek difference in Euripides, and is translated here for the first time.[15] It remains very much in lecture format—there is only one footnote, and it contains many passages which were clearly written for oral performance. Reinhardt was a famously expressive lecturer, and even in a written version his histrionic flair can be discerned.[16] The essay displays many typical insights and concerns: Reinhardt's interest in ancient philosophy surfaces at the start of the essay;[17] his intellectual debt to Nietzsche,

[13] In saying this, I find I echo Reinhardt, p. 46, the earliest contributor to this volume, yet I still believe it to be true.

[14] It is clear, though, that some ancient views of the tragedians, particularly the caricatures of them in Aristophanes' *Frogs*, die hard, and their plays are criticized differently accordingly. What would criticism of Sophocles' *Philoctetes* have been like if it had come down to us under Euripides' name, for example? See also n. 37 below.

[15] See translators' note. For other Reinhardt remarks on E., see e.g. Reinhardt 1979, 5–6.

[16] See Lloyd-Jones's Introduction to Reinhardt 1979 (Lloyd-Jones 1979*b*), xvii.

[17] Reinhardt wrote three books on Posidonius and one on Parmenides, although, as Lloyd-Jones points out (1979*b*, xvi), his work on Posidonius was flawed. Professor Dillon has pointed out to me that much of what he says about ancient theories of mind at the start of this essay is not now generally accepted.

and his particular interest in religion and the interaction of men and gods are highly important to his theme;[18] his great knowledge of, and love for, German literature is in evidence;[19] his method of concentrating on particular scenes, characteristic of his book on Sophocles, is used to great effect here. Reinhardt is clearly a child of his time: the traumatic events of the first half of the twentieth century explicitly inform his understanding of the fifth century BC; and though it is greatly to Reinhardt's credit that he draws distinctions and makes contrasts between modern phenomena and ancient thinking (note especially his critique of Wilamowitz's view of Phaedra),[20] we may still feel that his view of Euripides is overly coloured by modern European views of intellectuals and intellectualism.[21] Not all his comparisons between the three great dramatists seem wholly valid; and yet some are striking, and they all stimulate the reader to consider what, if anything, can really be said to be different in Euripides. The breadth of reading and the sensitivity of criticism in this essay continue to impress. Apart from the central argument that Euripides differs radically from his predecessors, which has been very influential, some of Reinhardt's remarks, even those made very much in passing, have proved very fruitful: for example, his comments on Euripidean music are now beginning to be followed up;[22] and his focus on the escapism of the Euripidean chorus has been shared and explored further.[23] His use of what one might call counterfactual criticism in his discussion of the end of the *Orestes* is a good example of how effective this approach can be when used with restraint.

It is interesting to compare Winnington-Ingram's essay with Reinhardt's, whose description of the intellectual atmosphere of the later fifth century Winnington-Ingram seems broadly to accept.[24] Both wish to see Euripides as epitomizing an intellectual movement; and both take examples from his work and argue that they illustrate an attitude to the gods and to dramatic conventions and techniques

---

[18] Lloyd-Jones 1979*b*, xv–xvi, xx, xxiv.   [19] Lloyd-Jones 1979*b*, xv.

[20] Lloyd-Jones 1979*b*, xviii–xix, and see pp. 25–6 below.

[21] For perceptive remarks on ancient and modern intellectuals and intellectualism, see Zanker 1995.

[22] Two papers in Banff, by Eric Csapo and Peter Wilson, touched on aspects of Euripidean music: this is another area which deserves more exploration.

[23] Padel 1974.

[24] Winnington-Ingram 1969*a*, 127 (pp. 47–8 below), though his 'world of clever ideas . . . and of clever men for whom nothing remained unquestioned' sounds much less tortured than Reinhardt's version.

which is self-consciously 'modern' and quite different from Aeschylus
or Sophocles. Both, but particularly Winnington-Ingram, find rapid
and deliberately bewildering changes of tone in Euripides' works;
Winnington-Ingram in some cases sees no need to find much more
explanation for such changes than 'sheer cleverness' (p. 129, p. 48
below), though in others, for example his discussion of the Euripidean
Electra, he has a more subtle approach. In some of these discussions,
as with Reinhardt's essay, one may feel that certain expressions and
ideas belong more to the author's time and milieu than to the fifth
century.[25] Sometimes the audience Winnington-Ingram posits seems
more like that of the Royal Court than that of the theatre of
Dionysus,[26] but it is striking that, unlike many scholars, he does
not view the audience as a monolith, and that he is interested
in audience response as well as authorial intention, which is an
important feature of much more recent work.[27] Once again, even
though some may feel that the differences between Euripides and the
other dramatists may be exaggerated or expressed too much in terms
of ludic play at the expense of other possible explanations, many of
his observations are still fresh and useful, many of the passages he
cites are worthy of note, and as part of his discussion of Euripides'
search for novelty in dramatic technique he includes an intelligent
and worthwhile early treatment of the important and difficult subject
of metatragedy. Written in his customary lively and elegant style,
this essay remains full of challenging insights and important
questions.

The difficulty of assessing some of Euripides' changes of tone,
particularly those associated with his scenes of formal debate, is dealt
with at greater length and with considerable success by Christopher
Collard,[28] who rightly warns against isolating them from their
dramatic setting. Apart from its valuable discussions of individual

[25] For a perceptive and sympathetic account of aspects of Winnington-Ingram's
background and scholarship see Easterling's excellent foreword to the second edition
of Winnington-Ingram 1948, v–xii.

[26] e.g. 129 'a young intellectual in the audience'; 130 'Then an Aristophanes may
have turned to his neighbour and whispered that a *deus* was due *ex machina*' (pp. 50
and 52 below).

[27] Focus on the audience is implicit in performance criticism (see above). For a
nuanced and culturally aware view of ancient audience responses, see Lada 1993
and 1996.

[28] Collard 1975*a*, here reprinted with his addendum from McAuslan and
Walcot 1993.

passages, this essay represents one of the best examinations of the importance of form and its relationship to content, and so redefines the two earlier essays' references to Euripides 'flouting convention' by assessing more carefully what, if anything, might be conventional in these important parts of the plays.[29] The essay well displays Collard's remarkable gift for saying a lot in a short space.[30]

Desmond Conacher, in a characteristically judicious and fair-minded essay, takes a more general view of rhetoric in Euripides and focuses on its relationship to the concept of characterization in Greek tragedy as a whole and particularly in Euripides, who, as he rightly says, is particularly suitable as the subject of such a study, since he is 'admittedly the most "rhetorical" of the Greek tragic poets and yet also the one providing the most clearly-marked tragic themes and the subtlest psychological effects'.[31] Characterization in the tragedians is an important and complex subject which continues to attract a good deal of attention, and this essay represents an important contribution to that debate.[32] Whatever the reader's own view of the moral status of the characters in *Alcestis*, it is hard to find much to disagree with in Conacher's critique of Dale on character in tragedy; and his treatment of Phaedra's speech in *Hippolytus* is a particularly clear and convincing argument for the view (important for the interpretation of this vexed and difficult passage) that the speech is not a representation of Euripides' words but of Phaedra's.[33] The essay has in common with Collard's its close examination of rhetorical conventions and how they are manipulated to create effects vital to the poet's dramatic purpose. The rather sterile criterion of relevance is not so often used in recent criticism as it once was: richness of discourse and theme and polysemy of language have more pride of place; essays such as Conacher's, which seek to account for what is in the text rather than reject it because it does not seem to fit,

---

[29] The study of the *agōn* has since been carried further by Lloyd 1992, though I am not sure I agree with Collard's addendum that Lloyd's narrower interpretation of what constitutes an *agōn* is preferable. Individual *agōnes* have also been extensively studied: on *Tro.*, see Lloyd 1984, Croally 1994, and now Meridor 2000, and on *Hec.* see Mossman 1995, 94–141.

[30] This is particularly evident in Collard 1981, which contains a series of excellent annotated bibliographies as well as many important insights.

[31] Conacher 1981, 4 and p. 82 below.

[32] For more recent treatments see e.g. the important Pelling 1990, Mossman 1995, 94–141, and now Gill 1996.

[33] On this passage see also Goff 1990, 96–7, Cairns 1992, Craik 1993, with much earlier bibliography, Furley 1996, McClure 1999, 127–35.

have contributed greatly to this change and therefore to the reputation of Euripides.[34]

The next essay relates closely to the subjects of Reinhardt and
Winnington-Ingram in particular, and in many respects constitutes
a corrective to their views of Euripides (taken further—and often
taken for granted—by many subsequent critics). Lefkowitz examines
Euripides' attitude to religion and its reporting by comic poets,
biographers, and modern scholars. Her emphasis is very much on
the unwisdom of taking out of context remarks made by desperate
Euripidean characters and attributing the views expressed to the poet
(Winnington-Ingram's apparent acceptance, partial and qualified
though it may be, of the portrayal of Euripides in Aristophanes is
particularly to be contrasted here). Lefkowitz, like Reinhardt, discusses
Hecuba's prayer to Zeus in *Trojan Women* (pp. 106–8); but unlike
Reinhardt, she seeks to make sense of it in its literary context rather
than simply commenting on its bizarre effect.[35] In general Lefkowitz
shares with Conacher the desire to see the plays as organic wholes
and not to interpret individual passages out of context. Lefkowitz's
essay is also important for its treatment of Euripides alongside
Homer: a subject of recurring interest.[36] She also makes the important
point, which could also be made in relation to other areas besides
religion, such as for example dramatic technique, that Euripides is
often seen as avant-garde because critics overestimate the conservatism and homogeneity of Sophocles.[37]

Another concern of Conacher's, namely characterization, is
broadly the subject of Stahl's wide-ranging paper. This constitutes
an important and convincing defence of the idea that Euripidean
characterization is not wholly ancillary to the plot; that sometimes it is
precisely the characterization which carries the weight of Euripides'

[34] This should have repercussions for textual criticism as well: yet some passages
are still being excised for 'irrelevance' when there may in fact be good reason for their
presence: see Goldhill 1986*b*, and, on Kovacs 1998 on *Electra* 907 ff., see Mossman
2001. See also Heath's essay on the concept of 'varietas', Ch. 11, pp. 218 ff.

[35] It is interesting that she and Winnington-Ingram (e.g. 1948, 57) are somewhat
closer in their approach to Teiresias' speech in *Bacchae*: Winnington-Ingram is much
more willing to rule out a novelty-seeking Euripides in some plays than in others, and
Bacchae is one (like *Hippolytus*) where he is most willing to seek for serious meaning.

[36] See e.g. Stinton 1965, Garner 1990, Croally 1994, 192–207, and Mossman 1995,
19–29.

[37] That is to say, critics who are primarily discussing Euripides are sometimes in
danger of constructing an artificial 'Sophocles' against which Euripides is set: when
Sophocles is the primary focus of interest this is less the case.

thought. Stahl concentrates on a number of passages where, without practical impact on the plot, characters seem to build emotional bridges, however temporary, between one another, with a powerful effect on the audience.[38] This is in stark contrast, he says, with the harsh world of the plays outside these scenes, which he relates to the picture of turmoil drawn by Reinhardt:[39] the impossibility of these emotional links is clear, and yet for all their impossibility the characters' desires and aspirations illuminate the plays. This essay is particularly satisfying for its discernment of a high level of serious-ness in Euripidean drama from its beginnings right through to the late plays (Stahl's final example is from *Iphigeneia in Aulis*). Among an abundance of ironic readings of Euripides which depict him as always in search of novelty at all costs (of the essays in this collection, Winnington-Ingram perhaps goes furthest down that road, but he is far more moderate and sensitive than some), it is refreshing to find appreciation of the portrayals of emotion for which Euripides was famous in antiquity, and impressive to find so clearly stated the excellence of the dramatic technique which produces them.[40]

The final general essay on Euripides also brings out his emotional seriousness, and makes a particularly fitting conclusion to the first phase of the collection. Pietro Pucci, in a rich and suggestive piece, discusses the important subject of the cathartic and memorializing function of Euripides' poetry and the complex nature of its representation. Interestingly, in the context of the clash between Reinhardt and Winnington-Ingram and Lefkowitz on Euripides' cultural predilections, Pucci finds resonances in Euripides' use of the language of healing to describe the effects of poetry, not only with Gorgias, but also with Homer and Hesiod; his insistence on the power of *logos* and on the gulf between the signifier and the signified have both had many interesting subsequent exponents, as has his concentration on scenes of sacrifice (albeit broadly interpreted).[41]

[38] Mastronarde 1979 examines similar moments from a more linguistic perspective.

[39] See p. 125. See the translator's note to Reinhardt for the ambiguity in that essay between 'intellectual crisis' and 'crisis of meaning'.

[40] Dramatic technique has also recently been a major concern of many of the single-play studies mentioned in n. 7, and of e.g. Goward 1999.

[41] The death of Hippolytus, for example, is not exactly presented as a sacrifice in a strict sense. The influence of Derrida, as well as of Girard, is obviously strong in this essay, but the essay blends old and new types of criticism in its inclusion of a careful discussion of Aristotle. Discussion of the power of *logos* has become an important

Pucci's discussions of individual passages are also satisfying, especially his reading of the messenger speech of *Hecuba*. As well as showing sensitivity in its application of modern theory to ancient texts, this is a fascinating rationale of Aristotle's description of Euripides as *tragikōtatos* ('most tragic').

The remaining ten essays are devoted to individual plays, though many of the same concerns which inform the general essays resurface in them.[42] Richard Buxton's essay on *Alcestis* is a case in point, though he goes beyond the questions of characterization which dominate most discussions of this play.[43] His discussion of the use and symbolism of the house door is one of the most interesting available discussions of a point of Euripidean stagecraft; in all its five sections his article sites the play firmly in the context of Greek religious beliefs and social customs and thus contributes greatly to our understanding of it. He also never loses sight of the important issue of genre, without assuming that the play's status as a non-satyric fourth play relegates it to the second rank as a work of art. He, too, rejects overly ironical readings, and provides convincing support for this rejection by setting the play firmly in its cultural context.

Buxton, in treating five aspects of the play, makes clear an interpretation of the whole; Easterling centres her essay on *Medea* around the infanticide, that defining dramatic moment from which we began, but frames her discussion of the child murders themselves with an account of the play as a whole which embraces many important issues: characterization, structure and stagecraft, and rhetoric. Particularly illuminating are the contrasts she makes with Seneca's *Medea*, as well as her cautious but suggestive comparisons with modern cases of infanticide.

strand in tragic criticism, and with good reason: see e.g. Goldhill 1986a and now Goldhill and Osborne 1999; on the intersection of fictional representation and sacrifice see Burkert 1983, esp. 3–7 and 168–79. Sacrifice in Euripides is also discussed by e.g. Foley 1985. Pucci's references to Freud and his vision of Euripides' own psychological processes in creating his plays have on the whole been less overtly influential: but see Goldhill in Easterling 1997, 340–3.

[42] It has not been possible to include an essay on each play, which has inevitably led to some hard choices: excellent work is available on every play, though not always in a format suitable for this collection. Perhaps particularly regrettable is the absence of an essay on *Cyclops*: the reader is referred to Seaford's excellent commentary (1984).

[43] *Alcestis* is also discussed at some length by Pucci and by Stahl.

Winnington-Ingram's essay on *Hippolytus* originally appeared in the *Entretiens Hardt*. As is customary in those publications, the discussion which followed his original paper is preserved and reprinted after the essay (though for reasons of space we were unable to reproduce it here). The paper was warmly received: 'a profound and illuminating analysis', the chair, Günther Zuntz, called it, and it still has important and provocative arguments to present. The issue of characterization in *Hippolytus* becomes more than simply a question of dramatic technique; it embraces questions of free will and determinism of the highest importance. Here we have 'intra-dramatic' characterization (to adapt Stahl's terminology): character is seen actually as a potential cause of events. Here Winnington-Ingram's penchant for psychological criticism, carefully grounded in the text, is to the fore, and here it is at its most impressive, convincing, and self-aware.[44] Once again, as in Conacher's essay, Phaedra's speech is a key passage (and it was the focus of much of the discussion after Winnington-Ingram's paper was read for the first time, too);[45] but Winnington-Ingram also discusses with great perception the role of the gods and the theme of escape in the play.[46]

The reception of Euripides, as we noted above, is a topic of particular interest at present; Malcolm Heath's essay remains one of the most valuable examples of a reading which, through a meticulous examination of the *Rezeptionsgeschichte* of a play, casts new light on the text by showing how modern critical responses are shaped by the opinions of previous generations of critics. The clarity with which Heath discerns critical trends and the qualities of his chosen

---

[44] See also e.g. Winnington-Ingram 1983, 101–31, and 1948, 71–87 on Pentheus with Easterling's preface, x–xii. This is much more controlled and productive psychologizing than the quotation from Wilamowitz on Phaedra to which Reinhardt objects: see below, pp. 25–6.

[45] More detail on the nature of the bad *aidōs* was sought; Winnington-Ingram expressed the view that it was not possible to find specific incidences of bad *aidōs* in the play, but that Phaedra was using the expression to indicate that she had doubts about the nature of the concept in general: '*aidōs* is playing a dubious part in the action . . . The really important aspect of *aidōs* in the earlier part of the play is the effort that Phaedra makes, out of shame, to conceal her passion for Hippolytus. I suggest that Euripides saw that this concealment—this "bottling up"—although the outcome of her nobility, was at the same time something psychologically harmful . . . Another way of looking at it is to say that *aidōs* betrays her all along the line; it betrays her when it causes her to be silent, and equally betrays her when it causes her to speak' (194, see pp. 206 ff. below). See also n. 33 above. The classic treatment of speech and silence in *Hippolytus* is Knox 1952; see also Goff 1990, 1–26.

[46] See n. 23 above.

text—*Hecuba*—which appealed to or repelled succeeding generations is admirable, and his conclusion that 'an understanding of the history of a text's interpretation can help us to see more clearly and more critically the assumptions which underlie our own interpretations' (p. 260) can be applied to Euripides' oeuvre as a whole.[47] It is indeed perhaps particularly desirable that it should be applied to this most controversial and polarizing of authors.

Zeitlin's essay on *Electra* (like *Hecuba*, a difficult and controversial play) also throws new light on a complex text, this time, though, by immersing itself in ancient culture as opposed to later critics' opinions.[48] It uses the festival of Hera at Argos as a key to reinterpreting the characterization of Electra, and also as a starting point for making sense of Euripidean 'realism', often abused, but an essential part of his dramatic technique. The essay also makes sense of the religious content of the choral odes and points to their relevance to the action, as well as exploring the poet's use of corrupt religious motifs, reminiscent of, but significantly different from, Aeschylus' handling of the myth.[49]

A similar awareness of the importance of siting Euripides' plays in the culture which produced them is at the heart of Jacqueline de Romilly's essay on the rejection of suicide in *Heracles*. She elaborates the comparison, already found in Reinhardt's essay, between Sophocles' *Ajax* and Euripides' *Heracles*, and in doing so successfully suggests a real contrast between the two authors through their respective portrayals of the heroes. She also insists upon close reading of the text under scrutiny as a necessary complement to the more

[47] This is particularly true because he focuses on two issues—unity and the acceptability of violence—which critics have often been divided over with regard to other plays as well (for example, unity in respect of *Heracles* and *Andromache*, and the acceptability of the type of violence in *Electra*).

[48] Some of the most important developments in tragic criticism have taken shape through the application of extra-textual information about Greek religion, art, and culture to tragic texts. Taking only the example of *Medea*, it is striking what significant refinements in our understanding of this play have been made by essays such as Schein 1990 (an examination of the theme of *philia*: see also on Sophocles Whitlock Blundell 1989) and Sourvinou-Inwood 1997.

[49] Zeitlin, though, is not trying to draw the same kind of conclusions from her comparisons with Aeschylus and Sophocles as those critics in this volume who wish to generalize about what is 'Euripidean'. Rather she is exploring the intertextuality between the different versions of Orestes' homecoming created by the three tragic poets.

general study of ancient culture. The resulting essay is a contribution both to the study of Euripides and to the history of ideas.

Close reading is also a feature of Mastronarde's essay on *Ion*. Indeed, his reinterpretation of the parodos of *Ion* illustrates very clearly some important shifts in Euripidean criticism. Of it he writes (p. 300): 'This description [of the temple at Delphi and its sculptures] may be considered evidence of Euripides' interest in the fine arts (significant for those who believe he was a painter as well as a poet); it may be excused as an archaeological curiosity or condemned as a pretty irrelevancy.' He then goes on to provide a brilliant interpretation of the parodos, and of the subsequent description of the tent in the messenger speech. Mastronarde clearly shows that these passages make a vital and integral contribution to Euripides' design, emphasizing the bringing of order out of chaos and mirroring the internal struggles of the major characters. So from two passages which had previously been the focus of an obsession with relating Euripides' works to ancient conjectures about his life, and of incomprehension of his descriptive 'realism', Mastronarde wrests a holistic and serious interpretation of the play without excessive resort to the ironizing explanations which Euripides' 'happy ending' plays persistently attract. This reading has its implications also for Euripides' treatment of the gods in the play, also handled in a measured manner by Mastronarde.

'The *Orestes* is the most Euripidean of all Euripidean plays', says Zeitlin at the start of her second essay in this volume. This perception is one shared with Reinhardt, who also discusses *Orestes* at length, and by Winnington-Ingram and Collard. Zeitlin, however, goes further than they in suggesting a 'post-modern' aspect to *Orestes* and in discerning 'a combination of literary allusions which creates . . . a *palimpsestic* text, where one layer can be deciphered under another' (p. 314) throughout the play. This treatment of the concept of allusion goes further than her earlier piece on *Electra* in reading a Euripidean text, not just in the light of an earlier Aeschylean one, but as part of a whole complex web of texts, including other Euripidean plays. She describes the result as 'a Dionysiac "chaos of forms" ' (p. 318), which points towards Segal's concept of Dionysiac poetics,[50] and relates also to Pucci's poetics of sorrow[51] in that the form of the text and its content are held to reflect each other, as it were in an endless series of

---

[50] See Segal 1982, 339–47.   [51] See Pucci 1980, esp. 21–58.

mirrors. Zeitlin also makes use of modern psychoanalytic theory to characterize Orestes and the society in which Euripides portrays him. In this essay, the characters are described as eternally playing out a variety of different roles, as reading from unexpected scripts provided by Euripides' mythological innovations: metatheatre is both part of the essay's subject and part of its mode of expression.

Foley's essay on *Bacchae* shares Zeitlin's interest in role-play. This ground-breaking study of Dionysiac metatheatre has, together with Segal 1982,[52] influenced many interpretations of many plays.[53] Foley's concentration on metatheatre works particularly effectively for *Bacchae*, however, and her argument that Dionysus uses the weapons of the theatre to destroy Pentheus is convincing and well substantiated. Her discussion of Euripides' relationship to comedy, and use of comic techniques in this theatrical onslaught against Pentheus, is particularly valuable: her essay shows how the two genres mingle and define each other. Her comparison of the structure of the latter part of the play to the festival of Dionysus at which it was performed adds an extra dimension to the metatheatrical language employed;[54] and her discussion of the impact of the smiling mask and other visual elements during the performance of the play adds a further dimension to this wide-ranging and multi-layered interpretation.

Finally, Irene de Jong applies the principles of narratology to three Euripidean messenger speeches, focusing on three off-stage characters who die without appearing. This essay is important for a number of reasons: it has important and suggestive things to say about each of the plays it discusses;[55] it makes interesting use of the theories of drama of Pfister and Elam, rather underused by critics of

---

[52] See Segal 1982, 215–71, esp. n. 1 for the relationship between Foley's approach and Segal's. Segal traces the progress of this strand of scholarship in the useful Afterword added to Segal 1982 in the 1997 edition, 369–78. The whole Afterword is an extremely useful overview of scholarship on Dionysus, the *Bacchae* and related matters. See also Easterling's Foreword to the second edition of Winnington-Ingram 1948.

[53] Studies which discern Dionysiac patterns in other tragedies include e.g. Schlesier 1988, 1993, Seaford 1993. On metatragedy see Foley 1985, Zeitlin 1990, Bierl 1991, and Segal's Afterword for more bibliography.

[54] Goldhill's (1987) analysis of Sophocles' *Ajax* and *Philoctetes* in the light of his discussion of the dramatic festival similarly shows the immense potential of this type of approach.

[55] Esp. *And.* and *El.*: it might be said to have inspired e.g. Phillippo 1995 and Mossman 1996, and makes an important contribution to the debate on the characterization of Orestes in *El.*

Greek tragedy;[56] and it forces the reader to examine messenger speeches, those high points of Euripidean poetic visualization, more closely than is often done. The use of narratology is a highly interesting experimental approach which has had an impact on the reading of tragedy in general, as it has on other classical texts, and may well have more in the future.

As I said in the Preface, although many approaches are represented here, many others are not, and could not be, if only for reasons of space. It is hoped that this small selection will further the understanding of Euripides, and be representative of some possible critical lines of attack, as well as helping to illustrate the path criticism has taken over the last few decades. It is not intended to imply that these essays, by virtue of their 'classic' status, are somehow no longer current. On the contrary, in literary criticism, 'sometimes fairly, sometimes not, the new defines itself against the established. To that extent it might be said to depend on what it seeks to displace.'[57] It is the editor's hope that all these essays represent ideas and arguments about Euripides which are sufficiently important to continue to inspire debate for the foreseeable future. Their common subject matter, the most tragic of poets,[58] should ensure that they do.

---

[56] Though see now Goward 1999, which takes further some of the approaches used in de Jong's subsequent book (1991). She comes to the interesting conclusion that (121): 'although Euripides certainly produces remarkably new kinds of tragedy . . . these movements inevitably result from a reworking—however radical—of tragedy's traditional narrative resources'. More might still be done here, it seems to me, especially on the later plays. Could the theory of 'focus' developed by Heath 1987 be elaborated further with profit? Dramaturgy clearly has many of the complexities of narrative, but they have yet to be as meticulously described.

[57] Dollimore in Wells 1990, 405.   [58] Aristotle, *Poetics* 1453[a]29.

I

The Intellectual Crisis in Euripides

KARL REINHARDT

Whether Mind is determined, or pre-determined, or given, or projected by the subject, or obtained from Being, or rooted in nature as an essential feature of life, or resolved in God, or disclosed as a favour, whether it is structured or amorphous, mystic or mythical, eternal or lost for ever—it is not to be expected that any example of the sort of crisis into which Mind has strayed in the modern world is to be found in the world of antiquity.

Admittedly in Greek there is the word *nous* ('mind') and, deriving from that, the word *noetic*; there are, admittedly, very diverse doctrines of *nous*, for example, around the middle of the fifth century, the cosmological teaching of Anaxagoras, or, in the late Hellenistic Stoa, the theory of macrocosmic universal intelligence; but nowhere is reason or the mind attacked by radical doubt, stricken by loss, or restored after it. In Heraclitus, reason, or the mind, is the 'common denominator': 'In order to speak with reason one must rely on what is common to all' (the divine element in man recognized by all).

As has been remarked before by Hazel and David Harvey, the translators of Reinhardt 1979, Reinhardt's German style is by no means easy (xi): he is fond of long and complex series of antitheses and of idiosyncratic vocabulary. The usual problems of his style are exaggerated further by the remaining traces of orality in this particular essay. We have chosen to try to preserve the flavour of the original rather than attempt a smoother but less faithful rendering. There is an ambiguity, which Reinhardt exploits extensively here, in the German word 'Sinn', which can mean, among other things, either 'intellect, mind' and so on, or 'meaning'. This is particularly at issue in the first part of the essay. We were unable to reproduce it exactly, and so have varied our approach and made explicit whichever meaning seemed to be uppermost. In the opening section, for example, we have chosen to use 'Mind', which seemed to fit best with Reinhardt's discussion of *nous*. Following the example of Harvey and Harvey, we have replaced Reinhardt's translations (and occasionally even some of his paraphrases) with more literal English versions, and the occasional minor slip has been corrected. We would like to thank John Dillon, Sir Hugh Lloyd-Jones, Gillian Martin, and Christopher Pelling for helpful advice and comment.

Anaxagoras proclaimed the principle of the discerning, differentiat-
ing, organizing, understanding Mind in the world, of *krisis* as
opposed to that which melts away into the infinitely mixed and
chaotic particulate matter. He revealed Mind as something unadul-
terable—superior to all else. In Plato the *nous* is the supersensory
knowledge directed towards the Forms: by separating, it unites, not
to say, redeems. Finally, in the later works, in the creation myth of
Timaios, the world is created by the demiurge as a graded copy of the
eternal and the perfect, in the contemplation of the eternal and real,
in the realm of the evolving and the ephemeral, creatively wrested
from the obstacle of blind compulsion (*anankē*): 'For the world has a
mixed origin through the combination of *anankē* and *nous*' (*Timaeus*
48a1–2). The world is conceived as the most perfect of what is
possible on earth. Of all the doctrines concerning *nous*, that of the late
Plato is the most dualistic. A rejection of meaninglessness, which
runs through Plato's entire life, which frequently appeared in his
confessions of spiritual torment and helplessness from which the
Form provided escape, becomes finally the most tremendous *apologia*
of the imperfect world. 'If this world is beautiful and the demiurge is
good, then he was clearly looking to the eternal; but if it is what
might only be termed sacrilege, then at what it has become (*Timaeus*
29a2–4).' Who would care to measure the abyss of this 'if'? Between
the two worlds—that of Anaxagoras and that of Plato—lies a
breakdown of far-reaching effect—of that more in a moment. In
Aristotle, who did not experience this breakdown, dualism disappears, all Nature becomes rational, its structuring purposeful,
directed towards an end—reason absolutely everywhere! In Neopla-
tonism reason is elevated to unimaginable heights, in the Hermetic
or Gnostic philosophy it sinks to unspeakable depths—*nous* itself
remains exalted beyond all question. Admittedly in the Athens of the
Hellenistic period the school of the Sceptics emerges, but even they
refute only the sects of the dogmatists; they themselves are
restrained, they draw, as we like to say, no 'existential' conclusions.
In antiquity there is not even a remotely comparable analogy to the
decline of meaning, the loss of the centre, etc., in which so many of
our artists and analysts of art and culture wallow—apart, perhaps,
for one brief exception, which is like an intermezzo. The exception is
confined to Athens and to the period between 450 and 400 and is
known as the epoch of the Sophists.

Of modern European nihilism or pessimism suffice it to say—for the youngsters among us—that it falls into two periods. In the first, the artists, beginning with Leopardi and continuing through to Flaubert and the *fin de siècle*, were in the van; pessimist and artist were practically one and the same; even Schopenhauer's pessimism was to some extent artistic pessimism. The first nihilism was that which Nietzsche, as a symptom of decadence, imagined that he personally had both taken to extremes and overcome. At the beginning of the twentieth century he was replaced by a series of new philosophic ambassadors of very different status and with very different messages to proclaim—it is difficult to bring oneself to list them next to one another—think, for example, of Bergson's 'élan vital', of Stefan George, of the apostles of German expressionism (for this was ecstatic and religious: 'Mankind is good'), of Rilke, of the 'precursors of the new France', as Ernst Robert Curtius summarized them— enough, the first nihilism bowed out or was discarded only to break out again in the 1920s in an even more radical form than ever before. The unwilling prophet—he never considered himself as such—of this new, labyrinthine nihilism, irreligious yet invested with religious frenzy, was Franz Kafka.

Whilst we at home swore literary oaths of eternal friendship and thrashed ourselves politically, then glimpsed salvation in the madness of heroes and racism, then immersed ourselves in the needs of those returning home, his posthumous fame waited to conquer America's youth and then returned freshly imported over to ours. I remember vividly the student production of *The Trial* in Gide's dramatization in Chicago in the summer of 1949. An American student had just brought the text over from Paris and translated it during the crossing. The effect on young minds exceeded all expectations. The image of the prisoner's cell, the situation of being imprisoned, or of the trap, is perceived with real fervour by the younger generation as fitting them like a glove; Kafka, indeed, had already written in a letter from 1921: 'Everything is an illusion—family, the office, friends, the street—everything an illusion, more immediate or more distant— woman; the most immediate truth, however, is that you are banging your head against the wall of a windowless cell that has no door.' With these words the entire 'cell situation' up to Sartre's *Huis Clos* is anticipated.

Existence as a prison is also present in antiquity. In Plato's Allegory of the Cave the earthly world resembles an underground dungeon, humanity is in chains—but so that the soul can raise itself up to the enlightened realm of the Forms. In the Gnostic philosophy of late antiquity the world is depicted as a cave—but looking up to the Redeemer. Hands are stretched out to the modern nihilisms and imprisonments, too, ready to redeem them. Nietzsche fled from his 'European disease', as he called it, to what he called his 'health', which he glorified as 'life' and which he finally proclaimed to be the most awe-inspiring of all sacraments in the eternal resurrection. The ancient Athenians would certainly have shaken their heads gravely over his tempter god Dionysus to whom he sang his lonely dithyrambs when on the threshold of his mental derangement. The later works of Gottfried Benn, however differently his language sounds, show consciousness of his connection with Nietzsche in his nihilistic aestheticism. In Nietzsche, to mention only one of the many examples, in the Zarathustra parable 'The Soothsayer', we hear biblical tones: 'A decree went out, a belief went with it: All is empty. All is the same. All was.'

In Benn we have the approximately corresponding:

> The world wiped out by thought. And space and ages
> And everything that wove and weighed mankind
> Merely the function of infinities—
> The myth lied.

'Wove' the fabrications, the ideologies. 'Weighed' the values. 'Function': that is where modern physics comes in. Then the summary: the 'Myth'—the thinking of mankind—'lied'.

> Whence, whither—not night, not morning,
> No Evoe, no requiem,
> You would like to borrow a catchword—
> But from whom?

'Whence, whither—', history, the utopias. 'Not night, not morning': no hope. 'No Evoe, no requiem'—the heathen or Nietzschian affirmation of life, the Christian affirmation of death. The diametrically opposed expression exhausts all possibilities. A 'catchword': nothing of one's own, not even something borrowed, just something one could speak about, play one's part! . . . The conclusion: 'You would like . . . But . . .'. What does this deliberately revoking 'but' remind one of? I would suggest Goethe's *Mignonlied*:

> I would like to show you all my soul
> But fate will not have it.

And Mignon cannot speak either: 'But an oath seals my lips.' But how changed, not to say destitute, compared with the Mignon tragedy, is the hopelessness in Benn. What a monstrous fall!

The nihilism of Benn and Nietzsche is historically orientated, that of Kafka is immediate, rising darkly from sources of which I am unable to speak.

In more recent American literature—in so far as I am informed— one usually wrestles one's way through the feverish jungle of senselessness to a broken and entombed humanity, a cowed, timid, makeshift, consumptive humanism. Damaged existence gets by— moving helplessly under a rough exterior.

Let these reminders about the modern intellectual crisis (for the younger members of the audience) be sufficient.

With the Greeks the question of the intellect is bound up with the question of the gods. If the gods waver, the intellect wavers until it finds an anchor in some new godliness. The mortal is not sufficient. If reason totters, society must have become ripe for it. That is the case in the Athens of the sophistic Enlightenment. For the first time there are representatives of the mind, intellectuals as we might call them, both professional itinerants—the Sophists—and amateurs among the open-minded aristocracy and the elite of the democracy. Each powerfully attracts the other, there is no stinting of the highest praise, the master Protagoras teaches: 'Man is the measure of all things.' Central to all practical and theoretical questions is the problem of education. The basis of education is morality. But morality is also the most constraining thing for the emancipated mind. The powers of conservatism find once again their greatest expression as they come to blows with the radical rethinking in all areas.

Euripidean theatre is the barometer of the crisis. The young generation stands against the old. But both get a chance to speak through their poets almost simultaneously. Sophocles dies between 406 and 405 at almost 90. Euripides, less than twenty years younger, dies one year earlier. In the Athens of the Peloponnesian War they are played alongside one another through plague, siege, and party struggles. The highly developed theatrical art and the indestructible enthusiasm for the theatre enjoys, criticizes and crowns them both, even if Euripides was treated with very much more caution. He won only five victories.

In that respect, the Athenian democracy seems not dissimilar to our own Western one. But one thing we must not overlook: there are no revolutionaries as we understand them. There were fanatical party struggles, outside Athens shockingly bloody ones, there was no lack of terror, but by comparison with the underminingly explosive spirit of European revolutions it all remains quite harmless. Also, the economic and social foundations, compared with the modern ones, remained unchanged. The social question did not become an all-consuming philosophy of life. There was no lack of thoughts of reform, even radical ones, but there was no compulsion to find Utopia, the tyrannical picture of a better future, the Moloch of the Good to which the hypnotized present must sacrifice its children. The bond between technology, the masses, and profaned Christian inheritance did not exist—popular passions were whipped up by the demagogues, so that the lives of contemporaries were made a misery and yet, it must be said, there was less hypocrisy. Everything in this Athens was public and open to a degree which never ceases to astound us. Criticism was a universal passion, not the privilege of a press that continually makes up our minds for us. It leaps on to centre stage, not only in comedy, which it dominates, but also, ultimately, in tragedy. We see how human hypocrisy in Euripidean theatre is exposed in ever more colourful disguises, and how, finally, venerable old Sophocles joins in the same theme. The citizens of Athens who attended court with the same passionate enthusiasm that they brought to the theatre, watched it all with critical pleasure. For theatre and court they have the same name: both are *agōn*, 'contest'. 'The scene changes to a court of law': how often does this happen, not to our unadulterated delight, even in such romantic adventure and intrigue plays as Euripides' *Helen* (412; see how from 894 ff. he struggles for the decision, the *krisis*, at 997!).

Towards the end of the century a restoration set in, that counter movement which began with Socrates falling victim to it. Philosophic thought also takes the opposite direction through the condemnation of Socrates. With that the intellectual crisis disappeared once again from the show place of history. A phenomenon such as the Sophistic movement—a sort of youth crisis, considered historically—never reappeared in the ancient world, despite all philosophizing. The unthinkable was no longer enticing. In the place of the heroic came the rational struggle against pain and fear, in the place of the ancient cults and myths came the philosophical god of the world, of reason and of destiny, the old gods dwindled into popular gods and their believers behaved towards intellectuals like exoterics towards esoterics. Thus peace between intellect and tradition was concluded once and for all.

The question: do the gods exist? is posed often enough in Euripidean theatre, linked to a greater or lesser degree with questions of conscience in matters of morality. In the *Thesmophoriazusai* (*Women at the Festival of Demeter*) of the year 411 the women accuse the poet of atheism. The consequences are far-reaching. One of them complains (446 ff.):

My husband fell in the war in Cyprus and left me with five small children whom, with great difficulty, I have supported by making wreaths in the myrtle market. Up to now I have made only a half miserable living. But now this person, through his tragedies, has made men believe that there are no gods, so we don't sell half as many as we did.

(For there was no festival of the gods, no sacrifice, no prayer, for which one did not wear a wreath.)

If there are no gods, what happens to morality? At the same time the question can be posed the other way round: if morality exists, what happens to the gods? A fragment from the *Oinomaos* runs (577 Nauck): 'Whenever I see miscreant mortals come to grief, I say: the race of the gods exists.' The second part of the equation is not given. In the *Iphigenia among the Taurians* Orestes complains (570–5):

The wise gods, as they are called, are no more truthful than winged dreams. Much confusion dwells among the gods, as it does among mortals. The man who is prudent and trusts in the words of soothsayers comes to ruin, just as does the man who follows wise men.

In the drama Orestes' nihilism seems to be given the lie by the improbably happy outcome. Nevertheless the question is posed temptingly and behind the happy outcome there is nothing more than the Euripidean theatrical *deus ex machina* who is so helpful to the story.

At the end of *Heracles* the suffering hero acknowledges, after he has killed his own children in the madness which Hera inflicted upon him (1341–6):

But that the gods indulge in forbidden love and that they bind one another's hands [*Both points criticize Homeric myths of Zeus*], that I have never believed, and never will, nor that one god can be master of another. God, if he is a true god, is not in want of anything. Those are the wretched tales of poets.

In both the last verses something of the criticism of the old Enlightenment philosopher Xenophanes is repeated. But in the old rhapsode the account was clear: the censure of the Homeric gods serves the praise of his almighty spiritual god. The Euripidean Heracles, on the other hand, says it as he comes to himself before the corpses of his children. If his madness did not come from a god, where did it come from? If it did come from a god, were they truly a god? The poetry turns against itself. What in Xenophanes was criticism of the Homeric gods is extended to the whole question of godhead. If one of the greatest Euripidean tragedies ends with such an acknowledgement, then the question of the relationship between human tragedy and godly power, the arc between the two cornerstones of Attic tragedy, is deliberately veiled in ambiguous twilight. Euripides cannot resist driving the play with the holiest of plays to the point where, beyond the limits of art, there are momentary glimpses of senselessness.

No less confusing is Hecuba's prayer in the *Trojan Women* (884 ff.). If Heracles' protest is reminiscent of the rhapsode critic Xenophanes, this is reminiscent of the philosopher of nature Diogenes of Apollonia, who was in vogue at that time. Traditional or Aeschylean forms of prayer: 'Whoever you may be, incomprehensible Zeus; be you . . .', and further: 'I pray to you, for, striding along soundless paths, you guide all things mortal in your righteousness', are mingled with the speculative philosophy of nature and the profoundly contradictory, as in 'O you, who bear the earth and sit enthroned upon it'. What is meant is the air, the soul-giving, all-penetrating element, the divine in the world of Diogenes. But then, when it is further said about this—or Zeus: 'Be you a necessity (*anankē*) of nature (*physis*) or the reason (*nous*) of mortals', then the listener can scarcely be expected to complete the derivation of human reason from cosmic reason—rather Necessity thus contrasts with Reason, *anankē* with *nous* (see Plato!) as well as 'nature' with 'mortals'; both combine in an expression that diametrically opposes them, embracing all possibilities. Thus Menelaus too finds it an incredible new prayer, which he listens to with some consternation. For, apart from the fact that one cannot pray to such a god, the refutation of the god's apparently confirmed righteousness follows hot on the heels of the deceived old lady's prayer. The prayer, spoken at the beginning of one of the main *agōnes*—it is about the stoning of Helen—is, according to the intention of the dramatist, an unsolvable riddle masquerading as profundity. The just god cannot become a two-headed Janus. The prayer form is also stylistically overstrained. The traditional and the (so-called) enlightened divinities, heaped one upon the other, as if they were compatible, end up equally absurd, a prelude to the entire ensuing *agōn*, which annuls its own mythical assumptions.

The archaic gods could abandon man without becoming less real for doing so. In spite of their Homeric brightness, they remained veiled in darkness, impenetrable to man. When Aeschylus' Cassandra is deserted at her death by her god, the soothsayer Apollo, the mysteriousness of the god is deeply shocking. When Euripides' Hippolytus is deserted by his adored goddess, the virginal Artemis, as he suffers the tortures of death, it seems not dissimilar. But the difference is that this desertion is no longer acceptable, that here, in all the sympathy that the goddess feels, in all that is moving in the blind devotion unto death of her faithful admirer, something turbulent is aroused: is it a mystery worth honouring when the gods so deny themselves to their worshippers? Is not the mortal, the purer his devotion, the more betrayed? The goddess may see no corpse, may shed no tears. This much is demanded by her nature and her cult. There is scarcely another scene which so cries out in condemnation under the cloak of the sacred and moving. The fact that the scene is so poetic makes it even more two-faced. And how perfidious that the goddess herself morally justifies her desertion! She would gladly have it otherwise! 'But amongst the gods the law prevails: no god interferes with the will of another, we always refrain from that.' She excuses herself with Aphrodite and Zeus. In the Euripidean gods—so incarnate do they appear—there is a subjective human streak: they deceive, are vengeful towards, betray and desert mortals—in the poor mortals' belief in the gods. Or, in so far as they embody powers, like Aphrodite, the mortals fall victim to their own impotence.

The mystery shifts from god to man. The gods are, and behave, as in the lays and legends which have been handed down. They love their protégés, detest their detractors, desert their poor victims, order matricide just as before. But, the mortals! If one drew up a register of everything that exists among the mortals in Euripides and what did not exist in Aeschylus and Sophocles, then on the Euripidean side, there would be—admittedly not in intensity and fate, but certainly in human potential—a not inconsiderable preponderance.

Sophocles' *Ajax* shows how an archaic hero in god-imposed madness massacres the flocks in his own camp instead of his enemies, and, robbed of his honour, hurls himself onto his sword. But that a victorious hero, fighting for justice in the world, a son of Zeus, and the greatest benefactor of mankind, should in god-imposed madness heroically kill his own children in the mistaken belief that he is killing his enemies, and, in his despair, instead of taking his own life, persuade himself to persist with his life—however broken that life may be—such a compelling failure did not exist before the *Heracles* of Euripides.

Similar points could be made about Medea, Kreousa, Phaedra, Orestes, Agamemnon, indeed almost all Euripidean theatre. The archaic relationship between men and the gods, which is not suspended, but continued on the special stage of the *theologeion*, is complemented by a new broad field inviting exploration: the field of struggles, aberrations, deceptive ploys, and paradoxes of the psyche. Liberated, laid bare, and exposed, the poor soul steps out of the sphere of influence of the divine-demonic to which it was subject, a step just as moving as it is startling.

The interpreters of the nineteenth century may be proud of the fact that in this they rediscovered what they called 'the psychological'. If one wishes to be comfortable with this description, however, one reservation must be stated: the psychological in Euripidean drama is not to be confused with the psychological element of the psychological novel, of realism or of naturalistic drama. In 1891, one year after Ibsen's *Hedda Gabler*, Wilamowitz may have characterized Euripides' Phaedra as: 'No ordinary woman: . . . She is through and through a woman of the polite world, recognizes and fulfils her duties: she has her husband and children, relations and social status and is well aware of the consideration that she must observe towards all. Her reputation is spotless. But she feels no inner relationship to her children and her husband, let alone to anything else. Her life lacks the blessing of work [compare Ibsen's Nora!] and she is too intelligent to find satisfaction in idleness and empty sociability . . . So she is ripe for passion. Suddenly, in her stepson, she is confronted by a being who astonishes her simply because she does not understand him . . . She dreams of a life for herself at his side, free of the chains of convention, a life of freedom and emotion such as she has never known. Plucking flowers with him at the stream's edge [compare Hedda's fantasy of the vine leaves in the hair of her beloved], riding and hunting at his side: that would give her existence some meaning. So run her emotions. Reason is not silent. She knows that she cannot, will not, take the false step . . . What she fears is not the sin; heaven forbid! She believes, after all, that she cannot help being in love. What she fears is disgrace. Her role was her life. She was the blameless wife because it behoved her to be so; because it behoves her, she will also die: it is impossible for her, Phaedra, Minos' daughter, Queen of Athens, to create a scandal . . .'

How does it go in Ibsen?

BRACK. Yes, Hedda—then comes the scandal.
HEDDA [the general's daughter]. The scandal!
BRACK. Yes, the scandal—of which you are so mortally afraid.

The correspondence was too overwhelming for one to be able to notice the anachronisms creeping in: 'polite world', 'social status', 'inner relationship', 'blessing of work'(!), 'empty sociability', 'chains of convention', 'give her existence some meaning', . . .

But Ibsen's psychology is the bourgeois psychology of the doctor or the lawyer, his criticism is of society and milieu and, consequently, optimistic. What occurs in *Medea* or in *Hippolytus* is more disturbing than Ibsen in his entirety: the disintegration of all convention, the impotence of virtue, the absurdity of honour . . . The psychological drama of the nineteenth century sought the individual; individuality was in itself worth while, if every individual could be confirmed in himself in accordance with his experience. Antiquity shows the heroic as it fragments in the light of the new cognition. Euripides gainsays the reasoned optimism of the sophists no less than the optimism born of Socratic knowledge of virtue. The damage which he uncovers is as rich in confusing aspects as it is irremediable.

The spiritual struggle between the loving mother and the avenger, between insight and passion, in the *Medea*, which was performed in 431, may be regarded as the breakthrough of psychology in the theatre. But what does this struggle signify? Is it supposed to present to our gaze what 'woman' is capable of in good and evil? Does feminine self-destruction contrast with thoughtless masculine egoism? But why then does the play end with her triumph? The enchantress turned daemon is transported away as the victor on her grandfather Helios' dragon chariot. The miracle of the theatrical machine, formerly concerned with the revelation of a divinity, helps the horror story to its final effect. Or is there, as Wilamowitz assumed, a forgotten myth of the goddess of death hidden somewhere behind it? In either case, would the conclusion have had nothing to do with the actual drama? In explanation of this the same Wilamowitz again turns to milieu. If *Medea* is seen as a drama of marriage or the soul, would the meaning be a new 'realism'? A slice of 'life' (also a meaning)? Truth instead of falsehood, convention? A didactic play?

In the legend Jason was the adventurous, bold hero and terrible avenger. In Euripides he becomes one of the weakest, morally speaking, as do so many of the heroes in his works. Medea, in the legend, was the acquisition, the uncanny Undine, the criminal sorceress in love and loathing. In Euripides she, too, disintegrates, but in the opposite way: as a criminal she becomes her own victim—she becomes sentimental. A child murderess, she becomes a piteous mother. As she becomes human, she dwindles into absurdity.

The messenger concludes the luridly histrionic report of the tortured death of Jason's young bride with the commonplace, 'Not for the first time, I think what is mortal is a shadow'; the prologue of Sophocles' *Ajax* concluded with the same sentence. There Odysseus said: 'I see that the mortal is no more than a shadow—before the gods.' 'Therefore beware presumption,' warned Athena, 'but the gods love those who are mindful of themselves.' The Messenger in *Antigone* concluded in a similarly formal manner: the greatest evil is stupidity ($\dot{\alpha}\beta o\nu\lambda\acute{\iota}\alpha$). Whence the end of *The Bride of Messina*. In Euripides, in spite of the formal similarity, there is no trace of this spirit. Instead his messenger: 'I tell you boldly: those who consider themselves clever, those who brood in their minds are those who are most punished! For no mortal is happy ($\epsilon\dot{\nu}\delta\alpha\acute{\iota}\mu\omega\nu$), one is more successful [favoured by *tychē*], the other less so . . .'. Who are the optimists who imagine that they can achieve bliss through reason ($\lambda\acute{o}\gamma o\iota$)? The pupils of the sophists? Or those of Socrates? No matter, it is they who are punished. And why? Because they are the greatest illusionists. The sting with which the commonplace ends does not invite one to seek a *fabula docet* except, perhaps, a pessimistic one.

The more traditional the gods, the less discovered the mortals. Enigmatic beings. They seek security, maxims, old and new rules, according to which they would like to live their lives, believe they do lead their lives, indulge in impotent protest, query only too frequently justice and injustice and stray into an increasingly torrential whirlpool of self-contradiction, hopelessness, error, delusion of self and of others, of the perverse and the absurd. More and more often virtue tends to change to crime. In this it is not only kings veiled in rags who act, as Aristophanes caricatured them, to everyone's delight: the substance, the very marrow of heroic morality is eroded. A couple of youths, a boy, three girls who sacrifice themselves with emotional enthusiasm for their fatherland or all Greece, cannot contrive to alter anything of the impression of the decay of everything previously seen to be uplifting. Things are particularly bad for the old. A dark chapter. It should not be forgotten that the old, even in Attic theatre, had previously been held to be worthy of respect.

Judgemental morality is not touched upon. Like all nihilistically inclined intellectuals and artists Euripides is also a *moralist*. The noble person's sense of justice, dignity, freedom (not, however, as something to be won, but rather as a dowry of nobility), humanity, sympathy, loyalty and patriotism to the point of self-sacrifice provide the standards by which gods and men are measured and found wanting. The heroic, courageous instincts win approval—also love, selfless love that is, of spouse, siblings, and friends. Love as passion is temptation of the worst sort. But as the foundation on which morality stands, or was supposed to stand, starts to sway, so morality, and whatever is done in its name, sways with it into the danger zone of absurdity. The poet who has become godless sits in judgement over the disaster of his godlessness.

The characters in his plays also refer to morality; nothing is more familiar to them. However much the overall picture of his plays reflects the decadence of the age, concurring with Thucydides, there are no professed villains, no Richard III, no Iago. Weakness, lack of character, lies, falsehood, egoism, arrogance, unscrupulousness, ossification—the carnival procession of spiritual affliction struts across the stage in the pompous finery of moral self-assertion. Almost even worse than the passions, so blindly do they rage, are the examples of shrivelling, atrophy, weakness, and cowardice. Rationalist deconstructions of morality and religion such as were popular in the circles of the thoughtless, as in the *Sisyphus* of the aristocrat Critias who, after the conquest of Athens, was to become one of the thirty 'tyrants', do not occur. Yet, so much the richer, shimmering in all colours, is the involuntary self-revelation of the self-assertive.

The *agōn* also, the battle of words, which previously, in its archaic form, followed the Homeric model, a heroic struggle for heroic honour and heroic fame, is included in the spreading distortions and confusions. The more the *agōn* becomes the art form of theatre, in which the equally balanced *pro* and *contra* of Protagoras, along with the rhetoric of justice, steps onto the stage, the more its meaning also changes. One of the impressive proofs among the sophists for the superiority of the mind, the double speeches (*Dissoi logoi*) in Euripidean tragedy thrust themselves into the foremost ranks of the provocative. The optimism of the sophistic *technē* becomes reversed into the pessimistic play of its application. The human as it ought to be completely loses its footing, seized by the intellectual.

The former reigning powers, *daimōn* and *moira*, swept along in the general drive towards meaninglessness, become in external events *tychē*. *Tychē* was that which, in life and politics, resisted all rational optimism. It is that which thwarts all plans, even in Thucydides. Confused play of chance and the destruction of all human façades are the complementary forms of disintegration.

In part, the intellect, which no longer finds fulfilment in tragic events, flees for recovery, so to speak, to topical allusion and political leanings. As a patriot and political commentator Euripides, as in so much else, seems to turn back to Aeschylus. In Aeschylus, however, the political and patriotic remained subservient to the tragic, the religious. In the new freedom which it wins, however, the political threatens first to become almost superficial, in order then to elevate itself to a new, almost unheard-of extent, to indictment and warning. The tendentious plays of the Archidamian War, *Herakleidai* and *Hiketides*, were followed by the *Trojan Women* of 415. Franz Werfel translated it as an indictment of war shortly before the First World War. In view of the outcome of the Sicilian expedition, the original has been called one of the greatest poetic predictions. Also partially directed against war is the *Helen* of 412. The Trojan War fought over an illusion: in this way the palinode of the choral lyricist Stesichorus to Helen—'The legend is untrue, you did not come to Troy'—is changed into the political. The Euripidean chorus sings (1151): 'Fools, who obtain virtue for yourselves through war and the blade of the mighty spear, ignorantly ($\dot{\alpha}\mu\alpha\theta\hat{\omega}\varsigma$) trying to end suffering by death' [instead of through *logoi* (by rational means)]. In the post-humous *Iphigenia in Aulis*, performed after 406, the plot, the sacrifice of Iphigenia, is only prevented from ending in the sheerest absurdity by the fact that in the second part, the transformation of the childish, trembling girl into the self-sacrificing heroine achieves a drastic general change into the heroic under the slogan: the battle of the united Hellenes against the hubris of the barbarians! But for it to

have come thus far, the heroic, even in its model Achilles, must first
have become so questionable that one despairs of its restoration.

The wealth of themes of the choral songs and the wide-sweeping
monodies seems to be untouched by the symptoms of the crisis
depicted. The music seems to offer security against the looming disintegration. The choruses seek and achieve spiritual uplift, inspiration,
or flow broadly along rich in imagery and melodic plaintiveness. The
dissonance between the critical intellect and exaggerated emotion
seems to do the mythical themes which they bring with them little or
no harm. And yet here, too, there are signs of a break. Euripidean
lyric no longer concentrates on the tragic event, it intensifies, it no
longer interprets, it breaks out, flies over land and sea, raves, dances
among the gods, wishes the world were otherwise, becomes escapist,
longs to be elsewhere, generalizes. It resembles to no small extent the
yearnings and complaints of a prisoner. If the Athenian prisoners in
the quarries of Syracuse did not sing the incantations of Aeschylus,
nor the observances and acceptance of suffering of Sophocles, to
relieve their lot, but the songs of Euripides, then this betrays not only
how easily they were absorbed, something to which Aristophanes
also testifies, but also why. He was also famous as a composer.

Let the hymn to the Aphrodite of the gardens in *Medea* serve as
an example of escape into the realms of the lyrical and sublime
(*Med.* 824 ff.):

By the waters of the fair-flowing Cephisus, where they say Aphrodite drinks
and breathes fragrant warm breezes over the land, and for ever winds
sweet-scented wreaths of roses in her hair, and sends her winged boys [*lit.:
the Erōtes, also in a transferred, intellectual, significance*] to sit beside Wisdom
(σοφία), to create with her every kind of excellence (ἀρετή).

Aphrodite surrounded by Cupids is a favourite motif of contemporary
vase painting. What is Euripidean is the change towards the spiritual;
σοφία is high culture, as in fragment 897 Nauck.

Attic sacred landscape is also praised by Sophocles, as in *Oedipus at
Colonus* 668 ff. It is praised in such a way that it almost sounds
Euripidean to us. But there the praise is relevant to the plot, which
once again turns into a ritual play. The hill of Colonus, the grave
of Oedipus, is holy ground. The garden of Aphrodite is, in the
horror of the *Medea*, a charming idyll and a digressive song of praise
to Athens.

Another example.

In the aged Aeschylus the chorus of old men hints in a bitter proverb at the lot of old age which, in war, makes it like a child; frailty
thrusts itself into the coded word: *Agamemnon* 72 ff. In the aged
Sophocles the chorus of ancients submits to the burden of the years;
youth and sad old age have their measure: *Oedipus at Colonus* 1211 ff.
In the ageing Euripides the chorus of ancients wishes for its return
to the remembered joys of youth. Would that murderous old age
might fly away in waves and ether! The world is topsy-turvy: virtue
deserves twice as much youth. Only one thing old age does not steal
from me: the cult of the Graces and the Muses: *Heracles* 637 ff.

In the end the confusion of meaning and the paradoxes penetrate
the music as well. Cassandra, in the madness of pain, breaks into
jubilant marriage-hymns in the *Trojan Women* 308 ff. The monody
in which she finally becomes pathological on top of everything else,
achieves the pinnacle of virtuosity. Euripides was also the first to
introduce children's monodies to the stage. A late example of the
virtuosity of his new style of monodies is the Phrygian's monody in
his *Orestes*. The elements of mannerism and mimicry break into the
realms of the lyrical-musical.

It cannot be denied that this break with tradition brought with it at
the same time an unparalleled liberation for the poetic imagination.
It opened up possibilities for the theatre which, under its religious
servitude, had been closed to it. The free-wheeling *tychē* could conjure
up miraculous encounters, confusions, ways of being carried off
and romantically reunited in which people—husbands and wives,
brothers and sisters—could meet, in a quite new, exciting, touching,
and charming way. Recognition, *anagnōrisis*, formerly bound to the
leadership of the gods or to the Delphic command 'Know thyself!'
becomes the freely floating play under the autonomous direction of
the artist, becomes the artistic form which outdoes itself in more and
more fresh inventions. The gods, as a counterforce to be evaluated
by a purely aesthetic measure, are swallowed up in them in order to
make them more exciting, more witty. Human will, no longer steered
or punished by the will of some god or daemon, creates a new genre
for itself: the intrigue, in whose constellations, dependent only on
man and *tychē*, the falterers can be made fools of in yet different
ways, the innocent move us in yet different ways from those of
the tragically crumpling witnesses and victims of incomprehensible
powers. The *Antigone* of Sophocles moves us in one way, Euripides'
Alcestis in another. Antigone, obedient to the unwritten law, suffers

death for the sake of the gods and her dead brother. To be able to comprehend this, familiarity with Attic cult is required. Alcestis, obedient to her love, suffers death for the sake of her living husband. To some she might appear more moving as a human being.

The loss of the old relationship has, however, an even more liberating effect on the wealth of matter and form which only now becomes usable for the theatre. Only now does the treasure of local legends, the Greek *Thousand and One Nights* from which Ovid's *Metamorphoses* derives, reach the stage unimpeded. The way in which Euripides builds a bridge between local legend and his own domain, the psychological-pathological, was to be of even greater significance for world literature. It was his discovery that local legend and local cult can, beyond their religious content, be psychologically-poetically interesting, dramatically fascinating. His *Alcestis*—a Thessalian legend; his *Hippolytus*—a legend from the Argolid; his *Iphigenia among the Taurians*—an Attic legend; testify to his intuition. Finally, from a Theban legend he derives his *Bacchae*, the only extant tragedy of Dionysian frenzy.

But probably of even greater significance is the fact that, alongside Sophocles, a new style of theatre, a new concept of theatre arises— theatre which is produced as such with its own strongly emphasized conventions. It was a considerable determining factor in what was understood by 'tragedy' until the eighteenth century.

Enough of this jumping about. If, in order finally to sketch an entire drama with a few strokes, I turn to the *Orestes*, I choose it not because I regard it as one of the most commendable, but rather as one of the most difficult tragedies of this difficult dramatist, and therefore nevertheless consider it enlightening. Produced in 408, it represents, along with the *Bacchae* and the *Iphigenia in Aulis*, the final stage of the style.

The tragedy of the *Orestes* encapsulates the problem of guilt as it achieves its form in Greek literature. After the *Oresteia*, the two *Electras* and the *Iphigenia among the Taurians*, one might have thought that the theme would have been exhausted. Then this difficult dramatist takes up the theme one last time and steers it down a new path. He makes a surprising choice of dramatic moment. The action takes place in Argos (following Aeschylus) on the sixth day after the funeral of Clytemnestra. That was the length of time it took for the murder to react upon the murderer and at the same time upon his environment. The interaction between the spiritual problem and the social problem, that was new.

Outside the palace of the long since murdered Agamemnon and the recently murdered Clytemnestra lies a sick-bed. On it lies the sleeping Orestes. Electra, tending him devotedly, speaks the prologue. The chorus are women of Argos who are friendly with her. Everything, the choruses included, is united in aiming at wretchedness and sympathy.

The madness of Orestes, we hear, began the night after the burial. In the night three women appeared to him—he will neither name nor describe them—'woe betide me! how they pursue, persecute me!' Since then he has been lying there on his sick-bed. The murder of Aegisthus recedes completely, arouses no interest.

While Orestes still sleeps, something is being prepared on the quiet. Helen is living in the palace, sent ahead by Menelaus, who, having been delayed for so long, is returning from Troy. As she dare not allow herself to be seen by the embittered people of Argos, pursued by the hatred of the war victims, she is naïve enough to ask her niece Electra to deliver in her (Helen's) place her grave offering for her sister Clytemnestra. Electra, who is unable to look upon her mother's grave because of her feeling of guilt, directs her to her little daughter Hermione, who is living with her mother in the royal household in order to await her father. The relatives begin to gather around the sleeping Orestes. Hermione, sweet and good, goes with the offerings to the grave. Scarcely has Helen returned to the palace when Electra curses her: 'Did you see the way she cut off the ends of her hair (as an offering for the grave), retaining her beauty? She remains what she was. May the gods hate you for the way in which you have plunged me, him (Orestes), and all Greece into misery' (128 ff.).

The fortunate, who are unchanged, are separate from those who have changed, become guilty, the tortured and abandoned. The state of being outcast is accompanied and supported by the choruses, which run through all the registers of sympathy.

Orestes continues to sleep. Already the leader of the chorus fears that he has passed away. Then he awakens, strengthened like the waking Philoctetes after the great sleep and illness scene in Sophocles (211 ff.):

ORESTES. Dear magic potion of sleep, ally in sickness! How sweetly you came to me in my moment of need! O Lethe, goddess of forgetfulness of troubles,

to whom the wretched pray, how wise you are! Where have I come from?
What brought me here? I know nothing more, I abandoned consciousness.

He has every reason not to remember. Quite different from the
bodily suffering and the physical loss of heroism in the case of the
ailing Philoctetes, his suffering is the guilt which again and again
he seeks, in vain, to thrust away from himself. Remembering, he
succumbs to it once more (284 ff.):

ORESTES. You agreed to it, but our mother's blood is on my head! I blame
Apollo, who urged me to this most infamous action, encouraged me in
word, but not in deed. Certainly, my own father, if I had asked him face to
face, ought I to kill my mother? would have prayed me many times by this
beard not to plunge in the sword and slaughter my mother, since it could
not bring him back to life, and it loaded me, poor wretch, with so much
misery.

One moment he hides himself in his blankets, covering himself out
of shame and remorse, the next he leaps up, hallucinating, hounded
by the Erinyes, gesticulating as if he were striking his persecutors
with Apollo's arrows. No merciful sister could be more caring and
touching than Electra, who supports and soothes the confused, weak
Orestes, who for five days has eaten and drunk nothing and has not
bathed himself.

Inner distress is now compounded by external trouble. Argos has
expelled the murderers. They are under guard. On this day, at this
hour, the people's assembly will decide their fate.

The exiles pin all their hopes on Menelaus, who is soon to arrive.
The chorus greets him as a happy, indulgent conqueror as he enters.
He has already heard, enquires about Orestes, whom he does not
recognize (380 ff.):

ORESTES. I am Orestes, for whom you ask. I will gladly lay my sufferings out
before you; I clasp your knees as the first act of my supplication, letting fall
prayers instead of a suppliant's olive-branch! Rescue me from my troubles:
you have arrived just in the nick of time!
MENELAUS. Gods, what do I see? What corpse is this before me?
ORESTES. Quite right. I am dead of misery, and yet still living . . .
MENELAUS. You glare terribly with your sunken eyes.
ORESTES. My body has gone, only my name remains.

(The tragic pathos leads up to the epigram. In this, Euripides is the
forerunner of Seneca; similar is *Helen* 286: 'I am dead in appearance
but not in fact.')

In order to make being hemmed in on all sides even more of a torture, old Tyndareus, the father of Clytemnestra, has to burst in, in the middle of the meeting between Orestes and Menelaus. In shame and remorse Orestes seeks to cover himself again. Must he look into the eyes of the man whose daughter he has killed, the honourable old man who was so tender and so kind to him, his grandson, when he was a child, who kissed him, fondled him!

The old man comes—walking reverence. He wants to bring offerings for the grave of the dead woman: 'Where, where is Menelaus, my friend?' Menelaus: 'Greetings, Honoured of Zeus!' Tyndareus: 'Greetings, son-in-law!' Then he falls back: 'How dreadful it is, surely, not to know the future. The matricide, the poisonous worm, slithers flashing pestilence outside my house! Menelaus! You speak to him?' Menelaus: 'To my brother's son! How could I not?' Tyndareus: 'O . . . [after long reasoning] His madness is proof of the punishment of the gods. Is any other testimony necessary? Do not argue with the gods! Let Argos stone him!'

Tyndareus as a questionably noble old man is akin to the father of Admetus, to Teiresias or Cadmus in the *Bacchae*. He preaches the law, the *nomos*. If only Orestes had stuck to *nomos* and exiled Clytemnestra! What she did was dreadful. I am unlucky in my daughters, otherwise I cannot complain. In his case, *nomos* masks that which, in Menelaus, is masked by the 'possible', the *dynaton*: his true face.

Argumentatively, he asks as if before the court (507 ff.):

I shall ask you, Menelaus, only this: suppose Orestes' wedded wife murders him, and his son in turn kills his mother, and again his son makes murder atone for murder, when will there ever be an end to these troubles?

(The argument is reminiscent of that in Sophocles' *Electra*: the consequences of bloody revenge if it were raised to the level of *nomos* (581), but here, applied to pure matricide, it also becomes a caricature linguistically.)

That is why our ancient fathers in all wisdom established this law: let the one stained with blood be banished from the sight of our eyes and our presence. Let exile punish him, but not death!

It is part of the psychology of the feeling of guilt that the same person who fell apart under the burden of his guilt becomes a quite different one as soon as he is reproached for this same guilt by another, ill-disposed, person. Then he defends himself, he speaks his mind, he presents his own reckoning. So Orestes is no longer recognizable in his demeanour towards old Tyndareus.

Just to give just an indication of the content: 'Away with you, old man! I am more the son of my father than my mother—your daughter!' (He uses the same argument as Apollo in the *Eumenides*.) 'The way your daughter carried on—it was not honourable! I know that in saying this I dishonour myself—her secret paramour was Aegisthus! I killed him. My mother was only a makeweight to my sacrifice. For this, however, you threaten to have me stoned—hear what salvation I gave to all Greece by this deed! If all criminal women could shelter behind their motherhood it would be made easy for them to murder their husbands. I have put an end to this law, this *nomos*, with my dreadful deed! You yourself, old man, who fathered this daughter, have brought this misery upon me! Surely you see: Telemachus did not kill Odysseus' wife. But I have obeyed the Delphic Apollo whose infallible words we mortals all obey. Blame him! He sinned, not I!'

Nomos against *nomos*, morality against morality. *Nomos* becomes a none-too-edifying shield of virtue from behind which the attacked mounts his counter-attack.

And what does the old man say to this? Now he lets his mask drop. 'What! Do you now become insolent as well? Do you dare to come at me with insults? Just you wait! Whether the people of Argos will it or no, I will so stir them up against you that they will decide on death by stoning for you—and your sister who incited you to do it! A welcome addition to my grave offering!'

So much for the tender old man calling upon *nomos*! Trembling with agitation he hastens to the people's assembly.

But how does the returning Menelaus, crowned with victory, respond to the hopes placed in him? When he saw his nephew immersed in his misery, he was, at first, full of sympathy, declared himself ready to help in any way. One has a duty to stand up for one's nearest and dearest to the death—and to destroy the enemy. Aristocratic morality demands this. But there is an 'if': if God provides the possibility, the δυνάσθαι, for it. May the gods grant it to me!

The *dynaton* ('the possible'), the argument of political realism, also plays its questionable role in the Melian Dialogue of Thucydides (5. 89). The Athenian envoys refuse to tolerate the moral arguments of justice and injustice, but demand 'rather that that should come to pass which is for you yourselves, as for us, according to our true thinking, possible (*dynata*); as, amongst those of us who know, it is surely no secret that the concept "just" in a human judgement can only be applied when each side is equally under pressure, whereas the "possible" is demanded by the superior and conceded by the weak.'

The *dynaton* also stands opposed to morality in the diplomatic speech of Menelaus. For—unfortunately, the might of my army is small, we have suffered heavy losses; to *fight* against Argos—impossible! It is true that it is as difficult to extinguish popular passion as raging fire. Yielding, waiting for the opportunity, that is the way in which one's objective may be reached. People also feel sympathy. Only with cunning (σοφία), not with might (βία), can I try to rescue you from the more powerful. Admittedly, it was never our intention to pacify Argos. Nevertheless, we must attempt to do so.

Preserving his noble bearing he goes off. Orestes, shouting after him: 'O you, commander only for the sake of a woman, most cowardly in support of your nearest kin! You are giving me up! You were friendless, father, in your need! *Oimoi*! I am betrayed! All hope gone of escaping the Argives!' (718 ff.).

Then to the two despairing creatures comes their only loyal friend, Pylades. Whilst Orestes lies captive and ill in Argos, Pylades' father Strophios in Phokis has outlawed him for having been an accessory to the matricide. He returns, he does not shy away from the judgement of the Argives, it is the Phokians who have jurisdiction over him. They decide, together, Orestes supported by Pylades, to enter the assembly of the people of Argos. Orestes will defend himself. His courage, his nobility will have their effect (783). Orestes: 'Onward, then! It would be cowardly to die without honour!'

After a choral song which changes from the most joyful anticipation of regained *aretē* to the double misery of the most pitiful matricide (following the example of Aeschylus), Electra enters, desolate at finding her brother missing. But just at that moment comes the messenger to report. The people's assembly took its typical course. Some of it reminds one of the trial which is best known to us from this period: the people's trial of Socrates, nine years after the performance of *Orestes*.

First to speak is Talthybius, the heroic herald of Agamemnon: a type of the time-server, since as a herald, as an official, he always complies with the current ruler. (Athens was proud of being a democracy, not a state run by officials.) Then Diomedes (measured).

His proposal is for exile. Then an unnamed demagogue of the worst kind speaks. He demands death by stoning. His demand is supported by—Tyndareus. Out of personal rancour ancient aristocracy joins forces with the most extreme radicalism. Then a simple, decent, awkward husbandman speaks. His appeal is that Orestes should be garlanded on behalf of the state because of his liberating deed. Finally, the accused has his say. He defends himself not ineffectively, but when it comes to the vote, the demagogue wins.

Nobility availed you nothing, the Pythian Apollo did not help at all, concludes the messenger regretfully.

The mythical holy court of justice presiding over Orestes on the Areopagus, as Aeschylus represented it on the stage in the *Eumenides*, is replaced in Euripides by a mirror in a frame of heroic proportions reflecting much comment on contemporary issues. The former was glorifying in its belief in the triumph of justice, this is the opposite.

But there is another thing which one seeks in the report in vain: where is Menelaus? Only one little sentence refers to Menelaus— how easy it is to miss it! (931): 'And nobody else spoke'. In what circumstances could a modern dramatist risk throwing light upon a character through such a discreet omission? How safely Euripides could rely on the keen apprehension of his Athenians! Menelaus keeps quiet as a mouse. So that was what was behind his call for the 'possible'! We have experienced this 'keeping quiet', it occurs in various forms. You would look for it in vain in our modern theatre.

Unfortunately, Menelaus' failure is not just cowardice, Orestes was not mistaken (1058): his uncle has hopes of Agamemnon's throne if the heir to the throne, Orestes, is condemned to death!

All that Orestes has achieved through his courageous defence is that the death penalty demanded for the political criminal will be so modified that it will be left to both brother and sister to take their own lives on this day. How, is up to them.

So, now, there they stand, driven victims, surrounded by an inescapability which leaves nothing to be desired, if what we seek is the imprisoned, hopeless person, the person 'in an extreme situation'. Internally they are plagued by guilty consciences; externally, they suffer inhumanity, failure on the part of kinsfolk, opportunism, vengefulness, incitement of the mob, alienation, hostility of all around them . . . This is not the inescapability of destiny, as in *King Oedipus*, where abandonment, oracle, and seer were still half-mythical motifs and the gods as the rationale behind it all left no doubt.

In this inescapable situation, not the work of the gods, but of man alone, what does the nobly born aristocrat do?

The first thing that he does is take his destiny heroically upon himself, he does not succumb, he does not lose his dignified bearing, not *he*, never *he*. The heroically aristocratic, the decisive part of his consciousness, fills a lavishly constructed moving scene in the theatre. The moralist has a penchant for the tear-jerker (1018 ff.).

ELECTRA. Ah! brother, I see you already at your graveside, at your funeral pyre—I mourn for you! [*She bursts into cries of mourning for the dead*] Alas, alas for you! I see you for the last time! The sight drives me mad!

ORESTES. Can you not be quiet? Instead of woman's tears, accept what is imposed, hard as it is!

ELECTRA. How can I be quiet? If it is no longer possible for us, poor wretches, to gaze on this immortal light!

ORESTES. Do not you too kill me! I have enough death from the Argives! Let my present troubles be!

ELECTRA. Your youth! Your destiny! Your untimely death! Orestes! You ought to live, and you are no more!

ORESTES. By the gods, do not surround me with cowardice, bringing me to tears by reminding me of my troubles!

ELECTRA. We will die! It is impossible not to mourn, for the loss of precious life is pitiable for all mortals.

ORESTES. This is the day! Now is the time to make the noose fast up above, or to sharpen the sword.

ELECTRA. You, brother, kill me, so that no Argive may do so, putting to shame the house of Agamemnon.

ORESTES [*bitterly*]. My mother's blood is enough. I will not kill you. Die by your own hand however you like!

ELECTRA. Yes! I will not lag behind you at the sword's point! But—let me throw my arms around your neck!

ORESTES. Enjoy that empty comfort, if it is comfort to embrace those who stand before death.

ELECTRA. O my dearest! O longed-for, sweetest of names to your sister, and one nature in two bodies!

ORESTES. You soften my resolve. Let me requite the tenderness of your embrace! Why am I ashamed? My sister's breast, this dear embrace, these words can stand in place of marriage and children for both of us, poor wretches.

ELECTRA. Ah! If only one sword might strike us both down, if it were right, and one cedarwood coffin receive our bones.

In his way Euripides outdoes the great brother-sister scene in
Sophocles' *Electra* ('Then receive me into your abode!', 1165). He
outdoes it by making each turn to the other and through setting
hardness against softness, horror against tenderness.

Love between brother and sister, Agamemnon's blood in both,
drives them to one another in the intoxication of death. I will prove
my noble birth to the city, cries Orestes, and will thrust my sword
into my entrails! You emulate my daring! And you, Pylades, be our
executor and bury us both by our father's grave!

Following the dispute over precedence between the siblings comes
the similar dispute between Orestes and Pylades. Twice Orestes
prepares to bid him farewell and twice his friend contradicts him,
refusing to survive his friend. The second farewell, even more
emotional, is even more pointed in its increased pathos (1083 ff.):

ORESTES. Farewell I say to you, not you to me. We, the dead, are deprived of
farewells.
PYLADES. How little you understand my thoughts!

How, he asks, am I to see my homeland again? Was I your friend
in good fortune, only to leave you in misfortune? 'How am I to see
my homeland again?' is the same heroic argument with which
Sophocles' Ajax determined his death (460).

The drama could end with that. There is no shortage of dramas,
old and new, which end not very differently. A noble, exalted dispute
over precedence, wrenching itself out of despair, as to who should die
and sacrifice himself for the other, would remain the answer for the
merciless inner reversal as well as the external reversal. From the
point of view of length, too, what has happened up to now (up to
1097, to which a short conclusion might be added) would suffice.
The *Alcestis* and the *Herakleidai* are scarcely any longer.

In Attic theatre the customary final scenes are either *exodos*,
procession, after the display of the corpses, or *deus ex machina*. How
might an Athenian spectator who has reached this point expect the
play to end, in the light of his knowledge of the theatre? He might
expect brother and sister to go into the palace, that he might hear the
death rattle of the embracing siblings, or Electra's scream, he might
expect Pylades to follow them, a messenger to step forward as
Exangelos, the horrific ending to be described in pathetic language,
whereupon the interior of the palace will be revealed with the corpses
lying heaped upon one another; he might expect that they will be

carried out and that the chorus, gloomily lamenting, will follow them. That would be a normal *exodos*.

Or—the other possibility—at the last moment a god, Apollo, might appear on the balcony of the gods, the *theologeion*, hold his protective hand over the condemned and command the people to set them free, and give the delivered captives instruction. That would be a conclusion like, for example, those of the Euripidean plays of intrigue.

Neither ending comes about. Instead something quite out of the way happens.

The drama is divided into two apparently quite different parts, a first part which in spite of all criticism is, on the whole, tragic and moving, and a second—of what sort, we shall see. If one has committed oneself to the first, one would never provide oneself with the second. It seems to lack any preparation such as that which precedes the big turning points in the dramas of Aeschylus and Sophocles: hints of a concealed element which suddenly bursts on the scene.

The surprise ignites like a small spark in the loyal friendship of Pylades, spreads to the two siblings, and engulfs all three like a raging inferno. It begins thus (1098 ff.):

PYLADES. But as we are dying, let us discuss together how Menelaus might share our misfortune.
ORESTES. Dearest friend, if only I could see that before I die!

But how? How can they get at Menelaus? Nothing easier, says Pylades. Let's murder Helen! She's in the palace, isn't she? After all, we have nothing more to hope for for ourselves.

ORESTES. I am right at my last breath; I want to die having accomplished something against my enemies, so that I can pay back those who betrayed me, and those who made me wretched may groan themselves. I am Agamemnon's son, who was thought fit to lead all Hellas, not a tyrant,[1] though he had the strength of a god in him; I will not shame him with a slave's death, but I will give up my life like a freeborn man, and take revenge on Menelaus! (1163 ff.)

How often did the wish: if I am to die, let it be nobly! fall from the lips of heroes! So it did again, a short time before this play, in the *Helen* (*Helen* 298; 841). Although, here, it is bound up with enigmatic vindictiveness, that too is not, sadly, beyond the realm of the heroic. Just think of Achilles! But how the absurd is underlined

---

[1] The same compliment is bestowed on him at *Helen* 395.

here even in the expression! 'Birth', 'shame', 'slave', 'freeborn' and, finally, spat out, the hated name: Menelaus! He who feels himself to be a hero is the creature who, instead of yielding to his destiny, first has to perpetrate something horrendous. So the first part in which the siblings are the sufferers is followed by a second part in which they are the activists. A play of intrigue follows the drama of suffering.

And behold! loving Electra is there again and the girl is not hanging back behind the boys, either. It is she who gives the other two the idea of seizing Hermione, who has been sent out and is expected back, of using her as a hostage, of holding a sword to her throat before her father's eyes when he comes to take his revenge upon the murderous pair for the death of Helen!

ORESTES. O what a manly spirit have you, yet a body so fitting a true woman: how much worthier are you to live, not die! Pylades, this is the wife you will lose, poor wretch—but if you live, what a blessed marriage will be yours! (1204 ff.)

Never for one moment in the whole crime do they lose the consciousness of their heroic morality.

At the end of their conspiracy the three direct an alternating prayer to the soul of the dead Agamemnon. In form and content it is reminiscent of the great *kommos* in the *Choephoroi* of Aeschylus. The echoes are too marked to be missed (1225 ff.):

ORESTES. O father, you who dwell in the house of dark night, I, Orestes, your son, call upon you to come to our aid. For I suffer unjustly on your account, and I am betrayed by your brother, though I acted justly; I want to kill his wife—be our help in this!
ELECTRA. O father, come, if inside the earth you hear your children call, dying in your cause.
PYLADES. Kinsman of my father, hear my prayers too, Agamemnon, save your children.

Where now is the Orestes who had solemnly declared that Agamemnon would have beseeched him not to kill his mother?

In the *Choephoroi* the children prayed to their dead father for atonement for murder commanded by the god. Here they pray for help for a murder which is psychologically comprehensible but, seen in human terms, utterly repulsive. And yet, here again, Orestes finds himself in agreement with aristocratic morality. His behaviour is all of a piece with the little Attic song which was sung in the noble *symposia*: 'Then the crab said, as he took the snake in his claw: the friend must be straight and not plot crookedness!' But unfortunately he takes Helen and Hermione in his claw, because Menelaus cannot be got at in any other way.

When one hears the siblings' prayer one is tempted to ask: is this supposed to be a parody? A dig at Aeschylus? It is no more parody than all the rest. It is the degeneration of the heroic and religious heritage taken to absurdity. The piety of the cult of the dead and the ancestors becomes a thing that masks the instincts for revenge of those who are driven to extremes, for the sake of their justification and glorification. So the dead Agamemnon also refrains this time from offering his hand. The trio which in the *Choephoroi* succeeded in conjuring his power from the hereafter, hovers gruesomely in the imagination. For, in addition to everything else, after so much heroic expectation of death, there is mingled in all this madness the crazy hope of fame, public honour, and gratitude on the part of all the Greeks for freeing them from the universally detested Helen.

The deed follows the plan. With drawn swords the two youths burst into the palace. In breathless suspense Electra waits, listening, at the door—as in Sophocles. But at the same time she divides the two halves of the chorus to right and left to watch over the proceedings. This produces a chorus piece with divided roles—almost as in *Don Giovanni*. At last the expected scream of fear from Helen rings out: 'Menelaus, I am dying! Where are you?' The Sophoclean 'Strike again!' is surpassed by a breathless, pleading litany which is suddenly interrupted: the unsuspecting Hermione returns at that very moment from Clytemnestra's grave. She too has heard a noise which has made her fearful. Electra calms her, saying that Orestes is pleading at Helen's feet for his and Electra's lives! Support us! Hermione: Gladly! Scarcely has she entered the palace when she cries from inside: Heavens! Who are these? Orestes (from inside): Silence! You have come to save us, not yourself! Electra, outside the door: An axe to her neck! The chorus thereupon sings loudly in order not to arouse suspicion amongst the Argives. Then, in the role of the Exangelos, a Phrygian bodyguard of Helen's comes out, singing in broken Greek so that at first nothing he says can be understood.

I cannot enumerate here all the stage motifs which are concentrated at this point in the narrowest space. Let me refer to just one. Euripides furnishes the crime committed at random with stage devices which in the *Choephoroi* of Aeschylus presented the matricide

which had been ordained. In Aeschylus a dying scream from inside
does not indicate which of the two has fallen, Orestes or Aegisthus.
The chorus huddles in fear at the side, the stage empties. Then a slave
hurtles out of the central doorway, shouts and rattles at the side
entrance. He finds it locked and laments: '*Oimoi! Panoimoi!* The
master is dead! Thrice *oimoi!* Aegisthus is dead! Open up! Break open
the womens' house! Fetch a crowbar! We need strong arms! Not to
help him—he is dead. *Iou, Iou,* my cries fall on deaf ears. Where is
Clytemnestra?' In intensifying contrast the vulgar enters into the
tragic style. In Euripides, instead of the slave, the Phrygian appears;
instead of the Aeschylean lament he is given a great monody freely
composed throughout, a quite grotesque *mimos* bursting with asiatic
motifs, exotic images, screaming, whimpering, whining . . . The
interplay with the main and subsidiary entrances is surpassed by an
astonishing effect: the Phrygian does not come out of the gate but
hoists himself high up between the triglyphs and wriggles out of the
entablature of the palace front. This was the only way in which he
could escape from the raging youths. The leap from the roof timbers
was a brilliant coup for the actor. In later performances—for the
Orestes became popular—the dangerous leap was replaced by a few
lines with which the actor was permitted to enter through the doorway; the ancient commentators remarked on it.

Tragedy begins to be permeated by the affectations of the theatrical. As musical *mimos* the singing barbarian is comparable to
Antigone's singing number as she climbs a ladder up to the tower, led
by her tutor, in the *Phoenician Women,* or Ion sweeping the temple.
The history of clambering or bustling about while singing in the
theatre has not yet been written. Interest here is directed as much
to the dance-like gestures as to the horror which is emerging from
the torrent of ornate expressions from the Phrygian. The language
contains reminiscences of Aeschylus, whose Egyptian Herald in the
Hiketides is unmistakable. No reminiscences, no affectation.

CHORUS LEADER. And where were you then? Have you long since fled
 in fear?
PHRYGIAN. In Phrygian, Phrygian manner I was stirring the air, the air,
 with a well-made fan of feathers, by Helen's hair, Helen's, by her cheek in
 the eastern custom. (1425 ff.)

Amidst a lot of mimicry it emerges that Pylades pursued the servants
and locked them in the stables and corners of the palace, the

unsuspecting Helen led Orestes to the hearth of the house, the two of them stepped in front of her like wild boars: 'Die! die! Your husband is killing you!' She flees and then Hermione enters. Whilst the two throw themselves on her, Helen has disappeared as if by magic. Orestes comes out of the palace, threatening the whimpering barbarian with his naked sword, scornfully lets him go and hastens back in again to seek the vanished Helen. Menelaus turns up with his retinue, finds the door barred and gives orders for it to be broken open to free his daughter from the power of the murderers. He believes that Helen has been killed. Then Orestes appears on the roof, threatens to crush Menelaus with a cornice if he attacks the doorway, smoke and flames rise up, Orestes and Pylades on the roof threaten to slaughter Hermione, who is kneeling between them with Orestes holding his sword above her neck, before the very eyes of her father, if he does not accede to their demands. Menelaus rages, curses, wails, and promises them what they want. But now Orestes, crazy in his triumph over his enemy, is out of control: he shouts to Electra to set the house on fire, and to Pylades to set fire to the roof. Menelaus, foaming with rage, calls upon the gods for help and Apollo appears on the *theologeion*. From the mouth of the god Menelaus learns that Helen has been translated to the gods. In an instant everything makes sense. Helen had to be so beautiful to be stolen and, through the Trojan War, relieve the earth of so many wicked people. You, Orestes, take yourself off to Athens so that you can be acquitted by the court of Areopagus (just as Aeschylus says) and delivered from the goddesses of revenge. But the one whom you are holding beneath your naked sword, Orestes, you are ordained by fate to marry! Give your sister to Pylades. But, Orestes, leave the people of Argos to me, who commanded you to kill your mother.

Menelaus: O daughter of Zeus, Helen! I hail you! Orestes! I bestow my daughter upon you! Noble one, born of nobility, be happy with her as I am with you!

Apollo: Enough of this discord! Now honour the most beautiful of the goddesses, Eirene! But I shall accompany Helen along starry paths to the house of Zeus where she will be enthroned eternally with Zeus and Hera, Heracles and Hebe, reconciled with the Tyndarids, a saviour and protector for sailors.

When Apollo *ex machina* commands the madman to marry the girl whom he was just on the point of beheading and the said madman consents to do so, then it is difficult for us to take the solution seriously. The girl isn't even asked. Is the dramatist bowing ironically to theatrical convention? Is the solution so absurd that the theatre is nullifying itself? The conclusion shows how it ought to be—and isn't. 'Measureless confusion exists in the godly as in the human sphere.' 'Though this be madness, yet there is method in't', Polonius would say. And yet this is—man. Where is the sense in it? It is part of the greatness of Euripides that he liked to pose the question but not to provide the answer.

His last tragedy, the *Bacchae*, also, he triumphantly forged from the very impossibility of a solution. In that play he presented the god of the theatre himself as a stranger, an alien on the stage, through whose mask and seductive, sinister quality, reason and unreason and everything human is wrecked. The horrendous revenge of the god of enchantment for the resistance of a tyrannically assertive reason—that of the unhappy Pentheus—a poor reason which succumbs to sexual desire even in that very assertion; the dramatist has withdrawn behind this sanctimonious, all too sanctimoniously dramatized legend—or shall we call it a *griphos* (a riddle)? People are puzzling over it to this day.

2

Euripides: Poiētēs Sophos

R. P. WINNINGTON-INGRAM

Sophos ('wise') and its cognates take up nearly three columns in Allen and Italie's *A Concordance to Euripides*. The frequency with which *sophos* and *sophia* ('wisdom') occur in Euripides is at once a mark of the age and a mark of his mind.

The extant plays, by which alone we can judge him, belong (with a single exception)[1] to the last third of the fifth century, to the period of the Peloponnesian War, but also to the age of the sophists. The influence of the sophistic movement upon the poet has been by no means neglected by critics.[2] He has been called 'the philosopher on the stage', and indeed his plays contain numerous echoes of contemporary philosophical ideas. Perhaps, however, the notion has been overdone. It is arguable that, despite this top-dressing of philosophy, Euripides was the least philosophic of the three tragedians,[3] though, being a Greek, he had a mental range and a capacity for general thought beyond the ordinary measure of dramatists. But one can be clever without being a philosopher. It is with other kinds of cleverness that this article is concerned; and it was cleverness of every kind that the sophistic movement encouraged and propagated. This was the Enlightenment[4] or, if you prefer, 'Enlightenment'—a world of clever

---

[1] Leaving the *Rhesus* out of consideration.

[2] I have borrowed, for my more limited enquiry, the title of a book by D. F. W. van Lennep (1935), which is a comprehensive treatment of the poet's work with a particular interest in the influence of the sophistic movement.

[3] This may sound a paradox, but I am fortified by a comparison which Professor E. A. Havelock has made (1957, 33) between, on the one hand, the philosophic breadth with which the evolutionary view of the development of society is handled in the *Prometheus* and in the *Antigone* and, on the other, the rhetorical version of similar ideas which Euripides puts into the mouth of Theseus in his *Supplices*. For the details, see pp. 52–83.

[4] For an admirable account see Dodds, 1951, 179–206. Dodds rightly stresses that the beginnings of the Enlightenment long preceded the Sophistic Movement; and he shows how rationalism bred reaction, partly under the influence of war. This age

ideas (with which in the main I am not concerned) and of clever men for whom nothing remained unquestioned. In this world—we hardly need the testimony of Aristophanes to tell us this, though he tells it in unmistakable terms—Euripides was a poet of the avant-garde. He was *sophos* and addressed himself, in part, to *sophoi* ('the wise').

And the word is constantly on the lips of his characters. It is hard, if not impossible, to say when this echoes the tones of intellectual conversation in Athens and when it betrays the idiosyncrasy of the poet. The tendency, for instance, to state or re-state moral values in terms of *sophia* and *amathia* ('ignorance') is likely to have character-ized sophistic thinking,[5] whereas the way in which Euripides is pre-pared to turn the most incongruous characters, permanently or temporarily, into 'sophists'[6] betokens his sometimes cavalier attitude to characterization. In the *Bacchae* the true nature of *sophia* is an issue of the play,[7] but an ironical twist is given to the debate by Teiresias, the clever man who declines to play the sophist with the gods and then goes on to give a dazzling exhibition of sophistry and sophistication. If I say that Euripides was a sophisticated poet, it would no doubt be well to define the term, but I shrink from the task. It is an odd development of language that a word which began as a term of disparagement is now so often used as a term of praise. Perhaps one might say, with truth, that Euripides is, or can be, sophisticated in both the good and the bad senses of the word. It is the main purpose of this article to consider the sheer cleverness of Euripides in two lights: to consider him as a

---

indeed, like all ages, blended new and old in a proportion desperately hard to determine. Should we not, then, be cautious in ascribing to an ancient author mental attitudes familiar from the modern world? It depends upon the common ground; and so sober and judicious a scholar as Professor W. K. C. Guthrie has recently said of the Athenian Enlightenment (Guthrie 1968, 22): 'I need not expatiate on the amount of common ground that exists between this moral climate and our own: the relativism, the abandonment or reversal of previously accepted standards, the permissiveness, the widespread diversity of opinion.'

[5] e.g. *Heracld.* 881 (cf. 965); *Phoen.* 499; *Or.* 417, 490 ff. (cf. Winnington-Ingram 1969b, 53). For *sophia* in moral contexts prior to Euripides see O'Brien 1967, 24, but the sharp confrontation of the *kalon-* ('noble') and *sophon-*standards is new and characteristic.

[6] For Menelaus in the *Orestes* pp. 57–8 below. Jocasta in the *Phoenissae* is hardly a sophist, yet *sophos* and similar words are constantly on her lips (65, 86, 394, 414, 453, 460, 530, 569 f., 584): she has been made the standard-bearer.

[7] Cf. Winnington-Ingram 1966, 34–7 (and 1948, 88 f., 162, 167).

sophisticated poet and (closely related but not identical) as a poet in pursuit of novelty.[8]

Euripides, who wrote plays of different sorts, was sophisticated at different levels; and it is obvious that the less seriously his thought and feelings were engaged the more scope, the more excuse, there was for sophistication. Sometimes, certainly, and in some sorts of play, he wrote to amuse—to amuse himself and his clever friends in the audience—to amuse and perhaps to shock. 'What has come over Apollo? I must give him a piece of my mind,' says the young Ion, when he has heard Creusa's story about her 'friend'.[9] Raping virgins and leaving them in the lurch? Begetting children and (so Ion thinks) leaving them to die? The temple-servant goes on to preach his little sermon, the temple-treasurer to say that, if Apollo and Poseidon and Zeus had to pay fines for rape, they would empty the treasures of their temples. How seriously is this meant to be taken? It is, surely, a piece of cleverness intended to amuse: it is sophisticated fun, or wit. This is not to deny that Euripides was critical of Apollo or that he thought immoral stories about the gods were dangerous. But for serious criticism we must look elsewhere in the play. We must look to Creusa's monody,[10] in which she recalls the scene of her childhood, singing how the radiant golden-haired god of music found her gathering flowers, took her by the hand into the cave and lay with her, while she cried out for her mother. This monody was written by a great poet who could enter into the feelings of a young girl and could use a consummate gift for lyric poetry so as to bring the brilliant attributes of the god into ironic contrast with the cruelty of his act. To do so was indeed clever and original (and no one but Euripides could have written the song), but it was not in any sense sophisticated. It *was* sophisticated, however, at the end of the play, to make Athena explain the non-appearance of an embarrassed Apollo.[11] And it was sophisticated, at the end of another play (*Electra*),[12] not merely to accuse the Delphic god of uttering a foolish oracle, but to put the criticism into the mouth of a fellow-god.[13]

---

[8] This aspect of Euripides has recently been well treated by Webster 1968, 27–45, to which I make references below.   [9] *Ion* 436 ff.

[10] *Ion* 881 ff. See also p. 59 below.   [11] *Ion* 1557 f.

[12] *El.* 1245 f., cf. 1302.

[13] But new in divine circles. The recent apotheosis of the Dioscuri was hardly a matter which the clever Euripides could take seriously, and there is perhaps a tone of faint ridicule in references to it, here and elsewhere.

'Phoebus,' says Castor to Orestes, 'Phoebus—he is my patron, so I keep silence. He is clever, but there was nothing clever about his oracle to you.'

If Apollo is harshly treated by Euripides, this may have been partly because he saw an irritating and harmful falsity in the prestige of the Delphic oracle; partly no doubt it reflects that general animus against the gods which pervades his theatre. The topic is too large for discussion here. There are the real—and really frightening—gods like Dionysus and Aphrodite, who are treated seriously in the action, though they may be satirized in their mythological character, with a satire which can itself be serious. The significance of Hera in the *Heracles*—the degree of reality which she represents—has been much debated, but, certainly, when words of justice are accumulated to prepare the entry of Iris and Lyssa,[14] this is serious satire against the divine government of the world. When, however, Lyssa, the goddess of frenzy, shrinks from her task and is rebuked by Iris for her *sōphrosynē*,[15] the element of sheer cleverness has crept in. *Lussa sōphronousa* ('madness being sensible'): there could be no more sophisticated conception, nothing more calculated to delight a young intellectual in the audience.

In all these judgments, where high themes are involved, there is bound to be a subjective factor. Let us come down to earth and consider technique. To a sophisticated poet—a 'modern' writing for 'moderns'—Aeschylus was fair game. In the *Electra* Euripides ridiculed the recognition-scene of the *Choephori*: the lock, the footprints, the fabric.[16] Critics have shaken their heads, as they asked themselves why he should have done such a thing, in such apparently bad taste. He may indeed have had some respectable reasons connected with the dramatic shape and characterization of his own play: a

---

[14] *Her.* 733, 739 f., 756, 772, 776, 813; contrast 842.   [15] *Her.* 855, 857.

[16] *El.* 524 ff. (fully discussed by Denniston 1939). Cf. Lloyd-Jones 1961, 177–81, from whom (180) I quote: 'I see no good reason to doubt that in this scene Euripides amused himself at the expense of what seemed to him the primitive technique of his predecessor.' We need not deny that Electra has a motive. Her first objection—her first example of the old man's 'silliness' (524)—is expressed in 525 f.: the idea that her brave brother would come in secret; it is only then that she proceeds to demolish the evidence. Adams 1935, 120, may well be right when he says: 'Where the Aeschylean Electra would believe but cannot, the Euripidean would disbelieve but is afraid,' but he goes too far in saying: 'It is Electra attacking the evidence, not Euripides attacking the *Choephoroe*.' It is both.

recognition which he wished to delay, an Electra reluctant to face the unheroic truth about her brother. But this is not a sufficient answer. Nor is it enough to point to the ironical (and amusing?) fact that Electra turns out to be wrong and the Paedagogus right.[17] This was not the only occasion on which Euripides implied a criticism of Aeschylean technique: there is a couple of lines in the *Phoenissae*[18] which undoubtedly hit at the central scene of the *Septem*, and there is a passage in the *Supplices*[19] which may be aimed at a lost Aeschylean messenger speech. The question remains, therefore, why Euripides should have done such a thing. It has been thought malicious, but no one can tell us why he should have felt malice towards an eminent predecessor so long dead. It is not malice so much as an exhibition of cleverness. It was clever to score points at the expense of the archaic technique of the older poet;[20] and these points will have been appreciated by the young Aristophanes, who, some years later, was to put Aeschylus and Euripides together upon the comic stage. Wilamowitz, who did not approve, chided Euripides[21] for behaving like the caricature of himself in the *Frogs*, but perhaps the attitude of the Aristophanic Euripides may not have been so remote from the Euripides of real life as we are accustomed to think.[22]

If Aeschylus was fair game, so too were the stage conventions within which he worked so happily, and within which Euripides, often so unhappily, had to work. These conventions—notably the constant presence of the chorus, the flexible treatment of place and time—depended upon a willingness on the part of the audience to

[17] As wrong as Menelaus at *Or.* 1556–60. Are 'rationalists' ever right in Euripides?

[18] *Phoen.* 751 f., cf. Fraenkel 1963, 56 and n. 1. Euripides has already described the Argive champions, by a more 'modern' and naturalistic method, in the highly original scene between Antigone and the Paedagogus; and it would be pointless to give the names of the Thebans.

[19] *Suppl.* 846–56. Cf. Fraenkel 1963, who cites Wilamowitz 1923, i. 202. One could, but need not, see criticism of Aeschylus at *El.* 671 ff.

[20] There is some reason to suppose that the *Choephori* had been revived in the late 420s, cf. Newiger 1961, 422 ff.

[21] Wilamowitz 1896, 2. 169: 'er hat sich benommen wie Voltaire gegen Maffeis Merope, oder besser, als wäre er sein eigenes Zerrbild in den Fröschen'.

[22] Cf. Lloyd-Jones 1961, 180: 'It is dangerous to talk as if the caricatures of Aeschylus and Euripides in the *Frogs* were meant for exact portraits. But if we could know what Euripides really thought of Aeschylus, it might be in some ways closer to the attitude of the Aristophanic Euripides than to that of . . .' (I omit the name of the scholar in question). It could have been part of the fun for part of the audience that Euripides is made to say, with comic exaggeration, the sort of things that he actually used to say.

exclude those realistic considerations which would destroy them. There is reason to suppose that, in the later fifth century, the goodwill that had once been forthcoming was no longer to be taken for granted in all quarters; that realism was creeping in, with a demand for clarity (*to saphes*) and plausibility (*to pithanon*). We may take an example from Sophocles.[23] Electra is warned not to betray her joy; there is no fear of that, she says, since her ancient hatred is engrained upon her. A reference, as the editors rightly say, to her unchanging mask. It is significant that in this relatively late play Sophocles thought it necessary or suitable to excuse a lack of realism which would have passed unnoticed in the mid-fifth century. No one would suspect Sophocles of an ulterior motive. But can we be so sure that Euripides is never amusing himself and others at the expense of stage conventions?

A crucial, if minor, case is to be found in the *Orestes*. Three actors only were available to the Greek tragedians; and this conventional restriction resulted from time to time in arrangements which lacked plausibility. Tecmessa has to be silent throughout the second half of the *Ajax*; in the *Ion* Xuthus has to be dispatched on not very plausible business.[24] So, in the *Orestes*, Pylades, who has played a prominent part in organizing the intrigue, is represented, when it gets under way, by a mute person. Well and good: the audience was used to it, and there was plenty of excitement to distract. But Euripides causes Menelaus to address a question to the silent Pylades which Orestes answers for him: 'his silence gives consent'.[25] There is no dramatic necessity for this question to be asked nor is any dramatic purpose served by it. It is completely gratuitous, which makes it hard to believe that the poet is not hitting at the three-actor rule. But how, it may be asked, did the audience know that Pylades was in fact taken by a mute person? The answer is that they did not know—until he was addressed and failed to reply. Then an Aristophanes may have turned to his neighbour and whispered that a *deus* was due *ex machina*; and some thirty lines later Apollo, for whom the third actor had been held in reserve, duly appears.[26]

A minor, if revealing, instance. The basic dramatic convention was the presence of the chorus. This could be awkward when an

---

[23] Soph. *El.* 1296 f., 1309 ff.   [24] *Ion* 1125 ff.
[25] *Orestes* 1592 (φησὶν σιωπῶν).
[26] For the closing scene see p. 58 below.

intrigue was in progress; and all students of Euripides are aware that, from time to time, he calls attention to this awkward presence instead of glossing it over.[27] A tribute to realism? Perhaps. When, however, in the *Orestes*, Electra tells the Chorus to go away and not wake up the hero, it is, as Kitto says, 'a new experience for this ancient institution',[28] and we may be entitled to find it amusing. Again, the chorus is continuously present, but (by a fairly strict convention) confined to the orchestra and not permitted to approach or enter the stage-building. When, in the *Agamemnon*, the Elders hear the death-cry of the king but cannot intervene, the difficulty which confronted Aeschylus arose out of the situation:[29] the poet did not create it for himself. In the *Hippolytus*, however, Euripides makes Phaedra tell the Chorus to listen at the door, which they cannot do; they remind her that she is close to it and say she must listen for herself.[30] It seems oddly dragged in. While we dare not suppose that at this tense moment of a serious play the poet is aiming to provoke a smile, it is not quite out of the question that he is indicating how much more realistically he could have produced the scene, if the convention had allowed.

It was the choral convention, largely, that necessitated the flexible treatment of place and time, the agreement to be vague which was threatened by the demand for clarity. When, in the *Helen*, the Egyptian king explains that he has buried his father outside the front door so that he can salute him as he goes in and out of the palace, is this a tribute to realism? Or is it a hit at the conventional treatment of locality in the *Choephori*, where the scene shifts unobtrusively from

[27] At *Med.* 1275 ff. the non-entry of the Chorus is emphasized by their being overheard from within; at *Hipp.* 776 ff., less strongly, by the imperative of 777. On *Hipp.* 575 ff. see below. Barrett 1964 on *Hipp.* 710–12 gives a full list of cases in which silence is requested or required of a chorus. It would be interesting to know if the Chorus of the *Ion* was the first to disobey.

[28] 'Not only does the general situation not readily accommodate a chorus, but as Orestes is asleep on the stage, its arrival is actually a nuisance. Euripides boldly makes capital out of this by allowing Electra to treat the chorus as a nuisance; it becomes fifteen sympathetic but untimely visitors who are earnestly implored to stop singing and to go home again' (Kitto 1961, 346). When, at *IT* 64–6, Iphigenia looks in vain for the Chorus, who have not yet arrived, this may have struck some as amusing, but I do not press the point.

[29] On Aeschylus' handling of the difficulty see Winnington-Ingram 1954, 23–30.

[30] *Hipp.* 575 ff. Barrett 1964 ad loc. does his best for his author: 'Request and refusal in fact underline the lack of verisimilitude; but their purpose is to draw out the scene and so let the tension build up as we wait to hear the worst.' The convention is reviewed by Arnott 1962, 34–40, who discusses this passage on p. 36.

tomb to palace-front?[31] Since the tone of the *Helen* is often light, and since Euripides does elsewhere make game of the archaic Aeschylus, the second explanation seems more likely to be correct. As to time, it is telescoped by Euripides, as by the other dramatists, in a perfectly acceptable manner and, in particular, the singing of a choral ode may represent whatever duration (within the day) the action requires. There is, however, one very odd case. In the *Electra*, Orestes and Pylades have gone off to murder Aegisthus, and the Chorus sings its ode. The normal thing would be to bring on a messenger at the end of the ode to tell the story, but Euripides, for whatever reason, frustrates expectation.[32] He gives us, before the messenger, a short dialogue between Electra and the coryphaeus which is on original lines. Electra, who has no great confidence in this brother, is on tenter-hooks. Sounds have been heard from afar, but the outcome is not clear.[33] She contemplates suicide, and the coryphaeus urges her to wait. 'Impossible,' she says, 'We are beaten, for where are the messengers?' 'They will come,' replies the coryphaeus; and the very next line is spoken by a messenger, though only seven lines have elapsed since the last reference to the remoteness of the noise. The passage contributes something, though nothing new, to the characterization of Electra; it is lively and novel, but one may still ask why Euripides thought good to introduce a telescoping of time which is quite without parallel.[34] The messenger was a formal convention of Greek tragedy.[35] Can it be that Euripides was thinking of the inevitable promptitude with which tragic messengers arrive? 'Where are the messengers?' asks Electra. She need not worry: the

---

[31] In effect, the first half is played at the tomb, the second half before the palace, but there is, strictly, no change of scene: the tomb is apostrophized at 722–4, and 264 ff. imply the vicinity of the palace.   [32] *El.* 747 ff.

[33] The sounds—a low rumbling noise—are first heard by the Chorus, who summon Electra. She too has heard the cries: τηλόθεν μέν, ἀλλ' ὅμως. The coryphaeus replies: μακρὰν γὰρ ἕρπει γῆρυς, ἐμφανής γε μήν ('Distant, but still audible', 'The sound travels far, but is clear all the same').

[34] In tragedy. In comedy cf., for example, the *Acharnians*, where Amphitheus leaves for Sparta at 132 and returns (out of breath, though for a different reason) at 175, without an intervening ode.

[35] Euripides was well aware of the conventional nature of such speeches. *Ion* 1106 ff. is quite the wrong moment, realistically considered, for a long speech, but the poet proceeds to give us one of his longest (1122–1228), complete with an elaborate description of the banqueting-tent. It is lamely (or humorously) justified in terms of feminine curiosity. But the audience liked messenger-speeches and Euripides was good at writing them: we may be glad that he wrote this one.

death of a king in tragedy cannot fail to be followed, promptly, by a messenger's speech.[36]

What has been said so far may strike the reader as repugnant or even abhorrent. Here we have Euripides, one of the world's great tragedians, and he seems to spend his time making sophisticated jokes at the expense of gods, of Aeschylus, and of stage conventions. A sophisticated poet: thus, a coterie poet? An Alexandrian before his time?[37] And therefore, in the strict sense, an unpopular poet, seeking the plaudits of the sophisticated few? Such a competitor would not have lasted long in the emulous world of fifth-century tragedy, nor have we good reason to suppose that Euripides lacked popular appeal.[38] He may have obtained few first prizes (he had to compete against Sophocles), but he got his choruses, he got fame and the backhanded accolade of Aristophanes. So far from despising popular success, he saw the ways—certain ways—to popular favour and pursued them. He had a gift for pathos and a gift for theatrical intrigue; and both were to the taste of the day. What is often said of Sophocles—that he was primarily a man of the theatre—may be even more true of Euripides. At the same time he was a great tragedian; and at the same time he was an intellectual of the avant-garde, who could not resist the temptation to amuse himself, to amuse his fellow-intellectuals, and of course to infuriate the old-fashioned and conventional. There is about the Aristophanic Euripides—of the *Acharnians*, the *Thesmophoriazusae* and the *Frogs*—an intolerable superiority. Allow for comic exaggeration, and for the tradition of *alazoneia* ('braggartry') essential to Old Comedy, and perhaps we are left with something authentically Euripidean.

It is hard to pin down Euripides. But then it is hard to pin down the late-fifth-century audience, which included Nicias and Alcibiades, Agathon and Sophocles, and thousands of undistinguished Athenians

---

[36] 'The Messenger does, in fact, arrive with remarkable speed, close on the heels of the cries, without even an intervening choral ode to gloss over the lack of realism' (Denniston 1939). But what is the point of οὔτοι βασιλέα φαῦλον κτανεῖν? 'A king, unlike an ordinary person, has his attendants, and these have to be disposed of' (Denniston 1939)? This, by explaining the 'delay', would call attention to its absence. Or does it mean: the killing of a king is no small matter—and therefore bound to be signalized by a messenger-speech?

[37] And in certain aspects he was indeed a forerunner not only of New Comedy but of Callimachus.

[38] For a judicious review of the evidence see Stevens 1956, 87–94.

of all ages, all temperaments, and all tastes. One thing is certain that, collectively and on the average, this was not the audience of the mid-fifth century. For one thing far more tragedies had been written, produced and seen. Tragedies had been produced in competition since 533 BC. Between 480 and 430 some five hundred had been staged; and a middle-aged man in the audience of Euripides might well have seen two hundred or more, in which familiar stories had been treated again and again. If he was conservatively-minded, he wanted the new tragedies to be just like the old; and he admired Sophocles because, on the whole, he wrote the older style of play. Young men and doubtless many of the middle-aged (and not only the intelligentsia) were restive, ever anxious 'to hear some new thing'. They welcomed novelty. They welcomed the novelties of Euripides and Agathon.

Agathon, so Aristotle tells us,[39] invented a new plot not drawn from myth, with imaginary characters. Dramatists, however, stuck mainly to the old stories. Even so, says Aristotle,[40] the poet must use invention; and it has not escaped the notice of interpreters that Euripides has, from time to time, a free and innovating way with the traditional plots.

The story of the Pelopidae was famous. We do not know how often it had been treated before and after Aeschylus, but one can imagine that to write a new play about Orestes, Electra and the matricide in the penultimate decade of the fifth century might well present a challenge to the dramatist. Euripides transferred the action from the palace to a small farm in the hills. Electra is married—has been married off—to a peasant; and, since the peasant has refrained from consummating the marriage, she is in the anomalous position of a virgin wife—a novel situation which Euripides exploits.[41] Orestes slips unobtrusively across the frontier, to the disgust of his sister; and ways have to be found to bring first Aegisthus and then Clytemnestra out of this remote spot to be murdered. It is novel and ingenious,[42] and we need not suppose that it was only the sophisticated who enjoyed it, though some people will have felt that it lowered the dignity of tragedy. (And Sophocles was to show, some years later,[43]

---

[39] *Poet.* 1451^{b}21.   [40] *Poet.* 1453^{b}25.

[41] We should not forget that the audience of the *Electra* was also the audience of the *Lysistrata*; the implications of *El.* 215 ff. are obvious.

[42] Cf. Webster 1968, 39 ff.

[43] The debate on the chronology of the two *Electras* continues. See Vögler 1967 and H. Lloyd-Jones' review (1969a, 36–8). Despite Vögler and Lloyd-Jones, I still

that it was still possible to write a brilliant *Electra* on more traditional lines.)

Having treated the matricide in the *Electra*, Euripides went on, in the *Orestes*, to deal with the next phase of the story, to show what happened to Orestes and Electra after the murders. The first decision he took was to reverse the roles: it should now be Orestes, as it was then Electra, who is blind to all sense of reality, with a more realistic sibling. Then, by a bold anachronism, he made the people of Argos play a part, threatening to execute the murderers by judicial process. But Menelaus and Helen have arrived. A traditional Helen, who comes for murder or apotheosis, but first earns her keep in the prologue, where her little scene with Electra is a gem of felinity; the claws of adulteress and virgin are both out.[44] (Euripides was a misogynist or else he was the first feminist or else the charges cancel out.) With Menelaus the question is whether he will or will not act to save the nephew who has avenged his brother. Before it is decided, and to the surprise of all, there enters old Tyndareus, the father of Helen and Clytemnestra.[45] Confronted with his grandfather and his uncle, Orestes (one may suggest) plays his cards badly. He pins his hopes on Menelaus and appeals to traditional sentiment, to the bond of *philia* ('kinship'), but Menelaus (whom Aristotle thought inexcusably bad)[46] is a cold calculating sophistical politician who would like the throne for himself. Tyndareus is a stern old man, a traditionalist[47]—and like so many traditionalists rather sentimental: he cannot understand how Orestes could have resisted the appeal of Clytemnestra's breast, the mere thought of which reduces him to tears.[48] His strong disapproval of his scandalous daughter was, however, something on which Orestes could have built, but instead he is rude to the old man and clever, and so forfeits his one real

incline to maintain the priority of Euripides, but the issue is far too complex for discussion here.

[44] *Orestes* 71–135. For 72 Electra has to wait for her revenge but gets it at 99. A typical touch is 128 f.

[45] 'Not a frequent visitor to the Athenian stage': so Kitto 1961, 346, who has good comments on the debate.

[46] And thought it worth saying twice: *Poet.* 1454[a]29, 1461[b]21. Menelaus is not only a sophist, but a man of elegance (349). He is particularly horrified by the squalor of Orestes' outward appearance (385 ff.), which must have amused those who had seen the shipwrecked Menelaus of the *Helen.*

[47] On the contrast between Menelaus and Tyndareus see Winnington-Ingram 1969*b*, 53. [48] *Or.* 526 ff.

chance of support. However that may be, Orestes and Electra were
condemned; and this leads to an exciting intrigue, in which Pylades
plays a more prominent role than was doubtless usual in these plays.
Helen is murdered: at least we are made to think so, but then learn
that she disappeared into thin air. The story is told in a monody by
a Phrygian eunuch who escapes from the palace. Hermione is kid-
napped and, with a knife at her throat, used to blackmail Menelaus.
The palace is set on fire. What will Menelaus do? Capitulate, or lose
his daughter and the palace on which he has set his heart? The
action is poised in suspense, when Apollo appears *ex machina* above
the stage-building and restores the play to traditional mythology. It is
a skilful, exciting, and successful drama,[49] which enjoyed a well-
deserved popularity in the Hellenistic world. It is full of novelty and
has at least one interesting technical innovation, to which reference
has already been made. We return to technique.

For, if Euripides sought novelty of plot or situation, he was
particularly concerned, like all practising dramatists, with questions
of technique. When Sophocles and Euripides met in the agora (they
probably dined in different circles), they will not have talked about
justice and the gods, but rather about stichomythia, monodies, and
the use of the machine. One technical problem which faced both
Sophocles and Euripides was that of the messenger speech. The Greek
theatre observed, broadly, the unity of place; events occurring at
a distance or even within the house[50] had to be reported, and the
traditional technique, going back no doubt to the first beginnings of
tragedy, was the speech of a messenger or some character who could
serve as such.[51] But, in the working out of a plot, it might be necessary
or convenient for off-stage events to be conveyed to the audience
on more than one occasion. Second messengers are not avoided, but
their speeches tend to be short; two full-scale messenger-speeches are
rare.[52] In the *Orestes*, there has already been one long messenger
speech on traditional lines, describing the trial of Orestes. How then
is the audience to be told what happened to Helen within the palace?

---

[49] It is perhaps rather surprising that a play of this character has been regarded as
a serious treatment of the ethics of matricide or a serious response to the *Electra* of
Sophocles.   [50] Subject to use of the eccyclema.
[51] Cf. di Gregorio 1967 and Lloyd-Jones' review (1969*b*, 38 f.).
[52] In *IT* the two speeches—of the Boukolos (260 ff.) and of the Messenger
(1327 ff.)—are widely separated. In the *Bacch.* Euripides makes a special effect of the
parallelism between the two speeches (677 ff., 1043 ff.).

The solution found by Euripides was a *singing* messenger.[53] The song of the Phrygian eunuch was a twofold novelty: it was not only a new kind of messenger speech but also a new use for the monody.

Fashions in music and metre changed like everything else; and Euripides was naturally in the van, like his friend Timotheus.[54] To 'modern' music reactions will have been as diverse then as they are today. We no longer have the music, whether of Sophocles or Euripides, and can say little about it. One thing is clear, however, that a fashion developed for *soli* sung by an actor, and, though these were sometimes organized in strophe and antistrophe, there was a tendency for them to break away into a freer form.[55] Euripides wrote such monodies in his later plays with great brilliance and to diverse effect. The longest and most original is the song of the Phrygian, exotic and exciting. Reference has already been made to the monody of Creusa in the *Ion*, in which she tells the story of her rape by Apollo: it is vivid and also extremely poignant. There is another musical number in the same play which well illustrates the originality and inventiveness of the poet.

The play opens with a prologue speech by Hermes, from whom we learn, among other things, that Ion (not yet so called) had been brought up a foundling in the temple at Delphi and given a responsible position as guardian of the treasures. Hermes withdraws, when he sees Ion coming out. He is coming out to sweep the approach to the sanctuary, before the proceedings of the day begin. He does not come alone. There are Delphians in attendance, whom he dispatches after a few lines to fetch water from the Castalian spring. There may be several reasons for their presence,[56] but one is that they are needed to carry things. Ion needs a broom and water-jugs as well as his bow and arrows; and he can hardly have entered carrying everything, like a Xanthias in comedy. There is a little procession: Ion with his bow (and for Apollo's son to appear in the temple-doorway with the attribute of Apollo is a point in itself), followed by a little band of Delphians carrying the rest of the equipment. The opening part of his solo is declaimed in processional anapaests. Then, when he has sent his attendants away, he puts down the bow, picks up a broom, and

---

[53] A messenger so picturesque and full of possibilities that, assuming 1503–36 are genuine, Euripides could not refrain from adding a scene between him and Orestes which does not quite fit the dramatic situation. See, however, Gredley 1968, 409–19.

[54] On Timotheus see Webster 1967, 17 ff.   [55] Cf. Webster 1967, 285 f.

[56] To enhance the status of Ion, for instance.

begins to sing—and of course to dance: a broom-dance that mimes the sweeping of the stylobate.[57] The structure is formal, strophe and antistrophe with refrains (or ephymnia); and since refrains were probably a feature of the hymn-style, and since the metre is hieratic,[58] the effect is at once realistic and ritualistic. Then formal structure is abandoned, and Ion sings the rest of his song in free lyric anapaests. First he pours water out of the pots: more mime, more ballet. Then comes a famous scene which was recognized by an ancient critic[59] as giving scope to the actor, as he dashes for his bow and looks up to the sky, threatening the birds that defile the sanctuary with their droppings.[60] At the end of his monody Ion moves away. The Chorus enters; and we soon realize that they are not only the servants of Creusa but sightseers from Athens who have never been to Delphi before and are full of a naive enjoyment at what they see. These brilliantly written scenes are full of points, visual, verbal and dramatic, which could be studied at length. My present purpose is merely to call attention to the lightness of touch, to the novelty, to the cleverness and inventiveness which the poet shows.

The foregoing remarks and illustrations have indicated a possible approach to Euripides which, I suggest, should neither be neglected nor over-emphasized. Let me now try to put the matter into focus. I began by speaking about Euripides as a sophisticated writer addressing himself to other sophisticated persons, having and giving sophisticated fun, if fun is the right word: there may be touches of restiveness and resentment. This is an aspect of the poet which no sensible critic would wish to stress too much, but which ought not to be ruled out of court by those who like to take their Euripides seriously all the time. The number of people in the audience who

[57] Webster 1968, 31, suggests that this 'would have been accepted as a brilliant modernization of the ball-dance in Sophocles' *Nausicaa*'. Naturally we cannot say how often special dances had been introduced in lost tragedies, but Webster gives a salutary warning (1968, 27) 'that what seems to us to be Euripidean innovation may in fact be traditional in the sense that he borrowed it from an earlier play of Sophocles'. Equally, of course, he may be repeating an innovation of his own.

[58] 'These lines of molossi may be a Delphic hymn, known to Athenian visitors, a touch of local colour' (Owen 1939 on *Ion* 125–7). Collocations of long syllables (in different metres?) are not uncommonly found in religious poetry. The metrical problems are sometimes considerable, and the subject deserves careful study.

[59] Demetrius, *On Style* 195.

[60] I trust it will not be thought indelicate, if I point out that the birds in question are not sparrows, but an eagle and a swan.

enjoyed a hit at Aeschylus may not have been large, but need not have been small.[61] Cleverness may be suspect, but the flattering implication that you yourself are clever has its appeal, as Aristophanes—and Bernard Shaw—well knew. The number of people who sought, who demanded, or who enjoyed, novelty in the theatre may well have been large. Clearly, this is a much more important aspect of Euripides than his esoteric wit. He recognized and met the demand for novelty, not only because it was congenial to his temperament, but because it was one way to the popular favour he did not despise.

Indeed it may well be asked how far Euripides led and how far he followed popular taste. The rhetoric which pervades his theatre was not a personal idiosyncrasy, but an addiction of the Athenian people. If he tended to open his plays (in the so-called playbill prologues) with a lucid statement, it was not merely that he himself shrank from lengthy and indirect expositions[62] but that the Athenian audience— or a large section of it—now demanded lucidity (*to saphes*) as well as cleverness (*to sophon*), being accustomed in the law-courts to be presented with a clear statement of the facts of the case. They were tired of waiting while an Aeschylus pursued a traditional craft of gradual exposition. Equally, they were tired of always knowing what was going to happen. And so Euripides gave them his exciting intrigues, full of unexpected turns and of suspense carried to the ultimate point, right up to the appearance of a *deus ex machina*.[63] I have already suggested that Euripides knew his strong points and exploited them. It is a minimal explanation of the *Hecuba* that he gave the people first the pathos of Polyxena, then the excitement of Hecuba's vengeance for Polydorus. The explanation is minimal, since Euripides had so much more to give to those who were equipped to take it. But, whatever he gave, he gave with a personal flavour, with a twist of his own mind, which some liked and some disliked, while others did not know quite what to think.

There is Euripides at his most sophisticated, who may or may not amuse us, who is an interesting phenomenon in the history of thought and writing, but not of the first consequence. There is Euripides the restless innovator and experimenter, popular and

---

[61] Though, according to Professor K. J. Dover's acute observation in his edition of Aristophanes' *Clouds* (1968, 253), they were likely to have been under forty!

[62] Which did not in any case suit his attitude to the mythical past.

[63] e.g. in the *Orestes* (what will Menelaus do?); in the *IT* (what will the wind do?).

unpopular, leading taste and following it, but in all things a highly professional playwright, a practitioner, even a cool practitioner, with a detachment which is sometimes disconcerting. And there is Euripides the great poet and dramatist, who is not the subject of this article—the Euripides who wrote the *Hippolytus* and the *Bacchae*. It is a question, partly, of kinds of play; and it will have been observed that my illustrations have been taken mainly from plays which are generally recognized to be less than tragic in their tone and treatment (and which are relatively late). The work of Euripides, however, defies precise classification. Elements of his greatness may be found in any kind of play—his knowledge of the human mind; his sympathy (intermittent, perhaps, but genuine) with human predicaments; his insight into the forces which mould human society, into moral values and social standards (and the ways in which people can be led astray by false standards); his sense of the devastating, destructive power of blind emotion, his capacity to convey it and sometimes, but not always, to render it tragic. Where we find these things must often be a matter of subjective judgment.

Let us glance quickly again at the *Ion*. After the prologue speech of Hermes, after the brilliant ballet of Ion's monody, after the chorus of sightseers, we have a long scene between Ion and Creusa (itself a technical tour de force in the exacting form of stichomythia),[64] which is a dialogue not only of fantastic skill but of great psychological insight and a certain tenderness, as sympathy develops between the pair who do not yet know that they are mother and son. Yet the characterization built up with such subtlety in this scene—and indeed in the whole first half of the play—seems to go for little when the intrigue develops.[65] Euripides is after other game—after another audience perhaps; and we have something to enjoy, but something of

---

[64] It is in fact the longest passage of stichomythia in extant tragedy.

[65] Cf. Conacher 1967, 283: 'From now on, the Queen's actions, and the ironic situations in which they place her, will be all that interest us in Creusa—a far cry from the pathetic and, despite the improbable plot, potentially tragic characterization hitherto presented.' This seems to me so true that I am slightly sceptical of the same writer's attempt (214) to trace 'a clear line of development' in the hero of the *Orestes*. Webster (1968, 44) speaks of 'the gentle heart-broken Kreousa changing into an inefficient murderess, or the physically starved and mentally crazed Orestes turning into an efficient criminal'; he finds evidence in this of an instability in the characters which, in his view, marks the later plays of Euripides, affecting the action and corresponding to a change in metrical texture. The point is an interesting one. The simple explanation, in some cases, may however be that, when intrigue comes in by the door, psychology flies out at the window.

a different kind. One more illustration, from a very different kind of play. The *Troades* has been called a pageant of the miseries of war, and was inspired perhaps by the sufferings of the Melians. In a series of scenes focused upon Hecuba poignant emotions are aroused, and there is a certain unity of tone (though also of course the bravura of Cassandra's mad marriage-song—another monody). Then, with the entry of Menelaus and Helen, there is a complete change of tone. There is a debate; we become interested, and in very interesting things: in Helen's life in Troy, in moral and philosophical issues, in the question (to which there is an ironical answer) of what Menelaus is going to do. The pageant of miseries is then resumed.

If there are elements of greatness in less serious plays, we must be prepared to find discordant, if not repugnant, features in the greatest tragedies. Of the *Bacchae* I once wrote that, in this play at least, Euripides 'saw his aims clearly and controlled them firmly';[66] and, broadly, I should not wish to go back on this opinion. On reflection, however, if there is any part of that great play which seems not perfectly assimilated to the grand design, it is the Teiresias scene. It has its relevance of course to that design.[67] But may it not be that Euripides became a little too much interested in Teiresias and in satirizing the type which he took him to represent?[68] This is a personal reaction, a subjective qualm, but it makes me wonder whether, in the words of Oscar Wilde, Euripides was not capable of resisting everything except temptation—the temptation to be clever.

---

[66] Winnington-Ingram 1948, 6.   [67] Ib. 57, 163, 169 f.

[68] Ib. 41–58 *passim*. Tyrrell compared him to 'a Broad Church dean'. But where did Euripides hear such sermons? Perhaps he has grafted the ecclesiastical attitudes of a Delphic exegete on to the lecture-room style—the mannerisms, the linguistic subtleties, the ingenious 'modernisms'—of a sophist.

3
Formal Debates in Euripides' Drama[1]

C. COLLARD

The prime dramatic character of Greek tragedy is agonistic. Its myths for the most part show men struggling toward some goal, in conflict with one another, or against some force of circumstance or destiny, which is often personified in a god. Tragedy is at the same time a dramatic form restricted severely by theatrical conditions. The number of its speaking actors is held to three. It avoids the staging of any physical action like an assault or battle, let alone catastrophe, or death—for whatever reasons of narrative tradition, aesthetic convention, or simple impracticability. Despite certain ritual or symbolic aids to representation such as music, dance, and gesture, it is in consequence a drama of extreme, sometimes exclusive, verbal concentration. Exposition, development, climax, resolution, action and reaction—all movement occurs in the narrow room of at most three stage persons at any one time debating to confirm or change their attitudes or intentions—often, with a single character so placed debating within himself, in monologue or soliloquy, or in relief or opposition to another voice. My subject here is this last *mise-en-scène*: the deliberate working up of the ordinary exchange between characters into the opposition of one character to one or two others in a formal debate.

Jacqueline Duchemin has claimed[2] that tragedy's agonistic character—and particularly its formal debates—are in part its natural inheritance from a long popular or pastoral tradition of dramatic poetry—a primitive mimetic poetry, she means, of alternating or amoibaic form, which represents two contrasted characters or interests. She notes that debates as an established dramatic form, the *agōn*

---

[1] A paper read to the Liverpool Branch of the Classical Association in March 1974. I have condensed the main text but added the notes.

[2] Duchemin 1969, 247–75, a supplement to her analytical study Duchemin 1945, esp. pp. 11–37.

of tragedy, appear first in Sophocles and Euripides (that is, in the surviving plays, the earliest of which, the *Ajax*, is generally put at c.450 BC); but they are absent from Aeschylus. Earlier, she had drawn attention to two other literary forms strongly reliant on the formal opposition of characters or forces. One of these, comedy, developed its idiosyncratic *agōn* well before the formal debate became established in tragedy; Duchemin's other analogy, the historians' use of contrast as mode in dramatic narrative or reported argument, is less cogent from the point of synchronism, but indicative in a general way of her truth. The spoken word, and especially the reported argument, is as natural to Greek historiography as it is to Greek poetry, let alone poetic drama, when we consider the chief place of oral epic in time and influence in the Greek literary tradition. Duchemin therefore sees Aeschylus' use of alternating and pointed dialogue, especially stichomythia, as the linear ancestor of the more stylized exchanges in Sophocles and Euripides; she suggests that, while the sudden appearance of formal debates in Sophocles and Euripides around 450 is chiefly through the influence of contemporary developments in sophistic argument and rhetorical technique, it is certainly not due entirely to the sophists or rhetors. Rather, tragedy owes much to the sophists, but may itself have influenced them, from the time of its own sudden growth in Aeschylus' lifetime; it may actually have provided some kind of model for their agonistic discourses or ἀντιλογίαι.

I begin with these general remarks because, despite warnings by sensitive critics,[3] there is still an instinctive temptation to isolate Euripides' formal debates from their dramatic setting. The temptation stems from their often rigidly antithetical and symmetrical appearance in the printed text; I doubt whether these symmetries are quite so immediate to a theatre audience, but an audience is as likely as a reader to pick up the measured matching of arguments within the debates; and Euripides sometimes gives the impression of presenting and matching debating points for their own sake. Older critics of Euripides told us that our instinct is right, and that the poet is guilty

---

[3] Since Tietze's important corrective to older views of Euripidean rhetoric (1933), I would name: Dale 1954, xxvii–xxix (cf. 1969, 151f., 274f.); Clemen 1961, 45–7; Strohm 1957, 3–49 (the richest and most sympathetic study of the *agōn*, to which this paper is more widely in great debt than the particular acknowledgements may suggest); Stinton 1965, 38f. For other literature on the Euripidean formal debate see: Schwinge 1968a, 33 n. 1 ('symmetry'); Lesky 1972, 507 n. 4 (dissertations), and Collard 1975b, commentary on lines 87–262: C (general).

of self-indulgent digression for the sake of rhetorical display, at the cost of dramatic continuity and relevance. Besides, Euripides' formal debates tend to compare badly with those of Sophocles. In this poet the debates are less rigid in structure; they are more naturally accommodated to episodic development; they are always more circumstantial in their argumentation; there is a sense of firm dramatic control as well as harmony of style.[4] Yet debates in Sophocles are often not less evidently 'formal' than in Euripides; at the end of *Ajax*, for example, Menelaus forbids Teucer to bury his brother, in a long rhesis (1052–90); Teucer replies in kind (1093–1117), but then debate gives way to angry argument; the episode ends without resolution, and after a stasimon the final episode (1223 ff.) begins with another formal exchange between Teucer and Agamemnon, running on into the reconciliation worked by the selfless broker Odysseus. There is no stiffness, no lack of circumstance, no feeling of abstraction about these debates, in this earliest surviving play of Sophocles as in the last, the *Oedipus at Colonus*: here, in the long central episode (720–1043), formal exchanges, in rhesis and dialogue, first between Creon and Oedipus, second between Theseus, Creon, and Oedipus, surround a central passage of vigorous action as Creon abducts Antigone and Ismene and then threatens Oedipus—but Sophocles gives the whole episode fluent variety. Form never dominates. Unitary structures, 'blocks' of action or matter, are avoided, for the long speeches are kept at differing lengths and dialogue never settles into stichomythia; there is constant shift in focus and mood, in the pace of argument as well as of action, fitting the busy movement of the characters onto, from, and across the stage.

What is 'formality', then, that it marks off one scene from another, distinguishing organized debate from ordinary exchange? The easier and less satisfactory distinction is purely according to form, less satisfactory because it subjects to taxonomy something not originally specific. Nor can taxonomic description be rigid: formal debates are too various and loose in structure, despite frequent responsion or symmetry between their various elements in position, length, or even content.[5] The only constant features are long 'set' speeches from

[4] Debates in Sophocles, perhaps for these very qualities, have had little separate discussion, but see Webster 1969, 148–55, and Long 1968, 155–60; both note other literature.

[5] It was the major achievement of Tietze (1933) and Duchemin (1945 and 1969) to insist on the irregularity, rather than the regularity, of formal debates.

each of, or all the antagonists—for sometimes there are three, not two, participants—but the length, structure, and style of these speeches are very flexible. Other elements vary even more, and may indeed be altogether absent, so that, at the barest, two opposing speeches stand almost on their own, with little introduction, or consequence, dramatic or thematic. These other elements are, first, animated dialogue, stichomythic or irregular in form, sometimes very long, preceding or following the two main speeches, or, very rarely, between them; second, shorter single speeches by the participants, usually at the end of the debate; and last, brief interventions by the chorus, normally two lines in length, to mark important divisions in the whole structure—that is, they punctuate the debate at the end of the long set speeches, where they tend to have a flatly neutral or sententious character.

The further definition of 'formality' relates to content and style. It is something more, however, than the concentration of the long speeches, or the whole debate, on a single issue toward which the parties have opposite views or intentions. We might describe many dialogue scenes in those terms, most of all those in which one character makes a long appeal to another and receives acceptance or rejection in reasoned terms, quite often in a long reply. It is rather that an issue, or the problems inherent in a crisis, become the subject of a debate through their explicit proposition by one of the participants, in Euripides sometimes through a positive challenge to argument. Indeed, Euripides commonly signals a formal debate with such words as ἀγών, ἀγωνίζεσθαι, ἄμιλλα λόγων ('argument, debate; to argue, to debate; contest of words'). Such headlines, or combative premisses, mark out Euripides' formal debates most obviously from those of Sophocles; and they show his more deliberate recourse to the modes, even formulas, of forensic debate or sophistic argument. So, for example, Tyndareus reviles Orestes for the matricide:

What argument could there be about wisdom with Orestes here? If what is good and what is not good are clear to all, was ever man more fool than he, who did not look for justice nor had resort to Greece's common law? (*Or.* 491–5)[6]

---

[6] 491 πρὸς τόνδε σοφίας τίς ἂν ἀγὼν ἥκοι πέρι; ('What argument could there be about wisdom with Orestes here?') Porson: πρὸς τόνδ᾽ ἀγών τις σοφίας ἥκει πέρι ('Some argument . . . is coming with this man' (unmetrically)) *codd.* Dramatic context and the logic of the argument (cf. below, p. 78) bar Bothe's ἀσοφίας ('about unwisdom') and it must be struck from Murray's OCT.

Such headlines often draw responses which accept the ground of argument marked out by the opponent, as Orestes takes up this attack by Tyndareus:

Old man, I truly fear to speak against you when I am likely to outrage you. I know, for killing my mother I am impure, but under another head, pure, in that I have avenged my father. (*Or.* 544–7)

Even to define formal debates risks isolating them still further in criticism from their dramatic setting. Their success as scenes depends very much on the skill of their introduction to the stage, in the incident from which they spring, and in the harmony of their theme with the main direction of the plot, in terms of the motives or feelings they expose. They can reveal the grounds of disagreement or hostility, present or past (for they are often necessarily retrospective, like the arguments of Theseus and Hippolytus (*Hipp.* 902–1089), or, in *Electra* (998–1146), between Clytemnestra and Electra). In leading to conflict subsequently dramatized or reported by a messenger, we might expect them to occur either at the start of a play or at a critical turn of the action; indeed, most do occur before the climax. Or they may expose the history of a conflict already fought to its end, and so have no outcome except to deepen enmity or confirm hatred, as in the debate between Hecuba and Polymestor at the end of *Hecuba* (1129–1292). Or they may, exceptionally, end in agreement, rather than continuing or exacerbated hostility: so the final scene of *Heracles* in which Theseus argues the hero into enduring life, in continued proof of his ἀρετή ('heroic nature') (1214–1404: see below). Or they may have a more subtle function, as the debate between Admetus and Pheres in *Alcestis* (614–740) serves to reveal Admetus' helpless and angry disillusion after his wife's death. Or, in this same dramatic intention, they may tend to dispose the audience's sympathies towards one or other of the disputants. Here, it is worth noting that the 'winner' of a debate, where victory in it means success for a policy, or 'moral victor', whose just or sympathetic case is rewarded by victory in a subsequent conflict—the 'winner' normally speaks second, and there is no come-back for the first speaker in a reasoned speech of rebuttal, only retaliation with abuse in fast and often colloquial stichomythia.[7]

---

[7] On the order of speakers in formal debates see Schlesinger 1937, 69 f., and, e.g., Dale 1954 on *Alc.* 697.

The starkest debate, least 'natural' in effect, will be one between two characters which pre-empts the dramatic room of a whole episode, thrust abruptly on an audience. The only surviving debate which risks this impression is that in the early *Alcestis* (614–740). Indeed, Euripides moves steadily throughout his work away from two-character debates cast rigidly in block-form towards the greater freedom of three-person scenes incorporating debates, rather than debates simply among three participants.[8] Conflicts most of the debates remain, usually without resolution, and they still most often precede the climax, but there is a refinement in their quality. They tend to show more of the internal constitution of the debaters, in a way consistent with their general role in the action (and this we might expect when we recognize the dovetailing of the debates into episodes): they circumstantiate inflexibility of attitudes, usually in one only of the debaters. The recognition of this more precise but subtle function is due to Strohm,[9] whose book was published before the nature and mode of characterization in Greek tragedy received its newest discussion.

In the early plays, Euripides frequently presents the issues of 'suppliant' drama in a formal debate,[10] which resembles a trial, either of the suppliant or of his persecutor, sometimes of both together. Trial-scenes are as common in the late plays, where the expansion from two to three characters increases variety and flexibility, in stage-movement of the parties, their disposition and sympathies, but also in emotional range. Scenes in which one of two debaters is judge, perhaps even also prosecutor, of the other, are strong but simple drama; it is enough to think again, and only, of Theseus and Hippolytus (*Hipp.* 902–1089). There is at once greater richness, however, in scenes where two debaters plead before a third person who judges them, like Eurystheus' herald and Iolaus before Demophon at the start of *Heraclidae* (111–287), Helen arguing for her life against Hecuba before Menelaus in *Troades* (860–1059)—or where the third party waits helplessly on the outcome of a debate in which one of the debaters has power of decision, like Andromache the beneficiary of Peleus' worsting Menelaus (*And.* 547–765), or in *Phoenissae* (435–637: see below), Jocasta the victim of Polynices' and Eteocles' sterile confrontation. Trial-scenes inevitably are formal debates and

[8] Strohm 1957, 44 f.   [9] Strohm 1957, 46 f.
[10] Strohm 1957, 16 ff.; cf. Gould 1973, 89 n. 76, etc.

feel most successful as drama, for they accommodate convincingly the strongest single external influence on the tragic *agōn* as a whole, the law-court *plaidoyer*. The Athenian audience no doubt responded as readily as we to courtroom drama, because of its immediacy to our own experience and our easy identification with the emotions of the stage-persons—and because the formalities of forensic debate by their very familiarity seem less obtrusive, less interruptive of the illusion of tragic myth. That is something of a paradox, but it relates to the further problem of apparently incongruous intellectual content of these debates which I touch below. In trial-debates the speeches are shot through, exactly as they were in the law-courts of contemporary Athens, with all manner of emotional colour and narrative, or special pleading; and they are carefully organized with calculated switches from attack to defence, pre-emptions of the opponent's argument, appeals to probability, sententious or self-righteous recourse to moral truths.[11] The imagination of transfer from δικαστήριον ('law-court') to σκηνή ('stage') is completed by the accompanying dialogue, carefully phased, where it precedes the long speeches, in its range from methodical question and answer to sudden accelerations in pace as a crack in the defence is widened, or, after the main speeches, impassioned charge and rebuttal, recrimination, hostility and defiance, which are the regular stuff to end formal debates, gain theatricality from the forensic ambience.

If in trial-scenes the mere illusion conspires with the formality, perhaps even artificiality, of some debates, in other places Euripides seems to yield to extraneous pressures in allowing the long speeches to develop a momentum of their own, as a character pursues an argument for its own sake and not that of the basic issue. Sometimes there is damage to the consistency of these persons' ἤθη καὶ διάνοια ('character and thought'), but A. M. Dale wisely told us how to take such excursions as Euripides' own instinctive response to the 'rhetoric of his dramatic situation'.[12] We need to recognize there the poet's intellectual personality breaking poetic convention in an unprecedented way. This greater immediacy, like the whole illusion of the trial-scene, stands with the rhetorical cast Euripides gives not only most speeches in formal debates, but many other long speeches in scenes of quite differing temper (it helps create the impression that

---

[11] For these technical devices see Duchemin 1945, 167–216.
[12] Dale 1954, xxvii–xxix.

there are many more formal contrasts of argument than there actually are). So the easy yielding of any speech to technical analysis, or to taxonomic description with rhetorical labels, must not *de suo* induce its further misappreciation on grounds of irrelevant or digressive content as one governed entirely by its own ends, self-contained and self-indulgent.

The rest of this paper illustrates very selectively the development in Euripides' use of debates between his early and late plays, in the general ways I have described. Some other aspects of debates are left to implicit example.

First three early plays, in which Euripides sets an agonistic scene, or formal debate, at their very end, in order to show a conflict or hatred which lasts beyond the action the whole play has resolved: *Medea, Heraclidae, Hecuba*. Medea, her cruel vengeance taken, escaping on the μηχανή ('machine') in her magic chariot, calls down in triumph to the helpless and embittered Jason (*Med.* 1317 ff.). She rejects his accusation of the children's murder, defiantly refusing him their burial. There are short rheseis, of unequal length, and fierce stichomythia (1323–88), then a final curiously dissonant exchange, in anapaests, half-abusive, half-pathetic; familiar idioms of lamenting parents help the play to its end on a note of tragedy (1389–1414).

This agonistic setting for the final display of Medea's fury is comparable with the end of *Heraclidae*, which shows Alcmena cruelly insistent on the death of captive Eurystheus in vengeance for his persecution of Heracles and the family (*Hcld.* 928 ff.).[13] While Alcmena is clearly the prosecutor (and judge), and Eurystheus the defendant, yet the premiss of her attack is contested before Eurystheus speaks. Euripides brings out the repellent vindictiveness of Alcmena by showing her ride down the moral objection that she flouts the law (of Athens, where they now are), which forbids the execution of captives. Such an objection cannot come from the equally immoral Eurystheus, so that it is raised by a third party, hesitantly by one of Alcmena's own side and, not less significantly, by a servant. Nor is it raised in a rhesis, only in a dialogue between the servant and Alcmena (961–74),[14] which divides her speech of accusation

---

[13] The interpretation of this scene is made hard by major textual uncertainty: see Zuntz 1963, 125 ff., and 1947, 48 ff.

[14] For the distribution of 961–74 between Alcmena and her servant (Barnes, Tyrwhitt) see Zuntz 1963, 125 ff.

(941–60) from Eurystheus' speech in defence (983–1017). Form is adapted to accommodate the priority in dramatic logic. Or, Euripides' conception of the scene required separation of two issues both meriting exposition by formal contrast, the general problem of rights over captives and Eurystheus' particular excuse to Alcmena of being made the agent of Hera's cruelty. So Euripides wrote one loosely agonistic scene, from which the formality of plaintiff and defendant still comes strongly out.[15] That Eurystheus picks up the servant's moral objection, at the end of his speech, in his ambiguous appeal for a life which he admits is justly forfeit (1009 ff.), is in character with his special pleading. It does not lessen the impact of this extraordinary conflict: the former victim is now callous in revenge, the former persecutor now helplessly protests—just as the end of *Medea* reverses the sympathies the play's whole course has fostered. How could Jason merit such vengeance? Is justice truly justice in the hands of Alcmena?

Like Medea, like Alcmena, Hecuba too is extreme in vengeance. The end of the play, it has to be admitted, is weak in dramatic logic. It is hard to know whether Euripides uses the trial-scene (*Hc.* 1129 ff.) to help out this weakness theatrically, or the debate is his chief purpose. The treacherous Polymestor has been lured into the women's tent by Hecuba, with Agamemnon's acquiescence, and blinded; and his sons have been killed. Polymestor returns to the stage, stumbling about in a frenzy of pain, crying his fury in a broken dochmiac song, groping for Hecuba (1056–1107). The noise brings Agamemnon, who is aghast at Hecuba's vengeance, but prevents Polymestor falling on her. 'Stop,' says Agamemnon, 'put away your savagery and speak, that I may listen to you and her in turn and decide the justice of your suffering' (1129–31).

This headline to the ensuing *agōn* is not a little forced, because when Hecuba got Agamemnon's complicity in luring Polymestor to the tent, she gave him a long explanation (760–802) how she sent her son Polydorus for safety to live with Polymestor, together with much gold; and how the discovery of Polydorus' body points to Polymestor as traitor, thief, and murderer. Now, Polymestor, as the unsympathetic defendant, speaks first, and a remarkable speech it is: a specious narrative of how he killed the Trojan Polydorus to prevent an enemy of Agamemnon growing strong behind his back, and then

---

[15] Cf. Duchemin 1945, 76 and 121.

an account, *misericordiae causa*, of the horrible vengeance Hecuba took on him inside the tent (1132–82). In its richly evocative language this is more a messenger-speech than a law-court defence, but Hecuba rebuts it with a conventionally methodical demolition of Polymestor's case (1187–1237).

Agamemnon's role as judge in this trial is artificial: he has already conceded Hecuba the justice of her revenge. Besides, this is no ordinary trial, a debate *post factum*, but one in which both opponents have done murder and injured the other, in which they argue their cases after both have acted in them. Agamemnon thus serves only dramatic realism, in a simple way, compounding the illusion of a stage trial which upholds the justice and immunity of Hecuba, and she is vindicated when Agamemnon banishes Polymestor, the formal act which ends the play. Without Agamemnon we would have a scene like the end of *Medea* or *Heraclidae*, when unquenchable hatred crushes its now pathetic victim. Hecuba and Polymestor come out from Agamemnon's verdict only for a bitter stichomythia (1252–79) in which Hecuba's triumph is turned to ashes when Polymestor prophesies her transformation into a dog and her daughter Cassandra's death from Clytemnestra. Euripides' penchant for aetiology (Hecuba's death and transfiguration at the headland Cynossema: 1271–3) invades even stichomythia here, its function a weak corroboration of the plot's veracity; but it also provides in its harsh meaning for Hecuba Polymestor's only satisfaction for his punishment at her hands. Once again, as in *Medea* and *Heraclidae*, it brings a readjustment of sympathies in the play's last words; it makes us re-examine the extremity of Hecuba's vengeance.

The *Heracles* too, from Euripides' 'middle' period, has a final debate (1214–1404), but one which achieves harmony rather than confirms estrangement. This outcome is implicit from the start in the long-standing friendship of the disputants, Heracles and Theseus. The *agōn* between the two is a contest of will; Theseus forces Heracles to resist the suicide that tempts him as punishment for, and escape from, the shame of having killed his children: he must be true to his ἀρετή ('heroic nature'), must live to surmount dishonour. This is a long scene in which the formality of debate is skilfully concealed. There are four long speeches, two shorter ones by Theseus each preceding a longer one by Heracles, but the central pair are the important ones; and Theseus as 'winner' speaks, as usual, second. Formal variety matches shifting emphasis in theme. Theseus' first speech (1214–28), with its charge to Heracles to brace up, is not answered at once: a stichomythic dialogue (1229–54), in which Theseus presses home this encouragement, avoids the immediate formal opposition of rhesis to rhesis. Heracles' first speech (1255–1310) half takes up Theseus' charge, half moves to new argument; Theseus' second speech (1313–39) has the same form: its first half insists again on Heracles' holding firm, its second half anticipates his concession with its promise of Athenian reward. Similarly again in Heracles' last speech (1340–93), his concession, the formal conclusion of the debate, gives way to pathetic farewells to his father, wife, and dead children. The whole scene thus gets a natural forward movement, avoiding rigidity and 'block-form' for the debate.

In this fluent handling of a debate the *Heracles* has the accomplished style of a late play. The first debate in *Hecuba* (216–443), even earlier than *Heracles*, is also of interest for the greater variety the form enjoys in later Euripides. In a lyric scene Hecuba and Polyxena together lament the daughter's imminent sacrifice to Achilles' ghost (154–215): so two of the participants to the debate, whose sympathies are close and who form one side of it, are shown together before the entry of the third, Odysseus, to fetch the girl (216 ff.). Argument between Hecuba and Odysseus for the girl's life begins at once, but cannot affect what is determined. The victim Polyxena listens in silence, then accepts. Further, the unsympathetic party speaks second here, for good dramatic reasons: the tragedy of the helpless victim is emphasized.

Thus the scene in *Hecuba*, in which a debate is easily incorporated; the episode runs out on one of Euripides' favourite motifs, the voluntary death of a sacrificial heroine. Look now at the strikingly similar course of a scene in *Phoenissae*, which shows perfected technique (435–637).[16] It too has a lyric prelude, in which Jocasta welcomes Polynices on his return to Thebes. She sings a monody (301–54) which conveys passionately an aged mother's yearning for her estranged sons' reunion in happiness. A dialogue between Polynices and Jocasta (357–434) introduces the debate, associating these two participants and building sympathy for Polynices as the wronged exile. His final words to Jocasta are the headline to the debate proper: 'it lies with you, mother, to resolve these wrongs, reconciling

---

[16] For the affinities cf. Duchemin 1945, 122.

kin to amity, and to end the suffering for me, yourself, and the whole city' (435–7).[17]

Three lines from the chorus announce Eteocles' entry, and twice repeat the key-word 'reconciliation'. Eteocles' first words give the debate a familiar start: 'Mother, I am here; it is a favour to you that I have come. What must I do? Let someone start the talking' (446–7). Briefly, Jocasta enjoins the brothers to drop their hostility and to present and receive each other's arguments fairly: 'Let some god be judge and reconcile the wrong', she ends (467–8). Thus, dexterously, Euripides withdraws the third participant, indeed the promoter of the debate, from the position of judge into that of witness and, finally, victim. The brothers argue: Polynices the simple justice of his case, to be restored to Thebes where Eteocles broke their agreement (469–96); Eteocles his greed for sovereignty once enjoyed, unashamedly (499–525). Now Jocasta adds a long plea for reconciliation in which she matches the arguments of her two sons (528–85). Helpless victim Jocasta may be, but Euripides uses her as an independently strong voice in the debate—in the way an audience might react. A clever speech, this: it satisfies the internal logic of the debate proper, answering the general questions it raises; but it also suits the dramatic and ethical needs of the scene. Jocasta has brought the brothers into debate: her speech shows the possible accommodation of their mutual stubbornness and in that throws up the tragedy of what follows. For at once Eteocles rejects further argument (588–93); and the closing dialogue, in the deliberately faster rhythm of tetrameters (594 ff.), typically inflames incompatible stances into implacable enmity. This is well-chosen variation in tempo, matching διάνοια ('thought'), but the quality of the scene goes beyond careful development and pace. Jocasta lays bare Polynices' motives before the debate proper begins; his antagonist, Eteocles, enters only at the start, for he needs no preparation: he is not an exile seeking reparation and his motives are otherwise straightforward. Euripides purposely builds this sudden and vivid conflict of two quite differing personalities, their contrast starker because Eteocles has a rugged selfishness; so it exposes Jocasta's helplessness more cruelly.

Groupings of three participants similar to that in *Phoenissae*, where the sympathy of two is matched against the inflexibility of the third, are found also in *Bacchae* (170–369) and the *Aulic Iphigenia*

[17] 438–42 are an interpolation: Fraenkel 1963, 25 f.

(1098–1275). In *Bacchae* the overtones are more resonant than in *Phoenissae*, the sense of theatre more telling. After the parodos evoking the power of Dionysus, the aged Cadmus and Tiresias affirm their worship of the god in an uneven but natural sequence of short speeches and dialogue (170–214). Then Pentheus enters to deliver a tirade against the Lydian stranger (215–62), blind in his prejudice as he is stage-blind to the old men in their Dionysiac livery. A sure dramatic imagination conceived this argument, in which antagonisms of conviction and submission, of wisdom and arrogance, have countervailing and ironic theatrical contrasts between physical weakness and strength, age and youth. There is no dialogue in the debate, no stichomythic widening of the gulf argument cannot bridge: after the long, responding speeches of Pentheus and Tiresias come irregular shorter rheseis from both sides when Pentheus, isolated by his inflexibility, can retreat only to harsher threats.[18]

The debate in the *Aulic Iphigenia* similarly fills an episode but is even more tersely expressive. Clytemnestra has found out Agamemnon's intention to sacrifice Iphigenia; with her weeping daughter she comes out to confront Agamemnon with his deception (1098 ff.). Iphigenia listens silently to their exchange, as irregular in form as the emotions it depicts. Then Clytemnestra launches into a long repudiation of the sacrifice (1146–1208). The rhesis of Iphigenia follows, supplicating Agamemnon for her life (1211–52); this is a pleading speech, but it deploys pathos, evoking situations of filial love and its return, methodically, like arguments. Both these speeches are set off by distichs from the chorus, but not Agamemnon's reply, for that closes the episode (1255–75). Its brevity, too, is the measure of the scene's success. Agamemnon admits his misery, but also his inability to resist the pressure from both gods and Greeks to punish Troy. The shortness of his answer and the speed of his exit mark his discomfort; and there is no final angry stichomythia to the debate to weaken the impact. The scene leaves an impression of naturalness, therefore— nothing too rigid in the opposition of arguments, though they have been presented and countered in formal style, for these have been subjective and emotional pleas to which surrender or defiance are equally impossible.

---

[18] The sensitive appreciation of the episode by Winnington-Ingram 1948, 40–58, recognizes the real but deftly concealed formality of argument; for the long speeches see pp. 45–53.

Helen shows the same grouping of three participants but in a situation of much lighter charge (857 ff.). Helen and Menelaus plead together, each in long speeches (894–943, 947–95),[19] for the help of Theonoe in escaping her brother Theoclymenus. Theonoe is thus in the role of judge. But the debate is remarkable in two ways. It has extraordinary compactness and symmetry: it begins and ends with a rhesis by Theonoe, its arbiter, and these two speeches (865–93, 998–1029) enclose the two by the appellants, there being no other dialogue. Further, it lacks all hostility, even contrast in argument, for the appellants make common cause for the judge's favour. It is significant here that of the three plays usually classed together as romantic melodramas or intrigues, *Ion*, the *Tauric Iphigenia*, and *Helen*, only *Helen* has this fully formal debate: that in *Ion* (517–675) is very loose in structure, and the *Iphigenia* has only an 'embryonic' *agōn* (674–722).[20] There are no conflicts or explicit animosities between characters in these plays which lend themselves to exposition in the usual way of formal debates. If Euripides does intend contrast with debate-form in *Helen*, and does not simply stage the scene for its own effect or to emphasize formally the crisis, the contrast is subsidiary and ethical: it lies in the differing tones of Helen, who mixes supplication with the claims of right, and of Menelaus, who rests his case straightly and sturdily on right alone.[21]

The very long second episode of the *Orestes* (348–806) is the most subtly contrived of all scenes incorporating a formal debate, and makes the best conclusion to this paper. The chorus sing of the misery and madness in Agamemnon's family. Menelaus enters on his return from Troy (348); he is aware of Agamemnon's and Clytemnestra's death—and of Orestes' condition. Orestes at once engages him in dialogue, entreating his protection against death by public vote for the matricide (380–455). Menelaus' reply is prevented by the entry of Tyndareus, whose joy at greeting him is cut short by finding him in Orestes' company (456–80). A very brief dialogue (481–91) headlines the debate which now follows between Tyndareus and Orestes: the prize is the sympathy of Menelaus, who relapses into the role of third party, or silent judge; he must decide whether to honour his obligations to Orestes as his nephew, or to respect his father-in-law Tyndareus' disgust for Orestes. In this introductory dialogue

---

[19] For the structure of these two speeches, and of the episode as a whole, see Ludwig 1954, 43–50 and 100–4.   [20] See Duchemin 1945, 76–8 and 121.
[21] Cf. Duchemin 1945, 118; Ludwig 1954, 48 ff.; Lesky 1972, 419 f.

Menelaus protests to Tyndareus that it is the Greek way always to honour kinship; Tyndareus retorts that it is also the Greek way not to put oneself above the law, as Orestes has done. Then Menelaus: 'Wise men reject slavish servitude to necessity.' Tyndareus: 'Well, you go on in that belief; it's not going to be mine.' Menelaus: 'Your anger is as little wise as old age generally.' Tyndareus: 'What argument could there be about wisdom with Orestes here?'[22] This is the extraordinary start to the debate about wisdom, σοφίας ἀγών, between Tyndareus and Orestes: Menelaus, initially sympathetic to his nephew, has prompted its theme, but takes no part in it; and when it is done he comes out with his sympathy for Orestes almost destroyed.

For Tyndareus' long rhesis (491–541) develops naturally from the relation between wisdom, or sense, and law, into an attack on Orestes' lawlessness, which he invites Menelaus not to condone; and Tyndareus strengthens the honesty of his case by admitting the lawlessness of his own two daughters, Helen and Clytemnestra. Orestes' answer (544–604) protests the rightness of his matricide, putting down a lawless woman (and he hits at Tyndareus on Tyndareus' own admissions); and Orestes blames Apollo's command, who now deserts him.

Tyndareus and Orestes argue, without concession. After their speeches, there is no exacerbation, only a stiffly angry rejection of Orestes' plea by Tyndareus; he will go to the assembly, he says, to incite its condemnation of Orestes to death. With Tyndareus' second and briefer speech (607–29), the debate proper ends. Orestes turns to renew his case to Menelaus, but finds him reflecting, in doubt where he earlier defended Orestes to Tyndareus. So Orestes pleads again (640–79), formally marking out his case, claiming a return for Menelaus' debt to Agamemnon in the Trojan war, and for Menelaus' duty to the family. Menelaus' reply (682–715) is subjective and evasive, half promising help, half expressing helplessness: this is no considered reply, no argued rejection. He goes out immediately, much as Agamemnon runs from Clytemnestra and Iphigenia (*IA* 1275).

Now Orestes is deserted, his friend Pylades comes in, still within this one episode, to give it a logical climax in a mood of despair and yet hopeful excitement (725–806): two old friends, alone again, find

---

[22] Cf. n. 6 above.

for Orestes a new strength: he resolves to confront the assembly while it deliberates his execution, and defend himself before it.

The cleverness of this scene is its richly convincing dramatic sequence, the introduction and interplay of three persons in a variation upon a straightforward debate with three participants. The power of decision over Orestes' life lies with Menelaus, who veers from instinctive sympathy, from actual defence of Orestes, to desertion—but the moment, the process of this change is artfully concealed by the place and order of the forces: for the set debate is between Tyndareus and Orestes, and Menelaus responds only with doubt. The same artful disposition of formal elements makes his final speech appear none the less as the delayed judgement in the debate. Menelaus and Orestes begin the episode in dialogue; Tyndareus arrives and Menelaus listens to his σοφίας ἀγών ('argument about wisdom') with Orestes; then Orestes and Menelaus confront one another again. This in a sequence of rigid dialogue, formal debate comprising two rheseis, then two rheseis again—but while Orestes' second rhesis, to Menelaus, is formal in method, agonistic in tone, Menelaus' final speech is not a rebuttal of argument but a natural confession of helplessness. So Euripides avoids a stiffly abrupt end to the debate, working a smooth transition to the episode's climax between Pylades and Orestes. This is his mastery of form.

ADDENDUM

The text of 1975 has not been changed, apart from a few small corrections to references; to have rewritten it would have been false to its original conception as a lecture (see n. 1).

The paper has generally been cited with approval, but not everything has gone unquestioned. I would, I think, now concede something to criticism on two points: (1) that I have applied the term 'formal debate' rather too widely, by including scenes which have many, but not all, of the compositional elements typifying the *agōn* as narrowly defined at pp. 66–7 and 70–1 of the paper (see in particular Lloyd 1992); my now more circumspect approach may be seen in the discussion of *Hecuba* 216–443 (p. 74 of this paper) in my *Hecuba* (Collard 1991, ad loc.); and (2) that I have sometimes used inappropriate criteria of rhetorical relevance or texture, e.g. at pp. 65–6 (see in particular Heath 1987, 130–7, whose own position is given by, e.g., p. 131, 'rhetorical ethos is a matter of assuming in a given speech the *persona* which best suits and supports the thought there expressed'; and Goldhill 1986*a*, 230 ff.). I might defend myself against those criticisms by observing that my intention in the paper was to evaluate the 'formal debate' as a dramatic form in its totality— something recognized by Conacher 1981, 3–25 and pp. 81–101 below, who (esp. at 94–101) has very useful supplementary remarks on the *agōn*; to his generally wider treatment of rhetoric in drama should be added especially Buxton 1982, with (pp. 162 ff.) remarks on the *agōn*; and on Euripides, Knox 1985, 327–30.

Two details:

n. 6: the text of *Or.* 491 continues to exercise editors. Bothe is followed by Willink 1986, who dismisses Porson as involving 'too much alteration' and 'inferior'. West 1987 changes to πρὸς τόνδ' ἀγών τις τοῦ σοφοῦ γ' ἥκει πέρι ('What has an intelligence contest to do with this fellow?'), σοφοῦ like Porson giving the *agōn* the positive headline ('wisdom') which I am sure it must have. The line is obelized by Diggle (1994).

n. 17: *Pho.* 438–42 are retained as authentic by both Craik 1988 and Mastronarde 1988.

4

Rhetoric and Relevance in
Euripidean Drama

D. J. CONACHER

The highly rhetorical nature of Greek Tragedy in general, and the
agonistic character of much Sophoclean and Euripidean Tragedy
in particular, have nowadays become so well recognized that most
Classicists accept the fact and its implications: this was the convention within which, for whatever reason,[1] the Greek poets composed
their tragedies (at least in the latter half of the fifth century) and
modern critical judgments as to what is probable and relevant in any
given dramatic speech or debate, and what is consistent with the
overall characterization of the speaker, must undergo drastic revision
when applied to Greek Tragedy. Indeed, now the pendulum has
swung the other way. When one reads critics like Dawe on Aeschylus,
Tycho Wilamowitz (admittedly a bit ahead of his time) on Sophocles,
Zürcher and (more moderately) A. M. Dale on Euripides, one finds so
much emphasis on the effects of the individual speech or scene, that
it is now the critic who looks too closely for the larger dramatic
relevance of various speeches or (God forbid!) some consistent thread
of characterization in their speakers, who is under fire.[2] The present

An earlier version of this paper was delivered at a 'Workshop on Euripidean Tragedy'
(supported by the Social Sciences and Humanities Research Council of Canada and by
the University of Victoria) held at Victoria, BC, October 6–8, 1978.

[1] Jacqueline Duchemin (cited by Christopher Collard in his interesting paper, Collard
1975a, 58: above, pp. 64–80, claims that this characteristic of Tragedy was inherited
from a pastoral tradition of dramatic poetry composed in alternating form. See the
supplement to Duchemin 1945, Duchemin 1969, 247–76. I prefer the more general
explanation given in Duchemin's original study, 236–8, that the antithetical form
sprang from 'des tendances les plus profonds de l'esprit grecque et en particulier l'esprit
athénien', which Sophocles and especially Euripides developed in their individual ways.

[2] See Dawe 1963, 30; Wilamowitz 1917, *passim*; Dale 1954, xxii–xxix (and articles
noted below, nn. 6 and 7). The whole question of 'characterization' in Greek Tragedy
has been much debated in recent years; the reader is referred to two excellent studies,

paper should not be regarded as an attempt to put the critical clock
back, as it were, but rather to find some compromise between the
extremely 'atomistic' approach just described, which allows only a
vague cohesive force to the overall tragic theme, and the more old-
fashioned approach of the formal critic, who expects every speech to
be uttered with a view to furthering the dramatic action, developing
the theme or exhibiting the character of the speaker. Since Euripides
is admittedly the most 'rhetorical' of the Greek tragic poets and yet
also the one providing the most clearly-marked tragic themes and
the subtlest psychological effects (in individual scenes if not in overall
characterization), his work seems the most suitable in which to pursue
the question of 'rhetoric and dramatic relevance'. To what degree,
and in what ways, did Euripides seek to make those set speeches and
debates whose immediate effect (both rhetorical and dramatic) is most
obvious, contribute to the larger dramatic meanings of the play? Or
was the poet and his audience content to take their tragedies scene
by scene, even speech by speech, for their own isolated effects, with
no more than a general requirement that some large tragic idea
('The King has offended the gods in such and such a way; the King
must die!') should suffice to provide a unifying coherence to the
tragic action?

Two overlapping issues are raised in considering the question of
'rhetoric and relevance' in Tragedy: one concerns the kind of relation
which we may expect to find between the content of a given speech

assessing recent critical trends, by Charles Garton, 1957, 247–54 and 1972, 389–413.
In most of the studies referred to at the beginning of this note and in Garton's
review articles, the reaction against the excesses of 'psychological' or 'individualizing'
critics commenting on characterization in Greek Tragedy is very marked; this
basically healthy and well-substantiated reaction has been further developed by Jones
1962, e.g., in his attack on the 'baneful' concept of 'the tragic hero', pp. 16 ff., and in
various comments by Hugh Lloyd-Jones (see, for example, his comments on
'character' in Aeschylus in Lloyd-Jones 1964, 370–1, and in the Introduction to his
translation of Aeschylus' *Agamemnon* (Lloyd-Jones 1979*a*), 6–7). Two recent articles
by P. E. Easterling, 1973, 3–19, and 1977, 121–9, have attempted to select what is
valuable in the attacks on the 'psychologizing critics' while still insisting on the
presence of individualized and credible dramatic personalities in the works of
Aeschylus and Sophocles. Finally, John Gould in an excellent article, Gould 1978,
43–67, seeks to put 'the new criticism' on character in Greek Tragedy in a fresh
perspective by discussing the various ways in which 'the framing process of dramatic
language and dramatic form', as used by the three tragedians, affect our perception of
dramatic personality in the particular medium in which various 'dramatic persons'
exist (see ibid. 44). I shall have occasion below to indicate agreements and dis-
agreements with Gould's study where it impinges on certain points to be made in the
present paper.

or debate and the theme of the play as a whole; the other concerns the degree, if any, to which we may expect a speech to be 'in character', to tell us something significant about the speaker, especially if that speaker is a central figure in the play. I shall try to address these issues separately, though they are not, of course, wholly separable. As a sort of Prologue, I should like to consider certain comments of A. M. Dale in her Introduction to Euripides' *Alcestis*. Assailing with some justice the excessive interest of critics in the character and psychology of Admetus in this play, Miss Dale maintains that apart from the King's ὁσιότης ('piety') mentioned at v. 10, Euripides had no particular interest in the sort of person Admetus was.

For in a well constructed Euripidean Tragedy, what controls a succession of situations is not a firmly conceived unity of character but the shape of the whole action, and what determines the development and finesse of each situation is . . . the rhetoric of the situation—what Aristotle calls διάνοια.[3]

Miss Dale would replace the question, 'What would X, being such a man, be likely to say in such a situation?' with the question, 'Suppose a man involved in such a situation, how should he best acquit himself? How gain his point? Move his hearers . . . ?'

The aim of rhetoric [Miss Dale continues] is Persuasion, Πειθώ, and the poet is, as it were, a kind of λογογράφος ('speech-writer') who promises to do his best for each of his clients in turn as the situations change and succeed one another.

Now, in venturing to criticize some of the more extreme features of Miss Dale's view on the characterization of Admetus in *Alcestis*, I should make it clear that I think that her interpretation of the play as a whole is, for the most part, sound. The *Alcestis* is more concerned with the irony of the situation, 'the irony of human intentions measured against their outcome',[4] than with an estimate of, or judgment on, Admetus' character. Its central theme is, as Miss Dale says, 'summed up in his [Admetus'] words, ἄρτι μανθάνω ('too late, I learn') . . . What Admetus realizes too late is that this life of which he has cheated Destiny is a useless possession.'[5]

What does trouble me in Miss Dale's interpretation is the, to my mind, gratuitous removal of *all* interest in the sort of person Admetus is, her doctrinaire refusal to allow anything of what he says, or of

---

[3] Dale 1954, xxvii. For the following three quotations, see ibid. xxviii.
[4] Ibid. xxv.   [5] Ibid. xxii.

what others say about him, to tell us anything about what sort of man he is. In another short essay, 'The Creation of Dramatic Characters', Miss Dale warns against allowing attitudes of mind, religious and moral beliefs of other generations and cultures, to influence our impressions of a play's characters: only the dramatist's words and their implications provide real justification for such impressions.[6] It seems to me that in the *Alcestis*, Euripides does supply us with 'words and their implications' which do, in fact convey a somewhat unfavourable, even satirical 'characterization' of Admetus, particularly in his own speeches in the *agōn* ('dramatized debate') with Pheres, where, according to Miss Dale's account of the poet's role as λογογράφος ('speech-writer'), we would least expect to find it. All that I shall be arguing for here is not that such 'characterization' is central to some sort of πάθει/μάθος ('learning through suffering') theme (such as one might argue in the case of Creon in *Antigone*) but rather that Admetus himself, for a certain blindness or insensitivity which he shows throughout the course of the *present* action, is included in the 'dry mock' which Dale has rightly concluded to be the dominant note in the play.

The allegedly naive reaction of modern readers to Admetus, as he mournfully watches Alcestis die in his place and as he berates his father Pheres for allowing Alcestis to sacrifice herself for him, when Pheres might have done so himself, is to feel that the King is in a somewhat disadvantageous, not to say invidious, position. We are warned by the critics, however, that such a reaction may be *merely* modern and sentimental: it may never even have occurred to a fifth-century Greek in the audience. We find in the play, however, evidence that such a thought could, and in fact did, occur to a fifth-century Greek, namely Euripides, when he allows Pheres (admittedly in a moment of anger) to say, without contradiction, that Admetus will have ill-renown (ἀκούσῃ . . . κακά, 705) for the shame of 'having killed his wife' (ταύτην κατακτάς, 696), and allows Admetus later (954–60) to fear that this is precisely what his enemies *will* say of him. This is evidence also, by the way, that the poet means us to understand that even in the mythical times and circumstances of the play Admetus could (and so *would*) be viewed in the unfavourable light to which some critics ask us to close our eyes.

<hr />

[6] Dale 1969, 278.

Having established that this unfavourable view of Admetus is at least a possible one for a fifth-century Greek and that the playwright does not expect us to regard it as impossible (or even improbable) in the dramatic time and circumstances of the play, one might still argue that the playwright did not wish *us* to think of Admetus in this light: there are all manner of extenuating circumstances and possibly it is only Admetus' enemies who might be expected to take the uncharitable view. If this were the case, then surely the poet must avoid giving the 'sympathetic' characters, and *particularly Admetus himself*, any lines which would make us think of the more invidious aspects of his position, that he in fact has caused and accepted his wife's death by letting her die for him. In this case, surely the last words which he should put into the King's mouth during the death scene of Alcestis is the plea, twice repeated, that his wife should not *betray* him ($\mu\grave{\eta}$ $\pi\rho o\delta\hat{\omega}s$, 250; $\mu\grave{\eta}$ $\pi\rho\acute{o}s$ $\langle\sigma\epsilon\rangle$ $\theta\epsilon\hat{\omega}v$ $\tau\lambda\hat{\eta}s$ $\mu\epsilon$ $\pi\rho o\delta o\hat{v}v\alpha\iota$, 275) ('Betray me not!' 250; 'Don't, I beseech you by the gods, have the heart to abandon me!' 275) by dying.

The purist will reply, 'But this is just the sort of thing which the rhetorical-dramatic convention requires of the husband at the moment of his wife's untimely death.' Precisely, but it also happens to be the last thing which someone in Admetus' particular position *can* say, with any conviction: Euripides seems to me to be exploiting, for ironic effect at Admetus' expense, the conflict between the conventional and the particular aspects of the situation. However, this inference is, I am aware, debatable: it is at best an interpretation, not a dramatic certainty.

Be that as it may, ironic mockery of Admetus is surely developed, with devastating effect, in the speech given to him in the Pheres scene. Even before he knows he is unwelcome, Pheres sets the tone for this effect when he praises his son's union with Alcestis as a model of profitable marriage (627–8). Now let us look at Admetus' tirade against Pheres in some detail, for if, as Miss Dale insists, Euripides like a good logographer is concerned to let the speaker made the best case for himself on each occasion, then surely he has failed badly here: Admetus scores so many points *against* himself.

We may, perhaps, pass over the rather obvious irony of Admetus' initial amazement at Pheres' audacity in mourning one whom he has himself allowed to die, and accept as merely an ironic overtone Admetus' use (v. 646) of the word $\acute{o}\theta v\epsilon\acute{\iota}\alpha v$ ('not a blood relation') of Alcestis, the same unusual and ambiguous term as he has earlier

used when he sought to 'deny' to Heracles that the dead woman in
his house was even a member of his own family. But surely the most
telling shaft which Admetus lets fly against himself is the one which
comes near the end of his speech, when he has formally repudiated
his parents (itself a fearful thing for a Greek to do) and all duties
toward them:

My hands will never bury *you*, since, as far as it lay in *your* power, I've
perished. But since I live by chancing on (τυχών) another saviour, I say
that I am *that one*'s son and loving guardian of her old age   (665–8)

γηροτρόφον ('old-age-tending'; 668) as a description of Admetus
vis-à-vis Alcestis who, χάριν αὐτοῦ ('for his sake'), will never reach
old age! I find it impossible not to believe that here the poet (far from
doing his best for his client Admetus, as Dale would have it) is here
indulging in a bitter irony at the speaker's own expense. And if this
is the case here, it may well be the case in the less obvious instance
cited. Dare one suggest that the insensitive lack of perception which
Admetus' unconscious irony reveals, reflects onstage the blindness
which he has earlier shown in choosing survival under conditions
which he will find intolerable?[7]

    There is, indeed, quite another way (rather less doctrinaire than
Miss Dale's) of looking at the rhetorical aspect of Tragedy and of Greek
literature generally. J. H. Finley, for example, reminds us that the art
of rhetoric implied more than skill in language and argumentation: it
implied an ability to understand broad laws of individual and social
conduct. 'The common ground [between Euripides and Thucydides]',
he adds, 'is that in both alike the concrete issues at hand are looked

---

[7] Something of the theoretical background of Miss Dale's view of 'character' in
Greek Tragedy appears in Dale 1969, 139–55. Space forbids a detailed critique of this
interesting article. The (in my view) excessive restrictions which Miss Dale imposes on
the function of 'character' in Greek Tragedy, according to Aristotle, spring from a
possible misinterpretation of *Poetics* 1450[b]8 (compare, with her interpretation, Lucas'
(1968) note ad loc.), from a refusal to allow to *dianoia* in Aristotle's discussion of Greek
Tragedy any of the 'intellectual' aspect which it has in the *Ethics*, and from a failure to
give adequate attention to Aristotle's reminder (at *Poetics* 1449[b]36 ff.) that *ēthos* and
dianoia (which together provide an approximation of the English concept of
'character': cf. Dale, 143, 145–6) jointly determine the quality of actions in Tragedy.
However, one can agree with her modest claim that the various Aristotelian distinctions which she discusses are 'some sort of reflection of actual differences between
Greek and more modern tragedy' (ibid. 146). It is mainly in considering the degree of
those differences (as exemplified in our discussions of the *Alcestis*) that I venture to
differ from Miss Dale.

on as not, so to speak, interpretable in and through themselves but only through the more universal laws they exemplify.'[8] The same awareness of a certain universalizing quality in Euripidean rhetoric (a quality which suggests interest in larger themes, even while depicting the cut and thrust of furious debate) is present also in Friis Johansen's comments on Euripides' use of 'general reflections' in his speeches. Contrasting this with Sophocles' 'reluctance against working in two separate levels of thought', he remarks: 'Euripides never seems to have doubted the necessity and desirability of a superstructure of general thought and action.'[9] Now this 'generalizing element' in Euripidean rhetoric did not, of course, always find expression in relation to the larger theme of the play (as opposed to the individual scene) but I would suggest that sometimes this was the case. There is a tendency even among critics who, like Lucas and Zürcher, find something approving to say about Euripides' psychological subtlety, or about his concern for the motives of his characters, always to concentrate (with some justice) on individual scenes.[10] So, too, even recent defenders, such as Hans Strohm, of Euripides' dramaturgy in connection with his 'rhetoric', have dwelt mainly on his increasing skill in incorporating his 'debates' into properly dramatic scenes; Collard develops Strohm's approach, which he cites with approval, though he also speaks in very general terms of the success of agonistic scenes in Euripides as depending in part on 'the harmony of their themes with the main direction of the plot . . .'.[11] However, it is with the subtler, more detailed connections between the 'generalizing' rhetorical passages in Euripides and both the themes of their plays and our overall impression of the characters who speak them that we shall be concerned in the rest of this discussion.

John Gould has suggested that one result of this 'pervasive intellectualism' (his term for the 'generalizing element' noted above) surrounding many Euripidean characters is that these characters 'seem not to be grounded in the common sensible feel of life but to move restlessly in the thinner air of uncertain abstraction'.[12] This effect he contrasts (unfavorably, in this regard) with 'the general shape and feel . . . of concrete reality and of present circumstances' which he

---

[8] Finley 1967, 52.   [9] Friis Johansen 1959, 174.
[10] See below, p. 93 and n. 19.
[11] See Collard 1975a, 66 ff.; pp. 68 ff. above. For Strohm's view on the matter (cited by Collard, ibid. 59, 62 and nn. ad loc.; pp. 65, 69 above), see Strohm 1957, 44–6.   [12] Gould 1978, 53.

finds in the Sophoclean *agōn* (the scene at Sophocles' *Electra* 516–609 is his particular example). As far as this comparison with Sophocles is concerned, one must admit the justice of Gould's observation concerning the effect on characterization of the generalizing aspect of speeches in Euripides. I would argue, however, that even some of the most abstract and 'philosophic' speeches which Euripides appears to 'put in the mouths' of his characters are often more relevant to a fuller understanding of those characters and to their part in the dramatic action than this critic would have us believe. A brief discussion of two scenes from Euripides' *Hippolytus* (which Gould also selects to illustrate *his* points) may serve to substantiate this view and to distinguish it from Gould's rather different opinion on the matter.

The 'philosophical discourse' of Phaedra at *Hippolytus* 373–430 is certainly one of the finest and most interesting speeches, considered in and for itself, in all Euripides. Here indeed the poet has done his duty well as Phaedra's logographer, providing her with a speech admirably suited to her situation. Yet the speech is clearly something more than this. On the one hand, it blends most expertly certain ethical generalizations with their precise application, made by the speaker herself, to Phaedra's own case. This feature saves the speech from appearing, in places, to be merely an exposition of Euripides' own views as some (Bruno Snell, for example) have argued, but this much Miss Dale's 'speech-writer' for Phaedra in her immediate situation might well have achieved. On the other hand, however, the speech provides us with certain information about Phaedra which, while it is certainly not characterization for its own sake, will be most relevant to our reactions to two coming events in the play of which neither we nor the speaker are yet aware.

Phaedra begins with a little disquisition on the cause of human disaster ($\hat{\eta}$ διέφθαρται βίος, 376): first, not ignorance (for many of us *do* have sound moral judgment, εὖ φρονεῖν, 378) but the distractions of pleasure prevent man from doing the good they know; then αἰδώς, *in the bad sense* of diffidence or indecisiveness[13] is also the

---

[13] Here I follow Barrett's interpretation of 'the bad αἰδώς' in his notes to vv. 381–5 and 385–6 in his edition of *Hippolytus* (Oxford, 1964), though I must admit to continuing uncertainty about the matter. Barrett's explanation is, at any rate, the most convincing among the several divergent views offered by scholars (see especially his references to other ancient passages on the ambivalence of αἰδώς, including Plutarch's explanation (*De Virtut. Mor.* 448 f.) of our *Hippolytus* passage. Barrett's

bane of houses ($\H{a}\chi\theta os$ $o\H{\iota}\kappa\omega\nu$, 386). From this philosophical basis,
Phaedra turns to her own case (388 ff.): having failed to overcome
her love (for though she 'knows what's right' she cannot do it), she
will commit suicide and the rest of the speech (403–30) shows clearly
that it is the fear of scandal, which is the cause of her decision.

The second half of this demonstration goes from the particular to
the general (the reverse of the earlier sequence):

> May all men know my deeds, if noble;
> If shameful, may few witness them.   (403–4)

From this spring-board, Phaedra embarks on a general condemnation of adultery in noble houses as the source of similar corruption in
society in general. The passage ends with a characteristic rhetorical
flourish:

> How can the false ones on their spouses look
> Not fearing the very walls will shriek their guilt!   (405–18)

The peroration (419–30) arises from Phaedra's personal fear, with
this significant statement:

> This it is that kills me, friends, the fear lest I
> be caught shaming my husband and the children whom
> I bore!
>
> (419–21)

Again the particular fear is generalized into a fine rhetorical statement
about $\epsilon\H{\upsilon}\kappa\lambda\epsilon\iota a$ ('reputation') and about the horror of family disgrace
when at last the dread secret is revealed. As before, a vivid image
caps the sequence:

> Time, in its passing, shows the evil ones
> Like mirrors set before a maiden's face:
> 'Mid such as these may I be never seen!   (428–30)

As I have suggested, the speech is a model of Euripidean rhetoric in
its blend of philosophic generalizations and of their particular
applications to the speaker's fears and resolutions. But besides this
immediate application, the speech is most relevant to two scenes
which are yet to come. When Hippolytus gives his great indictment

interpretation also has the advantage, which he presses, of fitting in well with
Phaedra's own situation: her difficulty in 'fighting down her love as she knows she
should', whether by suicide (on which she appears to decide later in the speech, but
which—fatally, for Hippolytus—she postpones fulfilling), or by any other means.

of Phaedra with all womankind, we judge the extent of his injustice from the evidence of nobility which Phaedra has provided in the present speech, and since Hippolytus' tirade marks the turning-point in the play, and leads directly to his own undoing, we feel a certain justification (ironic and tragic, however 'unfair') about his downfall. Secondly, Phaedra's great emphasis on εὔκλεια ('reputation') does more than explain, as Phaedra intends, the Queen's decision to slay herself. Not so much innocence as good *reputation* is all-important: the Queen's *total* commitment to this as a family obligation renders probable, in proper Aristotelian fashion, the extreme measures (suicide and the false incrimination of Hippolytus) which she eventually takes to protect it. Thus I would maintain that here the poet has not only provided Phaedra (as Miss Dale would expect) with a speech admirably suited to her conscious needs in her immediate situation; he has also provided the audience with a passage essential to the understanding of Phaedra (insofar as her character will be relevant to the coming action) and of the tragic meaning of the play.[14]

Such defences of the relevance behind the rhetoric of such speeches as Phaedra's are, as I have already indicated, by no means generally accepted today. Thus Gould comments as follows on the speech we have just discussed:

I do not think that we make any particular headway in understanding the movement of the scene by looking for Phaedra's 'purposes' in uttering this *epideixis* ('exhibition speech'): when Mr Barrett says that the disquisition here is by Phaedra and not by Euripides, I have the feeling that the critical cat is out of the bag. A speech such as this presents, in the Euripidean theatre, a facet of the action, arrested and illuminated by rational analysis: the movement of the verse in Phaedra's speech is antithetical and inferential, with scarcely a flicker of the emotional distraction and the restless, defensive evasion which she displayed in the earlier part of the scene.[15]

---

[14] An indication that the dramatist himself regarded at least certain aspects of both Phaedra's and Hippolytus' flights of rhetoric as dramatically relevant is provided by the rhetorical *clausulae* which he has each of the characters aim (indirectly) at the other. 'Let someone teach them (women) to be chaste (σωφρονεῖν) or let me trample on them forever!' cries Hippolytus (667–8) at the end of his speech castigating Phaedra and all womankind. 'In dying,' cries Phaedra before her suicide. 'I will become a bane to that other one as well . . . he will learn at last to moderate his utterance!' (σωφρονεῖν μαθήσεται, 731, an almost untranslatable expression in the context). The degree to which Phaedra and Hippolytus respectively can claim σωφροσύνη ('moderation', 'self-control'), and the degree to which each falls short of it, has been amply demonstrated in their two great speeches at 373 ff. and 616 ff., respectively.

[15] Gould 1978, 55–6.

Gould's rejection of any such formulation of 'personal motivation' as I have attempted for this speech rests mainly on its rhetorical form and the contrast which its dispassionate rationality provides with the emotional utterances of Phaedra in the preceding scene. I have discussed elsewhere this highly artificial (but extremely effective) Euripidean device (most observable in the *Alcestis*, the *Medea* and the *Hippolytus*) for showing two conflicting aspects of a character's personality in juxtaposition;[16] however, the lack of 'realism' involved in this Euripidean exploitation of Greek dramatic convention need not imply that the 'rational aspect' of a character thus displayed is any less valid or credible than the emotional aspect. The formal parallel between Phaedra's speech here and Medea's speech to the women of Corinth at *Medea* 214 ff. (which also follows an emotional outburst from the same speaker, in that instance off-stage) further arouses Gould's suspicions concerning the 'in character' nature of Phaedra's great speech: if we 'psychologize' Medea's calm speech, he argues, we must take it as 'Machiavellian dissembling', and since such an interpretation does not work in the case of the 'parallel' speech of Phaedra, he rejects the 'in character', or 'psychological' (to use Gould's term) interpretation for both speeches. But surely this conclusion involves a *non sequitur*: the contexts of the two speeches are quite different. It is not *simply* the 'tone of reasonableness' which leads us to the possible suspicions that Medea is 'dissembling'; she has an axe to grind in her reasonable persuasion of the Chorus, whereas Phaedra has not; nor does Phaedra, in her reasonable speech, suppress anything which she has revealed in her hysterical outbursts, while Medea does (*viz.* the wish for the death of her children along with their father, at vv. 112–14). Neither Phaedra nor Medea can be expected to be hysterical all the time. All that we are entitled to expect of the formal similarity between the 'Phaedra-sequence' in the *Hippolytus* and the 'Medea-sequence' in the *Medea* is that the poet is using the same dramatic device for similar purposes: to provide us (in addition to some intrinsically 'interesting' philo-sophizing) with information relevant to the dramatic situation—information, which may (and usually does) include some revelations about the characters themselves, in passionate and in rational mood. There is no reason why *what* is revealed should be similar.

[16] Conacher 1972, 199–203.

Another highly rhetorical passage in the *Hippolytus* is the *agōn* between Hippolytus and Theseus (902–1101) and here, too, in my opinion, Euripides is remarkably successful in relating the immediate rhetorical effects to dramatic meanings of wider significance. I have discussed elsewhere, from this point of view, the preliminary exchanges (902–42) between Hippolytus and Theseus in this scene;[17] here I shall restrict myself to discussion of Hippolytus' speech of self-defence against Theseus' accusations based on Phaedra's lying suicide note naming Hippolytus as her seducer.

The speech is a model of forensic rhetoric, complete with exordium, brief narration of the alleged offence, proofs of innocence, and refutations of anticipated rebuttals (both nicely based on $\tau\grave{\alpha}$ $\epsilon\emph{i}\kappa\acute{o}\tau\alpha$, 'the probabilities' of the situation), and a resounding peroration, ending with a clever and ironically significant play on words in the speaker's favour. But before we conclude that this speech too has been written by Miss Dale's ubiquitous $\lambda o\gamma o\gamma\rho\acute{\alpha}\phi os$ ('speech-writer'), we should note again the recurrent terms and self-characterizing touches which, like thematic hooks, relate the speech to the tragic characterization of Hippolytus throughout the play. Thus Hippolytus spoils the conventional *captatio benevolentiae* of the exordium with characteristic haughtiness ('unaccustomed as I am to public speaking' acquires the unfortunate addendum, 'for only the vulgar can speak before the mob', 988–9). Among the 'improbabilities' of his alleged fall from grace is included a tactless reminder of Phaedra's limited charms ('Was she, after all, so beautiful?' 1009–19). Finally, the repeated occurrences of the term $\sigma\acute{\omega}\phi\rho\omega\nu$ ('temperate, chaste'), in one form or another (995, 1007, 1013, 1034), provide sinister reminders that this 'virtue', linked with Hippolytus' $\sigma\epsilon\mu\nu\acute{o}\tau\eta s$ ('haughtiness'), has been played up throughout as the catastrophic element in this tragedy.[18]

The *Hippolytus* is, to be sure, one of Euripides' best constructed (some would say, 'most Sophoclean') plays. A brief glance at his *Electra*, an extremely 'rhetorical' play, may indicate the wisdom of lowering one's sails somewhat in one's claims for Euripidean 'relevance', or at least of sailing rather more closely to the wind of rhetoric. Here I am thinking particularly of Electra's own great 'set speeches', her vaunt over the head of the slain Aegisthus (907–56)

---

[17] Conacher 1972, 206–7.
[18] For a contrasting view of the Hippolytus–Theseus *agōn* in the *Hippolytus* see Gould 1978, 57–8.

and her indictment of Clytemnestra at 1060–85, in the one formal *agōn* in the play.

Aegisthus is assailed for his adultery, for his ignominy in marriage (as 'Clytemnestra's husband', 931) and for his presumption in thinking to be *someone* (τις εἶναι, ... 939) on the basis of wealth and pretty looks rather than on natural nobility. The speech lends itself well to effective gnomic passages, e.g.

> Money's worth nothing, save for brief companionship.
> Not wealth but one's nature (φύσις) is enduring:
> for that stands ever by one and defeats one's woes.
> Wealth blossoms but a little while, then flies the coop,
> Taking its base companions with it. (940–4)

All this, one might argue, has little to do with either Aegisthus' major crimes or their avenging. Yet the whole drift of Electra's assault on Aegisthus is consistent with the sordid frustrations and deprivations (of 'substance' and marital status) which are at the heart of Electra's woe. So, too, Electra's indictment of Clytemnestra (1060–85) dwells mainly on her mother's infidelities, thus allowing the poet to frame her arguments with moralizing maxims on the proper—and the improper—behaviour of wives in wartime:

> Any woman who adorns her beauty (ἐς κάλλος ἀσκεῖ) when
> her man's away, strike her off as a harlot!
>
> (1072–3)
>
> Evil behaviour provides a model—'gainst which the good
> may shine!
>
> (1084–5)

Yet once again, however much these topics are pursued 'for their own sake', in flights of fancy rhetoric, the topics themselves are close to Electra's own bitter heart and to her own jealous motives in pursuing the mother-murder.

Critics unwilling to accept the possibility of 'unitary characterization' in Greek Tragedy (that is, the intentional presentation of an individual consistently illustrating the same or similar characteristics in a variety of situations throughout the play) go to surprising lengths to deny this description to Euripides' presentation of Electra. Zürcher, for example, describes this Electra as 'zwar psychologisch, nicht aber charakterologische motiviert'.[19] He believes that Electra is provided

---

[19] Zürcher 1947, 131. (I am indebted to Charles Garton, 1972, 403 and 408, for this and the following citation of Zürcher.)

with certain character traits in accordance with the various situations in which she finds herself throughout the play which do, in effect, add up to a fairly constant *ēthos* ('character'). This *ēthos*, it is alleged, 'appears as a natural result of the situation at various points...' and participates in shaping the action without governing it.[20] Now it is true that Euripides' 'characterization' of Electra cannot be said to 'govern the action' in any basic sense: the myth of the return of Orestes, his recognition by Electra and the subsequent vengeance on Aegisthus and Clytemnestra, which forms as it were the *ur*-plot of this and other 'Electra and Orestes' plays, precedes any conception of Electra on which Euripides may have decided. But for the rest Zürcher's formulation seems perversely to put the matter the wrong way around. Euripides, with a clear conception from the start of the kind of Electra which he wished to present, surely devised scenes and their 'occasion' (witness the novel introduction of Electra's vaunt over the slain Aegisthus) which would best illustrate the character (in an admittedly restricted sense) and motivation of Electra throughout. What is of particular interest for our study here is that he effected this largely through the most rhetorical parts of the play: Electra's 'set-speeches', including that of the *agōn*, which still produce, along with this 'character-deployment', their usual Euripidean quota, and more, of 'everyday topics' not normally associated with this heroic theme.

So much must suffice, within the limits of the present paper, concerning the 'characterizing' aspects of rhetorical passages in Euripides, though similar demonstrations could, I think, be attempted with respect to certain other Euripidean plays, most notably, perhaps, the *Medea*. Let us turn now to the examination of a few Euripidean '*agōn*-scenes' whose relevance to the theme and action of the play has been particularly questioned by the critics.

Jacqueline Duchemin, in her useful book, *L'ΑΓΩΝ dans la Tragédie Grecque*, remarks on the tendency of Euripidean *agōnes* to show increasingly less connection with the theme and action of their respective plays.[21] This is, on the whole, true—and certainly true of Euripides in contrast with Sophocles; nevertheless, Duchemin does seem to me often to underestimate what connection there actually is. Thus in the case of the *Helen's agōn* (one of the few which, *pace*

[20] Zürcher 1947, 134.   [21] Duchemin 1945, 124 ff.

Hans Strohm,[22] actually do affect the action of their plays),
Duchemin wrongly attributes the success of Helen's and Menelaus'
plea to Theonoe not to their arguments but to the fact that Theonoe
had from the beginning decided not to betray the pair to the Egyptian
King:[23] a strange conclusion in view of Theonoe's line, in her opening
speech, 'Who, then will go and reveal this man's presence to my
brother, so that *my* safety may be secured?' (892–3).[24] Duchemin also
finds it 'extraordinary' that in this *agōn* the two antithetical speeches
(by Helen and Menelaus) defend the same case in perfect agreement[25]
but had she pursued the matter further, she might have noticed that
it is actually the contrasts between these speeches which provide one
of the organic links with the rest of the play. While this is not a play
involving 'tragic characterization' in any depth, nevertheless we have
already been given clear if superficial impressions of both pleaders in
the *agōn*: Helen as a melancholy and reflective beauty (contrasting
ironically with other 'Helens' of Euripides), pondering the causes,
whether natural or supernatural, of her undeserved reputation;
Menelaus, a man of action, presented in possibly mock-heroic
manner, whose brain-cudgelling over the problem of 'the two Helens'
suggests a certain lack of philosophic subtlety. Their two pleas reflect
nicely these contrasting personalities, Helen's plea being a complex
blend of the ethical and the theological ('How shameful if you, a

[22] Cf. Strohm 1957, ch. 1, *passim*, esp. pp. 37–8, who argues for the unproductive
nature of the Euripidean *agōn*. Another possible exception is the first *agōn* in Euripides'
Supplices (110–262), which has at least the 'negative result' of deciding Theseus (at
this point in the play) against accepting the Argive supplication.

[23] Duchemin 1945, 128.

[24] The authenticity of these verses (*Hel.* 892–3) as they stand, has, it is true, been
questioned by several scholars, e.g. Wilamowitz (who regards the verses as an
interpolation); Zuntz (who argues for a sizeable lacuna after v. 891); see Dale's note ad
loc., in her edition of the play (Dale 1967). I accept Dale's defence of both these verses
as they stand and her rejection of any lacuna here: the verses are faultless in
themselves, intelligible as they stand (even if they do not fit some scholars' views of
what Theonoe might be expected to say at this point) and could be addressed to one of
the Chorus. Kannicht in his edition of the play (Kannicht 1969) obelizes v. 892; in his
note he develops Zuntz's argument for a lacuna but adds no compelling arguments of
his own. However, even if Zuntz's strenuous argument (Zuntz 1960, 206 ff.) for a
lacuna after v. 891 be sound, my point, above, about the importance of Helen's and
Menelaus' pleas to Theonoe is in no way invalidated: Zuntz believes that, in the
(incompletely transcribed) conclusion of Theonoe's speech here, she is simply expressing the danger to herself of failing to reveal Menelaus' presence to her brother. Zuntz
concludes: 'Helen's and Menelaus' appeal are felt by no means to be a mere rhetorical
exercise when it is realized that success is anything but a foregone conclusion'
(1960, 210).   [25] Duchemin 1945, 128 n. 4: cf. also pp. 75, 118.

priestess, should know all *divine* matters . . . and yet not know what is just!' 922–3); Menelaus', a blunt (if slightly confused) soldier's appeal for his rights . . . and a promise of bloodshed all around if he doesn't get them. There is, moreover, another (this time ironic) connection between the content of this *agōn* and the subsequent action. Helen argues, successfully, that Theonoe should not perform base and unjust favours (χάριτας πονηρὰς, 902) for her brother Theoclymenos by delivering to him what is not rightly his (namely, herself, Helen); in the sequel, it is Helen who will exploit 'base χάρις' ('favour'), when she secures Theoclymenos' aid in the feigned 'sea-burial' of Menelaus, with the false promise, χάρις . . . ἀντὶ χάριτος (1234) ('favour for favour'), of what is not, and never will be his (namely herself, Helen). These connections are, perhaps, superficial, and suited to the somewhat improbable action of the *Helen*; nevertheless, they indicate the playwright's awareness, as he composes his rhetorical *agōn*, of what is going on in the rest of the play.

Let us consider next three agonistic passages in Euripides' *Hecuba*, each of which makes its separate rhetorical impact in its immediate context. In the first, Hecuba pleads with Odysseus for the life of her daughter, doomed to be sacrificed to the shade of Achilles; in the second, Hecuba pleads with her victorious enemy, Agamemnon, for aid in vengeance on Polymestor, the Thracian King who has treacherously slain her son, Polydoros; in the third, Hecuba defends herself before Agamemnon against Polydoros' indictment of her for the slaughter of his children. Can we find, in addition to the separate effects of these scenes, any connections between them which relate to the larger theme of the play?[26]

In the first scene, Hecuba is seeking a favour from Odysseus, namely that he should save the life of her daughter in return for a favour she once did him in saving *his* life, when he might have been captured by the Trojans. (The Greek concept of *charis*, 'favour', traditionally contained this reciprocal element.) Hecuba concludes her plea with a significant *sententia* ('wise sentiment') on 'persuasion'. Odysseus' *stature* among the Greeks (she tells him) will persuade them, *even if he speaks badly*:

For the same argument coming from men of repute and from men of *no* repute has very different weight. (294–5)

---

[26] Only the first and third of these passages is, properly speaking, in the form of an *agōn*. For the limited dramatic relevance which Duchemin finds in them, see Duchemin 1945, 128–30.

Odysseus rejects Hecuba's plea based on *charis*, stating that the personal favour which he owes to her is outweighed by the *political* favour which is owed to Achilles, for the latter carries implications for other warriors who may be asked to die for their country. *Greeks*, Odysseus reminds her scornfully, understand this principle of honouring their heroic dead, and so prosper; barbarians do neither.

As the play progresses, the suffering Queen is crushed not only by the sacrifice of Polyxena but by the further blow of Polydoros' murder. Hecuba's earlier appeal to Odysseus was based on *just* claims of favour for favour; now, in her desperation, she resorts to an ignoble use of the *charis*-argument: she begs her victorious enemy Agamemnon for aid in avenging Polydoros in return for erotic favours from her daughter Cassandra (vv. 826–30). This time, Hecuba's gnomic utterance on Persuasion (*Peitho*) occurs in the middle of her speech and is now adapted to the base use to which she is about to put the art of rhetoric:

Why do we mortals labour at all other arts. . . . and yet spend neither sweat nor gold to learn Persuasion, man's only mistress, by which we might achieve whatever we might wish . . .? (814–19)

(A *cri de cœur* reminding us of the base descriptions of rhetoric urged by certain sophistic opponents of 'Socrates' in Plato's *Gorgias*.)[27]

In the last of our three scenes from the *Hecuba*, the Queen's pronouncement on Rhetoric comes at the *beginning* of her defence before Agamemnon in the *agōn* between her and her victim Polymestor. It is now her enemy Polymestor who has had recourse to the *charis*-argument: he now claims vengeance on Hecuba for murdering *his* children in return for his favour to Agamemnon for murdering the young Trojan prince. Once again, the changed circumstances produce a significant difference in Hecuba's view of the art of Persuasion:

Never (she cries) should words have greater power than deeds! Only if men do good should they have power of speech! (1187–9)

Polymestor's 'favour-for-favour' claim on Agamemnon, Hecuba neatly rebuts by taking a leaf out of Odysseus' book. Odysseus has

---

[27] e.g. by 'Polus', at Plato, *Gorgias* 466a ff.

scornfully shown her the gulf between Greeks and barbarians when
she has pressed her claims of gratitude on him:

Base one! [she now cries to Polymestor] How could your *barbarian* race be
friend to Greeks? What favour urge on them?   (1199 ff.)

Hecuba has learned her lesson well.

In these three passage, Euripides rings the changes on several well-
worn rhetorical ploys concerning *charis* ('favour') and the art of
rhetoric itself. In so doing, he shows us also how men's values, like
their use of rhetoric, change tragically with the vicissitudes of
fortune and this, I would maintain, is an essential element in the
tragedy of Queen Hecuba, as it is presented in this play.

In a section entitled '*L'agōn hors d'œuvre*',[28] Duchemin describes
the adaptation of the *agōn* by Euripides to a new use: that of presenting
his own ideas, on topics of contemporary interest, in debates of a
sophistic type between two people defending opposed points of view.
At the extreme end of this development, Duchemin places the debate
on 'Democracy versus Tyranny' in Euripides' *Supplices*. In between,
she places such scenes as that between Ion and his newly found
'father' Xouthos (*Ion* 517–65), in which Ion unsuccessfully urges
various reasons why he should remain as a temple-boy at Delphi
instead of assuming his position as a young prince at Athens. Here
she finds that, though the subject of the debate does arise from the
action, the theoretical discussion has only a 'quite intellectual' link
with the situation of personages involved. Now it is quite true that in
Ion's long speech (584–647) the speaker develops several set and
'detachable' topics, some of them favoured elsewhere by Euripides
and other tragic poets: such are 'the unpopularity of foreigners at
"autochthonous" Athens' (589–94; cf. *Medea* 222 ff., 252 ff.); the hard
lot of ambitious young men in a keenly competitive state (596–606);
the fear-ridden life of the τύραννος ('tyrant') versus the peaceful life
of the private citizen (621 ff.; cf. *Hipp.* 1016–20; Sophocles, *OT* 584–
99; Shakespeare, *Henry V*, Act IV, Sc. 1). But Duchemin fails to point
out the very real links which this speech does contain with the
thematic material of the play, including Ion's own ambiguous situation and his own characteristic reactions to it, both here and
elsewhere in the action. The myth of Athens' autochthonous origins
has already received considerable attention (265–93) and it is to form

[28] Duchemin 1945, 132–5.

the basis of the Chorus' and the old Tutor's encouragement of Creousa to murder the young interloper. Secondly, in the midst of his 'political' worries about moving to Athens, Ion expresses a touching concern for the childless Queen Creousa's feelings which his presence at Athens as the King's son might evoke. This surely reaffirms the instinctive sympathy between Ion and his unknown mother, Creousa, which has been such a prominent feature of their first encounter (see 237–369, passim) and which is to add a piquant irony to the two murder plots (mother versus son and son versus mother) and their happy *denouement* later on. Once again, it would appear that Euripides has done much to atone for the rhetorical excursions which he does make in this agonistic speech.

Let us turn to a 'political' play of Euripides, his *Supplices*, where the agonistic passages have been singled out as lacking both dramatic relevance and any concern for 'character' in the utterances of the principle *persona* ('character in a play'), Theseus. The first *agōn* of the play occurs (87–262) between Theseus and Adrastus as they debate the issue of Adrastus' supplication: namely, whether Athens should force Thebes to return the bodies of the Argive heroes slain in battle. Illustrating his view of the 'inherent contradiction between the *agōn*-form and natural drama', Collard comments (in his recent edition of the play): 'When the debaters argue "politics", they rationalize Adrastus' defeat and Theseus' rejection of the suppliants according to attitudes and premises which rely less on the tragic world of myth than on contemporary Greece or Athens: their immediacy develops naturally from the *agōn*-form's essential independence.'[29] Of Theseus in this context, Collard remarks: 'His words are informed by the needs of the *agōn*, what A. M. Dale well described in the general context of Tragic character-drawing as "the trend of the action and the rhetoric of the situation". It matters less in *Supplices* that we need to balance attitudinizing in an *agōn* against a whole portrait, because Theseus is important not as an individual, a "character" with feelings, faults or destiny, but as a symbol, a representative, a catalyst of the action.'[30]

Now we may readily grant that neither the character nor the destiny of Theseus is the central concern of this tragedy. Nevertheless, Theseus is more than a symbol through whom the appropriate rhetoric is piped. Both major decisions in this play are made by

[29] Collard 1975b, vol. I, p. 28.   [30] 1975b, 30.

Theseus, decisions which involve 'choice' and so (as Aristotle would tell us) 'character'.[31] Paradoxically, *both* Theseus' decisions, first to reject, then to accept Adrastus' supplication turn on his attitude to the gods and on the 'world view' which this entails, though it takes his mother's advice to open his eyes to the true issue. Ironically, the major expression of this 'world view' (which is maintained consistently throughout the play) is to be found in a passage which is most in danger of being mistaken for a mere rhetorical *excursus* on a contemporary theme. Theseus begins his formal rejection of Adrastus' plea with a little disquisition (vv. 195–213) on man's social evolution. Theseus praises 'whichever of the gods' it was who first separated man from his bestial existence by giving him intelligence whence he acquired successive arts and may successfully conduct his life. Significantly, Theseus' list of the arts ends with the divine art of augury which Adrastus neglected when he ignored the warnings of his prophet and joined bad allies in an unjust war. Thus it is Adrastus' infringement of the rules of 'the well-ordered universe' in which Theseus believes which results in the initial rejection of the Argive suppliants, but when Aithra opens her son's eyes to the greater wrongs now being done the suppliants, he goes to war with the Thebans in defence of that same 'well-ordered universe'. This is the point of his repeated claims to the Theban Herald later that he is championing the ancient law of the gods (νόμος παλαιὸς δαιμόνων, 563) and the international law of all the Greeks (Πανελλήνων νόμος, 671) in insisting, by force if necessary, that the Thebans allow burial of the enemy dead.

This is perhaps about as much as we can claim, in the way of 'dramatic relevance' and 'in-character opinions' for Theseus' speech to Adrastus and his debate with the Theban Herald. Those parts of the former speech which deal with ambitious war-mongering 'hawks', who plague the state (232–7) and which describe and evaluate the three orders of society (238–45) are, of course, nothing more than political *topoi* ('common-places') based on contemporary circumstances which have 'nothing (or at any rate very little) to do with the case'. The same is true of the celebrated debate, 'Tyranny versus Democracy', which forms the main substance of the second *agōn*, that between the Herald and Theseus. This passage, which reads almost like a set piece from a rhetorician's school, has only the most

---

[31] Cf. Aristotle, *Poetics* 1450[b]8–9; cf. 1449[b]36–1450[a]2.

general kind of connection with the dramatic situation (e.g. the con-trast between 'good' democratic Athens and 'bad' despotic Thebes), and contains various rhetorical criticisms and defences of each constitution which are quite irrelevant to it.

I have purposely concluded this discussion of Euripidean rhetoric with mention of a passage which is least amenable to the kinds of defence, in terms of dramatic relevance and appropriateness, which I have urged in other, more debatable examples. I am not concerned in this paper with any special pleading for Euripides; indeed, I am sure that readers of the dramatist will think of various other passages, and not all of them from the so-called 'political plays', which could be assailed almost as effectively, on this score, as the 'Theban Herald debate' in *The Suppliants*. All I have sought to establish is that, gen-erally speaking, Euripidean rhetoric is not as dramatically inorganic as many scholars have argued, and that many passages which have been assessed simply as set pieces of sophistic debate also contain much that is relevant to the major themes and even to significant revelations of character (in relation to the dramatic action) in the plays to which they belong.

5

'Impiety' and 'Atheism' in Euripides' Dramas

MARY R. LEFKOWITZ

In the surviving plays of Aeschylus and Sophocles the gods appear to
men only rarely. In the *Eumenides* Apollo and Athena intervene to
bring acquittal to Orestes. In Sophocles' *Philoctetes* Heracles appears
ex machina to ensure that the hero returns to Troy, and we learn from
a messenger how the gods have summoned the aged Oedipus to a
hero's tomb. In Sophocles' *Ajax* Athena drives Ajax mad and taunts
him cruelly. *Prometheus Bound* (assuming that it is by Aeschylus)
might seem to be an exception, since all but one of its characters are
gods. But nonetheless the intervention of the gods in the life of the
one human character, Io, brings pain and trouble as well as promise
of benefit. Io has been driven mad because she has refused to obey the
dreams that tell her to go to the meadow where Zeus wants to have
intercourse with her. The god does not make his request in person,
and it is only in the course of her wanderings that Io learns how Zeus
will bring a gentle end to her sufferings. Her informant is another
god, Zeus' adversary Prometheus, who answers her questions at
times grudgingly (778), and in ways that are not immediately clear
to her (775).[1]

Of the three dramatists, it is Euripides who makes his audience
most keenly aware of the gods' interest in human affairs. Nine of his
nineteen surviving plays conclude with scenes where gods speak

---

[1] Gods also appeared in Aeschylus' *Prometheus Luomenos* (p. 306 Radt),
Psychostasia (p. 375), *Oreithyia* (fr. 281), *Xantriai* (or *Semele?*, fr. 168). Athena speaks
angrily in Soph.'s *Aias Lokros* (fr. 10c) and Apollo points out victims to Artemis in
Niobe (fr. 441a); Demeter speaks in the *Triptolemus* (fr. 598) and Thetis in the
Syndeipnoi (fr. 562). Schmidt 1963, 69–78 lists examples of epiphanies in myth
and cult.

from the stage machine;[2] in four plays gods speak the prologue;[3] Iris
and Lyssa appear, dramatically—and with terrifying effectiveness—
in the middle of the *Heracles*. Only six plays have no gods as characters, though in four of these the audience hears about or sees a
miraculous event that could only have been brought about by a god:
Medea appears with the bodies of her children in the chariot of Helios;
in the *Heraclidae* we learn how in the midst of the battle against
Eurystheus (Heracles' persecutor) Heracles and his bride Hebe, the
goddess of youthful vigour, appear as a pair of stars near the chariot
of old Iolaus, Heracles' nephew, and make him young again, just for
the day of the battle (851–8); as Agamemnon prepares to sacrifice his
daughter Iphigenia, the goddess Artemis makes the girl disappear and
puts a deer in her place (*IA* 1580–95). In the *Hecuba* the murderer of
Hecuba's son Polymestor is told by Dionysus that Hecuba, who has
blinded him and murdered his children will be turned into a dog whose
tomb will be a landmark for sailors (1265–74). Only in two plays, the
satyr play *Cyclops* and the *Phoenissae*, does no miracle occur.

Yet despite the frequency with which Euripides portrays in his
dramas the gods and their actions, he is thought of as the poet who
more than any other asks his audiences, ancient and modern, to
question the nature of the gods and even their existence.[4] The notion
that the poet himself had doubts about traditional religion, even to
the point of being atheistic, derives from his own dramas, or rather
from Aristophanes' and other comic poets' versions of them.[5] In the
Thesmophoriazusae, a woman claims that Euripides has spoiled her
livelihood (selling wreaths for statues of the gods) because 'by
working in tragedies he has persuaded men that the gods do not
exist' (οὐκ εἶναι θεούς, 450–1). Perhaps she is alluding here, as
Christoph Riedweg has suggested, to the striking lines in Euripides'

---

[2] Gods *ex machina* in *Hipp.*, *Suppl.*, *El.*, *Ion*, *IT*, *Hel.*, *Or.*, *Ba.*, *Rhes.*, cf. *Antiope*;
cf. Barrett 1964, 395; Taplin 1977, 444–5. Possibly also *Phaethon*, *Rhadymanthys*
(PSI 1286 = Hypothesis 14 Austin), *Erechtheus*, *Phrixus*, *Archelaus* (cf. test. 7, Harder
1985, 174).   [3] Gods speak in the prologues of *Alc.*, *Hipp.*, *Tro.* *Ba.*
[4] e.g. Segal 1982, 335–6, 'the monumentalising effect of these lines (*Ba.* 1325–6)
again puts the truth about divinity in the form of an absence'; cf. Foley 1985, 258,
'Euripides can find no order outside ritual and myth and rational speech, yet in the end
the order provided by art, ritual, and speech remains in an uncertain relation to the
reality of the contemporary world'; cf. Goldhill 1986*a*, 234; Michelini 1987, 315–20;
Dunn 1996, 26–44. On the development (from Romanticism) of this modern attitude,
see esp. Schlesier 1986, 35–50; Lloyd-Jones 1983, 151–5; Michelini 1987, 108.
[5] Cf. Lefkowitz 1987, 149–66; Riedweg 1990*a*, 39 n. 2.

Bellerophontes, where the speaker, probably Bellerophontes himself,
denies the existence of the gods:[6]

> φησίν τις εἶναι δῆτ' ἐν οὐρανῷ θεούς;
> οὐκ εἰσίν, οὐκ εἴσ', εἴ τις ἀνθρώπων θέλει
> μὴ τῷ παλαιῷ μῶρος ὢν χρῆσθαι λόγῳ.

Does anyone say that there are gods in heaven? No, they do not exist;
they don't exist, unless someone is a fool and wants to rely on the old
story.   (Frag. 286. 1–3 N²)

The comic Euripides in the *Frogs* prays to 'other, private gods': 'Ether,
my food; Pivot of my tongue, Comprehension, and Nostrils keen to
scent' (888–93). In the *Thesmophoriazusae* he tells a story of creation
in which Ether, rather than Earth, is the mother of all living things
(14–15). In the *Frogs*, according to his adversary Aeschylus, he is 'an
enemy of the gods' (836).

    In antiquity being atheistic or impious (the terms are not syn-
onymous)[7] signified an inability to distinguish right from wrong.
Consequently, Aristophanes' Euripides is a notably 'deft' (δεξιός,
Ran. 71, *Thesm.* 9) and wordy poet, capable of verbal play that his
interlocutors cannot follow (e.g. *Thesm.* 5–11). In the *Thesmophoriazusae* Euripides' aged in-law (275–6) and in the *Frogs* Dionysus
(102, 1471), in order to get out of commitments that they have made
to him, use his own famous lines from the *Hippolytus*: 'my tongue
swore it, but my mind foreswore the oath' (612). Aeschylus accuses
him of writing about incest (850), putting whores like Phaedra and
Stheneboea on the stage (1043), and not setting an appropriate
moral standard, which is 'to hide what is shameful, not to bring it on
the stage or to write about it. Little boys have a teacher to tell them
[what is right]; grown men have poets' (1053–5). Euripides, claims
Aristophanes' Aeschylus, has caused a general moral decline in
Athens, not only by portraying immorality on the stage, but by his
rhetoric:

For what evils is he *not* responsible? Hasn't he exhibited procuresses, and
women who bear children in temples, and have intercourse with their
brothers, and state that life is not life?   (1078–82)

---

[6] As always, the lines are quoted out of context: Bellerophontes' impiety was
punished by Zeus at the end of the play; see Riedweg 1990*a*, 46–50 and Riedweg
1990*b*, 130.   [7] Cf. Winiarczyk 1984, 182–3.

This atheistic and immoral Euripides bears a close resemblance to the Socrates in the *Clouds*,[8] who is carried about in his basket in the air, praying to new gods that have no established cult, Air, Ether, and Clouds (264–5), and who can produce a Worse Argument that 'can plead an unjust cause and overturn the better argument' (884–5, cf. Pl. *Apol.* 19b). As the writer of the Hippocratic treatise *On the Sacred Disease* observes, because magicians and wonder-workers try to usurp the gods' function by bringing down the moon, eclipsing the sun, and changing the weather, 'I think that they are impious (δυσσεβεῖν) and that they do not believe that the gods exist (οὐ νομίζειν θεοὺς εἶναι)[9] nor that the gods have any powers nor that the gods would refrain from any of the most extreme actions' (*Morb. Sac.* ch. iv). As Plato has Socrates say in the *Apology*, people assume that philosophers 'search for what is in the air and beneath the earth' (*Apol.* 23d) and 'do not believe in the gods' (θεοὺς μὴ νομίζειν) and 'make the worse appear the better cause' (cf. 18c).

But although Euripides' 'philosophizing' made him seem impious, at least to the comic poets and the biographers who used their works as 'evidence', I believe that it can be shown that any character in Euripides who expresses 'philosophical' notions about the gods does so out of desperation, and that ultimately, the gods in that play will prove—not always to the characters' satisfaction—that the gods still retain their traditional powers. Perhaps understandably, modern scholars often seem uncomfortable with such an austere notion of divinity. But let us review the passages where characters in plays criticize the gods or question their motives or even their existence,[10] considering the nature of the gods' behaviour in the dramas where characters complain of them, and comparing (wherever possible) Euripides' portrayal of the gods with those of Homer and of the other dramatists.

---

[8] Aristophanes, in the first version of his *Clouds*, even has a character claim that Socrates composed those hyper-wordy plays for Euripides, the 'clever ones' (σοφάς, fr. 392 K–A). Other comic poets also alleged that Socrates collaborated with Euripides; Aristophanes' contemporary Teleclides wrote of 'Euripideses nailed together by Socrates' (1 219 K, cf. also Callias, fr. 15 K–A) and of Euripides' father-in-law Mnesilochus (possibly the poet's old in-law in the *Thesm.*) cooking up a new play for Euripides, and Socrates supplying him with firewood (39, 40 K, cf. DL 2. 18, and Lefkowitz 1987, 152).

[9] This phrase is synonymous with οὐ θεοὺς νομίζειν, cf. Fahr 1969, 164–7.

[10] Not including the notorious fragment of the *Sisyphus* (Critias, fr. 1 N) sometimes attributed to Eur., cf. Winiarczyk 1987, 35–45.

Hecuba, in a famous passage, speaks lines that according to at least one ancient commentator, 'derive from the sayings of Anaxagoras' (ὁρμῶνται δὲ ἐκ τῶν Ἀναξαγορείων λόγων, schol. *Tro.* 884):[11]

> ὦ γῆς ὄχημα κἀπὶ γῆς ἔχων ἕδραν,
> ὅστις ποτ' εἶ σύ, δυστόπαστος εἰδέναι,
> Ζεύς, εἴτ' ἀνάγκη φύσεος εἴτε νοῦς βροτῶν,
> προσηυξάμην σε· πάντα γὰρ δι' ἀψόφου
> βαίνων κελεύθου κατὰ δίκην τὰ θνήτ' ἄγεις.

conveyor of the earth and you who have a base on earth, whoever you are, most difficult to know, Zeus, or necessity of nature or the mind of men, I address you in prayer. For as you go along your silent path, you direct all mortal affairs according to justice.　(884–8)

To ask a god by what name he or she prefers to be addressed is an act of piety, whose purpose is to make the prayer effective by getting power over or at least pleasing the god.[12] Like the chorus in Aesch. *Ag.* 160–6, who say 'Zeus, whoever he may be', Hecuba does not doubt that Zeus exists, but rather indicates that she is not sure exactly who he is, since he is 'most difficult to know'.[13] Although it seems to have been in no way impious to speak of Zeus as the controlling force in the universe,[14] because Euripides has Menelaus observe that she seems to have 'invented new prayers to the gods' (εὐχὰς ὡς ἐκαίνισας θεῶν, 889), scholars have assumed that she might be thought of as unconventional, or even impious, like Socrates, who was accused by Meletus of believing in 'other new forms of divinity' (ἕτερα δαιμόνια καινά, *Apol.* 24b). Her third suggestion, that Zeus might be 'the mind of man', encouraged the ancient commentators to propose that Euripides was thinking specifically of Anaxagoras' theory that Mind controls everything in the universe (59 B 12 D–K). But the allusion, if it is one, is not precise. Similar notions were expressed by other philosophers at the time.

---

[11] Cf. Lefkowitz 1987, 154, 163–4.

[12] Cf. Fraenkel 1962, II. 100; Kannicht 1969, II. 296; Dodds 1960 on 893–4.

[13] But cf. how in Euripides even so traditional a question as 'Zeus, or if you prefer to be called Hades' (fr. 912 N), was judged to be 'philosophical' by a commentator on his work: 'he has caught Anaxagoras' world-view concisely and accurately in three words'; and provokes the claim that 'elsewhere he is uncertain about the established order in heavenly affairs' (Satyrus 37 iii).

[14] Cf. esp. Aesch. fr. 70 Radt; Derveni Papyrus apud West 1983, 26–9.

For example, the eclectic Diogenes of Apollonia,[15] a contemporary of Anaxagoras, speaks of the air that is 'life and intelligence' ($\psi \upsilon \chi \grave{\eta} \ \kappa \alpha \grave{\iota}$ $\nu \acute{o} \eta \sigma \iota s$) to men and beasts (64 B 4 D–K): 'what men call air is what has intelligence ($\nu \acute{o} \eta \sigma \iota s$), and all of them are governed by it and it controls everything' (69 B 5 D–K).[16] In any case, in her vague allusions to the language of the philosophers, Hecuba does not completely abandon conventional anthropomorphic terminology:[17] Zeus who is the conveyance of the earth also has 'a seat upon the earth',[18] and 'he goes along a silent path and guides human affairs with justice'. In calling Zeus' movements 'silent', Euripides might have in mind the music of the spheres, which is inaudible to man (Philolaus 58 B 35 D–K), but the idea that men are unaware of, and thus surprised by, Zeus' enactment of his justice also goes back to Solon, who compares the justice of Zeus to a sudden spring storm (fr. 13. 17–25).[19]

Although Aristophanes and the ancient commentators did not hesitate to ascribe to Euripides himself the notions expressed by characters in his plays, we must keep in mind that in this passage from the *Trojan Women* it is, of course, Hecuba and not Euripides who is speaking. Troy has fallen, and she, along with the other women have been assigned as slaves to Greek masters. Hecuba has just seen her grandson Astyanax led away to be hurled to his death from the walls of Troy—an act that even moves the Greek herald Talthybius to pity (787). Now Menelaus has come to get Helen; the Greeks have given him permission to kill her, but he wants to wait till he returns to Greece. It is at this point that Hecuba utters her prayer. She and the women of Troy (857–81, 1071–6) doubt here and throughout the play that the gods care about the fate of Troy (cf. also 469–71,

---

[15] Cf. Lee 1976, 224; on Diogenes, cf. Kirk, Raven, and Schofield 1983, 444; Barnes 1982, 580, 646 n. 10.

[16] Cf. also 'in each of us our mind is god', a line attributed both to Euripides (fr. 1018 N) and Menander (Monostich. 588 Jaekel), cited by schol. *Tr.* 884. Matthiessen 1968, 699–700 (followed by Barlow 1986, 209), identifies Zeus here with $\alpha \grave{\iota} \theta \acute{\eta} \rho$ ('ether'), as in frr. 877, 941, cf. 330 N (parodied in Ar. *Ran.* 100, 311; *Thesm.* 272). But Eur. combines 'Anaxagorean' ideas with traditional terminology in Eur.'s *Chrysippus*, fr. 839 N = 59 A 112 D–K, about 'great Earth and Zeus' $\alpha \grave{\iota} \theta \acute{\eta} \rho$, who is the begetter of men and of gods' (cf. frr. 944, 1023, 1004 N); Zeus inhabits the air in fr. 487 N, cf. Empedocles 31 B 142 D–K.   [17] Cf. Scodel 1980, 93–5.

[18] Cf. Scodel 1980, 94 n. 33, who compares the divine (Poseidon, Zeus, Artemis) epithet $\gamma \alpha \iota \acute{\eta} o \chi o s$ ('earth-carrying').

[19] Lee 1976 ad loc. compares Solon's description of Dike who silently ($\sigma \iota \gamma \hat{\omega} \sigma \alpha$) takes in all that happens and eventually takes her revenge (4. 15–16 W); cf. also Solon fr. 17 W where the mind of the immortals is always invisible ($\grave{\alpha} \phi \alpha \nu \acute{\eta} s$) to men.

1240–5, 1280–1). But the audience knows that the gods have not forgotten about Troy. They realize, as the Trojan women cannot, since the scene took place in the prologue, before Hecuba and the other women of Troy came on stage, that Zeus and his daughter Athena, with the help of Zeus' brother Poseidon, have already set in motion the forces that will bring about the revenge against the Greeks that Hecuba desires. Thus if Euripides has put Anaxagorean notions into Hecuba's mouth, it is only to show that even though she suspects that the gods have abandoned her and the cause of justice, Zeus remains in control of the cosmos, not only in the form of the 'mind of man', but (though also imperceptibly to mortals) through the powerful agency of his immortal daughter and brother.[20]

Ancient biographers believed that Euripides was a pupil of his younger contemporary the sophist Prodicus, who like Anaxagoras and Protagoras was said to have been tried in Athens for impiety; according to the Suda, like Socrates Prodicus 'died in Athens by drinking hemlock on the grounds that he corrupted the youth' (P 2365: I. iv. 201 Adler). In the commentaries that have come down to us, no particular passages are identifed as 'Prodicean', but modern scholars have thought that the lines in the *Bacchae* where Tiresias describes the gods Demeter and Dionysus show the influence of Prodicus' ideas.[21] In the drama, Tiresias tries to persuade the hostile Pentheus not to reject the cult of Dionysus and to acknowledge both the existence and the power of the god:

For there are two things that are of the greatest importance for men: the goddess Demeter—she is the earth, by whatever name you wish to call her; she nourishes mortals with dry food; and after her comes the son of Semele, who discovered the wet drink of the vine and brought it to mortals . . .   (275–80)

Prodicus wrote: 'the ancients thought that the sun and moon and rivers and springs and in general everything that helps our life were gods because of the help they received from them, as the Egyptians call the Nile a god, and on account of this they called bread Demeter, wine Dionysus, water Poseidon, fire Hephaestus, and every useful thing [by the name of a god]' (77 B 5. 13–17 D–K). That men gave the names of gods to useful things apparently was for Prodicus not a mere

[20] Riedweg 1990*a*, 51–3.
[21] Cf. Dodds 1960, 104–5; Lefkowitz 1987, 158, 164. On other 'allusions', see esp. O'Brien 1988, 31 n. 4.

façon de parler; recent papyrus discoveries have confirmed that Prodicus claimed that the gods of popular belief did not exist.[22] Tiresias, on the other hand, does not go so far as saying that bread *is* Demeter or wine *is* Dionysus; he only claims that they are important gods because they have given men such useful gifts.

We ought also to ask how much conviction Tiresias' 'modernistic' arguments carry in the context of the drama. Tiresias tells Pentheus that it is not necessary literally to believe that Dionysus as a baby was sewn into the thigh of his father Zeus, but explains that the story was concocted out of a confusion in words (286–9). Cadmus likes Tiresias' rationalistic arguments (330), and urges his grandson Pentheus to say that Dionysus is a god, even if, as Pentheus alleges (332–3), he is not. But, apparently, it is not enough for Cadmus to don the god's apparel, or to say that he should be made much of because he is the son of his daughter Semele, or even to have made Semele's grave into a sacred area, since at the end of the play, Cadmus will be exiled from the city he has founded and be turned into a snake.

Tiresias (or Prodicus') arguments thus prove worthless. What the god wants is not gratitude for his services to men, but public recognition that he was born the son of Zeus (47), which involves accepting the bizarre story of his birth. In fact, whenever the god manifests himself during the action of the play, he has nothing to do with his practical gift to men of wine. Rather, the women who have come with his cult from Asia sing twice of the miraculous way in which he was taken as an embryo from his mother's corpse and enclosed in Zeus' thigh with golden pins (88–100, 521–9). As we have seen, the god is not satisfied with mere conformity or lip service, nor is the notion of private, personal belief in any way involved; what the god wants is honour. As he tells Cadmus when he appears *ex machina* at the end of the play to prophesy what will happen to him and his family:

I Dionysus am telling you this, because I was not born from a mortal father but from Zeus. If you had understood how to be sensible, when you didn't want to, you would be happy to have the son of Zeus as an ally.   (1340–4)

'Being sensible' (σωφρονεῖν) about Dionysus means not going along with sophistic arguments, as the chorus says: 'being wise is not

---

[22] e.g., *PHerc.* 1428 fr. 19; cf. Henrichs 1975, 110 n. 64; 1984, 145 n. 24. Testimonia in Winiarczyk 1984, 177.

wisdom (τὸ σοφὸν δ' οὐ σοφία) nor is [wisdom] thinking more than
mortal thoughts' (395–6).

Can Euripides in the *Bacchae* be recommending the pious acceptance of irrationalism? Walter Burkert has characterized these lines as
an expression of the paradox that the state that produced Socrates
condemned him and other rationalists to death: 'Pentheus, the sensible defender of rational order, is drawn to a wretched end; irrationalism rises against enlightenment.'[23] But to speak of Pentheus as a
'sensible defender of rational order' does not correspond with the
facts of the play, where Pentheus' conduct is neither sensible nor
rational; as the messenger states from his more objective standpoint:
'I fear your quick judgments, master, your sharp temper and your
too imperious bearing' (670–1). The issue, as Euripides describes it, is
not irrationalism vs. enlightenment, but whether or not it is desirable
to have the cult of the god Dionysus in Thebes. From the beginning
Euripides makes it clear that the dances and rituals of the god will
bring at best a mixed blessing to the city. Participants in his rites are
required to act contrary to the conventional rules of behaviour: they
must wear a strange get-up that strikes Pentheus as absurd and
foolish (250–2), and the rites of Dionysus are celebrated mainly at
night, a time that Pentheus, like most Greek men, considers 'treacherous and corrupt for women' (487). Nonetheless, the consequences of
rejecting the cult are even worse: the god drives the women mad, so
that they abandon their homes and live in the mountains and
behave like wild beasts. To portray such undesirable alternatives
does not amount to condemnation of the gods; as Achilles says in the
grim context of the last book of the *Iliad*, from his two jars of good and
evil Zeus offers man a mixture, or all evil (524–33).[24] As a dramatist,
Euripides' purpose is to describe ancient myth in realistic and vivid
terms; and his lesson, if anything, as in other Greek religious ritual, is
to do honour to the gods and, in the process, to remind men of their
mortal limitations.[25]

It is important to remember that to Euripides' contemporaries,
honouring the gods did not mean liking them, or applauding their
actions; on the contrary, the Athenian dramatists seem concerned to
portray them in all the emotions that the gods manifest towards

---

[23] Burkert 1985, 317.
[24] Cf. Eur. fr. 661 N from the beginning of the *Stheneboea*.
[25] Cf. Dodds 1960, xlv–xlvi.

mortals: cruelty, neglect, anger, loyalty, and occasionally, even affection, especially for one of their own children. It is characteristic of mortals to complain that the gods do not play by human rules, and to state openly that humans are notably kinder and more forgiving. When Hippolytus refuses to honour Aphrodite, his slave prays to her statue: 'queen Cypris, you must forgive him; if a man talks foolishly with intense passion because of his youth, pretend not to hear it. For gods ought to be wiser (σοφωτέρους) than mortals' (*Hipp.* 117–20). But, as Euripides will say again in the *Bacchae*, human wisdom is not wisdom, so far as the gods are concerned. Aphrodite has told us in the prologue that:

I give preference to men who honour my power, and I destroy those who adopt a proud attitude towards me. For the gods as well [as men] have this trait: they take pleasure in being honoured by men. (5–8)

Aphrodite would not resent that Hippolytus honours Artemis, if he gave due honour also to her, but instead 'he says I am the worst of divinities; he refuses to have intercourse and does not touch marriage' (13–14). And so she will exact her vengeance on him, without expending much effort, in one day. Note again that his 'wronging her' (ἃ δ᾽ εἰς ἔμ᾽ ἡμάρτηκε, 21) does not consist simply in his not having paid due respect, by placing a wreath on her statue, as he did for his patron Artemis; he must also acknowledge her power by submitting to the demands of sexuality.

Why didn't his patron Artemis try to defend him? Speaking *ex machina* at the end of the play, she explains that she could not save him because there is a law among the gods, set down by Zeus, that none will oppose the set purpose of another; otherwise she would not have let the mortal dearest to her die: 'the gods get no pleasure from the death of pious men—it is the evil we destroy, children and house and all' (1340–1). She promises Hippolytus that she will avenge him by killing with her own arrows whoever happens to be dearest to Aphrodite, and by giving him 'very great honours in the city of Troezen': girls before their marriage will dedicate a lock of their hair to him, and will sing of him and of Phaedra's passion for him.[26]

---

[26] On Artemis' 'indirect' revenge, cf. de Romilly 1961, 32 ff. Since preserving one's name, like song itself (cf. Eur. *Tro.* 1242–5), bestows a kind of immortality even on dead men and women, gods at the end of plays, either in person or through prophecy, frequently grant eponymous honours, either in the form of rituals or place-names; Wilson 1968, 70 n. 8 lists *El.* 1273, *Or.* 1646, *Hel.* 1670, *HF* 1328, *IT* 1453, *Hec.* 1275, *Antiope* fr. 48. 80–5 ed. Kambitsis 1972; to which might be added the first

In a religion where there is no possibility of an afterlife, heroic honour and lasting fame are the highest compensation one can expect, especially if they can be combined with the possibility of revenge, in a moral system that enjoins one to help one's friends and harm one's enemies. No one asks Artemis, as the Corinthian women ask Medea, whether her intended victim—whoever he is—deserves to die, so that she can harm Aphrodite; how else could one harm a being who is immortal and ageless except by destroying some perishable being that she loves? In the *Homeric Hymn to Demeter*, the goddess prevents the crops from growing, and allows humans, even in the site of her cult, Eleusis, to perish of starvation, so that the gods will get no sacrifices, because only in that way can she get Zeus to restore her daughter to her.

The contrast between divine and mortal existence is brought out most poignantly in Hippolytus' final speech to Artemis. The goddess says she must leave because she cannot look upon the dead or pollute her sight with dying gasps (1427–9), just as Apollo says he must leave Admetus' house because Alcestis is about to die (22). So Hippolytus bids her farewell: 'easily you leave this long relationship' (1441). As Homer has Achilles say to Priam when he comes to get his son Hector's body, 'this is what the gods have allotted to miserable mortals, to live in sorrow, while they themselves are without cares' (*Il.* 24. 525–6). Artemis, like the gods in the last book of the *Iliad*, feels pity for mortals, and makes them feel pity for each other; but the same gods 'will human suffering and never share it'.[27]

If in Euripides' dramas the gods do not behave very differently from the way they behave in heroic epic, why is it that the human characters in the dramas, and consequently Euripides' audiences, express proportionately more doubts and resentment of them? I will suggest that they do so not because the nature of divinity has altered, or that the poet is trying to get his audiences to question the gods' traditional nature, but that increased fears and resentments expressed by the characters are an aspect of Euripides' celebrated realism. None of Euripides' characters, not even the children of gods, like Achilles or Helen, are so noble as his or her counterparts in Homer, or as capable

---

Hipp. (fr. 446 N = fr. U, 44–5 Barrett 1964, with n. on 1423–30), Alope's fountain (p. 390 N), and Andromeda's galaxy (p. 392 N).

[27] Macleod 1982, 132. Cf. also Desch 1986, 22; Kovacs 1987a, 69–71; Stevens 1971, 242; Denniston 1939, 210. Cf. fr. 177 N: 'Dionysus, because he is a god, is never a support to mortals.'

of seeing the suffering they have brought to their enemies, or so knowledgeable about the future.

In Euripides' *Heracles* Amphitryon is an old man, physically very weak and afraid of death; it is hard to remember that he was once a famous hero, whose form was assumed by Zeus himself in order to deceive Amphitryon's faithful wife Alcmena, Heracles' mother. It is this attenuated Amphitryon, whose only weapon is words, who blames Zeus for his neglect of his human family:

Zeus, in vain I had you as a comrade in marriage; in vain we have made famous our partnership in our son. You are less of a friend than you seemed to be. Even though I am a mortal I surpass you in virtue, even though you are a great god. For I have not betrayed the children of Heracles. You knew how to come to bed as a secret lover, seizing another man's bed when no one offered it to you, but you do not know how to save your friends. You are a stupid kind of god (ἀμαθής τις εἶ θεός), or by nature you are unjust. (339–47)

Other characters doubt the existence of the gods, when they have suffered a complete reverse of fortune: Hecuba, as we have seen, in the ruins of Troy, is uncertain who controls the universe; in the *Ion* Creusa claims that Apollo is unjust, and does not rescue the mother of his son, or answer her questions through his oracle (384–7). But as Ion (who will prove to be her son, although she does not yet know it) has said, the gods are under no obligation to answer mortals' questions if they do not choose to do so, however many sacrifices they might be offered: 'if we pursue the gods by force when they are unwilling, we have obtained unavailing benefits; but if the gods bestow gifts willingly, we are helped' (374–80).

Sometimes the god does what the mortal asks. In Euripides' *Antiope* Amphion claims that

if Zeus was our father, he will rescue us and with us punish our enemy . . . I say this to you who dwell in the bright plain of heaven, do not marry for your pleasure and then prove useless to the children you have begotten; it is not fair (καλόν) to act like that, but you should be an ally to your friends. (GLP 10 Page = fr. 48. 2–3, 10–14 Kambitsis)

In an exciting reversal of fortune (fr. 48. 67–116 Kambitsis), Zeus sends his orders through Hermes and saves the day. In the *Heracles* for a short while Zeus seems to have responded to Amphitryon's rebuke. Heracles comes, rescues his family, and kills their persecutor. But then his divine enemy Hera intervenes, and has her minion Iris come with Lyssa ('Madness') to drive Heracles insane so that he murders his wife and children. Lyssa herself protests that she takes no pleasure in attacking men she likes, and reminds Iris that Heracles has restored the shrines of the gods that had been attacked by impious men. But the rule of non-interference that Artemis described to Hippolytus remains in force, and Lyssa, though still reluctant, has no choice.

At that point the chorus, who have just exclaimed that 'the gods know about unjust men and listen to the pious' (772–4) must hear how Heracles has slaughtered the family he has just saved; and how he would have murdered his father had not Athena thrown a stone at him. Heracles, after he sees what he has done, says to Amphitryon: 'Zeus, whoever Zeus is, begot me and Hera hated me (don't be angry at me, old man; I think of you as my father rather than Zeus)' (1264–5).[28] Gods beget sons, but they do not look after them as a human parent would; the contrast demonstrates once again that the gods live without care and do not share in our sorrows. To the gods' attitude toward mortal suffering, we need only compare the conduct of Heracles' nephew Iolaus in his old age towards Heracles' second set of children:

I have joined his children in exile as an exile; I am reluctant to betray them, lest some mortal say, 'Look at this! When the children's father is dead, Iolaus, who is their relative, doesn't protect them!'   (*Heracl.* 26–30)

Perhaps the greatest privilege of being human is the ability humans have to care for one another, and to forgive; in this respect alone men are superior to gods.

The notion that human beings, despite their ignorance and weakness, are at least more compassionate than gods is not exclusive to Euripides.[29] In *Iliad* 24, the god Hermes, pretending to be a Greek soldier, assures Priam that he will not harm him, but rather protect him, since he reminds him of his own father (370–1). He tells Priam

---

[28] The formula 'whoever Zeus is' as used here (and *Or.* 418) struck Dodds 1960, on *Ba.* 893–4, as 'sceptical and bitter', perhaps because it is not accompanied by a prayer, as in *Tr.* 884; cf. Willink 1986, 155, 'consistent with piety', and West 1987, 212, 'a Euripidean cliché'. Cf. also *Hel.* 1137, with Kannicht 1969, II. 296. But the beginning of *Melanippe the Wise* was taken by ancient commentators as evidence of supposed impiety: 'Zeus, whoever Zeus may be, I don't know except from stories' (fr. 480) was said to have caused a commotion in the audience, so that Euripides changed it to 'Zeus begot Hellen, as the story goes' (fr. 481, but cf. fr. 591. 4 N²).

[29] Cf. Heath 1987, 51; Matthiessen 1968, 703–4.

in his appeal to remind Achilles of his own family (466–7). But it is Achilles, the slayer of so many of Priam's sons, not Hermes, who shows that he understands what Priam has suffered, because his own father Peleus has only one son, who like Priam's sons, will not live to keep his father company in his old age (540).[30] It is the necessity of eventual loss that makes human beings aware of the value of affection: as he is about to die, Sophocles' Oedipus says to his daughters Antigone and Ismene: 'you could not have had more love than you have had from me, and now you must live the rest of your lives without me' (*OC* 1617–19).

But it is Sophocles, not Euripides, who emphasizes the isolation of human beings from the gods, if in no other way than by *not* using the device of the *deus ex machina*. As Oedipus lingers embracing his daughters and weeping, the god's terrifying voice is heard shouting to him over and over again: 'you there, Oedipus, why are we waiting to go; long since your affairs have been delayed' (1627–8). In Sophocles' *Women of Trachis*, absence of compassion makes the dying Heracles, despite his suffering, begin to resemble a god. His son Hyllus, who will not be transformed into an immortal, is left with the duty of carrying out Heracles' orders, to burn his father alive, and to marry Iole, the woman who has caused the death of both his father and mother. Hyllus, in his speech at the end of the play, asks his slaves to carry Heracles out:[31]

grant me much forgiveness (συγγνωμοσύνην) for this, and recognize the great lack of compassion (ἀγνωμοσύνην) for what is being done; these gods who beget us and are called fathers gaze on such suffering. No one sees what is to come, but what is now happening brings sorrow to us and disgrace to the gods, the cruellest suffering experienced by man to [Heracles] who must suffer this disaster.   (1264–74)

The audience knows, as Hyllus does not, that Heracles, once his mortality is burned away, will be turned into a god, but the poet ends the play without reminding us of the one positive result of all this suffering. Instead, the last words of the play (whether spoken by Hyllus or by the chorus),[32] emphasize that so far as the human participants in the drama are concerned, Zeus is the cause of all the troubles they have witnessed: 'many sorrows, and strange; of these

---

[30] On the motif, see Macleod 1982, 118, 124. Cf. 504, where Priam says that he is more pitiable than Peleus, because he has no sons left.
[31] Cf. Easterling 1982, 230–1.   [32] Cf. Easterling 1982, 231–2.

there is none that is not Zeus' (1277–8). How different the effect
might have been if, as in Euripides' *Antiope*, Hermes had appeared
ex machina and explained to Hyllus and the others what would
happen in the future!

Since no one in antiquity assumed that because he described the
gods as uncaring Sophocles was being impious, why should we continue to ask whether Euripides was being either impious or ironical in
his portrayal of the gods? Is it because, as Bernard Knox has suggested, his gods resemble mortals so much that they are unworthy of
belief?[33] But, as I have tried to show, Euripides' gods resemble
mortals only in certain ways: they love their friends and hate their
enemies; they like honour and recognition. In other respects they are
very much unlike mortals: they do not feel pity; they do not act out of
compassion for mortals, as a mortal would for his fellow man, but in
order to see that justice is done, in their terms, which sometimes
includes a human notion of justice, but at other times involves
ensuring the working out a family curse, or taking revenge for some
wrong against them, like deprivation of their proper honours.

Why worship gods like these? The question is not easy to answer,
because except for Aristophanes, we do not know what Euripides'
contemporaries thought about the portrayal of the gods in his plays.
We cannot attribute to the poet himself what a character says
(however eloquently) in a particular situation. It is Heracles, not
Euripides, who complains of Hera's malice: 'Who could pray to such
a goddess? Because she hated ($\phi\theta o\nu o\hat{\upsilon}\sigma\alpha$) Zeus on account of a
liaison with a woman she destroyed the benefactors of Greece, who
are in no way responsible' (*HF* 1307–10). It is the nature of Zeus'
justice that the innocent must suffer (cf. Solon 13. 31–2); as the elders
of Thebes say to Antigone, 'you are paying for one of your father's
sufferings' (Soph. *Ant.* 856). But in the end, Heracles will in fact fare
better than Antigone, because he will be made a god, but even
Antigone will not die 'desolate and unlamented', as she imagines
(879–82).[34] It is not the voice of the poet speaking through his chorus,
but the women of Troy who complain of the gods in the *Trojan
Women*. In a choral song they speak of the past, when Zeus fell in love
with Ganymede, and compare it to the present, when Eros the god of
passion brought not honour but ruin, through Helen, to Troy, and
death to their own husbands and children, 'gone is the affection of

[33] Knox 1985, 317.   [34] Cf. Desch 1986, 16–17.

the gods for Troy' (821–59).[35] That they are not aware of the gods' plans to punish the Greeks does not mean that the crimes the Greeks committed during the sack of Troy will not be avenged; as Poseidon says in the prologue:

Any mortal is a fool if he sacks cities, temples, and tombs, the shrines of the dead; once he renders them desolate, he himself will perish afterwards. (95–7)

In the *Iliad*, where the gods are openly involved in the world of men, it is somewhat easier for mortals to see that the gods are concerned about them. When Zeus sends Hermes to tell Priam that his son's body will be returned to him, undamaged, 'because the blessed gods care for your son even though he is dead, because he was dear to them', Priam is able to reply: 'it is good to give appropriate gifts to the gods, since my son, if he ever was, never forgot to give [gifts] in the halls of the gods, who hold Olympus' (24. 422–7).[36] In the *Trojan Women*, if Euripides had allowed the chorus to learn that the gods were about to destroy the Greek fleet, or even if they had been able to believe Cassandra's prediction that Agamemnon would be murdered on his return, they might, like Priam, have been able to conclude, even in the midst of their loss and suffering, that the gods were at least in some measure just. But in Euripides it is primarily mortals with divine relatives who receive such privileged information, like Peleus from his wife Thetis, Orestes from his uncle Castor, Cadmus from his grandson Dionysus, and Ion from Athena, who is sent by his father Apollo.[37]

The *Trojan Women* ends with a sad reflection by the chorus on the consequences for them of the action of the play: 'alas my city; nonetheless, turn and walk towards the Greek ships' (1331–2). But other plays end with general reflections on human life that might be thought to be addressed directly to the audience, in order to allow them to reflect on the meaning for themselves of the drama that they have just seen enacted.[38] Of these, five plays have an abstract, interchangeable exodus that comments on the nature of the gods,

[35] Cf. fr. 1028 N about Zeus bringing sorrow to both Trojans and Greeks, though without context.   [36] Cf. Macleod 1982, 121.

[37] Cf. Barrett 1964, 395, who observes that 'the physical position of the *deus ex machina* may reinforce remoteness', and Harder 1985, 230, who notes that no *deus ex machina*, even Artemis in the *Hipp.*, ever addresses a person on the stage with a familiar phrase like ὦ παῖ ('my child').

[38] Cf. Roberts 1987, 59–60; Dunn 1996, 16; Schlesier 1983, 279.

and it is here, perhaps, that we may look for some indication of what Euripides meant his audiences to think about the gods in his plays:

πολλαὶ μορφαὶ τῶν δαιμονίων,
πολλὰ δ' ἀέλπτως κραίνουσι θεοί·
καὶ τὰ δοκηθέντ' οὐκ ἐτελέσθη,
τῶν δ' ἀδοκήτων πόρον ηὗρε θεός.
τοιόνδ' ἀπέβη τόδε πρᾶγμα.

Many are the forms of divinity; the gods bring many things to pass unexpectedly. And what we thought would happen did not come to pass, but the god found a means to bring about what we did not imagine. That is how this action went.

The description of the gods must have the most general possible application in these lines, since they were appended to plays with both sad and happy endings: to the grim tragedies *Medea*, *Bacchae* and, in two manuscripts, *Hippolytus*; to two plays in which catastrophe is survived, *Andromache* and *Helen*, and also to the *Alcestis*, which replaced the satyr play in its trilogy.

Though in most cases there is no external reason to doubt the authenticity of these lines, scholars have suggested that these and other moralizing 'tail-pieces' were added by actors.[39] For example, Barrett in his commentary on the *Hippolytus* calls the repeated lines about the forms of divinity 'an extraordinarily undistinguished platitude', appropriate only for the *Alcestis*, only 'tolerable' for the *Andromache*, *Helen*, and *Bacchae*, and 'grossly out-of-place' in the *Medea*, even with its different first line.[40] But if the lines can be seen to suit the *Bacchae*, why not the *Medea*? In both dramas a mother kills her son, and in both the outcome of the action is not exactly what the actors in the play (let alone the audience) expected in the beginning. In the *Bacchae*, Pentheus cannot stop the worship or the followers of the god he thought so powerless; the same god compels him to dress in the costume of the female worshippers which he finds so abhorrent and leads him to his death. In the *Medea* the Nurse is afraid that Medea will harm someone (93), and hopes that it will be her enemies rather than her friends; at the end of the play she has killed both friends and enemies. Although powerless and alone at first, she

---

[39] See esp. Roberts 1987, 51–4.
[40] Barrett 1964, 417. See also Dale 1954, 130; Page 1938, 181; Stevens 1971, 246; Dunn 1996, 17–18. But contrast Roberts 1987, 57–8.

escapes with the help of her divine grandfather, the Sun: 'but the god
found a means to bring about what we did not imagine'.

If modern critics have considered the interchangeable exodus lines
unsuitable for the *Medea*, it is perhaps because they have not
sufficiently acknowledged the power of divine agency in the *Medea*,
which helps to bring about an ending that punishes not only Jason
(1352), but Medea herself (1249), and bestows upon her children
heroic honours (1382–3), such as Hippolytus receives from Artemis.[41] Dodds in his commentary on the *Bacchae* thought the lines
'appropriate to any play having a marked *peripeteia*';[42] as Kirk
observes, 'the formal yet familiar quality [of the coda] stresses the
ritualistic origins of the drama, the inevitability of the human
predicament, and the inscrutable power of the gods'.[43]

Specifically, the aspect of the 'human predicament' that these lines
describe is ignorance: men are taken unawares ($\dot{a}\epsilon\lambda\pi\tau\omega s$) by the
gods' actions, and cannot anticipate their outcome ($\delta o\kappa\eta\theta\acute{\epsilon}\nu\tau a/$
$\dot{a}\delta o\kappa\acute{\eta}\tau\omega\nu$).[44] The gods, by contrast, have knowledge of both the
past and the future, and also, they have the power to assume
different shapes ($\pi o\lambda\lambda a\grave{\iota}\ \mu o\rho\phi a\acute{\iota}$), to bring about what they want,
and to find a means to accomplish what men thought impossible
($\pi\acute{o}\rho o\nu\ \eta\hat{\upsilon}\rho\epsilon\ \theta\epsilon\acute{o}s$). There is perhaps no more concise statement of
unpredictability of human life, and of the weakness of the human
condition. If the gods appear in these lines to be more austere and
capricious than they do in the *Iliad*, it is because the nature of drama
does not provide the same opportunity for us to observe them on Mt.
Olympus and hear their conversations and plans, and we are left to
judge them exclusively by their effect, for better or worse, on the lives
of the human characters of myth.

Occasionally a mortal in one of Euripides' plays will try to deny, in
the face of the myth's gruesome 'facts', that the gods could behave as
badly as people think. Heracles, who has made hasty judgements
earlier in the drama (586), asserts that the 'poets' miserable stories'
about the gods cannot be true. Like Xenophanes (21 B 11, A 32. 23–5
D–K), he believes that a god would not commit adultery, bind his
father, or want to have power over another god, 'because the god,

[41] Cf. Lloyd-Jones 1983, 171.   [42] Cf. Dodds 1960 on 1388, p. 242.
[43] Cf. Kirk 1979, 140.
[44] Cf. Dio Cassius 78 [79]. 4. 1–10. 2, where the lines are seen in retrospect to have
predicted the assassination of Caracalla.

if he is truly a god, needs nothing' (*HF* 1340–6).[45] Hecuba insists that
Hera and Athena could not have been so foolish as to ask a
barbarian's opinion, or have any need of a beauty contest (*Tro.* 969–
77). But in each play the audience has already seen the gods
ex machina in the act of 'needing' something, in both cases revenge for
personal wrongs done them. Whatever these or other well-meaning
mortals would like them to be, 'the powers which govern the world
and man's destiny are unpredictable, implacable (though we must
try to placate them), more often hostile than favourable, extremely
rough in their justice, and [in the *Heracles*] downright malignant'.[46]
There is no reason to imagine that Euripides is using these
characters' suggestions to recommend to his audience that they
adopt a 'new creed'.[47]

I do not see why the notion of divine behaviour expressed in the
coda, even though it is stated so simply, should not be taken
seriously. The lines suggest that the gods deserve respect and honour
because of their supreme power, which is made manifest to men,
especially in the ritual of drama, by what we would now call
miracles: Dionysus is born from Zeus' thigh, he makes ivy grow
around his mother's tomb, he causes the palace to fall down, and
makes Pentheus do what would have been unthinkable for him at
the beginning of the play, to dress like a woman, wear the fawnskin,
and carry the thyrsus in the god's honour. Dionysus also undergoes
a series of metamorphoses; first, he appears as a mortal (4–5), then he
seems to Pentheus to be a bull (920–3); the women hear his voice as
a god but do not see him; finally he appears *ex machina* as himself.[48]

---

[45] Cf. Bond 1981, 400; Desch 1986, 20; fr. 292. 7 N, 'if the gods do something
shameful, they aren't gods'. Contrast Schlesier 1985, 25–6 and 1986, 41, who, by
emphasizing the positive elements of the drama, seeks to make Eur. espouse a new
and more beneficent theodicy. The old notion (see bibliog. in Schlesier 1985, 12) that
this passage constitutes a serious critique of the gods and their traditional roles in
myth is restated by Halleran 1986, 179–80.

[46] Cf. Stinton 1976, 83–4; Kovacs 1987*a*, 110–11. Cf. also how Iphigenia tries to
attribute to men's 'notions' the human sacrifices Artemis desires (*IT* 380–91), not only
in the context of the play but in other myths. The chorus of the *Electra* would prefer
not to believe that the gods would have reversed the course of the sun because of a
human crime (737–44), but the action of the play shows that the gods will go to
extraordinary lengths to enforce their justice. Cf. esp. Spira 1960, *passim*; but contrast
Schmidt 1963, who regards the *deus ex machina* as a purely technical device.

[47] As suggested by Yunis 1988, 155–66; cf. Bain 1990, 222–3; also Gregory
1991, 148.

[48] Cf. also how Hera assumes the form of a priestess in Aesch. *Xantriai* (fr. 168, cf.
above, n. 1); Athena imitates Aphrodite's voice in *Rhes.* 637–9. Changes of shape are

Euripides was not the first (or last) Greek poet vividly to describe the miraculous, and (to men) capricious and cruel, behaviour of the gods.[49] In the *Homeric Hymn to Dionysus* the god seems first to be a young boy; then vines and ivy grow on the ship, and wine flows; a lion appears, and a bear. The sailors jump into the sea and become dolphins, but the god takes pity on the helmsman, who had seen that he was a god and had tried without success to persuade his companions to release him (16–23). As in the *Bacchae*, the god in revealing his identity, emphasizes the story of his birth: 'courage, since you have been pleasing to me; I am Dionysus the thunderer whom Semele, daughter of Cadmus, bore after lying with Zeus' (55–7). Cadmus in the *Bacchae* is not so fortunate as the helmsman, but then why should the god do what he (or the audience) expects?

---

frequent in myth but for practical reasons rare in dramatic performance; Io can wear a mask with cow's horns in *PV* 588 (see Griffith 1983, 198–9), but the audience learns about Iolaus' rejuvenation from a messenger (*Heracl.* 857–8).

[49] Cf. Schlesier 1986, 45.

6

On 'Extra-Dramatic' Communication of Characters in Euripides[1]

H. P. STAHL

The title of my paper is intended to emphasize two things. By 'extra-dramatic', I want to indicate that the scenes to be considered do not participate in the dramatic action proper of the tragedy in which they appear, and so in some sense can be said to move outside the plot; but, at the same time, I also want to suggest that the dramatic structure of the plays can in each case provide a useful point of reference for a methodical comprehension of the phenomenon I have in mind.

I have chosen the term 'communication' because it can signify a close human relationship that finds expression through exchange of words, as for example in dramatic dialogue. 'Communication' does not entail any restriction regarding the kind of persons who communicate. In the Euripidean passages the persons involved frequently address each other as *philoi*, but the common English translation, which is 'friend', would unduly limit my reader's expectations. For the observations which follow are in no way tied to a particular word or a particular bond between human beings. Even *philos* and *philia* (which, unlike our 'friendship', can indicate not only the ties between friends, but the familial relationships of father and son or brother and sister as well) are too narrow terms. With regard to my special subject, I should therefore not use 'friendship', or, if at all, in an extended sense, meaning any close human relationship.

Before closing in any further on the target of this paper, I would first like to outline the complex background against which Euripides has

---

[1] Part of this article (translated into English by W. Zukowski and reviewed by the author) was a *Habilitationsvortrag* ('Zum "ausserdramatischen" Motiv der Freundschaft bei Euripides'), held before the Geisteswissenschaftliche Fakultät der Westfälischen Wilhelms-Universität zu Münster (Westfalen) on 19 June 1964.

set it off. One ingredient of this background is for instance the *philia* mentioned above, in its traditional and common Greek sense. For the characters whom we shall consider, *philia* is one of the basic relations that tie them to their environment, a notion immanent in their thinking and inseparable from their set of fundamental ideas.

In presenting a simplified sketch of the environmental relations so basic to the characters in the play, I must paradoxically start out with a negative statement: it would be wrong to attribute to characters in a Euripidean play a complete (or even halfway complete) understanding of the world and their position in it. The world proves utterly incomprehensible to them. The more they strive intellectually to understand it, the more elusive it becomes. This is true of all facets of life, but of the gods above all. And it is especially true of those gods who seem to lend man a helping hand. Thus, Orestes says in reference to the sooth-saying god Apollo (*IT* 570 ff.):

Nor are the gods whom we call wise less deceptive than winged dreams.

And three lines later he mentions

the man who, though not imprudent, followed the bidding of seers, and is undone: how undone to those who know!

'Those who know': Orestes, of course, in the first place refers to himself and his experience of the god's deceptiveness, but the phrase also encompasses the spectators who have witnessed his experience.

Since trust in and reliance upon divine guidance no longer seem justified, men are obviously left to their own faculties. This is implicit in Orestes' allusion to the prudent man who despite his good sense confides in the prophecies of the god. Since, however, the events which involve men are capable of many interpretations, it is increasingly doubtful whether man can accomplish plans of his own. If the course of events (*ta pragmata*) appears to form a movement of its own, the possibility of influencing it is withdrawn. In this area, too—as in that of divine guidance—a point is reached where man resigns action. What wonder that, when unexpected good fortune comes, *Tychē* is hailed as the guide—Tyche, which is the whim of chance and by definition incalculable? (*Ion* 1512 ff.):

O you who have already brought about change for countless mortals, so that they experience suffering and afterwards good fortune—Tychē, what a plumb-line of life we have followed . . .!

'Plumb-line' and 'chance' in a single statement: clearly, the concrete experience of life can only be expressed by a paradox—the intellect must keep silent.

Where in a world thus constituted is there room for the man of action, for the dramatic deed? There can be none. Studies of Euripides' dramaturgy confirm that he sought increasingly to withdraw from his characters the possibility of action.[2] The people of his plays become passive; external action is replaced by internal reaction. Viewed from the angle of their dramatic structure, the plays reveal that humanity is always a step behind events (a development which can equally well be illustrated from the historical account given by the poet's contemporary Thucydides).

But if the conduct of the gods, as well as the course of events, is inaccessible to human understanding, where can a man find his bearings? On what can he depend? On other men, his neighbors, his friends? Basically, this question must be answered in the negative, since disappointment rather than a justification of the confidence bestowed is the usual outcome of such reliance, as must be stated once more. Medea's despairing question, when she finds herself betrayed by her husband, recurs frequently in altered form (*Medea* 516–19):

Why, O Zeus, have you given to men unmistakable criteria for detecting false gold, yet men have no mark ingrown on their bodies by which the villainous can be recognized?

And the murderer of a child entrusted to his protection addresses his victim's unfortunate mother with the words (*Hecuba* 957–60):

Alas, there is nothing on which we can rely—neither glory, nor, when we prosper, that we shall not fare ill. The gods themselves confuse and thoroughly disorder our lots to the end that we will revere them because of our inability to attain knowledge.

The dissembler expresses ideas which are thoroughly in accord with the experience of Euripides' dramatic characters. His lament over the fact that in life there is nothing reliable seems to mark him out of all as the trustworthy man *par excellence*. How could anyone see through him or even unmask him?

---

[2] Strohm 1957, 152.

There are numerous examples in Euripidean tragedy of bitter disappointment over betrayal by a supposed friend. A discriminating investigation[3] has even shown that the baffling enemy need not at all be a particular individual—as was the case with the infanticide just mentioned—but that Euripides more and more frequently brings the anonymous masses into the play as the adversary of his heroes. But in the face of amorphous anonymity vigorous action directed toward a specific goal is an impossibility. Here again, we encounter the passivity of Euripidean characters.

To sum up: gods who lead astray; events determined by chance; untrustworthy and deceitful men; anonymous crowds—this is the world in which humanity finds itself: a room with many doors, none of which can be opened. With ample justification one may speak of a *Sinneskrise*,[4] a crisis of meaning, in Euripides.

From this background sketch of the relations between the central figures and the world around them, one fact of great importance to our subject emerges: that in the whirlpool of uncertainty and loss of direction not only a single bond like that of friendship—be it in the English sense or in the wider one of Greek *philia*—is lost, but also any close human relationship appears in jeopardy. We may already surmise that, when a Euripidean character does gain certainty of human closeness, he will not win it by any active exertion of his own powers. Rather, if such certainty comes at all, we shall expect it to do so as something which comes to pass and befalls men quite unexpectedly.

In the following pages I wish to show that, in fact, such certainty of the closeness of a fellow human being is occasionally expressed in Euripides, and I shall try to describe the manner in which the artist employs this feature to heighten and intensify the tragic aspects of his plays.

I now return to the concept of the 'extra-dramatic', and to the selection of the scenes which I wish to set before the reader.

Scholarship has been much occupied with the dramatic structure of Euripides' work (we immediately think of names like Solmsen, Zürcher, Friedrich, Strohm, *et al.*). Investigations of this sort have sometimes led to charges of excessively schematic organization of

---

[3] Diller 1960, 89 ff.   [4] Reinhardt 1960, 227 ff. and above, pp. 16–46.

individual tragedies (especially of the so-called intrigue-dramas). Above all, one grave reproach held against our author deserves mentioning here: he has been accused of concentrating on plot at the expense of the delineation of character. That is, he has been said to disregard the unity of character and to provide the people of his plays only with such traits and qualities as are necessary to further the action—or, to put it more briefly, to make the *dramatis persona* a function of the plot.[5]

We may dispense with discussion of the truth or falsehood of theses like these (and with the more general question of the validity of such lines of interpretation), since the problem before us is not affected by them. I have nevertheless introduced them for two reasons: (1) because through them I have been led to the category of the 'extra-dramatic'; (2) because the existence of these investigations has determined my choice of scenes.

The sort of communication we will be dealing with is in a way exhibited also in the so-called intrigue-dramas—where a character in extreme difficulty finds help and support from another character, together with whom he plans the intrigue in order to surmount the emergency that now involves them together. Usually, the rediscovery of a loved one previously lost leads to a common duet of rejoicing in which the suffering of the solitary past, anxiety over the threatening future, and joy at the nearness of the one who has been found again are mingled together. However, the certainty of human closeness expressed in such scenes clearly is not without a dramatic function. Indeed, it is necessary for the course of the intrigue-drama that first a uniting bond between friends or near ones should be established or reconfirmed so they can act together for a common end. Thus, a character's discovery that he can rely upon his fellow-man could, in these instances, be regarded simply as a function of the dramatic plot.

Accordingly, I have set aside the intrigue-dramas and have chosen only scenes and descriptions which have no importance for the progress of the plot. By thus limiting the range of inquiry, I believe I have at the same time gained an advantage: in the presentation of a static situation which contains no impulse to movement in the sense of dramaturgic progress the power immanent in linguistic expression is possibly stronger, since the words serve no purpose other than

---

[5] Zürcher 1947, 180: the person 'verhält sich einfach so, wie es der Fortgang oder das Ziel des Dramas erheischt'.

description of human feeling or pure communication of inner experience.

I wish to illustrate the phenomenon I have in mind first from the *Alcestis* of 438 BC.

In this play we find a theatrical adaptation of the old folk-tale (*Märchen*) in which a man is able to redeem himself from dying by placing the life of another at Death's disposal. To this basic plot is added the burlesque feature that Death does not even get possession of the substitute victim when all is done, since a hero of superhuman might snatches her from him in a wrestling-match at the grave.

The first, or tragic, part is what interests us in our present inquiry. The victim is Alcestis who, on her wedding-day, voluntarily pledged to surrender her life for that of her threatened husband Admetus. Years have passed since the pledge was given, and today is the day on which she must depart. We find her on her death-bed in her last conversation with her husband.

The leave-taking is movingly depicted, but remarkably static— conventional, one is tempted to say. Admetus promises never to remarry and to be both father and mother to their children. He hopes that Alcestis will often appear to him in dreams.

All these are features which could be said to be determined by dramatic necessity: for Admetus must be characterized as a good husband so that his recovery of his noble wife in the second part of the play will seem fitting. His request that his wife should wait for him in the kingdom of death until he comes to her at the conclusion of his now prolonged life can be regarded in the same fashion: the dramatic plot demands that Admetus continue to live.

Up to this point, I would agree that there can be no question of a psychological depiction of the characters;[6] indeed, I would go further and assert that there is not supposed to be any, since without the play's static first part, its second part, which is not at all static, would lose its meaning.

In the final lines of the conversation, i.e. already in the *stichomythia*, individualizing emotion, indicated once before in the antecedent lyrical passage (see 278 ff.), makes its decisive appearance in the constellation we have so far observed. At the end of the almost

[6] Zürcher 1947, 24 ff.

functional discussion of Alcestis' last wishes, Admetus abruptly breaks out (380):

Alas, what shall I do alone and without you?

Alcestis' reference to time which mitigates all things does not impede him (382):

Take me with you, by the gods, take me below.

And suddenly the recognition (384):

Oh God, what a wife you rob me of!

This is no longer the Admetus who was to join his wife in the underworld after an admittedly sorrowful but long life—it is the man who, later in the play (897 ff.), must be forcibly restrained from throwing himself upon the corpse in the grave in order to unite himself with his wife in death (386):

I am undone, my wife, if you forsake me.

What is happening here? Obviously, Admetus recognizes that the death of his wife is identical with the loss of his own existence ('if you . . . then I'). Thus, there is a movement towards her on his part, a removal of a borderline that has been separating them.

And how does Alcestis react to her husband's new closeness, to this new dimension which can have no importance in the realm of actuality and cannot change anything about her fate? (387)

You may speak of me as nothing, I am no longer alive.

This is equivalent to no answer at all. We get the impression that Alcestis is not being reached by Admetus at all, that she does not even learn any more about the certainty of his affection. The possibility of 'togetherness' remains unfulfilled; in the sphere of high tragedy, any effect is precluded.

Ten years after the *Alcestis*, the *Hippolytus* was produced. Hippolytus, the young hunting companion of the chaste goddess Artemis, has rejected the faked proposal (invented, of course, by the old Nurse) of his stepmother Phaedra. Phaedra kills herself and leaves behind a letter to her husband Theseus, in which she accuses her stepson of having raped her.

In his first passion, Theseus, invoking his father, the god Poseidon, curses his son and prays for his death. The curse must take effect, since Poseidon has promised Theseus the fulfilment of three wishes. The confrontation of father and son over the body of Phaedra is the high point of a tragic misunderstanding. In a passage cited above, Medea lamented that there was a 'clear, infallible' test for false coinage, but not for the character of a man. Now, Theseus believes he possesses such absolute and unfailing proof of his son's viciousness. He uses the word *saphes* which was used by Medea also (925):

Alas, there ought to have been established for mortals an unfailing criterion of friends and a means of judging the hearts of men [to determine] who is upright and who is not a friend.

He means that he has previously misjudged his son's character; now, however, he imagines he possesses irrefutable certainty about what that character is (972):

Why should I still wrangle with you in words, since the corpse is present as a witness giving most certain evidence?

Can there be any evidence more manifest or more unerring than the dead Phaedra provides?

Still later, when Theseus learns that Hippolytus has been assailed by Poseidon and is at the point of death, he wishes to see him to convict him of his guilt by the new evidence of divine punishment—which, in fact, has no bearing on anything but the fulfilment of Theseus' own curse (1267).

Before the dying youth is brought forth, however, Theseus learns the truth from the goddess Artemis. Thus, when they meet again, father and son are both victims of Phaedra's revenge—or, to express it in terms of the divine powers involved, of the wrath of Aphrodite who wished to destroy Artemis' chaste young devotee.

The dying youth seems even more isolated and lonely than Alcestis. His divine patroness can do nothing to save him. The only consolation she can offer (if it is any) is to assure him that she will take vengeance on Aphrodite and for her part, too, kill a human dear to that goddess. From Hippolytus, however, she must now take her leave, since it is not permissible for the gods to be present at a man's death.

Lightly you abandon a long communion,

says Hippolytus (1441). The brutality of divine blessedness, untouched by suffering, is illustrated by the manner in which Artemis delegates what according to our feeling should be her own task, to the mortal father: *he* is bidden to take the dying youth in his arms; the two humans are asked to extend reconciliation to one another—which, evidently, the gods cannot do.

Thus, after the goddess' departure, after the dramatic action has run its course, there remain two men united in suffering: the son absolves his father of guilt for his death; Theseus holds his dying son lovingly in his arms. The whole is, as it were, a contrast to the scene over Phaedra's body, a moment of genuine recognition. Theseus says (1452):

Oh dearest one, how noble you show yourself to your father!

Thus, at this point the motif of human closeness recurs: 'dearest one', *o philtate*, is Theseus' address to his son. And once more he expresses his new understanding (1454):

Alas, for your pious, noble heart!

Here, too, as in the *Alcestis*, a bridge seems to be laid between the two men, a communication established that was never reached before; but Hippolytus' answer shows that he is already in the grip of another world:

Farewell, my father, you too, many times farewell.[7]

Once again we see that the dying one can hardly be touched any more by the closeness of the other. Theseus says (1456):

Do not forsake me, child, bear up and endure.

Hippolytus says:

My struggle has been borne, father, I am dead. Veil my head as quickly as you can.

As Alcestis put it,

You may speak of me as nothing, I am no longer alive.

---

[7] 1453, transposed with 1455 by von Wilamowitz, followed by Murray and Barrett. Though it does not matter for our present inquiry, I wish to point out that there is probably no need for transposing. Commentators feel that Hippolytus' 'Goodbye to you, too' in 1453 can only follow Theseus' goodbye to Hippolytus or an equivalent to a goodbye which they find in 1454. They overlook the fact that, ever since exchanging 'goodbye' with Artemis (1437; 1440: χαίρουσα καὶ σὺ στεῖχε), Hippolytus has been wishing to take leave of his father, too (already in 1444 darkness approaches him), but has been kept from doing so because of his promise to Artemis (λύω δὲ νεῖκος πατρί, 'I relinquish the quarrel with my father', 1442) and Theseus' own repeatedly expressed desire for absolution and reconciliation. It is only consistent that, with their reconciliation established, Hippolytus presses for a last goodbye to his father before losing consciousness (ὡς τάχος, 'as quickly as you can', 1458).

In neither case can the dying person's situation be altered in the least by the movement of the other in his direction and the removal of the former barrier between them. To be sure, there is the growth of a certainty, even a very intimate certainty; but it remains—in the former case as well as in the present one—lost and powerless in the tragic space, devoid of any fulfilment in the realm of actuality. Its essence seems to consist only in the fact that (despite all the impossibility of fulfilment, despite its very purposelessness) it has been there for a moment, and that it came quite unexpectedly if one considers the isolation and loneliness that preceded it.

Let us pause for a moment, before turning to another play. When we compare the structure of the two death-scenes, we discover a remarkable similarity between them. In both cases, the action of the play has reached its goal; in the dramatic course of events a resting-point has been reached. This extra-dramatic resting-point is then expanded to an entire scene of the strongest internal and (as we cannot but call it) individually molded emotion. A voice for the sorrow and suffering is found in the souls of the untragic ones, the sympathetic and new-found friends, who in this manner are themselves integrated into the sphere of tragic experience. It is, however, precisely this unexpected display of sympathy which throws into bolder relief the isolation and loneliness of the dying tragical victim.

In both cases the internal emotion is heightened by the fact that the course of external events is changed, in the imagination of the survivor, and reshaped into unreality (a sort of contrary-to-fact movement). Admetus wishes to accompany his wife in death; Theseus bids his son bear up. Each time, this would involve a different outcome to the play than that which actually occurs.

Also common to both is the abruptness with which the survivor comes to recognize the significance for himself of the impending loss. This too is psychologically convincing. Both Admetus and Theseus knew well in advance (and, in one way or another, even approved of) what was about to happen; but only the moment of parting is able to change the event, which so far has only been imagined, to an experience which puts their own existence into question.

How much Euripides put into the extra-dramatic scene of the *Hippolytus* can be determined from the following. The *Hippolytus*, as we possess it, is the second working of the same material by our author. In the first version—as Seneca's *Phaedra*, to which Racine adhered on this point, allows us to conjecture—it is highly probable that the second encounter between father and dying son did not take place. The earlier misunderstanding-scene between father and son, which we examined above, also belongs to the new version and not the old. (On this point Seneca—and, following him once more, Racine—held to the second version.) Presumably, in place of the two Theseus–Hippolytus scenes, the first version contained two scenes between Theseus and Phaedra: in the first, Phaedra slandered her stepson; in the second, she revealed the truth before her own death.

Euripides' artistic interest in the extra-dramatic final scene can further be illustrated by a 'parallel', which at first sight may look like an opposite rather than a parallel.

As the reconciliation scene at the end of the *Hippolytus* forms a pendant to the earlier scene which contained the argument of father and son at Phaedra's corpse, so the final scene of the *Medea* proves to be a dramaturgically comparable pendant to an earlier scene (866 ff.). Here, however, the (fictitious) reconciliation comes first, and the quarrel last. But the human revelation of the extra-dramatic final scene is no less compelling.

Medea is still convinced that she is not to blame for what she did. Rather, she seems to feel that the guilt lies with Jason (1364) and that her horrible deed is a clear consequence of his perjury and deceit (cf. 1392). Therefore the revenging deity will not listen to his complaints (1391). Medea only ('as must be done') returned the blow he had struck at her (τῆς σῆς γὰρ ὡς χρὴ καρδίας ἀνθηψάμην, 1360; cf. 1372), and so, in her strangely consistent reasoning, she still claims to be the loving mother: the dead children are 'dearest', φίλτατα, 'to their mother, not to you' (μητρί γε, σοὶ δ' οὔ, 1397; her claim is uttered at the point of highest agitation, in the broken anapaestic *stichomythia*).

The extra-dramatic scene, this time, breathes purest, self-righteous hostility; the place of the sympathizing friend is taken by a hateful superior; the contrary-to-fact movement of wishful thinking is replaced by Medea's joyful prediction of the sufferings that will actually accompany Jason through the rest of his life ('so far, you don't have reason to lament: wait for old age!', 1396), and delight is taken in the prospect of his miserable death, which Medea regally defines as a punishment of his behavior towards her ('a bitter ending you experience of your marriage with me', 1388). As in the scenes we interpreted earlier the sympathizers would do everything to see the tragic victim live on, so Medea does everything—she even inflicts incurable wounds upon herself—to harm Jason. The message, extraordinary as it may sound, is in both cases a purely human one. We should not minimize the horrors Euripides finds inherent in human nature by saying that Medea here substitutes for the not human *deus ex machina*. We would never say so about Theseus, although he, too, could be said to fill, at least partially, the place from which Artemis, *dea ex machina*, had withdrawn.

That the *Hippolytus* II has gained a great deal by being remolded towards a new climax hardly needs to be stressed. What is of methodical interest to the present inquiry is the very fact (which is not my finding) that the final scene has been newly composed. For it provides supporting evidence for the great emphasis I place on such extra-dramatic passages as the high points of the tragedies.[8]

For further illustration of the structural features we have thus far considered, we proceed over a space of more than twenty years to the posthumously produced *Iphigenia at Aulis*.

The underlying situation is as follows: the Greek host has assembled at Aulis in preparation for a punitive expedition against Troy, because Helen, the wife of Menelaus, has been abducted by the Trojan prince Paris.

A calm keeps the army in the harbor of Aulis, and the seer Calchas discloses that the voyage cannot be continued before the commander Agamemnon has sacrificed his daughter Iphigenia to the goddess Artemis. Agamemnon, concerned for his glory, makes use of a stratagem. He sends a letter to his wife Clytemnestra, enjoining her to send his daughter to Aulis to be married to Achilles, the foremost of the Greek heroes.

All this has occurred before the play commences. In the play itself we encounter a completely different Agamemnon. He regrets his intrigue and tries to undo it by writing a second letter to his wife. The

---

[8] Perhaps it should be added that these scenes cannot at all be regarded as 'retarding moments', as the rejoicing duets in the intrigue-dramas often can, where the tension is heightened by the fact that the newly found, in their happiness, tend to forget the danger they are in.

letter, however, is intercepted and opened by his suspicious brother Menelaus who confronts its author with it.

In invective and viciousness, the quarrel between the two brothers surpasses all bounds. Among other things, the fact again plays its part that there is no accurate means of testing a man's character unambiguously (expressed by the word *saphes* (333) which we have mentioned before). Agamemnon is upbraided for his unpleasant hunger for military glory and his change of heart regarding the sacrifice of his daughter, Menelaus for his jealousy as a cuckolded husband. A theme of Homeric heroic epic is deliberately debased to the level of a family row.

In the midst of the quarrel a messenger suddenly arrives with the news of Iphigenia's (*and* Clytemnestra's) imminent arrival. The coming meeting with his wife, as well as the now more concrete threat to his daughter, causes Agamemnon's collapse. And now Menelaus says (471):

Brother, give me your right hand.

Agamemnon rejoins:

I do so. For yours is the victory, and I am wretched.

Agamemnon regards his brother's gesture as a final demand for surrender, and submits because he feels himself overwhelmed by events.

Such, however, is not Menelaus' meaning. Rather, on his side, he has not felt able to avoid the sight presented to his view by his deeply afflicted brother, lamenting over the news. The motif of sudden recognition, which we have commented on before, is thus duplicated here. Menelaus feels the recognition is equivalent to a process of maturation on his part (489 ff.):

I was a young fool, until, viewing the matter from close by, I recognized what it means to kill a child.

'Viewing the matter from close by'—this is the catch-word for the experience which starts at the moment when what was long intended turns into actuality. The reality is not what man had imagined it would be.

Thus, once again, a movement takes place towards the other, and a bridge is laid between two men who were formerly separated and mutually antagonistic. A true change of heart, caused by the other person's suffering, and again a change of heart which seeks to depart from the course prescribed for the play: for if Menelaus renounced his claim to vengeance, the Trojan war would not take place.

To be sure, on this occasion the other is more manifestly being reached, he does perceive the certainty of the affection offered him so unexpectedly. Agamemnon thanks his brother—but his gratitude is joyless since the situation will remain unchanged. For there will be others who also know of the oracle. The ambitious Odysseus and the common soldiery as well (here we encounter the anonymous crowd in the role of antagonist), they all will refuse to abandon the campaign and forgo their chance for glory, but will exact the sacrifice by force.

Thus, another feature of the scenes we interpreted earlier is seen to have been retained. The certainty of the other's sympathy cannot be transformed into practical help or effective action. On the contrary: on the one hand, the sympathy itself was communicated in a renunciation of action (i.e. in Menelaus' renunciation of the campaign)—and on the other hand the two brothers, despite their new fellowship, have no means by which to oppose effectively the threatening crowd. The circle is closed; the course of the play has returned to the point it had already reached at the scene's beginning. Since external events have not been changed, the scene has been, so to speak, 'extra-dramatic'.

I wish to give a final example from the same tragedy.

Later in the play, Achilles, the involuntary bridegroom, rebels against the sacrifice of Iphigenia—not because he pities the girl, but because the generals have misused his name: Achilles' honor ought not to be stained by a maiden's murder!

Achilles speaks out against the sacrifice in the assembly. But he is shouted down and almost stoned by the furious host (above all by his own troops), reviled as a woman's slave. At this time, he unexpectedly takes the betrothal seriously—in his own peculiar fashion: with the aid of a few loyal followers, he proposes to defend Iphigenia against overwhelming odds, even though the struggle is hopeless from the beginning.

At this moment, however, and in Achilles' presence, Iphigenia announces her decision to offer herself voluntarily as a sacrificial victim. In doing so, she—after all the human (and only too human) motives which have been mentioned up to this point—reaches out for the heroic motive suggested by her father and makes it her own. In passing, I should remark that, although Iphigenia is not unaffected by the hero's presence, there is no thought here at all of any stirring of passion in her for Achilles such as Racine delineates. She intends to liberate Hellas and to prevent Greek wives and Greek marriages from being dishonored by barbarians (1374 ff.).

Objectively considered, in view of all that has preceded, such an interpretation of the expedition is plainly absurd. Subjectively, it makes possible the heroic self-fulfilment of a young woman who does not share the base motives of her environment. One is tempted to ask whether, for the dramatic deed (a very passive 'deed' in this case, anyway), a state of illusion is needed.

And how does Achilles conduct himself? (1404 ff.):

Agamemnon's daughter, a god would make me blessed, had I your hand in marriage!

And again:

Desire to be your husband grips me more, since I have seen your nature.

As in the three scenes we considered earlier, the bridging of the antithesis of 'I' and 'Thou' is connected with a process of recognition, a sudden insight into the situation and nature of the other: 'since I have seen your nature'. Achilles asks Iphigenia for her hand, he wishes to rescue her from death and Aulis and to take her home as his wife.

The change of heart—from the earlier motive of insulted honor— again threatens to disrupt the outcome of the drama; for if Achilles did as he intends, the Trojan war would—again—not take place. As in the other scenes, reality is transformed into unreality in the soul of the new sympathizer and reshaped in a sort of contrary-to-fact movement.

The point which my investigation has just reached calls for an interruption. For the result affords one of those rare cuts through the history of Greek literature, which, without resulting in cheap clichés, can reveal a surprising continuity.

What I wish to introduce here is an 'extra-dramatic scene' from the *Iliad*. When Achilles' wrath against Agamemnon has made him withdraw from fighting, the Greeks suffer such heavy losses that they send an embassy to Achilles' tents, consisting of smart Odysseus, fatherly friend Phoenix, and square fighter Ajax. The scene (truly a 'scene' in the dramatic sense, with three subtly characterizing addresses by the envoys and three answers spoken by Achilles) is 'extra-dramatic', because the envoys return as empty-handed as they arrived and nothing has changed in the external situation. But internally the conversation moves through the different environmental relations by which a Homeric hero is defined, and even up to that borderline on the other side of which the negation of the heroic ideal is located. Even the closest friend, Phoenix, is far too conventional (Achilles will blame him for this attitude) ever to cross this border (in this respect, there can be no parallel to the Euripidean close one). But the hero of heroes himself performs the contrary-to-fact movement so characteristic of the Euripidean scenes. Achilles, denouncing war and honor (equal portions and equal honor fall to coward and brave man, 9. 318 f.), picks up the plot and leads it on into unreality: he will go home, marry (but not Agamemnon's daughter), enjoy his father's possessions. For Troy's wealth 'is to me not of equal worth with my life' (401), which, once lost, cannot be regained (408). Therefore he chooses the long life rather than *kleos esthlon* or *aphthiton* ('good' or 'unfading glory', 412 ff.).

If Achilles' intention became reality, the Trojan War would have to be discontinued ('I would advise you others, too, to sail home', 417 f.). Of course this will not happen, and thus the main effect the scene leaves us with is our insight into Achilles' soul: even the deathbound warrior and Homeric hero *par excellence* can have an almost Euripidean difficulty in finding his bearings. Having read book 9, we will never forget his doubts and his desire to live on—in whatever situation we may find him later. The fact that he has once seriously considered the unheroic alternative to his glorious destiny (and that in terms of a free choice), illuminates his existence as that of a human being in a way similar to that we found in Euripides' extra-dramatic scenes.

I return from Homeric Achilles to his Euripidean 'bride'. Naturally, as before, the unexpected certainty that one has a new friend can have no effect on actuality; it can only be communicated and expressed in its tragic 'thereness'. Iphigenia says (1418 ff.):

Yet you, my friend (*o xene*), do not die or kill anyone on my account. But allow me to save Hellas, if I am able.

Of all the scenes with which we have dealt, this seems to me to express in purest form the tragic dilemma which the certainty of human closeness often involves for Euripides: for only by relinquishing her life does Iphigenia gain her new friend—or rather, her bridegroom. In case she wished to make use of this friendship to prolong her existence, she would have to destroy its necessary conditions and thus forfeit the friendship itself.

To sum up: in all the uncertainty and unreliability of the surrounding world, the certainty of another human being's closeness can fall to the lot of men in Euripides—but it cannot be counted on. Pentheus for example, in the *Bacchae*, dies friendless, killed by the human being supposedly closest to him: his own mother. If closeness or friendship occurs in the cases we have considered, it does so unexpectedly and without being able to alter the tragic situation. It is like a flash of light, a recognition (though hardly accomplished) that a sympathizer is there; full of restraint, it is hardly more than a gesture, certainly not a consolation. Its occurrence is basically as accidental for the character visited by it as is the deliverance in the untragic chance-dramas. Still, despite all the ambiguities which adhere to it as to all environmental relations in Euripides, it renders one thing unmistakably clear: that the one whom the new friend is no longer able to help is a human being, and, indeed, one in utter loneliness, about to meet the extreme situation of annihilation. In this may lie its poetic function.

This emphasis on human tragedy is brought about by the use of dramaturgic resting-points. Of course, as I have sought to show, while the external events of the drama have come to rest, the two communicating characters pick up the plot and, in a contrary-to-fact movement, lead it on into unreality. Because of the fact that the play's course is continued internally, within the souls of the participants, one may speak even here of a dramaturgy—an internal dramaturgy as it were. It is for this reason that in the title of my paper—'On "Extra-Dramatic" Communication of Characters in Euripides'—I have put the word 'extra-dramatic' in quotation marks.

7

Euripides: The Monument and the Sacrifice

PIETRO PUCCI

Aristotle (*Poet.* 1453[a]19) defines Euripides as the *Tragikōtatos* ('the most tragic') among the Greek tragedians. The context makes clear why Aristotle considers Euripides the most 'tragic' poet: in the words of a recent commentator, Euripides 'reaches in the highest degree the goal that according to Aristotle should be aimed at by tragedy, i.e. to arouse strong feelings of pity and terror in the audience'.[1] The Aristotelian text alone justifies research aiming at illustrating the rhetoric of pity and fear in the plays of Euripides.

In a book soon to be published,[A] I have undertaken such a task: in this paper I would like to summarize some of the results of my analysis and to touch upon some problems that emerge from Euripides' writing as of a kind prompted by pity and aiming at arousing pity in the audience. I shall first show that such writing has a declared and specific function, that of healing—as a Euripidean character says—the hateful griefs of men and that writing that excites pity has a 'remedial' function: in this precise point Euripides anticipates the Aristotelian idea of catharsis.[2]

NOTE: newly added notes (1998) are indicated by capital letters.

[1] Gallavotti 1974, 152.

[A] Pucci 1980.

[2] A pioneering and bold essay on the *tekhnē alupias* ('the art against grief') in Euripides and contemporary thinkers is Diano 1961, 117 ff. The author analyses fr. 964 and other Euripidean passages in which the *tekhnē alupias* takes the shape of a 'meditation on death', of an exercise in preparing oneself for death (*meletē thanatou*).

I comprehend Diano's notion of *tekhnē alupias* within the discourse of pity. For the *sophos* ('wise man') who imagines his own death produces a self-affecting representation whose dynamics are not unlike that of a pitying discourse affecting the self.

De Romilly 1961 points very clearly at pathos and pity as the main feelings and effects produced by Euripides' drama. On p. 16 she writes, 'on serait tenté de penser

We shall then discover that this remedial discourse is characterized by upsetting properties: though at the end this discourse *seems*
capable of producing a healthy state of mind, it is initially dangerous,
'a loss' as another character defines it, and therefore, possibly poisonous. Through an analysis of the dynamics that control pity, we shall
be able to understand the necessity of this unstable balance.

Remedial discourse develops on the Euripidean stage through an
action whereby, as Aristotle notices, the characters very often end in
utter ruin and unhappiness. That this very representation of catastrophe should be remedial and should heal the hateful griefs of men
is not the least paradoxical aspect of Euripides' writing; but there is no
reason to be surprised. His tragic action leads the characters to the
consummation of human sacrifices: Medea, for instance, sacrifices her
sons, Heracles his sons, Dionysus sacrifices Pentheus through the
maddened bacchants, etc. Accordingly, Euripides' writing functions
in analogy with the performance of a sacrifice; the sacrifice is the
violent ritual through which men achieve a remedy, placate their consciousness, establish order in chaos, compensate for losses and ruins.[3]

Euripides' writing, therefore, inasmuch as it is a representation of
sacrifices, functions in accordance with the analogous properties and
effects of the real sacrifices. Euripides' tragic representations are
marked by analogous loss and violence while simultaneously retrieving analogous gain and remedy.

I have outlined the successive arguments of this paper in order
to make clear the steps that lead me to privilege the images of the
sacrifice and of the monument. But the reader will perceive also a
certain insistence, throughout this paper, on the notion of representation. The reason for this emphasis will become clear in the
course of my arguments, but I wish to stress now the general sense of
this emphasis. Both the 'sacrifice' and the 'monument' in Euripides'
text remain 'representation', i.e. rhetorical, mimetical and fictional
enactment of both rituals. This point may seem obvious and banal
from the vantage point of a naive and unquestioning attitude toward

qu'il [Euripide] a renoncé aux grandes scènes de violence, pour insister sur celles de
souffrance, qu'il a negligé le heurt, *le drama*, mais pour renforcer ses consequences, le
pathos'. On p. 86: 'Tout se passe . . . comme si de ces deux sentiments [crainte et
pitié] . . . l'un était l'apanage du théâtre d'Eschyle, l'autre de celui d'Euripide . . .'.

[3] I am referring to two recent books: Girard 1972 and Burkert 1972, which, in
different ways, stress the unique importance of sacrifice in religious and social life, and
describe its remedial effects in Greek society. For Greek tragedy in particular see
Burkert 1966, 87 ff.

'representation'. But if 'representation' is not simply the 'mirroring' of actions and things, if 'representation,' on the contrary, implies always a detour—a movement away from the immediacy of actions— and an addition to the univocal simplicity of things, this notion ceases to be obvious and raises some intriguing problems. Thus, for instance, it is arguable whether the 'real' sacrifice is itself framed in a representational, theatrical structure; but it cannot be denied that Euripides' sacrifices are only represented, acted, imagined. This point is of paramount importance, for this fictional quality does not simply reduce the force of impact that a real sacrifice has, but it introduces also a representational displacement having its own force, which constantly threatens to jeopardize the effects that are expected by the enactment of the sacrifice.

Let us begin by analysing a passage from the *Medea*, where the Nurse ponders on the therapeutic power of songs. This passage (190 ff.) contains an elaborated theorizing about the function of poetic songs: though this theorizing exceeds in importance the Nurse's immediate concerns, it is not inconsistent with the dramatic context. The Nurse feels deep pity for Medea's despondency and prostration: the old woman comes out to tell Heaven and Earth of the calamities that have befallen her mistress. Her feeling of pity is frustrated to some extent by Medea's unwillingness to listen to friendly advice and solace (*Medea* 28–9). Analogously the chorus of Corinthian women feel frustrated that they are unable to reach Medea with their compassion and consolation (*Medea* 173–9). Finally they invite the Nurse to call Medea out in order to comfort her. It is at this point that the Nurse underlines the difficulty of persuading Medea, all the while theorizing on the therapeutic effects of songs: 'It would be right, I think, to consider foolish and not at all wise those men of the past who discovered (*hēuronto*) songs for festivities, banquets and dinner parties, merry music for life (*biōi terpnas akoas*). But none has discovered (*hēureto*) how to stop men's hateful griefs (*stugious . . . brotōn . . . lupas*) by means of poetry and songs of many notes,[4] the

---

[4]   στυγίους δὲ βροτῶν οὐδεὶς λύπας
       ηὕρετο μούσῃ καὶ πολυχόρδοις
       ᾠδαῖς παύειν . . .

In accordance with the rhythm *brotōn* should qualify *stugious lupas*, 'hateful griefs of men', but translators often take *brotōn* with *oudeis*: 'no one of them', with reference to *tous prosthe brotous* ('the men of the past') of line 191.

hateful griefs which cause death and misfortunes ruining the families. And yet it is a gain if men heal these (*kaitoi tade men kerdos akeisthai* | . . . *brotous*) by means of songs.[B] But where are pleasant banquets, why raise vainly the song? For the abundance of the feast offers already a pleasure of its own to men' (*Medea* 190 ff.)

This passage raises various problems of interpretation: I should like to begin to unravel them by focusing my attention on what seems to me the central notion of the Nurse's theorizing, namely, that there is a 'gain' (*kerdos*) in healing (*akeisthai*) hateful griefs by means of song. The notion of *akos* ('remedy') recalls the medicinal power of the songs and words and it is consonant with the notion of *pharmakon* ('medicine') used by Gorgias in stressing the seductive and corrupting power of the *logos*.[5] In using these words *akos* and *kerdos* the Nurse expresses herself in philosophically modern terminology, although the general notion that poetry is pleasurable and induces

[B] Another possible translation of the sentence is analogous to that of David Kovacs in his Loeb edition and translation of the *Medea* (1994): 'It is because of these griefs that death and terrible disasters overthrow houses. It would have been a gain for mortals to cure these ills by song.' In this translation, if I follow it correctly, the Nurse states that the old poets did not discover the therapeutic song and yet it would have been a gain if they had done it. In this way, while the text follows a certain logical progression, it leaves undecided whether some recent poet, in modern times, did discover this therapeutic song.

I prefer to translate: 'and yet it is a gain to heal these ills by song' with a positive rather than a contrary-to-fact conditional clause, for the following reasons.

(1) Since the Greek has the ellipse of the verb 'to be', one is authorized to translate either as Kovacs or as I propose. Yet the ellipse of the verb 'to be' is most frequent in the present indicative (Kühner and Gerth 1898, II.1, pp. 41–2, esp. Anm. 2). Here, in order to translate as a contrary-to-fact condition, one would probably wish to have the particle *an*, even after the impersonal form *kerdos* (*ēn*): see Smyth 1956, § 2315.

(2) If the text leaves uncertain, or even doubtful that such a therapeutic song is possible, in what sense were these old poets 'foolish and not at all wise'? Their foolishness is explained and stressed only if this therapeutic song that they did not discover is in fact possible, existing, and a reachable gain. Otherwise the Nurse's argument, with its polemical and vehement tone, would turn out to be extremely weak, for there is no serious foolishness in producing songs for festive occasions: the songs may be unnecessary, as the Nurse says, or harmful.

(3) It is difficult to believe that such a reflection on the therapeutic power of the song (poetry) is placed here at the beginning of the play without referring to the poetry itself that embeds it. At the time of Euripides, this therapeutic notion is popularized by Gorgias, and, as my examples show, is upheld by Euripides. Here Euripides indicates, I believe, the terms and the tenets of his poetic wisdom (*sophia*). For he would certainly not reprove the foolishness and silliness of the past poets if he were, like them, unable to discover a therapeutic song.

[5] See Gorgias, *Apol. of Hel.* 14, where the action of the *logos* ('word') is explained by a full analogy with that of the *pharmakon*: as the *pharmakon* acts on the nature of the body, so the *logos* acts on the disposition of the soul.

'forgetfulness of evils and rest from cares' is for us at least as old as Homer and Hesiod.[6] The terminological novelty is not gratuitous or showy; on the one hand, the text suggests that the *terpsis* (pleasure) that the epic poet boasts of producing (*Od.* 1. 345–7 etc.) may be considered just as superfluous as the merry music (*terpnas akoas*) that unnecessarily resounds on occasions of festivity and banquets. On the other hand, the word *akos*, together with *pharmakon* (both words are used by Euripides in similar conceptual frames)[7] transfers the

---

[6] For Homer see esp. *Od.* 1. 337 ff. For Hesiod see *Theogony* 52 ff.:

λησμοσύνην τε κακῶν ἄμπαυμά τε μερμηράων

(Forgetfulness of evils and ceasing from troubles)

and *Theogony* 98 ff. where the same principle is applied to the art of the poet itself. As I have shown in my book (Pucci 1977) Hesiod's argument is complex and rigorous, implying the deflective power of the word (*Theogony* 103) and therefore, among other things, the upsetting 'logic' which controls poetry, source at once of memory and forgetfulness, truth and lies, etc.

Notice in Euripides' and Hesiod's passages the same word: *pauein*, *ampauma* ('stop', 'ceasing').

[7] The word *akos* 'remedy' to describe the healing power of the word, is used in the *Andromache* (121) where the *logos* is compared to the juice of roots used as a medicine: 'if I were able to find (lit. to cut) a remedy (*akos*) for the inextricable griefs . . .'. As the scholiast explains, the idea of cutting refers to the technical *rhizotomein* 'to cut, find medical roots'. Aeschylus uses a parallel phrase (*Agamemnon* 16 f.):

ὅταν δ' ἀείδειν ἢ μινύρεσθαι δοκῶ
ὕπνου τόδ' ἀντίμολπον ἐντέμνων ἄκος

(and when I sing or hum a tune finding [lit. tapping] a remedy-song against sleep . . .)

The implication here is that through singing or humming the watchman fights against sleep. Other examples in Euripides:

εἰσὶν . . . λόγοι θελκτήριοι· φανήσεταί τι τῆσδε
φάρμακον νόσου.   (*Hipp.* 478–9)

(there are speeches that charm: a remedy will appear for this disease)

. . . ἀλλ' ἐπ' ἄλλη φάρμακον κεῖται νόσῳ.
λυπουμένῳ μὲν μῦθος εὐμενὴς φίλων,
ἄγαν δὲ μωραίνοντι νουθετήματα   (fr. 962)

(There are different remedies for different diseases: benevolent speech of friends for one who suffers, but advice for one being excessively foolish).

See also 1079. In Aeschylus we find parallel statements only in the *Prometheus* 378, 249. Democritus (DK 11, pp. 152–68 B 31) presents a parallel statement about *sophia* ('wisdom'):

. . . ἰατρικὴ μὲν
γὰρ κατὰ Δημόκριτον σώματος νόσους ἀκέεται, σοφίη δὲ
ψυχὴν παθῶν ἀφαιρεῖται.

(Medicine according to Democritus heals the diseases of the body, wisdom frees the soul from passions).

idea of discourse into a medical sphere; the comparison of discourse
to a medicine, a drug, a medical remedy, initiates a complex metaphorical chain of ideas suggesting that the *logos* functions as an
entity that is external, and heterogeneous to the entity called soul or
consciousness; it functions as a supplement, adding drugs or sub-
tracting something by medical means. The *logos* therefore is not only
other than the soul and the world of being that we associate with the
soul; its representation either falls short of that world or exceeds it.[8]

Furthermore, the medical metaphor suggests the possible danger
or painfulness of all remedies: this point may well explain why the
text speaks of a 'gain' in healing hateful grief, as if the advantage and
profit of curing diseases were not self-evident and could not be taken
for granted. For if the medicine is truly painful, the advantage of the
cure is not quite so obvious.

In fact, the word *kerdos* recalls here the possibility of a 'loss' and
indeed, the polarity, gain : loss qualifies the feeling of pity and the
remedial discourse prompted by pity in Euripides.

In the *Hecuba*, after the sacrifice of Polyxena, Talthybios appears
on stage to narrate the heroic death of Polyxena to her mother
Hecuba. He qualifies his own report to Hecuba as a 'second gain of
tears' (*dipla . . . dakrua kerdanai*) derived from his 'pity' for the girl
(*Hecuba* 518–19):

$$\delta\iota\pi\lambda\hat{a} \ \mu\epsilon \ \chi\rho\acute{\eta}\zeta\epsilon\iota\varsigma \ \delta\acute{a}\kappa\rho\upsilon\alpha \ \kappa\epsilon\rho\delta\hat{a}\nu\alpha\iota, \ \gamma\acute{\upsilon}\nu\alpha\iota,$$
$$\sigma\hat{\eta}\varsigma \ \pi\alpha\iota\delta\grave{o}\varsigma \ o\check{\iota}\kappa\tau\omega\cdot$$

He then recalls on which occasions he experienced such a double
gain of tears: first 'gain' was felt when he assisted at the slaughter of
Polyxena (*pros taphōi . . . hot' ōlluto* 520); and he 'profits' a second
time now in reporting the grievous news: 'now in telling the grievous
news I will drench my face with tears' (*nun . . . gar legōn kaka tenxō
tod' omma* 519–20).[9] This 'gain of tears', obtained through pity,

---

The 'gain' of a pitying or self-pitying discourse is not represented by Euripides only
by the imagery of medicine (*akos, pharmakon* etc.) but by other expressions: see for
instance the *kharis goōn* (the joy of laments) in *Supplices* 79; the pleasure (*philon*) to
sing aloud [my past] happiness (*Troades* 472 f). In this later passage the connection
with self-pity is explicit. 'Thus,' Hecuba goes on, 'I will throw greater pity (*oikton*)
against my misfortunes.'

[8] On the upsetting dynamics of the '*pharmakon*' in Gorgias and Plato, see Derrida
1972.

[9] The paradox 'gain of tears' recalls the famous Homeric description of Andromache,
dakruoen gelasasa ('smiling in tears', *Il.* 6. 484); but Talthybios' expression in Euripides
is heavier and more prosaic: it sounds 'hedonistic' in stressing the personal, contrived

capitalizes on the slaughter of Polyxena, but also transforms it: the girl's beauty and poise before death evokes for Talthybios the beauty of a statue (560–1). Pity builds a consoling monument.[c]

The oxymoronic and artificial expression *dipla . . . dakrua kerdanai* shows clearly the paradox of this gain: the profit of tears elicits a strange cluster of images where the gain (consolation, purging of distress) and loss (pain and suffering) jar with each other. This oxymoronic compression of ideas is repeated and mirrored in several analogous images which describe the simultaneous presence of a loss and a gain. For instance in the *Supplices* (79 ff.), the chorus of suppliant maids describe their plaintive cry as the 'insatiate, painful pleasure of laments':

$$\text{ἄπληστος ἄδε μ' ἐξάγει χάρις γόων}$$
$$\text{πολύπονος, ὡς ἐξ ἀλιβάτου πέτρας}$$
$$\text{ὑγρὰ ῥέουσα σταγὼν}$$
$$\text{ἄπαυστος αἰεί·}$$

This insatiable delight (*kharis*) of lamenting, full of grief, thrust me out of myself, just as spring-water runs down the high cliff, ever unending.

Here, clearly, the corresponding terms for 'loss' and 'gain' are 'grief' (*gooi* and *poluponos*), and 'pleasure', 'grace', 'beauty' (*kharis*).

We may now turn to Euripides' *Electra* 290 to find the statement that pity constitutes indeed a 'loss' for the pitier. Orestes is pondering on the strange feeling of pity: a feeling that can affect even a stranger and painfully sting the mind. Yet, he says, this feeling moves only the mind of educated people and this is the 'loss' or 'penalty' (*oud' azēmion*)

---

advantage of the pitier, and 'rationalistic' by implying a theory and a poetics of pity, of which we are outlining the profile.

[c] Though most interpreters and translators render the paradoxical meaning of the text as I do (Collard 1991: 'To weep twice in pity for your child: this is the reward you desire for me'; Sheppard 1949: 'You bid me take a double meed of tears . . .' etc.), some interpreters take the verb *kerdainein* (to gain) as ironical and translate it with what would be its opposite meaning, as Kovacs for instance does (1995): 'Lady, your request means that I must twice pay the penalty of tears shed in pity for your daughter . . .'. There is no support for *kerdainein* in this sense: the only example in LSJ, Xenophon, *Apology* 9, is, as in Euripides' *Hecuba*, an intended paradox, since, when Socrates states that he prefers to die rather than 'to gain a much worse life (than death)', he ironically underlines by the verb 'to gain' his own paradoxical preference, the common humanity preferring of course to live at any cost. To translate as Kovacs does implies deciding that the verb is used ironically, then hiding its irony and/or paradoxical force by rendering the verb with its opposite meaning, and accordingly flattening Euripides' bold image, his intellectual provocation, and obscuring the poetics that emerge through the notion of the gain, the pleasure of tears.

that they must pay for their excessive *sophia* (wisdom). To suffer for others' griefs (*sunalgein*) is then a 'loss' or 'penalty' for the sensitive and educated judgment.

If we combine the two texts, that of Talthybios and that of Orestes, we may describe part of the process that is implicit in the imagination or feeling that we call pity. As the pitier feels the grief produced by his *sunalgein*, he realizes a 'loss', or a penalty, but in the process his pity may become also a gain, a consolation. Analogously the self-pitier will find at once pleasure and pain in his lament as we read in *Suppl.* 79 ff., *Troades* 474 ff., etc.

Remedial discourse, in this instance that we have chosen, namely that of a pitying discourse, emerges as the discourse of the other, and in its process becomes, as we shall see, the discourse of the self. It is just within this ambivalence that it can be a loss and a gain, a pain and a pleasure.

The passage from the *Hecuba* illustrates yet another point: Talthybios by feeling pity and expressing it achieves a gain, but Hecuba too, by sensing through Talthybios' pity and eulogy the nobility of her daughter, achieves the same gain. His words affect her as she learns about the noble behaviour of her daughter (591 f.):

you [Polyxena] have removed my excessive cry (*stenein*) in that your nobility has been reported to me.

Talthybios' eulogy has the added effect of reducing and assuaging Hecuba's tears as well.

It is important here to open a parenthesis. According to Talthybios, he receives the same gain of tears twice, at the actual slaughter of Polyxena and at the moment in which he recounts that killing. The text therefore implies that the remedy produced by a real sacrifice, and the remedy produced by the discourse which re-enacts it, have the same effect. If this is true, the text forces us to accept one of the following alternatives: either the compassionate representation does not add anything to the real event, or the sacrifice itself is a theatrical happening that is already inscribed in a representational pattern and is surrounded by pity. This second assumption seems to be confirmed by the description of the sacrifice in the text of the *Hecuba*.

This leads us back to the significance of the Nurse's theorizing utterance in *Medea* (190 ff.). It is in general assumed that this passage, while consistent with the dramatic situation, describes also what for Euripides is the essence of tragedy. Our analysis of the crucial expression 'gain of healing grief' confirms this last point, but it also qualifies very precisely what Euripides thought tragedy should be. For, if we press the consonance and the complementarity between the *Medea*'s text and the other two passages from the *Hecuba* and the *Electra*, we must conclude that Euripides presents tragedy as a song aiming at the paradoxical *kerdos* (gain) of tears as medicine for grief.

Nevertheless, this explanation is not sufficient: the remedy described above should not be confused with that provided by conventional themes of consolation. The Corinthian women, for instance, think that they may 'relax the deep passion' of Medea's rage (176–7) by the platitudes of consolatory speeches: unhappiness in love is a common lot (155 ff.); Zeus will help to restore justice (148 ff.), etc. No, these are not the remedies of Euripides' drugstore: Euripides' song promises healthy effect only through an administration of violent and painful remedies: the patients, Euripides himself and his audience, must undergo the most distressing experience, a derangement of the mind struck by the brutality and senselessness of suffering. Only then, paradoxically, does the healthy effect emerge.

Euripides' tragedy follows the dynamics and principles of a therapeutic practice (invented by a *sophos*, 'wise man') of which he speaks in fr. 964 (2 ff.):

. . . I was imagining in my mind cares, calamities, inflicting on myself exile from my fatherland and premature death and other ways of evil, so that if I had to suffer some of the things that I was imagining in my mind, I would not be stung more sharply by the novelty of the event.

The language of this passage is instructive: the remedy is grounded on imagining, i.e. in representing and making present to the mind all possible evils (*edoxazon . . . phreni*) of which this *sophos* is actually exempt. It is therefore appropriate that he should say that he is adding (*prostitheis*) the imagining of these evils to his mind, and that he should use this imagination as a weapon (*eballomēn*) against the real evils that might threaten him. The text makes clear the vicarious aspect (supplementarity) of this imagination that by adding that which is not there *exceeds* all presence. It is this representation, this imagining that is enacted by the tragic *logos* and that should finally be a *kerdos*.

In another passage of Euripides we find the same metaphor in a parallel context: Hecuba in the *Troades* cries (472–3):

My pleasure (*philon*) is first to sing aloud (*exaisai*) about my past happiness. Thus I will throw (*embalō*) greater pity (*oikton*) against my misfortunes (*tois kakois*).

Hecuba's doom is the enemy against which she throws as a weapon her own pity. This counteracting the *kaka* (evils) with pity is pleasurable, gratifying (*philon*); it lulls the grief.

Hecuba adopts the same remedy that Aristotle has analysed in describing the effects of mournings and laments (*Rhet.* 1. 11. 11 ff.): through an appropriate discourse the mourner is able to evoke the presence of his dead beloved. Distress results from the absence of the loved one, but pleasure lies in remembering him just as he was. Analogously Hecuba should be able to lull the pain of her present situation by evoking her joyous and prosperous past. Yet, since she describes her pleasure as resulting from a song that produces greater pity, she remains aware that her recollection will not wipe away the sense of her present situation. For pity will emerge from the comparison of her past and new experience.

Hecuba's recollection of her past happiness will initially increase her pain. It is extraordinary that Euripides should like to deepen her experience of pain and grief, as if the sea of afflictions by which she is distressed were not yet sufficient. She is shown inflicting on herself an additional dosage of anguish, while looking beforehand at the advantage she will receive. The experience of the audience is parallel: they will suffer more intensely for Hecuba, but simultaneously receive the balm, the remedy that is implicit in pity.

This self-inflicted additional pain and the awareness of its possible advantage characterizes even the tone of voice of such Euripidean characters as Hecuba, Medea, Creusa, etc. They voice bluntly and forcefully their own suffering but simultaneously they show awareness that a possible remedy may ensue from their cries. Consequently, the tone of their voice has a specific loudness, an excessive resonance as if these characters were in fact listening to themselves and to the effects that they produce on their listeners.

Some of the evidence we have reviewed supports the argument that pain and pleasure, loss and gain are the simultaneous and inextricable effects of Euripides' tragic discourse. But if so, how can his tragedy be therapeutic? For in the *Medea* (190 ff.) the Nurse assumes that it would be wise to invent a profitable song that can heal the grief of life. She does not mention any 'loss' or 'penalty'.

Through the Nurse, therefore, Euripides states the ambitious goal of his art: to repress the negative terms, loss and pain, by means of a rhetorical experience of these same terms and thereby reach the gain and the pleasure: that is, a 'presence'.

By 'presence' I mean the univocal signified, the *mimēma* of the real thing or of the emotion that the classical view of language presupposes to emerge from discourse. Aristotle in *Rhetoric* I. II. II ff. writes that lovers 'rejoice not only if the beloved is present (*parontos*), but they love also if the beloved is absent (*apontos*) by recalling him to mind. This is why even when his absence is painful, and even in mourning and laments there is some pleasure: distress results from the absence of the loved one, but pleasure lies in remembering him and, as it were, in beholding his actions and personality. And therefore this has been rightly said: 'thus he spoke and he stirred in all a desire for laments' (*Il.* 23. 108).' With this last line Aristotle summons up the episode in which Achilles stirs desire to lament in his companions, by telling them that Patroclus' ghost had appeared to him. Aristotle seems to take Achilles' conversation with Patroclus' ghost as an example of a mourner's recollection. He therefore connects the lover and the mourner's experience: love increases Achilles' distress for Patroclus' absence and death makes that absence ultimate.

In the translation I have transcribed the Greek words for 'presence' and 'absence' in order to stress the terms on which Aristotle's argument pivots: against the physical absence of the beloved, the recollection (the talking, the letters of the lovers, etc.) recovers at least momentarily the presence of the absent beloved. The words, therefore, recover a presence, carry in the mind of the speaker the present or past life of what is now remote.

What is brought into the foreground of the mind is not the physical person of the beloved, but his live image; yet this image acquires such an intensity that the speaker really sees and hears him. Aristotle seems to stress that force and concreteness of this presence of the beloved when he alludes to the scene in which Patroclus' *psychē* appears to Achilles and converses with him. As Achilles says, Patroclus' *psychē* appears extraordinarily similar to the man himself (*Il.* 23. 105–7). Aristotle seems therefore to suggest that the discourse of the lover recollecting the person of his beloved constitutes a real entity, something analogous to the '*psychē*' of the beloved himself: like the *psychē*, this discourse is alive, present, carrying exactly the marks of the beloved, shaping his traits and voice just as he is. If the classical view of language considers the *logos* as a *psychē*, so to speak, of the world of being, of the nature of things, a live ghost reproducing Being exactly as it is, a *mimema* that mirrors it, then we perceive the sense of 'presence' that is implied in language.[10]

Modern criticism has attacked this classical view of the *logos*, of the representation: 'presence' would always appear in the discourse only belatedly, i.e. in the wake of the discourse itself, which does not in fact mirror any 'original' model, any 'original' signified. But I cannot here reproduce the arguments of J. Derrida, and illustrate how meaning takes shape through a play of differentiations, in the gaps and lags that mark language as difference, spacement and deferral.[11] Nor is it necessary here to reproduce such arguments: the text of Euripides declares, if we interpret correctly its paradoxical statements, that presence can emerge only with absence, and therefore that the gain of a presence is always in some way frustrated. The medical metaphors that we have illustrated imply that the *mimēma*, the representation, the medical song adds itself as an external hetero-geneous entity to the soul: the remedial representation therefore, as otherness from the mind, i.e. addition and supplementarity, appears to be uncontrollable. This is the dangerous aspect of the discourse: for the remedial discourse functions initially as a loss and, accord-ingly, as a poison: the gruesome meditations that the *sophos* inflicts on his mind are painful and poisonous before becoming remedial. The predicament in which the remedial *logos* finds itself is therefore the following: since the initial effect of this discourse is negative and poisonous the administration of this discourse must be carefully controlled and its effect must be cleverly turned into beneficial results. The therapeutic process that is here implied constitutes the specific detour and deferral of Euripides' language; in this process the remedy appears to be a deferred and controlled poison, the gain ensues from

---

[10] Aristotle in the passage quoted does not speak explicitly of a presence of the beloved in the words of the mourner; this presence nevertheless results from the opposition of the terms he uses and from considering Achilles' conversation with Patroclus' ghost, a discourse of remembrance.

In his theoretical works, Aristotle defines language as conventional signs (*sumbola*) of the emotions or impression of the soul (*pathēmata tēs psykhēs, De Interpret.* 16[a]5 ff.). He accounts for the difference from language to language, but at the same time he upholds the universality of these *pathēmata*. In other passages, his definition of language puts in contact directly language and the world of things: see for instance *Soph. El.* 1. 165a7: *tois onomasin anti tōn pragmatōn khrōmetha sumbolois*, 'we use the names as tokens for the things', where the nouns are directly signs or symbols of *pragmata*.   [11] Derrida 1967.

a shrewdly stored and manipulated loss, and the pleasure results from an artful articulation and economy of pain. One is reminded here of the upsetting dynamics of pleasure and pain that Freud has outlined in *Beyond the Pleasure Principle* and that Derrida has taken as an instructive instance of deferral.

As it is clear from the previous passage, the two facets of the remedial discourse, the poisonous and the healthy one, are opposite and polarized only in accordance with traditional logic; in fact as we are suggesting, they emerge from an odd economy of the same discourse; one facet looming always, as a threat, over the other. Accordingly, the instability of this balance jeopardizes the success of the remedial discourse. Only if it were possible for the writer to open up a neat separation between loss and gain, between poison and remedy, would he control the upsetting dynamics of difference and deferral that mark the remedial discourse. The writer indeed aims at this goal the very moment he erects a logical opposition between loss and gain, pain and pleasure, the one being thought of as opposite and exclusive of the other. Yet the 'paradox' that we have seen: 'pleasure and pain of laments' shows us that the logical opposition and separation between pleasure and pain, gain and loss constitute a form of domestication.

There is no doubt which term, paradox or opposition, is more reassuring. By the strategy implicit in the latter terms, the movement of deferral and difference is controlled, the instability frozen, the upsetting economy of the drug mastered. In this frame and by being so framed the discourse would appear univocally as a remedy, pointing only at its remedial effects; simultaneously this discourse would be the expression of the mind that has full control over it.

The dynamics of this process would entail that the deferral is controlled and a presence emerges. It is obvious for instance that the *sophos* who imagines all sorts of evils for himself must handle his own imagination—which is initially poisonous—with a complex and contradictory strategy. On the one hand he must forget that his imagination is a fiction: for only if he really suffers from these evils that he adds to or inflicts on his mind, will he become immunized. He must therefore let the poison invade and affect his soul. On the other hand, he must always gain control of his imagining, otherwise he could become obsessed by it, he could become morose and melancholic and his imagining could remain a poison. The *sophos* therefore must handle his own imagining as an entity that though inflicted on himself, as a foreign drug, ceases to be other than himself and can be perfectly controlled. His imagination must become present to him, identical to the strategy of his own mind, without any excess or displacing power.

My arguments have suggested that the upsetting dynamics of the therapeutic discourse depend finally on the unstable movement of representation, of imagining, in a word, of the *logos* itself. We are dealing with a special *logos* that by affecting the mind with a peculiar force, aims at procuring a defense against evil, at retrieving some pleasure in the midst of pain, at insuring the control and the presence of the self just when the self is repeating the discourse of the other, of death, and anguish. We may come closer to grasp the mechanics of this special discourse if we analyse the way in which the discourse of pity functions.

In the famous passage on the tragic catharsis, Aristotle considers pity and fear as fully parallel emotions; but in the *Rhetoric* he sees that pity arises from fear. Thus in *Rhet.* 2.5.12 he writes that 'all things are to be feared when, happening to others or threatening them, they excite pity'. More explicitly in 2.8.13 he asserts that 'all the things that are dreaded (*phobountai*) for ourselves, excite our pity when they happen to others'. Of course, as we find ourselves in the grip of fear facing others' pains, several types of reactions and discourses are possible, and pity is only one of them. But it is important to stress these points, viz. that pity emerges from beholding others in the grip of some deadly *kaka* (evils), while we are still exempt from it; that pity bridges, so to speak, the distance between self and other and makes the other the sign or the premonition of what we would suffer; that pity therefore stings us as an anguish that we receive from others, a pain that is greater by the extent to which we fear the same for ourselves. This pain inflicted by pity is deeper if we love the person whom we perceive in the grip of a deadly evil, because we desire what is good for the person we love, but also because we fear the loss of this person as a loss for ourselves.

If we keep these points in mind we should realize the first remedial effects of the discourse of pity: though it emerges from our fear, this discourse replaces fear, and though it emerges as the discourse of the other, it ends as our own discourse.

Before we analyse the precise way in which these effects function, let us recall that we find a Euripidean text, unfortunately difficult, that theorizes on pity and on fear of death. In *IT* 484 f., Orestes reacts against Iphigenia's compassionate expressions and upholds a heroic attitude whereby he condemns pity and compassion:

I do not consider it wise (*sophon*) that whoever is about to die be ready to overcome the fear of death (*to deima toulethrou nikan*) by pity (*oiktōi*).[12]

That pity, therefore, may replace fear of the deadly *kakon* and prevail over it, is clearly spelled out in this passage, even if Orestes, in accordance with heroic ethics, rejects such a practice.

The process by which we overcome our dread of some deadly *kakon* by means of pity, starts as we gaze with dismay at the sufferings of others. Take for instance the Nurse's opening utterance in the *Medea* (1 ff.) that presents a compassionate view of her mistress. As the Nurse is trapped by the griefs of Medea, she beholds them in fear: she enters, so to speak, into Medea's mind and diction. In fact she recites a sophisticated, lofty and almost lyrical speech, many expressions of which return later in Medea's own utterances.

As the Nurse speaks and relates Medea's grief she affects herself and moves herself to anguish. This phenomenon cannot be fully understood without referring to the self-affecting power of the voice. The voice is perceived as the most direct and immediate 'expression' of our soul or consciousness. In fact we could say with Derrida that consciousness is already the metaphysical 'presence' foisted on us by the voice. The Nurse, then, using Medea's language, affects herself and voices her own anguish for her mistress' misfortunes. In this process, through the self-affecting power of the voice, a new rhetorical frame of mind emerges. First, the Nurse perceives her discourse as her own, that is as a discourse that she can control since it is the expression of her own consciousness. Consequently, and we touch here upon the second point, the Nurse is allowed to feel that her anguish is a spontaneous emotion, induced by her free will; and

---

[12] I translate according to the manuscripts' reading: *thanein* ('die'). Most editors, on the contrary, accept Seidler's conjecture *ktenein* instead of *thanein* and read therefore: 'I do not consider it wise that whoever is about to kill someone wishes to overcome the latter's fear of death by pitying him.' See Platnauer in his commentary (1960) who, however hesitantly, prefers the manuscripts' reading *thanein*.

Also the expression *oiktōi deima nikan* is ambiguous: either 'to drown his fear of death in pitiful cries' or 'to overcome his fear of death by the help of someone else's pity'. In the former sense the text could imply the force of self-pity. It is suitable here to make clear that self-pity functions with the same strategy as pity. He who pities himself, in fact, introduces an unconscious split into himself: a part of him corresponds to the pitying voice, the other part corresponds to that which is in the grip of anguish and for which the pitying voice feels pity.

finally, she experiences grief only through the sign, through her imagination. In this way she gains control over Medea, that is, over the source of her fear and anguish, feels master of her own expression and emotions and suffers only vicariously. No doubt she finds this discourse remedial. We may recall here Freud's famous passage in *Beyond the Pleasure Principle* where he studies the motivations behind children's games. One explanation Freud gives for the child's dramatization of unpleasurable experience is that at the onset the child is in a passive situation—he is overpowered by the unpleasurable experience; but by repeating it, unpleasurable though it was, he takes an active part and masters the pain.

It would be easy to show how the Nurse in the *Medea* gains control over her own discourse and seems to reach a presence—how for instance, in the first fifteen lines she evokes the 'presence' of harmony as source of 'deliverance, preservation' (*sōtēria*) and how this 'presence' guides her regretful recollection of the past; or how in the next passage, she shares grief (*sunalgei*) with Medea by depicting her prostration with hyperbolic expressions that simultaneously betray the Nurse's own annoyance at the excessive seigniorial temper of the masters (*turannoi*). Similarly it would be easy to show that the Nurse finally beholds her own consciousness, and feels her anguish as a spontaneous emotion, an evidence of her noble mind (see lines 54–5 when she explains that noble (*khrēstoisi*) slaves feel pity for their masters); the initial fear now jars with the 'presence' of a noble consciousness.

But this analysis would take us far and I prefer to exemplify the nature of this gain granted by the discourse of pity, in passages in which the gain is embodied in the images of the monument and the sacrifice and pertains to the art of the poet itself.

The poet finds himself in a rhetorical frame of mind that is analogous to that of the Nurse or that of Talthybios: his discourse prompted by pity and trying to secure a remedy, a gain, a pleasure reveals the same strange economy. For the poet shows an irrepressible propensity to dig with extreme cruelty into the misery of human existence and to subject himself to the poison of death. Not unlike the *sophos* of fr. 964, the poet imagines exiles, premature deaths and murders to prepare himself, and gain control over suffering. He administers to himself the poison of death in order to be cured of the fear of death. This therapeutic advantage is gained by feeling anguish for an imagined death: this anguish is preferred to any fear of death, for by this imagining, through the tragic representation that prompts pity, the poet succeeds in gaining control over death. He aims at gaining a presence in the form of a consciousness that is completely master of its imagination: ideally, between his consciousness and his representation there should be no gaps or excesses, no replacing entity, the one mirroring the other. Since he who pities finds himself noble and wise, so Euripides' consciousness will contemplate its nobility and wisdom; and since remedial discourse hides fear, it should ideally gain control over the 'other', over violence. Analogously, as this discourse seems to be the expression of the healthy and controlling consciousness, it should be able to repress the difference, the detour, and the deferral of remedial language and imagination.

By the concrete illustrations that follow I hope to support the model so far outlined. Nevertheless we should be aware that the recovery of a presence is illusory. In fact, remedial discourse can never efface loss, pain, otherness, the dead lags and gaps in all language. Discourse remains irreconcilably marked by excess (supplementarity) and deferral: in the case of Euripides' discourse, remedial imagination involves a therapeutic process within which medicine and poison have a strange and upsetting similarity, a difference in sameness, which the poet tries vainly to control.

This last statement would apply more pertinently to the word *pharmakon* which designates at once medicine and poison; but as we have seen, the ambivalence of *akos* is *implicitly* the same. Rather we should appreciate the optimistic gesture whereby Euripides describes the therapeutic process of the *logos* by a word, *akos*, that designates the successful stage of the medical cure.[13]

The Euripidean tragic *logos* is concerned with the suspension of grief through the manipulation of a discourse that grants remedy.

---

[13] Beside the parallelism between *akos* and *pharmakon*, one should not neglect to observe the function that *pharmaka* have in Euripides' tragic discourse. That we read about the 'remedy' of poetic songs in the *Medea* is certainly not a matter of chance. Medea, just like Creusa, possesses *pharmaka* of ambivalent nature: on the one hand, she knows 'such *pharmaka*' that will make Aegeus a prosperous father (*Medea* 718): *toiad' oida pharmaka*; on the other hand, she knows 'such *pharmaka*' that will destroy the daughter of Creon (789): *toioisde khrisō pharmakois dōrēmata* ('with such poisons will I anoint the gifts'). Notice in this last instance that the poisoner presents herself as a donor, masking her deadly action beneath the role of a generous giver. This ambivalence of Medea's *pharmaka* corresponds to the ambivalence of Euripides' remedy: Euripides' writing is inscribed in a set of medicinal images that bespeak the same concrete dynamics as that of Medea's actions.

Nothing better illustrates this point than the first and the last lines of
the *Medea*: the Nurse opens the drama with the words: 'Would that
(*eith' ōphel'*) such and such had not happened' by which she means
all the past events of Medea's involvement with Jason; and Jason
closes the drama with the line: 'Would that (*ophelon*) I had never
begot [my children] nor seen them destroyed by you' (1413–14).
The whole plot of the *Medea* is embraced by two laments that show
frustration on the one hand, and the inanity of regret on the other.
Yet if the desire that things had not happened is inane, the expression
itself of that desire becomes consoling and remedial.

Two important figures mirror the process of Euripides' remedial
discourse of pity, the monument and the sacrifice. To be sure the
sacrifice is more than a 'figure': as Burkert and Girard have shown,[14]
the sacrifice is at the heart of Greek theatre. As the sacrifice enacts
destruction and restitution, violence and peace, it is emblematic of
the attributes that Euripides grants to his own remedial discourse,
loss and gain. As I have shown, these attributes are grounded on the
representation itself, in the imagining of pity, in the dynamics of the
remedial discourse that the *sophos* tries to control. In these dynamics,
the sacrifice turns out to be a sort of self-induced violence, and the
pleasurable result of the sacrifice consists in the capability of controlling that violence. I say self-induced from the point of view of the
writer, since I am referring to the representation of violence and of
the deadly evil that Euripides stages in order to retrieve a remedy for
himself and the audience.

At this juncture, the reader will notice that my approach to the
problem of sacrifice in Greek tragedy differs from that of Girard. For
Girard reads the texts of Greek tragedy mainly as anthropological
sources in which he discovers significant support for his views of the
sacrifice, as an expression of desacralizing and sacred violence. I am
on the contrary focusing on the force of representation that encompasses also the representation of the sacrifice. The dynamics of the
discourse of pity are instructive in understanding also the representation of the sacrifice, for in this case too the power of the sword
opens an unstable movement between violence and peace, death and
life, analogous to that of loss and gain in the discourse prompted by
pity. More important, the Euripidean sacrifice is represented in such
a way as to be itself a source of pity rather than the enactment of a

---

[14] See n. 3 above.

shivering violence. To some extent therefore the representation of sacrifice in Euripides provokes a 'gain of tears', just as the sacrifice of Polyxena brings forth pity in Talthybios.

It is not the sight of the blood, nor the shivering that grips all the sacrificers as the knife strikes the victim, nor the desacralizing and sacred violence of slaughtering the human victim that triggers a remedy in tragedy. The sacrificial act in tragedy is never acted on stage but always reported. It is always fictionally acted behind the scene—from where we hear the screams of the victims; it is always reported and couched in an interpreting messenger's utterance (*angelia*). We have seen that Talthybios does not distinguish between 'the gain of tears' that he receives at the moment in which he takes part in the sacrifice and the 'gain of tears' he receives in reporting it. In both moments he feels only pity, not the sacredness of the act, nor its liberating violence. He feels only pity, i.e. a compassionate anguish for the other's deadly evil, as if, in experiencing the sacrifice, he were affected by the theatricality of the ritual.[15]

All this does not mean to deny the connection of tragedy with the sacrificial ritual of the goat (Dionysus, as Burkert has maintained) or to question Burkert's assertion that 'the essence of the sacrifice still pervades tragedy even in its maturity';[16] on the contrary, my

---

[15] Various and difficult problems arise at this point: are all Euripidean narratives of sacrifices marked by the same theatricality and impregnated by the same sentiments of compassion and pity? Or do some of his texts transmit the sense of sacred violence, of the unanimous assault on the victim? Is the sacrifice itself—I mean the real ritual of sacrifice—immune from theatricality and the representational frame? Can the ritual retrieve what Girard sees in the 'original' sacrifice?

It is impossible to answer all these questions here. Let it suffice to notice that Euripides' most sacred representation of sacrifice, that of Pentheus, contains a strong streak of compassion. While the messenger describes the action of the god with religious awe and fearsome respect, without commenting on it (*Bacchae* 1048 ff.), he describes the Bacchants themselves in terms that show his entire dissociation from them and arouses pity for the fate of Pentheus. His disavowal of the sacrifice corresponds to the hostility that the men in Thebes feel for the Bacchants, as we are induced to believe from various hints (716 ff., 781 ff.). His reporting of Pentheus' suppliant words (1118–21) stresses the full consciousness of the victim and the irresponsible madness of the sacrificers who appear to be in his eyes not only *emmaneis* by the god (1094), but more precisely crazed and possessed by an abnormal state of mind that he describes clinically (1122–3). In the next scenes of the play, order and peace are not established by the sacrifice itself, but by the process of regaining 'sanity': the scene between Cadmus and Agave shows that the 'human' borders are again retrieved by the pity of the former and by the disavowal of the sacrifice of the latter.

As concerns the ritual itself, one should read the various hints that Burkert 1972 offers on the 'theatricality' of the ritual. See for instance p. 52 and *passim*.

[16] Burkert 1966, 116.

argument tends to support both points and to define Euripides' tragic sacrifice as the staging of a violence that 'repeats' the ritual one but simultaneously, being a self-inflicted, fictional and represented action, displaces its meaning and efficacy.

It is on the force of this displacement that we must concentrate our attention, trying to understand how the social and ritual effect of the sacrifice is displaced into a self-affecting and remedial violence whose dynamics function in accordance with the pattern that I have out-lined for the discourse of pity. Furthermore we must see how the remedy that is expected to derive from this representation fails to work and remains always, simultaneously, a poison. We have already mentioned the case of Talthybios in the *Hecuba*. The herald of the Greeks is struck by pity for the death of Polyxena and receives—as he says—a double gain from his pity. He equates the naked body of Polyxena, ready to be slaughtered, to a beautiful statue (*agalma*). This word alone mirrors the complex way of domestication and control that are at work in this image: even before being slaughtered Polyxena appears to Talthybios in the permanent beauty of a statue (*agalma*) which is generally offered to the gods and which represents them. The shivering that should grasp everybody at the mortal stroke to the poor body of Polyxena is replaced by an image that evokes already restitution, honour and immortality. A gain. The violence that should unite the Greeks in the performance of the slaughter is replaced by such a feeling of pity that Neoptolemos barely has courage to strike. The monument is erected before the sacrifice, the restitution is given before the loss, immortality is evoked before destruction.

This illustration shows exactly how Euripides' remedial repres-entation functions: the *sophos* inflicts a painful imagining on himself while looking beforehand at the gain, at the profit, at painlessness. So Talthybios sees his own nobility before seeing himself as an executioner.

Furthermore, the image of the statue gives meaning to the other-wise arbitrary sacrifice of Polyxena: the capricious will of Achilles' ghost, with whom the Greeks comply only out of necessity, receives some sense. With the complicity of Polyxena's heroic behaviour, Talthybios glosses over the senselessness and arbitrariness of the sacrifice and contemplates an ideal form, a lasting sign of beauty.

But the monument remains a sign of death and nothing can efface the absence of life (from the effigy). So that Hecuba, after Talthybios' reporting, expresses her feeling in a somewhat jarring statement (589–92):

And now I cannot efface from my mind your [Polyxena's] suffering so as not to weep. Yet you have taken away the excess of my weeping in that your nobility has been reported to me.

The statue erected by Talthybios cannot efface for Hecuba her daughter's death (*pathos . . . exaleipsasthai*).

The unstable meaning of the monument is dramatically felt by Admetus in the *Alcestis*. At the moment in which he faces the noble sacrifice of his wife he imagines that he will find joy (*terpsis* 313), however cool, from a statue of Alcestis in his bed. Admetus' strange idea of placing a statue in his bed stems probably from the archaic view that statues or figurines represent the double of the real person, his or her *psychē*. In Aeschylus' *Agamemnon* (410–26) both the figurines of Helen and her presence in Menelaus' dreams are mentioned as forms of Helen's double, or forms whereby to evoke her presence while she is in reality absent.[17] More generally, Admetus senses his house as a building and a center from which Alcestis cannot be absent. Consequently, the house will remain a permanent place of mourning, a sort of enlarged shrine for the *psychē* of the sacrificed victim,[18] and Alcestis will of course be there in the forms allowed her by death (354 ff.). But immediately after the funeral Admetus stops before his house and starts a long lament in which he declares the inanity of the monuments that should have ensured the presence of a double, of Alcestis' *psychē* (861 ff.):

> O me! hateful gates,
> hateful view of my empty house
> O me, O me . . .

It would take too long to elaborate the themes of this *kommos* in which Admetus realizes that his soul is prisoner of Alcestis and of death, not the contrary, and that he cannot live any longer without her. He has accepted her sacrifice as master (*kurios*) of the house to ensure its preservation and prosperity but now he realizes that her sacrifice was

---

[17] Vernant 1966, 256 ff. has studied the symbolism of the stone-figure and of the figurines as representations of the double (*psychē*) and has shown their relevance to the *Alcestis* text.

[18] Euripides 'made even Alcestis' death a sacrifice, Thanatos a sacrificial priest, *hiereus thanontōn* (25)' (Burkert 1966, 116).

useless. He wants to die and go where she is (866 ff., 895 ff.). As the
monument bespeaks only death, it becomes unbearable.

In the *Alcestis* Euripides demystifies the symbolic force of the
monument, for in this play death is overcome by no less a remedy
than by Alcestis' resurrection. But in other plays the monument,
either in connection with the sacrifice or not, becomes the image of
permanence. We may turn to the passage of the *Troades* in which
Hecuba places the little corpse of Astyanax in the shield of Hector and
recites a funeral oration.[19] She rises above the havoc of Troy and
the victory of the Greeks by voicing an epigram for the shame of the
conquerors (1188–91):

What would the poet (*mousopoios*) write on your grave?
'The Greeks slaughtered the child, being afraid of him?'
Shameful epigram for Greece!

We have here an indicting statement, a discourse of protest. This
epigram condemns the history of the Greeks from the time of the
Trojan Wars to Euripides' own time, given that Hecuba's words are
probably intended to refer also to the Athenian cruelty on the occasion of the Melian affair. The poet whom Hecuba evokes represents
the mind of Euripides. His voice therefore acquires the monumental
proportion and the lasting force of that history.

The text of the epigram and Hecuba's funeral oration elicit simultaneously a profound pity. The old queen of Troy recounts the unfortunate short life of Astyanax (1167 ff.) and takes him as the symbol
of Troy's vain efforts and doomed heroism. Everything has been
fruitless, and Hecuba dwells even on Astyanax's untruth (1181) when
he was promising to bury Hecuba. The truth of all this is contained in
that grave inscription, in that tomb which unites in death Hector and
the last hope of Troy, Astyanax. The poet who writes that inscription
is Euripides himself and the sense of the whole play might well be
described as his funeral oration inscribed on the tomb of Troy. The
voice of the poet acquires therefore the monumental proportion and
everlasting force of a grave inscription.

The permanence of the voice, the beauty of the monument, and
the victory over death constitute the presence recovered by Euripides'
song. His voice contrasts the havoc of destruction and the terror of

[19] On the dramatically gratuitous return of Astyanax' body to Hecuba, see the
perceptive page by de Romilly 1961, 26: she shows that Euripides manages to have
the body of the child on the stage only for the sake of a moving and pathetic scene.

death with a hedonistic self-gratifying celebration of death. Euripides' language starts with the inescapable void contained within the monument, namely death. In fact he starts out appropriately with the void of his own language itself: 'Would that such and such had never happened' indicates precisely and explicitly that the function of his language is to evoke the inescapability of the *kakon*. But he fills that void with a rhetorical performance that in itself becomes a presence in the form of a voice that decries death and gains control over it.

Yet nothing can ever efface death, void and absence from the monument. For the monument is equally the 'sign' of life in death and the 'sign' of death in life. The monument partakes of the function of the sign, as the Homeric *sēma* illustrates, because the monument stands to replace and to signify a lost life, just as the linguistic sign replaces and signifies the world of being. The monument stands as a stony and dead entity that recalls life; analogously the linguistic sign is an inert chain of semiotic matter recalling the world of being. In neither case life flows ever in them: nowhere does the semiotic chain plunge into being. For this reason the monument has been so often chosen as the privileged metaphor to indicate the 'difference' of the linguistic sign. Indeed we have only to continue to read the text of *Troades* to realize how the shield of Hector does not contain any everlasting inscription, but only the impression, the trace, or mark (*tupos*) of Hector's vain toils in defending Troy. Hecuba turns to this monument, the shield, and exclaims (1194 f.):

You, that protected (*sōizousa*) the handsome arm of Hector, you have lost your best guard (*phulak'*).

The shield that had to defy history with its engraved inscription is now lost since Hector is not there to guard it (1196 f.):

How sweetly the imprint (*tupos*) rests on your handle and the (trace of) sweat on the well-turned border . . .

Another inscription (*tupos*) lies on the shield of Hector, not the poetic one that would sing forever the pitiful fall of Troy, but the imprint of Hector's arm, the sign of his vain sweat, of his vain toils. Hecuba finds the shield sweet to touch, now that she had described it as a monument defying history, as the tomb of Astyanax, as the perennial memory (*mnēma*) of glory and pity; but a few lines before, when the shield had been handed to her, she had felt only sadness and pain in beholding it (1156 f.).

The monument that should immortalize the sacrifice of Astyanax and Troy with a perennial inscription carries on the contrary an inscription that is the mark of an absence. Accordingly, the voice of the poet, that melts with Hecuba's, does not retrieve a presence but betokens at once death and destruction. Thus the monument reproduces the same instability that marks the therapeutic process of the remedial *logos*. A strange result! For the monument should block this unstable detour, this odd economy and deferral by means of its own solidity and stability: but the monument is erected and installed within this detour; like Niobe's rock, it bespeaks at once permanence and absence.[20]

It would take too long to analyse all the sacrificial rituals that are staged in Euripides' plays: I consider here first the sacrifice of Hippolytus, condemned to death by a revengeful goddess and honoured after his death by sacrificial honours.[21]

At the end of the *Hippolytus*, when the sacrifice of the young man is consummated, Euripides unfolds a scene of great pity. Here Hippolytus is dying and Artemis descends from Heaven to witness his innocence (1400, 1402, etc.) and to pity him. First Artemis promises to take revenge on a favourite of Aphrodite and then she establishes, as a sort of compensation, everlasting honours for Hippolytus (1423 ff.):

To you, unhappy man, for the sake of this doom, I'll grant (*dōsō*) the greatest honours in Troezenia: for virgin girls before their wedding shall cut off their hair; and through all ages you shall reap the fullest grief of their tears (*penthē megista dakruōn karpoumenōi*). And forever the poetic thought (*mousopoios merimna*) of virgins shall be in your honour, nor shall Phaedra's love for you be forgotten or fall in silence.

We remark first of all how tears of pity, and songs of pity constitute the honour (*timē*) for Hippolytus, or even more positively the fruit,

---

[20] It would be interesting to consider the image of Niobe's rock and the parallel image of the stream that pours from a mountain's rock. The image of Niobe's rock appears in the last book of the *Iliad* (24. 602 ff.) as an example of permanent mourning (617); the metaphor of the stream springing from a rock at *Iliad* 16. 3–4 to illustrate Patroclus' crying as he feels pity and anguish for the doom of the Greeks. This last image occurs many times in Greek literature and in Euripides in particular (*Supplices* 79 ff., *Andromache* 116). The Nurse of the *Medea* describes her mistress' prostration with terms that recall Niobe's rock (*Medea* 24–9).

[21] 'What is more general and more important: any sort of killing in tragedy may be termed *thuein* ("sacrifice") as early as Aeschylus and the intoxication of killing is called *bakkheuein* ("act like a bacchant")' (Burkert 1966, 116).

the enjoyment, the gain (*karpoumenōi*) that he reaps from his sacrifice. By utterly losing himself he gains everlasting pity, institutionalized both in a ritual—the cutting of the hair—and in a poetic song. That Hippolytus should feel consoled and compensated by the knowledge that poetic song shall celebrate Phaedra's love for him, would be a bitter irony, if this poetic song were not indeed that which we are listening to now, this very play by Euripides. We do not even feel the irony of this compensation and gain because we are already possessed by the pity elicited by the play. Thus, just as Hippolytus dies, Euripides, through the divine words of Artemis, forces us to look at his own play as the everlasting gain for Hippolytus' death. The voice of Artemis, full of pity, itself in anticipating the repetition of the song from age to age, melts with the voice of the poet, so that her tribute—of pity—to the fallen hero is also the tribute of Euripides looking forward to the permanence of his own voice.

Just as Artemis establishes the honour of ritual offerings and songs to compensate for the loss of Hippolytus, the poet aims at compensating for a loss within his own writing: his gift, his immortal song of tears will serve him as a compensation for the senselessness of his death. This immortality is affirmed not only by Artemis but also, explicitly, in the final lines of the Chorus which anticipate 'repeated onsets of weeping' (*pollōn dakruōn estai pitulos* 1465). In contemplating the immortality of his song and his role as a donor, the poet has achieved a presence. The image of the donor is crucial: for the donor finds himself in a privileged position as he offers a gift and therefore makes the other indebted to himself. The poet donates to Hippolytus (and to the audience) the honour of his own perennial song and graciously, spontaneously, celebrates him. Here the discourse of pity seems to reach that metaphysical goal we have outlined: though it is prompted by fear of death, and though it starts as the discourse of the other, as a loss, this discourse seems to end as a spontaneous expression of the poet, as a gracious and noble tribute of his mind, a ritual gesture that encompasses death and controls it. And, as a donor, the poet is indeed fully master of his own representation.

Yet it is easy to scramble this presence, which is nothing more than the evocation of a permanence that defies death and a consciousness that is master of its own representation. We do not need to question the metaphysical premises that sustain the role of a divine donor. For our text makes plain that neither the immortal song, nor the ritual offering, can really compensate for the loss of

Hippolytus. Both are intended to gratify him and console him for his suffering but they are not sufficient to satisfy Artemis. She already foresees taking revenge on Aphrodite by killing someone dear to that goddess (1417 ff.). Hippolytus' sacrifice does not stop any chain of violence, does not bring back any order or rule; on the contrary, it is part of a chain of 'vendettas', of reciprocal violence.

Artemis foresees two courses of action in order to compensate for the loss of Hippolytus: on the one hand, the vendetta against Aphrodite; on the other, the gracious offering of song and ritual performances. As the role of the poet is mirrored by that of Artemis, the poet finds himself in the same posture, as a violent avenger and gracious donor of immortal tears. Why should not Artemis content herself with the lavish tribute of honours to Hippolytus? For, finally, she decrees immortal recognition to the fallen hero. The answer is simple: Artemis' gift of honour hides her necessary complicity in the murder of Hippolytus: her late appearance can only function as a weak atonement for her neglect and neutrality, however justified by Zeus' law.

Analogously, the poet appears to be an odd donor if it is true that his act of donating hides his indebtedness to the song of Hippolytus.[22] For Euripides is able to contemplate the noble and permanent tribute of his song, just in the act of representing Hippolytus' slaughter: he contemplates his consciousness as master of its representation while he repeats the ritual killing of Hippolytus and offers him as a victim to the Muses. He extols the noble offering of his song, while also intoxicating the audience by this song: true to the double meaning of *dosis*, Euripides' gift is also a poison. Indeed the remedial song should really embalm and enshrine the victim in a monument, control the play of difference, and appear to be the noble tribute of a consciousness that has mastered violence. But we discover that something exceeds forever the presence of such a consciousness, of such noble meaning, and makes the remedial discourse also a poisonous one.

The sacrifice that Medea enacts upon her children is instructive on two accounts: it shows us again that the 'gain' reaped by the sacrificer is simultaneously a 'loss', and it teaches us about the intriguing multiplication and proliferation of sacrifices.

---

[22] On the indebtedness that the sacrificers feel and try to atone for by the ritual, see Burkert 1966, 24.

When in the last scene of the play, Medea faces Jason and defends the murder of her children, she raises the question of the advantage she has obtained from that sacrifice. In this critical moment the whole meaning of her action will be oriented by the answer she gives to this question. It is in this decisive moment that the text presents an extraordinary ambiguity (1361–2):

JASON. You, too, grieve and share fully my pain.
MEDEA. Be well assured: my grief is a profit (*luei*) if you cannot laugh at me.

With this interpretation of *luei*, Medea's gain appears to be illusory since it is limited to her recognition that, while she suffers just as he does, she has nevertheless punished him. Since Medea's revenge implies that Jason must grieve for the loss of the children just as she does, her revenge is a loss for her too. Yet *luei* can also mean 'annuls' and Medea's line can also be interpreted to say: 'This annuls my pain: that you cannot laugh at me.' With this interpretation of *luei* Medea would hurl to Jason the triumphing assessment of her full, absolute gain: her motherly grief for the loss of the children is effaced by her joy for the victory over Jason. No grammatical or stylistical subtlety can settle the ambivalence: the polysemy is textual. Though the examples of *luō* in the *Medea* would back here the meaning 'it is a gain' (see Verrall's 1881 commentary), the other meaning is in principle possible and, in the light of Medea's apotheosis, is far from being absurd or indefensible. Nothing can eliminate from this text the ambivalence whereby Medea is made to say simultaneously, in the same line, that her revenge is an illusory gain, a loss for herself too, or that her revenge is an absolute gain.

This extraordinary ambivalence epitomizes at the end of the play the contradictory statements that mark Medea's assessments of her loss and gain throughout the play. Something in the text exceeds or falls short of a unique, simple statement. This excess or this default prevents Medea's language from stating her gain or her loss: in fact, she implies both at once. Meaning oscillates with an unresolvable tension between gain and loss, remedy and poison, pleasure and pain. We call this unresolvable tension 'difference'.

The 'gain' Medea fails to point out explicitly in this critical moment corresponds to the 'gain' that the tragic song should insure to the listeners. The discourse fails to become identical with a recomposed self, an immunized consciousness, a self-sufficient mind. What we are left with is the endless repetition of the sacrifices that Medea establishes for her children. The unresolvable tension will continue forever.

We may come to the second point. While preparing herself for the murder Medea terms it a secret 'sacrifice' (1054). At the end of the play, she states that she will bury the corpses of her children in the temenos of Hera's temple in Corinth and establish a 'solemn festival forever in atonement (or because) of this impious murder' (1382 ff.).

We can fortunately control the exactness of Medea's last words. An annual sacrifice was performed in Corinth in the temple of Hera in atonement for the murder of Medea's children. We know (see Burkert 1966) that seven Corinthian boys and seven girls were interned for a year in the sanctuary of Hera where the tombs of Medea's children were shown. They wore black clothes. The climax and conclusion of their service was a sacrifice of a black she-goat, which obviously died as a substitute for the black-clad children; they were free of their obligation.[D]

No doubt, then, that the play is a sort of sacred representation of the primal violence which is the *aition*, i.e. the cause and the motivation of the Corinthian ritual sacrifice. The *Medea* of Euripides records and dramatizes the event that is annually commemorated by the ritual at the temple of Hera in Corinth. In this sense the play takes in some of the functions of the sacrifice.

To this extent, therefore, the play, just like the ritual sacrifice, has a cathartic power and functions as a remedy, a gain, a purification. In representing Medea's violence the play succeeds in gaining control over it. There are some affinities between the play and the ritual sacrifice which are obvious. The ritual sacrifice substitutes the black-clad children with a black she-goat and the play stages the murder of the children only, fictionally. Though on different lines the 'primal violence' is brought back only symbolically, through a symbolic replacement and through a representation, a rhetorical performance. Because of this power of replacement, deferral and representation, the primal violence is evoked but simultaneously also removed and substituted.

[D] I should add that even in the sacrificial *aition* there is an important difference, to the extent that the children are not killed by Medea but by the women of Corinth (Eur. *Medea Schol.* 264; and see Page 1938, pp. xxii–xxiv and xxviii). Burkert 1966 ends his illustration of the *Medea* passage by terming Medea's mention of the sacrifice (*emoisi thumasin* 1054) a 'metaphor' (p. 119).

But, as we have anticipated, this primal violence, cause and motivation for establishing annual sacrifices in Corinth, appears in Euripides' text to be already a sacrifice. As Medea bids her farewell to the children, she defines the murder of her children as a secret 'sacrifice'. The consequences of this metaphor are far-reaching both for the notion of ritual sacrifice and for the tragic remedy. We cannot pursue here all the lines that are opened to us, and we limit ourselves to two points. First, if we have to believe Euripides' text, there is not a primal violence that would be the beginning and the origin of the sacrifice. The murder of Medea's children is already a sacrifice and the annual sacrifices in Corinth do not commemorate anything other than a sacrifice. The original event therefore appears in either case only as 'representation' both in the sense of 'fiction' and in that of reintroducing a meaning. We realize that the 'original' event is already a 'script', a stage 'script' or a ritual 'script'. If then, the 'primal' violence of the sacrifice is already a 'script', a repetition of some kind, we should uncover a more precise parallelism between the two scripts, the stage and the ritual one. And in fact a sort of parallelism exists between the sacrifice and the discourse of pity. Medea sacrifices her sons as 'signs' of her motherhood and of their belonging to the hated Jason. To this extent they are dear to her and simultaneously stand for her wretchedness. In sacrificing her sons, Medea destroys the otherness, as it were, of her suffering, by actively inflicting suffering on herself. She should gain control over the otherness of her pain.

At any rate, Medea fails to receive the therapeutic and ritual advantage from her action: the text is indecisive in its most crucial point. That is why Medea then establishes new sacrifices to commemorate her earlier sacrifice. The proliferation of the therapeutic acts of violence is endless.

Euripides' writing fulfils indeed the role of a sacrifice: in HF 1023 the old men of the chorus recall that Procne murdered her child; they describe this slaughter as a 'sacrifice to the Muses' (thuomenon Mousais 1023). This crucial text is odd and critics have often been unable to interpret it.[23] Possibly a naive interpretation may not be wrong after all. Literally the text intimates that Itys becomes for his mother Procne the ceaseless theme of her complaints once she is changed

---

[23] In his commentary on the Heracles, Wilamowitz (1895: vol. III, p. 222) writes that it is unknown for what reason the murder of Procne is called a sacrifice to the Muses, and he adds that the fact that the Nightingale sings Itys forever does not justify this rare expression.

into a nightingale. And since Procne the nightingale constitutes a stock simile for endless weeping in poetic texts, Euripides in bold expression may term the murder of Itys as 'a sacrifice to the Muses'.[E]

The murders that are produced on the tragic stage are sacrifices to the Muses. Again, literally, Euripides may imply that the tragic art itself constitutes an offering to the Muses in order to obtain their continuous favour. But more deeply Euripides identifies tragic writing with the violence and the function of the sacrifice. He declares explicitly the violence of poetic representation, the violence of writing. This violence has various aspects. Indeed, a thematic aspect: the violence of Euripides' writing implies that intoxicating and outrageous representation of violence while looking beforehand at its beneficial effects. As if the poet could somehow bracket violence, he looks beyond violence at the moment in which his song becomes a lasting tribute of honour, a song that is monument, permanence, that signifies and contains death. Just because the sacrifice to the Muses experiences the slaughter only in the imagination, it needs to increase endlessly the outrageousness of violence. There is no doubt that the gruesome and intoxicating meditation of the *sophos* aiming at immunizing himself characterizes pertinently Euripides' tragic writing: paraphrasing Nietzsche, we might say that the whole mystery, *kharis* and fullness of life is submitted to the strategy of retrieving a remedy, a safety, a deliverance (*sōtēria*).

Beside this, we have seen the specific forms of Euripides' writing that are consonant with the violence of the sign, of representation. On the one hand the remedial representation intoxicates the mind and produces an initial loss. As Orestes says, we feel this loss even when we pity foreigners. The loss is inherent to all signs as the loss of what is one's own, identical, etc., and is unavoidable in the structure of supplementarity. In Euripides, this loss is inscribed in a medical metaphor that implies the similarity between remedy and poison.

Furthermore, we have pointed out the violence of Euripides' writing as it aims at gaining control over language, at handling the remedy as a healthy and reassuring tool. This violence could be described as the assault against difference, the other, the arbitrariness, in view of presence, self, and meaning. This violence shows

---

[E] This interpretation may find some support in the story that Pindar, having arrived at Delphi, would have defined his 'paean' as his 'sacrifice' to the god (*Schol. Vet. in Pind. Carmina* Drachmann, p. 3).

conspicuously in the images we have analysed: that of a donor that hides his indebtedness, that of a sacrifice that seeks for a *new* victim while the present victim is still alive.

The sacrifice to the Muses, the representation of violence can never gain full control over violence, over the other, can never fill up the void of the monument, the absence of death.[24]

[24] [Postscript to original publication] I wish to thank the scholars who contributed to the present form of this paper by their discussion and suggestions, and especially Christian Wolf, Charles Segal, Jacqueline de Romilly, Ann Bergren (who made possible the Princeton Conference on Structuralism and Post-Structuralism), Eugenio Donato, James Siegel, and of course, the editors of this issue of *Arethusa*, John Peradotto in particular for his many stylistic suggestions.

8

Euripides' Alkestis: Five Aspects of an Interpretation

R. G. A. BUXTON

This article is intended to be a contribution towards an overall understanding of *Alkestis*. I discuss five topics which seem to me to be of major importance for our interpretation of the play. Whereas many previous treatments have concentrated on matters of characterization, especially relating to Admetos, the emphasis of my own account will be different. Only the fourth of my sections will engage with the debate over character. For the rest, I shall be analysing the changing significance of the door in the visual stage action (Section I), the boundary between life and death (Section II), the role of Herakles (Section III), and the tone of the work as a whole (Section V).

I. THE DOOR OF THE HOUSE

The *skēnē* represents Admetos' palace at Pherai. In the centre is the door, the visual focus for most of the significant actions in the plot.

According to a stage direction in some manuscripts, the play begins with the emergence of Apollo from the house. While it is impossible to demonstrate the correctness of such a direction, it is surely incontrovertible that such a beginning is symbolically appropriate. Apollo's identification with the fortunes of Admetos is now over: the presence of the god from above is to be replaced by that of the god from below. Thus at the end of the first scene, Apollo leaves by the side exit, but Thanatos enters the palace through the central doorway.[1]

---

[1] Apollo emerges from house: see Hourmouziades 1965, 162–3. Symbolism of Apollo leaving and Thanatos entering the house: Dingel 1967, 213, followed by Rivier 1972, at 130. (There is virtually nothing on *Alk*. in Haight 1950.)

When the chorus arrive they notice (98 ff.) that outside the door there is no sign either of hair cut in mourning or of a vessel of water— needed, after a death, so that those emerging can purify themselves before resuming contact with normality outside.[2] The reason for these absences is of course that Alkestis is still alive. When she has emerged, spoken and died, she is carried back into the house; and the house-door then takes on the significance which had been prefigured as Thanatos passed through it: it becomes the point of transition between the polluted interior and the non-polluted world outside.

With the arrival of Herakles on his way north, the door's significance is intensified. In order to treat Herakles properly, i.e. as a ξένος ('stranger, guest-friend') and φίλος ('friend; person who is near or dear') should treat his ξένος and φίλος, Admetos must persuade him to enter the house—in spite of the evidence from Admetos' appearance that this is a place of mourning. (Incidentally, it is surely quite likely that a vessel of water *has* now been placed on stage outside the door.) The pivot of Admetos' persuasion of Herakles is linguistic: the woman who has died was ὀθνεῖος, 'no blood relation' (532–3).[3] For the first of two occasions in the play, a man gets his φίλος to enter the house by deception, but for the best of motives.

After the carrying-out of Alkestis and the argument with Pheres, the next scene, between Herakles and the servant, goes back to the linguistic point which I have just mentioned, but with a different word in question. 'Why so gloomy?', asks Herakles; 'the πῆμα ('pain, grief') is θυραῖον' (778); 'the woman who died was θυραῖος' (805). 'She was only too θυραῖος', replies the servant (811). Herakles: 'These don't sound like θυραῖα πήματα' (814); and later, when he knows the true identity of the deceased: 'He persuaded me by saying it was a θυραῖον κῆδος ('grief, funeral rites, dead person') he was taking to the tomb' (828). θυραῖος—etymologically, 'at, connected with, the door' (hence Hermes, that quintessential boundary-crosser, can be Hermes Thuraios).[4] But just as 'Go and see who's at the door' means 'Go and see who's *outside* the door', so θυραῖος can mean 'one connected with the outside', 'an outsider'.[5] And a wife is an

---

[2] Schol. *Alk.* 98, 99; Aristoph. *Ekkl.* 1033; Pollux 8. 65–6; cf. Kurtz and Boardman 1971, 146, and Parker 1983, 35.   [3] See Steidle 1968, 146, with n. 76.

[4] Hermes Thuraios: cf. Farnell 1896, v. 66 n. 23, and Eitrem in *RE* 8. 777.

[5] Linguistic connections between words meaning 'door' and 'outside': see Benveniste 1973, 255–6.

'outsider', brought across the threshold into the husband's house from outside.

It is exactly this reference which becomes poignantly explicit in the next scene. Admetos, having just buried Alkestis, returns to confront the house-door, now hateful to him because of yet another range of associations which the door has.

> ἰώ, στυγναὶ
> πρόσοδοι, στυγναὶ δ' ὄψεις χήρων
> μελάθρων ... (861 ff.)
> ὦ σχῆμα δόμων, πῶς εἰσέλθω; (911)

(Alas, hateful approach, hateful sight of this house of bereavement! (861 ff.)
O form [perhaps: 'familiar form'] of my house! How can I enter? (911)

He is reminded of that other time when he passed through the house-door, when he and Alkestis, white-robed instead of black, surrounded not by lamentation but by marriage songs, together entered the house, with Admetos holding her hand—that is, her wrist—in his (917).[6]

As the door was a boundary-marker in the case of a death, so it was in the case of a wedding. A Greek wedding dramatized in ritual terms the transition of a woman from the οἶκος ('house') of her father to the οἶκος, or more specifically the bedroom, of her husband. The crossing of the threshold of the new οἶκος was one aspect of this transition. There was, as far as I know, nothing comparable to the Roman custom[7] of carrying the bride over the threshold (so marking the danger and significance of the passage); and the door of the θάλαμος or bridal chamber seems if anything to have been of more importance (it was outside *that* door that a θυρωρός ('door-keeper') was posted);[8] nevertheless, the crossing of the threshold of the house itself *was* marked in Greece, since it was there that the couple were welcomed by the groom's parents.[9]

---

[6] Groom holds bride χεῖρ' ἐπὶ καρπῷ ('hand upon wrist'): see Jenkins 1983; the significance of the gesture in *Alk.* is noted by Foley 1985, 87–8.

[7] Bride carried over threshold in Rome: refs. listed by Ogle 1911, at 253.

[8] θυρωρός: Sappho fr. 110 LP; Pollux 3. 42; Hesych. s.v.; see also Theoc. 15. 77 with Gow ad loc. We may add that the literary lover/suitor only got as far as the *house*-door, which was where he sang his *paraklausithuron*; cf. Copley 1956.

[9] Welcome by groom's parents: schol. Eur. *Phoin.* 344 (mother); Sabouroff loutrophoros, illustration and refs. in Jenkins 1983 = Daremberg/Saglio s.v. 'matrimonium', fig. 4866 (mother and father); Berlin cup, Beazley *ARV*² 831, 20 (mother); Louvre pyxis, Beazley *ARV*² 924, 33 = Pfuhl 1923, pl. 580 with pp. 568–9 (? mother and father).

Recalling his marriage, Admetos describes his present dilemma:

$$\pi\hat{\omega}\varsigma \ \gamma\grave{\alpha}\rho \ \delta\acute{o}\mu\omega\nu \ \tau\hat{\omega}\nu\delta' \ \epsilon\grave{\iota}\sigma\acute{o}\delta\sigma\nu\varsigma \ \grave{\alpha}\nu\acute{\epsilon}\xi\sigma\mu\alpha\iota; \quad (941)$$
$$\grave{\eta} \ \mu\grave{\epsilon}\nu \ \gamma\grave{\alpha}\rho \ \acute{\epsilon}\nu\delta\sigma\nu \ \grave{\epsilon}\xi\epsilon\lambda\hat{\alpha} \ \mu' \ \grave{\epsilon}\rho\eta\mu\acute{\iota}\alpha \quad\quad (944)$$

How shall I bear to go into this house?   (941)
The desolation [or: 'loneliness'] within will drive me out.   (944)

$\acute{\epsilon}\xi\omega\theta\epsilon\nu \ \delta\acute{\epsilon}$ (950): 'But outside' there will be weddings, social gatherings of women of Alkestis' age—and that too will be intolerable. Apollo's unique gift to him has resulted in a unique dilemma.

But when all is said and done, *Alkestis* is not a tragedy, it is a non-satyric fourth play. And so we have the scene where Herakles returns with a veiled woman (see Section II). He reproaches Admetos for entertaining him as if concerned only for $\theta\nu\rho\alpha\acute{\iota}\sigma\nu \ \pi\acute{\eta}\mu\alpha\tau\sigma\varsigma$ ('a foreign grief', 1014—a line unnecessarily deleted by Méridier following Lachmann) and he urges Admetos to take the woman into the house. When Admetos at last relents, Herakles goes further: Admetos must lead her in *with his own right hand*—enacting, of course, the entry of a bridal couple (1115). For the second time a $\phi\acute{\iota}\lambda\sigma\varsigma$ is deceiving a $\phi\acute{\iota}\lambda\sigma\varsigma$ in order to be kind—although there is in this case perhaps a fine balance between our sense of the pain of the deceived $\phi\acute{\iota}\lambda\sigma\varsigma$ and our anticipation of his joy. But eventually Admetos looks at Alkestis' face; and what came perilously close to being a bitter parody of part of a wedding ceremony turns into a resolemnization of the union which only death has put asunder. From the beginning of the play the significance of the action of entering the house has varied as the house itself has successively become a place of death, hospitality, mourning, and marriage. At the end, the restored stability of the house is sealed by a definitive re-entry of Admetos and Alkestis over the threshold, as man and wife.

II. LIFE AND DEATH

The relations between life and death in *Alkestis* are complex;[10] and perhaps the most interesting aspect of this complexity is the fact that, for virtually the whole of the play, Alkestis herself is presented as being between life and death. Before going inside the house, Thanatos

---

[10] Good remarks on this in Burnett 1965, repr. in E. Segal 1983, 254–71, esp. 269.

says that the person whose hair his sword has 'consecrated'
(ἁγνίσῃ, 76) by cutting it is thenceforth ἱερός ('dedicated, holy')
to the gods below: so begins Alkestis' separation from life. In
practically their first words the chorus express doubt about whether
Alkestis is alive or dead (80 ff.). When a servant-girl comes out of the
house, and the chorus ask her, 'Is she alive or dead?', they are told:

καὶ ζῶσαν εἰπεῖν καὶ θανοῦσαν ἔστι σοι   (141)

It is possible to tell you that she is both alive and dead.

By her actions—washing herself as a preliminary to putting on the
clothes in which she will die; praying to the Hearth and adorning the
altars of the other gods; bidding farewell to her bed, children and
servants—Alkestis shows that she is in the process of dying. It is not a
physiological, 'Hippokratean' process ('seventh day: great chill; acute
fever; much sweat; death'); rather it is a social process, involving
severance from all the cultural ties which bind a person to life.[11] The
counterpart to the social process of dying is the belief that death is
not instantaneous, but a journey: so Alkestis sees a two-oared boat,
and Charon calls, τί μέλλεις; ('Why do you hesitate?', 252, 255).
The reference to Charon is significant: he, like Thanatos,[12] is an
intermediate agent of death. Perhaps this makes the ultimate rescue
more imaginatively credible: the dead woman has not yet been
definitively incarcerated in Hades. Furthermore, although she dies at
line 391, Alkestis in a way remains, even after that, between life and
death. We have already been told (348 ff.) of Admetos' plan to give
his wife a kind of continued existence by creating a life-like statue of
her; and when Herakles arrives and asks, 'How is your wife?',
Admetos' reply ἔστιν τε κοὐκέτ᾽ ἔστιν ('She is alive, and no longer
alive', 521) seems to perpetuate in a linguistic manner this ambiguity
of Alkestis' status. And even at the very end of the play, when Death
has been defeated, Alkestis is still not yet fully alive. As throughout
the play, so at its end, she is poised on the boundary between life and
death. To see how this can be so, it will be necessary to explore two
themes: veiling and silence.

On the evidence of Admetos' words at 1050 ('She is young, *to judge
from her clothing and appearance*') the scholiast inferred that Alkestis
was veiled; and he was surely right. At 1121 Herakles instructs

---

[11] On death as a process see now Garland 1985, 13.
[12] See Dale's commentary (1954) on 871.

Admetos: βλέψον πρὸς αὐτήν ('Look at her')—and here Herakles will have unveiled her. (Compare *Herakles Mainomenos* 1227, where Theseus, unveiling Herakles, tells him: βλέψον πρὸς ἡμᾶς ('Look at me'). The veil in *Alkestis* is powerful from the sheerly dramatic point of view, in that it makes possible the tense persuasion of Admetos by Herakles, which depends on Admetos' inability correctly to identify a woman—just as Admetos earlier persuaded Herakles when Herakles failed correctly to identify a woman.

But there is more to veiling than that. A veil often marks out an individual who is in a marginal or transitional state. Those in mourning veiled themselves.[13] Those in the abnormal state of being polluted might cover their heads.[14] And of course veiling might mark a transition with quite different emotional resonances: as Kassandra says in *Agamemnon*, 'My oracle will no longer peep out from a veil like a newly-married bride' (1178–9). That the bridal veil signals a transition is evident enough; but there is uncertainty over details. We know that the bride was veiled at the meal at her father's house,[15] but when did she *unveil*? In his recent account of the Anakalupteria or Ceremony of Unveiling, Oakley[16] followed Deubner[17] in placing it at the house of the bride's father, i.e. *before* the procession to the new house. However, not only is it more plausible on general grounds of ritual symbolism that the bride made the transition from house to house veiled,[18] but there is a considerable number of vases showing the bride in the bridal procession with her head still veiled, even if her face is visible.[19] Whenever the unveiling took place, it is clear that the moment when the groom saw the bride's face was an important one in the wedding ritual (one name for the gifts presented to the bride at the Anakalupteria was ὀπτήρια, 'to do with seeing');[20] and

---

[13] Hom. *Il.* 24. 93–4, *Od.* 8. 92; *Hom. H. Dem.* 40 ff.; Plato, *Phd.* 117c; etc.

[14] *Her. Main.* 1160–2, with Bond's commentary (1981) ad loc.

[15] Luc. *Symp.* 8: πάνυ ἀκριβῶς ἐγκεκαλυμμένη ('very carefully veiled'). An *onos* from Eretria (Beazley *ARV*² 1250–1, 34, Arias/Hirmer *HGVP* pl. 203) shows Alkestis veiled in the company of women—possibly before the wedding.

[16] Oakley 1982.   [17] Deubner 1900.

[18] So rightly Roussel 1950, at 10.

[19] For vases depicting wedding processions see Haspels 1930; Boardman 1952, at 34–5; Krauskopf 1977. Examples of 'veiled' bride—i.e. bride with head covered—in bridal procession: Sabouroff loutrophoros, Berlin cup and Louvre pyxis as cited in n. 9 above; hydria from Orvieto (in Florence, Mus. Nat.) showing Peleus and Thetis on marriage chariot, Beazley *ABV* 260, 30; pelike in Louvre showing veiled bride being led χεῖρ' ἐπὶ καρπῷ ('hand upon wrist'), Beazley *ARV*² 250, 15.

[20] Pollux 2. 59, 3. 36, cf. Deubner 1900, 148.

realizing the importance of the moment of seeing the bride may sharpen our awareness of what is at stake in the unveiling in Euripides' play.

What, then, of the veiled Alkestis? She is in a doubly transitional state. Firstly, she is still between death and life, between the other world and this.[21] Secondly, her new arrival at Admetos' οἶκος is like the prelude to a second marriage. There is no reason to believe that Alkestis' unveiling *before entering the house* represents a direct transcription of wedding ritual. Rather it would seem that the symbolism of unveiling is borrowed and adapted to fit the specific dramatic requirements of the play. Alkestis must unveil on stage (i.e. outside the house) because Admetos must recognize her on stage.

I have repeatedly spoken of Alkestis as a character poised between life and death. It remains to consider one last aspect of this point. 'You may speak to her', Herakles tells Admetos, 'but it is not yet *themis* ("lawful") for you to hear her addressing you, until she has been deconsecrated from the gods below, when the third dawn comes' (1132; 1144–6). The connection between silence, covering the head, and real or symbolic death is not unfamiliar to us. We think perhaps of Benedictine monks, who wear the hood over the head at all times when forbidden to speak; but when they take their final vows, they lie still and prostrate on a pall (not only physically resembling the dead but explicitly 'dying to the world') and have the hood pinned under the chin; they must then keep silence until the hood is unpinned—at Communion, on the third day afterwards.[22] From ancient Greece we have several examples of a congruence between veiling and silence. Aischylos' Niobe sits veiled and silent until the third day;[23] and his Achilles seems to have covered his head and been silent in both *Phrygians* and *Myrmidons*—his silence persisting in the latter case, apparently, till the third day.[24] Euripides' Phaidra

---

[21] Eurydike too is veiled during her transition from death to life: see the 5-cent. relief of Orpheus, Eurydike and Hermes (known from Roman copies, cf. Thompson 1952, 60 ff., with pl. 17a, and Harrison 1964, 76 ff., with pl. 12d).

[22] There are further links between the hood and 'death': the monk is surrounded, when prostrate, by 'catafalque' candles; and monks are buried with the hood *up*. (I am indebted for guidance here to Dr Ian Hamnett.)

[23] *Life* of Aischylos, 6 (= Aisch. fr. 243a M); see Taplin 1972, at 60–2.

[24] The 'third day' detail (cf. Aisch. fr. 212a M) is accepted for *Myrmidons* by Taplin 1972, 64. In *Phrygians* Achilles' motive for veiling seems to have been grief; in *Myrmidons* it may have been because of his self-imposed marginality; see Taplin 1972, 76.

is veiled and silent at one point in *Hippolytos* through shame at her polluting state; and it is her third day without food.[25] In *Alkestis* the congruence is only partial: the silence persists for three days *after* the unveiling. This is partly a matter of dramatic necessity: as we observed earlier, she *has* to unveil, but there is no compelling reason for her to speak. But her silence is appropriate in ritual terms too, since it marks her unusually anomalous condition. The words of a person in any state of pollution might be harmful to others: as Orestes says in *Eumenides*, 'the law is that the murderer be ἄφθογγος ('without speech') until purified'.[26] But this applies *a fortiori* to Alkestis: she has died and been buried. Plutarch notes that anyone for whom carrying-out and burial had been performed, as though he were dead, was considered impure by the Greeks, and they would not let such a person associate with themselves or approach a temple; and Hesychios refers to a ceremony of re-enacted birth designed to admit the δευτερόποτμος ('one who, though supposed dead, reappears alive') back to life.[27] Did a symbolic silence figure in the ritual for managing such a rare and anomalous case, and was Euripides adapting that silence in *Alkestis*? There is, I think, no evidence; and the silence could just as easily have been Euripidean invention, appropriate because of Alkestis' still-dangerous link with the dead. Or could he, here too, have been borrowing from the wedding ritual? When the bride was veiled before the Anakalupteria, did she also have to keep silent, being restored to normal communication only after the unveiling? According to Pollux, an alternative name for the Anakalupteria gifts was προσφθεγκτήρια, 'gifts of salutation'.[28] In any case, we would be dealing, not with a simple 'reflection' of ritual, but with its adaptation to the needs of a given dramatic context.

Even at the end, then, Alkestis is not yet fully alive. Through her fate, the relation between life and death is shown to be in certain respects ambiguous. Now closely related to this ambiguity is what seems to be an outright paradox. The plot is based on the assumption that Death will inevitably get what is due to him: if Admetos does not

---

[25] Eur. *Hipp.* 275.

[26] *Eum.* 448 ff. For the converse see *Eum.* 276-7 and esp. 287: when Orestes' pollution has gone, he speaks ἀφ' ἁγνοῦ στόματος ('from a pure mouth'). NB. also Eur. *IT* 951 and 956 for the silence surrounding the polluted Orestes at Athens.

[27] The revived dead: Plu. *Quaest. Rom.* 264f–265a, Hesych. s.v. δευτερόποτμος. See Betts 1965, and Parker 1983, 61.　　　　　　　　　　　　　　[28] Pollux 3. 36.

die, someone else must. Furthermore, there is in the course of the work a series of references to the *fixity* of the boundary between life and death: (*a*) the fate of Asklepios (3–4, 122 ff.; cf. 970) who raised the dead and was thunderbolted for it; (*b*) the emphatic words of Herakles at 528 ('Most people reckon there is a big difference between being alive and being dead'); (*c*) the attitude of the chorus: 'There is no way round Necessity' (962 ff.), 'You will not raise the dead' (985–6).[29] And yet *Alkestis* ends with the defeat of Thanatos and the restoration of Alkestis. Is the boundary between life and death not, then, fixed, as we have been led to believe? On this paradox two things should be said.

First we must consider who it is that is apparently threatening the boundary between life and death. Of all the figures in Greek myth, Herakles is the one who seems to be licensed most regularly to push beyond boundaries. In particular, he breaks the confines of mortality in two ways: downwardly, by invading Hades and stealing Kerberos; and upwardly, by achieving acceptance into Olympos. In *Alkestis* the boundary between life and death is not abolished or redrawn: 'after' the action of the play, things will remain as they are. It is just that, in one exceptional case, the exceptional hero *par excellence* is able to intervene and postpone (but not, we imagine, cancel) the death of Alkestis.

This leads us to the second point. In the house of Admetos, normal life has at last, we must assume, been re-established. Normal life— and normal death: the recent suspension of normal relationships between life and death has, presumably, come to an end. From the beginning of the play, the relationship between life and death has been in an unusual state, with both the main characters poised in different ways between the two; finally, the usual distance between the extremes is restored.[30] Perhaps one respect in which *Alkestis*

---

[29] A word needs to be added about Admetos' assertion (357 ff.) that, had he the voice of Orpheus, he would have gone down to charm the powers of the underworld. One implication is, of course, that Admetos does *not* have the voice of Orpheus; hence the outlook in Admetos' own case would seem (as with the references to Asklepios) to be made even more pessimistic. On the other hand, it is not clear what version of the Orpheus/Eurydike story had the greater currency in Euripides' time—did he look back and lose her, or was his mission successful? If the latter alternative were being evoked, the reference to Orpheus might offer a small glimmer of hope that the boundary between life and death *can* be affected by human entreaty.

[30] Justina Gregory appropriately describes Herakles in this play as 'the restorer of differences', 1979, at 267.

asserts itself as a 'fourth play' rather than a tragedy is that, at its conclusion, at least one ambiguity is resolved instead of being left open-ended.

III. HERAKLES

In order to appreciate Herakles' role in *Alkestis* it will be useful first to remind ourselves about his place within Greek mythology as a whole, and the literary tradition in particular.[31]

Herakles was the great 'helper' to whom one could appeal in time of trouble. Myths about him range widely: from the East to the far West, from (as we mentioned) the underworld to Olympos. In other ways too he is associated with the limits of humanity: he is repeatedly connected with animals, which he kills or controls; he has to deal with centaurs (incompletely human) and with Amazons (abnormally human). Sometimes, it is true, Herakles is situated in the social rather than the natural world, as when he sacks the cities of Troy and Oichalia. But here once more he is hardly a comfortably socialized being: he is a disrupter of civilization, a hero whose boundless violence can be a potential threat to order as well as (when he slays monsters) a supporter of it.

Literary representations of the hero are heterogeneous. It will be convenient to take three examples.

(*a*) Praise-poetry. In Pindar Herakles has an honoured place as a representative of athleticism, of ἀρετή ('excellence'), and of a willingness to strive in order to deserve the reward of victory. In return for his exertions he attained peace and rest on Olympos, with Hebe by his side (*Nem.* 1. 69 ff.). Such ambivalence as there is in the Pindaric Herakles[32] fades before the presentation of the hero as a shining example to emulate.

(*b*) Tragedy. Here Herakles is a much more paradoxical and ambiguous figure. In *Trachiniai*, for instance, he is the monster-slayer who is himself a monster, the mighty hero who is brought so low as to be subservient to the weak (Omphale, Deianira): in *Herakles Mainomenos* he is the hero who is both son of a god and son of a man. In general tragedy explores the darker and more problematic side of

---

[31] One may consult Brelich 1958; Galinsky 1972; and Silk 1985.
[32] Cf. Silk 1985, 7.

Herakles—he is a defender of civilization, yet he can kill his own wife and children, and is only just prevented from killing his father.

(c) Comedy. Once more, of course, we have a different emphasis. Athenaios (411a) gives us a picture of the gluttonous Herakles: 'Epicharmos, for example, says in his *Busiris*: "First, if you should see him eating, you would die. His gullet thunders inside, his jaw rattles, his molar crackles, his canine gnashes, he sizzles at the nostrils, and he waggles his ears." '[33] And in Ion's satyr-play *Omphale* the audience heard that 'not content with the steaks, he ate the charcoal from the grill as well' (Athen. 411b).

Where do we locate *Alkestis* in all this? The Herakles of this play combines the three types which we have reviewed. The mighty athlete praised by Pindar is the heroic figure who strides boldly out to wrestle with Death. The fact that it is *with Death* that Herakles fights reminds us of the tragic Herakles, whose exploits so often have the profoundest implications for humanity and for the boundary between life and death. And the scene in which the bewildered servant reports the drunken misbehaviour of his unruly guest reminds us of the Herakles of comedy. But it is important that we do not misrepresent the balance between the three aspects of Herakles in *Alkestis*. In particular, we must realize that there is nothing tragic about Herakles' own position. He is on his way to Thrace to perform one of his labours; that is, he is *in the middle* of his labours. His situation is therefore unproblematic: only when his labours are over, as in *Herakles Mainomenos*, will his fate become precarious. In *Alkestis* he is merely in transit. The only tragic or near-tragic events with which he comes into contact are events in the life of the Thessalian household in which he is entertained.

One other question is worth asking before we leave Herakles: why is he not polluted either by entering the house of Admetos when the corpse is still inside, or by his wrestling match with Death? On the first point, no one in the play expresses any criticism of Admetos for exposing Herakles to possible pollution, so we can only conclude that no such pollution was felt to have been incurred—presumably because pollution most strongly affected the deceased's immediate kin, a group to which Herakles clearly did not belong.[34] As for the

---

[33] Trans. slightly adapted from Gulick 1930, Loeb edn.
[34] See Garland 1985, 41 on the varying relationship between pollution and degrees of kinship in Greece.

second point, I suggest that the reason why Apollo (like Artemis in *Hippolytos*) feels compelled to avoid a house where Death is present, while Herakles can go so far as to wrestle with Death, is that, in religious terms, the distance between Apollo and Death is greater than that between Herakles and Death: Apollo is a god of the above, Death a god of the below, and Herakles a figure whose activities span both spheres. With a splendidly structuralist logic, Herakles can operate where Apollo fears to tread.

IV. ADMETOS AND HOSPITALITY

The issue of how we are to take the character of Admetos has come virtually to dominate criticism of the play. On the one hand, there are scholars who detect numerous hints that Admetos' willingness to accept his wife's sacrifice is represented by Euripides in a negative light.[35] On the other hand, there are those who prefer a 'naïve' reading, accepting the lines at face value rather than looking between and behind them. My own view coincides with the latter approach, and in particular with the excellent discussion by Burnett.[36] I shall confine myself here to some specific comments in support of a 'non-ironical' reading of *Alkestis*.

A small but significant detail occurs in the scene where the servant tells the chorus about Alkestis' moving farewell to her children, marriage bed and household slaves. Although the chorus are full of praise for Alkestis (150–1), they express sympathy for Admetos too:

ὦ τλῆμον, οἵας οἷος ὢν ἁμαρτάνεις   (144)

Poor man! What a husband you are! What a wife you have lost!

It would have been perfectly possible for Euripides to have written a play in which Admetos appeared as unpleasantly insensitive as is Jason in *Medea*; but that is not what he has done. Again, nothing in

---

[35] An example is Smith 1960, who sees the play's apparently positive verdict on Admetos undercut by 'a running commentary which hints at kinds of motivation and qualities of character beneath the surface' (134); on this reading Admetos emerges as 'self-centred, cowardly, and short-sighted' (129). For similarly unflattering views of Admetos see von Fritz 1962, 256–321, esp. 310; and Schwinge 1968a, 109.

[36] Burnett 1965. Another non-ironist is that fine Euripidean A. Rivier; see Rivier 1972, with sequel, Rivier 1973.

the farewell scene between husband and wife can lead us to regard
Admetos as a hypocrite, or to regard his grief as insincere. As a result
of his generosity to a god, he has been given a gift; and the gifts of the
gods, as Paris reminded Hektor (Il. 3. 65), are not to be cast away.
Apollo's gift to Admetos was life; and one of the play's paradoxes is
that this 'life' is no life at all without the person who made the life
possible. But, for most of Alkestis, the result of the paradox is
sympathy for Admetos, not censure of him. For most of Alkestis the
question, 'What do we make of a man who allows his wife to die so
that he himself may live?' is simply not asked, because that is not
what the play is mainly about.

The positive presentation of Admetos is maintained in the episode
where he deceives Herakles into accepting hospitality. How are we to
evaluate his decision to withhold the truth because he does not wish
to fail in his obligations as a ξένος ('guest-friend')? Euripides does not
present it as absurd or foolish. On the contrary, it is—as Herakles
himself later recognizes (855 ff.)—the act of a noble man and a true
friend. In a society such as that of ancient Greece, where travellers
were bereft of all the social ties which made existence practicable when
they were at home, the institution of ξενία ('guest-friendship') was of
enormous practical and emotional significance. Hence it was sanc-
tioned by Zeus (Xenios) himself; and its obligations could be ignored
only at great peril: in myth, those who break ξενία invariably suffer
for it, whether they are behaving as a wicked host in their own house
(Tantalos) or as a wicked guest in the house of another (Paris). In
presenting Admetos as a good ξένος Euripides was reflecting a fundamental custom of Greek society; although the chorus is at first critical
of Admetos, his explanation—he absolutely refuses to turn away a
friend—convinces them, and they sing an ode in praise of his nobility.

Then, with a sharp contrast so typical of Euripides, we have the
bitter scene between Admetos and Pheres. Now for the first time
Euripides confronts us with the moral issue implicit in the starting-
point of the plot, namely: what do we make of a man who allows his
wife to die so that he himself may live? So far we have seen Admetos
only as loving husband and noble host; now suddenly we are forced
to look at the other side of the coin—to see him as a murderer:

σὺ γοῦν ἀναιδῶς διεμάχου τὸ μὴ θανεῖν,
καὶ ζῆς παρελθὼν τὴν πεπρωμένην τύχην,
ταύτην κατακτάς·   (694–6)

Shamelessly you strove to avoid death, and you are living past your appointed fate—having killed her.

Whether this scene can outweigh the positive evaluation of Admetos which the play has given us so far is perhaps something which each individual reader or spectator must answer for him-/herself; in my own view it certainly does not. The scene makes Admetos more complex, and therefore more interesting. We see his grief take a new direction, leading him to be fiercely aggressive to his own father. Hence his isolation becomes even more complete. The ground is thus prepared for the truly distressing scene at 861 ff. when Admetos, returning after the funeral, comes face to face with the empty house. Here once more, as in the early part of the play, we must surely take Admetos' grief as sincere: there is more than a hint of real tragedy in his ἄρτι μανθάνω ('(Only) now do I realize it', 940).

How, finally, does the last scene of the play affect our view of Admetos? It is interesting that Herakles gently but firmly expresses criticism of Admetos for concealing the truth: μέμφομαι μέν, μέμφομαι ('I blame you, I blame you', 1017). The suggestion seems to be that true friendship in fact lies in something more than a mechanical returning of χάρις ('favour') for χάρις: it should involve a willingness to trust another person and to confide in them. But it is one of the numerous paradoxes of *Alkestis* that Herakles, in the very moment of blaming his φίλος ('friend') for deceiving him, proceeds immediately to use deceit; and this brings us to the persuasion of Admetos by Herakles.

It has been said that Admetos' agreement to accept what he believes to be 'another woman' into his house is designed by Euripides to seem heavily ironical in view of his earlier promise (328 ff.) not to remarry. It is of course hard to disprove such a suggestion conclusively; but certain considerations tell against it. Firstly, the resistance of Admetos is extremely lengthy. At line 1020 Herakles instructs him to look after the woman, but only at line 1108 does Admetos consent to her entry into the house; and not until 1118—almost exactly a hundred lines since the original instruction was given—does he reluctantly agree to take her in himself. Given the compression and stylization of stichomythia—one may compare the handful of lines in which Klytaimnestra persuades Agamemnon in *Agamemnon*—Euripides can hardly be said to have portrayed

Admetos acquiescing readily. Secondly, there is that much more
pressure on Admetos to accept because to refuse would be to refuse a
χάρις to a friend—and throughout the play we have seen and heard
of several such favours which have been presented in a positive light,
most notably Alkestis' χάρις of life to Admetos and Admetos' χάρις
of hospitality to Herakles. Thirdly, does it not make a difference that,
because of what the audience knows but Admetos does not, the
audience *wants* him to acquiesce? The desired outcome, the outcome
which will restore the relationship torn by Alkestis' self-sacrifice and
Admetos' grief, the outcome which will enable Herakles worthily to
reciprocate Admetos' gift of hospitality—that outcome depends on
Admetos' giving way. Often enough in his other works Euripides uses
irony to expose the reality behind human pretension; but there is no
reason why we should deny him the right to be unironical if that was
what the drama required.

V. THE TONE OF *ALKESTIS*: TRAGEDY? COMEDY? 'FOURTH PLAY'?

Alkestis is unique amongst the surviving works of the Greek
tragedians in that it is the only one of which we know both that it
was put on fourth and that it was not a satyr-play. Scholars have
tried to accommodate this uniqueness by inventing the term 'pro-
satyric'; but this does little more than remind us that there is an
unusual phenomenon which needs explanation.[37] However, the
impulse to coin such a term is not wholly misguided, since it reflects
the importance of our being able to reconstruct the category—the
mental 'heading'—to which the original audience would have
ascribed the play. After all, some sense of what the Athenians
would have expected from *Alkestis* is necessary before we can judge
how far Euripides met, or perhaps challenged, those expectations.
But how do we proceed if we have no other work which we can be
certain is a non-satyric fourth play?

Faute de mieux we may consider satyr-plays themselves. To answer
the question, 'What would the audience have expected from a

---

[37] Sutton suggests other possible candidates for the category 'pro-satyric'; see
Sutton 1980, 184–90.

fifth-century satyr-play?', we have to rely mainly on Sophokles' *Ichneutai* and Euripides' *Kuklops*, the only two examples to have survived in anything like complete form. The subject of *Ichneutai* is the theft of the cattle of Apollo by baby Hermes; helping in the quest for the lost beasts are Silenos and his sons the Satyrs. In other words the plot is, like the plots of tragedy, taken from the mythical past, but bursting into it is a disruptive and indeed farcical element. *Kuklops* too is set in the mythical past, and includes many of the features familiar from *Odyssey* 9: Polyphemos' cannibalism; Odysseus' trick with the name; the blinding; the escape. But into this traditional world of myth there bursts, as before, an element of disruptive farce: once again it is the lustful and cowardly Satyrs with their pot-bellied old father. Amongst many amusing moments perhaps the best is when Polyphemos, hopelessly drunk, ominously announces that he prefers boys to women, and carries off the alarmed Silenos into his cave to be his Ganymedes.

The rest of our evidence about satyr-plays,[38] meagre though it is, does not invalidate the assumption that the audience awaiting the start of such a work was expecting something set in the mythical past, but with a disruptively comical element breaking in to disturb the seriousness. But what about *non*-satyric fourth plays? While we really cannot be dogmatic about audience-expectations in this case, it is at any rate interesting that in *Alkestis* too we find a combination of a mythical setting with an element of disruptive comedy, as Herakles totters on to the stage after enjoying himself in Admetos' wine store.

Alkestis is indeed a quite remarkably variegated work. It has many features in common with tragedy: an οἶκος ('house') is disrupted; a character is caught in dilemmas (be hospitable, or mourn; accept the gift of life and live emptily, or die and render the gift meaningless); events come to a crisis; a father and son are driven to a bitter scene of mutual recrimination; someone learns the truth too late. On the other hand, Herakles' riotous good spirits, and the loving reconciliation at the end, may make us think rather of comedy. But it has to be said that the serious part of the play far exceeds the light-hearted. Could it be that Euripides was surprising his audience in 438 by providing something darker and more thought-provoking than they

---

[38] Recently collected and analysed by Richard Seaford in the introduction to his edn. of *Cyclops* (Seaford 1984).

were expecting from a fourth play? We have no way of answering the
question for certain. It is better simply to rejoice in the particular—
indeed unique—range of emotions and tones which make up this
rich and complex masterpiece.[39]

[39] This is an expanded version of a paper given at the Hellenic Society Colloquium
for Prof. Winnington-Ingram; my thanks are due to the audience for their
constructive comments, and in particular to Ian Jenkins for subsequent assistance.
The same material also formed the basis of a lecture given in Greek in the Department
of Classical Philology at Ioannina; the ensuing discussion was of great value to me,
particularly the contributions by Mary Mantziou, Katerina Synodinou, Andreas
Katsouris and D. Sakalis. The present paper is substantially the same as that which
appears in *Dodoni: Philologia*, 14 (1985), 75–90, and is printed here with the kind
permission of the editors of that journal.

9

The Infanticide in Euripides' Medea

P. E. EASTERLING

In many respects Euripides' *Medea* is not a problematic play. It is a singularly bold, clear-cut, assured piece of writing, the concentration and dramatic intensity of which are readily felt by reader or audience and command the respect even of those who find the subject matter repellent or who cavil at the Aegeus scene and the dragon chariot. But its starkness makes it deeply disturbing; and this unease is reflected in the critical literature on the play. The language, though consistently powerful, lacks the rich expansiveness of *Hippolytus* or *Bacchae*, almost never allowing us to range in imagination away from the immediate painful situation; it is typical that one of the most prominent of the recurring images is of Medea as a wild beast.[1] Then there is the striking absence of a cosmic frame of reference: we are given no sense of divine motivation or sanction or control. Medea is admittedly grand-daughter of the Sun, but the fact has no theological significance: its function is to symbolize her sense of her heroic identity and—at a different level—to motivate the final scene. The most uncompromising feature of all is Euripides' handling of the story, his design which makes the murder of the children the centrepiece of the play.

This horrific act is something from which we naturally recoil. 'No sane person', we say, 'would do such a thing', and indeed Euripides' many imitators have tended to present Medea's behaviour as that of a madwoman.[2] Or 'no civilized person would do it'; Sir Denys Page, for example, writes, 'The murder of children . . . is mere brutality: if it moves us at all, it does so towards incredulity and horror. Such an act is outside our experience, we—and the fifth-century Athenian—know nothing of it.'[3] Doubts have been felt in particular about

---

[1] 92; (103); 187 ff.; 1342 f.; 1358 f.; 1407.   [2] Cf. Friedrich 1968, 209.
[3] Page 1938, xiv.

Medea's great speech at 1021 ff. in which she wrestles with her conflicting feelings of injured pride and love for her children: is Euripides
merely playing with our emotions through a rhetorical handling of
the situation, exploiting the dramatic effectiveness of Medea's debate
with herself rather than having an eye to what a person would really
do in such circumstances?[4] Or conversely, is this conflict in Medea's
soul the real high point of the drama, of more tragic importance than
the violent act itself?[5] Or is it possible, as has recently been suggested,
that we retain some sympathy with Medea right through to her final
triumph, so that the final scene is the real climax of the play?[6] Clearly
an important question to be faced by any critic who wishes to interpret *Medea* is whether Euripides is exploring the realities of human
behaviour or creating only an illusion of reality out of a sequence of
essentially melodramatic actions.

'Real life' in drama is not, of course, the same phenomenon as
real life outside. Distortion or suppression of documentary fact and
neglect—within certain limits—even of probability are part of the
dramatist's stock-in-trade which we accept at the same time as believing in the truthfulness of his situations. Thus it is no fundamental
failure on Euripides' part that he abandons probability in his treatment of the chorus. It is highly unlikely that these respectable ladies
of Corinth would really have stood ineffectually by when Medea
announced her intention to kill their king and princess and then her
own children. In real life they would have taken steps to have Medea
taken into custody, or at the very least would have gone to warn the
royal family and Jason. But we accept their inactivity because these
women are not at the centre of the play: they are peripheral figures
whose role is not to do and suffer but to comment, sympathize,
support or disapprove. The advantages of providing Medea with a
sympathetic and understanding audience within the play far
outweigh any loss of naturalism. A much graver breach is committed
by Seneca, when he makes Medea after killing the children toss the
corpses down to Jason.[7] The whole motivation of the mother who
murders her children is unintelligible if she is willing to surrender
their corpses to the husband whom she is punishing. Similarly, in

---

[4] 'She has her struggle with her maternal feelings—a theatrical struggle rather
than a psychologically convincing one', Kitto 1961, 195.

[5] Cf. Pohlenz 1954, I. 255 ff.   [6] So Steidle 1968, 165.

[7] If modern editors are right in so interpreting 'recipe iam natos parens' ('Now,
father, take back your sons', *Medea* 1024).

Corneille's *Médée* there is no conviction at all in the scene where *Jason* thinks of killing the children to punish Medea.[8]

It is worth considering how Euripides manipulates the story in order to force us to take Medea seriously. The barbarian sorceress with a melodramatic criminal record who could so easily be a monster must become a tragic character, a paradigm, in some sense, of humanity. The Nurse's opening speech alludes briefly to that record: Medea is in exile for persuading the daughters of Pelias to kill their father, but there is no suggestion that she is shunned or feared by the Corinthians; the Nurse says she 'pleases' them (11 f.) and the friendly words of the chorus (137, 178 ff.) imply that she is an accepted, even a respected, figure. According to a scholiast on Pindar (*O.* 13. 74) Medea served the Corinthians by stopping a famine in their city; but Euripides makes no explicit mention of a story which on the face of it looks ideally suited to his purpose, for the good reason that it would introduce distracting complications into the scene with Creon. Unlike Seneca and Corneille, he clearly wanted to avoid giving the situation even the vaguest political dimension: there are to be no outside pressures on Creon, and he is to have no obligations to Medea for past services. So Euripides with fine sleight-of-hand contrives to imply that Medea's status at Corinth is one of some dignity, but without explaining why; later it becomes clear that she has a reputation as a wise woman, but the picture that is very lightly sketched in (for example in the scene with Aegeus) is as close to that of a respectable religious authority as to that of an outlandish witch.[9]

Medea as foreigner is another theme which is delicately handled by Euripides. At the most superficial level the fact that she is a barbarian from Colchis must have helped a Greek audience to accept both her past crimes and her expertise as a powerful sorceress, but we should be rash to conclude that it offered them an adequate explanation of the child murder. If Medea is to be seen as a distinct-ively oriental type ('because she was a foreigner she could kill her children')[10] why does Euripides make her talk like a Greek, argue like a Greek, and to all appearances *feel* like a Greek? It is hard to believe, particularly in view of the astonishingly crass words he gives to Jason at 536 ff., that Euripides was seriously imputing moral superiority to the Greeks, implying that only a foreigner could or would murder her own kin. On the contrary, he seems to exploit the theme of Medea's

---

[8] *Médée* Act v. Sc. v.   [9] Cf. Conacher 1967, 186–7, 190.   [10] Page 1938, xxi.

foreignness in order to emphasize her vulnerability and isolation and also to make a searching analysis of the nature of civilization and barbarism, a deep preoccupation of this play, to which we shall return.

Similarly, the record of Medea's past crimes is used—initially at any rate—more to arouse than to alienate the audience's sympathy. Euripides does not suppress the murder of Apsyrtus (166–7) or the killing of Pelias (9), though he is careful not to dwell on the grisly details of dismemberment and boiling. The subdued recall of these past horrors no doubt foreshadows the violence to come; but one of its main functions is to make clear that Medea has sacrificed literally everything for Jason, thus emphasizing his special ingratitude and her special defencelessness: she has not merely abandoned her family, she has betrayed them for Jason's sake. Nor does Euripides allow any character to raise the question of the legal relationship between Jason and Medea. None of them suggests[11] that Jason was perfectly entitled to abandon Medea without bad faith because as a foreigner she could not be his legitimate wife. Like other dramatists in other plays[12] Euripides permits himself a certain vagueness in legal matters, relying on the fact that the story is set in the heroic age, not in fifth-century Athens, however strongly the social comment may strike us as contemporary. This is one of those questions which in real life would be crucially important, but which it suits a dramatist to suppress. The essential situation is perfectly clear-cut: Jason and Medea are to be regarded as permanently pledged,[13] so that when Jason abandons Medea he *is* breaking faith (and even he does not deny it).

Euripides has taken pains, therefore, to present the situation in such a way that we are obliged to take Medea seriously. The structure of the first part of the play and the detail of these early scenes seem to be aimed at the same objective, the audience's full response to Medea as a tragic character.

The prologue from 46 ff., the entry of the children, can fairly be described as a 'mirror scene', a tightly self-contained presentation in miniature of the course that the action is going to take. It has very little direct connection with the immediately following scene, beyond

---

[11] Although at least one critic has done so (Murray 1910, vii f.).
[12] e.g. Sophocles on the edict in *Antigone*. Cf. Hester 1971, 19–21.
[13] The theme of their oaths is given repeated stress: 21 ff.; 160 ff.; 168 ff.; 208 ff.; 438 ff. (and the whole *stasimon*); 492 ff.; 1392.

the fact that the chorus ask the Nurse to coax Medea out of the house and she does actually emerge at 214, the beginning of the first episode; its main function seems rather to be prophetic, like the short scene in *Hippolytus* where the old servant reproves Hippolytus for his neglect of Aphrodite (88–120). Here the Nurse three times expresses her fear for the children's safety at their mother's hands (90 ff.; 100 ff.; 116 ff.), having already glancingly introduced the theme in her opening speech: 'She hates the children and takes no pleasure in seeing them. I am afraid she may make some new [i.e. sinister] plan' (36 f.). Medea's own curses reinforce this sense of foreboding: 'O cursed children of a hateful mother, may you perish with your father, and the whole house go to ruin!' (112 ff.). And the children themselves appear, fresh from their games, to impress their significance on the audience. From the start, then, it is made clear that this is not just a quarrel between man and wife, but a family drama in which the future and even the safety of the children are at stake. Medea herself is presented in all the alarming violence of her passion, but framed by the sympathy of Nurse and chorus, and therefore to be seen by the audience as a victim, even if also as a potential criminal.

When Medea comes out to talk to the chorus all the wildness has gone and she develops her arguments with complete composure. The focus of the dramatic interest is now this commanding personality in a sequence of encounters, first with the chorus, then with three men who in different ways have power to affect her life. With the chorus she is at her most frank and open, winning their whole-hearted support with her account of the miseries of a woman's life. At this stage the audience, too, must readily give her their sympathy, but complications already begin to arise. How much, we may ask, of what she says to the chorus is special pleading, designed to make them promise to keep her secret? As always with Medea it is hard to be sure; and here we meet for the first time the subtle complexity of Euripides' character-portrayal. At least her description of the constraints on women is deeply convincing, but when she complains of her special lack of resource as a foreigner with 'no mother, no *brother*, no kinsman' to support her (257 f.) we perhaps remember that it was she herself who caused her brother's death and betrayed her family. These words lead straight into her plea for collusion on the part of the chorus if she finds some way of punishing her husband: 'for woman is fearful and timid in other respects and a coward when it comes to looking on steel, but when her marriage is treated with contempt there is no bloodier purpose than hers' (263 ff.). We are left in no doubt that this is a formidable woman; and, despite all that she has said in this scene about the limitations of the feminine role, it is clear that she herself is capable of overcoming them. When she makes her famous claim (250 f.) that she would rather stand three times in the battle line than bear one child she wins our respect—she is talking, of course, about the emotional hazards of being a mother, not just about the physical pain and danger of childbearing—but even so, not many women would say what Medea says; these words may come back to our minds at the end of the scene with Creon.

With the king we see the full exposure of Medea's cleverness, her *sophia*. Creon is explicit that he is exiling her because he fears what her cleverness may devise to harm his family; Medea's response is a dazzling virtuoso display of the very quality he fears. First she argues that her cleverness could not possibly be used to harm *him*, next exerts extreme emotional pressure by appealing to his feelings as a father,[14] and finally makes a disarmingly modest request: just one day's grace, time for making the necessary arrangements for going into exile. But as soon as he has left and Medea has got her way there is a striking change of tone: now we see all the contempt of the clever person for the fool. 'Do you think I would have fawned on that man if I had not had some profit or plan in mind?' (368 f.). Now in a highly professional way she discusses the possible modes of murder she might choose: shall it be fire, or sword, or poison, her speciality? This could easily be bloodcurdling for bloodcurdling's sake as in Seneca and Corneille, who both make much of her gruesome rites and incantations. In Euripides the effect is less gothic; indeed a main function of this detail seems to be to emphasize Medea's cleverness: in her own view of herself her magical skill is part of her heroic *aretē*.

This speech at 364 ff. (and particularly the last section from 392) illuminates a most important aspect of Euripides' Medea. She sees herself not just as a woman wronged, but as a great personage in the heroic mould of an Ajax or an Achilles: she owes it to herself and to her high pedigree to allow no enemy to triumph over her. The granddaughter of Helios must face 'the test of courage': νῦν ἀγών

---

[14] Schlesinger 1966, 42, makes much of Creon's remark at 329 that his children are dearer to him than anything else in life. This is certainly important, in that it gives Medea her cue for exploiting Creon and keeps the theme of children in the foreground, but can we say that it actually gives her the idea of killing her children?

εὐψυχίας, language that an Ajax or an Achilles might perfectly well use. In this context Medea standing in the battle line becomes fully intelligible. The scene ends on a less grandiose, more sinister, note: 'We are women, helpless when it comes to good deeds, but skilled practitioners of all kinds of evil' (408 f.).[15] There is a clash here between Medea's self-image as a hero of the old style braving a great ordeal and her awareness of the destructiveness of thwarted female passion. We see very clearly that her cleverness is a potent force for evil as well as for good. The tragedy is that she does stand out above the limited or shabby people around her, does have a sharper moral awareness and far greater distinction and force of personality, yet the audience cannot help but shudder at the ruthlessness of her anger and passion for vengeance.

In her first scene with Jason, Medea is at her most sympathetic, because here we are allowed to see the full extent of the provocation she has been suffering. Jason is a status-seeker, embarrassed by his barbarian wife who refuses to go quietly, anxious to have her out of the way but insensitive enough to talk about exile being a hardship, crassly patronizing in his offer of material help. Medea's theme is simple: 'I saved you';[16] and she is right. All her past acts of betrayal were committed in the cause of Jason and her love for him; and now he is guilty of the greatest betrayal of all, the breaking of those dearly-bought oaths. The only extenuation would have been if their union had been childless: but they *have* children (παίδων γεγώτων at 490 carries the strongest possible emphasis). Jason's answer only confirms our sense of his outrageousness. He is sophistical in his argument that it was Cypris, not Medea, who saved him, ludicrously arrogant when he recalls the benefits he has conferred on his wife by bringing her to civilized Greece from her benighted barbarian home, patently self-deceptive[17] when he pretends that his only interest in the new marriage is the welfare of his existing family. Once more the importance of children is made very prominent, particularly at 565, when Jason implies that he needs a family more than Medea does. Medea's final taunt turns into a sinister threat which recalls the

---

[15] The rhyme (ἀμηχανώταται . . . σοφώταται, 'most helpless . . . most skilled') adds to the sonorousness of this ending.

[16] 476; 515: powerful use of ring-composition.

[17] The chorus are not deceived (578; 637 ff.); and Jason's words to the princess (reported by the Messenger at 1151 ff.) suggest that he was enjoying his role as royal bridegroom.

concluding lines of the two previous scenes: we are reminded that she is still planning revenge, though the encounter with Jason has done nothing to further the action in any practical sense and Medea still has no idea where she can go when she has punished her victims.

Then Aegeus arrives unexpectedly to answer her need. Aegeus is merely passing through Corinth on his way from the Delphic oracle to consult Pittheus, his old friend who is king of Troezen. The casualness of his arrival has been criticized from Aristotle[18] onwards, but as with Io's visit to the place of Prometheus' punishment in *Prometheus Bound* such casualness is readily acceptable to an audience provided that the scene itself is dramatically significant, and provided that it is seen to be part of a structural pattern. Here there is a clearly discernible design: three contrasting visits to Medea, of which the third offers a close parallel to the first.[19] Both the scene with Creon and the scene with Aegeus show Medea using her wits to get what she wants from a person in authority; but whereas Creon was all suspicion and misgivings Aegeus is full of honourable and rather naive trust. Medea is equal to either situation; and the most interesting link between the two scenes is in her choice of persuasive argument. With Creon it is his feelings as a parent she exploits, with Aegeus his longing to be a parent. Once more her cleverness succeeds: she now has a refuge in Athens, and she can afford to make a detailed plan of vengeance.

Her speech at 764 ff. is the most remarkable in the play. It starts with her triumphant exultation and her plot for the murder of the princess and Creon, then leads without preparation into the terrible revelation that she intends to kill her children. Her own explanation makes the best starting point for a discussion of this speech. She sees the murder of her children as a means of *punishing her enemies*. The deed will be 'most unholy', but she will do it because her enemies' laughter is not to be tolerated. The penalty that is worse than death for her enemy Jason will be to have no children, neither Medea's nor any borne to him by the princess. And so 'let no one think me cowardly or weak, or peaceable, but of quite the opposite temper: dire to my enemies and kindly to my friends. For it is such people who live in the highest esteem.' This is the kind of language with which she exults in her success over Aegeus: 'now I shall win the victory over my enemies' (764–7), language that recalls the end of the scene with

---

[18] *Poetics* 1461^{b}21. At least Euripides has warned us to expect *someone* to arrive (390–4).   [19] Cf. Lucas 1959, 197.

Creon with its image of the heroic Medea facing the 'test of courage'. These are all words that belong to the traditional code, in which the laughter of enemies is the ultimate disgrace and harming enemies and helping friends is the duty of a hero. But Medea's appropriation of the code seems hideously out of place in a situation where the enemy is her husband and the means of punishing him is to be an act of bloodthirsty treachery followed by the murder of her own children.

The essential relevance of the scene with Aegeus must be its stress on the value and importance of children. Euripides does not make clear exactly when Medea arrives at the details of her plan, and we cannot say that the encounter with Aegeus gives her the idea to kill the children; it is enough that after the scene with Aegeus she has the idea very fully worked out: this will be Jason's consummate punishment, to be robbed of his future. Her announcement comes as a surprise, but it is not factitious: the prologue's prophetic warnings and the prominence of the theme of parents and children in all three of Medea's encounters have effectively prepared the way.[20] This technique is perhaps subtler than the version preferred by Seneca, an episode in which Medea sees how much Jason loves his children and says 'Now I have him.'[21] Euripides' Medea does not need to be shown evidence of Jason's fatherly love: she simply knows that even a man as selfish and coarse-grained as Jason, who for the moment is quite absorbed in his young bride and his new social status and content for his whole family to go into exile, can still be profoundly hurt by the loss of his children.

Even more than the scene with Aegeus it is the child murder itself that has caused the greatest critical unease. Perhaps this is because society so much abhors the murder of children that it refuses to regard it as anything but the rarest and most outrageous of deviations. Hence the attempt to explain Medea's act as something quite outside the experience of civilized people. In general we tend not to look on murder as such with the same disbelief; and it comes as a surprise to find from modern statistics that a large proportion of murder victims are in fact children—nearly one-third of the total in the United Kingdom between 1957 and 1968,[22] nearly half in

---

[20] Cf. Ebener 1961, 224.

[21] *Medea* 549–50: 'sic natos amat? | bene est, tenetur, vulneri patet locus' ('Is this how much he loves his sons? Good, he's caught: the place to wound him is exposed.').

[22] Cf. Gibson and Klein 1969. I am grateful to my colleague Mrs A. M. Morris for a criminologist's view of the problem of child murder.

Denmark in recent times[23]—and that the killers are predominantly
their parents. Often the killing of children is accompanied by suicide
on the part of the parents, but one parent may kill a child or children
as a means of hurting the marriage partner. May it not be that in
Medea we find Euripides exhibiting the same psychological sureness
of touch as in his studies of Phaedra and Electra and Pentheus, or as
in the scene where Cadmus brings Agave back to reality?[24]

Medea is trying to achieve the punishment of Jason; the death of
the princess and Creon is not enough, because through her children
Medea can still be hurt or insulted (by the 'laughter of her enemies'),
if *they* are hurt or insulted. With them alive and in his care Jason can
still look to the future through them. There is no question of Medea's
admitting to a wish to punish the children: she calls them 'most
beloved' (795) and her deed 'most unholy' (796): only in the prologue
does she curse them and the Nurse say she 'hates the children'
(presumably because they represent her vulnerability to Jason).
Indeed she thinks she is being loyal to her dear ones and winning
glory by her actions (809 f.), heroic language which a psychologist
would probably describe as an 'altruistic' and 'protective' rational-
ization of the child murder. It seems that very often the parents who
kill their children convince themselves that the children would in
their own interests be better dead.[25]

The scene of false reconciliation between Medea and Jason makes
magnificent theatre; it also has a subtle importance in its relation to
the rest of the play.[26] It emphasizes the link between the two stages of
Medea's revenge by showing the children who are to be victims of the
culminating deed innocently bearing the poisoned gifts which will
make them the agents of the first murder, with Jason as their accom-
plice. From 894 ff. the children are the focus of the action; and seeing
them in Jason's embraces and hearing his confident words about
their future, Medea twice breaks down, though each time she resource-
fully contrives to explain her tears in a sense which furthers her
deception of Jason. The episode has a complex function: it confirms
our awareness of the children's importance to Jason and at the same
time prepares for the moving passage (1029 ff.) where Medea
imagines the future that the children will never have. Moreover

---

[23] Cf. Harder 1967, 197 ff.
[24] Cf. Devereux 1970, 35–48 for a study of this scene.
[25] Harder 1967, 235 ff.   [26] Cf. Lesky 1972, 307; Steidle 1968, 156 f.

her self-mastery here, according to Steidle's persuasive analysis,[27] foreshadows the success of her resolve in the following scene. Certainly it must now seem clear to the audience, as it does to the chorus, that the children are bound to die: 'Now no longer have I any hope left for the children's lives, no longer. They go already to their deaths' (976 ff.).

Now Medea learns that the first part of her plan has worked and the children have been allowed to stay in Corinth; she must say good-bye to them, ostensibly because she is going into exile, but we know that she confronts the essential issue. Time is short, and without the death of the children her revenge will not be complete; but can she face the deed? The speech at 1021 ff. in which she expresses the struggle between her maternal love and her desire for revenge has been tirelessly discussed:[28] is it the tragic climax of the play, showing Medea caught in a conflict on the outcome of which we hang in suspense, or is the inevitability that she will kill her children strongly felt all through the speech, and the climax reached only in the final scene? Recent critics have been particularly concerned with the structural question and also with the apparent inconsistency of Medea's motivation. Within the space of a few lines she moves from the statement that she will take the children with her into exile (1058) to the assertion that there is no escape: they are certain to be killed in Corinth, and she must therefore do the deed (1059–64).

The detail of the speech suggests that despite a certain rhetorical formalism of manner Euripides keeps close to observed patterns of human behaviour. The reality of Medea's love for her children is evoked in her very precise recall of the hopes she used to cherish for their future and hers (1024–35) and in her response to the extra-ordinarily powerful appeal of their bright eyes and soft skin (1070–5). But the reality of her obsessive need to triumph over her enemies is also made inescapably clear (1049–55; 1059–60), the need to hurt Jason as deeply as anyone can ever be hurt, which has been fully explored earlier in the play, both in the betrayed wife's passion for vengeance and in the heroic self-image which makes Medea a far from ordinary but none the less convincing and tragic figure.

Euripides needs to make us believe in Medea's maternal feeling not because we are to think there is a real hope that she may change her mind for good, but in order to achieve the full depth of tragic

[27] See n. 26 above.   [28] Cf. Lesky 1972, 311 f.

seriousness. The deed she contemplates is so horrific that we cannot accept it unless we are given evidence that it has cost a profound struggle. Comparison with Seneca illustrates very well the difference between tragic and melodramatic treatment of the situation. Seneca's Medea carries conviction only as a raving madwoman, whose moments of maternal feeling (938 ff.) show none of the Euripidean Medea's precise awareness of what children mean to a mother. In any case, her softer emotions soon give way to visions of Furies accompanying the dismembered Apsyrtus, to whom Medea sacrifices one of the children, keeping the other to be killed in full view of Jason and the citizens. With her intended victim at her side she expresses a fleeting sense of remorse, but this is soon lost in the joy of gloating over Jason; of the child's presumed agony she seems (like Seneca) to be unaware:

> quid, misera, feci? misera? paeniteat licet,
> feci. voluptas magna me invitam subit,
> et ecce crescit. derat hoc unum mihi,
> spectator iste. (990–3)

wretched woman, what have I done? Did I say wretched? I may repent, but I did the deed. A great sense of pleasure comes over me against my will, and it is growing. There was just one thing missing: he should have been there to see it.

Euripides' master-stroke in this speech is Medea's announcement at 1059 ff. that there is no going back: the poison must have done its work by now and the princess must already be dead. We can assume that the treacherous murder of the princess and Creon will in reality mean danger for the children from the outraged royal family (as Jason later confirms, 1303 ff.). Medea's reaction, when she faces the fact that the murder must have happened, is to treat this danger as inescapable, although a moment earlier she has been speaking of taking the children away with her. She is filled, in fact, with a sudden sense that she is caught in the tide of events and has no longer any choice. This is the atmosphere of sudden urgency in which we are told that the murder of children is often committed: the parent becomes convinced of a threat to the children that clinches the feeling that they would be better dead.[29] Such an interpretation seems much more relevant to Medea's case than any of the others that have been put forward, of which the latest is that the children were too young to accompany their mother in a hasty escape.[30]

[29] Cf. Harder 1967, especially p. 237, and Bender 1934, 41.
[30] Steidle 1968, 159 ff.

The sense of urgency is brought to a desperate climax in Medea's speech after the Messenger has told his story and urged her to fly. There is no word now of triumph over her enemies or of her own situation at all beyond her need to steel herself: her whole concentration is on the children. She must act 'as swiftly as possible', 'without delay'; since they are bound to be killed, she who loves them must be the one to do the deed, not some 'other more hostile hand' (1239 ff.). The murder itself is represented by means of cries from the children and the chorus, but without any word from Medea; nowhere is there any hint of the gloating of Seneca's Medea as she raises the knife: 'perfruere lento scelere, ne propera, dolor' ('Take your crime slowly, my grief, and enjoy it to the full', 1016).

The gloating (but never over the children) is to come in the stark final scene where Medea triumphs over Jason from the chariot, prophesying an evil death for him, refusing to let him even touch the children's bodies. The brute fact of Jason's loss moves us now; but it is Medea who speaks with prophetic authority. Clearly she has the role of the 'god from the machine' who so often in Euripides makes the final dispositions. This is one of the most alarming features of the play, the fact that there is no comparatively distant and objective divine figure to speak with the voice of authority, relating these events to real life through their link with some cult or institution and thereby restoring a sense of normality after the frightful extremes of the action. Medea makes a link between this story and a festival at Corinth (1381 ff.); but she offers no relief whatever from the horror of the situation.

The powerful effect of this final scene depends on Euripides' use of the supernatural device of the dragon chariot, which transforms Medea's status from that of runaway criminal to something outside ordinary human experience. It was a bold dramatic experiment, but Euripides was justified in making it, granted that the effect could be adequately and not absurdly represented on the Greek stage. There has been criticism of the contrast between this very blatant use of the supernatural and the realistic tone of the rest of the action,[31] but some kind of miraculous device was needed if Euripides was to contrive a final confrontation between Jason and Medea in which Medea should at last have her triumph. The whole plot in fact rests

---

[31] R. Lattimore, for instance, regards the chariot as 'preposterous', merely a 'taxi to get from Corinth to Athens' (Lattimore 1958, 108).

on unrealistic data which we accept without qualm: for example, Medea's relationship to Helios (a frequently stressed motif which helps to prepare for the chariot) and the remarkable nature of her magical power. Yet throughout we are invited to take Medea seriously as a real human being, and even this final scene is perfectly consistent with the rest of the play in its handling of her motivation; it is only the spectacle of her in the chariot, high above Jason, taking with her the children's bodies that he may not touch, that makes her seem to have been transformed, in Murray's words, 'into a sort of living Curse . . . Her wrongs and her hate fill the sky'.[32]

The sense that Euripides seems to be making out of all this is as comfortless as the conclusions to which he points in *Hippolytus* or *Bacchae*. What a vulnerable thing is civilization, when man's passions are so powerfully destructive. When he makes the insensitive Jason praise Greek society and values and when he gives the barbarian witch the ideals of a traditional Greek hero he is surely suggesting that there is no safe dividing line: civilized life is always most precariously poised, continually threatened from within.

One of the play's recurrent themes is that of song and the Muses: it comes in that curious passage at the end of the *parodos* where the Nurse meditatively wonders why poets have not devised songs to cure human miseries instead of accompanying their pleasures (190 ff.); in the first *stasimon* when the chorus reflect how poetry has always represented the man's side of things (421 ff.); most prominently in the great passage in praise of Athens after the departure of Aegeus (824 ff.). Athens, city of the Muses, the ideal of civilized splendour, where *Sophia* and the Loves are in harmony: is this merely a fine compliment to an Athenian audience, or is it related more intimately to the deeper meaning of the play? All these passages draw attention to the ambivalence of human intelligence and creativity, which is potentially a source of beauty and harmony, but liable, too, to break out in destructive violence under the influence of passion. Medea in her *sophia* exemplifies this ambivalence: we see her great expertise and intellectual power turned, because of her betrayed love for Jason, to destructive—and self-destructive—ends. And her heroic sense of identity is used to bring out the tragic nature of what she does and suffers.

[32] Murray 1910, xi f.

IO

Hippolytus: A Study in Causation

R. P. WINNINGTON-INGRAM

Why did the events happen as they did? This is no problem to Aphrodite or to Artemis. Bitter enemies though they may be, on one point they are agreed—that what takes place is the work of a god; and the responsibility which Aphrodite claims in the Prologue is endorsed by Artemis in the closing scene. Yet the human characters seem to choose their courses and to work out their disasters on the plane of human circumstance and motive, so that Wilamowitz could say: 'Aphrodite is not necessary for our understanding of the action.' (Though I should myself prefer to ask whether the action is not necessary to our understanding of Aphrodite.) Another critic finds it the very purpose of the play to demonstrate that human freedom is illusory. Various views have been held by various scholars; and at the moment I do not wish to express one of my own. Though I would ask a question. Where else does Euripides use a god or gods as the spokesmen of his deepest insight? (In the *Bacchae* do we not learn far more about Dionysus from the Chorus and the Messengers than from anything Dionysus himself says?) However that may be, the degree of truth which may reside in the utterances of the two goddesses can only be determined by close study of the action as a whole.

I have chosen my original question as the starting-point for a survey which will range widely. The play is rich, complex, subtly-patterned (as are few of Euripides): in a brief paper one can only single out certain aspects and certain details, hoping that the selection does not too seriously falsify the total work of art. I shall from time to time give warnings against over-simplification, but I know that I shall myself be guilty of this critical fault, which I hope may be corrected in the discussion that follows.

Aphrodite and Artemis. The symmetry of the two goddesses, whose appearances frame the disastrous action, is a striking formal device, which must be significant. Here are two divine powers—one of sexual passion, the other of sexual purity. With the two principal characters they form a pattern. It may be useful at the outset to make clear that this pattern is not a simple one. This is no clash between two characters who are, severally, adherents of one and the other goddess. In the first *Hippolytus* it seems as though Phaedra was as committed to the camp of Aphrodite as Hippolytus to that of Artemis, but in our play she has no such loyalty. Nor is there a clash between the goddesses in the soul of either character. While there is psychological conflict in Phaedra, it is not precisely a conflict between what Aphrodite and Artemis stand for; and there is no conflict in Hippolytus at all. And that is interesting, if we compare the *Hippolytus* with the *Bacchae*. Dionysus takes his revenge by releasing in those who have rejected him the instincts which they have repressed. That is what happened to Agave and her sisters. The case of Pentheus is even more relevant, if (as I think) he is represented as having repressed his sexual instinct. In our play it is not Hippolytus but Phaedra who represses—or attempts to repress—her instincts, not out of puritanism, but out of respect for social obligations. Hippolytus is untouched by sex, and his ruin is not worked out in terms of his own conflicts, which do not exist. There was no psychological reason whatever why Hippolytus should not have gone on indefinitely with his young friends, breaking in horses, hunting, eating hearty meals, competing in the games, and communing with Artemis in the pure meadows. It was a life eminently and (at least while youth lasted) indefinitely satisfactory within the closed circle in which he sought to live. Why then does he come to grief? Was it through external causes only—through Phaedra, through Aphrodite? Or did he contribute to his own undoing? If so, it was not through any inner discord in his own heart.

Like Euripides, I have been careful to bring Hippolytus first upon the stage, particularly since Phaedra will hold it for so long! Hippolytus in the perfection of his harmonious life. Ascetic in point of sex alone, he goes off to eat a hearty meal (112)—to be succeeded by Phaedra, who out of love is starving herself to death and reduced to the extremity of bodily weakness. Why then did Phaedra come to grief? She was a woman of fine intelligence and admirable principles. Yet her efforts to master her disgraceful passion were vain, and she was led into a series of disastrous actions. Why? Because Aphrodite is irresistible, ἢν πολλὴ ῥυῇ ('if she flows in full force')? Because in the face of passion intelligence and resolution are futile? And Socrates was wrong when he equated virtue with knowledge?

As a key to the interpretation of the play as a whole, these formulations suffer from their exclusive relevance to Phaedra. Even in relation to Phaedra they strike me as inadequate by reason of an excessive generality. The devastating power of emotion in human life—that is indeed something by which Euripides was obsessed, not least during the period in which he wrote the *Hippolytus*; and he was hardly sanguine about the ability of men, individually or collectively, to control this power by intelligence. But Euripides is not merely concerned to show Phaedra being worsted by emotion—another of a class with Medea and Hecuba—but also to show *why*, in the specific circumstances of her case, she was so worsted.

Why human beings fail to carry out their virtuous resolutions was a question to which Phaedra herself had given some attention. (373 ff.) 'Women of Trozen . . . in time gone by I have reflected in the long watches of the night on how man's life is ruined. And it seems to me that it is not in the nature of their intelligence (κατὰ γνώμης φύσιν) that they go wrong—for many have sound sense (τὸ εὖ φρονεῖν). No, one must look at it this way. We know quite clearly what is good, but we do not carry it out, some from inertia, others because they put some other pleasure before the right. And life has many pleasures.' This passage has been discussed acutely by Professor Snell,[1] who finds in it not only a reaction to the Socratic paradox that virtue is knowledge but evidence for dating the first formulation of that paradox. I have no wish to challenge this conclusion, which seems plausible, if not certain. Where I join issue with him is in his assertion that the passage is only loosely, if at all, related to the situation of Phaedra. He can of course point out that the force which frustrated Phaedra's good resolutions was her love for Hippolytus— a passion, a sickness, a madness. Whereas she goes on: 'Life has many pleasures. Long gossips and leisure—that delightful but dangerous thing. And modesty (αἰδώς).' And she proceeds to distinguish between two kinds of 'modesty' or 'shame'—one which is honourable, the other 'a burden on the house'. But Snell's argument is surely double-edged. For, if (on the face of it) these factors—inertia, the pleasures of gossip and idleness and modesty, are not relevant to the passion of Phaedra, are they not also strange examples to select in order to illustrate the principle of *video meliora proboque; deteriora sequor* and to refute the Socratic paradox? It would seem singularly

---

[1] Snell 1948, 125 ff.

incompetent on the part of Euripides to choose instances which do not fit either his dramatic or his undramatic concerns.

I think there is a simple explanation. If Euripides had been arguing with Socrates in the market-place, these would be strange examples to select. Yet it is natural for Phaedra—a woman speaking to women (cf. 405 ff., and particularly 395-7)—to select them, for they are part (one might almost say the whole) of her experience.[2] We can see then what Euripides is doing. As Phaedra follows her train of thought, the dramatist is revealing to his audience something of dramatic importance. He is revealing her environment; and that, I suggest, is an essential factor in the causation of the tragedy.

Human beings are the product of heredity and environment. That is how we might put it, but there is nothing specifically modern in the idea. For the Greeks there was φύσις, the hereditary endowment; and there was τροφή and παιδεία, a notion which extends from the upbringing of children to the whole trend of the cultural environment. One aspect in which this distinction greatly occupied the thoughts of the contemporaries of Euripides was in the sophistic antithesis between φύσις, 'nature', and νόμος, 'custom' (a theme to which we shall recur). Euripides, who was aware that no human being can be fully accounted for without reference to his heredity and environment, has given Phaedra both.

When she has decided to reveal her love for Hippolytus to the Nurse, she cannot bring herself to make the revelation directly. The first step is to indicate that she is in love. The way she does it is too subtle for the Nurse, who does not see the point of these references to Pasiphae and Ariadne. 'You mean the love she had for the bull' (338)? The references are meant for us: they are meant to bring home to us the heredity of Phaedra; and that is the meaning of her remark (343): ἐκεῖθεν ἡμεῖς οὐ νεωστὶ δυστυχεῖς—the roots of her misfortunes are in the past. It is not a question of inherited guilt, but of inherited sexuality.[3] In fact, both the principal characters have hereditary backgrounds relevant to their character and behaviour. Hippolytus is the son of an Amazon (a fact emphasized at salient

---

[2] 'The woman speaks, the queen, her life brings these pleasures with it' (Wilamowitz 1880, 516 and 1891, 203). The inclusion of αἰδώς among pleasures is a difficulty. It may be that, as Wilamowitz says (1891, 203), there is 'a slight zeugma'. That anything has gone seriously wrong with the text I do not believe.

[3] Pasiphae's bull is no less a symbol of sex than that which came out of the sea to destroy Hippolytus.

points in the play); and the poet intends, as has often been suggested, to indicate that it is from his mother that he has inherited his peculiar temperament. Phaedra is daughter of the woman that loved a bull and sister of Ariadne. This too is surely the point of the repeated references to Crete—to remind us of this background. When the secret is out, the Chorus end their short song of horror with the words: (372) ὦ τάλαινα παῖ Κρησία, 'Unhappy child of Crete'. What happened to this ill-starred child of Crete, Pasiphae's daughter, when she came to Greece? What environment did she find? That, I suggest, is just precisely what is told us in the long speech which Phaedra now makes.

The audience liked such speeches, and Euripides liked writing them. They may strike us as undramatic, but we should not be in too great a hurry to discount them as rhetorical exercises. The form is rhetorical, but the content is often (I do not say always) closely relevant to the drama. This is certainly true of Phaedra's speech. It opens with a generalization about the failure of human beings, despite their intelligence, to act rightly. But this turns out to be illustrated with emotional factors, with 'pleasures', which are part of her experience. More than that, they give a picture of her life (corresponding to the picture which we gain elsewhere of the life of Hippolytus) and so provide a background to the account she now gives of her struggles. Phaedra is a lady, a queen, and belongs essentially to the palace.[4] There she lives surrounded by her servants. She has nothing to do, but passes her time in sweet idleness, in long gossiping conversations and (as we have seen) introspective reflections upon human life. She lives in a house upon which αἰδώς lies like a burden (but more of this hereafter). Is it excessively and inadmissibly 'psychological' to suggest that Euripides knew well that these were fatal conditions and that, despite the clearness of her intelligence and the sincerity of her intentions, Phaedra was defeated from the start. 'Secondly', she says (398 ff.), 'I took thought how I might bear my insane passion nobly, overcoming it with self-control (τῷ σωφρονεῖν)'. An impossible task, surely, for an idle brooding queen: for one devil she expelled, seven were waiting to take its place. And of course she found it impossible. 'Thirdly, when I did not succeed in mastering Cypris by these means . . .'

---

[4] A point brought out earlier in the play by contrast both with Hippolytus and with the Chorus (cf. 121 ff.).

My point is simply this. Euripides is not demonstrating that passion *in abstracto* is too strong for intelligence *in abstracto*, but showing how, given certain antecedents and circumstances, it is too strong. Given certain circumstances. But the idle palace does not constitute the whole environment of Phaedra. Among the environmental factors which determine our lives can be counted (can they not?) the moral standards of the society and class to which we belong. Phaedra had her moral code and her ideals: σωφροσύνη—εὔκλεια—αἰδώς ('self-control—good repute—*aidōs*').

About εὔκλεια ('good repute') and its paramount importance this aristocrat—or should we say this typical Greek?—had no doubts (unfortunately). By αἰδώς she was puzzled (385 ff.):

> δισσαὶ δ'εἰσίν, ἡ μὲν οὐ κακή,
> ἡ δ' ἄχθος οἴκων. εἰ δ' ὁ καιρὸς ἦν σαφής,
> οὐκ ἂν δύ' ἤστην ταῦτ' ἔχοντε γράμματα.

There are two kinds, one not bad, the other a burden on a house. If we could be sure of what was opportune, there would not be two of them spelt with the same letters.

What is the good and what the bad *aidōs?* And are they both illustrated in the play? The passage has been much discussed.[5] It has been suggested that the bad *aidōs* was that respect for the suppliant which caused (if it did cause) Phaedra to reveal her secret to the Nurse. This did indeed lead ultimately to disaster. But Phaedra was not to know this yet. There is no sign whatever that she regrets the revelation; she is still firm in her resolution to die, already taken. The *aidōs* of Phaedra towards the Nurse cannot in any case be the ἄχθος οἴκων ('burden on a house') here—because it was the cause of action; and Phaedra is giving the reasons why people (why women) fail to act.

A passage in the *Ion* may throw light. 'Listen then to my story', says Creusa (336 f.), '—but no, I am ashamed (αἰδούμεθα)'. And Ion replies: οὐ τἄρα πράξεις οὐδέν· ἀργὸς ἡ θεός ('Then you will not accomplish anything; that goddess is lazy'). Phaedra is puzzled. She has been brought up to regard a proper modesty as a virtue, particularly in a woman, particularly in an aristocrat, and yet she feels that this modesty, this reserve, this fear of criticism, can be indulged to the point of obstructing virtuous action. That is all Phaedra means.

---

[5] e.g. Dodds 1925, 102, and 1929, 97 ff.; von Erffa 1937, 166 ff.; Snell 1948.

But just as, in the references to inertia, gossip and leisure, Euripides is depicting the environment which has contributed psychologically to Phaedra's plight, so too with *aidōs*, except that *aidōs* is a mental attitude, a moral standard and an ideal. *Aidōs* was the feeling of modest shame, which dictated silence. It was the shame that Phaedra felt (244), when she had revealed her love obliquely through fantasy (208 ff.). She was ashamed, because, however oblique the revelation and however little understood, it was a betrayal of the first of her resolutions: (394) σιγᾶν τήνδε καὶ κρύπτειν νόσον ('to be silent and conceal this sickness'). Hence (240): ποῖ παρεπλάγχθην γνώμης ἀγαθῆς; ('how far have I swerved from my noble resolution?'). It was a noble resolution. But at what cost could repression succeed, if at all? Euripides knew the human mind well enough to answer that question. The answer is given by the neurotic state in which Phaedra is presented to us at her first entry,[6] torn between her shame and her longing to reveal herself. Paradoxically, then, it is the noble *aidōs* of Phaedra that has contributed to the state of mind (and body) which makes possible the whole disastrous sequence. No wonder that (at 247 ff.) she feels the choice too much for her; and we see her death, not (as she would later—402—have us see it) as κράτιστον . . . βουλευμάτων ('the best of plans'), but in the light of an abdication of choice: ἀλλὰ κρατεῖ μὴ γιγνώσκοντ᾽ ἀπολέσθαι ('it is best to lose all consciousness and die').

In this interpretation of that passage I am confirmed by Mr Bernard Knox (in his original and important 1952 article), who points out that this attitude of mind foreshadows the crucial abdication of choice by Phaedra, when she allows the Nurse to take charge of her affairs. But, before we come to that scene, *aidōs* has a different role to play, in close partnership with another article in Phaedra's code. Εὔκλεια ('good repute') has recently been described[7] as 'the most important Leitmotiv in the play'. This may be going too far, but the theme is certainly of primary importance, particularly in the later phases of Phaedra's catastrophe. It first emerges at 329 ff. It emerges in the form of a dilemma. The Nurse is pleading with her and has adopted the posture of a suppliant. Why does Phaedra yield? There can be no doubt that the fundamental reason is the deep longing that she has to make the revelation. But the way must be eased for her. It is eased by the Nurse's suppliance, so that Phaedra can represent her

---

[6] Well described by Dodds.   [7] Strohm 1957, 104 n. 1.

yielding as an act of *aidōs*, even of εὐσέβεια ('reverence': σέβας γὰρ χειρὸς αἰδοῦμαι τὸ σόν, 'for I respect the reverent power of your hand', 335). But it is eased also by the Nurse's argument, which is bound to move her. 'It will kill you to hear', says Phaedra (329); 'yet what I am doing does me honour'—ἐκ τῶν γὰρ αἰσχρῶν ἐσθλὰ μηχανώμεθα ('for I am devising nobility from shame'). 'Then speak, and your honour will shine the brighter (τιμιωτέρα φανῇ).' Phaedra is exposed to a dilemma inherent in her ideal: if honour is everything, what is the point of virtuous action, if it is known to none—neither in your life-time nor after your death? In revealing her love and her honourable resistance, not only to the Nurse but to the women of Trozen, Phaedra can (in the words of Mr Knox, who has dealt admirably with this topic) 'have her cake and eat it too'. She makes her long speech, which breathes the spirit of her sense of honour (cf. 403 f., 407 ff., 419 ff.); and she receives the tribute of the Chorus (431 f.). Little harm seems to have been done, and some good.

I must pass rapidly over the following scene. Under the assaults of the Nurse Phaedra still clings to her ideal of εὔκλεια ('good repute') (488 f., cf. 498 f., 503 ff.). But the very violence of her reaction is a sign that she is weakening. The Nurse sees that the time has come to go to Hippolytus. She speaks of a magical cure for Phaedra's love. 'I am afraid . . . that you will tell the son of Theseus'. And, because she longs for this in the very depths of her soul, she lets the Nurse go in—yet without herself taking any positive decision or accepting any responsibility.

When Phaedra addresses the Chorus (373 ff.), she can still die—and will be honoured for it. When Hippolytus has been told and has spoken, she *must* die (599 f.): but how can she now die with honour? It is in Phaedra's last scene that the theme attains its greatest prominence.[8] 'Leave it to me, my child', the Nurse had said (521): ταῦτ' ἐγὼ θήσω καλῶς ('I will arrange these matters well'); and Phaedra, like a child, had left it to her. But καλῶς ('well') to the Nurse meant one thing only—that the life of her beloved child should be saved. This was her one standard of value (cf. 252 ff.), in comparison with which all moral considerations counted for nothing. The result she produced was οὐ καλόν ('not good') by any standard. At 706 ff.

---

[8] Note that within 30 lines we have εὐκλεεῖς, καλῶς, οὐ καλῶς, καλῶς, εὐκλεᾶ ('of good repute', 'well', 'not well', 'well', 'of good repute'): 687, 694, 706, 709, 717.

Phaedra resumes control over her own destiny, with the words: ἐγὼ γὰρ τἀμὰ θήσομαι καλῶς ('I will arrange my own affairs well'). And by καλῶς ('well') she means 'honourably'. By applying her standards of honour, will she produce a result which is less disastrous? Or even one which is truly honourable? In fact her sense of honour leads her into an act of cruel deceit by which her honour has been tarnished down the ages. Which is ironical.

But Phaedra's mind is never simple. At 335 she responded simultaneously to the appeal of the suppliant, to the desire for outward recognition, and to the deepest cravings of her love-stricken heart. Now, in the closing lines of her part (728 ff.), love comes once more to the forefront—but turned into hatred and the desire to make Hippolytus suffer as she has suffered. This note is heard once and once only. It may be that, as W. Zürcher[9] has suggested, this is 'Motivtrennung', a technique which he finds in other plays, by which different impulses ascribed to the same character are kept, as it were, insulated from one another. In view of the psychological complexity of the earlier scene, however, I am inclined to think that Euripides has deliberately reserved this theme for the climax—to let us see in the last moment a deeper level of Phaedra's mind. In any case, we see once more in combination within her the instinctive and the conventional springs of action and once more (I would suggest) the conventional serving the purposes of the instinctive.

In this long account of Phaedra I may be thought to have fallen into more than one heresy. To some my account may have seemed too psychological: I offer no defence except that I believe the psychology is to be found in Euripides, in the form and language of the play. If, however, I have given the impression that this is primarily a play about Phaedra (a view which has been maintained), I plead not guilty. A case can indeed be made for regarding Hippolytus as the principal hero, but I think that Professor Lesky is right, when he says:[10] 'our play is the tragedy of a double destiny', and that the role of Phaedra is of far from subordinate importance. The reason why I have devoted so much time to it is that, of the two leading roles, it is the more subtle and complex; and that, in order to develop my main theme (of which I assure you I have not lost sight) it was necessary to examine in some detail the causes of Phaedra's behaviour, as I conceive Euripides to have revealed them.

---

[9] Zürcher 1947, 86.   [10] Lesky 1972, 323 (1964, 167).

Let us return to the goddesses. 'Aphrodite', says Mr Knox, 'tells us not only what will happen but announces her responsibility and explains her motives. It is a complete explanation and one which (even if it were not confirmed in every particular by another goddess at the end of the play) we are bound to accept'. It is indeed confirmed by Artemis: but what does she say? She says in effect (1301 ff.): 'Phaedra was driven mad by Aphrodite; she tried to overcome Cypris by her intelligence (γνώμη), but was destroyed by the craft of the Nurse against her will'. I would not go all the way with the late Professor Norwood in pouring scorn on the intellectual incompetence and moral obtuseness of Artemis. But is it not clear that she is giving a grossly over-simplified version of a highly complex affair— a version designed to give the maximum of pain to Theseus. (οὐχ ἑκοῦσα, 'not willingly': was that true? how far was it true? Euripides can tell us, but not Artemis.) What does Aphrodite say? Her preparations, she tells us, are far advanced (22 f.). If I may put it rather grotesquely, those preparations turn out to have been very elaborate indeed. She has caused Phaedra to fall in love with Hippolytus: well and good, that is within her province. Phaedra's inheritance of passion can also count as within her province. But, if she is to be responsible for the whole action, she must also have placed Phaedra in the fatal environment of the palace and (more important still) provided her, through the wider social environment, with a set of moral ideas which proved inadequate to the situation. For all these things played a part in her downfall. Aphrodite goes on to say that she will make the truth known to Theseus, and that Theseus will curse his son and kill him. But this involves the Nurse, her single-minded devotion to her mistress, and *her* moral limitations. It involves Theseus being what Theseus was—and a relationship (or rather a complete lack of relationship) between Theseus and Hippolytus, who himself has more aspects than the scorn of Aphrodite for which he is so cruelly punished.

This is rather a grotesque way of putting it; and I may seem to be grudging the dramatist the mechanics of his plot. But I think it goes deeper than that. There is a depth and solidity in this tragedy upon the human plane that cannot adequately be expressed by two angry and sexually preoccupied goddesses. There are comments upon human life and human nature which are quite out of their range. Let us return to Phaedra and Hippolytus.

We have seen the importance of social factors in the tragedy of Phaedra: environment and ideals—εὔκλεια, σωφροσύνη, αἰδώς ('good repute, self-control, modesty'). What is the case with Hippolytus? Take αἰδώς, for instance. It is in its origins a social emotion, a social virtue; and it was as such that it was felt and exercised by Phaedra. But when Hippolytus speaks of an Αἰδώς which waters his sacred meadow, the abstraction must symbolize an innate quality, like the sōphrosynē ('self-control') which alone qualifies a man to cull its flowers (79 f.):

> ὅστις διδακτὸν μηδέν, ἀλλ' ἐν τῇ φύσει
> τὸ σωφρονεῖν εἴληχεν ἐς τὰ πάνθ' ὁμῶς.

those who have nothing taught, but in whose nature virtue (self-control) in all things always has been assigned a place.

Is sōphrosynē φύσει or νόμῳ ('by nature or by nurture')? Can virtue be taught? In the age of the sophists these questions were much in the air and must have been raised in the minds of the audience by this play. Is there a sōphrosynē that comes by nature—and a sōphrosynē that is the product of convention? And does the former stand the test better than the latter? This is a possible formula on which to interpret the play.[11] But here again we must beware of over-simplification.

Can virtue—can sōphrosynē—be taught? Is it the product of nature or of nurture? Hippolytus believes that it is a gift of nature; and, so far as he himself is concerned, he is broadly right, for his chastity is a matter of temperament. Yet that is not the whole story, even of Hippolytus: or why should he first be introduced to us, not merely as the Amazon's son, but as the product of chaste Pittheus' education (ἁγνοῦ Πιτθέως παιδεύματα, 11)? If Pittheus is largely ἔξω τοῦ δράματος ('outside the play'), Hippolytus' present social environment is not. He is first seen by us as a member of a kōmos ('band of revellers', 55), and he is escorted on his last journey by his ὁμήλικες ('friends of similar age', 1098). He has his friends and his social life (cf. 987, 997 ff.).[12] He has surrounded himself with a circle of

---

[11] Cf. Pohlenz 1954, 269 f.
[12] This speech is an excellent example of how dramatic points can emerge from conventional rhetoric. Note particularly the turn given to the forensic cliché at 986 f. 1016 ff. is a commonplace, but the reference to the games contributes to the picture of Hippolytus.

like-minded contemporaries; and by this environment his innate
qualities are fostered and confirmed![13] Phaedra has a φύσις
('nature') which is both passionate and intelligent; and, if she was
in some sense chaste by convention, it was convention equally that
helped to destroy her chastity. Since nature and convention—innate
characteristics and social influences—*both* make their contribution
to the virtues and the disasters of *both* Hippolytus and Phaedra, I
doubt if we can find in the play some simple formula for the right
kind of *sōphrosynē*.

Having said this, we must not deny the moral failure of Phaedra,
the moral triumph of Hippolytus. There is a point at which Phaedra
gives the wrong answer. We come back now to the theme of εὔκλεια
('good repute'), for this too is a link between Phaedra and Hippolytus.
Phaedra is virtuous, but she would have her virtue known. She
reveals it, with results so disastrous that she can only save her
honour by an evil act. When the Nurse has urged submission to
desire, Phaedra rebukes her for her specious words (488 f.):

> οὐ γὰρ τὰ τοῖσιν ὠσὶ τερπνὰ χρὴ λέγειν,
> ἀλλ' ἐξ ὅτου τις εὐκλεὴς γενήσεται.

One should not say things to delight the ears, but what will lead to good
repute.

She does not (as at 427) speak of γνώμη δικαία κἀγαθή ('a just
and noble resolution'), but only of εὔκλεια ('good repute'). Perhaps
she does not distinguish clearly between them at all, and that was the
moral trap into which she fell. Hippolytus too has his honour at
stake. He finds himself indeed in the position envisaged by Glaucon in
Republic 361c: μηδὲν γὰρ ἀδικῶν δόξαν ἐχέτω τὴν μεγίστην
ἀδικίας ('although he has done nothing wrong, let him have the
greatest possible reputation for wrongdoing')—a position from
which he could only extricate himself by breaking his oath, which
he refuses to do. He is touched to tears by his plight (1071): εἰ δὴ
κακός γε φαίνομαι δοκῶ τέ σοι ('if I seem wicked and you think
me so'), but he does not make his honour an excuse for a breach of
eusebeia ('piety'). He sticks to his principles. It is Artemis who ensures
that the man of virtue and piety (1419, cf. 1454) receives his honour
in the end.

---

[13] We may compare *Ion* 643 ff. On *Ion* and *Hippolytus*, see Matthaei 1918, 83.

Looked at in this light, Hippolytus does indeed emerge with greater moral credit than Phaedra. I should be surprised, however, if this moral verdict was among the primary purposes of Euripides, whose detachment from his characters is so marked, and who was even less interested than most great writers in awarding certificates of merit.

Time does not allow me to study the role of Hippolytus in the same detail as that of Phaedra. Besides, I am rather frightened of the subject: it can rouse strong emotions. Those to whom, by reason of temperament or religion, Hippolytus makes a strong appeal, may resent any account of him which appears detached and even in some points critical. So I will be brief and (I hope) tactful.

That critic would indeed be deaf to poetry who could deny the beauty of the life of Hippolytus, as Euripides has depicted it; he would be insensitive, if he did not see that in the devotion of Hippolytus to Artemis there was something of the stuff of true religion.[14] If the beauty and the religion are not felt, then the pathos and the irony go for nothing, when the beauty is crudely destroyed and the man of religion is brought low by the operation of divinities. It is of the essence of the life and religion of Hippolytus that they are limited and narrowly enclosed. His religion cuts him off, for good or ill, from a large part of mature human experience. His life is led, with extreme satisfaction, in a small closed circle, among those of similar bent. For these limitations he receives a rich reward. He can ask for nothing better—and to be nothing better than what he is. But is there not a state of mind, of which mystics are warned, called spiritual pride? And may not the *semnotēs* of Hippolytus, which frightened his servant and antagonized his father, be something akin to spiritual pride? Further, when the worshipper identifies himself so closely with the worshipped, is there not another danger? (1080) πολλῷ γε μᾶλλον σαυτὸν ἤσκησας σέβειν ('You schooled yourself far more in self-regard') . . . Certainly we must not take the taunts of Theseus at their face-value. But this taunt follows two of the most striking lines in the play. (1078 f.)

εἴθ᾽ ἦν ἐμαυτὸν προσβλέπειν ἐναντίον
στάνθ᾽, ὡς ἐδάκρυσ᾽ οἷα πάσχομεν κακά.

If only I could stand facing myself and look at myself, so that I could weep at the evils I am suffering.

[14] Cf. Festugière 1960, 10 ff.

Opinions will differ, but I cannot help feeling that Euripides is suggesting that there was some element of *self*-contemplation and *self*-worship in the devotee of Artemis. Did Hippolytus die in some degree a martyr to his own idea of himself? I shudder away from this hypothesis, and turn to that point in the play where he can truly be said to have contributed to his own destruction. For, when the closed circle is broken, he finds himself in just those circumstances with which his nature and way of life have most unfitted him to deal. That he should be horrified and revolted by the proposals of the Nurse is both natural and proper, but his tirade against women which Phaedra hears is not only harsh but crude and childish, spoken (as one critic has put it)[15] 'from the depths of inexperience'. And by turning Phaedra's love to hate it helps to bring about his death.

The dialogue with Theseus has no direct bearing upon his fate, since the curse has already been pronounced, but from it we gain the same impression of Hippolytus as a man belonging to a world apart, striving incompetently to communicate without common ground. This brings us to another factor in the causation of the events. They fell out as they did, because Theseus was the man he was. Of course Aphrodite played a part. As Theseus gives lyrical expression to his love for the dead Phaedra, we see the goddess working in him to further her purposes. He was a man of passion. It was because he was also a man of action that he sought release of emotion in an immediate act by cursing his son. It was because he was a man of action, well qualified to deal with such as Sinis (976 ff.), that there was a complete incompatibility between him and his bastard son (whom Aphrodite had caused him to beget).[16] It was because of this incompatibility that he was predisposed to believe in the guilt of Hippolytus. M. Rivier has put it well:[17] 'Entre le père et le fils la mésentente est totale, et sans doute préexistait-elle à la crise.' Had Theseus stopped to think? But he was not a thinking man. And that too contributed to the disaster.

And so we come back to the goddesses and their claims. Broadly, what I have been trying to do in this compressed and incomplete survey of the play is to show something of the depth and solidity, in

---

[15] Lucas 1946, 68.
[16] Hippolytus read books! The only γράμματα ('letters') that Theseus ever read were written by Phaedra. Hence the irony of 954. [17] Rivier 1944, 68.

terms of human psychology and human society, which Euripides has given to the action which he presents. When we compare them with the concrete details of the play, the explanations which the goddesses give are thin and over-simple. They suit the context of power-politics upon Olympus better than they suit the complexities of human life. It might seem, then, that what the goddesses provide is not so much an adequate account of the tragedy as its raw material, and that Euripides, by framing the action, as he has done, between Aphrodite and Artemis, has used an artistic device which turns out to be significant, but rather less significant than might at first appear. Nevertheless, I think it would be wrong to look at the matter in this way.

Clearly it is quite impossible at the tail end of a lecture (which has already gone on too long) to embark upon a discussion of the nature and functions of Euripidean gods. Gods play many roles—different roles in different kinds of play; and different kinds of gods play different kinds of role. And it is no accident, in my view, that in what many regard as the two greatest plays of Euripides—the *Hippolytus* and the *Bacchae*—the gods who appear in them and work in them are also forces which are manifestly seen to be moulding human life. Whether Euripides believed in the objective existence of Dionysus and Aphrodite apart from the manifestations of their power I do not know and I do not suppose that anybody will ever know. And I do not greatly care. Enough that they are real, that they are powerful, that they are superhuman, and that they involve man in tragedy. It is by the tragedy that we understand the gods, not by the gods that we understand the tragedy. It is by the tragedy that we understand the conditions that are imposed upon human life and the limitations under which we live.

Mr Knox has argued that the tendency of the *Hippolytus* is to demonstrate that human freedom is illusory. I think that is too strong, too positive a conclusion. But the facts to which Mr Knox appeals are true facts. Analysing the play on rather different lines from those which I have chosen, he points out, with great acuteness, a pattern which strikes me as valid and illuminating. He shows how each of the characters is confronted with the alternatives of speech and silence; how they choose—or evade choice; how they change their minds; how they apply or refuse to apply the faculty of reason. 'The alternatives . . . first and second thoughts, passion and judgement, silence and speech, are chosen and rejected in a complicated pattern which shows the independent operation of . . . separate human wills producing a result desired by none of them.' I think he has demonstrated beyond doubt that this pattern was deliberately developed by Euripides. (I have myself tried to show some other patterns inherent in the play.) And, although I feel that he lays too much stress on Aphrodite as an 'external directing force', when he speaks, on the other hand, of 'the futility of human choice and action' he is not far off the mark. Nor is Professor Norwood, when he speaks[18] of 'the grim muddle that we make of life, no less by our virtues than by our faults'. The tragedy, as always perhaps in Euripides, lies in what an English poet has called 'the wearisome condition of humanity'. It is no wonder that human beings are restive under this condition and would have things other than they are. I come to one last theme—one last pattern—in the play.

Escape. It is remarkable how insistently this theme runs through the tragedy. During the suicide of Phaedra, the Chorus sing their famous ode: (732 ff.) ἠλιβάτοις ὑπὸ κευθμῶσι γενοίμαν ('if only I could be in the hidden hollows of the high cliffs'). But this they cannot do: they must wait and watch, while an even more terrible event unfolds. Phaedra longs (208 ff.) to be in the meadows and the forests, where Hippolytus is. But it is only through a sick fantasy that she can escape from the reality of her hopeless love. When she finally escapes, it is only into death (828 f.):

$$\text{ὄρνις γὰρ ὥς τις ἐκ χερῶν ἄφαντος εἶ,}$$
$$\text{πήδημ' ἐς Ἅιδου κραιπνὸν ὁρμήσασά μοι.}^{19}$$

For like a bird you have vanished from my hands in your swift and nimble leap to Hades' house

Not even Hippolytus, in pursuit of an ideal, can with impunity pick and choose (104) and turn his back on what he does not care for. For his way of life is in some sense also an escape, but the element which he would exclude from his life is as remorseless in its revenge as the bull which drives him to destruction on the sea-shore (1226 ff.). Nor can Theseus banish him (1053) πέραν γε πόντου καὶ τόπων Ἀτλαντικῶν ('beyond the sea and the Atlantic regions')—that is, out of the whole human world, where Aphrodite holds sway (3)[20]—out to the Garden of the Hesperides (743–7)

---

[18] Norwood 1954, 110.   [19] A reminiscence of 732 f.?

[20] (3 f.): ὅσοι τε Πόντου τερμόνων τ' Ἀτλαντικῶν | ναίουσιν εἴσω φῶς ὁρῶντες ἡλίου. | ('All those who dwell within the sea and the Atlantic limits and see the light of the sun').

ἵν' ὁ ποντο-
μέδων πορφυρέας λίμνας
ναύταις οὐκέθ' ὁδὸν νέμει,
σεμνὸν τέρμονα κυρῶν
οὐρανοῦ τὸν "Ατλας ἔχει,

Where the sea-lord of the dark waters no longer permits a way for sailors, reaching the holy boundary of heaven which Atlas keeps,

where happiness is to be found, but for the gods alone (751).

Of this total reality from which there is no escape the gods are symbols. Artemis and Aphrodite stand in their place, not only as the major instinctive forces operating in the tragedy, but as proper and artistically satisfying representatives of the realities which condition human life.

What can the gods do for men, except destroy them? The chorus which begins with: ἦ μέγα μοι τὰ θεῶν μελεδήμαθ' ὅταν φρένας ἔλθῃ λύπας παραιρεῖ ('The care of the gods [for mortals], when it comes to my mind, greatly assuages my sorrow', 1102) works round to μανίω θεοῖσιν ('I rage against the gods', 1146). What can Artemis do for Hippolytus? In life she gave him joy and an object of devotion. In death she can restore his reputation and deplore his destruction. But it is Hippolytus, not Artemis, that dwells on the beauty of their unequal partnership. Of the two specific consolations which she offers one is an act of vengeance which will show her as cruel as her rival; the other a commemoration which is not without irony, for the virgins of Trozen will sing of him when they are about to pass to the maturity which he rejected and they will sing of Phaedra's love. The end of the play belongs to Theseus and Hippolytus. With the reconciliation between them a gleam of light irradiates the tragedy. Human beings can at least forgive one another, even if the gods cannot forgive (117 ff.).

II

'Iure principem locum tenet':
Euripides' Hecuba

MALCOLM HEATH

I

Among the *Carmina Burana* there is a song (no. 16) on the Wheel
of Fortune, the last stanza of which reminds the king, enthroned
at the pinnacle of Fortune's cycle, of the monitory inscription
beneath him:

> Rex sedet in vertice,
> Caveat ruinam;
> Nam sub axe legimus
> Hecubam reginam.

Hecuba, once queen of Troy, then a slave, who sees her daughter
sacrificed to honour the destroyer of her sons, her last surviving son
treacherously murdered and callously exposed unburied by his
supposed protector—Hecuba provides an outstanding illustration
of the fragility of human good fortune. If, then, by tragedy we mean
the Aristotelian turn from good to bad fortune, evocative of fear and
pity, Hecuba's story is surely paradigmatically tragic.

For the critics of the Renaissance *Hecuba* was indeed a paradigmatic tragedy, perhaps the outstanding piece in the Greek tragic
corpus. Caspar Stiblinus, whose annotated edition of Euripides was
published at Basel in 1562, began his introduction to *Hecuba* by
noting that it stood first in the traditional ordering of Euripides' plays,
followed by manuscripts and in the printed editions of the time; it
is this primacy of place which, he says, the play deserves: 'iure
principem locum tenet'. In the sixteenth century, that was far from
an eccentric judgement. But few critics in more recent years have
been willing to describe the play as a work of outstanding merit.

Hecuba has found its defenders; but to most critics over the last two centuries it has seemed a flawed, and to many a fatally flawed, piece of work.

In this paper I propose to give a summary account of the history of *Hecuba*'s reception. I shall try to explain why the play was so highly regarded by sixteenth-century critics, and to trace its subsequent decline from that status. I want to do this for two reasons. First, I think that the story is an interesting one in its own right. Secondly, I think that it has implications for our own approach to the play. It can be argued that the preoccupations of recent criticism of *Hecuba*—both the problems which it raises and the solutions which it proposes—are the product of the history which I shall be recounting. It can also be argued, I believe, that we have been misled by that history, and that we would do well to recover perspectives which our Renaissance colleagues would have taken for granted. I shall return to these contemporary points at the end of the paper; I begin with the historical survey.

II

Let us begin at the beginning. We do not know when *Hecuba* was first performed. *Clouds* provides a slightly unstable *terminus ante quem* of 423; attempts to deduce a *terminus post quem* are not persuasive, but about 424 seems a reasonable conclusion to draw from metrical evidence.[1] Nor do we know how the play (or, more precisely, the tetralogy of which it was part—which is also unknown to us) fared in competition. The only index we have to its contemporary reception is Aristophanes. The play has a small, but not a negligible, presence in his works; it is certainly not one of his favourites. *Clouds* 1165–6 clearly allude to *Hec.* 172–4, and *Clouds* 718 may allude to *Hec.* 159 ff.; at a somewhat later date, the opening lines are parodied in a fragment of *Gerytades* (156 KA).[2] Other allusions are doubtful.[3]

---

[1] The Delian celebrations of 426/5 (cf. Thuc. 3. 104) have been linked to lines 485–6; but see Wilamowitz 1895, I. 140–2. To see an allusion to Sphacteria in 650–1 is absurd. For the metrical data, and an overly credulous treatment of the external evidence, see Ceadel 1941, 75.

[2] Post-416 (there is a reference to Agathon); Usener conjectures 407.

[3] Fr. 1 KA shows no particular verbal similarity; so, in view of the frequence of the formula, it may be mere coincidence that the beginning of *Hecuba* gives the closest parallel. *Frogs* 1331 ff. is probably meant to refer to a Euripidean cliché rather

In the fourth century there is little evidence of attention to the play in literary sources. No use is made of the play, so far as I am aware, in comedy. Plato does not cite it. Aristotle does quote 864–5 as one of a number of illustrative passages in *Rhet.* 1394^{b}4–6; but it is not probable that there was a reference in the *Poetics*,[4] so that his assessment remains a matter of conjecture—for which, of course, the *Poetics* does afford some evidence. There is no didascalic evidence that the play was revived on the stage,[5] but Demosthenes cites (again) the opening lines in a satirical attack on Aeschines in a way which suggests that his victim had, or could plausibly be thought of as having, acted in it, and which presupposes its familiarity (Dem. 18. 267); and there is evidence of histrionic interpolation.[6]

We get, therefore, the impression of a play enjoying a continued life, but one by no means at the forefront of attention; this picture will not require revision until very late antiquity. The play's relative unimportance[7] is surprising when one reflects on the pre-eminence it achieved in the Byzantine period—it was the first play in the Euripidean triad. Quotations provide one index of the play's popularity; a quick census reveals several trends. The select plays are increasingly dominant over the others; within the others the proportion of alphabetical to lost plays is fairly constant. Within the select plays the triad achieves an early prominence much increased in late antiquity; but *Hecuba* does not share either in the early dominance of the triad or in its late increase.[8] Quotations, of course, are not an ideal index; they are likely to underestimate the dominance of the select plays, since quotations can be transmitted independently of the plays from which they are taken. Papyri confirm that the early dominance of select plays over others was greater than quotations suggest; the prominence of *Orestes* and

---

than a specific passage, although *Hecuba* 68 ff. is the closest extant parallel (as the scholia note).

[4] Valla's reading at 1456^{a}17 is accepted only by Else among recent commentators (Else 1957, 544–8); and he observes that the reference would in any case probably be to *Tro.* (547 n. 99).

[5] An unknown poet won at the Lenaea of 363 with a *Hecuba* (adesp. F1h Snell).

[6] Cf. Biehl 1957, 55–69 and—speculatively—Bremer 1971, 232–50.

[7] It is interesting that Dio Chrysostom quotes *Hec.* 607 as from a comedy (*Or.* 32. 86).

[8] I report here the results of my own informal census of quotations.

Phoenissae is likewise reflected very early in the papyri, while *Hecuba* lags behind.[9]

In so far as the play was read and admired, what in it was valued? The opening of the play was evidently found striking. We have noted citations of the first lines in Aristophanes and Demosthenes; they reappear in Strabo, Lucian, Hermogenes and Libanius.[10] Hecuba's laments we have noted in Aristophanes; 162–3 is loosely quoted by Dionysius of Halicarnassus to illustrate the effect of spondees, and by the rhetor Alexander to illustrate the difference between genuine *aporia* and the rhetorical figure.[11] Polyxena's dignity naturally excites admiration. Her reply to Odysseus (342 ff.) is admired in the scholia for the 'heroic character' which her outspokenness displays. The messenger's report of her death is quoted by Philo, pseudo-Lucian, Galen, Clement of Alexander, Pliny and pseudo-Hermogenes.[12] Pseudo-Lucian praises 568–9 as 'dignified'; pseudo-Hermogenes agrees, but sees a lapse into bad taste in 570, a judgement found also in the scholia.[13]

Indeed, character and decorum are recurrent concerns in the scholia. A note on 825 defends Hecuba against the charge of prostituting her daughter;[14] this is a reply to the view reflected in a scholion to Sophocles, *Ajax* 520. A note on 601 defends Hecuba's philosophising as appropriate to a character of royal status;[15] it is probable that Theon had this passage in mind when he criticised Euripides for making Hecuba philosophise inopportunely.[16] When Agamemnon's care to explain his reasons at 889 ff. is criticised as unkingly, it is not altogether clear whether the criticism is of Agamemnon (as Hecuba criticises him in 864), or of Euripides for

---

[9] On the *Hecuba* papyri see Matthiessen 1974, 108–12; cf. Bremer 1984, I. 281–8.

[10] Strabo 14. 5. 4; Lucian, *Nec.* 1; Hermogenes, *Id.* 2. 4 (but this is simply a quotation of Demosthenes); Libanius, *Decl.* 23. 61; also in the scholia to Apthonius and John Doxapatres (*RG* II. 53 and 496 Walz).

[11] DH *Comp.* 17; Alexander III. 12. 20 Spengel.

[12] 548–51 in Philo VI. 633 Cohn–Wendland; 568–74 in [Lucian] *Dem. enc.* 47; Galen XIV. 236, XVIII/2. 8 Köhn; Clement, *Strom.* 2. 33, and *Paed.* 2. 10 with scholia (I. 332 Stählin); Pliny, *Ep.* 4. 11; [Hermog.] *Inv.* 4. 12.

[13] 361. 26–362. 2 Dindorf.   [14] 66. 21–3 Schwartz.

[15] 370. 22–4 Dindorf. On 603, one view (reminiscent of the Pindaric scholia) is that Euripides is admitting to an untimely digression (371. 8–11 Dindorf); a better account is given in 371. 16–18 Dindorf.

[16] Theon II. 60. 29–30 Spengel; *Tro.* 884 ff. is also possible. Cf. Eustathius on *Il.* 13. 292 (III. 467. 8–13 van der Valk).

portraying an unkingly king.[17] Another focus of concern is dramatic
plausibility. A number of difficulties are raised in the scholia, and
attempts are made to resolve them. Where does Hecuba make her
entry?[18] What exactly did Achilles' apparition demand?[19] How did the
blinded Polymestor identify Agamemnon?[20] Most significant (for the
play's subsequent history, at least) was the problem of an army in
the Chersonese sacrificing at Achilles' tomb in the Troad; a cenotaph
is mooted.[21] The implausibility of the story which Euripides invents
to put Odysseus in Hecuba's debt is noted; no defence is offered.[22] An
implausibility is detected also in 280 (for Hecuba will be separated
from Polyxena even if her life is spared); but this is rightly seen as a
rhetorical device on Hecuba's part, as is the claim to have lost fifty
children in 421 and the misrepresentation of Polymestor in 1219.[23]
As to the play's structure, the only comment is that the duplication
of Hecuba's loss doubles the pathos of the tragedy.[24]

The play is most frequently cited for its gnomic content. We
noticed Aristotle quoting 864–5 to illustrate the idea of gnome and
enthymeme; the same lines were quoted by Libanius,[25] as well as by
the anthologists. Stobaeus quotes a range of gnomes on justice,
persuasion, good breeding, honour, the transience of fortune and
the behaviour appropriate in good and bad fortune.[26] As we saw,

---

[17] 71. 12–14 Schwartz.

[18] On 53 (17. 30–18. 23 Schwartz). An attempt is made to visualise the stage action
in order to grapple with the possible inconsistency (for the idea, cf. Aristotle, *Poet.*
1455^{a}22–9); cf. on 59 (19. 3–5), 99 (22. 20–2), 680 (61. 18–19).

[19] On 95 (21. 26–7).   [20] On 1114 (83. 4–6).

[21] On 521 (50. 27–9 Schwartz; but he has a mutilated version of the note, and
one must consult Dindorf 348. 25–349. 1, and 243. 14–18, for the attempted
resolutions).

[22] On 241 (32. 3–5 Schwartz); cf. SE *Od.* 4. 255. For Euripides' adaptation of myth
cf. on 3 (12. 5–9 Schwartz). Anachronisms: 254 (32. 16–17), 573 (54. 2–8); and cf. on
1186 (497. 32–498. 2 Dindorf).

[23] Cf. 33. 19–21, 42. 29–33, 87. 23–4 Schwartz (and 502. 25–503. 3 Dindorf).

[24] On 80 (20. 13–15 Schwartz). Some miscellaneous notes: on 689 (62. 13–14),
reduplication excites emotion; Anon. Seg. (i. 457. 20–2 Spengel) remarks on the
pathetic effect of address to the dead (cf. 558 ff., 684, 694, 707). The notes on 414 and
426 (42. 15–24, 43. 8–10 Schwartz) show a better appreciation of that exchange than
Diggle's OCT.   [25] Libanius, *Or.* 25. 3.

[26] Stobaeus quotes 227–8, 282–5, 293–5 (cf. Gellius 11. 4. 21–2: versus . . . verbis,
sententia, brevitate, insignes illustresque, 'verses outstanding and famous for their
words, their meaning and their brevity'), 306–8 (cf. Aristides ii. 704 Dindorf), 332–3,
395–8, 379–81, 600–2, 622, 663, 805, 814, 831–2, 836, 844–5, 846–7, 864–5, 956–7,
1178–82, 1183–6, 1238–9, 1250–1. *Hecuba* is one of the most frequently quoted plays
in Stobaeus, even though (by comparison with his contemporaries) he has a bias to
non-select plays; but *Archelaus*, *Antiope* and *Andromache* are more frequent.

objection can be raised where such material is introduced inopportunely or out of character; but in general it is valued. A note on 1187 expresses admiration for the philosophical content of *Hecuba*'s opening.[27] It may be recalled that one of the features of *Phoenissae* singled out for praise in the hypothesis is its wealth of excellent gnomes.[28] That the play was seen as rich in edifying and quotable matter goes a long way towards explaining its Byzantine pre-eminence;[29] the play was eminently suitable for use in schools. The play's high rhetorical content, and numerous reflections on rhetoric and persuasion, reinforce this usefulness.[30] This does not, of course, explain why that pre-eminence was achieved so late; that I am unable to explain.

III

Whatever the reason for the late establishment of *Hecuba*'s pre-eminence, once established it was bound to be passed on to the Renaissance. As the first play in the Byzantine triad of Euripides it was the first Greek tragedy to be read by students; it was thus the tragedy most widely and best known in the original. But also, and as a consequence of that, it was the first and most frequently translated Greek tragedy, both into Latin and into vernacular languages; this ensured its wider dissemination.[31] These accidental factors of transmission might be thought sufficient to account for the success which the play enjoyed in the sixteenth century;[32] and no doubt the play was as useful to Renaissance as to Byzantine educators. But there is more to it than this. The play was attractive to the sixteenth

[27] 86. 28–9 Schwartz.
[28] Cf. S Soph. *El.* 539: critics should not be so preoccupied with minor errors and inconsistencies in a poem that they lose sight of what is really important, i.e. 'what is heroic and beneficial to us when we encounter it'.
[29] It is the most frequently quoted play, for example, in Eustathius: see Miller 1940, 422–8.   [30] On the rhetoric, see Matthiessen 1974, 111–12.
[31] For details of early translations, see Waszink's introduction to Erasmus' translation, in Waszink 1969, 195–212. The play is also one of the first Greek tragedies for which we have evidence of performance in modern times: Waszink (207) mentions performances at Louvain in 1506 or 1514, and at Wittemberg, under the direction of Melanchthon, who lectured on the play in 1525/6.
[32] Cf. Wilson 1973, 87.

century, both thematically[33] and aesthetically. Those who read the play had previously read attentively and admiringly Seneca's tragedies; and they found in it familiar and welcome features: a ghost, vengeance, horrific bloodshed, rhetoric and pointed sententiousness.[34] For the aesthetic aspect, we may return to Caspar Stiblinus. He was not a casual reader, to be over-influenced by the accidents of first exposure; and he goes out of his way to praise *Hecuba*, for in general he was sparing of evaluative comment in his prefaces—apart from *Hecuba* he singles out only *Heracles* for particular praise, and *Electra* (not published until 1545, its place in the Euripidean canon still open to question) for adverse comment.[35] His comments, therefore, are more than a routine puff and merit, though brief, closer attention.

What Stiblinus says is this: 'This play, on account of its subject-matter's variety and more than tragic atrocity, rightly holds first place' (38). The two key terms—variety and atrocity—reappear in his more elaborate praise of *Heracles* (626), a play 'not inferior to any of the preceding ones in respect of the economy of its writing, the seriousness and variety of its subject-matter, or the deadly and atrocious changes of fortune, of the kind that tragedies claim as their own'. With this one might compare, for example, William Gager's preface to his own neo-Latin tragedy *Meleager*, published in 1592; he explains that he opted to present Atalanta and Oeneus in the way he has to increase 'the variety and atrocity' of the tragedy's subject-matter. It seems that this pair of terms will bring us to the heart of the tragic aesthetics of the sixteenth century; we shall consider each in turn.

First, variety. In *Hecuba* this is promoted, obviously, by the double action. The events of the Polyxena and Polymestor actions are diverse, as are the emotional demands which each makes on the audience. This juxtaposition of contrasting material may be found aesthetically interesting *per se*. That it involves a doubling of the

---

[33] This aspect is emphasised by Mueller 1980, 21–2, 25–6, 105.

[34] For Seneca's influence see Charlton 1946; Braden 1985. Seneca was widely preferred to the Greek tragedians in the sixteenth century.

[35] *Electra*'s first editor, though convinced of the play's authenticity by manuscript evidence and ancient attestation, conceded that it had faults, especially of structure (Victorius 1545, 4); and Stiblinus counts this (Stiblinus 1562, 659–60) among grounds for doubting—though not for denying—the work's authenticity.

action is not a problem for sixteenth-century critics; there is, in fact, very little adverse comment on the play's structure in this period. The only instance that I have discovered is Giraldi Cinthio's; and what worries him is not the combination of the Polyxena and the Polymestor actions, but the fact that the latter contains two instances of *peripeteia* (Hecuba's discovery of Polydorus' body and the entrapment of Polymestor), which he thinks appropriate only in a tragedy that ends happily for one party.[36] Nobody suggests that there is a problem about the unity of the play. From this one might conclude that sixteenth-century critics were indifferent to the structure of plays;[37] but that is clearly untrue. I have mentioned the questionable status of *Electra*; what most distressed its first editor, and what prompted Stiblinus to doubt its authenticity, was precisely the play's 'frigid and incoherent' economy.[38] Contemporary poetic theory recognised the importance of this issue.[39] We should look, rather, at the kind of theory of appropriate literary economy with which the critics of this period worked.

Everyone agreed that a play's plot should be unified—that is, that it should comprise a single and complete sequence of causally connected events. But a distinction was recognised between the structure of a plot and the structure of the text in which that plot is realised. It was not thought that the text ought to be restricted to the realisation of its unified plot; on the contrary, it was thought to be an advantage if a narrative or dramatic text is 'amplified' or 'dilated' by the insertion of extraneous material. For such digressions refresh the reader, returning him to the plot in a more attentive frame of mind; and they provide ornament and variety, which are aesthetically rewarding. Thus, for example, Viperanus insists uncompromisingly on unity in his discussion of plot:[40]

So if the plot is a composition of fictional actions, then the plots of single poems will also be single, and in a unified plot, the actions (or parts of an

---

[36] See Giraldi Cinthio 1554, in Guerrieri Crocetti 1973, 196–7; cf. Aristotle, *Poet.* 1453^{a}30–3.

[37] See, for example, Stone 1974, 67–71. Stone's emphasis on the humanists' interest in style and moral content is justified, but he is too dismissive of their interest in dramatic structure.   [38] See n. 35 above.

[39] e.g.: 'Tragedy requires that everything should be well disposed and ordered': de Laudun Daigaliers 1579, v. 4, quoted from Lawton 1949, 91 ff.

[40] Viperanus 1579, 30–1.

action) will be similar. Just as an orator's speech should be constructed, like a living organism, from limbs that are suited to one another and properly connected, so a poem should consist of parts that are not different, but similar and conjoined; for if you portray actions that are diverse in kind and discrepant, they will no more be congruous with each other than an assemblage of the limbs of different animals . . . In poetry everything should be in harmony and contribute equally, as it were, to a certain concord. Nothing should be inserted that does not have either a necessary or a probable coherence with something else. And the whole should be connected in such a way that nothing can be removed or altered or transferred to another place without destroying the whole structure of the plot.

But, having imposed these seemingly unqualified restrictions on the content of a poem, he goes on to add (34):

But in the actual realisation of the plot, much is often inserted for purposes of ornamentation or amplification; writers on this art designate these things by the Greek word *episodia*.

And of epic he says (75):

Even if an epic poem embraces a plurality of actions, it still constitutes a unified plot, like a unified body composed of many limbs. Indeed, an epic poem (for which either no time-limit is set, or else one sufficiently long for the imitation) should be amplified with many episodes, to ensure that it does not (if it is not dilated by any digressions) become sterile and unadorned, and thus bare of all the charm and grace which the variety of episodes does most to confer.

This doctrine could be illustrated from many other sixteenth- and seventeenth-century poetics; and Scaliger cites *Hecuba* to illustrate just this manner of treating the tragic *argumentum*: 'So one should take an extremely concise subject-matter, and make it as varied and manifold as possible. For example, Hecuba in Thrace . . .'—and he goes on to summarise the plot.[41] These critics do not explain in detail how *Hecuba* will be read in the light of this theory. But it is obvious that one could construe the Polyxena action as an 'episode'

---

[41] Scaliger 1561, III, c. 97. Compare Pontanus 1597, 110: the plot should be 'unified and extremely concise, and dilated and amplified by concise episodes and embellished by a variety of events and persons'. Cf. 58, on epic. Similarly Vossius 1647a, 37 insists on the utmost simplicity in the conception of the plot; but then (40) one should see to the episodes and digressions 'by which the narrative should be dilated, so that it has greater amplitude and gives greater pleasure by its variety'.

diversifying and ornamenting the unified sequence of events involving Polydorus and Polymestor, an episode which, being materially related to the plot and formally interwoven with it, is unobjectionable despite its structural superfluity.

Atrocity, the term paired with variety in Stiblinus' assessment of the play, was definitive of tragedy in the sixteenth century; as one critic pointedly expresses it: 'The more tragedies are cruel, the more they excel.'[42] For Scaliger 'the events of tragedy are grand, atrocious . . .'; it is not necessary for a tragedy to have an unhappy ending: 'only the events it contains should be atrocious'.[43] What are these atrocious events? Scaliger provides a catalogue of violence and emotional extremity: 'the edicts of kings, murders, acts of desperation, suicides, exiles, bereavements, parricides, incests, fires, fights, blindings, weeping, wailing, lamentation, funerals, funeral speeches, funeral laments.' *Hecuba* abounds in such things; to quote Stiblinus at slightly greater length:

This play, on account of its subject-matter's variety and more than tragic atrocity, rightly holds first place. It contains the captivity of Hecuba, the sacrifice of Polyxena, the cruel murder of Polydorus, the blinding of Polymestor, and the wretched butchery and death of his children.

But we should not overlook the attractions of moral extremity. When Gager introduced into his *Meleager* 'Atalante . . . recoiling from her husband, Oeneus proud and contemptuous of the Gods, and putting a sudden end to his life' to increase the variety and atrocity of his play, it was (presumably) Oeneus who was responsible for the latter. His suicide, of course, provides additional bloodshed; one thinks of the slaughters with which many vernacular plays of the time conclude.[44] But Oeneus is also a monstrously impious character; his first lines are closely modelled on the vaunts of Seneca's Atreus.[45]

[42] de Laudun Daigaliers 1579.

[43] Scaliger 1561, VI, c. 97. It is odd that later in the chapter he comments: 'Since tragedy has an unhappy ending, and *Hecuba* is a tragedy, Hecuba should be more sorrowful at the end than in the beginning. But that does not happen at all: vengeance makes her a little less sad.'

[44] Robert Garnier, in his preface to *Porcie* (1568), says that his invention of the Nurse's suicide was designed 'to steep the catastrophe in blood'.

[45] Par diis superbis gradior, et caelo tenus, | Inter tyrannos, arduum caput effero, 'I walk as an equal to the proud gods and carry my head high as the heaven among kings', cf. Seneca, *Thyestes* 885–6: aequalis astris gradior . . . 'I walk on a level with the stars'.

This wickedness surely contributes a frisson of horror; again, one can think of contemporary vernacular tragedies in which much of the effect derives from the presentation of extreme evil. This feature, too, is present in the climax of *Hecuba*, the moral depravity of Polymestor enhancing our sense of horror.

But the wickedness of Polymestor is integral to a third feature of the play valuable according to sixteenth-century tragic aesthetics: its moral utility. It was generally accepted that the function of tragedy was to instruct—to instruct and to give pleasure, or to instruct by giving pleasure. Stiblinus is careful in introducing each play to point out its *scopus*, the moral lesson (or, more often, lessons) which it contains. In *Hecuba*, the queen's fate reminds us of the instability of human fortune, and this inculcates due restraint in prosperity (39):

These savage tricks of fate and lamentable changes of fortune should warn those elated by their great success to recall themselves to moderation, and not to allow themselves to be carried away by their wealth and power: things of that kind, bestowed by blind fortune's whim, are suddenly snatched away and given to others; they do not stay fixed in any one place.

And the fate of Polymestor should act as a deterrent:

This most conspicuous example deters us from insane, insatiable desire for material possessions, which is ever the cause of terrible disasters and urges mortals to impious wars: it drives them to undertake any and every crime, and in defiance of nature's own laws it repays the greatest acts of kindness with cruel robbery.

These are commonplaces of sixteenth-century writing on tragedy. Indeed, deterrence was the basis for one of the two main interpretations of tragic catharsis current at the time: the emotions which impel us to criminal acts are expelled by the fear and pity excited in us when we see the tragic consequences of those acts.[46] (The other main interpretation of catharsis was the converse of tragedy's inculcation of moderation in good fortune; by putting before us images of human misfortune tragedy accustoms us to the insecurity

---

[46] e.g. Lombardi 1550, 98; Giraldi Cinthio 1554, 182; Viperanus 1579, 93–4; Pontanus 1597, 108; and elsewhere. Cf. Stiblinus 1562, 168, on *Medea*: 'Immoderate and illicit love is the cause of many evils. Example lies to hand. And the *scopus* of this play is none other than to deter us by this horrifying example from immoderate loves and dishonourable lusts.'

of our human prosperity, so that we are less profoundly distressed by the misfortunes which befall us.)[47]

Polymestor's sufferings are wholly deserved, and Stiblinus has no moral qualms concerning Hecuba's act of vengeance. I do not know, in fact, of any adverse judgement on Hecuba's vengeance in this period; that is the more striking when one recalls that the moral ambiguity of revenge was a recurrent theme in vernacular tragedy. In this respect Stiblinus' treatment of *Hecuba* is significantly different from his treatment of *Medea*. He realises that Jason, just as much as Polymestor, deserved punishment;[48] but he regards Medea's act with the utmost horror (170). It is Medea's killing of her own children that revolts; Hecuba's vengeance is quite different. So far from being revolted, Stiblinus proposes the circumspect calm with which she goes about retaliation as a model.[49] Furthermore, he sees the vengeance as religiously edifying; the poet exhibits, in Polymestor's just punishment, the workings of Providence.[50] Here, too, Stiblinus finds in Hecuba one of the categories of tragic utility standard in sixteenth-century criticism; thus Melanchthon:[51]

So this is the main subject-matter of all tragedies. This is the opinion they aim to fix in our minds: that there exists an everlasting Mind, that always marks out acts of atrocious wickedness with exemplary punishment, but gives the moderate and just a more tranquil life.

We are now in a position to reconstruct a sixteenth-century reading of the play. The basic premise of its plot is the downfall of the Trojan royal house; this premise is embodied for us in the sad figure

---

[47] Robortello 1548, 53; this interpretation was also followed by Minturno and Castelvetro. For a useful survey of interpretations of catharsis, see Halliwell 1986, 350–6.

[48] Stiblinus 1562, 165: he begins the preface with an outline of the whole story of Jason and Medea designed to make clearer Jason's ingratitude and the justice of Medea's wrath.

[49] Stiblinus 1562, 39: 'Hecuba's mature and shrewd judgement in taking vengeance on Polymestor, by which she does not hurry the punishment or rush upon him violently, carried away by her anger . . . tells us that in difficult matters we should be slow, circumspect and cautious: in every matter haste is fraught with peril, but delay is safe.' Cf. Vossius 1647*b*, 51.

[50] Stiblinus 1562, 39: 'With the loss of his sight and the death of his children, he has paid a just penalty for his deed. In this passage the poet aims incidentally to warn that there is an everlasting Mind that governs the world and avenges atrocious crimes with terrible punishments, but generously rewards honest deeds.'

[51] Melanchthon 1545, in Bretschneider 1834, v. 567 ff. Cf. Camerarius 1568.

of Hecuba. It is both pitiful (and pity, as one of the tragic emotions, is a constituent of the proper pleasure of tragedy), and also instructive, reminding us of the transience of good fortune and preparing us to meet misfortune with resolution. It is the downfall of the Trojan royal house which tempts Polymestor to commit an atrocious crime against one of its, now apparently defenceless, members; and the plot, strictly conceived, of the play is the discovery and avenging of that murder—a perfectly unified series of events. Polymestor's bloody fate excites horror; horror is the other tragic emotion,[52] so that this fulfils the 'characteristic pleasure' (*oikeia hēdonē*) of tragedy. The outcome also deters us from similar crimes, and reminds us of the providential guidance of human affairs; thus it, too, is instructive. Into this unified structure is introduced, by way of digression, the sacrifice of Polyxena. This moving episode, as well as offering a noble example of self-sacrifice, is inherently attractive, enriching the play as a whole by diversifying its emotional demands upon us. That fully justifies its insertion.

IV

We have seen, then, how *Hecuba* fulfils what were, for sixteenth-century critics, the three fundamental requirements of tragedy: variety, atrocity, utility. Our next task must be to trace the decline of the play's reputation in the seventeenth and eighteenth centuries. Interestingly, we will find the same three headings applicable.

First of all, changing ideals of dramatic structure show *Hecuba*'s variety in a less favourable light. Critics of the seventeenth century increasingly insist on restricting the text of a narrative or dramatic work to the realisation of its plot. For example, Heinsius had cited the dispute over the burial of Ajax in Sophocles' play to illustrate the concept of episode: 'It is appropriately related to the subject-matter, but is also outside the subject-matter, and placed there by the poet for the sake of amplification.'[53] For Corneille the same scenes, understood in exactly the same way as 'outside the subject-matter', call into question the structural integrity of the

---

[52] Aristotle's *phobos* was more often rendered 'terror' (e.g. Micyllus in Stiblinus 1562, 672, Pontanus 1597, 108–9) or 'horror' (e.g. Heinsius 1611, 12, 18) than 'fear' (*metus*) in the sixteenth and early seventeenth centuries.

[53] Heinsius 1611, 49–50.

play:[54]

I do not know what pleasure the Athenians derived from the argument
between Menelaus and Teucer over the burial of Ajax, whom Sophocles
caused to die in the fourth act; but I do know that in our own times the
dispute between the same Ajax and Odysseus over the arms of Achilles after
his death wearied the audience, even though it came from a fine hand.

Corneille's point is that a play should end when its action is
complete;[55] the 'dilation' of a play by additional matter not part of
that action cannot, on such a view, be tolerated.

Although Corneille speaks here of the extension of a play beyond
the completion of its action, the same is true, on emergent neoclassical principles, of episodic matter inserted into a play. André
Dacier, for example, will admit 'episodes' only in the more restrictive
sense of incomplete but necessary parts of the action of a play; they
must be 'proper to the Subject, and drawn from the ground of the
Fable; . . . so join'd with the Principal Action, that one is the
necessary Consequence of the other, either truly or probably. And to
conclude, they are in themselves imperfect Members, which do not
make a compleat and finish'd Body; for an Episode, which makes a
Compleat Action, can't be one part of a Principal Action.'[56] For:

When any Action, which does not make a part of a Principal one, is mixed
with the Fable, it may be all left out, without making any Breach, or

---

[54] Corneille 1660, in Barnwell 1965, 12. In a work first published in 1657
d'Aubignac had taken *Ajax* as a paradigm (d'Aubignac 1715, I. 327–40); on the other
hand, Rapin found the argument over the corpse is 'frigid and listless' (Rapin 1674, II.
194). The high standing of this play in the Renaissance is another challenge to
modern evaluative assumptions; indeed, as late as 1741, a critic could waver between
Oedipus and *Ajax* when choosing the best of Sophocles' plays (Hauptmann 1741;
cf. also Stollius 1728, 239 n. 5).

[55] Cf. Corneille 1660, 12: 'When the action is necessarily complete, nothing further
must be added; for when the end-point is reached, the auditor expects nothing more,
and all the rest is tedious.' Cf. 112, from the 'Examen' of *Horace* (1660): 'The unity of
the hero's peril in tragedy determines the unity of action; when he is secure, the piece
is finished.' Racine defends his *Britannicus* in this respect in the first preface (1670, in
Picard 1950, 386); but note also his attack on Rotrou's *Antigone* in the preface to *La
Thébaïde* (1676, ibid. 115).

[56] Dacier 1692, 134; the following quotation is from 151–2. Cf. Dennis 1696, in
Hooker 1939, I. 58: to ensure that episodes do not corrupt unity of action 'they are to
have three Qualities. First, they are to be deriv'd from the first Plan of the Action.
Secondly, They are to have a necessary or probable Dependence one upon another.
Thirdly, Not one of them is to be an Action in itself, but only a necessary Part of an
Action extended by probable Circumstances.'

destroying the Action, which makes the Subject of the Poem, which is thereby made better, since it loses only that which was improper and corrupted its Unity. An Episodick Fable then is, a Fable which has something which is improper, foreign, and superadded, and which may be retrench'd without the Fable's losing anything.

What is required here is not the exclusion of diverse incident from tragedy, but its causal integration into the action. Simplicity and unity were distinct issues. At the same time that some plays were criticised for their lack of unity, Greek tragedy in general was characterised as more simple than modern. This was sometimes meant as praise. Racine, for example, argued that verisimilitude was impaired by the modern practice of cramming too much incident into a short period of time; the ancient taste for simplicity, exemplified by such plays as *Oedipus* and *Ajax*, was artistically superior, although it made correspondingly greater demands on the skills of the dramatist, who had to sustain an audience's interest without the benefit of a constantly varied pattern of events.[57] More often the modern technique was preferred. Although Voltaire found fault with Corneille for introducing the erotic sub-plot of Theseus and Dirce into his *Oedipe*, on the grounds that it was not causally subordinate to—indeed, tended to usurp the place of—the main action, he was sure that Corneille was right in principle to eschew the 'simplicity, or rather barrenness' of Sophocles' plot.[58] Dryden's Neander argues that the use of 'underplots' gives English tragedy a 'variety and copiousness' superior to 'the barrenness of the French plots', given that 'the Unity of Action is sufficiently preserv'd if all the imperfect actions of the Play are conducing to the main design'.[59] Variety was permissible, therefore, and even desirable; but it was no longer permissible to achieve variety by digression from the main action.

A further point should be noted. Unity of action was increasingly interpreted, in the the seventeenth and early eighteenth centuries, in terms of unity of personal focus. It was not, of course, thought to be a sufficient condition of unity that the plot be about 'a single person'; Aristotle's strictures (*Poet.* 1451^a16–22) were too well-known. But it

[57] Racine, preface to Bérénice (1671), Picard 1950, 466. Cf. Barnwell 1982, 133–78.   [58] Voltaire, 'Lettres sur *Oedipe*' (1719), in Moland 1877, II. 29.
[59] Dryden 1668, in Ker 1900, I. 70–1, cf. 40–1; note also Blair 1783, 488–90, preferring modern richness to Greek simplicity.

might still be thought a necessary condition. For Corneille it was not, in fact, an absolute necessity that a play move fear and pity 'by the means of a primary actor'; but it was part of 'the perfection of tragedy'.[60] Dacier, misunderstanding Aristotle's metaphorical use of *prōtagonistein* in *Poet.* 1449[a]17–18 to mean that Aeschylus invented the idea of the principal character, explains:[61]

Aeschylus having added a second Person, 'twas necessary, in order to preserve the unity of the Action in Tragedy, that one of these Persons should have the chief character, and the other should be one of his Retinue, or dependent on him; for if these two Persons had both been Heroes, so equal, that the part of one had not been subordinate to the other, there had been no unity of Action.

This trend was most explicitly formulated by La Motte in the 1720s. He argued that what he called 'unity of interest' is a more fundamental notion in dramatic criticism than unity of action:[62]

If a number of characters have diverse interests in the same event, and if they are all worthy of my entering into their feelings, then there is unity of action, but not unity of interest; for in this case I often lose sight of one to follow the others, and I have hopes and fears (so to speak) on too many sides.

It is true that Voltaire maintained, in his reply to La Motte, the necessity of the traditional unities and the superfluity of unity of interest; but that was because he thought it already entailed by the unity of action:[63]

When one reads our better French tragedies, one always finds that the principal characters have diverse interests; but in every case these diverse interests all relate to that of the principal character, and so there is unity of action. If, on the other hand, all these different interests do not all relate to a principal actor, if there are not lines converging on a common centre, then the interest is double; and so too is what in the theatre is known as the action.

---

[60] Corneille 1660, 36; cf. 83, from the 'Examen' of *Clitandre* (1660): 'As for its construction, that is so disordered that one has difficulty in divining who are the primary actors.'

[61] Dacier 1692, 47 (ch. 4 n. 37). Cf. Dryden 1668, 72–3, and 'The Grounds of Criticism in Tragedy' (1679), in Ker 1900, 216.

[62] A. Houdart de La Motte, 'Discours a l'occasion des Machabées', in Jullien 1859, 455. (This is the preface to his tragedy *Les Machabées*; the play was first published in 1722, and the 'Discours' was published in 1730.)

[63] Voltaire, preface to *Oedipe* (1730), Moland 1877, II. 52.

These new elements in the theory of dramatic unity will, when applied to *Hecuba*, generate the concern over the structure of that play which exercised its critics and commentators in the eighteenth century. But discussion of the play's structure was too closely involved with other considerations to be surveyed in isolation; before we look at this debate, therefore, we must complete our account of its context.

A second element which had been admired in *Hecuba*, and which now began to excite dismay, was its atrocity. Again Corneille provides a useful pointer to changing fashions. In his early *Clitandre* (published 1632) Dorise puts out one of the eyes of her pursuer Pymante in full view of the audience; in *Oedipe* (1659) he has to keep the blinded Oedipus out of sight to spare his audience's sensibilities.[64] In the *Discours* he discusses the necessity of concealing or omitting whatever is so cruel or horrific as to make the audience recoil in disbelief. He confesses to feeling a certain *délicatesse* towards the death of Clytaemnestra at her own son's hands; he suggests that the story would be more tolerable if Orestes, out of a 'respectful tenderness' towards his mother, intended to kill only Aegisthus, but struck her accidentally as she interposed to protect her lover. Corneille's concealment of the blinded Oedipus was imitated by Voltaire and La Motte; and the Orestes myth was reconstructed along the lines of Corneille's proposal by Crébillon and Voltaire.[65] Corneille naturally cites Horace's injunction that Medea should not kill her children in full view of the audience (*AP* 185). Conservative critics could appeal from the precepts of Horace to the practice of the Greek tragedians and of Seneca.[66] But the general trend was against them, and brought the ancient practice into disrepute. Over and over again in the criticism of this period the Greek taste for excessive horror is censured, Oedipus and Orestes being standard examples.[67] Dryden's modernist Eugenius contrasts unfavourably the ancient preference

---

[64] Corneille, 'Examen' of *Oedipe*, in Barnwell 1965, 155.

[65] Corneille, 'Trois Discours', in Barnwell 1965, 47–50. For the mitigation of the matricide by other dramatists and further indications of neoclassical sensibilities, see Mueller 1980, 65–75.

[66] Thus (e.g.) Pontanus 1597, III; Masenius 1661, III. 18.

[67] Dacier 1693, 162, is offended by the matricide in *Electra*; likewise Morvan de Bellegarde 1702, 216, cf. 209, 235; Voltaire, 'Discours sur la tragédie' (1731), in Moland 1877, II. 318, gives a list of examples including Oedipus and Orestes; Racine 1808, VI. 331–571, mentions Oedipus; and so forth.

for 'Lust, Cruelty, Revenge, Ambition, and those bloody actions they
produc'd; which were more capable of raising horrour then compassion in an audience' with the modern use of tenderer passions;
and his Lisideius praises the French for adhering to Horace's opinion:
that is, 'those actions which by reason of their cruelty will cause
aversion in us, or by reason of their impossibility, unbelief, ought
either wholly to be avoided by a poet, or only delivered by narration'.[68] Rapin's double-edged compliment to English tragedy—'the
English have more of Genius for Tragedy than other People, as well
by the Spirit of their Nation which delights in Cruelty, as also by the
Character of their Language which is proper for great Expressions'—
caused an embarrassment to English critics such as Rymer and
Addison for which the counter-claim that French tragedians erred in
the opposite extreme provided only partial relief.[69] Racine went so far
as to argue that there is no need for there to be 'bloodshed and
deaths' in tragedy at all: 'it is enough that the action should be
grand, that the the the actors should be heroic, that the passions should
be stirred, and that all is imbued with that sense of majestic sadness
that constitutes the whole pleasure of tragedy'.[70] Not all would have
concurred; French critics, including Voltaire, agreed that the French
stage was too extreme in its avoidance of bloodshed and horror. But
it is clear, even so, that we are a long way from the tastes of the
sixteenth century.

[68] Dryden 1668, 54, 65. Eugenius' preference for love-scenes reflects a continuing
debate about the suitability of love as an interest in tragedy: see the references in
Hooker's edition of Dennis (1939), I. 438–9. Richard West includes in the 'Epilogue' to
his English adaptation of *Hecuba* (London 1726) ironical self-criticism for his failure to
exploit love-interest: Neoptolemus should have fallen in love with Polyxena; Hecuba
herself 'should have confess'd a Flame'. In his preface he cites Fénelon's attack on love
in tragedy (see Fénelon's 'Lettre sur l'Eloquence écrite à l'Académie Françoise' (1716),
in Fénelon 1718, 341–3).
[69] Rapin 1674, II. 20. Cf. Rymer's preface to the English translation (1674), in
Zimansky 1956, 3–4; in 'A Short View of Tragedy' (1692) he is happier to echo
Rapin's reservations about the dominance of love-interest in French tragedy
(Zimansky 1956, 117). Addison says, in *Spectator* No. 44 (20 April 1711), in Bond
1965, 187: 'But among all our Methods of moving Pity and Terrour, there is none so
absurd and barbarous, and what exposes us to the Contempt and Ridicule of our
Neighbours, than that dreadful butchering of one another which is so very frequent
upon the English stage.' Addison goes on to suggest that the French have gone too far
in concealment: Horace 'never design'd to banish all kinds of Death from the Stage,
but only such as had too much Horrour in them, and which would have a better
Effect upon the Audience when transacted behind the Scenes' (190). Cf. Green 1941,
187–93.   [70] Racine in Picard 1950, 465. Compare Aristotle, *Poet.* ch. 14.

Neoclassical critics were as much concerned with the moral utility of tragedy as their Renaissance predecessors. Corneille may claim, provocatively, in the opening words of his first *Discours* that the sole function of dramatic poetry is to give pleasure; but he goes on to concede that a play composed to give pleasure according to the rules of art cannot fail to be morally instructive. Apart from overt moral comment (to be used sparingly) and catharsis (Corneille follows the deterrent interpretation, but does not think that it really occurs), the ancient poets instructed only through 'the simple depiction of vices and virtues'; modern tragedians have the more potent resource of a morally instructive catastrophe, rewarding virtue and punishing vice. This did not, in Corneille's view, have the status of a rule; but it was a practice favoured by the taste of contemporary audiences, and one which poets would do well to adhere to.[71] There were those, more rigorous than Corneille, for whom the reward of virtue and punishment of vice was a necessary principle of art; and it could be seen as a flaw in ancient tragedy that this 'poetic justice' was not observed.[72] The same point could be turned against the theory, of course; and in this case it proved harder to discredit ancient practice, since many critics persisted in rejecting the whole notion as absurdly contrary to the very spirit of tragedy.

Even Addison, who attacked poetic justice as a 'ridiculous Doctrine', had to acknowledge a distinction between protecting the innocent from suffering—a practice inconsistent with the tragic effects of fear and pity—and ensuring that the wicked do not escape unpunished; to neglect the latter is morally dangerous.[73] But this raises further questions. Deserved suffering is not tragic, because it excites no pity; this was universally agreed.[74] But if the punishment of wickedness is intrinsically untragic, then the moral requirement

[71] Corneille 1660, I, 3–4 and (for catharsis) 32.

[72] Dryden's Eugenius comments on the Greeks' failure to observe poetic justice (1668, 50). For references see Hooker 1939, II. 435–8.

[73] Addison, *Spectator* No. 40 (16 April 1711), in Bond 1965, 168; the distinction is made in No. 548 (28 Nov. 1712), Bond 1965, 465, in response to Dennis' reply to the earlier discussion.

[74] So Corneille 1660, 31, 33; Racine, first preface to *Andromaque* (1668), in Picard 1950, 242; Dryden in Ker 1900, 210; Dennis, 'The Impartial Critick' (1693), in Hooker 1939, 19; and many others. Du Bos comments that in real life we would feel a 'compassion machinale', but believes that our emotions towards imitations are less tyrannical (du Bos 1719, I. 114–15); like Johnson, he insists that the spectator is not subject to 'illusion' in the theatre.

that wickedness be punished in tragedy can hardly be more than conditional: if there is a wicked character, he must be punished. But should there be wicked characters? Since their punishment is not *per se* tragic, one has no reason to make one's characters more wicked than the causality of the play's genuinely tragic misfortunes demand; otherwise one would violate Aristotle's exclusion of unnecessary wickedness (*Poet.* 1454^{a}28–9). But in the best kind of tragedy the misfortune is, according to Aristotle, the consequence of some *hamartia*, a venial error of the primary tragic character; so there is no art in using a wicked adversary figure to bring about the tragic change of fortune. This leaves little scope for the representation of extreme evil in a well-made tragedy; accordingly it could be made a point of complaint against the Greeks that they introduced wicked characters in order to achieve effects of horror, rather than the genuinely tragic emotions of fear and pity.[75] It will follow that Euripides' treatment of Polymestor is faulty. For if Polymestor's fate is meant to be tragic, his wickedness should have been mitigated; and if it is not mitigated, then the sufferings with which the play reaches its climax, being deserved, cannot excite pity, and are therefore not tragic.

V

Before we review critical discussion of Euripides' play in this period, it is worth mentioning that there is some (though limited) scope for illustrating the points made in the previous section from sixteenth- and early seventeenth-century adaptations.

We have remarked, for example, that the structure of *Hecuba* was not, for Renaissance critics, a problem; the developments which turned it into a problem are reflected in adaptations. Seneca had spliced together Euripides' *Hecuba* and *Trojan Women* to produce his own *Trojan Women*, taking one strand from each (Polyxena and Astyanax) and alternating them. Robert Garnier opted for a fuller conflation in his *La Troade* (1578), prefixing (among other innovations) the Cassandra element of Euripides' *Trojan Women* to Seneca's kernel, and placing the Polymestor element of *Hecuba* in the final act.

[75] See Morvan de Bellegarde 1702, 212.

The prefix has no further consequences; the discovery of Polydorus' body is sprung on Hecuba (and the audience) by the Chorus without any kind of preparation after the deaths of Astyanax and Polyxena have been reported by a Messenger and Talthybius respectively. The effect is severely disjointed.

Spangenburg's *Hecuba* (1605) is more nearly a translation of Euripides' play. But (among other changes) he has a first act showing how news of Troy's fall reaches Thrace, and how Polydorus is murdered by Polymestor.[76] His version of *Ajax* is much more elaborately done. This begins with the Trojans plotting against Achilles, and takes us through the ambush in which Achilles dies, the battle over his body (a spectacular affair, with Amazons), the debate over and adjudication of the arms, and Ajax's consequent resolution on revenge; only then does he get to Sophocles' prologue.

A similar expansiveness is found in Benserade's *La Mort d'Achille* (1635). In the opening scenes of this play Priam, Hecuba and Polyxena come to plead with Achilles for the return of Hector's corpse. At first obdurate, Achilles yields to Polyxena; in the subsequent act the Trojans try to exploit his love for her to ensure his neutrality. But he returns to the fighting to avenge an insult on Troilus, and in return for Troilus' body he demands Polyxena; Paris and Deiphobus therefore set a trap and kill him. The last act deals with the aftermath—the dispute over Achilles' arms and the suicide of Ajax. In his preface Benserade records that he had been criticised for adding 'a detached piece' to his plot; he argues that the importance attached to Achilles' arms serves chiefly to reflect credit on his hero, so that the unity of the action is not impaired.[77] The terms of this unconvincing argument, and the very fact that Benserade had to defend his play against attack, suggest that critical standards were changing; it was in fact this play which Corneille mentioned disparagingly as an example of poor dramatic

[76] Medusa, a daughter of Priam, is shipwrecked *en route* to captivity, and comes ashore where Polydorus has been lamenting his long absence from Troy; there is a recognition, and they go to consult Polymestor. Greek sailors then reach shore; there is a comic scene, but at the end they reflect grimly on Medusa's fate if she has taken refuge with Polymestor. Polydorus is next seen asking Polymestor for the treasure, so that he can go to Greece to help his captive countrymen; Polymestor tries to dissuade him but, when he finds that he cannot, kills him. Nothing more is heard of Medusa; the next act begins with Polydorus' ghost. Spangenburg's *Hecuba* can be found in Daehnhardt 1896.

[77] Isaac de Benserade, quoted by Lancaster 1929, II/1. 146.

technique in the passage already quoted in connection with Sophocles' *Ajax*.[78]

Sallebray's *La Troade* (1639) illustrates this new outlook.[79] This builds on Garnier's play of the same title, and has the same diversity of incident; but it achieves a less disjointed effect by bringing the relationship between Agamemnon and Cassandra into the foreground as a continuing thread of plot into which the other incidents—Astyanax, Polyxena and Polymestor—enter as complications. The result is not perfect; Agamemnon's passion is not very interesting and leads nowhere in particular, so that it seems more like an underplot to a series of still unconnected tragic incidents. Nevertheless, the attempt to rework Garnier's rich material shows what the nascent neoclassical taste would like to do to the looser plotting of its forebears.

Changing attitudes to atrocity and wickedness are in evidence also. Garnier's *Les Juifves* (1583) includes a scene modelled on the Polymestor element of *Hecuba*: the defeated Jewish king Sedecie is blinded after seeing his sons killed before his eyes.[80] In Spangenburg's adaptation of *Hecuba* the death of Polyxena and the blinding of Polymestor are seen on stage, as well as being reported. This is unthinkable in Sallebray's play. There we find Polymestor admitting that his punishment was deserved before he dies of his wounds; this served to mitigate in some degree his extreme evil. A *Polymneste* was produced in 1696, by Charles-Claude Genest;[81] it has not survived, but it is seems probable that Polymestor's wickedness was mitigated in some such way.

In West's adaptation, which failed when performed at Drury Lane in 1726, the prologue is replaced by a dialogue between Polymestor and his henchmen, who report seeing the ghost after disposing of the corpse. The role of the Chorus is taken over by a maid, Iphis, and (when she has gone to prepare Polyxena's body) by another maid, Ismene. West is careful to establish in the opening scene that Achilles' tomb is to hand. Polymestor's prophecy is much compressed, the details of Hecuba's transformation and all foreshadowing of Agamemnon's downfall being omitted. Agamemnon enlarges on Polymestor's exile and the justice of his sufferings.[82]

---

[78] See text to n. 54 above.

[79] See Lancaster 1929, II/I. 159; Phillippo and Supple 1995.

[80] See Mueller 1980, 178–9.   [81] Lancaster 1929, IV/I. 401.

[82] I have not been able to consult the pamphlets issued in connection with this production (nos. 4061–2 in Arnott and Robinson 1970).

Thereafter numerous reworkings of the Polyxena story can be found.[83] It may, under the influence of Seneca, be combined with the death of Astyanax, as in J. E. Schlegel's *Die Trojanerinnen* (1745),[84] but the Polymestor story disappears. This reflects the prevailing critical judgement of the play; and to that I now return.

VI

We have remarked on a number of features of the critical context within which discussion of *Hecuba* will develop in the seventeenth and eighteenth centuries. First, conceptions of dramatic unity had changed since the Renaissance; it was now felt that a text should not be elaborated beyond the unified plot, either by extension or by episodic insertion, and the unity of that plot was increasingly felt to be bound up with its unity of personal focus. Secondly, a more delicate sensibility rejected the horror and cruelty which sixteenth-century critics had thought essential to tragedy. Thirdly, there was now little scope for the representation of extreme wickedness in tragedy. We must next see how these ideas were worked out in actual discussion of *Hecuba*. We will find, not surprisingly, that it was the second part of the play which drew most criticism. Initially this criticism was directed not towards questions of unity and connectedness of plot, but towards the unsatisfactory content of the second action; concern about unity emerged in due course.

La Mesnardiere provides a convenient starting point. *Hecuba* is mentioned very frequently in his *Poetique* (1640). He finds the action outstandingly pitiful (47, 77–8)—even excessively so, the queen's sufferings being raised to a pitch which the audience will find morally intolerable (320–3); he examines in detail the ways in which Polyxena's character is designed to increase our feelings of pity (91–4). But he finds the end of the play unsatisfactory. This is not because it lacks connection; he praises the coincidental discovery of Polydorus' body as an instance of 'astonishing verisimilitude', used to excite wonder (40). But the tragedian should reserve the most affecting events for the end of the play (47–8), and the sufferings of Polymestor, being deserved, excite horror, not pity; and horror,

---

[83] See Heinemann 1920, II. 87–101.   [84] Revised from his *Hekuba* of 1737.

although not wholly out of place in tragedy, is not one of the
definitively tragic emotions, and is a less humane and less agreeable
sensation than pity (cf. 18–27). There is also a lapse in decorum in his
soiling the hands of an 'august princess' with his blood (79).[85]

Bellegarde, in 1702, echoes La Mesnardiere's remarks, but in a
significantly modified form. He emphasises that the events of a
tragedy must form a single causally continuous chain, and comments that the last event in the chain should be the most tragic;
but he adds: 'If at the end of a tragedy two grand actions are
exhibited, the soul is divided and is left in a state of uncertainty, not
knowing in which emotions it is to fix itself'—and it is this fault
which, he says, critics (he mentions no names) have found with
Hecuba: Hecuba's lamentations over the body of her son are
exquisitely touching; the play should have ended at that point;
although Polymestor deserves his cruel treatment, the 'sad spectacle'
which it presents diminishes the sorrow evoked by Hecuba's
misfortunes. Though he agrees with La Mesnardiere, therefore,
that the second action is less affecting than the first, this criticism is
now more closely bound up with an objection to the doubling of
the action.[86]

It is somewhat surprising that J. J. Reiske did not take up this
objection in the important attack on the play which he published in
1743. He lists ten points in which it contravenes the rules of art.[87]
These are mostly technical: unity of place is broken; the prologue is

---

[85] Matters of decorum absorb a lot of La Mesnardiere's attention. Elsewhere he
criticises as a fault of style the lack of courtesy which the Greeks show towards
Hecuba (La Mesnardiere 1640, 296–7); only Talthybius treats her generously—an
example of a minor character sharing the elevation appropriate to all tragic
characters (246–7). Agamemnon, by contrast, displays an unkingly timidity, and it
was ungracious of Euripides so to portray him (241). As for Hecuba's reference to
Cassandra in her appeal to the king, that is too disgraceful even for 'the vilest
character in the whole of comedy' (303). Hecuba's rhetoric is also inappropriate
(378–9). While Polymestor's prophecy is a legitimate device in principle, he should
not be able to give so much detail (259).

[86] Morvan de Bellegarde 1702, 213. Bellegarde is extensively, and often confusedly,
dependent on La Mesnardiere. For example, his claim that it is acceptable for a play to
end bloodily if the hero sheds his own, but not if he sheds others', blood (209) is
excessively cryptic unless read with La Mesnardiere's analysis of the three kinds of
'spectacle funeste' (1640, 241–7).

[87] Reiske 1743, 535–51; see also his further reflections on this discussion in the
preface to Reiske 1754. Ammon 1789, lx–lxi, examines Reiske's points briefly and
concludes that all the objections can be 'considerably weakened', even if they cannot
be refuted.

undramatic; the chorus is badly handled; there are various improbabilities and lapses from taste.[88] The most significant objection is the tenth. Reiske says that he cannot understand what effect Euripides was trying to achieve. Aristotle established that in tragedy the sufferings of the wholly innocent revolt, and do not move to pity, while the deserved sufferings of the wholly impious excite joy rather than pity. Yet the first part of Hecuba is devoted to the death of the innocent Polyxena, and the second part to the punishment of the impious Polymestor. Had the actions been placed in the opposite order, the audience would at least have come away with a lively sense of pity;[89] as it is, the emotion is effaced by the play's ending.

Prévost, in his 'Examen' of *Hecuba*, argued that dramatic unity is a necessary virtue, since the division of attention diminishes interest. In a well-made play, everything is directed towards the overcoming of a single obstacle ('Odysseus undertakes to bring back Philoctetes to the siege of Troy; will he succeed?'); but *Hecuba* lacks that 'unity of enterprise', since Hecuba faces two successive challenges, preventing the death of Polyxena and avenging the death of Polydorus. Thus the play has a double action; and this diminishes our interest in it—although there are many compensating beauties of detail.[90]

Prévost's comments were reported by C. D. Beck in 1788.[91] But he takes a different view of the play's structure. Prévost had argued that the double action, quite apart from the intrinsic harm to our attention, prevented Euripides from developing either part of the play adequately; and it was to this that he attributed the faulty characterisation of Polymestor—he is too wicked to excite pity, and in a more extended treatment Euripides would have made him show signs of remorse.[92] Beck suggests that the question of pity for

---

[88] The first of these points is the old problem of the location of Achilles' tomb; this had been extensively discussed. Prologue and Chorus, too, were generally controversial matters.

[89] Remembering, perhaps, Aristotle's qualification 'or better than that, rather than worse' (*Poet.* 1453^{a}16–17).

[90] Prévost 1785, IV. 480–504. Cf. Lawson 1758, 377–8, on the 'unity of design' necessary to oratory: 'The same Remark extends equally to Poesy; and the *Hecuba* of Euripides is in like Manner defective, containing two distinct Actions, faulty thus joined, separately very beautiful. The Rule is indeed founded in Nature. We can contemplate but one Object at once; this engageth our whole Attention; and although its several Appendages and Relations may please by adding an agreeable Variety, yet the Mind still seeketh to dwell on this one, and the chief Object must predominate, must govern, and reign through the whole.'   [91] Beck 1788, 1064.

[92] Prévost 1785, 499–500, 503.

Polymestor is irrelevant; the audience is meant to feel none, since it is Hecuba's misfortunes which should concern them throughout. Considered as an account of Hecuba's sufferings, he thinks, the action is unified, even though it comprises two parts. The proposal would hardly have satisfied the play's critics. It does nothing to justify the unnecessary wickedness of Polymestor or to vindicate the tragic force of his downfall; it therefore leaves a significant part of the play unaccounted for. And it does not show that Hecuba's sufferings constitute a single action, in the traditional sense of a series of causally consequent events. Beck seems, in fact, to be assuming, despite Aristotle's warnings, that an action is single if it is about one person.[93] This at least provides evidence of the tendency to equate unity of action with unity of personal focus.

Beck himself was not satisfied by this defence; four years later he returned to *Hecuba* in a much less compromising mood. The play's plot is double, and the second part weakens our sense of pity, since the fate of an impious man is not pitiful. The play is not really a tragedy; it just contains a great deal of bloodshed. Beck suggests, like Reiske, that the play would have been improved if Polyxena's action had been placed second; but he is much more appreciative of that action than Reiske. Hecuba's character he does not find very moving; she is not consistent; many of her utterances are frigid. To Polyxena he responds much more warmly: 'Polyxena has a manly spirit; her single fate moves us more than Hecuba's manifold calamities.'[94] There is still here an inclination to a single focus; but the romantic figure of Polyxena seems a more appropriate focus. It is presumably no coincidence that this is the period when *Antigone* began to achieve its pre-eminence in critical estimation.[95]

Porson, in 1792, admitted the emotional power of the play, but he was disturbed by the flawed unity of action. Of this flaw, however, he gives a surprising account. It would have been better if the play had ended with the joint funeral of Polyxena and Polydorus. These two deaths he thinks sufficiently closely connected that the one seems to

---

[93] Thus he does not think that *Trojan Women* is unified, attention being divided between the different women (1079).

[94] Beck 1792, 7. This was the only volume published of a projected new edition of Euripides; it contains also *Orestes*, *Phoenissae* and *Medea*. None of the plays of the triad is highly regarded: *Orestes*, too, is not really a tragedy, but 'a play embellished with many tragic passages and remarkable changes of fortune' (74).

[95] See Steiner 1984, 1.

follow on the other in accordance with probability; it is only the
arrival of Polymestor and its sequel that destroy the unity of action.
It destroys the unity of place also; had the episode of Polymestor been
omitted, Euripides could have set the scene in the Troad, but the
attempt to combine two actions in a single plot has led him into
inconsistency.[96]

A. J. E. Pflugk, in his edition of 1829, mounted a vigorous defence
of the play. He states the common objection to the play's double
action, and asks what it amounts to. The principle of unity, he
suggests, does not exclude a plurality of events, but requires only
that they be directed to a single end (*finis*). This is, of course,
conventional; it is precisely the lack of a single end to which
exception is taken. Pflugk's next move is less conventional: the only
reason why a single end is required is that the completion of one
action, when two are combined, exhausts our capacity for emotional
response and leaves us less attentive and less responsive to what
follows. But in *Hecuba*, he argues, this effect is avoided. Sheer
calamity is not tragic; tragedy should excite grief without causing us
to despair. But Polyxena's death is merely calamitous, and if the play
had ended there we would have found it intolerably painful. We
therefore expect and need a second action after the death of Polyxena
to console and restore us.[97]

This unconventional approach moved Hermann to scorn.[98] Pflugk
had suggested that Polymestor's prophecies bring the play to an
appropriately tragic end; we are filled with horror at the thought of
Hecuba, after so much suffering, undergoing so foul a transformation, and of Agamemnon, at the peak of his success, coming to so
miserable an end. But this, Hermann remarks, destroys the consolation which, on Pflugk's reading, the second part of the play is
designed to supply. That reading is in any case absurd; what
consolation is there for the loss of a daughter in avenging the loss of a
son? Moreover Pflugk has misunderstood Polyxena's action. He has
assumed that Hecuba is the principal character in that action; that,
indeed, was Euripides' intention, but as the play stands it is Polyxena,
not Hecuba, who absorbs our attention. So this action does not move
us to despair; rather, we are inspired by Polyxena's courage and

---

[96] Porson 1792, 19–21 = Porson 1814, 18–20.   [97] Pflugk 1829, 4–6.
[98] Hermann 1831, xi–xxvi.

nobility.[99] Hermann allows no mitigation of the play's structural
flaw. The two actions are causally independent, and should therefore
have been treated in separate plays. Polyxena's action, extended to
an appropriate length, would make a fine tragedy. Polymestor's
action is less tractable. Were he to be afflicted with pangs of
conscience and fear of punishment, we would be able to feel some
sympathy. But as his action stands, there is nothing tragic about it at
all. It is impossible to feel fear or pity for him. One may be pleased that
he has suffered as he deserves, but that is not an appropriate emotion
for tragedy; and our pleasure is in any case dispelled by our lack of
sympathy for Hecuba, whose actions, though her case is just, are
revolting. This sort of thing can only affect the crudest kind of
spectator, who is moved to pity, grief and horror only by the sight of
the worst atrocities. One might almost suspect, Hermann concludes,
that Euripides thought tragic what is merely abhorrent.

VII

In an essay on Euripides published in 1796, Friedrich Jacobs was able
to trace the structural faults which exercised his contemporaries in
their reading of *Hecuba* to fundamental traits of Euripidean dramatic
technique. Aeschylus, he says, elevates the spirit by setting the
powers of man's moral nature over against an all-powerful fate;
Sophocles tempers the Aeschylean effect with a sympathy founded
on the character and condition of the tragic agent. Euripidean
tragedy, devoid of elevation, aims only to excite emotion; and it
arouses emotions by the mere accumulation of tragic events. Thus
Euripides' technique is simply to pile one blow on another, regardless
of intrinsic connection, until the play reaches its prescribed length;
this destroys 'the beautiful unity that is art's triumph'. *Hecuba* is
only one instance out of many.[100]

Elsewhere in the same collection of essays, Jacobs' friend J. C. F.
Manso contrasted Greek with modern German tragedy in much

---

[99] Cf. Boeckh 1886, 667: 'This is the tragic action, to the essence of which it is
immaterial whether the outcome is happy or unhappy: indeed, in so far as in each
case a satisfaction of the moral sense must be achieved if the realisation of a higher
Idea is to be manifested in tragedy, then the outcome must be happy, even in the
greatest unhappiness.'

[100] F. Jacobs, 'Euripides', in Dyk and Schaz 1792, v. 360–1, cf. 363–4, 379, 400.

the same way that Jacobs contrasted Euripides and Sophocles. In Greek tragedy, he says, it is often the magnitude of misfortune that is used to excite sympathy, rather than character; this is as true of *Oedipus* as of *Hecuba*.[101] Indeed, Manso finds Greek tragedy more generally deficient in its handling of character; he misses the 'sustained study of the heart and profound reflection' found in modern drama.[102] Hegel, despite his admiration for Greek tragedy, agreed:[103]

At its plastic height in Greece tragedy remains one-sided by making the validity of the substance and necessity of ethical life its essential basis and by leaving undeveloped the individuality of the *dramatis personae* and the depths of their personal life . . . Modern tragedy adopts into its own sphere from the start the principle of subjectivity. Therefore it takes for its proper subject-matter and contents the subjective inner life of the character who is not, as in classical tragedy, a purely individual embodiment of ethical powers.

Hegel was, of course, aware that the subjectivity of modern tragedy runs corresponding risks (123–33). But he still believed this deficiency of Greek tragedy to be the chief reason why it had failed to achieve Shakespeare's universality of appeal; modern audiences 'demand a greater depth of subjective inner life and a breadth of individual characterisation' (1177).

This is an issue which goes to the heart of Hegelian aesthetics. Character—'man in his concrete spirituality and individuality'—is for Hegel 'the proper centre of the ideal artistic representation' (236). Such a view would not have commended itself to the would-be Aristotelians of the Renaissance, nor to their neoclassical successors (recall *Poet.* 1450[a]39–44). But its rationale within Hegel's own system is clear enough. The end or aim of an action may be—and in art, should be—some fundamental principle: 'the essential needs of the human heart, the inherently necessary aims of action, justified and rational in themselves, and precisely therefore the universal, eternal powers of spiritual existence' (220). These are such things as love within the family, political loyalty, religion. But such powers do not set events in motion without human agency; they must be present in individuals as a motivating passion or—to use Hegel's

---

[101] J. C. F. Manso, 'Über einige Verschiedenheiten in dem griechischen und deutschen Trauerspiele', in Dyk and Schaz 1792, II. 269.

[102] Manso in Dyk and Schaz 1792, 260; cf. the discussion of rhetorical vs. naturalistic dialogue (263–4).   [103] Hegel 1975, 1222–3.

term—'pathos' (225–35). This pathos is then one element of the complex, concrete individuality that is character (236–44). In tragedy, more specifically, the action is set in motion by the individual's total but one-sided commitment to some aspect of these universal powers. Because it is one-sided, such a commitment must lead to the infringing of other and equally justified powers, and hence to a conflict in which each party is both justified in itself and, in its violation of the other, guilty. Such conflicts are inevitable under the finite conditions of human existence; but they involve a disruption of the ethical order, which must in the end reassert itself. And because the agent's one-sided commitment is total, such a resolution of the conflict can only mean his (or her) destruction (1197):[104]

> However justified the tragic character, however necessary the tragic collision, the third thing required is the tragic resolution of this conflict. By this means eternal justice is exercised on individuals and their aims in the sense that it restores the substance and unity of ethical life with the downfall of the individual who has disturbed its repose.

Therein lies the tragedy.

It is crucial to this interpretation of tragedy that misfortune and suffering as such are not tragic, however harrowing they may be. Misfortune and suffering may result from contingent external circumstances: 'a truly tragic suffering, on the contrary, is only inflicted on the individual agents as a consequence of their own deed which is both legitimate and, owing to the resulting collision, blameworthy, and for which the whole self is answerable' (1198). It is precisely this complaint that underlies the charge brought by Manso against Greek, and by Jacobs against Euripidean, tragedy: that our sympathy is demanded by great or manifold misfortune as such, by an accumulation of 'tragic' events which, if not grounded in the character and free action of the sufferer, are not genuinely tragic.

The free action of the tragic agent and its interplay with necessity are fundamental to tragedy on the theory just outlined. Hegelian tragedy springs from the exercise of a freedom which, being human and therefore finite, leads to an inevitable and inevitably ruinous collision with the moral order: 'what a man has really to fear is not an external power and oppression by it, but the might of the ethical

---

[104] The whole discussion (1194–9) is important.

order which is one determinant of his free reason and is at the same
time that eternal and inviolable something which he summons up
against himself if he once turns against it' (1198). Hegel develops
this theme in his own way; but it is, in essence, common to the
aestheticians of his time. A. W. Schlegel writes:[105]

Inward liberty and external necessity are the two poles of the tragic
world . . . As the feeling of an internal power of self-determination elevates
the man above the unlimited dominion of impulse and the instincts of
nature, in a word, absolves him from nature's guardianship, so the
necessity, which alongside her he must recognize, is no mere natural
necessity, but one lying beyond the world of sense in the abyss of infinitude;
consequently it exhibits itself as the unfathomable power of Destiny.

The 'inexpressible melancholy' which overpowers us when we
contemplate our aspiration for the infinite 'baffled by the limits of
our finite being' is 'the tragic tone of mind' (45).

Here, too, we can find a parallel to Jacobs' criticism of Euripidean
tragedy, and can see how radical it really is. Aeschylus and
Sophocles both (in distinctive ways) show the tragic agent's
freedom—'the powers of man's moral nature'—confronting the
necessity of fate. Euripides does not; he merely heaps misfortunes on
a passive victim's head (360–1, cf. 366–7). This objection is widely
shared. Schlegel again: in Euripides 'fate is seldom the invisible spirit
of the whole composition, the fundamental thought of the tragic
world . . . Euripides has drawn it down from the region of the infinite;
and with him inevitable necessity not infrequently degenerates into
the caprice of chance. Accordingly he can no longer apply it to its
proper purpose, namely, by contrast with it, to heighten the moral
liberty of man' (113–14). Boeckh, who agrees that tragedy shows
man 'in the struggle of his freedom with the universal power that
confronts him and determines his fate' likewise finds that in Euripides
fate is merely 'the caprice of chance'.[106] This is precisely to question
Euripides' status as a genuine tragedian.

Let us reconsider *Hecuba* in this light. The structural weakness of
the play is agreed: its action is not unified; there are two, causally
independent actions. Hecuba is involved in both; but is she the
principal character in both? In the first part of the play, clearly, she
suffers a blow from without that has no foundation in her character,

---

[105] Schlegel 1808, 67.   [106] Boeckh 1886, 667, 677.

in an exercise of free choice.[107] This is true, in a sense, of Polyxena as well. But her courageous response transforms her death from a blow suffered from without into an assertion of her own character and freedom. So we have a dilemma: if Hecuba is the principal character of the first action, it is not genuinely tragic; if Polyxena (as the dialectic of freedom and necessity would prompt us to conclude), then the play cannot possess unity of personal focus—which compounds the basic structural flaw. As for the second action, we have on the one hand Polymestor; but his motives are wholly squalid. On the other hand we have Hecuba. Her retaliation is an exercise of freedom, and it is in defence of a valid universal principle. But it is compromised as a tragic action by the means used which (for modern, enlightened sentiment) are neither elevated nor elevating— it is vicious and revolting. 'Who', asks Manso, 'does not turn aside when Hecuba gouges out her enemy's eyes?'[108] Schlegel certainly did (137):

The two actions have nothing in common with each other but their connexion with Hecuba. The first half possesses great beauties of that particular kind in which Euripides is pre-eminently successful: pictures of tender youth, female innocence, and noble resignation to an easy death . . . But the second half most revoltingly effaces these soft impressions.

And so, presumably, did Hegel, who found Philoctetes' festering ulcer, and his shrieks of agony, too much to bear (1183). The limits to atrocity are still firmly in place.[109]

One further consideration will complete the picture: the transformation of the concept of tragic utility. Hegel, in his discussion of the aim of art, insists that art is not to be understood instrumentally—as a

---

[107] Cf. Kirkwood 1947, 63 n. 6 (quoted n. 115 below).

[108] Manso in Dyk and Schaz 1792, 268.

[109] J. A. Hartung, who made a vigorous defence of the play, protests: the blinded Polymestor is indeed a foul spectacle; but what of Lear? Modern urbanity is foreign to Greek tragedy, and out of place on the tragic stage (Hartung 1843, i. 522). As for Hecuba's vengeance, it is indeed abhorrent to us; but Greeks had a different view of revenge, and Hecuba can be seen as acting out of *pietas*, as well as anger, in punishing the impious Polymestor (508, 520). The notion that a tragic character must perish in pursuit of some ideal if he or she is to be a worthy object of pity is wholly unfounded (497). Equally absurd is Hermann's objection to the punishment of a villain in tragedy: consider *Macbeth, Choephori, Electra* (530–1). Complaints about the play's double action are idle; all subsequent dramatists have recognised the need to enrich tragedy with a variety of action (508). Hartung's essay is refreshingly iconoclastic, and is rich in acute and stimulating observations; but as a sustained and coherent argument it must rate less highly.

'useful tool' for realising an end independent of art. Art is, in that sense, autonomous (55). It follows that the traditional notion of utility has to be replaced. Art does not exist to instruct us, or to improve us morally. Rather, it is to be understood on a par with religion and philosophy. It is the task of philosophy to supersede the oppositions which underlie the contradictions into which a culture has been led: 'i.e. to show that neither the one alternative in its abstraction, nor the other in the like one-sidedness, possesses truth, but that they are both self-dissolving; that truth lies only in the reconciliation and mediation of both' (54–5). Analogously, 'we must maintain that art's vocation is to unveil the truth in the form of sensuous artistic configuration, to set forth the reconciled opposition just mentioned, and so to have its end and aim in itself, in this very setting forth and unveiling' (55).

Again, the details are Hegel's own and need not be pursued further here. But the basic idea is common. Art—and therefore tragedy—has acquired (in principle, at least) a metaphysical vocation considerably more profound than older didactic approaches had envisaged: it unveils truth.[110] Thus for Boeckh 'the essence of tragedy is the presentation of an action; but the inner kernel of the action, its soul, is a thought, which manifests itself in the action.' As for Hegel, the end of art is to present absolute truth in an individualised and sensuously particularised form, so for Boeckh the action of a work like *Antigone* is the living embodiment of an ethical truth, the symbol of a 'necessary and eternal Idea'.[111] In practice this may not amount to so marked an advance on traditional exegesis as the rather pompous language of the Idealists makes it sound. The ethical idea of *Antigone*, on Boeckh's account, is that moderation is best; that looks suspiciously like the moral commonplaces in which sixteenth-century interpreters had dealt. The most conspicuous change in practice is that, whereas a commentator like Stiblinus would have been happy to list all sorts of different moral lessons, Boeckh insists on the unity of the play's 'idea'; we are, of course, talking here of the *Grundgedanke* familiar also from Boeckh's Pindaric criticism.[112]

---

[110] Manso in Dyk and Schaz 1792, 265 complains that the Greeks did not write tragedy 'from the depths of philosophy'.   [111] Boeckh 1886, 90, 666.

[112] For a discussion of this concept within Boeckh's theory of literary unity, see Heath 1986, 85–98. In Hegel, too, we find the notion of a unified thematic content, paraphrasable (like the *Grundgedanke*), and yet having no poetic validity until realised

Thus the increasingly far-reaching requirements of unity have advanced through unity of action and unity of personal focus to thematic unity. Still, however banal one may find the products of such interpretation, Boeckh insists that without an inner idea, a play is no genuine work of art; it may instruct or amuse, but cannot elevate the spirit.[113] Here, too, we find that we have returned to Jacobs' complaint: Euripides, accumulating 'tragic' events without regard for spiritual elevation, is not only failing to write tragedy: he is failing in the artist's most fundamental obligation.

VIII

I want to turn now to twentieth-century criticism of *Hecuba*. The mass of material, together with the increasing rapidity of methodological change and of change in the premises, both cultural and scholarly, of interpretation, make it difficult to produce a reasonably coherent synoptic account, as we have tried to do for Renaissance, Neoclassical and Idealist criticism. It would be foolish, certainly, to overlook the genuine diversity of recent work on the play. But it is possible, even so, to discern beneath that diversity some broad areas of consensus among most (although not all) recent critics; within these areas differences are largely of detail and emphasis—although, inevitably, those differences tend for us to be more salient than the areas of tacit agreement. I shall now offer a summary of this consensus. Such a summary will of course oversimplify the position of any individual critic; but it will, I hope, be more than a caricature.

It is, I think, universally accepted that the play's plot-structure is problematic, in that it combines two unconnected, or loosely connected, actions—the sacrifice of Polyxena and the avenging of Polydorus. Critics recognise that Euripides has mitigated this lack of connection by adroit transition between the two parts of the play, and in particular by the formal subordination of Polyxena's action to that of Polydorus;[114] but these are primarily technical points. Much

---

in the text (1975, 95–6); yet, as I point out in the article cited above, the idea has antecedents long before Idealist aesthetics.

[113] See the passage quoted in n. 99 above.

[114] Hadley 1894, xiii; Kirkwood 1947, 63; Friedrich 1953, 30–1; Méridier 1956, 175–6; Conacher 1967, 155. Norwood 1948, 216–19 finds the attempted mitigation unsuccessful, and is not alone in thinking the play's climax inadequate.

more critical effort is devoted to the quest for a more fundamental
unity beneath the play's apparent disunity of action. Most commonly
it is the figure of Hecuba herself that is thought to provide that unity.
It is not just that she is present and a focus of attention throughout;
the play may be read as designed specifically to exhibit her character
in its evolving reactions to the pressures placed upon her.[115] In this
way the play's double structure may readily be explained: it allows
us to observe Hecuba under different and escalating pressures. A
refinement of this approach is to argue that the exposition of
Hecuba's character and reactions takes place in part through a
significant contrast with Polyxena's response to her misfortunes;[116]
this view provides a fuller integration of the Polyxena action within
the overall structure of the play, and might be felt to do more justice
to the dramatic dominance of Polyxena within her action.[117] Other
critics have extended the context of relevant contrast to include the
Greeks, even to the point where the play has been described as a
group tragedy rather than the tragedy of Hecuba.[118] On any of these
readings, the play's structure is elucidated by the structure of its
personal focus. The significance of the play, its 'meaning', is then
held to reside in the implications of the character (or characters) thus
illustrated.[119] A consequential step is to shift the locus of unity
explicitly to the thematic level.[120] Formulations of the play's theme

---

[115] Hadley 1894, x–xi ('not a drama of episode, but a drama of character illustrated
by episode'); Perotta 1925, 280–1; Tierney 1946, xviii; Pohlenz 1954, 280; Méridier
1956, 176 ('cette unité n'est pas dans l'action elle-même, mais dans le développement
psychologique du rôle d'Hécube'). Qualified by Kirkwood 1947, 63 n. 6: 'Hecuba's
tragedy is not one of character in the same way as that of Sophocles' Oedipus or
Electra. One does not feel that what happens to Hecuba does so precisely because she is
the person that she is . . . but this does not alter the fact that in this play the person of
Hecuba is still the focus of the tragic idea, and its unifying element.' Unimpressed are
Heberden 1901, 9; Heinemann 1920, 87; Norwood 1948, 217.

[116] See especially Conacher 1967, 154–5 (elaborating Méautis 1944, 109); a related
approach has been developed recently by Nussbaum 1986, 397–421.

[117] But Zürcher 1947, 74, resists the idea that she is dominant.

[118] Arrowsmith 1959, 490, writes: 'The Hecuba is not the tragedy of an individual
but a group tragedy'. Abrahamson 1952, 120–9 had likewise emphasised the group
context (e.g. 129), though his assessment of the principals is harsher; compare
Arrowsmith 1959, 491 with Abrahamson 1952, 122. Kitto 1961, 216–221 also denies
that Hecuba and her character provide the main focus of interest or unity.

[119] Cf. Kirkwood 1947, 63 n. 6 (quoted above, n. 115).

[120] Here Kitto can rejoin the consensus: 'the separate actions are meant to point to
the one over-riding idea . . .' (1961, 221). Similarly Arrowsmith 1959, 490: 'The
Hecuba is not the tragedy of an individual but a group tragedy, its apparently random
and disconnected episodes bound together by a simple overriding idea . . .'.

vary.[121] But there is almost unvaried agreement that what is illustrated is a degeneration of character. Hecuba's moral character is warped and corrupted by extreme misfortune: only thus can one explain a vengeance that is seen by almost all critics as hideously and disproportionately cruel.[122] Indeed, the inhumanity of Hecuba's behaviour is seen as anticipating the literal dehumanisation fore-shadowed in Polymestor's prophecy.[123] This 'moral death'[124] is the tragedy of Hecuba; but it is also our tragedy: it depicts for us the precarious position of mankind's humanity in 'the dark chaos of a godless universe'.[125]

Such, then, is the general course of the mainstream of *Hecuba* criticism in the twentieth century. Where did this consensus come from? It will, I hope, be clear that the consensus is to a large extent the product of the history that we have been tracing.

First of all, we find the structure of the play's action problematic; our sixteenth-century colleagues would not have shared our puzzlement, which is the legacy of concepts of dramatic unity which began to develop only in the seventeenth century. Secondly, we are inclined to turn to the figure of Hecuba to resolve our

---

[121] See e.g. Grube 1941, 214; Kirkwood 1947, followed by Conacher 1967, but criticised by Buxton 1982, 183–4; Nussbaum 1986, 398, 405–6. By contrast Hogan 1972, 254–7, finds both that the character focus is inadequate to offset the weakness of the plot, and that the play is thematically confused and contradictory; he concludes that the play is melodrama, not tragedy. Gellie 1980, 41–4, similarly finds no coherence in the play's ideas, and denies that it is tragic.

[122] Hadley 1894, xii; Heinemann 1920, 87; Grube 1941, 83 ('the vengeance is so horrible that . . . we cannot but withdraw our sympathy from Hecuba'); Méautis 1944, 109; Kirkwood 1947, 67 ('the career of moral degeneration which will culminate in the brutality of her revenge on Polymestor'); Abrahamson 1952, 129; Kitto 1961, 219; Conacher 1967, 161–2; Buxton 1982, 182; Reckford 1985, 113–14, 118 ('she forfeits every shred of decency'); Nussbaum 1986, 408, 414–16. This is forcefully contested by Meridor 1978, 28–35; cf. also Erbse 1984, 56–7. At the end of her article Meridor leaves open the question of the play's tragic status; but Gellie 1980, who follows her view, concludes that the play is not tragic.

[123] Arrowsmith 1959, 490: 'a revenge so hideously brutal that we know, even before Polymestor . . . predicts her transformation . . . that her humanity has been destroyed'; cf. Méautis 1944, 112–15; Abrahamson 1952, 128; Conacher 1967, 163; Buxton 1982, 183; Reckford 1985, 123; Nussbaum 1986, 416. Contra: Meridor 1978, 32, followed by Gellie 1980, 38–41; Pucci 1980, 216–17 n. 39; Erbse 1984, 59.

[124] Conacher 1967, 160–1.

[125] Reckford 1985, 123. The theological implications of the play have in fact been explored less thoroughly than the anthropological implications; but see also Arrowsmith 1959, 492; Hogan 1972, 253; Nussbaum 1986, 402–3. Méautis 1944 is unusual in tracing a just providence in the play's conclusion.

problem; that instinct seems to reflect the demand for unity of personal focus that began to develop at about the same time. More specifically, it is to the character of Hecuba (or of Hecuba and those around her) that we first look for the play's integration; behind this move lies the late eighteenth-century preoccupation with character in drama. Our shift to thematic integration, too, seems to reflect the transformation of traditional concepts of literary utility into the expectation of a unifying theme or 'idea' in tragedy that was taking place at the same time; our sixteenth-century critic, expecting to find at the thematic level an irreducible plurality of instructive moral commonplaces, would have found this strange. It is true that we no longer share the tender dramatic sensibilities of our recent pre-decessors: atrocity has become tolerable once more; but we have inherited their enlightened ethical assumptions, and consequently interpret atrocities differently from sixteenth-century critics. We find it hard to see in Hecuba's revenge justice human or divine.

That an interpretation has been moulded by its history does not, of course, tell us either that it is right or that it is wrong; it is simply inevitable. But it is useful to be reminded of the historical contingency of our own perspective, and worth asking whether we have something to learn from predecessors whose response to the play antedated the trends in critical opinion which have conditioned our own response. In this case I believe that we do have something to learn.

Let us start, once again, with the question of the play's structure. The Renaissance critics assumed both that the locus of a play's unity was its plot, and that the unity imparted by a unified plot was not necessarily impaired if the play contained material digressive from that plot. On these assumptions the construction of *Hecuba* can be explained plausibly and economically. As I suggested earlier, the unified action is the causally consequent series of events concerned with the discovery and avenging of Polydorus' murder. Euripides is careful to establish that series as the primary object of our attention in the opening scene;[126] and the vengeance is the play's climax. The Polyxena action is then structurally subordinate, an episode. It achieves diversity; and it enhances the tragic effect, by diversifying

---

[126] So far, therefore, from being an undramatic dissolution of suspense, as was alleged by eighteenth-century critics such as Reiske (1743, 547–8) or Prévost (1785, 500–1), the prologue has a crucial structural role.

the emotional stimulus which the play provides. But it is not disruptive: it is drawn from closely related material; Polydorus' reference to Polyxena in the prologue ensures a smooth entry into the digression, helping to sustain an illusion of continuity; and it is cunningly made to lead back into the primary action, in that it leads (coincidentally) to the discovery of Polydorus' corpse. This seems wholly unobjectionable—indeed, given the assumptions stated above, laudable.[127]

That in itself affords *prima facie* evidence that those assumptions were built into the tragic aesthetics of the fifth century, out of which *Hecuba* was composed. Corroborative evidence can be found in ancient criticism. Admittedly, the claim that Aristotle would have approved of digression and digressive episode will not meet with universal agreement; but I believe that it is, nevertheless, true. This is, obviously, too large an issue to treat here. It can at least be said with confidence that Aristotle, in his account of dramatic unity, addresses himself solely to the level of plot; he says that, for a tragedy to be unified, it must dramatise a single, causally continuous series of events, but he significantly does not say that it must contain only the events of that series. I believe myself that in his discussion of epic he makes it clear that this restriction is not necessary; but that is disputed. Whatever one makes of Aristotle, it is at least certain that the bulk of critical opinion in antiquity sides with the Renaissance; one could look, for example, at Dionysius of Halicarnassus on Herodotus.[128] As for the favourite integrating devices of modern criticism, personal focus, character and theme, these are never given an integrating role in ancient criticism, at least before the later Neoplatonists, who did develop a theory of thematic integration. Aristotle never hints that theme or focus may unify, or indeed that they should themselves be unified; theme in any case plays a notoriously slender role in Aristotle's account of tragedy. And ancient critics approached the intellectual content of tragedy in much the same spirit of piecemeal didacticism as the critics of the Renaissance.

---

[127] The theory that Polyxena's action is causally integrated, inasmuch as the cumulative effect breaks Hecuba's morale and precipitates her cruelty, seems to me unduly speculative; as Kirkwood says (1947, 62): 'entirely hypothetical, and in a play one should not have to rely on hypothesis to fill so large a lacuna'.

[128] On unity in Aristotle and other ancient critics see Heath 1989; a preliminary discussion in Heath 1987, 98–111 also considers the general question of unity in Greek tragedy.

If, then, theme and focus are not available in ancient literary aesthetics as integrating devices, then (presumably) Aristotle and the sixteenth century were right to concentrate on unity of plot; and, given the structure of *Hecuba*, this reinforces the case for acquiescing in their tolerance of digression.

As for the ethical implications of Hecuba's vengeance, it must be emphasised that the judgements uttered within the play give every encouragement to Renaissance approval, none to modern disapproval, of Hecuba's actions; on this point it suffices to refer to Meridor's treatment of the question,[129] which seems to me the most radical and most persuasive departure from the modern consensus in the recent literature.

If we were to accept that, what would we make of the play's ending? I will offer two possibilities. First, it is possible that Euripides aimed to excite moral outrage and anger against Polymestor and, consequently, an unqualified sense of satisfaction at his deserved downfall. This provides, if not a 'happy ending', at least—as Pflugk suggested—a mitigation of the tragedy: which Euripides promptly and unexpectedly undercuts with Polymestor's prophecies. What Hermann saw as an incoherence in Pflugk's account can be seen as a calculated device on Euripides' part to intensify the tragic effect— partial relief followed by further and unrelieved gloom.[130] This is one interpretation; I do not think that it should be dismissed out of hand. A second possibility is more ambiguous. It will be conceded that we ought to feel satisfaction at Polymestor's fate; but this will certainly be compounded with physical, if not with moral, revulsion; what happens is, on any estimate, horrific. It may be compounded also with a certain pity for Polymestor. This will not be a moral pity; Polymestor's unrelieved nastiness precludes that. But the eighteenth-century critic du Bos spoke aptly of the 'compassion machinale' which we feel when confronted with extreme human suffering, irrespective of desert, in life, and it is arguable (though du Bos himself denied this) that we should give rein to this response in the theatre also.[131] Finally, I do not feel wholly confident, despite what has been said, that Hecuba's actions should be seen as morally unambiguous.

---

[129] Meridor 1978.

[130] Compare *OC*: Oedipus' heroisation is, again, not exactly happy, but it is a mitigation of the tragedy—and is undercut by the foreshadowing of Antigone's death.   [131] See n. 74 above.

There are attractions to a third view of the play's ending, according to which it would bear some resemblance to the end of *Medea*. There conflicting moral and emotional responses are evoked by the nature of Medea's vengeance. I myself feel that in *Medea* the final confrontation is handled in too perfunctory a way for its full potential to be realised; *Hecuba*, read in this way, seems to me the more powerful play. One pointer to this reading is to be found in *Hec.* 886–7: the precedents which Hecuba cites are hardly reassuring.[132] On the other hand Medea's vengeance does, as Hecuba's does not, evoke moral condemnation within the play, and that may justify Stiblinus' treatment of the two as on a different moral footing. I do not feel able to reach any firm conclusion here.

The second of these interpretations presupposes that we can, in drama, feel pity for those who suffer deservedly; this is an un-Aristotelian point of view.[133] But there is reason to suppose that Aristotle is being unduly restrictive; and the sacrifice of Polyxena is surely a powerful argument against his view that the sufferings of the wholly innocent excite a moral outrage that pre-empts the tragic responses of fear and pity.[134] It is true that many recent critics have been outraged by her death; but—significantly—their interest has been less in the audience's emotional response to Polyxena or to Hecuba than in the thematic implications of the Greeks' brutality.[135] This is, I think, a mistake. Odysseus' cynical evasion of his obligation to Hecuba does not endear him to us; but he makes a strong case for

---

[132] See Aesch. *Ch.* 585–61; Méautis 1944, 121 n. 1; Gould 1980, 55.

[133] Cf. esp. *Poet.* 1453[a]5; *Rhet.* 1386[b]26–37; *EE* 1233[b]24–6 (and see e.g. Nussbaum 1986, 384). There is disagreement over the meaning of the term *to philanthrōpon* in the *Poetics*; one view, hesitantly adopted by Halliwell 1986, 219 n. 25, interprets it as the 'humane sympathy' extended even to deserved misfortune; against this see Stinton 1975, 238 n. 2 (=1990, 165 n. 1) and (the fullest discussion) Moles 1984, 325–35.

[134] Polyxena's death can be accommodated by Stinton's more flexible theory, Polyxena's courage providing a 'compensating factor' (1975, 239–41). On Aristotle's position see Heath 1989, 80–8.

[135] e.g. Abrahamson 1952, 123–4; Conacher 1967, 152–4. This involves a firm rejection of Pohlenz's view (1954, 277–84) that Polyxena's sacrifice is in accordance with *nomos* ('law, custom'), unlike the murder of Polydorus. Kirkwood (1947, 64–5) is more cautious: the Greeks think they are following *nomos*, but the play's implicit judgement is adverse, though the play's purposes do not require a firm conclusion to be reached. Grube (1941, 83) concludes that an unambiguous evaluation of the moral problem is impossible. Adkins 1966, 195–200 sees no moral problem, which seems gross; see Hogan 1972 for discussion.

the Greek decision.[136] The sacrifice of a young girl is horrific: the Greeks were divided over it; and it moves pity precisely in those who have resolved to do it (see Neoptolemus' reactions at 566: 'unwilling and willing, out of pity for the maiden'). It is not, then, what one would choose to do. But once Achilles, who has undeniable claims on the Greeks, demands it, there is no morally straightforward way out of the dilemma; and Achilles' power over the winds leaves no way out at all.[137]

It has been urged, as grounds for doubting the real force of Achilles' demand, that the winds do not drop after the sacrifice.[138] But if Achilles refuses to allow the Greek fleet to depart until a sacrifice has been made, it does not follow that the Greeks will be free to depart as soon as the sacrifice has been made—at most, that Achilles will then cease to hinder their departure. There might be other hindrances; adverse winds, after all, are sometimes natural. And it is, at least, a striking coincidence that the winds continue adverse just long enough for Hecuba to execute vengeance (898–901, 1289–90). We know that the gods are at work to secure Polydorus' burial (49–50); is it too much to conjecture that, through the continued adverse weather, they are at work also to secure Polymestor's punishment? Agamemnon's words at 900–1 ('god does not send favourable winds') hint at this. The point is, perhaps, too speculative to be pressed. But it does have the merit of raising the question of the gods' involvement, and of suggesting a view of the play's world rather different from that of the secularised and theologically iconoclastic Euripides widely encountered in recent Euripidean criticism—a view somewhat closer to the Renaissance reading of the play as exhibiting divine justice and the workings of providence.[139]

---

[136] Hartung (1843, 513) observes that the obligation is invented to make Odysseus seem less justified, his arguments being sound (why that invention, if the arguments sufficed to condemn him?). This would give us a complex effect: the audience admires Polyxena, despises Odysseus, and pities Hecuba, but sees the force of necessity and, though appalled, cannot condemn.

[137] See Schlesinger 1937, 67–9; Grube 1941, 214, 217; Steidle 1968, 44 n. 2; Rosivach 1975, 360.

[138] Kitto 1961, 219 n. 2; Buxton 1982, 171 and n. 45; and cf. Hogan 1972, 252.

[139] Conacher 1967, 153, for example, appeals to the 'critical' Euripides as a premise in his discussion of the sacrifice. I do not, of course, want to deny that the Renaissance view was compromised by its tendency to interpret the text in Christian terms; but the preference for post-Christian interpretations that comes somewhat more naturally to

Hecuba refers to the gods in her appeal to Agamemnon. She invokes at once the strength of the gods and of Nomos ('Law'), lest Agamemnon should despise the plea of a powerless slave (798–800), and the critical importance of Nomos in human life, jeopardised if Agamemnon fails to stand to its defence (802–4). There is, indeed, some difficulty in interpreting this passage. Hecuba says: 'the gods are powerful, and so is *nomos*, which rules over them: for it is by *nomos* that we believe in the gods, and live distinguishing right from wrong.' It is clear that Hecuba is invoking *Nomos*, not *nomos*; having referred to the gods, she must reinforce her argument by referring to a power even greater and more fundamental to the order of the universe, not undercut it by asserting that our belief in those gods is merely conventional.[140] There is, however, an equivocation in these lines, which call to mind contemporary notions of *nomos* of a very different order, notions which would indeed have the effect of undercutting Hecuba's argument. It is difficult to believe that Euripides did not produce this effect deliberately; but it does not follow that he is using the equivocation to convey his own extradramatic opinions, or even to convey the falsity of Hecuba's trust within the dramatic world. It is characteristic of Euripides to make his characters formulate traditional ideas in a way that provocatively engages modern associations (for example, *Tro.* 884–8). But the point is (I think) the paradox as such which, like Euripides' rhetorical virtuosity, acts as a stylistic device, giving his writing an arresting surface, but not fundamentally threatening the traditional assumptions underlying his plots.[141]

There should, at any rate, be no denying that the plot of *Hecuba* does rest on traditional assumptions. Hecuba's confidence in the gods

us is no more commendable, and the conventional image of Euripides seems to owe something to a misleading assimilation of the sophistic movement to the Enlightenment.

[140] Contrast Reckford 1985, 120; Nussbaum 1986, 400. Heinimann sees that Hecuba is expressing trust in a divine world order, but thinks that Euripides is conveying his own belief that morality and religion are merely conventional through a deliberate ambiguity (Heinimann 1945, 121–2). Cf. Lanza 1963, 416–39; Conacher 1967, 161 n. 32; Hogan 1972, 247.

[141] This is not, of course, to suggest that Euripides was defending, rather than criticising, traditional theology; I simply do not think that theological debate was the province of the tragedian. What he did, rather, was to take certain traditional ideas for granted as the data of his plot, and exploit them for dramatic, and in particular for emotive, effect. I have discussed the question at greater length in Heath 1987, 49–64.

and Nomos is justified by the event: Polymestor does suffer his deserved punishment. That he suffers at her hands hardly weakens the case; the gods habitually work through human intermediaries in such cases.[142] The circumstances in which that human action become possible are significant. Polymestor could not reasonably have feared exposure, which—if it is not the work of the gods—must be seen as a most implausible coincidence. But coincidence is inartistic; the structure of the plot is superior if these events are interpreted theologically. We do in fact know that Polymestor's exposure came about as a consequence of divine actions (49–50), and although we are not told that his punishment was an aim of those actions, in a Greek tragedy it is scarcely unreasonable to suspect, indeed to assume, that the gods are at work to punish offences against them (cf. 790–7).[143] It is in strictly theological terms that the Chorus interpret Polymestor's fate as he goes unwittingly to meet it (1024–31). The doer suffers (cf. 1085–6); all is Aeschylean.

I believe, in sum, that the sixteenth-century consensus about the play was in many respects preferable to our own consensus: that it offers us a better understanding of the play's structure, and of its ethical and theological assumptions—or (what is arguably not the same thing) an understanding closer to that which Euripides might have expected of his fifth-century audiences. Even if I have carried no conviction in arguing this point, I hope at least to have established that an understanding of the history of a text's interpretation can help us to see more clearly and more critically the assumptions which underlie our own interpretations. If interpretation is to be, as I believe that it should be, a rigorously self-critical exercise, it is essential that we scrutinise the premises and prejudices to which we are prone to be unwittingly, and therefore uncritically, prey. The primary aim of this paper has been to promote that scrutiny.

---

[142] This does not protect the human from guilt (e.g. Clytaemnestra); so this would not help us in making a moral assessment of Hecuba's action.

[143] One might also consider the ease with which Polymestor is persuaded by the most unconvincing reasoning. This was regarded as implausible by Reiske. Cinthio likewise thought the presence of the children and the absence of guards needed explanation, and referred to the folly of the wicked; this point can be made more precisely (though still somewhat speculatively) in terms of *atē*.

12

The Argive Festival of Hera and Euripides' Electra

FROMA I. ZEITLIN

The chorus of peasant girls[1] in the *Electra* makes its entrance to inform Electra of the forthcoming celebration of the Heraia, the festival of Hera at Argos, and to invite her participation (167–74).[2] She declines their invitation, and, in the remainder of the play, no further allusion is made to the festival. Hera herself is only mentioned once, when Electra prays to the goddess, invoking her assistance in the accomplishment of vengeance (674).

The errand of the chorus, at first glance, seems to have no direct relevance to the plot of the play. It is a bold innovation to intrude realistic details of contemporary atmosphere into the archaic world of the myth, but one that is consistent with Euripides' technique of expanding and complicating the unitary concentration on the myth.[3]

---

[1] Denniston 1939, xxxi–xxxii, n. 1, believes that the chorus consists of 'fairly young women, as their excitement about the approaching festivities (167–97) indicates, though 173–4 does not prove they are unmarried. On the other hand, ὦ παῖ, "child" (197) suggests that they are appreciably older than Electra.' But it should be pointed out that at 761 the messenger bringing the report of Aegisthus' death addresses them as ὦ καλλίνικοι παρθένοι Μυκηνίδες, 'maidens of Mycenae, beautiful in triumph' (*kallinikoi parthenoi Mukēnides*).

[2] Textual references to the *Electra* will be cited from Murray 1908.

[3] For example, one has only to compare the Delphi of the *Eumenides* with that of Euripides in the *Ion* to gauge the difference in the Aeschylean and Euripidean approaches to tragic technique. In the austere Delphi of Aeschylus, the locale is briefly outlined with a few significant details at the beginning of the play, and only the characters essential to the drama are present. The Delphi of Euripides is alive with the hustle and bustle of temple servants, gaping sightseers, and local townspeople. The description of routine cult activity and of the aesthetic delights of Delphi's artistic treasures suggests a scene taken from contemporary life. Cf. also the realistic atmosphere of Delphi described in the *Andromache* (1085–1160).

This greater interest in peripheral details, in what one critic has termed the *Umwelt und Masse*,[4] has often led to unfavorable judgments on Euripidean trivializations and irrelevant distractions.[5] But closer attention to the structural elements in his plays and a greater willingness to judge Euripidean tragedy on its own terms rather than in comparison with its predecessors has yielded a deeper awareness of the complexities and ironies which are often manipulated in an oblique and unusual way.[6]

The brief allusion to the festival of Hera in the *Electra* is innovative and surprising, but it is only a minor disturbance in a play which rattles tradition in a host of other and more obvious ways. Hence, the festival is usually ignored in analyses of the play. When it is discussed, it may be dismissed as a gratuitous piece of realism,[7] or treated only as a part of the single scene in which it is mentioned.[8] One study, however, has looked for deeper implications with interesting results.[9]

The best approach towards understanding the part the festivel plays in the *Electra* might be the posing of three questions. First, what is the point of the chorus' errand and what is its impact upon the play? Secondly, what relationship does the celebration of a festival have with the remainder of the play? Finally, why did Euripides specifically choose the well-known festival of Hera? The answers to these three questions will, I believe, illuminate some important aspects of Euripidean technique.

THE ERRAND OF THE CHORUS

The errand of the chorus serves several different functions, for the initial encounter between the chorus and Electra is a skillful deployment of contrasts and ironies. Electra's rags and cropped

---

[4] Diller 1960, 87–105.

[5] See, for example, the remarks of Norwood 1954, 23–51.

[6] For example, see Strohm 1957, Arrowsmith 1964, now abridged and retitled 'Euripides' Theater of Ideas' in E. Segal 1968, 13–33, and Wolff 1965b. Wolff 1965a, 169–94, can justify the inclusion of external details and can demonstrate their dramatic and symbolic functions by the understanding of their resonance in the play. See also Förs 1964, 73–7.

Closer scrutiny of the themes and imagery of choral odes, which had been termed irrelevant or ornamental, encourages an appreciation of their place in the form and meaning of Euripidean drama. See e.g. Parry 1963 and O'Brien 1964, 13–39.

[7] Kitto 1961, 353 n. 1.

[8] e.g. Grube 1941, 301, Stoessel, 1956, 54, O'Brien 1964, 29, Conacher 1967, 205–11.

[9] Kubo 1966 devotes part of his discussion to the chorus as festive celebrants, but he is mainly interested in the costuming of the chorus and its impact on the play.

hair, contrasted with choral references to gold and to fine clothing (191–3), suggest the contrast between poverty and wealth, which is an important theme of the play,[10] and one which will be represented visually in the grand entrance of Clytemnestra into the poor surroundings of Electra's existence.[11] Secondly, the invitation to the festival immediately follows Electra's private lament, thus juxtaposing sorrow with joy and individual isolation with participation in the life of the community.

It has been pointed out more than once that Electra's menial chores and her rags are her own personal choice, which is attributable to 'the perverse pleasure she takes in enlarging upon her poverty',[12] and the significance of this scene is regarded as still another revelation of Electra's less than attractive character. One critic has called her the 'most ostentatious martyr in Greek tragedy', who 'complains of the clothes she must wear, the tasks she must perform, the hut she must live in, and her exclusion from the dances and sacred rites (304–13), but she is not compelled to fetch water: she does it [mainly] to show the gods how insolent Aegisthus is (57–8). She has just refused the chorus' invitation to the festival and their offer of fine clothing.'[13]

In Sophocles, Electra is forbidden to leave the palace even to attend a religious festival (S. *El.* 911–12). In Euripides, Electra's refusal may be self-imposed, but it should not be construed only as a 'subtle and deliberate suggestion of false self-pity'.[14] Her refusal is far more an outward token of her inner isolation, and, in Euripides' fifth-century outlook, that condition often includes isolation from the civic life of the *polis*.

A festival is an occasion of religious worship; it is also a time of joy and celebration, and it is a time when the bonds of social solidarity are strengthened and reaffirmed among the citizens.[15] The association of social, religious, and even political elements is especially true of cult life in Greece; it is particularly evident in the

---

[10] On the ironical manipulation of the theme of wealth see O'Brien 1964, 32–4.

[11] Kubo 1966, 23 suggests that the chorus at its entrance is already garbed in the rich ceremonial dress of the festival. If this hypothesis is correct, then the contrast between the chorus and Electra would also be a visual one, like the later contrast between Clytemnestra and her daughter.

[12] Grube 1941, 301.   [13] O'Brien 1964, 28–9. Cf. Conacher 1967, 205, 211.

[14] O'Brien 1964, 29 n. 26. Denniston 1939, xxxviii, interprets the refusal of Electra as a crude imitation of the Sophoclean motif.

[15] On the religious and sociological aspects of the festival see especially Caillois 1959, 97–127, Eliade 1959, 69–70, 85–91, and Cox 1969, 7–26, with excellent

cult of a divinity who is closely identified with the city itself as its civic symbol, as in the case of the worship of Hera at Argos[16] or of Athena at Athens. Participation, therefore, in a public festival is both an obligation and a cherished privilege for a member of the community.[17]

A true exile, like Iphigenia, longs for home, and her nostalgia is expressed through her lament that she cannot sing the hymn in honor of Hera at Argos (or weave the *peplos* ('robe') for Athena at Athens), she who is ἄγαμος ἄτεκνος ἄπολις ἄφιλος ('unwed, childless, deprived of city, deprived of friends' (*agamos ateknos apolis aphilos*): IT 220–4).[18] On the other hand, Electra's insistence on exclusion from participation in the festival, though her grounds for doing so may seem to us exaggerated and even somewhat untruthful, marks her own sense of exclusion from the experience of public celebration, which conflicts with her private grief, as well as her feeling of alienation from her community, which encompasses both the sphere of human society and the sphere of the divine.

For her condition *is* pitiable. Like her Aeschylean and Sophoclean counterparts, she is orphaned of her father, rejected by her mother, and bereft of her brother. She has already experienced detention in the palace like the Sophoclean Electra (19–24), and her current

bibliography. For Greek cult see especially Kerényi 1962, chs. 2 and 4. Plato well understood the varied functions of the festival and its religious and secular importance in the state (*Laws* 653d, 828–9). See also Morrow 1960, 352–5, 377–8, for remarks on the significance of the festival in Greek life.

[16] On the central role of Hera in Argos, cf. *Il.* 4. 51, 5. 908, A. *Suppl.* 299, Pi. *Nem.* 10. 2. Argos reckoned time by the years of the office of the priestesses of Hera (Thuc. 2. 2; 4. 133). See further in Nilsson 1955, I. 428, Farnell 1896, I. 186–7, Preller-Robert 1894, I. 160–74, Roscher 1886, 2075–7, and Waldstein 1902, I. 4–8.

[17] It was not lawful for a foreigner to sacrifice in the Heraion. See the story of Cleomenes' sacrilege in the temple, Herod. 6. 81.

[18] On several other occasions Euripidean characters allude to festivals, often in a context in which nostalgia for home or patriotic sentiments are expressed. In the *IT* (1096–1105), the chorus wishes it could join those assembled at Delos to celebrate the birth of Artemis in an obvious preference for the Greek Artemis over her Tauric counterpart. But in the *Hecuba* (455–74), the chorus of Trojan girls refers to the festivals of Artemis in Delos and Athena in Athens when they speculate on their eventual place of exile and their fate as captives.

In the *Helen* (1465–74), after Helen and Menelaus depart for the seashore, the chorus prays for a fair voyage so that Helen may dance at home again with the maidens before the temple of Pallas in Sparta or join in the nocturnal revels at the *Hyacinthia*, the chief festival of Sparta.

In the *Heracleidae*, before the messenger's report of the Athenian victory, the chorus prays to Athena for help in battle and reminds her of the nocturnal festival in her honor, which they celebrate with dance, song, and revels (777–83).

situation marks a further stage in maltreatment and abuse. For by her banishment from the palace, she is deprived of family, home, and social status, unlike the other Electras who are still members of the royal household. In her present situation, she could not be expected to lead the dance at the festival, the normal role of royalty at a public celebration (178).[19] Furthermore, cut off from her lawful inheritance, Electra is condemned to a life of poverty in a remote and isolated place far from the community of Argos.[20] To complete her social degradation, she must endure a humiliating misalliance; to her it is a θανάσιμος γάμος ('a marriage much like death' (*thanasimos gamos*): 247).[21] The citizens all know of her shame—they call her 'wretched Electra' (118–19). In her physical and emotional isolation, she also feels a spiritual isolation. She prays to the gods (135–9), but they do not heed her prayers and do not send her deliverance (198–200).

Her one defense in this situation is to maintain that marriage in name only, a fact which the farmer has already revealed in the prologue (43–53). But Euripides' ironical innovation in creating a married Electra, while, at the same time, preserving her traditional status of virgin, makes her a still greater social misfit, and only increases her bitterness and frustration. The choral invitation alludes to maidens summoned to dance at the festival (174), a painful reminder of her true condition and still another indication of the awkwardness of her ambiguous status.[22]

This marriage that is no marriage deprives her of the gratifications of sex and children; it deprives her of her proper social status and of

---

[19] *Oud' histasa chorous* (178). Denniston ad loc. rightly interprets this phrase as an allusion to her royal prerogative. Cf. also Hecuba's recollection of the role she played at the Trojan festivals (*Tro.* 147–52).

[20] The place is so remote that a mountaineer must bring the heralds' proclamation of the festival to the peasant women (169–74). In 297–9, the chorus claims that they live so far away that they have not even heard of the evils in the city.

Her poverty is not an illusion either. She must borrow finery from the women if she is to attend the festival (in true Cinderella fashion). In order to feed her guests on a suitable repast she must send to the Old Man for provisions (408–14; cf. 424–5).

[21] *Thanasimos gamos* is a potent phrase. (1) The marriage is a marriage of death because it is unconsummated and produces no issue. (2) Her marriage to the farmer is a substitute for the death Aegisthus had originally planned for her (27–30). (3) By her marriage she is 'dead' to her family, to her city, and to herself. Cf. 1092–3.

[22] Note Electra's subtle change of παρθενικαί, 'maidens' to νύμφαι 'brides' (179), an indication of her sensitivity on this point. Cf. 311: ἀναίνομαι γυναῖκας οὖσα παρθένος, 'I cannot talk to women since I am a maiden' (*anainomai gunaikas ousa parthenos*).

her normal role in the family and the community. It has made her
virtually an exile, for like Iphigenia, she too is ἄγαμος ἄτεκνος
ἄπολις ἄφιλος, 'unwed, childless, deprived of city, deprived of
friends'.[23] Her antagonism towards Clytemnestra is thereby intensified—towards the mother who abandoned her daughter by sanction-
ing the match, towards the woman, who lives, a queen, in royal
splendor, and whose marriage to Aegisthus, unlike Electra's own, is
not a fiction.[24] This is the note, a recurrent motif of the play, on
which Electra ends the scene:

$$\mu\acute{a}\tau\eta\rho\ \delta'\ \acute{e}\nu\ \lambda\acute{e}\kappa\tau\rho\text{ois}\ \phi\text{oví}\text{ois}$$
$$\ddot{a}\lambda\lambda\omega\ \sigma\acute{v}\gamma\gamma\alpha\mu\text{os}\ \text{oἰ}\kappa\epsilon\hat{i} \qquad (211-12)$$

My mother dwells united to another (sungamos) upon a bed stained with
murder.

In this context, it should also be kept in mind that Hera is pre-
eminently the goddess of marriage and of stable family life.[25]

Thus, everything the festival of Hera at Argos represents—the
social celebration on a religious occasion in honor of the goddess
who is the tutelary divinity of Argos, as well as the guardian of family
morality and well-being—seems wholly inappropriate to Electra's
sensibilities.

In short, Electra's refusal to join the festivities focuses and defines
the objective facts of her situation and also the subjective expression
of her emotions. But the confrontation between the chorus and

---

[23] Electra, in fact, calls herself an exile (209). On the importance of the theme of
exile in Euripides, see the excellent discussion of Wolff 1965b, 141–51.

There is an unfortunate tendency on the part of commentators to concentrate on
castigating Electra's self-pity and bitterness, while minimizing the real hardships she
must endure, both physically and spiritually. Euripides has created an intolerable
situation for her in every respect. Conacher 1967, 203 comments on Euripides'
intention to 'present the sort of Electra, who . . . will seek to slay her mother. Thus
Euripides presents, in its required setting, a deft and damning portrait of a
matricidal woman in action in which nearly every detail contributes to the required
characterization and situation, or else to the "realistic" . . . atmosphere, both social
and psychological, in which such a grim conception can be realized.' But his dramatic
analysis of the play focuses on her unpleasant personality and neglects any sympathy
for her situation, which the objective statements of the farmer and the reaction of the
chorus would justify. Steidle 1968, in his essay on this play, 63–90, seems to be the
only critic who follows through the full implications of Electra's situation.
[24] On Electra's hatred of her mother as her prime motivation see e.g. Rivier
1944, 137.
[25] Both the theme of marriage and the function of Hera as protectress of the
sanctity of marriage will be explored more fully below.

Electra over the issue of the festival is also organically integrated into the structure, issues, and motifs of the play. Several structural elements of the scene are proleptic of later developments, and three major themes which dominate the *Electra* are set forth—marriage and family, gold and wealth, sacrifice and celebration, and the last proves to encompass the first two.

THE MOTIF OF RITUAL—SACRIFICE AND CELEBRATION

The allusion to the festival of Hera is not an isolated reference to a religious occasion. On the contrary, the play is richly endowed with ritual activity and terminology. In their invitation to the festival, the chorus informs Electra of two facts. The Argives have proclaimed the forthcoming sacrifice to be performed in honor of Hera, and the maidens are gathering to participate in the festive dance. These two aspects of the festival—cult sacrifice and rites of celebration—together comprise the motif of ritual which pervades the play, unifies past and present, and determines the dramatic and imagistic structure of the play.

The theme of sacrifice emerges from the past in the actual sacrifice of Iphigenia at Aulis, and is hinted at in the murder of Agamemnon, which is expressed in language resonant of sacrificial death (123, 200). Three acts are performed in the play itself—the sacrifice of the lamb on Agamemnon's tomb in Orestes' funerary ritual (92; cf. 281), the murder of Aegisthus at the sacrifice in honor of the Nymphs (774–843), and the slaying of Clytemnestra as a sacrifice at the performance of a fictitious birth ritual of purification (1141–4, 1222–3, 1294).

The theme of celebration is best exemplified by the choral description of the golden lamb and the festivities of Argos, but it extends also to the celebrations of military and athletic victory, as well as to family celebrations in honor of the Nymphs and on the occasion of birth.[26]

---

[26] The birth ritual referred to in the play is not a ritual on behalf of the baby, but the ritual on behalf of the new mother. Electra sends word to her mother that she has delivered a male child (652). She specifies that it is ten days since she has given birth. The phrase is curious: δέχ' ἡλίους ἐν οἷσιν ἁγνεύει λεχώ, 'it is ten days since the parturient keeps pure' (654). It alludes to the natural pollution of the mother which lasts for ten days after birth. See Moulinier, 1952, 68. He explains ἁγνεύει ('keeps

With the exception of the funerary ritual performed by Orestes at
the beginning of the play and later by the Old Man, the other rituals
are either irregular or distorted or the mood of celebration itself
is displaced or converted into its opposite. The festival of Hera, in one
sense, stands as an objective yardstick of ritual regularity and normal
cult activity against which the other rituals of the play, when
measured, more clearly reveal their corrupted quality.

Rivier points out the contrast between the tranquil pastoral charm
of the setting and the violence of hatred and bloodshed, between
simple and unspoiled nature and the poisoned world of private
emotions.[27] A similar contrast exists between the formal festival of
Hera in which the chorus naturally delights and the flawed rituals of
the house of Atreus. Yet the same chorus, which had come to invite
Electra to the festival, maintains its festive role through the rich
ceremonial language and substance of its odes, but its role is now
adapted to one of observation of and commentary upon the dramatic
events. The extension of the celebratory tone to the unhealthy ritual
milieu of the play results in a curious incongruity between the high-
flown lyrics and the sordid behavior of the characters, an incongruity
which defines and intensifies Euripides' ironical treatment of the
myth. Only after the murder of Clytemnestra does the chorus shed its
mood of celebration and turn instead to ritual lament.

pure') as used in the negative sense—to refrain from performing an act which would
cause pollution. For ten days until the sacrifice and ablutions which would purify her,
the woman must avoid contacts that would increase her own pollution or
communicate it to others. During that time she is taboo and must keep herself apart
and refrain from entering any sacred or public place.

When Clytemnestra comes in response to her daughter's announcement of the
birth, this purification ritual is made more explicit. 'You have heard of my
λοχεύματα (locheumata, 'childbirth'). Make the sacrifice for me on the tenth day after
birth as ritual law requires. I am a new mother and do not know the procedure'
(1124–7). Commentators have assumed that the reference is to the ritual at which the
baby is named (e.g. Denniston 1939, 131–2). But the child is only mentioned in
connection with the specified time that has elapsed since his birth. In any case, it is
the father who names the child, not the grandmother and certainly not the midwife
(cf. Ion 661–3). The mother might be present at her daughter's confinement, and, like
the midwife, might officiate at the purification ceremony. In the absence of a midwife,
the mother is a likely substitute. On rituals after childbirth see Nilsson 1955, 1. 95,
Moulinier 1952, 63–4, 66–70, and Deubner 1952, 374–7, and Samter 1901, 59–62.
The naming of the child and the appropriate festivities took place on the same day as
the purification of the mother, so that it would be considered a day of celebration.

[27] Rivier 1944, 135–6.

The ritual that most closely parallels the present festival of Hera is the festival which once welcomed the entrance of the golden lamb into Argos. Both are public occasions celebrated by all the citizens of Argos. In each a herald announces the call to festivities (169–71; 706–7).[28] In each the luxury of gold and wealth is underlined, and in each there are dances and sacrifices. The chorus sings the ode describing the event of the past (699–745). The golden lamb was brought to Mycenae as a marvelous sight to behold. The chorus danced to celebrate the house of Atreus. The altars of hammered gold were spread with offerings, the fire of sacrifice gleamed in the city, and the sound of flutes was heard.

But it was then that the mood of celebration turned sour, when Thyestes stole the lamb through the seduction of his brother's wife, Aerope, thus violating the ties of kinship and marriage. It was then that Zeus changed the stars in their course and reversed the direction of the sun, in an inversion of the natural order in the universe, which, despite the skeptical attitude of the chorus towards the portent, reflects the horror at the inversion of the natural order in human relationships.

This choral ode is far from an ornamental intrusion into the play. The festival of the golden lamb is precisely suited to its context. It precedes the murder of Aegisthus at another ritual of celebration— the sacrifice in honor of the Nymphs. Thyestes' offense parallels the offense of his son Aegisthus. Each seduced the king's wife and usurped the throne.

The lamb itself has a schematic importance in the play. The golden lamb is the emblem of the wealth of the house, now enjoyed by Aegisthus and Clytemnestra as their royal prerogative, while Electra suffers in poverty and the tomb of Agamemnon is dishonored and deprived of offerings (314–31). Yet the lamb itself was the symbol of kingship for Argos in the past, and it is still the symbol of kingship in the present, both as Orestes' sacrifice on Agamemnon's tomb, the token by which he is recognized and regains his royal identity, and as the lamb for feasting brought by the Old Man.[29]

All these themes—gold, celebration, and family relationships— meet in the implications of the ode on the golden lamb as they did in

---

[28] This has been pointed out by Sheppard 1918, 140.
[29] On this point, see Kubo 1966, 20.

the first appearance of the chorus and their invitation to the festival
of Hera. In that earlier scene, the chorus chided Electra for her refusal
to participate in the celebration. The goddess is mighty (190). Does
Electra think that her tears rather than her worship of the gods will
vanquish her enemies? Not by groans, but by prayers to the gods in
reverence will she win the day of deliverance (193–7). At the end
of the ode on the golden lamb, the chorus speaks of the value of
terrifying myths, such as the cosmic reaction to Thyestes' crime, as a
stimulus to the worship of the gods (743–5), but Clytemnestra did not
remember the lesson of the myth. She committed adultery and slew
her husband, thus perpetuating the disorder of the house. The act
of matricide, a still more unnatural crime than the first two, which
Orestes and Electra are presently to execute, will demonstrate that
they too have failed to understand the import of the myth.[30]

In the two choral odes which precede and follow the stasimon on
the golden lamb, the women of the chorus direct their festive impulse
as celebrants of military and athletic victory.

The theme of ritual connected with victory is established at the
beginning of the play. Agamemnon is portrayed as a victorious
warrior, and the murderous welcome he receives is contrasted with
the celebration ordinarily accorded a military victor. First, the farmer
in the prologue begins with the history of Agamemnon who sailed
across to Troy. He juxtaposes the king's return as a conquering hero,
who set up trophies of the spoils of Troy (σκῦλα, skula) in the
temples, to his reception in the house, where he was slain in ambush
by his wife and her lover (6–10).[31] Electra, in her lament, makes a
similar complaint. Her father died in the treacherous toils of the net,
in the bath by the gash of the bitter axe, and bitter was his return
from Troy. His wife did not receive him with the victor's chaplet nor
with the customary garlands (157–66).[32]

The shield ode the chorus sings between the entrance of Orestes
and the reunion of brother and sister celebrates the recent heroic past
at Troy in the victory of Achilles, thereby linking the events of
Agamemnon's past with the coming events at Argos. O'Brien has

[30] Conacher 1967 suggests that 'the mythological expression of horror at Thyestes'
unnatural deed anticipates, perhaps, the horror of the coming matricide . . .' (212).
[31] On rituals following military victory see Rouse 1902, 95–148, and Woelcke
1911.   [32] For *mitrai* as victor's chaplets, cf. Pi. *Ol.* 9. 184, *Is.* 5. 62.

demonstrated the relevance of the ode to the context and interpretation of the play in its dark themes of violence, terror, death, and
the Gorgon.[33] But the ode also maintains the tone of celebration,
especially through gold imagery and allusions to the dance. The first
is reflected in the golden armor (444) and in the radiance of the sun
depicted in the center of the shield (464–5). The second is poetically
transferred to the ships winging their way to Troy accompanied by
dolphins and Nereids (434–7) and to the heavenly bands of stars,
which encircle the sun on the shield (467–8). The ode is also
thematically relevant to the play in its connection with the motif
of heroic victory. For the role Orestes is to play in this drama is also
that of the heroic victor who is to win both military and athletic
palms.[34]

The chorus applies the image of victory to Orestes (591) in the little
ode of celebration which follows the recognition of Orestes and which
also blends elements from its first two lyrics. They sing of the bright
day of Orestes' return which has shone at last in a repetition of the
sun that gleamed in the center of the shield (cf. 586 and 464). The
opening words (ἔμολες ἔμολες ὦ χρόνια ἀμέρα, 'you have come,
you have come, our long-awaited day': 585) recalls the parodos in
which they spoke of the man, the Mycenean mountaineer, who has
come with the news of the festival:

> ἔμολέ τις ἔμολεν γαλακτοπότας ἀνὴρ
> Μυκηναῖος ὀρειβάτας   (169–70)

He has come, some man has come, raised on milk, a Mycenean mountaineer.

The four sets of repeated words,[35] the triple reiteration of *theos*,
and the allusion to prayer (592) convey a hymnal quality with which
the chorus greets Orestes.

Orestes has come to win the crown for slaying Aegisthus (614;
cf. 581, 591, 675). When he prays to Zeus before his undertaking of
the murder of Aegisthus, he calls upon Zeus, first as *Patrōos* ('of the
Fathers') and then as *Tropaios* ('giver of victory'), to be the router of

---

[33] O'Brien 1964, 13–25.

[34] Sheppard 1918, 140 suggests that 'what looks like a celebration of Agamemnon
and Achilles is, in effect, a suggestion of the traditional, romantic, heroic view of
Orestes.'

[35] ἔμολες ἔμολες 585; θεὸς αὖ θεός 590; ἄνεχε χέρας ἄνεχε λόγον 592; τύχᾳ
σοι τύχᾳ 594 ('you have come, you have come' 585; 'a god, a god' 590; 'lift up your
hands, lift up your voice' 592; 'with fortune, with fortune' 594).

his foe (671; cf. 469). Electra would gladly die if she were to hear first the news that Aegisthus had taken a fatal fall in the wrestling match (685–7; cf. 751). If the good news comes, all the house would raise up the victory *ololygmos* ('song of triumph', 691). Orestes' disguise is that of a Thessalian stranger, who is on his way to sacrifice to Zeus at Olympia (781–2; cf. 862–3). In the aftermath of Aegisthus' murder, the king's retinue recognizes Orestes. They crown his head with garlands and raise up the victory battle cry in their joy (ἀλαλάζοντες, *alalazontes*: 855; cf. 843).

The messenger enters with news of the victory and addresses the girls of the chorus as *kallinikoi* maidens of Mycenae. Orestes has won and Aegisthus lies in the dust. One must give thanks to the gods (761–4). The chorus responds with a formal epinician song and calls for dancing and crowning with garlands. Now Electra, who had earlier refused to participate in the choral dance (178–80), willingly joins in the celebration with the members of the chorus. She raises up the victory song for her brother, the triumphant hero, and would crown his head (872, 882; cf. 887).[36] She draws father and son together as victors:

> ὦ καλλίνικε πατρὸς ἐκ νικηφόρου
> γεγώς Ὀρέστα, τῆς ὑπ᾽ Ἰλίῳ μάχης   (880–1)

Oh glorious victor (*kallinike*) born of a victorious father (*nikēphorou patros*) at the battle under the walls of Troy—Orestes.

She contrasts the trivial feat of an athletic contest with the feat of slaying the enemy Aegisthus in an act of war (883–5; cf. 862–3, 386–90), but later in her speech over Aegisthus' body, she repeats the athletic metaphor (953–6).

The outcome of the second contest (987) will no longer be a cause for rejoicing, but there is an echo of the theme of military victory at Clytemnestra's entrance. She comes on stage in sumptuous luxury to confront her ragged daughter. The temples are adorned with the spoils of Troy (σκῦλα, *skula*), but her share of the booty is the Phrygian slaves who accompany her, a small recompense for the daughter she lost at Aulis (1000–3). It is a brilliant entrance,

---

[36] Kubo 1966, 23–4 proposes, that 'if the scene is to be visualized in the way its epirrhematic form seems to require, the Heraean crowns are transferred from the chorus to Electra, and then from her to Orestes and Pylades' to be used for crowning the victors.

reminiscent of Agamemnon's fateful entrance in Aeschylus.[37] Her doom will also match his, for she too will be lured into the house to meet her death at a sacrifice on a joyous occasion.[38] The verbal echo from the *Agamemnon*, the repetition of the *skula* from the prologue's description of the king's death, and the choral ode whose subject is the murder of Agamemnon (1147–63) strengthen the parallels between the two events so that the opprobrium of the first murder is transferred to the second.[39]

But apart from this resemblance to the fate of Agamemnon, Clytemnestra's entrance is very similar to the initial entrance of the chorus. The luxury of gold and sumptuous dress is again contrasted with the ragged poverty of Electra.[40] The confrontation between mother and daughter takes up the themes exposed in the earlier meeting between the chorus and Electra, but in a more intense and more personal way. Moreover, the chorus had invited Electra to participate in a religious celebration; now she invites her mother to perform a ritual for her. Finally, the chorus, at the entrance of Clytemnestra, once again establishes the ceremonial milieu. For their address to the queen is phrased in the language of the cult hymn which is sung at a festival.[41]

The two aspects of the ritual motif—celebration and sacrifice— meet again as they did in the ode on the golden lamb which was followed by the sacrifice in honor of the Nymphs. In addition, a flawed ritual of the past is repeated in a present act of distorted sacrifice. For the discussion between Clytemnestra and her daughter, which precedes the queen's murder, focuses on the issue of Iphigenia's sacrifice at Aulis.[42]

[37] For example, in Aeschylus, Agamemnon enters with Phrygian captives as does Clytemnestra in this play. He receives a royal welcome as Clytemnestra does here (988–97). As in Aeschylus, Clytemnestra utters the command to step down from the wagon (cf. A. *Ag.* 906, 1039, and E. *El.* 998).

[38] On the development of the theme of sacrifice in Aeschylus, see Zeitlin 1965, 463– 508, and 1966, 645–53.   [39] On this point, see O'Brien 1964, 31 n. 31.

[40] Rivier 1944, 138 notes the contrast between Clytemnestra and Electra, but not its connection with the first entrance of the chorus.

[41] This point will be developed below.

[42] It is interesting to note that in Sophocles' *Electra*, the confrontation between mother and daughter also centers about the issue of Iphigenia's sacrifice at Aulis (S. *El.* 516–609). Discussion of a ritual of the past also precedes the performance of another ritual, for Electra has interrupted her mother's ritual preparations for an apotropaic sacrifice to Apollo Lykeios. The scene ends with Clytemnestra's request to

The play opened with funerary sacrifice to Agamemnon by Orestes and the lament of Electra. The play closes with the mother's death at a birth ritual and with lamentations. Now Electra can truly ask in what choral dance can she participate (1198). The dance she refused of her own free will is now closed to her; the self-imposed exile from Argos has become a reality (1311–15). Orestes begs her to embrace him and to raise up the dirge over him as one does for a dead man at his tomb (1325–6). The last celebration has turned to lamentation, and the chorus, who from its entrance, had set and maintained the festive mood, has participated in rituals which are far removed in spirit and execution from those of the regular festival of Hera. Celebration has proved an illusion and ritual sacrifice has become murder. Grief is the proper mood and the ritual of lament the proper ceremony.

THE FESTIVAL OF HERA AND THE *ELECTRA*

The chorus invites Electra to a festival and continues to perform a ceremonial function throughout the play, but this role need not be anchored to any specific festival. The question might still be asked: what is the relevance of the Argive festival of Hera to the play?

Electra to allow her to begin her sacrifice (630–1) to which Electra consents (632). But the whole import of the scene is different. Clytemnestra's defiant sacrifice and prayer to Apollo Lykeios for protection reveals her as a brazen woman with no outward sense of compassion or guilt. (See Jones 1962, 153, for an excellent analysis of Clytemnestra's ritual behavior in the Sophoclean play.) Clytemnestra's sacrifice is ironically doomed to failure. The temple of Apollo Lykeios is pointed out to Orestes as the first landmark of Argos by the Paedagogus at the opening of the play (6–7). It is Delphian Apollo who has sent Orestes upon his mission. The new entrance of the Paedagogus is an even finer ironic stroke. He comes with the false news of Orestes' death, an apparently immediate answer to the queen's prayer, but it will prove her destruction. Finally, just before the queen's murder, Electra prays to the same Apollo Lykeios (1376–83) for assistance in the act, and it is *her* prayer that is heeded.

In Euripides, the irony is of a different order. Electra, not her mother, initiates the ritual request, ostensibly for herself on the basis of their relationship, but the request is spurious. The effect of the scene, which telescopes the whole history of the house of Agamemnon—the sacrifice of Iphigenia, the echoes of the Aeschylean murder of Agamemnon, and the coming sacrificial death of Clytemnestra—suggests, not a progress towards justice, but a repetition of crime, guilt, and remorse.

The details of the *agōn* between mother and daughter will be further analyzed below.

Despite the scantiness of information about the details of the Heraia, an examination of the evidence we have suggests that Euripides seems to have used the events of the actual festival as an ironic counterpoint to the *mythos* of the play.

In addition to the athletic competitions normally staged at festivals and the more unusual martial processions of armed men,[43] an outstanding event of the Heraia was a special shield contest, the *agōn chalkeios*. The festival itself was sometimes called the Aspis ('Shield'), and the winner of the contest was proverbial for a man who received unusual honors.[44] In the light of the contest, the ode on the shield of Achilles assumes a still greater significance and serves as a relevant transition between the Heraia parodos and the central events of the play. Moreover, the prominence of the theme of military and athletic victory is thereby equally justifiable.

The chorus, in singing the shield ode and an epinician song to the victor, have recreated the circumstances of the Heraia, but in an entirely new context. For the epinician song is sung, not to celebrate the conclusion of an athletic contest, but to celebrate the accomplishment of murder, and the murder is one which has taken place at a sacrifice to which the author of the act was invited as a

---

[43] Aen. *Tact.* I. 17. 2: 'A public festival of the Argives took place outside the city, and the citizens formed an armed procession of men of military age.' LeBas-Foucart, *Inscr. du Pélop.* 112a, ἅρμα πολεμιστήριον ('war chariot', *harma polemistērion*).

[44] For a general discussion of the Heraia, see Farnell 1896, I. 186–9, Roscher 1886, I. 2075–7, P. Stengel, *RE*, Heraia s.v., 8. 416–18, Nilsson 1906, 42–5. For the textual evidence see Farnell 1896, I. 249–50.

The festival of Hera in Argos was called the Aspis: *CIG* 234, 1068, 2810, 3208; *IG* 3. 116, 129. For the *agōn chalkeios*, Hesychius s.v. Cf. Pi. *Nem.* 10. 22–3 and Schol. Pi. *Ol.* 7. 152: 'And in Argos a prize of bronze is given to the victor . . . and the prize is a brazen shield: the garlands are made of myrtle.'

The proverb is cited in Zenobius, *Paroem.* 6. 52: 'He is honoured just like a man who has won the shield in Argos' and 2. 3: 'you are worthy of the shield in Argos'.

Another interesting point which might connect the shield ode to the Heraia is that late tradition makes the famous Heraion (where the festival was celebrated) the place where Agamemnon was chosen leader of the expedition to Troy and the point of departure for the Greek host (Dictys Cretens. *Bell. Tro.* I. 16). It is thought that the metopes of the New Temple in the Heraion contained scenes of the Capture of Troy, while the western pedimental sculptures represented the departure of the heroes. See Paus. 2. 17. 3 and the discussion of Waldstein 1902, 146–53. The old temple accidentally burned in 423 BC, and the date for the completion of the new temple is set either around 416 or 410, according to Amandry 1952, 270–4. The date of Euripides' *Electra* is equally vexed (see Conacher's summary of the bibliography on the problem, 1967, 202–3 n. 9). The most that can be said is that the dates of the temple and of the *Electra* can overlap.

guest.[45] It is no less disturbing than the dance of Aegisthus on Agamemnon's grave and his gloating taunts (323–31), which are matched by Electra's speech over the corpse of the slain Aegisthus (907–56).

Secondly, the Heraia was also called the *Hekatombeia* because of the large number of sacrifices offered during the celebration.[46] When the chorus enter, they tell Electra that the Argives now proclaim the forthcoming sacrifice in honor of the goddess (171–3). I have already pointed out the importance of the sacrifice motif in the play and the abundance of sacrificial acts. The intrigues of the play are specifically built around the performance of sacrifice.

Moreover, the customary sacrifices at the festival of Hera consisted of cattle. *Bouthuteō* is used three times (635, 785, 805) and *bousphageō* once (627) with reference to Aesgisthus' sacrifice. Electra, before the murder of Clytemnestra, speaks of the sacrificial bull, Aegisthus (1142–4). In this same contest, Electra also refers to the ritual basket that is raised again (1142). The mention of the basket is not an arbitrary choice of a sacrificial detail, for we are told that a virgin girl, who was a basket-bearer (*kanēphoros*) at this festival, was the one who began the sacrifice, a cult role which Electra can readily fill.[47]

Earlier, Electra, in response to the chorus' admonition of the power of the goddess, had spoken of the futility of prayers to the gods (198–200). But the scene in which Electra, Orestes, and the Old Man plan their intrigues against the royal couple ended with their prayers to the gods for success in their enterprise. It is

---

[45] Adams 1935, 121, makes another point: 'That makes it seem the more horrible that he should not only strike down his victim from behind, but should even then make so miserable a job of it (842 ff). It is to emphasize by contrast the crude wretchedness of all this that Orestes is so emphatically compared by the Chorus and Electra to a Victor in the Games . . .'. On the motif of corrupted hospitality, see O'Brien 1964, 34–6.

[46] For the name *Hekatombeia* cf. Hesychius: '*agōn chalkeios*: the Hekatombeia in Argos'. Schol. Pi. *Ol*. 7. 152: 'There is a festival of Hera called also the Hekatombaia. For a hundred oxen are sacrificed to the goddess'. Cf. Pi. *Nem*. 10. 22–3: ἀγών τοι χάλκεος δᾶμον ὀτρύνει | ποτὶ βουθυσίαν Ἥρας ἀέθλων τε κρίσιν. 'The contest for bronze prizes lures | the people to Hera's sacrifice and the judgement of her games' (tr. Nisetich, 1980).

[47] Dion. Hal. *Ant. Rom*. 1. 21: 'An unmarried girl, called the *kanēphoros*, or "basket-bearer", performed the initial rites of the sacrifices, and there were choruses of virgins who praised the goddess in the songs of their country' (tr. E. Cary, Loeb, 1960).

Electra who ominously appeals to Hera, the goddess who rules over the altars of Mycenae (674).

Thus, in form, the two acts of murder which are set in a sacrificial milieu, maintain an implied connection with the festival of Hera, but the nature of the sacrifices themselves is even more closely related to the cult of the goddess.

For Clytemnestra herself seems to be presented as the priestess-goddess figure of Hera. The entrance of the queen is heralded by the chorus in a form that recalls a ritual cult hymn to the goddess. *Basileia*, 'queen', was one of the important cult epithets of the Argive Hera. Moreover, the ring composition, the elaborate phraseology, the pedigree of relationship with the divine Dioscuri, the reference to the local place of habitation, the formal greetings, χαῖρε and σεβίζω (*chaire* and *sebizō*, cf. 196–7), in addition to the term θεραπεύεσθαι (*therapeuesthai*), which denotes cult service to the gods (cf. 744) make the hymn form unmistakable.[48]

The most important event enacted at the festival was probably the ceremony of the *hieros gamos* ('sacred marriage'),[49] to which the priestess of Hera, probably accompanied by the image of the goddess, was driven in a wagon drawn by white oxen.[50] Clytemnestra enters the scene riding in a wagon, which, while it echoes the entrance of

---

[48] Hera *Basilis* (*basileia*), 'queen', at Argos: Kaibel, *Epigr.* 822, *CIG* 3. 172, Clem. Alex. *Strom.* I, p. 418.

Kubo 1966, 24 only hesitantly suggests a cult hymn. Cf. n. 47. On the hymn elements see Keyssner 1932, Meyer 1933, and Adami 1900, 215–47.

Also on Euripides' ironic use of the hymn form in the *Ion*, see Larue 1964, 126–36.

[49] On the *hieros gamos* in Argos see Farnell 1896, I. 187–8 and the evidence cited 244–5. Nilsson 1906, 44, points out that the direct evidence suggests a *hieros gamos*, but does not prove it beyond any doubt. Current opinion is inclined to accept the performance of this ritual at the Heraia, based on the evidence in Argos (see nn. 50 and 51) in conjunction with the more explicit evidence of the rite performed in related cults of Hera, especially in Knossos, Samos, and among the Italian Falerii. For the *hieros gamos* in connection with Hera in other cults, see Farnell 1896, I. 184–7, Eitrem, *RE* 8. 370–81, 392–8, Roscher 1886, I. 2098–2104, Kerényi 1950, 228–57, and Klinz 1933, 96–111. For the prevalence of this ritual in the ancient Near East, see Kramer 1969.

Furthermore, there is an Argive legend in which Zeus pursued Hera in the shape of a cuckoo, and the name of the mountain on which they first were united was called the *kokkygion* (Paus. 2. 36. 2; cf. 17. 4; Schol. Theocr. 15. 64). Pausanias saw the ritual couch of Hera in the precinct of the Heraion (Paus. 2. 17. 3), and the famous monumental statue of the goddess made by Polycleitus, which also stood in the temple, held a pomegranate in one hand and a scepter crowned with a cuckoo in the other (Paus. 2. 17. 4).

[50] On the wagon procession see Farnell 1896, I. 187. See too Palaephatus 51: 'A feature of the festival is the wagon drawn by white oxen and the priestess must ride in

Agamemnon in Aeschylus and sets up again the theme of gold and
luxury, can also represent this preliminary to the ritual of the Heraia.
The queen has agreed to officiate at the sacrifice for Electra, thus
performing a sacerdotal function, but she warns her daughter that
she must then hasten to the side of Aegisthus, for one must pay one's
debt of favour to one's husband: (*dounai charin*, 1138). Electra, in the
passage that follows, immediately declares that her mother will make
a marriage in the house of Hades with the man beside whom she
slept in life. This is the debt of favour she will pay:

> νυμφεύσῃ δὲ κἀν Ἅιδου δόμοις
> ᾧπερ ξυνηῦδες ἐν φάει. τοσήνδ᾽ ἐγὼ
> δώσω χάριν σοι, σὺ δὲ δίκην ἐμοὶ πατρός   (1144–6)

You will keep your nuptials in the house of death with the man you slept
beside in life. Such is the favour (*charin*) I will give you and in return you
shall give me justice for my father.

It is just two lines earlier that Electra says that the ritual basket of
grain is raised, the knife that slew the bull is whetted again, and
Clytemnestra will fall close beside him (1142–4).[51]

The procession of the *basileia*, the priestess-goddess, which is
thought to culminate in the propitious act of the *hieros gamos* is
converted into the ceremonial entrance of the *basileia*, adulteress and
slayer of her husband, who is to undergo a ritual death, and who
only then will wed her paramour in Hades. Electra, the humiliated
virgin, can play a ritual role for which she is well-qualified. It is a
devastating piece of irony.

While the distortion of the solemn ritual of the Heraia exposes
the distorted execution of justice, for Electra the manner and
circumstances of its accomplishment are a triumph of poetic justice.

it.' In the famous story of filial devotion (a marked contrast to Orestes and Electra),
Cleobis and Biton yoked themselves to their mother's wagon to bring her to the
Heraion so that she could perform her cult role as priestess of Hera at the festival
(Herod. I. 31).

Farnell 1896, I. 187, following Roscher, suggests that the priestess was probably
going to play the part of *numpheutria*, the attendant of the goddess at her nuptials.
Nilsson 1906, 43, following Deubner 1905, review of Eitrem 1905, 1401–5, thinks
that the priestess came simply in her capacity of cult officiant.

[51] In this connection, it is noteworthy that there was a special sacrifice called the
λέχερνα (*lecherna*), probably a prenuptial sacrifice, which was offered by the Argives
in honor of Hera. Hesychius s.v. 'Lecherna: the sacrifice accomplished for Hera by the
Argives'.

For the revenge of Electra, in its double ritual context, is thematically perfect. Both the fictitious ritual after birth and the travesty of the *hieros gamos* are the culmination of the theme of marriage, which embraces the relationship of mother and child and that of husband and wife.

Clytemnestra, despite her loving protestations on behalf of her daughter Iphigenia, is the unnatural mother.[52] Both Orestes and Electra are outcast children, abandoned by the one who bore them. Aegisthus, fearing the son's revenge, has put a price on Orestes' head, and his hatred of Electra is based on the fear that she will make a noble marriage and produce a male child, a potential avenger of Agamemnon's death. Electra's fiction of the birth of a male child is still expected to disquiet the royal pair, and she shrewdly calculates that just the news of the event will bring her mother unsummoned to her side.[53] Clytemnestra, at first reluctant to officiate at the rite, ultimately agrees to perform the ceremony for her daughter in an ironical assumption of a mother's role at the last.[54] Yet it is a mother's death which will be accomplished on the putative occasion of a child's birth and the executor of the deed will be her own child, the παῖς ποινάτωρ (*pais poinatōr*, 'avenging child'), who has returned, while the childless daughter will assist in the act.

Earlier, Aegisthus' fears were realized in the actual return of the child avenger. Without hesitation he correctly divines the meaning

[52] Note the callousness of Clytemnestra, who flaunts her wealth, claiming that the Phrygian handmaidens have compensated her in some measure for the loss of Iphigenia (1000–3) and her later admission that she could have overlooked Agamemnon's sacrifice of his daughter if he had not introduced Cassandra into the house (1086–7). O'Brien 1964, 35, interprets Clytemnestra's opening remarks as evidence that 'this is not the dissolute queen we have heard about, nor is it quite the woman whom Electra speared with the epigram, "Women love their men, not their children" (265)'. But a truly dedicated mother could never be compensated for the loss of a child.

[53] Kubo 1966, 15–18 points out the importance of the fact that Electra never directly summons her mother. He suggests the parallel of the 'myth of a cruel parent persecuting his or her daughter in fear of a possible grandchild . . . Her design becomes intelligible and mythically binding, when the audience can detect from the given clue an allusive mythical necessity. Clytaimnestra will come, precisely because she fits into the known mythical picture of a fearful and cruel parent who persecutes the daughter and grandchild' (18).

[54] O'Brien 1964, 26, sees Clytemnestra's coming as an act of graciousness, that she 'has been drawn to the cottage, appropriately, by mother love', but Clytemnestra only grudgingly agrees to perform the sacrifice and is in a hurry to join Aegisthus (1123–38).

of the ill omens at the sacrifice (831–3). When the plot was first conceived, Orestes inquired of the Old Man whether Aegisthus planned the sacrifice to the Nymphs in order to celebrate the rearing of children (*tropheia*) or in honor of an approaching birth (*pro mellontos tokou* 626). As O'Brien points out, Orestes, by an ironical word play, is the child in question, who repays *tropheia*, the wages paid back for rearing a child, while an imminent birth refers to the false report of a child born to Electra, which will lure her mother to the scene of her death.[55]

Orestes interprets the sacrifice to the Nymphs in their role of patronesses of children, but they are also patronesses of marriage and the home,[56] as Aegisthus makes clear when he appeals to them in his prayer at the sacrifice. He has often sacrificed to the Nymphs before to insure that he and Clytemnestra will enjoy continuing prosperity in the house and that their enemies will fare ill (805–7).

The sacrifice to the Nymphs is thus linked to the second sacrifice through the associations of children and marriage. Clytemnestra does not know Aegisthus is dead. She is impatient to join her

---

[55] O'Brien 1964, 26–7. Ballentine 1904, 105, in commenting on the literal meaning of the passage, suggests that 'the *tropheia* . . . seems to have been a sacrifice made to the Nymphs in return for their having safely brought up children to a certain age after birth. It was an expression of thanks for the care exercised by the Nymphs over the child during the time since birth. The usage of the word *tropheia* elsewhere shows that the reference is to care that has been given, not to that which is to be given; cf. Aesch. *Sept.* 472; Isoc. *Arch.* p. 138; Plat. *Rep.* 520b; [Lys.] *Andoc.* 49, etc.'

[56] On the Nymphs and their association with marriage see Ballentine 1904, 97–102. The comments of Mnaseas, an Alexandrine scholiast of the third century BC, on Pi. *Pyth.* 4. 104 are particularly apt: 'No marriage is accomplished without the Nymphs, but they honour these first for the sake of their contrivance, because they were considered guides of piety and holiness.' In addition to Ballentine's evidence, a more recently published papyrus fragment attributed to Aeschylus' *Semele* (355 M) demonstrates the functions of the Nymphs in this regard:

νύμφαι ναμερτεῖς, κ[υδραὶ θεα]ί, αἷσιν ἀγείρω
Ἰνάχου Ἀργείου ποταμοῦ παισὶν βιοδώροις,
αἵτε παρίστανται πᾶσιν βροτέοισιν ἐπ᾽ ἔργοις
εἰ [λαπίναις θαλίαις] τε καὶ εὐμόλποις ὑμ[εναίοις
καὶ τε[λέουσι κόρας ν]εολέκτρους ἀρτιγά[μους τε . . .]

'Nymphs who speak unerring truth, honoured goddesses are they for whom I gather offerings, the life-giving children of Inachus, the river of Argos. They are present at all the activities of men, at feasts and banquets and sweet songs of hymenaeals, and they initiate maidens lately bedded and new to marriage . . .'.

On this fragment and its attribution to the *Semele* see Latte 1968, 468–85. The speaker of these lines is supposedly Hera, disguised as a priestess. On Hera and the Nymphs in connection with marriage see also Ar. *Thes.* 973b–81.

husband at the sacrifice to the Nymphs in a show of wifely devotion, and it is in response to this statement that Electra speaks of her mother's forthcoming marriage (*numpheusēi*) to her lover in Hades.

The theme of distorted marriage is highly developed in the play. Helen's adultery launched the expedition to Troy (479–81; cf. 1027–9), Thyestes stole the golden lamb by his seduction of Aerope (719–22), and Iphigenia was lured to Aulis on the pretext of marriage to Achilles (1020–3). Euripides' innovation of a marriage for Electra allows a complex, ironical treatment, which juxtaposes the marriage of the daughter to that of the mother. Three elements of the marital relationship are exploited—the birth of children, social status, and sexual passion. On all three points Clytemnestra is gratified,[57] and Electra, emphatically, is not.

The emphasis on father-love, which is prominent in Aeschylus and Sophocles, is subordinated to Electra's obsession with her own situation, namely, a loveless marriage to a social inferior.[58] Electra's frustrations and suffering are due to her mother's domestic arrangements—her destruction of the marital bond with Agamemnon and her new liaison with Aegisthus. Clytemnestra's marriage to Aegisthus is shocking, unholy, disgraceful, adulterous, yet Electra's loathing of her mother is based partially on the fact that she is her mother's daughter. Euripides' portrait of Electra shrewdly suggests her thwarted sexuality, and given that temperament, the mock marriage is a still crueler punishment.[59] In the prologue, we learn that Aegisthus had first confined her to the house and refused to marry her off to any of her noble suitors, but he was afraid that she might produce a child out of wedlock, and therefore, changed his plans (19–24). Her speech over Aegisthus' body concentrates on her contempt for him as a man and on his sexual relationship with her mother, a constant refrain throughout the play.[60] Her suggestion of Clytemnestra's infidelity to Aegisthus (918–25) is not confirmed elsewhere in the play and seems instead to be her private fantasy. Even her plot against her mother exploits her obsession with her virginity. In her message to her mother, she stated that she had kept herself pure (*hagneuei* 654) for ten days, the proper procedure for

[57] We are told that Clytemnestra has borne children to Aegisthus (62–3).

[58] This subordination of the motive of father-love is noted by Rivier 1944, 137 and Solmsen 1968, 141–57 = 1932.

[59] See O'Brien 1964, 30–1 for further similarities between Clytemnestra and her daughter.   [60] On the speech over Aegisthus' corpse see O'Brien 1964, 31.

a new mother, but *hagneuei* is ambiguous. It can mean simply 'to remain chaste' (cf. 256), and that, of course, is Electra's true condition. Even in her remorse after her mother's death, marriage, and more specifically, the marriage bed, is uppermost in her thoughts 1199–1200).[61]

The tone of the *agōn* between mother and daughter is brilliantly worked out. For Clytemnestra, who thinks her daughter is now a gratified woman and mother, adapts her line of defense accordingly. She first brings up the sacrifice of Iphigenia, which is intended to play upon Electra's family loyalties and to appeal to Electra, the new mother, who can now appreciate the depth of maternal feeling (1018–19; cf. 1044–7). Moreover, Agamemnon enticed his daughter to Aulis with the false promise of marriage to Achilles and betrayed her hopes (1020–3), an offense which should provoke Electra's hostility.[62] He was willing to sacrifice his daughter, not for the common welfare, a pardonable excuse, but because of Helen the adulteress, who betrayed her husband (1024–9).

Clytemnestra freely admits that she could have forgiven Agamemnon for Iphigenia's death, but she could not overlook his introduction of Cassandra into the marriage bed.[63] Two brides under the same roof is an intolerable situation. Any woman could understand that. Why should there be a double standard for women? If a man can enjoy an extra-marital relationship, why can't a woman? (1032–40). The logical connection between Agamemnon's infidelity which postdated hers is weak,[64] but she is speaking in a confiding tone as one woman to another, whose own temperament and experience would bear out her contentions.

Electra's reply demolishes her mother's arguments and concentrates her rage on her mother's attractiveness and her sexuality. She can easily dispose of Clytemnestra's defense that her husband's offense against Iphigenia was a motivating factor by pointing out her mother's later mistreatment of her other children. She has made her

---

[61] The Dioscuri, in their predictions, seem to refer to Electra's obsession with marriage in all its aspects almost with a touch of malice. See 1311–13 and Orestes' remark (1340–1).

[62] In Sophocles, the marriage of Iphigenia to Achilles is not mentioned in the debate between mother and daughter.

[63] The word *lektra*, 'bed', is repeated three times in Clytemnestra's speech (1021, 1033, 1037) addressed to one who is *Elektra*, 'unbedded'.

[64] On the illogic of Clytemnestra's defense see Denniston 1939, 177.

surviving daughter's existence a living death, a far worse fate than that of Iphigenia (1086–93). Furthermore, Clytemnestra's misconduct preceded the news of Iphigenia's sacrifice. Agamemnon was no sooner gone from the house than the queen was primping and preening before the mirror, up to no good. She bought herself a lover with her children's inheritance (1069–80, 1089–90).

Clytemnestra interprets her daughter's response just as an indication of an excessive father-attachment (1102–3) and abandons the discussion. She is anxious to attend to Electra's request and to hasten back to her husband. Thus, Electra, who deems her own marriage a *thanasimos gamos* (247), in a more literal application, inflicts the same fate on her mother on the pretense of the performance of a birth ritual. The *hieros gamos*, far from fulfilling its promise of a propitious union and procreation, leads instead to death and to lament. The occasion of birth, which is also presided over by the goddess Hera,[65] is converted into its opposite.

Kubo, in his comments on the presentation of the chorus in the play, points out that the speeches of the *agōn* 'confront each other in one crucial point: the accusations of the two antagonists are essentially the same. The criminals violated the sanctity of marriage, destroyed the tie between parent and child. And the witness to this trial is the chorus [connected with] the Heraia, the cult [festival] founded in honor of the goddess who protects the sanctity of marriage and childbirth.'[66] The criminals to whom he refers are Agamemnon and Clytemnestra, but through the revenge of Electra, and Orestes, the pattern of violation continues, also in the presence of the same chorus. And this violation is revealed through the external form of intrigue built around the violation of ritual. The disordering of ritual, itself the supreme embodiment of order, objectifies the intrinsic disorder.

The repetition of this pattern may initially be satisfying to Electra, but the repetition of the pattern of Agamemnon's death implies a repetition of the same crime. O'Brien has marked the general similarities: 'Agamemnon dies by the guile of a woman and the hand of a man (9–10), but Clytemnestra also put her own hand on the weapon (1160). The pattern for Clytemnestra's death is the same: the guile of Electra, the hand of Orestes. But Electra too puts her hand on

---

[65] For the role of Hera Eileithyia, Hesychius s.v. Eileithyia: Hera in Argos.

[66] Kubo 1966, 24–5.

the weapon (1225) . . . The play depicts no erasure of evil, but
an exchange of like for like: *amoibai kakōn* (1147)', a fact which
is emphasized by 'superimposing the memory of the old wrong of
Agamemnon's death on the new wrong of the queen's death', in the
choral ode.[67] Beyond the implications of these parallels, the irony of
the dramatic events of the play, seen through the distortion of the
events of the Heraia, bears further witness to Euripides' negative
conception of the myth.

In conclusion, the festival of Hera, as a public celebration in Argos,
had, by contrast, at first objectified the alienation of Electra from
home, city, and normal family life and gave a new thrust to her
hostility. It established and focused the motif of sacrifice, which
unified past and present events, and which structured the intrigues
of the play. It stimulated the deceptive mood of celebration which
was framed by lamentations at the beginning and the end, and the
subtle inversion of its events enhanced the ironical presentation
of the myth. At the same time, the festival itself remained as an
exemplar of ritual regularity and proper cult worship against which
the distorted rituals of the play could be measured. Finally, by the
connection of Hera with the sanctity of marriage and childbirth, the
festival was thematically integrated into the issues of the drama.

After the murder of Clytemnestra, Electra asks: what dance can I
participate in now? What marriage can I make now? What husband
will receive me in his nuptial bed? (1198–1200). The Dioscuri later
answer her questions. She will marry Pylades, but at the cost of
separation from Orestes and exile from Argos. Orestes must also go
into exile; he has never even set foot in the city of Argos, his primary
goal.[68] The victory for both has been bought at a high price, a price
which is epitomized by the festival of Hera in Argos.

---

[67] O'Brien 1964, 31 and n. 31.

[68] Cf. the chorus' joyful statement: 'your brother shall set his foot (*embateusai*) in
the city', 595 and the words of the Dioscuri: 'you may not set foot (*embateuein*) in the
city any longer, since you killed your mother', 1250–1.

13

The Rejection of Suicide in the Heracles of Euripides

JACQUELINE DE ROMILLY

It is right to read a Greek tragedy closely. To understand its deep import, however, one should read all of them—and, moreover, read many other Greek texts, for they all hang together. I should like to offer as an example the *Heracles* of Euripides, and in particular the ending of that tragedy. This ending, in which the problem of suicide is discussed, may disappoint from the dramatic point of view,[1] but it is essential from the point of view of Euripides' thought. Its importance, however, really becomes clear only if we compare the scene both with the *Ajax* of Sophocles and with all Greek thinking about suicide.

Considered from this viewpoint, an analysis of the scene between Heracles and Theseus, with its stichomythia and its three speeches, ought therefore to allow us to define Euripides' originality. We will indicate its perspectives here, without going into the detail of particular textual problems, and contenting ourselves with indicating the accepted solutions in passing: after all, they do not much affect the overall interpretation, which is all we are concerned with here.

The link with Sophocles' *Ajax* is already apparent in the situation, which seems to impose suicide on both heroes. Both have committed murder, under the influence of an illusion created by a god. Ajax, believing he was massacring the army commanders, has in fact slaughtered their flocks: he awakes to find himself dishonoured. Heracles, thinking he was massacring the children of Eurystheus, has in fact slaughtered his own children: he awakes a criminal—and, what is more, without hope.

[1] Cf. Ehrenberg 1946, 144–66.

Beyond the parallel nature of the two situations, this slight difference is not insignificant: Euripides' hero is doomed to greater suffering, which is well in line with the taste for the pathetic which is reflected in the author's work in general. At the same time, this heightened suffering ought further to reinforce Heracles' desire for death, and so make his decision to live even more striking. In fact this suffering will continue even after he has made his decision, and the text is very insistent in this respect (1365: ἀθλίως ('wretchedly'); 1375: ὡς ἀθλίως; 1385: ἀθλίως; 1393: ἄθλιοι ('wretched ones').[2] It will still be present at Heracles' final departure, and will be conveyed by his tears, which he justifies to Theseus (cf. 1410 ff.).

Apart from this difference, however, the situations of the two heroes are much the same, and their reactions are also very similar. From the beginning, Heracles, like Ajax, sees refuge only in death.[3] Then, like Ajax, he is condemned to defend his wish to die in a sustained speech.

Ajax's speech (430–80) begins with the hero lamenting the dishonour that has befallen him—the dishonour that sets him against his father (cf. 440: ἄτιμος, 'dishonoured') and consigns him to ridicule (cf. 454: ἐπεγγελῶσιν, 'they exult').

Then Ajax wonders what he can do: going home and returning to combat are both out of the question. Finally he decides that honour demands he should die (473: αἰσχρόν, 'shameful'; 479: ἢ καλῶς ζῆν ἢ καλῶς τεθνηκέναι, 'either to live gloriously or to die gloriously'). Heracles, on the other hand, enumerates all his ordeals and evils, the murder of his children being only the last of the ordeals and the greatest of the evils.[4] In other words, we see again the difference that

---

[2] Nauck's correction for ἀθλίωι; the presence of the adjective ἀθλίου describing the dog of Hades is more suspect: it might have been suggested to the copyist by the repetition of the term throughout the passage. I do not believe that this suffering renders vain Heracles' ἀρετή ('virtue': cf. Adkins 1966).

[3] I do not believe it possible to retain the text κατθανεῖν ('to die') in line 1241; for it makes Theseus' incomprehension absurd: and it appears that καὶ θενεῖν (Parmentier) with the ambiguity attached to this word (knock at the door, strike a blow) would represent a considerable improvement. But in any case it is clear that Heracles is here announcing his suicide, and he makes it clear unambiguously in line 1247.

[4] It has sometimes been suggested that lines 1291–1300 (or at least 1291 and 1299) should be taken out of Heracles' tirade, bearing in mind that it is a contradiction to have Heracles say that he has been overwhelmed by woes since birth, and then to say that his misfortune is made worse by contrast with his former happiness. But there are two points of view here: trial follows unrelentingly on trial,

was evident from the start: for Ajax it is a matter of dishonour, and for Heracles one of suffering. The two endings will provide confirmation: where Ajax finds that life would be without honour, Heracles finds that it would be without profit (1301: τί δῆτά με ζῆν δεῖ; τί κέρδος ἕξομεν . . .; 'Why should I live, then? What profit will I have . . .?'). But apart from this difference the two texts are parallel, and Ajax's argument ('What can I do ?') corresponds to Heracles' ('Where can I go?'). One can only note that Sophocles has recourse to this theme, which is a sort of commonplace, solely to bring out more strongly the complete absence of hope. Euripides, on the other hand, introduces it to prepare the eventual response and solution: Theseus, the Athenian, the hospitable one, will in effect reply to Heracles that he need only come to Athens, where he will be purified, welcomed and honoured (1322–40).

The starting point is therefore presented in remarkably similar terms. But what leads to suicide in Sophocles leads to the rejection of suicide in Euripides. This rejection is achieved through two sets of reasons: those advanced by Theseus and those held by Heracles.

Where the reasons advanced by Theseus are concerned, one may be in some doubt. In the opening dialogue, he seems to appeal to Heracles' pride and self-respect. Heracles, as we shall see, will not be at all insensitive in that regard. On the other hand, these reasons do not reappear in his sustained speech as we have it. The question has been raised as to whether they were not in fact there originally, for a material accident seems to have occurred after line 1312, at the start of the speech. Something is missing. But what? A line?[5] Or even a possibly important sequence of lines, perhaps including that appeal to the hero's honour? The relative brevity of Theseus' speech (which has only twenty-eight lines whereas each of Heracles' has over fifty) may plead in favour of this latter hypothesis. It would, however, be unwise to take it as proven, and the text holds together very well without needing to resort to it. If the argument appealing to Heracles' courage has been suggested in the stichomythia, that is sufficient: the hero's pride is at stake, and gradually the feeling grows in him, to

but the outcome, formerly always happy, has become disastrous. As for the problem of the enclitic ἔστι (1293), a minor correction would be enough to deal with it: writing ἔσχ', for instance.

[5] Some believe the lacuna to be very short, perhaps just a single line (e.g. Drexler 1943, 333).

be asserted at the end as his deep personal conviction: 'I have
considered the matter' (1347: ἐσκεψάμην).[6] By means of a happy
allocation of thoughts, the author has therefore been able to give
Theseus only the argument set out in our text, that of τύχη
('fortune'), and leave the hero that of honour. In this case, the link
between the rejection of suicide and Heracles' courage is even closer:
Theseus offers support, he spurs on, he gives encouragement; but he
lets Heracles discover his true reasons himself.[7]

This argument from τύχη ('fortune'), by the way, is not as
insignificant as one might think.[8] It does indeed have a slightly
immoralist side, in that it evokes the misdeeds of the gods, as the
poets describe them; and in that sense Heracles' protestation is
justifiable. This protestation, which has been rather exaggeratedly
described as 'Platonism', fits in with the arguments that were at the
time fashionable and dear to Euripides.

But Theseus is not content to say, like the nurse in *Hippolytus*, for
instance,[9] that the gods' misdeeds excuse those of men. He considers
these misdeeds, like those of Heracles, to be misfortunes; and so the
misdeed then becomes a situation in which one finds oneself, without
having any hand in it: one suffers it, as Oedipus suffered being
parricidal and incestuous.[10] This interpretation, quite usual in the
thinking of antiquity, therefore serves for Theseus as a basis for a
moral rule, consisting of remaining serene with regard to anything
brought about by fate. The insistence of the text here is characteristic; the development is framed by the repetition of the word τύχη,
'fortune' (1314: ταῖς τύχαις; 1321: τὰς τύχας). Here we shall not go
into the problem of the general meaning of the tragedy;[11] it is well
known that interpretations such as Wilamowitz's, which see the
principle of the hero's misfortune in his soul and his character, are
opposed to others, like Chalk's,[12] for instance, which see in his
misfortune a purely external *peripeteia*: clearly Theseus presents

---

[6] This sense of ἐσκεψάμην is strongly stressed by Drexler 1943.
[7] This concurs with the general interpretation of the play in Chalk 1962,
7–18.   [8] Cf. Kamerbeek 1966, 1–16, esp. p. 9.
[9] Cf. *Hipp.* 440 ff., *Tro.* 947 ff. The comparison with *Hippolytus* is more interesting,
because there too it is a matter of dissuading Phaedra from dying the death to which
she aspires.
[10] With regard to this form of culpability in tragedy, see Saïd 1978.
[11] Cf. on this point Kamerbeek 1966.   [12] Chalk 1962, 7–18.

Heracles' madness in this light. For our purposes it is more important to note that the argument he extracts from it is not immaterial from the moral standpoint.

Moreover, it is not without effect on Heracles. For if the hero begins by rejecting the most shocking myths relating to the gods, he none the less accepts the idea of τύχη ('fortune'), and understands that yielding to it is in no way dishonourable. The text in which he declares himself resolved to live closes with the idea that, in spite of his tradition of heroism, τύχη is a fact: 'this time, clearly, fate must be obeyed' (1357: τῇ τύχῃ δουλευτέον). The word δουλευτέον (lit. 'one must be a slave') reminds us that that costs him dear. But he resolves to do it just the same.[13] Even on this point, Theseus' thoughts have not been useless.

In any case, they constitute a real moral doctrine, establishing the wise man's independence with regard to the blows struck by fate. The fact is all the more remarkable because in *Ajax* Tecmessa also certainly begins by talking about ἀναγκαία τύχη, 'a fate of compulsion' (485); but only extracts from it the idea of her own isolation and what Ajax owes her. Where she makes play with sentiment, Theseus develops a doctrine of general relevance. What is more, it is a doctrine which in a sense is already paving the way for Stoicism. To the wise man's serenity the Stoics will only have to add the idea of liberty to give Theseus' reasoning its true import.

However, it is not this argument which convinces Heracles, but the argument about courage, which is developed suddenly in Heracles' second speech, and is by far the more original.

Theseus, as we have seen, had already paved the way for him, still in a veiled fashion, in the stichomythia. In fact, his language was more suggestive of a critique delivered in the name of reason: suicide was presented there as ἀμαθία, 'stupidity' (1254):[14] the word evidently

---

[13] In his eyes, this fate remains a blow dealt by Hera (1393): ῞Ηρας μιᾷ πληγέντες ἄθλιοι τύχῃ, 'wretched ones, struck by one fate from Hera'. Something there does not fit with the opening statements against anthropomorphic gods. But it would be difficult for Heracles not to believe in at least the adulteries of Zeus and Hera's jealousy—and the myths to which Theseus alluded were graver and more remote.

[14] ἀμαθία certainly does not refer to Heracles' fit of madness, which would be the cause of his death (as some seem to understand it, e.g. Marie Delcourt). The word can be explained if it is compared with other Euripidean expressions intended to dismiss the idea of suicide: they will be quoted later. In fact, it is just as foolish to wish to die out of despair as it is to try and resist without any chance of success (*Heracles* 281–3). And it is another form of 'foolishness' not to want to save one's friends (347). All morality is a matter of judgement.

refers to any behaviour that is impulsive and unconsidered. But beneath the reprimand relating to intellect there already lay hidden both a moral reprimand and a call for courage. Heracles could not act like just anybody (1248: ἐπιτυχόντος ἀνθρώπου, 'a chance-met fellow'): he had to reject a suicide which did not befit a man who had endured so many trials (1250: πολλὰ δὴ τλάς, 'having endured much') and rendered so many services to mortals (1252: εὐεργέτης βροτοῖσι, 'a benefactor for mortals'). This was clearly making it understood that the true hero does not commit suicide.

Now that is the argument that convinces Heracles, and at the end of the scene he formulates this new *credo* with rare force. The most remarkable word is spoken at the start: Heracles does not want to be accused of cowardice (1348: δειλίαν). Living becomes an act of courage. Standing up against the blows of misfortune is like resisting enemy onslaughts. Cowardice, then, no longer means loving life too much, but means not having the courage to live: one cannot imagine a more comprehensive reversal of the usual definitions.

And this reversal is then illustrated by a formula so remarkable that it has shocked scholars. Ἐγκαρτερήσω θάνατον, 'I shall stand firm in the face of death', says Heracles (1351). Now, at *Andromache* 262, Hermione is astonished by the resistance of Andromache, who is not frightened by death: ἐγκαρτερεῖς δὴ θάνατον; 'you stand firm in the face of death?'; and those are the only two examples in classical Greek of the verb used transitively.[15] As in *Andromache* the expression means 'to face death bravely', whereas in *Heracles* the reverse is the case, scholars such as Wecklein have not hesitated to replace the word θάνατον in *Heracles* by its contrary, βίοτον ('life').[16] This reaction demonstrates how striking is the new sense Heracles gives to the expression. 'To stand firm in the face of death' no longer means to brave its danger, but to brave its temptation. Just as courage no longer consists of dying, but of living, so death is no longer the hard solution, but the easy solution, which one must be able to resist.

[15] The expression can be found also in Philostratus, *Life of Apollonius* 8. 26: in this case it concerns prisoners who are simply 'waiting for death'.

[16] Murray also accepted this correction. Wilamowitz thinks that the current text is not a copying error, but an adjustment reflecting the evolution of ideas. Why not then admit that this evolution happens specifically in *Heracles* itself?

This new attitude to suicide is never suggested in Sophocles. Tecmessa does attempt to show Ajax that nobility requires one to repay debts to those who have given help; but there is a great difference between that and saying that dying is cowardly! In fact neither Tecmessa, nor Agamemnon or Menelaus later, suggest in any way that Ajax's suicide could be criticized. So everything happens as though Heracles, at first so similar to Ajax, were suddenly emerging as an anti-Ajax. There has often been debate about the extent to which Heracles discovers a new virtue in the play;[17] in fact, one thing is certain: by intensifying his heroism in that sense, he allows Euripides to present a new doctrine concerning suicide, destined to know great success in the future.

The contrast is so clear[18] that it suggests the existence of a deliberate polemic. And Euripides can be admired for choosing the hero most worthy of incarnating courage to sustain his thesis, and for placing him moreover in the very situation most worthy of inspiring a wish to die. The choice of character is therefore brilliantly explicable. But it is also possible that this choice too is serving a preoccupation with polemic.

For after all Sophocles too devoted a play to Heracles; and he too showed him broken after his labours. In fact, similarities have been discovered in the two plays, even with regard to expression.[19] But to that must be added that *Trachiniae* deals with the death of Heracles. Heracles dies because he has put on the poisoned tunic sent to him by Deianeira. That is certainly not suicide. But it turns out that, by a strange distortion, this imposed death almost becomes a voluntary death. At the end of his tragedy, indeed, Sophocles has brought onto the stage a hero at the very height of his suffering, screaming for death, begging to be finished off no matter how. And finally, combining death by the tunic with the tradition of death on Mount Oeta,[20] Sophocles showed Heracles making his son Hyllus take him there and light the fatal pyre.

---

[17] With regard to this debate, see Chalk 1962, and the reply from Adkins 1966, 209–19. This reply consists in saying that Heracles, at the end of the play, formulates his resolve in the terms of traditional ἀρετή, 'virtue'. It is possible in any case to note that its content and application are radically new, which supposes at the very least a certain internalization of values.   [18] Cf. also Pohlenz 1954, I. 301.

[19] Cf. for instance *Trach.* 1101 ff., compared with *Heracles* 1353 ff.. These similarities have been very widely discussed; see among others Kroeker 1938.

[20] On the subject of this combination of traditions, cf. Linforth 1952, 255–67.

Euripides' *Heracles* therefore appears to be a combined response to Sophocles' *Ajax* and to his *Trachiniae*.[21] The suggested dates for these tragedies are consistent with that. And the contrast is so striking that it seems that one could use it to reinforce the arguments for placing both *Ajax* and *Trachiniae* before *Heracles*.[22]

In that case it would be a matter not just of reactions and literary taste, but of a deliberate conflict between two conceptions of heroism. In Euripides, heroism has become internalized. It has been argued, contested, submitted to the moralist's analysis; and in the course of these debates the duty to live has in the end proved to be worth more than the epic ideal in which only glory and death shone brilliantly.

This is confirmed by the fact that Euripides' theatre is always very guarded in the matter of suicide. Phaedra's suicide is sullied by crime. Evadne's, spectacular though it is, is described as a terrible act (1072: δεινὸν ἔργον); and the whole development of this scene tends to bring to light the sufferings which this death leaves behind her (for Iphis, for instance, in 1073: ἀπωλόμην δύστηνος 'I am lost, poor wretch'). Without reaching the heights of Heracles' proud declarations, the disquiet is clearly sensed. There are also several occasions when suicide is criticized as being unreasonable. Wilamowitz quotes *Orestes* 415, where Menelaus says to Orestes: 'do not speak of death, for it is not wise' (τοῦτο μὲν οὐ σοφόν), and fragment 1070 N, according to which anyone praising suicide 'is not to be numbered among the wise' (οὐκ ἐν σοφοῖσι). Similarly, although it is here a question of a voluntary death, rather than a suicide, Achilles declares to Iphigenia that he will not let her die as a result of her folly (*IA* 1430: ἀφροσύνῃ). The censure may therefore be perceived more or less clearly in all Euripides' theatre: *Heracles*, with its proud declarations, is the brilliant expression of a thesis, which the rest of the oeuvre rehearses in muted fashion.

But how original this thesis is! Even Seneca, who took up the idea of a Heracles finally agreeing to live, explained this agreement as

---

[21] Pohlenz (1954, I. 301) accepts this relationship between the *Trachiniae* and the *Heracles*.

[22] That is in any case the generally accepted chronology: Wilamowitz put *Trachiniae* late; he has been followed by some others (Schmid, Kitto, Perotta); but recent studies on the whole reach different conclusions; for the arguments against this late dating of *Trachiniae*, cf. Kamerbeek 1970, 27–8.

Heracles' concern not to bring about another death along with his own: no doubt Stoicism would have prevented Seneca from condemning suicide directly as Euripides does.

Now the importance of the thesis which emerges in *Heracles* can be seen even more clearly if it is put in its place in the series of Greek texts dealing with suicide. Before Euripides, to be a coward is normally to live. A fragment of Sophocles, for instance (fr. 952 Radt), says that anyone wishing to prolong a wretched life is cowardly or insane (δειλός ἐστιν ἢ δυσάλγητος φρένας, 'a coward or suffering in his wits'). After him, on the contrary, the cowardice of suicide becomes one of the great themes of Greek thought on suicide. Plato, for instance, who in the *Phaedo* took so many precautions against the temptation of philosophic suicide, also singled out in the *Laws* the rare cases when suicide could be acceptable: those cases apart, anyone is to be censured who commits suicide 'out of weakness, and cowardice due to a lack of courage' (873c: ἀργίᾳ δὲ καὶ ἀνανδρίας δειλίᾳ). Although the fourth-century philosophers were not all agreed on this point, or perhaps just because they were not, Aristotle took up the same idea in his *Nicomachean Ethics* (3. 1116ᵃ): 'dying to escape poverty, or sorrows of love, or any other suffering, is the deed not of a brave man but rather of a coward' (οὐκ ἀνδρείου, ἀλλὰ μᾶλλον δειλοῦ). Later the argument will appear again in Flavius Josephus (*BJ* 3. 25); and Plutarch will have his Cleomenes told: 'So, you wretch, you think that you will seem brave (ἀνδρεῖος) by committing the easiest act in the world, the act that anyone can manage, suicide, even though it would be an even more shameful escape than the first one (. . .). To shy away from trials, misfortunes, censure and the opinions of others—that is to be defeated by one's own cowardice' (*Cleomenes* 31. 7: μαλακίας). In the meantime the idea had passed into Latin.[23] Later it would be taken up by the moderns.[24]

The scene in Euripides' *Heracles* is therefore not of interest solely because of its contrast with *Ajax*. It is echoed in problems and debates

[23] Cf. Seneca, *Letters* 68 and 78: the first speaks of the cowardice involved in dying, the other of the bravery sometimes involved in living.

[24] Napoleon will repeat similar ideas: 'To give in to misery without resistance, to kill oneself to escape it, is to abandon the battlefield before achieving victory', or again, on the evening of the catastrophe: 'If I were to kill myself purely as an act of despair, it would be cowardly'.

which were long to be pursued.[25] If my analysis is accurate, it clearly demonstrates the way in which, at the end of the fifth century in Athens, ideas came into conflict, were adjusted and elaborated, and after this collective maturation were made ready to be taken up subsequently by the philosophers.

In short, this is one more proof that in the domain of Greek literature, where all texts are so closely linked, understanding of those texts always depends to a great extent both on constant comparisons and on the very history of ideas.

[25] Perhaps the difficulties and complications to be found in the text are even partly the result of alterations, cuts, or changes made by actors or later copyists.

14
Iconography and Imagery in Euripides' Ion

DONALD J. MASTRONARDE

Euripides' *Ion*,[1] like *Iphigeneia in Tauris* and *Helen*, the two extant plays closest both in spirit and in date of composition,[2] contains elements of romantic fairy-tale and melodrama, a recognition, and a happy ending. *Ion* in particular has been viewed as a precursor of New Comedy.[3] Nevertheless there are serious elements in all three plays. In *Helen* we find the riddling manipulation of appearance and reality, the recognition that men fight and suffer for phantoms, and a paradigm of the constructive force occasionally exerted by piety and good judgment in an uncertain universe. In *IT* the ignorance, confusion, and despair of the human condition are exemplified in Iphigeneia and Orestes before recognition comes and the protagonists

---

[1] For the major bibliography up to 1967 see Wassermann 1940, 587 n. 1; Burnett 1962, 101–3; Conacher 1967, 267 n. 1. The more recent contributions to the study of *Ion* include Radt 1968; Lembach 1971; Immerwahr 1972, 277–97; Willetts 1973, 201–9.

In my approach to the serious aspect of *Ion* I agree on many points with Burnett 1971, 101–29, and Wolff 1965a, 169–94. The present study also agrees on many points with the recent study of Athenian imagery in the play by Immerwahr, which R. S. Stroud kindly brought to my attention after the first version of this study was completed. In what follows I shall refer mainly to points on which we disagree, but Immerwahr's discussion is a very good one and it is to be hoped that it will be made more widely available in its English version. [Addendum. This essay is unchanged except for correction of typographical errors and minor additions in the notes set off by square brackets. Among works later than 1975 that elaborate some of the same themes touched upon here, see in particular Saxenhouse in Euben 1986, 252–73; Loraux 1993, esp. ch. 5 (transl. of Loraux 1984); Zeitlin 1993, 138–96.]

[2] See Dale 1967, xxiv–xxviii, for the metrical statistics, which are the best evidence and clearly indicate the grouping of these three plays within a few years *c*.412. The precise order of composition and the dates of first production of *IT* and of *Ion* are uncertain and do not matter to the interpretation of the plays; for speculation, see Webster 1967, 163.

[3] See, most recently, Knox 1970, 68–96 [repr. in Knox 1979, 250–74].

learn how to master the disorder of their world in order to win escape and salvation. Likewise in *Ion*, although there is undoubtedly some irony at the expense of Apollo (an irony which has dominated much of the criticism of the play),[4] the poet's central concern, I would suggest, is the human characters and their behavior under the stress of ignorance, despair, and strong emotions which are entirely human. It will be argued here that the play may in fact be viewed as a fable illustrating the intractability of human passions.[5] The two major characters, Ion and Kreousa, both win admiration and sympathy from the outset by their compassionate, refined, at times aristocratic bearing. But their civilization is only a veneer; beneath the surface lurk the primitive, rebellious emotions of the human soul, capable of turning both mother and son into bloodthirsty avengers, capable even of upsetting the scheme arranged by Apollo for their benefit and of nullifying the god's 'mercy'[6] and omniscience. Yet as the characters rebel against and disrupt the divine plan, they behave in a way the audience cannot easily or wholeheartedly condemn. The audience is invited, in fact, to sympathize with the humans and all their turmoil rather than with the emotionless calm of the Olympians. The tragedy of the human situation in *Ion* lies, as Christian Wolff well explains, in the fact that the very expression of their humanity brings closest to disaster.

An important element in the pattern of this fable is Euripides' use of iconography and imagery. The major purpose of this study is to

---

[4] For two quite different views typical of the critical debate, see Burnett 1962, 89–103, who gives a spirited and at times excessive defense of Apollo (her chapter in Burnett 1971 is more moderate, but still somewhat too favorable to Apollo), and Rosenmeyer 1963, 105–52, who reflects the tradition unfavorable to Apollo. I believe that Apollo is neither so good nor so bad as critics on the two sides of the debate have painted him (cf. the excellent remarks of Barlow 1971, 50); and both sides seem to me to misplace the emphasis of the play when they assume that Euripides in this play is most interested in the god Apollo and his nature. This is not to deny that the play at several points casts an ironic light on Apollo: though one of the Olympians, he has a hand in the event which creates so much confusion and disorder (the rape, carried out in a chthonic environment; cf. p. 302 [original 168] infra); though he is a god of prophecy, his own plan for the reunion of Ion and Kreousa is frustrated mainly because, though he can provide an innocent calm which Ion is reluctant to leave and a shimmering brilliance which dazzles Kreousa, he is ill-equipped to understand or deal with human emotions; and, of course, in the end a less flawed representative of Olympian order, Athena, must speak on his behalf. But it is not the purpose of this study (nor, I would argue, of the play) to define Euripides' attitude toward Apollo. [5] Cf. Burnett 1971, 128; Wolff 1965a, 189.

[6] A favorite word of Burnett's, but not really the right term for the favor which gods *occasionally* show toward men in Euripides.

show how some[7] of the imagery reinforces the play's serious theme. What distinguishes mankind from the gods is their earthly nature and the origin they share with the animal world. The major characters of this play are, moreover, paradigmatic specimens of mankind because they possess the fullest possible degree of primitive earthliness. They are not only autochthonous in a general sense as all genuine inhabitants of Attika were reputed to be; they are also members of a royal family whose founder, Erichthonios, was born directly from the earth. Erichthonios is mentioned as early in the play as lines 20–1, where Euripides has Hermes go into great detail about an ancestral custom of the Erechtheidai. The snakes which guard a royal infant (21–6) are not mentioned solely as preparation for the recognition tokens (1427 ff.); they are symbols of the dynasty's chthonic origins, for snakes are par excellence children of the earth—the paragons of autochthonism.[8] Serpents grow from blood which falls upon the earth;[9] earth-born creatures are often half-man, half-serpent;[10] serpents guard untouched springs (the waters of the earth) and caves (hollows in the earth) and must be overcome before man or god can take possession of unclaimed land;[11] from the teeth of serpents sown in the earth grow men of primitive violence.[12] Wherever snakes are mentioned in the play, they reinforce the theme of autochthonism and symbolize the earthly, primitive part of man's nature.

In addition to snakes, many other monsters of Greek mythology are earth-born. In particular, the Giants who rebelled against the Olympian gods and attacked them with rocks and fire were sons of Earth. They too are mentioned or alluded to in important contexts in the play, as will be seen. Snakes, Giants, monsters, and all the imagery of autochthonism and primitive violence serve to create one

---

[7] Some aspects of the imagery not treated here are discussed by Burnett, Wolff, Immerwahr, and Barlow.

[8] Cf. Hartmann, *RE* 2A[1] (1921) 509 s.v. Schlange: 'Für die Griechen war die S. in erster Linie das Tier der geheimnisvollen Erdentiefe.' Cf. also Küster 1913, 85–100; Eitrem, *RE* 11[1] (1921) 119–25 s.v. Kekrops.   [9] e.g. AR 4. 1513–17.

[10] e.g. Kekrops, and, in some versions, Erichthonios and Erechtheus; the Erinyes born from Earth impregnated by Ouranos' blood (Hes. *Th.* 185) have snakes for hair; the Giants, sons of Earth, came to be shown in art with serpents for legs from about 400 BC, but Typhoeus or Typhon, a monstrous son of Earth who also fights the Olympian order, has serpent-heads in Hes. *Th.* 820 ff. and appears in Greek art with snake-legs in the first half of the sixth century: see Vian 1952, 13–14, 20.

[11] e.g. Python at Delphi, slain by Apollo; the dragon which guarded the spring Dirke, slain by Kadmos.   [12] e.g. in the legends involving Kadmos and Jason.

side of the contrast which is central to the serious theme of *Ion*. The other side of that contrast is provided by symbols of serenity, order, civilization, or control and taming of what is wild and primitive. The symbols of order used by Euripides are ones familiar in Greek art.[13] Corresponding to these symbols we find in human behavior the refined veneer of politeness and compassion, which are part of the orderliness which civilization breeds in men. In the Olympian realm, on the other hand, we find the innocent serenity fostered by Apollo at Delphi and the god's scheme for the smooth and untroubled recognition of mother and son (ironically, however, the emotionless god is unsuccessful in his attempt to impose Olympian control upon human affairs)[14] as well as Athena's role as conqueror of Giants and as creator and ratifier of calm in the final scene. Just as the earth-born Giants rebelled against the serene Olympians, so in the human soul the primitive emotions which are the heritage of man's earthly origins constantly threaten to break through the veneer of civilized behavior. When the struggle within the human soul is viewed in these terms and when this struggle is admitted to be central to the serious theme of *Ion*, a coherent pattern of iconography and imagery directly supporting this theme becomes apparent.[15]

The monologue of Hermes which opens the play contains the precise narrative and genealogical detail which may be expected in Euripides. Genealogy is here not limited to Kreousa, Ion, and Xouthos; even Hermes himself is identified genealogically as grandson of Atlas, son of Maia and Zeus. Despite the corruption of lines 1–2 it is clear that Atlas' function as pillar of the heavens is referred to at the outset: this detail may be read, in my view, as an image of the order

---

[13] See infra, pp. 304–5 [169–71] and nn. 38 and 39.

[14] Cf. Willetts 1973, 207, commenting on that fact that by participating in the action Apollo is reduced to the human level and made prone to error.

[15] Parts of this pattern have been noticed by previous critics, but their interrelation and the connection with the serious theme of the play have not been clearly stated, though Immerwahr 1972 comes closer than earlier critics. Kamerbeek 1948, 271–83, has a paragraph (p. 281) on the assimilation of Kreousa's behavior to the θεομαχία ('fighting against the gods') of the Giants. Burnett 1971, 107–29, also uses the term θεόμαχος ('fighter against the gods') with reference to Kreousa (p. 122), discusses Ion as the new Erechtheus (pp. 105–9), and notes the symbolism of the poison used by Kreousa (pp. 119–20). Wolff 1965a notices the myths of violence (p. 177), lists the snake-imagery and remarks that there is a great deal of emphasis on birth from the earth (pp. 182–3). Conacher 1967, 282 and 284, notes the connection between the theme of autochthonism and Athenian xenophobia.

and stability[16] of the Olympian world, for this is not the only reference to the order of the heavens in the play, and so it contributes to a larger pattern. This interpretation of lines 1–2 is perhaps supported by the description of Delphi (5–7) as the navel of the earth—the center of an ordered world.[17] These details are the first hints of the symbolism of order, the order which belongs especially to the divine world surrounding Earth, but is also shared by Delphi as Ion knows it before this day and by Athens as a center of civilization fostered and protected by Athena. The first suggestion of earthly primitivism, on the other hand, comes in lines 20–6 (earth-born Erichthonios, serpents, and the Erechtheid custom). Then in line 29 Apollo is quoted as telling his brother to go 'to the autochthonous people of famed Athens'. Autochthonism[18] renders the Athenians very proud of their nationality, and in line 63 we find emphasis upon Xouthos' status as an outsider (an emphasis which prepares for later scenes).[19]

Ion's monody (82 ff.) reveals the youth's simple piety and innocence, qualities fostered by his nurture in an artificially secluded, sacral setting.[20] It is no accident, I would suggest, that Ion begins with an image of heavenly order: the appearance of Helios[21] and the orderly retreat of the stars (compare 1147 ff., discussed below). During the play Ion is gradually forced away from his secluded and highly

---

[16] A reader of the first version of this study suggests that the image in 1–2 is rather one of suffering. The use of ἐκτρίβων ('rub constantly, press hard') could support that view, but Hermes' tone does not invite me to put emphasis on that word, whereas παλαιὸν οἶκον ('ancient [so long-established, secure] house') recalls for me the phrase θεῶν ἕδος ἀσφαλὲς αἰεί ('always secure seat of the gods': *Od.* 6. 42; Hes. *Th.* 128; cf. Pindar, *N.* 6. 3).   [17] Cf. also lines 223, 461 f., 910.

[18] The question may arise whether autochthonism may not also be a source of Athenian civilization and order as well as a sign of primitivism and possible violence. The Athenians certainly took great pride in their autochthonism just as they took great pride in their political order and in their culture (as praise of Athens in the Greek poets, especially the tragedians, and the orators demonstrates). But the favor of Athena and of the Attic soil rather than the fact of being earth-born per se is usually seen as mainly responsible for Athens' glories: and in any case the animal/Giant imagery of the play and the unpleasant display of virulent xenophobia seem to me to place the major emphasis on the darker aspect of autochthonism.

[19] The prologue of *Ion* is a good example of the way Euripides carefully chooses the details of his apparently matter-of-fact introductory monologues in order to prepare for major and minor themes of a play. For a few more examples see ch. 2 of my dissertation (Mastronarde 1974) [or my note on *Phoin.* 5 in Mastronarde 1994].

[20] See Barlow 1971, 46–8. Likewise in *Phoinissai* Euripides uses the *teichoskopia* ('looking from the walls': *Phoin.* 88–201) to present Antigone's initial state of youth and innocence, the state from which she must grow later in the play.

[21] Cf. Immerwahr 1972, 288–9 for another approach to the symbolism of the sun (cf. n. 40 infra).

refined way of life. He is mild when ensconced in a pocket of Olympian calm, but when pulled into the turmoil of the human world of the Athenian royal family Ion shows signs of the underlying passions of his primitive human nature.

The parodos of *Ion* (184–237) is famous for its pretty description of the temple and its sculptures. This description may be considered evidence of Euripides' interest in the fine arts (significant for those who believe he was a painter as well as a poet); it may be excused as an archaeological curiosity[22] or condemned as a pretty irrelevancy.[23] Perhaps the most charitable interpretation so far advanced is Wolff's explanation that the mythological detail has a deliberate distancing effect and reinforces the theme of violence.[24] In terms of iconography, however, the scenes described in the parodos need no excuse, for they contribute in a vital way to the imagery of order vs. disorder which is so important to Euripides' meaning. Herakles' labors were interpreted not only as torments forced upon the hero by Hera, but also as creative feats which tamed the world and brought order and civilization out of savagery. Herakles is featured in the first scene described (190–200), where he is seen slaying the Hydra of Lerna—a snake-monster descended from Earth.[25] Lines 201–4 describe a comparable heroic feat: the conquest of the Chimaira by Bellerophon.[26] Iconographically interpreted, these are not simply images of violence, but *exempla* of the conquest of the savagery of primitive nature by a civilizing force. The same interpretation applies, moreover, to the scene described in the second strophe (205–18): the Gigantomachy, a theme very popular in Greek art.[27] In Euripides' depiction (as elsewhere) Athena is featured as one of the leading combatants among the Olympians, and her role in the battle against the sons of Earth will be alluded to again later in the play. Here and elsewhere in the play the Gigantomachy has a readily recognizable iconographic meaning: taming of the savage offspring of Earth, control of rebellious

---

[22] Many scholars have unnecessarily assumed that the artworks described were physically represented on stage: e.g. Owen 1939, 82–3. See, however, Hourmouziades 1965, 53–6.   [23] Cf. e.g. Wilamowitz 1926, 14–15.

[24] Wolff 1965a, 177–9.

[25] Euripides does not, of course, record the genealogy, but it would be known to his audience: Hydra was born of the rebellious son of earth, Typhon, and the snake-monster Echidna, a daughter of Earth (Hes. *Th.* 304–14).

[26] Chimaira is either the sister or daughter of Echidna: see Hes. *Th.* 319 and M. L. West's notes on 270–336 and 319.   [27] See Vian 1952 and 1951.

primitive forces by the representatives of calm and order[28]—themes directly relevant to the struggle within the human souls of the principal characters of *Ion*.

The close connection of the royal family of Attika with their native soil, first alluded to in the prologue, is emphasized again in the dialogue between Ion and Kreousa in the first episode. Ion is curious about three details in particular: Erichthonios' birth from Earth; the sacrifice of Erechtheus' daughters;[29] and the disappearance of Erechtheus himself into the earth (265–82). The converse motif, Xouthos' foreignness, receives ample treatment a few lines later (289–98). The first stasimon contributes little to the themes being studied here, but one may note that Athena is invoked under the name Nike in 457 (the name associated with her role in the defeat of the Giants).[30] Furthermore, the daughters of Aglauros are mentioned in connection with the Makrai Petrai, the site of the rape of Kreousa and the birth of Ion: an implicit comparison of the exposed infant (Ion, though the chorus does not know that) with the foundling Erichthonios is thus suggested; later a more open identification of Ion with his ancestors will be made. Again during the 'recognition' between Ion and Xouthos, Euripides plays with the motif of autochthonism and with the analogy between Ion and Erichthonios when the youth ironically concludes, 'Then I was born from Earth, Earth is my mother' and Xouthos replies with even greater irony, 'The soil does not give birth to children' (542).

The racial pride of the aboriginal Athenians is the first and foremost reason for Ion's reluctance to accept Xouthos' offer of a

---

[28] Cf. Vian 1952, 286–8.

[29] It would be interesting to know whether the maidens were sacrificed to Earth in any version of the story current at Euripides' time. In *Phoinissai* Menoikeus sacrifices himself to appease both Ares and Earth (*Phoin.* 931–41), but Earth has a special reason to be hostile to Thebes. The fragments of Euripides' *Erechtheus*, now readily available in Austin 1968, 22–40, indicate clearly that Erechtheus' daughter is sacrificed *on behalf of the Athenian nation*, but do not tell whether she was sacrificed to any particular divinity. Hyginus, *Fab.* 46 tells a version in which Chthonia is sacrificed to Poseidon, while Demaratos, *FGrHist* 42 F4, has the girl sacrificed to Persephone.

[30] Nike appears as a minor divinity distinct from Athena in Hes. *Th.* 383–403 (a daughter of Styx, who sides with Zeus in the Titanomachy) and in artistic representations of the Gigantomachy (see Vian 1952, 49, 71, 158 and *passim*). It is uncertain whether in origin Nike was a separate goddess whose nature was assumed by Athena or whether she arose as an emanation of one aspect of Athena: Bernert, *RE* 17[1] (1936) 295–6 s.v. Nike. In Athenian cult, at any rate, she was identified with Athena in Euripides' time.

home and an inheritance: 'They say the famed *earth-born* Athenians are *no immigrant race*' (589–90). The second stasimon and third episode demonstrate how right Ion is to fear resentment. The chorus condemns Ion as a foreigner (693) and Xouthos as a deceitful outsider (702–4); their virulent xenophobia makes them pray for Ion's death (719 ff.). Kreousa and the old servant enter with the words 'Erechtheus' and 'autochthonous' on their lips (725, 737). The passionate loyalty of chorus and servant prompts perverse statements: the chorus reports that Kreousa will never have a child (a remark refuted earlier by the oracle of Trophonios in 408–9 and later by Athena in 1589 ff.), and the old man perceives a long-planned scheme to usurp the Erechtheid throne. The veneer of polite civilization cracks as the old servant suggests violent revenge, but deliberation is delayed when Kreousa finally releases her pent-up sorrow and resentment in her monody and delivers a long explanation in the ensuing iambics (859–922, 936–69). Here again the chthonic environment of rape, birth, and exposure is alluded to (936–41, 949, 958). Although this environment was a locale for Apollo's action (the rape) as well as Kreousa's, it is charged with strong emotions only for the human woman of earth-born descent: it involves for her the mixture of horror and awe associated with the rape, the turmoil of the lonely birth, and the misery of her infant's exposure.

The stichomythia in which revenge is plotted is full of references to the Gigantomachy and the snake-motif. The old man's first suggestion is to attack the god's oracle with fire—a form of attack used by those who challenge the gods, including the Giants.[31] It is Kreousa who finds a way to attack Ion, but she reveals her plan in a dialogue which might seem perversely round-about and longwinded[32] if Euripides were not deliberately playing upon the complex of motifs involving Giants, serpents, and autochthonism. Kreousa starts with

---

[31] Before Pheidias the Giants are usually shown in art as hoplites, though they occasionally appear as savages without armor, employing rocks and branches for weapons: Vian 1952, 23–6. But with Pheidias the savage Giants become more popular (Vian 1952, 145–9) and the use of the torch as a weapon appears (Vian 1952, 146; cf. Vian 1951, no. 393 [beginning of 4th century]). The use of fire by an opponent of the gods is found much earlier in the Typhoeus-episode (Hes. *Th.* 820–68). As with snake-limbs (supra, n. 10), the use of fire seems to be a motif transferred to the Gigantomachy from other legends of savage or cosmic warfare. Kamerbeek 1948, 281 saw that the action suggested in *Ion* 974 is typical of rebellion against the gods, but he compares only the story (attested in late sources) of Phlegyas' attack on Apollo's temple.   [32] Note the comment of Rosenmeyer 1963, 116.

the Gigantomachy, then brings in the Gorgon (a child of Earth here provided with an unusual history different from the orthodox version involving Perseus),[33] Athena's defeat of the monster and creation of the Gorgon-breastplate (987–98). The second stage of her tale begins with Erichthonios and the gift of Athena handed down from Erichthonios to Erechtheus to Kreousa (999–1015): golden bracelets were given to the infant Erichthonios (cf. the golden snake-necklaces given to his descendants as babies). Whether or not these bracelets are imagined to have the form of coiling snakes,[34] they contain the blood of the earth-born Gorgon and the venom of the Gorgon's serpents (note line 1015). These two liquids hold separate the power of good and evil; as Anne Pippin Burnett has shown, it is significant for the serious theme of *Ion* that the good is unused while the evil is used.[35] It is the humans' own passions and emotions, the primitive force which is the inheritance of their earthly origin, which make them contrive potentially disastrous deeds, circumventing and

[33] Immerwahr 1972, 286 appears to accept the suggestion that the version alluded to here is a very old one: Ziegler, *RE* 7 (1912) 1641–2 s.v. Gorgo, believes that this version is original and the Perseus-version derived; Kerényi 1949, 299–312, argues that the Perseus-version is the original Gorgo-legend but that the Euripidean version with flaying of a monster is also very ancient. Vian 1952, 198–200, 209, 221–2, holds a view similar to Kerényi's but also believes that Athena's defeat of Gorgo was a major episode in the lost archaic epic dealing with the Gigantomachy; and several authorities believe that Euripides reflects an Attic version—Preller-Robert 1894, I. 76, 192; Cook 1940, III. 843–4; Rose 1958, 30. Only Farnell 1896, I. 286–8, emphasizes that Euripides' version is unknown before the fifth century and could naturally have arisen rather late as an attempt to explain Athena's attribute, the Gorgoneion.

The problem is further complicated by the somewhat labored progression of the text of *Ion* 991–7: Murray deletes 992–3, while others place the couplet after 997 (e.g. the Budé text [and now Diggle's OCT], which Kerényi accepts as the basis of his argument). Transposition produces a worse text, for then the question in 992 is quite superfluous and unnatural after the specific information in 995–6. Nor have I seen an argument adequate to justify the use of brackets. The verses should therefore be printed (with Wilamowitz) in their normal place and θώρακ' taken to mean 'breast' rather than 'breastplate' (cf. Owen's note ad loc.).

As for the mythological problem, I cannot accept Vian's theory that the Athena-Gorgo episode figured in the archaic epic version; and despite line 994 and the subtle inferences made by Kerényi and Vian, I have little faith in the antiquity of Euripides' version. It seems to me likely to be a fairly recent Attic variant or even an *ad hoc* innovation by Euripides (line 994 then serving to give it a specious prestige by making it an 'old story' in the imaginary world of the play).

[34] Euripides nowhere says this. But parallels do suggest connections between the bracelets and the necklaces: both are χρυσώματα ('golden objects'), 1030 and 1430; two snakes are attached to an infant's body in 21–6, while two bracelets are attached to an infant's body in 1001–9.   [35] Burnett 1971, 115–16.

overturning the more peaceful (but inhumane) plan of Apollo. It is quite proper that a scene laden with imagery of primitive violence should end with an amoral maxim in the mouth of a loyal servant acting on behalf of a previously refined and sympathetic queen, for the veneer of order and control is gone: 'It is fine to pay honor to morality when things are going well. But when one wishes to harm one's enemies, no sanction stands in the way' (1045–47).

The third stasimon again reflects the xenophobia of the proud Athenians as the chorus prays for success in the poisoning of the outsider (1056–60, 1069, 1073, 1087–9). But the fourth episode brings more symbols of order and civilization overcoming primitive violence as the murder-plot is foiled. These symbols occur in the long descriptive section of the messenger-speech (1122–1228), a passage of the play which has irritated or embarrassed critics of the play who have not seen the function of the iconography.[36] The description of the tent is not mere decoration, nor primarily a tool to create a distancing effect; it does set up a separate, almost sacral setting for the attempted murder and the salvation of Ion, as Burnett and Wolff explain,[37] but it is also vital to the imagery of the play. First the shape and orientation of the tent are fixed with careful measurements (1132–40). Then the description of the decoration begins. The roof (1143–58) consists of an offering made by Herakles when he defeated the Amazons.[38] Herakles' labor is a symbol of the taming of primitive savagery, for after the Persian Wars the Amazonomachy as well as the Centauromachy serves as an iconographic emblem of the triumph of moderation, order, and control over excess, disorder, and barbarity.[39] Woven into the fabric itself, moreover, is a picture of heavenly

[36] Wilamowitz 1926, 14–15 views the passage as decoration; Imhof 1966, 40–1, sees it mainly as evidence of the fully developed autonomy of traditional forms in late Euripides.   [37] Burnett 1971, 117; Wolff 1965a, 180.

[38] The Amazons, being both female and nomadic, are antithetical to conventional fifth-century Greek notions of civilization (male-dominated polis-civilization). For the representation of Amazons in fifth-century sculpture, see von Bothmer 1957, 208–23.

[39] After the defeat of the Persians, Greek (and particularly Athenian) confidence in the divine sanction of their civilization is evident in Aeschylus' Persai and Eumenides and in Herodotus. The same confidence apparently informed the sculptural decoration of some of the great temples of the fifth century, decorations which celebrate a triumph of civilization analogous to the triumph of Greeks over Persians: e.g. Herakles' labors and Centauromachy on the Temple of Zeus at Olympia; Amazonomachy and Centauromachy on the Parthenon. See Pollitt 1972, 22–36. Cf. also Vian 1952, 286–8, though he is inclined to doubt that after 480 the Giants were seen as analogous to the barbarian enemy because nothing in the art itself indicates identification of Giants with Persians.

order: earlier hints of the dwelling of the gods and its stability were brief (cf. 1–2, 82–5, 870, 1078–9); now the whole circuit of the sky is described—Ouranos with his stars, Helios and his chariot at dusk, Night and her chariot followed by stars, major constellations, and the Moon, and Dawn to complete the circle. All in the heavens is in order, untouched by the rebellious element that thrives on Earth.[40] The walls of the tent also present iconography which suggests the triumph of civilization and the taming of what is wild (1158–62): Greek ships face a barbarian fleet;[41] Centaurs (in battle with men?); hunting of deer and lion.[42] The final detail is the embroidery by the entrance to the tent (1163–5): Kekrops, another autochthonous king of Attika, here shown as half-man and half-serpent, with his daughters, the Aglaurides (mentioned earlier at lines 23 and 496). After the symbols of order and control Euripides thus places images which are ambiguous: Kekrops serves as a reminder of Athena's favor toward Athens and toward Ion,[43] but his physical appearance and the presence of his daughters also call to mind the earthly animal nature and the spirit of rebellion (suggested here by the Aglaurides, who disobeyed Athena's instructions) which linger in the blood of the Athenians and of Ion himself.

Ion's first speech in the exodos labels Kreousa openly as a serpent creature (1261 ff.). She is either an Echidna or a fiery-eyed snake and is no less dangerous than the dripping blood of the Gorgon.[44] The innocent, mild-mannered youth of the opening of the play is now

---

[40] Immerwahr 1972, 290 and 294 argues that Night dominates the tent because the action there is dark and murderous. But I believe it is mistaken to speak of Night as ruling or dominating the heavens: Ouranos is the first power mentioned (1147) and he is marshalling the heavenly bodies; Night comes, with no particular emphasis, in the midst of the description (1150); and Eos is ready to come forth (1158), insuring that the normal movement and order of the heavens is implied. Portrayal of the night-sky, with Helios on one side and Eos on the other, is in fact the natural way for an artist to present the entire circuit of the heavens.

See Immerwahr 1972, 292–3, for speculation that the tent would remind the audience of Xerxes' tent or of the Athenian Odeion. I cannot accept his suggestion (pp. 290 f.) that Athena at the end is to be thought of as rising like the moon.

[41] I assume, with Immerwahr 1972, 293, that the audience would be reminded of Salamis. See n. 39 supra for the analogy between the Greek victory and mythological themes.

[42] Hunting of wild beasts is another expression of man's subjugation of nature. The audience might also think of famous beasts whose conquest was a heroic labor: Nemean lion, Keryneian hind, etc.

[43] Immerwahr 1972, 294, takes into account only this positive aspect of Kekrops.

[44] Cf. Kamerbeek 1948, 281; Wolff 1965a, 182.

forced to interact in a human situation, and the expected traces of
primitive animality flare up in his soul. He acts like his attackers.
Now it is Ion who is accused of attacking with fire (1293; cf. 974);[45]
now it is Ion who is ready to suspend his usual morality in the case of
someone who is his enemy (1312–19 and 1334; cf. 1045–7). But violence is again averted, and soon recognition comes. The tokens include
an embroidery of the Gorgon edged with serpents (1421–3; cf. 989–
96) and the snake-necklace traditional among the Erechtheidai. Just
as an implicit connection had been made between the abandoned
infant (Ion) and Erichthonios, so now Ion is equated with Erechtheus
when Kreousa embraces him and says: 'Erechtheus grows young
again and the earth-born family no longer looks upon night but looks
up at the torch-light of the sun' (1465 ff.).[46]

By line 1515 the themes under study here are almost exhausted
and indeed the play could almost end[47] there: Ion and Kreousa have
ceased using violence against each other, and their human emotions
are now directed toward the happier activities of mutual love and
sympathy for each other's sufferings. But resistance to Apollo's
already-shaken plan for the reunion of Ion and Kreousa and for Ion's
inheritance of the Athenian throne is not yet at an end. Although
Kreousa is now content, Ion has qualms, first about his paternity and
then about the (to him) disturbing nature of Apollo's behavior
behind the scenes in this play. The last stage of the quelling of Ion's
'battling against the god' is effected by the appearance of Athena *ex
machina*. Her arrival is prepared for by the fact that Kreousa twice
affirms Apollo's paternity by swearing in the name of Athena: once
as Gorgophona (1478), once as Athena Nike 'who once fought by the
side of Zeus' chariot against the children of Earth' (1528).[48] It is a

---

[45] Wolff 1965a, 181–2 recognizes that these two passages are significantly related,
but he does not go far enough in interpreting the motif. Cf. n. 31 supra on the use of
fire as a weapon by those who rebel against the gods. The theme of fighting against a
god is again touched upon (very lightly) in 1385f.   [46] Cf. Burnett 1971, 109.

[47] Cf. Lesky 1972, 433f. There is something in the view (implied by Lesky) that
Ion's renewal of doubt is introduced by the poet in order to motivate Athena's
entrance (contrast the view that the goddess forcedly glosses over doubts that cannot
really be resolved—cf. Lembach 1971, 119–24). But that cannot be the whole story:
Ion at the end of the play is meant to be different from the innocent boy seen at the
outset, for he has moved into the domain of everyday human society (cf. Willetts
1973, 209).

[48] Alternatively, lines 1528f. may mean: 'By Athena Nike, who once in her chariot
fought beside Zeus against the children of Earth.' Vian 1952, 200 gives reasons for
preferring the interpretation given in the text.

fitting conclusion to the imagery and iconography studied here that the final[49] calming of the primitive passions within Kreousa and Ion coincides with the appearance of Athena, conqueror of monsters symbolic of those passions.

No single approach can exhaust the richness of a good Euripidean play, and what is offered here is only one approach to one aspect of *Ion*. If the interpretation of the imagery and iconography offered above is accepted, the play can be said to have, together with light and comic elements, a serious aspect—the exposure of the intractability of human passions. An auxiliary gain is that passages often considered irrelevant or ornamental are seen to be integral parts of the poetic composition. In poetic terms we are shown in *Ion* that a primitive element of animality lingers in the blood of the earth-born race of humans. Although this animal vitality and emotion can be tamed and expressed in very valuable positive forms not similarly discernible in the immortal gods (e.g. loyalty to kin and homeland, compassionate concern for suffering), this element is occasionally uncontrollable and is shown, within the world of the play, to upset even the careful plans of a god. The humans are like the Giants, rebelling against what the gods have contrived for them. I do not believe, however, that the audience is anywhere invited strongly to condemn the humans for their intractability or to praise the beneficence and mercy of the divine beings. The human situation is

---

[49] I believe that it is final; that is, I do not endorse the often-expressed view (the most recent exponent is Lembach 1971, 119–24) that a residue of doubt remains at the end of the play. Ion accepts Athena's assurance and apologizes for his previous restiveness in 1606–8. Much has been built at times on the supposition that Ion is silent from 1609 to the end (14 lines, but really only 10 before the withdrawal of the actors): cf. Lembach 1971, 122, who says the silence shows 'die tiefe Betroffenheit des frommen Jünglings . . . dem über seinen Gott die Augen aufgegangen sind', 'the profound perplexity of the pious youth . . . whose eyes have been opened as to his god'. If it were true that Ion is silent from 1609 on, his silence should hardly be made to carry such a burden of meaning, for it is very short and not explicitly brought to the attention of the audience, as it would be if it were significant: cf. in general Taplin 1972, 57–97. But, as many editors from Hermann to Wilamowitz to Owen have seen, Ion is not silent. Line 1618a should be addressed to Ion, and he must speak 1618b; he may have been the speaker of 1617a (cf. Owen ad loc.). Lembach 1971, 122 n. 1, following Verrall and Murray's note in the OCT apparatus, endorses the distribution and attribution offered by LP, which assign 1616a, all of 1617, and 1618b to Kreousa and 1616b and 1618a to Athena; but manuscript attribution (and, to a lesser extent, distribution) of lines is often untrustworthy in passages like this, 1617 cannot be spoken by only one person (note the second $\gamma\epsilon$ and Wilamowitz's comment), and neither $\dot{\epsilon}s$ $\theta\rho\acute{o}\nu o\upsilon s$ $\ddot{\iota}\zeta o\upsilon$ ('be seated on the throne') nor $\kappa\tau\hat{\eta}\mu\alpha$ ('possession, acquisition') fits Kreousa's situation at all well.

Euripides' focus. The conflict in the play should not, I think, be viewed as one between merciful divine champions and reluctant human beneficiaries.[50] It is rather a symbol for a conflict within the human soul: the very condition of being human requires the presence of those dangerous autochthonous forces which make men, for Euripides and for his audience, different from and more interesting than the gods.

---

[50] Burnett in her stimulating book (1971) seems to me to err in the bias of her interpretations toward praise of divine beneficence. In many of the plays she discusses the divine action does indeed in the end set things straight; but the audience's sympathy, I submit, is with the human characters. We sympathize with Megara and Amphitryon's complaints in *HF*; we cannot condemn Orestes' diffidence and despair in *IT* or Helen's in *Helen*; and we do not feel the warmth for Apollo which we are made to feel for Kreousa in *Ion*.

15

The Closet of Masks:
Role-Playing and Myth-Making in
the Orestes of Euripides

FROMA I. ZEITLIN

Of what interest would an Oedipus be who fell victim
to the fate of marrying, say, his aunt?

Bert States, *Irony and Drama*

The *Orestes* is the most Euripidean of all Euripidean plays, reflecting
his typical techniques, emphases, interests, and outlook. All the familiar signs are present and perceptible: for example, novelty of plot,
rapidity and multiplicity of action, sensationalism and theatrical
virtuosity, lyrical experimentation, increase in the cast of characters
on stage, comic and melodramatic elements, the illusion-reality game,
the ergon-logos paradox, the use of cliché and rhetoric, a focus on the
phenomenon of alienation, on the psychopathology of characters,
their natural victimage and their subsequent retaliatory reflex, the
secularization of myth, the questioning of inherited values, and
compensatory themes of *philia* and *sōtēria* ('friendship and deliverance'), etc. etc.

What marks the difference in this play is the extent to which these
implications are carried out, the outer limits to which these techniques are pushed; it is a question of intensification, escalation, a
question of a relentless drive towards the achievement of a theatrical
'style which deliberately exhausts (or tries to exhaust) its possibilities
and borders on its own caricature', to quote Borges' definition of his
own baroque technique.[1] Yet the aesthetic boldness of the play's
excesses moves it out beyond any formal definitions and limitations,
beyond parody, beyond outrage into another mode, one might say,

---

[1] Borges 1964, xviii.

to a new level of self-consciousness and authorial extravagance that does not seem to have existed before. And it is a play whose surface of seeming incoherence, instability and chaos is, in reality, under that kind of artistic control that brings about that fusion of form and content we call art, even as it always seems to be trying to escape from it.

Ironic, decadent, 'modern,' even 'post-modern': these are the labels usually applied to the play and they are all correct in that they insist in one way or another on the self-conscious awareness of a tradition which has reached the end of its organic development, that the artist uses every device at his disposal to convey a sense of historical discontinuity with its attendant ambivalence that marks it both as an emancipation from tradition and as a disinheritance and loss.[2] No poet is more involved with the realistic facts of a present laboring under its intellectual and spiritual discomforts even as he is deeply aware of the aesthetic and redemptive possibilities of myth and of the past (that often lie just out of reach and are consigned to nostalgia).

The *Orestes* is the play that most acutely embodies this dilemma by placing myth and reality in their most paradoxical and problematic confrontation whereby each can only mirror the other in an odd series of reflections but can never close up the distance, can never reconcile the fundamental otherness that separates them. Both the myth and the city imprison Orestes in this play, and if the invention of a new plot is the necessary response to the claustrophobic conditions of culture, it can neither effect Orestes' liberation on the literal level of the action nor can it itself attain its own liberation by moving away from myth and mythic pattern into the mode of fiction. For myth is the relatively closed and predetermined form while fiction is the mode of new possibilities marked by a receptivity to experimentation and change.[3]

In the conspicuous absence of Apollo, the myth-sustaining god, myth seems to generate fiction, to move from mythic fact to a fiction which is contrary to mythic fact, since in the normative tradition, Orestes did not, of course, kill Helen. Faced with the embarrassment of characters who seem to be reading from another script, the play

---

[2] On the issue of modernism and its range of various meanings, see, for example, the excellent discussion of Spears 1970, 3–33. On 'modernism' in Euripides (of which the *Orestes* is an extreme example) see especially Arrowsmith 1964. On connections of the *Orestes* with the modern drama of the absurd, see Parry 1969, 337–53.

[3] I use here the distinction drawn by Kermode 1966, 39, although his polarities are far too simple. Myths are open to transformation and change, while fictions are often pervaded with mythic patterns.

first permits the enactment of that fiction and then denies it. But a dialectic is established between the myth and its fictional mutant. While the new plot struggles to accommodate itself to the changed circumstances which prompted its invention in the first place, it both marks a radical break with the mythic tradition and, at the same time, asserts the irresistibility of the mythic paradigm.

Fictional freedom is really only an illusion; the borders of the imaginative territory, even as the borders of Argos, are closed. Fictional freedom brings about a repetition of myth, since, as we shall see, Orestes has no other script that he can play and still be Orestes. Yet the repetition or near repetition itself of the matricide, while psychologically necessary, also undermines the original myth. Redundancy impugns the uniqueness and hence the symbolic necessity of the first deed. It taints both the exemplar and its skewed imitation. Creative repetition in a linear series of development establishes connections, continuities, and progressions. Cyclic repetition inscribes the actions under the assurances of cosmic regularity. But repetition in a closed and circular set of circumstances implies a rut, a stutter, as it were, a meaningless pattern that arrests both the plot and the characters and fixes them in a mode that cannot be transcended. But more of this later.

The *Orestes* is a drama that for all its novelties and innovations is more preoccupied with and more consciously reflective of the past than any other play in the tragic repertory. First, mythic time itself is extended under the pressure of the contracting circumstances of the play from a unitary focus on the house of Atreus and the major members in it. From the very first line, Electra signals that she looks to the remoter past to try to understand the present miseries by beginning with Tantalus and passing down through Pelops before reaching Atreus and the more familiar details of the immediate family. The myth seems to extend itself also horizontally by including the collateral members of the family, Helen, Hermione, and Menelaus (who all function as both doublets and opposites of the primary group). But this extension is also vertical, since Euripides is actually calling upon another earlier mythic model for this elaboration, namely, the *Odyssey*, where Menelaus returns to Argos just after the funeral of Aegisthus and Clytemnestra (4. 544–8), just as he does here with the slight alteration of a six-day delay. One mythic level is thereby superimposed upon another, and what is more important still, one literary work lies beneath another.

For we must distinguish between myth as a formal but formless category of narrative and myth as embodied in distinctive literary form and endowed with specific shape and language according to its genre. Here is where myth cannot be viewed in Lévi-Straussian terms as simply a bundle of constructs and relations, but rather as the province of an individual poet who, while in active engagement with the mythic material of the tradition, himself is involved in a true act of mythopoesis, is actively involved in the business of literature with all that that implies.

The most striking feature of the *Orestes* is precisely its literariness. It is perhaps the first work of literature in which close sustained familiarity with other texts is imperative for any genuine appreciation of its meaning and achievement. Even as the play attempts to escape its mythic frame and freely formulate its own actions and reactions, it makes an appeal to all the literary resources that preceded it to create a style of such rich allusiveness and resonance, such density of texture, that, although one can track down a movement in this direction in a few earlier plays, we might speak here of a new type of literary consciousness.[4] No other characters in a Greek drama are so bookish, so learned, although they themselves are marvelously unaware of their erudition. Myth and the past are funneled through the technique of allusiveness to other plays which implies not only an artistic judgment but a judgment of the version of the myth created by the poet in question as well as a judgment on the uses of literature in general.

Certainly, it is not the myth of Orestes, but Aeschylus' *Oresteia*, as many have observed, which is the major model against which the *Orestes* is formulated as a reaction, for we have every reason to believe that the third play, the Aeschylean solution to the dilemma of Orestes, was his own invention for the largest part, an invention which rapidly assumed the authority of a civic myth that transcended its mythological and aesthetic limits to exemplify Athenian ideology (or fantasy) of fifty years previous. Nor is this the first time that Euripides has done battle with the Aeschylean elephant both as an artist and as a thinker. In two other plays, the *Electra* and the *Iphigenia in Tauris*, he also assumes the stance of a fascinated antagonist/rival to Aeschylean solutions which he rejects, modifies, or alters. And it is

---

[4] The *Phoenissae* displays similar ambitions for the Theban saga, but the techniques used are less disruptive.

significant too that there are also allusions in the *Orestes* to these two plays, effecting a kind of ironic dialectic among all the competing versions.

Every modern critic, in fact, who has taken on the *Orestes* in recent times, has drawn attention to the numerous echoes from other tragedies, whether they be precise verbal reminiscences or structural motifs or situations which may be repeated, inverted, combined or contrasted with each other. The *Oresteia* has received the closest scrutiny, as might be expected, but Sophocles enters the scene too with his own *Electra* and with his *Philoctetes* produced only the year before. References to other Euripidean plays have been detected—to his *Electra* and to his *Iphigenia in Tauris* as I have mentioned above and to his *Heracles*,[5] but also to his *Helen* and his *Andromache* which have not been observed, and the *Medea*, the play that provides the closest parallels, has received only limited attention.[6] In short, we have here an ironic retrospective of the poet's own repertory, distorted, jumbled, and reduced in scope and stature. Even more surprising, the *Odyssey* does not seem to be mentioned at all by the critics despite its major contribution to the formation of the innovative plot,[7] and many other allusions in the plays named above have gone unnoticed.

What is more, beyond the usual shared parallels such as the invocation to Agamemnon's spirit, different commentators independently find their own references to other works which they interpret with varying degrees of discrimination to delineate the extent of the radical shift in Orestes' new environment. But a tacit principle is generally observed, that a single discrete original be proposed for each reminiscence, which creates a one-to-one correspondence and effectively limits the resonance of the text. While it is often true that

[5] See esp. the important study of Christian Wolff, '*Orestes*', in Segal 1968, 132–49, who best formulates the ironic balance in the play between tradition and innovation. See also the excellent analysis of the Oresteian echoes in Burnett 1971, 205–22. For earlier treatments of literary allusions see Steiger 1898, 20 ff., Krausse 1905; Perotta 1928, 1–53; and Krieg 1934. Other scholars who have made more recent contributions include Reinhardt 1960, 227–56, and above, pp. 16–46, Chapouthier 1959, 14–16; Greenberg 1962, 157–92; Rawson 1972, 155–67; Burkert 1974, 97–109; and Erbse 1975, 453–9.

[6] Diller 1960, 95, picked up by Steidle 1968, 109 n. 70 and 110 n. 81. See also Strohm 1957, 126, picked up by Arnott 1973, 60.

[7] The *Proteus*, the lost satyr play, that formed a pendant to the *Oresteia*, may well have been important to our drama, but we have no idea of its contents or its treatment.

this principle is operative, there are many other instances when one allusion conceals another and perhaps another, and we find a combination of literary allusions which creates what I have termed a *palimpsestic* text, where one layer can be deciphered under another; each one makes its own contribution, but the total effect is one of a bewildering and cumulative complexity that establishes a series of new if often contradictory relations between the primary level of the text and the oscillating substratum that shifts beneath it.[8]

For instance, in the first part of the play, Orestes has recourse to a magic bow given to him by Apollo to ward off the Furies (268–71) and the scholiast informs us that this motif was borrowed from Stesichorus' version of the *Oresteia*. At the beginning of the same scene, Orestes lies sleeping in a brief respite from the attack of the Furies. He has been compared both to Heracles and to Philoctetes who are both placed in similar situations. The parallel to Philoctetes is especially close since in that play the chorus, like the one here, takes care not to wake him at the behest of the observer of the scene (*Ph.* 825–6, 843–8, 865–6: cf. *Or.* 136–51). But Philoctetes is also in possession of a magic bow, a fact that no one mentions in connection with this scene, and it seems to me quite likely that Apollo's bow can and does do double duty. As an echo of Stesichorus, it signals the more primitive Apollo who pre-dates Delphic Apollo and emphasizes the ironic inadequacy of the god's device in a world that has already experienced the *Oresteia* at a double anachronistic remove from the new atmosphere of this play. The incongruity is even more marked between the archaic remedy of a concrete material object and the new internalized and hallucinated Erinyes.[9] At the same time, the bow works too on the affective level, and a series of ironic parallels is established with the sick and isolated Philoctetes whom society has

[8] Richard Gordon has now drawn my attention to Genette's piece, 'Proust palimpseste' in Genette 1966, 39–67. His use of the term to describe the Proustian vision ('ce palimpseste du temps et de l'espace, ces vues discordantes sans cesse contrariées et sans cesse rapprochées par un inlassable mouvement de dissociation douloureuse et de synthèse impossible', 51) is far more metaphorical than mine since I am speaking of the superpositions of literary texts and motifs. Yet Genette ends too by recommending to the reader to approach the work of Proust as a palimpsest 'où se confondent et s'enchevêtrent plusieurs figures et plusieurs sens, toujours présents tous à la fois, et qui ne se laissent déchiffrer que tous ensemble, dans leur inextricable totalité' (67).

[9] See Burnett's remarks, 1971, 202, but I disagree with her interpretation that the bow is 'a visible proof . . . of his [Apollo's] readiness to aid this miserable Orestes' and that his [Orestes'] relinquishment of it is a sign of 'blind faithlessness' (203).

also rejected. Each received the bow as a gift from a divine or semi-divine figure whose unwelcome command they obeyed. But Philoctetes' bow is truly efficacious and is the focus of the drama; Orestes' weapon is useless, a stage prop that may or may not be real,[10] and is soon discarded and forgotten. Both Philoctetes and Orestes are confronted by a modern world of cynicism, expediency, and trickery, a world Philoctetes stubbornly refuses to join even at the expense of his heroic potential, and a *deus ex machina* must compel his re-entry. Orestes, on the other hand, joins that world with such enthusiasm that a *deus ex machina* must intervene to curtail it, and that enthusiasm is generated precisely by the desire to make his heroic name.[11] Orestes should play Neoptolemus, his age mate and true counterpart, each in search of a paternal role model to follow, rather than the adult Philoctetes, but he ends up as Odysseus, and perhaps it is not too far-fetched to see in his appeal to the politically shrewd Menelaus for a single day of injustice (646–51) as a mad distortion of Odysseus' plea to Neoptolemus to suspend his moral standards for just one day (*Phil.* 79–85).

Yet surely this same scene is also meant to play as an inverted reminiscence of the opening of the *Eumenides* where it is the Furies who sleep, while Orestes is seated upright under the protection of Apollo at Delphi. There Orestes is given new birth at the navel of the world and awakens into new consciousness. Here he is tended like a baby and comforted with a lullaby. There Night is the fearful mother, author of terrors whom the Erinyes solemnly invoke (*Eu.* 321–3, etc.), the archaic feminine principle that is to be superseded in the movement of the last play to clarification. Here prayer is made to Night, now the gentle mistress who brings sleep and oblivion (174–7, 211–14). There Clytemnestra's ghost wakes the Furies and Apollo dramatically evicts them from the shrine. Here, in a reduced and miniaturized version, the chorus of well-meaning women wakes Orestes by its concern and curiosity as to his condition, and it is

---

[10] The scholiast comments that a real bow was once used on stage but was later abandoned in favor of pantomimed action.

[11] The *Philoctetes* too is a play whose *praxis* tends towards the negation of its *mythos*, namely, that Neoptolemus and Philoctetes might not go to Troy. But the device of Heracles as *deus ex machina* redirects the *mythos* to its fulfilment. Despite its ambiguities, it corroborates and rescues the heroic image. In the *Orestes*, on the other hand, the *deus ex machina* negates and overturns the *praxis* in its arbitrary confirmation of the *mythos*.

Electra who would expel them from the scene (cf. 179, *Eu.* 179–85).
Orestes' sleep, his shocking appearance that terrifies all but Electra,
his attack of madness, indicate that he himself is the Erinys, as later
imagery will make clear.[12] Here in this scene Electra takes the other
divinity's role when she directly echoes Apollo's words in the
Eumenides by promising that she will not abandon Orestes (262;
cf. *Eu.* 64), but it would be well to remember that in this very context
just a few lines later, Orestes mistakes her for an Erinys (264).

In fact, it is an operative principle in this drama that roles can and
do shift from one actor to another, implying not only confusion of
moral categories, but also fundamental confusions of identity. Change
(*metabolē*) is sweet in everything, says Electra (234, cf. 976–81), and
we might add, nothing is more changeable than personality. The
principle works both ways, for if Electra is now Apollo, now Erinys,
perhaps there was no real difference after all, and Orestes makes this
point explicitly at the end of the play when he remarks that he
thought Apollo's voice was that of a demonic *alastōr* ('vengeance
spirit', 1669). Through this technique of unstable fusion and diver-
gence of categories, those firm polarities of Aeschylean drama are
undermined, mocked, and finally negated. And since those Aeschylean polarities once operated in the service of a vision that was
founded on a belief in hierarchic stability, Euripidean confusions
must be construed as more than mischievous impiety.

The Heracles allusion is not forgotten either and returns again, as
has been suggested,[13] in the scene between Orestes and Pylades when
the latter loyally proclaims his allegiance and tenderly escorts his
friend to the agora where the trial is to take place (790–5; cf. 879–
83). We are reminded of the redemptive act of Theseus towards his
sick and dispirited friend (*HF* 1394–1404). He leads him off to Athens
in return for Heracles' redemption of him from Hades in marked
contrast to the hopeless and temporary venture in this play, one that
is a brief abortive journey. There Theseus bravely and startlingly
defied the conventional restraints imposed by the other's pollution in
the face of Heracles' overwhelming *aidōs* at having slaughtered the
members of his own family (*HF* 1214–34, 1399–1400). The same
motif returns here, but at an earlier point in the play, reduced now to
a careless indifference to pieties in both Helen's and Menelaus' casual
approaches to both Electra and Orestes (75–6, 481–9). The *Heracles*

---

[12] See Smith 1967, 302–3.   [13] Erbse 1975, 443–5.

again provides a negative foil now for Menelaus, the obverse of Heracles returning home to find his suppliant family under similar circumstances, Menelaus who, in fact, is the doublet of Lycus, the refuser of supplication and the tyrannical usurper of the throne.

Another minor but revealing example is the mention of the Gorgon in the Phrygian slave scene (1520–1). It functions as a proper allusion to the myth of Perseus and Medusa. Yet the myth of the Gorgon has already been connected to Orestes. First, in the *Choephoroi*, the chorus draws a specific analogy between Orestes and Perseus just before he goes in to kill his mother and it makes another oblique reference to the myth by speaking of Orestes' deed after its accomplishment as a heroic decapitation of two serpents (*Cho.* 831–7, 1046–7). The myth of Perseus is not, in fact, operative in the *Choephoroi*; the last reference is instead an ironic cue for Orestes' first glimpse of the Furies (*Cho.* 1048–50). The serpent woman dead has proved deadlier still and has produced proliferations of herself still more baneful than she. Beyond that literary commentary on the myth, Euripides himself has reused the motif in his own *Electra*, for the Gorgon figures on the shield of Achilles in the first stasimon of the play (*El.* 461), and it has been shown by O'Brien to be a potent and important image throughout the play.[14] At the moment of killing Clytemnestra, Orestes shields his eyes from the sight, not out of primitive terror at the monster, but out of shame, of *aidōs* before his mother (*El.* 1221), thereby transposing the gesture into the domain of social norms. His own cry, 'what stranger, what god-fearing man will look upon my head, who have killed my mother?' (*El.* 1195–7), hints at the applicability of the Gorgon allusion to himself but it is veiled in the traditional language of the polluted homicide. Now here in the recurrence of the Gorgon motif in the *Orestes*, the echoes of the other literary allusions return to confront a new distortion. Orestes now openly identifies himself in mockery as the primitive Gorgon, the Erinys (cf. *Eu.* 48–9; *Or.* 261); he now truly resembles Clytemnestra of the earlier works, a connection that not only announces his affinities with his hated mother and with her moral outlook, but it also transfers the archetypal female image to the male.[15] At the same

---

[14] O'Brien 1964, 13–39.
[15] Cf. the *Ion* where the Gorgon theme undergoes a more complex development in connection with the archetype of the murderous mother.

time, the allusion is made comic by the exaggerated cowardice of the slave who quails before a heroic encounter with his adversary.

In the case of this almost hermetic text of the *Orestes*, we are justified, I think, in taking a truly hermeneutic approach, one, as Geoffrey Hartman says, that eschews the 'straight line', 'the stigmatic approach', but one that sees 'writing as a labyrinth, a topological puzzle, and textual crossword; the reader for his part must lose himself in a hermeneutic "infinitizing" that makes all rules of closure appear arbitrary'.[16] And we are justified too in following out all the possible implications of a text which presents itself to the investigator much as a rich and many layered site does to the archaeologist who respects the relationships between the strata he uncovers, marking both their continuities and discontinuities, marking too the random-ness of the selection of artifacts, and being alert to the possibility too that objects may be misplaced and the strata confused.

In this archaeological structure of the *Orestes*, the culture presents itself as a 'reserve of art', 'a reservoir of resonances', a collection of *literary* artifacts, and a series of symbols and signs that can be drawn upon economically as a kind of evocative shorthand. Yet several inferences can be made from this basic formulation. In so far as these allusions are fragmentary and sometimes apparently random, cul-ture itself is seen as open to fragmentation, already fragmented, for words, gestures, and acts can be drawn out of their original contexts for the purpose of play, distortion, and dissonance, for reduction of meaning, for parodistic echo, and, above all, for a kind of treasonous and deliberate misunderstanding.

There is a Dionysiac 'chaos of forms', of supersaturation, of too many options crowding in from the past[17] that results in the creation of a turbulent text, a turbulence which is matched by the chaotic and turbulent plot that moves abruptly from one event to another with a corresponding turbulent shift in moods and attitudes of the characters. It matches too the new proliferation of actors in various

---

[16] Hartman 1976, 216.

[17] Hartman in Cohen 1974, 95–105. He is speaking of our modern predicament, but with a suitable reduction in scale, his formulations are adaptable to the age of Euripidean theater. In fact, what he says of one aspect of our current *history* is precisely applicable to the *literary* play, the *Orestes*: 'There is no "mystery of form" [Emerson's phrase] when forms lose their representativeness or mediational virtue: when men, distorting rather than exploring art's common-wealth, its link with an interpretable fund of roles, fall back on narrow concepts of manliness and reenact those tragedies of revenge which society was founded to control' (100).

degrees of relationship and affinity that now overcrowds the stage at Argos, characters who themselves adopt a 'chaos of roles'.

There is a kind of 'sparagmos' effect which, if taken far enough, encourages the decomposition of language itself, strains its lexical resources, reverses relationships, divides signifiers from signifieds in willful and arbitrary ways, and which in the dialectic between past and present supports the major divisive tactic of the play, namely, the anachronism that locates the mythological *geste* of Orestes in the contemporary political arena that subverts it and makes it incomprehensible, willful, and arbitrary.[18] That dialectic, in fact, is a failed one signalled by Orestes' rhetorical failures and by the successive failures of each of his actions.[19] The 'basic strategy . . . [of the *Orestes*, like that] of the Genet play, is to produce the sensation of a world composed of constantly shifting surfaces, an "architecture of emptiness and words" (says Archibald in the *Blacks*), beneath which we pursue "a skillful vigorous course towards Absence".'[20]

The distortion and confusion of the temporal sequence that underlies the apparently progressive movement of the tightly plotted series of events on the stage can be characterized as the major controlling symbol of the play. The distortion and confusion, the palimpsestic effect, in fact, increases in the second part of the play when the characters, casting about for a totally novel device to break the claustrophobic deadlock of their earlier efforts to cope with the stubborn refusal of circumstances to conform to the mythic paradigm, resort to a series of other scripts.

---

[18] An examination of the *Orestes* from this point of view would require separate and lengthy treatment. The whole play can, on one level, be read as an inquiry into the breakdown of language, speech, semantics, and communication signalled from the beginning by Tantalus' punishment for his unbridled tongue (*akolaston glōssan*, 10). The major symbol of this process is the Phrygian slave's rendition of Greek as he plays the role of the messenger (see Wolff's analysis, in Segal 1968, 140–2). The deconstructive impulse is manifested in other ways as well. Things may not be as one says they are (*hōs legousi* used three times in Electra's prologue as a commentary on the mythical history of the house). Things are what one says they are (the perversion of vital social words like *dikē*, the dissonance of heroic vocabulary in the latter part of the play). Rhetoric is translated into action, wish fulfillment into reality (see p. 331 and n. 44 below). Things are and are not what one says they are (hypocrisy, self-contradiction). (On Orestes' double-speak, see also Burnett 1971, 216 n. 12.) To these larger rubrics add the pervasive technique of literary allusiveness which self-consciously transposes, distorts, and perverts language.

[19] 'Only the *Orestes* makes outright failure its subject, imitating it with a series of actions that one after another go astray or simply disintegrate.' Burnett 1971, 184. See her whole analysis, 183–95.   [20] States 1971, 119.

In the earlier part of the play, the jumbled echoes of the *Choephoroi* and *Eumenides* are predominant: the replay of the libation motif with a new cast of characters, followed by a revision of the opening of the *Eumenides* with the sleeping Orestes. If here, as I have pointed out above, Electra plays the parts of both Apollo and Erinys, Orestes subsequently does the same. He uses Apolline arguments of the *Eumenides* in his appeal to Tyndareus in the altarless suppliant scene (552–6), but next plays Erinys in the assembly where, as Burnett observes, he paraphrases their arguments in a defense of 'their necessary punitive force among men', marking an 'anti-Apolline' stance (940–2).[21] The bridge between the first and second parts of the play is the justly often noted invocation of Agamemnon by the three conspirators (1225–45), which perversely echoes the great *kommos* in the *Choephoroi* (*Cho.* 479–509).

This allusion, of course, signals the coming replay of the matricidal act, for Helen, the mother's sister, is the intended victim.[22] The affinities between the two women are first marked by their genealogy (which is emphasized by Tyndareus' presence on the stage), and by their marriage to brothers, next by their sexual appetites and their indulgence in adultery, and finally by the daughter Hermione, natural child of the first and adopted one of the second (64–5, 109, 1184, 1340). Hermione literally acts as liaison between the two since upon her falls the duty to bring the signs of Helen's devotion to Clytemnestra[23]—and note that Helen's first act upon her return is to re-establish her relationship with her dead sister. But the terms in which this new matricide is carried out are those of the *Agamemnon*. Again Burnett has drawn attention to the verbal echoes that create an affinity between Clytemnestra of that play and Electra and Orestes of this one. 'Like his Aeschylean mother, this Orestes feels no shame in speaking of his own dissimulation, and like her he will take pleasure in the shedding of kin blood (1122; cf. *Ag.* 1372 ff.).' They, like her, would add a second victim to the first, also a virgin; they too are *alastores, syllēptores* ('vengeance spirits, accomplices', 1230; cf. *Ag.* 1507). 'Having earlier begged his sister to be unlike her mother,

---

[21] Burnett 1971, 208.
[22] Perotta 1928, 1–53 draws attention to the repetition of 'matricide' in the assault on Helen, but the theme is more fully developed in Greenberg 1962, 160, 184, 186, and *passim*. This parallelism of action forms the basis of his entire interpretation.
[23] The scene recalls too Sophocles' *Electra* with Hermione now taking the role of the sister Chrysothemis as bearer of libations from mother and foil to Electra.

he now hails her for her masculine wit (1204) . . . and she seems to accept the tribute as she plans to "net" her prey (1315) and to hide her joy with her mother's pretence of grief (1319) . . . '[24] The murder, like that of Agamemnon, is carried out in images that relate it to ritual sacrifice. Burnett is perhaps correct here in suspecting also a profanation of the mysteries,[25] but it is also worth pointing out that nowhere else in Greek tragedy is so much blatant sacrificial language used throughout a play with such indiscriminate and careless prodigality, upholding the basic principle that when sacrificial imagery is used in tragedy, it warns the audience that murder imaged as sacrifice is to follow. But, at the same time, that very prodigality of reference divests the sacred words and gestures of their mystical power, reducing them to cliché, slogan, and absurdity.[26]

There is another important parallel, here an inverted parallel, of the *Agamemnon*, which has been overlooked, namely, the affinity between the Phrygian slave and Cassandra. The Phrygian slave is himself a polysemous symbol of the play; he is certainly, as has been pointed out and will be discussed below, a mirror of Orestes, but surely we can see in him the reverse doublet of the Trojan princess. He babbles in terror in a debased version of Cassandra's mad prophetic ravings as the new representative of Troy in Argos. The Trojan princess, in her new status as captive slave in Agamemnon's house, still stands outside it; she understands the present, past, and future, both near and remote, and foretells the death of Agamemnon as well as the circumstances of her own approaching death, a death she goes

---

[24] Burnett 1971, 210–11.   [25] Burnett 1971, 216 n. 11.

[26] With one exception, sacrificial language is applied to all the family murders or threats of murder alluded to in this play: the literal sacrifice of Iphigenia (658–9), the murder of Thyestes' children (814–18 cf. 1107–10), and that of Clytemnestra (842–43; 291; cf. 1236, 562–3). The attempt on Helen at the hearth of the house (1284–5; cf. 1107; 1493–4) even includes the gesture of pulling back the neck of the victim for the fatal blow (1471–3; cf. 1513) and Menelaus himself in his lament over her uses the same technical term (*sphagion*) as the other characters (1614). Hermione too is drawn into the same semantic sphere (1199, cf. 1193–4, 1596; 1345–56, 1349–50, 1575, 1671). Orestes terms his Furies priestesses of the underworld who are ready to kill him (260–1) and in the oddest metaphorical use of all, Electra claims that Apollo has sacrificed (*exethyse*) them as vengeance for the matricide (191–3). In the *Agamemnon*, it was Clytemnestra who used sacrificial imagery for the slaying of her husband (see Zeitlin 1965, 463–508). Here in the *Orestes* his death is the only one that is *not* imaged in these terms, a fact that increases the dissonance of their language even as they overecho and almost parody Clytemnestra's Aeschylean terminology.

to meet with a courage her new masters admire. The Phrygian slave rushes *out* of the house *after* the deed to tell what he saw with his own eyes but which he did not understand, and to cringe in terror for his life (1369–1530).

Here is a triple palimpsestic effect: the murder of Helen, a second matricide, under which lies the first one, the murder of Clytemnestra, and beneath that, the murder of Agamemnon (with subsidiary echoes of the murder of Aegisthus in Sophocles' *Electra* (*El.* 1409–12; cf. 1301–10)). As the plot progresses, the allusive associations suggest a regression through the trilogy back to the first play. In the *Oresteia*, each play provided a specific point in time. In the *Agamemnon*, the fates of Troy and Argos were linked through the returning vanquisher of Troy, and the suggestive language of the text connected Trojan and Argive in many ways, as, for example, in the parable of the lion cub (*Ag.* 717–36). There Cassandra herself was the mediator between Troy and Argos, and her murder by Clytemnestra drew the queen also into the net of guilt over Troy. In the second play, the immediacy of the Trojan war has passed and the king, long dead, was rehabilitated as the great military hero. Only the chorus of Trojan servant women remained to allude obliquely to the past, although their loyalties now lay firmly with the house and with Orestes (*Cho.* 75–83). In the last play, Troy is gone, recalled only once as a topographical location, the place from which Athena comes to Athens to judge Orestes' case (*Eu.* 397–402). Each new event, each progression of the trilogy has crowded out the one preceding. Concentration of interest narrows, the cast of human characters dwindles until one human being stands alone in the spotlight. Clytemnestra is only a ghost and appears only at the beginning of the play to yield her place to her supernatural surrogates. Iphigenia, Cassandra, Aegisthus, the children of Thyestes, the hereditary curse on the house are only memories. The emotional dynamics of personal relationships have been gradually purged away and the intellectual and theological issues, the abstract concept of justice and how it is to be executed, are now the focus. By contrast, at the beginning of the *Orestes*, Electra, the family archivist, extends the accursed heredity of the house as far back as it can go to the two preceding generations of Tantalus and Pelops (1–11). It was Pelops' act which inaugurated the curse (995–6; cf. 972); it is Tantalus, the first father, to whom she longs to flee (985), and it is with the poor victim children of Thyestes that she compares herself and her brother (1007–12; cf. 814–15).

Here in the *Orestes*, Troy, emblem of the recent past, is again an operative issue. Helen, only sung of in the *Agamemnon*, is here before our eyes. The play opens with the return from Troy of another hero, the paternal uncle. In this reading, Menelaus is both a doublet and opposite of Agamemnon. Agamemnon's susceptibility to oriental blandishments is here enlarged into the more fully barbarized figure of Menelaus with his luxurious pomp (349) and golden curls (485, 1532, 1754). But while Agamemnon proves naive and gullible, Menelaus is a shrewd politician. Like Agamemnon, he returns with a woman he loves, but, unlike his brother's situation, that woman is his wife, not his concubine. Far from maintaining the double standard by indulging in the *male* prerogative of sexual freedom (i.e. Cassandra), Menelaus actually violates it by forgiving his adulterous wife and reinstating her in her old position. Agamemnon, upon his return, is lured into the house to his death. Here it is the woman alone who is drawn into the trap. Moreover, Agamemnon's crime was to sacrifice his daughter. Here Menelaus will be in the position of trying to save his daughter. Orestes, in fact, assumes at the last his father's role as a sacrificer of a virgin daughter,[27] now in an effort to avenge himself on the father figure who failed him, who, in competition with him for the throne, looks back to Aegisthus and to Atreus before him. Orestes is, in fact, now at war with both parental figures.

But in the introduction of Helen and Menelaus under their own names upon the scene, there is still a further retrograde movement in literary time since for his new plot, Euripides, as mentioned earlier, has used a variant of the Homeric tradition in the *Odyssey*. The Phrygian slave's reference to Odysseus (1404; cf. 588) establishes the textual connection and the Odyssean parallels, arranged now in a new palimpsestic series of allusions, oscillate between Odysseus, Telemachus, and the Orestes of epic, the Orestes who in the *Odyssey*

---

[27] For Orestes, Agamemnon's sacrifice of Iphigenia was only further proof of the debt Menelaus owed to his brother and surviving children; he will not demand exact reparation: Menelaus need not kill Hermione (658–9), he declares, in wonderful ironic innocence of the act he will shortly agree to perform. That repetition will, in fact, apply not only to the obvious parallel between Hermione and Iphigenia, but it will be reduplicated in the attack upon Helen who will disappear at the crucial moment as in the variant version of the myth of Iphigenia (used before by Euripides in the *Iphigenia in Tauris* and soon to be used again in the *Iphigenia in Aulis*). Burnett 1971, 199–200 n. 15, comments that 'both Helen and Hermione are . . . associated with Iphigenia as being likewise innocent victims, for the poet calls them *skymnoi* (1387; 1493; cf. *Agam.* 141–3 of Artemis and her love of young animals, i.e. Iphigenia).'

is specifically posed as the positive model for Telemachus' coming of age, a comparison to which Orestes himself refers in 588–90.

First, recall the motif of Odysseus in Phaeacia who hopes to win reception from a king through the supplication of his wife Arete at the hearth (*Od.* 6. 310–15; 7. 141–54), and remember that Orestes' plot to kill Helen takes place at the same location in the house and hinges on a pretended repetition of that act of supplication (1408–15, 1437–43). Next, recall the meeting of Helen and Telemachus in Book 4 with its aftermath in Book 15. In the first context, Helen enters with her weaving implements (*Od.* 4. 131–5), and in the second, she gives him the gift of a robe she had made herself for him to bring back to his future bride (*Od.* 15. 125). Here in the *Orestes* (1436), Helen is weaving a robe as a funerary gift for Clytemnestra (although one can hardly resist noting that the last thing the dead Clytemnestra would seem to need is another robe). In the *Odyssey*, Telemachus' visit to Sparta coincides with the celebration of the double wedding of a brother-sister pair (*Od.* 4. 3–4), while our play ends, of course, with the prediction of a double wedding of a brother-sister pair (1654–9). Hermione is the bride in both versions, there to Neoptolemus, here to Orestes, and Apollo will be quick to annul the other betrothal (1654–7).

The conflations accumulate. Homeric Troy is recalled by the Phrygian slave's narrative of the battle within the house which combines Homeric and Aeschylean language and which alludes by name to the heroes Ajax and Hector (1479–80). Note too that Orestes himself plays the part of the magnanimous hero on the battlefield who spares the life of his enemy suppliant (1523–8). But in the skirmish within the house, the scene now shifts to Ithaca: the battle with the suitors is evoked first by the locking up of the servants to prevent their interference (1127, 1448–51) and then by the ensuing carnage (1482–9). In both the *Odyssey* and the *Orestes*, the key to success lies in planning and in treachery, and the Phrygian slave makes reference to that similarity by comparing wily Odysseus with Pylades, the son of Strophius, in a pun upon his father's name (1403–6).

But here the aim of the action is inverted; there the purpose is to kill the suitors who tried to impugn the loyalty of the faithful wife, here to slay the unfaithful wife, although this unfaithful wife bears an uncanny resemblance to the faithful wife. It is tempting to see in Helen at her loom at work on a funerary garment the figure of Penelope, the archetypal weaver of shrouds (1431–6). Like Penelope, the model housekeeper, Helen, Orestes suspects, has already begun to put things in order by taking inventory and placing a seal upon the household goods (1108).

But what has Orestes to do with Troy? Its events lie far outside his experience and his usual sphere of association. In so far as the Trojan references serve to unravel the *Oresteia* back to its beginning play, Troy establishes identifications between Orestes and his father of that drama. But in so far as Troy is represented in its Homeric terms, it might be said that Orestes looks to Troy and its epic symbolism as a model for heroic action. It might also be said that he looks to Ithaca for a positive re-enactment of his original Odyssean role in Argos. And if the main action in Odysseus' house is the reverse of the action here (i.e. the slaying of the unfaithful wife), the same principle is operative in both, namely, the principle of patriarchal marriage and the punishment of sexual transgressors, whatever their gender. Orestes earlier in the play himself suggests this Ithacan context to come when in defense of his position he reminds his grandfather at the climax of his misogynist tirade that Telemachus did not slay the wife of Odysseus, for she did not add a second husband to the first but remained at home, an uncorrupted companion for his bed (588–90).

What a marvelous ironic inversion! Orestes had served as paradigm to Telemachus; now, discredited, he needs Ithaca to revive his old emblematic self in a new guise, still more grandiose than the first. His new action will give him a new title, not the matricide, avenger of his father and his disinherited children, but slayer of Helen, avenger of all the fathers, brides, and orphaned children of Greece (1132–42; cf. 1584–90).[28]

But before I proceed with this line of thought, I would like to draw attention to a third palimpsestic effect, namely, the extraordinary relevance of the *Medea* as the closest and most compelling model.[29] First, the general theme of revenge as an act of desperation by a victim in a situation in which there seems to be 'no exit'.[30] Secondly,

---

[28] Beye 1975, 295–6, goes still further: 'Orestes' defense before the people of Argos turns on the symbolic value of his act (565 ff.), really his worth as living theater and symbol. His very act of defense is indeed theater. Pylades' arguments for murdering Helen (1132–4) . . . reinforce the idea of Orestes as emblematic. And ironically . . . Orestes is the first significant paradigmatic figure in extant Greek tragedy.'

[29] 'His [Euripides'] *Medea* left a deep and lasting impression in the minds of his Athenian audience; comic parodies, literary imitations and representations in the visual arts reflect its immediate impact . . .' Knox 1977, 193 and nn. 2, 3, 4.

[30] See Reckford's excellent essay (1968), 329–59.

the more specific motivation to action in the theme of betrayal by a
loved one ('betrayal' is a favorite word of both Medea and Orestes)
and the revenge taken on the traitor by assault upon his spouse and
his progeny. Thirdly, the appearance of the avenger on the rooftop,
holding the child in question and refusing to give back the body.[31]
Only Medea, of course, is her own *dea ex machina* and will make good
her escape, while wingless Orestes (cf. 1593) will be displaced and
superseded by the rightful owner of the upper space, the god Apollo,
and will discover that he has no true talent for accomplishing a
vengeance that was not in his original script. His first victim, Helen,
moved upward to divine status, ironically not totally unlike the final
status of Medea herself.[32] The second victim is to become Orestes'
own wife. More important still, he thought he was the Orestes-
Telemachus of the *Odyssey*, but turned out to be a debased Medea, a
Medea without her demonic concentration of mind and passion.

But this cross-sexual identification between Orestes and Medea
and the regressive movement that leads Orestes to try on again his
Odyssean mask, namely, to assume the role of an Orestes who was
never condemned for matricide, are the two most significant clues in
the play. Together they provide the keys to Orestes' behavior, which
is not simply a homicidal mania or a gratuitous self-indulgence or a
spontaneous involuntary reflex as various critics have proposed in
turn, but a wonderfully delusional attempt to re-establish for himself
and his dilemma that old world in which his myth was operative and
had meaning. His youthful naiveté and his bookish misreadings
reduce the myths of the past to slogans of misogyny and Homeric
heroism and he crudely transfers these into the present by updating

---

[31] Strictly speaking, the body Menelaus demands is that of Helen, while he has
hopes of saving his daughter. But in each case there is a request for the corpse in
order to give it burial that will not be granted (*Or.* 1585, cf. 1564–5; *Med.* 1377, cf.
1402–3). Both scenes begin with a command to open the doors of the house and that
too is refused (*Or.* 1560–1, 1567–8; *Med.* 1314–16).

Arnott 1973, 59–60 also remarks on the parallelism of the theatrical device in both
plays that misleads the audience by first drawing their attention to the doors in the
usual anticipation of witnessing the results of an act of violence and then raises their
eyes upward to the unexpected appearance of the character on the roof. But Arnott
attributes the same shock value to the repetition in the *Orestes* on the grounds that
twenty years later 'memories of its original impact would have faded enough for its
effective exploitation', while my point, of course, is precisely the opposite.

[32] An inversion too of Euripides' other Helen in the play of that name in which the
malevolent phantom disappears and the rightful innocent Helen is restored. Here the
guilty real Helen is absolved and katasterized as a reward.

them with the current slogans of patriotism and pan-Hellenism.[33] This naiveté emerges in a gloriously perverse idealism and it leads him to believe that a second matricide under these old-new circumstances will be more effective than the first one, will, in fact, wipe out the first. Blood will be washed out by blood, not as an act of compensation, but as one of extension. It will earn for him his first heroic laurels which he fully expects as a reward from society for his deed (1132–42; but cf. 565). The operative fantasy is that he will be praised again and held up as a model as he was in the *Odyssey*. But in actual fact, he ends up on the female side in tragedy, identified with Erinys, Gorgon, Clytemnestra, Medea, and even Hecuba. And of the characters in the current drama, his situation is closest to that of both Electra and Helen.[34]

The Phrygian slave is not only Orestes' own absurd and cowardly shadow figure, his own alter ego,[35] but as a eunuch, a figure neither male nor female (1528), a hybrid of both, he has a larger immediate value, first, as the best sign of the indeterminacy of genders in the various roles Orestes has consciously and unconsciously adopted for

[33] On the heroic vocabulary used in the intrigue scene, see Reinhardt 1960, 252, above, pp. 41–2, Burkert 1974, 102.

[34] 'The Helen of the prologue is a figure that repeats that of Orestes. Both are tools the gods seem to have laid aside, and both in consequence are unpopular among mortals, etc.' Burnett 1971, 201. Beyond the obvious affinities between Electra and Orestes, marked by the emphasis on their devotion to one another, there are also structural similarities: each meets the collateral family member, female confronts female and male male. Smith 1967, 302 notes that 'Helen and Menelaus produce the same effect on the children and as Menelaus exits, Orestes ridicules him behind his back as Electra does to Helen (125 ff. 717 ff.).' In still more general terms, it is the old, the very young and the women who find themselves in situations of 'no exit' like Orestes.

[35] 'This brief scene recapitulates the play. Orestes plays viciously at an indecision with which he is himself really afflicted. The slave in turn is a distorted reflection of the Orestes who had cried out for his life (644 ff., 677 ff.), and whatever pathos those cries had expressed is now grotesque ridicule. And the cause of that ridicule is Orestes himself. He taunts the slave, dangling the lure of life before him, as he himself has been taunted, bedeviled, and harassed—by circumstances, gods, men, and the impulses of his own mind. Orestes in his dejection had said to Menelaus that "we are enslaved to the gods, whatever the gods are" (418). He now acts out divine arbitrariness upon another slave, his image.' Wolff in Segal 1968, 137. See also Parry 1969, 345.
The Phrygian slave is also the doublet of Electra. Each has an unusual monody framed by choral passages, itself astrophic (1369–1502; 982–1012). Each is faced with imminent death, one by the decree of the assembly, the other by the violent pursuit of Orestes. Each yearns for escape to the upper air (1376–7; 982–3). The sea–air dichotomy is maintained, although in a different way (1377–9; 990–4), etc. See also Biehl 1965, 150, but he sees the two as antithetical rather than parallel.

himself, and more generally, as a concrete indication of the merging of the polar distinctions of sexual categories which are normally maintained in tragedy. The eunuch, therefore, speaks directly to the issue of the collapse of male values in this society, values which are subscribed to only by Pylades, Orestes, and the clearly anachronistic old farmer in the assembly (who himself, in his proposal of a crown instead of stoning for Orestes (923–5), is an echo of Euripides' *Electra*).[36] More specifically, the eunuch is also the inversion of Aeschylus' androgynous Clytemnestra, once a worthy adversary to Orestes, now reduced to the other side of androgyny, the weak effeminate male. Is it not significant that the *Oresteia* begins with an image of confusion in sexual categories and ends with firm hierarchical distinctions established between male and female, while this play, towards its end, resurrects the old image, inverts it, corrupts it, and by this inversion, affirms and even escalates the confusion? Moreover, since male values are the dominant values of the group, this collapse signals the collapse of the subsidiary polarities which are subsumed under the fundamental rubric of the male–female dichotomy. The Phrygian eunuch slave in confrontation with Orestes is then himself an emblem of the collapse of all the social polarities, of slave and free, Greek and barbarian, of inner and outer worlds. And the deflation of male values is also aptly represented in the image of the unsexed male; his impotence in fact and behavior is an instant metaphor of a generally deflated and impotent society.[37]

Orestes, deprived of his social role as defender of his father and his father's society, turns to a second action, first to avenge himself on the father figure who betrayed him and, as he claims, his father (1588), and then to undertake the larger project of making the world safe again for patriarchy. No one who is *philopatōr* could condemn him ('who loves his father', 1605). Otherwise, his myth doesn't play, and as an actor in this new drama he has been forced to create, he must repeat the act of matricide, since once he is in Argos, an Orestes, like a broken record, can perform one action and one action only,

[36] The farmer, of course, recalls the setting of the *Electra*. There Orestes has come to win the crown for slaying Aegisthus (614; cf. 581, 591, 675). On the importance of the *kallinikos* and the crown, see Zeitlin 1970, 656–7 and above, p. 272.

[37] On the symbolic value of impotence in another example of anomic literature, see Arrowsmith 1966, 309, and Zeitlin 1971, 673. The latter article makes some general comparisons between Petronius and Euripides, 678–80.

namely, he can kill mothers or mother surrogates and wives who are adulterous, and he can ally himself solely with paternal principles.

On the other hand, from the psychological point of view, this is a true case of repetition compulsion, for blocked from purification, expiation, and reconciliation, Orestes can only re-enact the trauma again and again. It has also been argued convincingly by Lichtenstein that repetition compulsion does not belong to the sphere of the 'death instinct' as formulated by Freud, but is rather a 'manifestation of the necessity for the maintenance of the "theme of identity". Identity in man requires a "repetitive doing" in order to safeguard the "sameness within change"' which Lichtenstein postulates is 'a fundamental aspect of identity', the first priority in human life.[38] Plot and person intersect as the plot runs down towards its own extinction at the assembly's decree of death for Orestes, subverting the course of his *mythos* which promised him salvation, not condemnation. In the midst of the multiple roles Orestes has tried to assume, repetition becomes the ironic guarantee of the salvation of Orestes' identity, a motive Orestes affirms indirectly at the moment of his acceptance of the plan by formally proclaiming himself the child of Agamemnon, the father who once ruled Greece (1166–7).[39]

But what is, in fact, most egregiously absent from this society is any strong allegiance to patriarchy, a point ironically emphasized by the artistic device of redundancy, since Orestes in this play, far from being fatherless, is overendowed with an embarrassing number of fathers. Electra refers back to Tantalus and Pelops with whom she tries to establish identifications from the beginning of the play (5–11, 971–1000; cf. 348). For Orestes there is the dead and silent Agamemnon (425–6) whom he earlier suspects would not even have approved of the deed (288–92); there is Apollo who is absent and does not defend him (419–20; 596–9). Menelaus, his uxorious paternal uncle, in the same structural position as the returning Agamemnon, has even looked forward to greeting Clytemnestra (372–3), and he

---

[38] Lichtenstein 1961, 235. See also Caldwell 1976, 417–18.

[39] The maintenance of identity through repetition of real or symbolic action is a characteristic feature of the economy of tragic representation. Cf., for example, Agamemnon's trampling on the *sacra* of Troy and his treading on the carpet before the palace in Argos, Oedipus' repeated role as riddle solver and interpreter of oracles and his double trespass on forbidden female territory, once through incest and once in the grove of the Erinyes, and Medea's career as a user of children as destructive instruments against fathers. Orestes' mythic role, however, does not span a lifetime of events but is normally centered around the single non-repeatable act of matricide.

betrays his affinities with the barbarian and sensual East where women rule. In fact, he is the least likely candidate in the world to be persuaded by the Apolline arguments of male biological superiority which Orestes absurdly addresses to Tyndareus in his hearing (552–7). Even more, he turns out to be not just the betrayer of kin, but an active hostile rival who has his own designs on the kingdom.

Tyndareus, his maternal grandfather, is the true surrogate father since he gave Orestes fosterage (462–5), but he is Orestes' most vigorous opponent. He speaks badly of his two adulterous daughters (518–22), but his vindictiveness Orestes later shrewdly observes is really due not to Orestes' violation of the law but to his personal anger over his daughter's murder (752–3). His presence on the stage, after all, is prompted by his self-imposed errand to pay his respects to Clytemnestra's tomb, a desire shared by his other daughter who is, to this extent, identified with him.[40] The redundancy of *two* eager visits by relatives to pour libations to Clytemnestra emphasizes the distance in mood between this play and the opening of the *Choephoroi* where the neglected tomb of Agamemnon provides the dramatic focus of the drive towards the restoration of the law of the father and the male patriline. Collaterally, Pylades, now given an authentic genealogical relationship to Orestes, is condemned by his father for his participation in the matricide and is banished from his native land (763–7), a sign that the social censure is not simply an Argive aberration.

The society itself, represented by the assembly, is filled with both his father's friends and comrades at Troy[41] and the supporters of Aegisthus. The argument against Orestes poses the matricide as a bad precedent for the safety of both parents, precisely the Erinyes' argument in the *Eumenides*. Even more, the aetiology of the already established institution of the law court refers back to the inverse crime, involving Danaus and his daughters, which concerned the killing of husbands, not of mothers. The principle of justice that

---

[40] From another point of view, I agree with Burnett's assessment that 'Helen is . . . the exact opposite of her father Tyndareus, who argues, like Creon, that principles must override the ties of blood', while she displays 'sisterly devotion' and 'thoughtless familial sympathy' (200–1).

[41] Wedd 1895, Introduction, xxvii, remarks 'that Talthybius, whom he [Euripides] represents as leading the attack on Orestes, was not only regarded by a general tradition as having rescued him at the time of his father's murder, but was in all probability represented by Stesichorus as actually helping him in the murder of Aegisthus and Clytemnestra'. If these resonances are alive in the play, Talthybius might serve as still another surrogate father figure who fails him.

substitutes a tribunal for a vendetta was built on the precedent of the opposite paradigm. Yet justice itself is not even mentioned as an issue in the assembly and Tyndareus, the archetypal father figure, entitled by his age to serve as spokesman for the institutions of the fathers (512), only pretends to support the principle of male superiority and public standards of female behavior in a show of concern only for the external forms. In a parallel hypocrisy, he only poses as the champion of civic justice, first, because his original arguments to Orestes on the rule of law are specious, as Grube pointed out,[42] and secondly, because he shifts to open advocacy of reciprocatory mob violence (612–14, 915–16).[43]

In short, the society provides no norms, the fathers no role models. If Orestes has learned anything from Tyndareus, it is duplicity, role-playing, lip service to ideology, intrigue, and vengefulness. If he has learned anything from Menelaus, it is a basic mistrust of paternal behavior. What is more, he has realized that if Menelaus' readiness to enjoy future happiness with his adulterous wife is condoned, his own original act of matricide is annulled and negated. Orestes may be an exemplar of 'modern' man in his sickness and instability of spirit, but he is also archaic man, who looks to the archaizing aspects of both the myth and values that underlay it in order to redeem himself. He becomes, in fact, a mythmaker in a world that has turned its back on myth. But his efforts are limited and distorted by his superficial socialization and his naiveté in relying on outworn ideologies of patriarchalism and patriotism. He has read his texts but he cannot discriminate between levels of meaning. Thus he acts out literally the standard rhetorical fantasy of killing Helen which many other characters in many Euripidean plays give utterance to at moments of despair. But they, of course, never act upon it any more than a chorus that yearns to take wings and fly away to some distant land ever expects to fulfill its dream.[44]

---

[42] Grube 1941, 384.

[43] Reinhardt 1960, 245–7, and above, pp. 35–7. See also Wolff in Segal 1968, 143. The best that can be said for Tyndareus is that he himself is unaware of his hypocrisies, of the feebleness of his arguments, and his own inconsistencies. In this reading, the spokesman for society has not succeeded in grasping its principles beyond the most superficial level of mechanical enunciation. But his rage at Orestes seems to me to suggest a more conscious corruption.

[44] On the negative portrait of Helen in Euripidean drama, see the collection of the evidence and the discussion of Vellacott 1975, 127–52. Helen in the *Orestes* still arouses strong and contradictory reactions from her literary critics. The pendulum

In short, Orestes' dilemma is that of the other desperate young men in Euripidean drama, including his counterpart in the *Electra*, namely, how to be a man in a world in which there are no men, in a society without fathers.[45]

In fact, *Society Without the Father* is the title of Alexander Mitscherlich's modern study in social psychology which investigates and describes the kind of personality which results from the breakdown of paternal and paternalistic authority, where society no longer provides an identification with a positive and realistic father figure. Although Mitscherlich's interest lies in this breakdown of authority under the impact of modern industrial and urban trends, it is remarkable how closely Orestes' personality in this play fits the clinical description.

The mature and well-integrated individual is one who has passed from the first stage of development in the 'imitation and unquestioning experience of things' to the next stage of 'identification with [role] models', and then, having incorporated those models and internalized them, successfully completes a positive development into a self-sustaining and critically conscious individual. Without this process of internalization, the individual is unstable. 'He is governed by . . .

swings widely from one extreme to the other—from Vellacott's view that 'the killing of Helen is the destruction of gentleness, warmth, and beauty, experienced by a people [the Athenians] who have suffered and inflicted a generation of ferocious war', 73, to Erbse's (1975) equally astounding justification of the murder of Helen on the grounds of her guilt and of the imperatives of the heroic code, 445–7. Burnett 1971 gives the best assessment of her positive and negative characteristics, 199–201.

The motif of longing for escape through ascent is actually very prominent in this play which is not surprising in view of the claustrophobic environment of the city. Electra feels herself already bound up with her race sprung of nobility and wishes to fly to the rock of Tantalus (982 ff.). The Phrygian slave also yearns to fly into the sky (1373–4). But these *adynata*, whose element of fantasy is even more conspicous in the realistic world of the *polis* (cf. 1593), ironically find their fulfillment in Helen's miraculous deliverance (1498, 1580, 1631, 1633, 1636).

[45] The *Electra* is particularly relevant to this theme. There the young man in search of an adequate male image is beset on the one hand by Electra's fantasies and inflated ideas of masculinity (the recognition scene, often read only as a parody of Aeschylus, makes clear her denial that she could ever fill Orestes' shoes; her speech over the dead Aegisthus is equally instructive) and, on the other hand, by a trivialized model—that of the standard war hero and of the athletic victor in the games. The identity Orestes assumes, that of a Thessalian, makes him a master butcher, and his putative destination, Olympia, suggests an athletic context which the later references to *kallinikos* ('beautiful in victory') confirm. Yet earlier he expressed only scorn for displays of physical prowess in athletics (386–90) and he yearns, like other Euripidean characters, for an objective touchstone by which to judge his fellow men (367–7).

external stimuli without being able to organize these in the sense of a consciousness, a self . . . He lives by the feeling of the moment', he has a 'basic mistrust', is given to scapegoating, to the release of aggressive drives, to psychical infantilism, and gives his loyalties only to a peer group. He has not 'grown into a system of values, ideas, and commandments guided by his personal models', but displays 'a manipulated conformity; he is an "echo person" '. Instead of a positive development into a tangible individual personality, there is simply 'role behavior that picks up slogans' to live by. He is, in fact, arrested at a stage of reliance on role-playing, role stereotypes, and role status. The result, Mitscherlich observes, is that 'compulsive role-playing in the service of an unconscious superego and compulsive drives that are practically unhampered by consideration for others often coexist in the same person', and there are often 'abrupt transitions from one [type of reaction] to the other', in psychoanalytical terms, 'from behavior guided by the superego to that guided by the id . . . True unification of the personality depends on incorporation of instinctual experiences into the identity feelings; it is this alone that makes it possible among the temptations of everyday life to prevent behavior from ending in real guilt, contempt, callousness, anti-social behavior, or "killing with a good conscience". ' And Mitscherlich goes on to quote Riesman's study of the 'other-directed' man for whom 'the requirements of civilization are not assimilated and firmly associated with the attainments of the ego, but are complied with only provisionally: the "other-directed man" . . . does not have a superego with permanent contents; . . . his principles do not evolve, but merely follow one another in catastrophic succession as the ideologies born of catastrophe require'. Moreover, in the collapse of real paternal authority, this kind of person whose 'model is that of a mythical idealized father, immune to error, temptation, anxiety', etc., is continually in search for a new father on whom to rely, here in Orestes' case, the idealized society of men who will applaud him for his version of heroism and patriotism.[46]

By playing a character in a drama where his role has been determined only by the facts of his myth, Orestes' response to Apollo's command was equally externalized. In this play, Orestes reveals no true understanding of the implications of his actions. He has not, like the Orestes of the *Choephoroi*, had the benefit of an author to give him

---

[46] Mitscherlich 1970, 14, 285, 53, 82, 186, 49, 300–1, and *passim*.

a four-hundred line *kommos* so that he could integrate the god's imperative into his own, so he could explore the full nature of the deed he was about to commit and thus fully accept his own personal responsibility. Hence he oscillates in the first part of the play between remorse and resentful feelings of victimage. He has only been an instrument of the gods; he has never understood. 'We are slaves to the gods, whatever gods may be' (418). And the proof of the pudding, of course, lies in his willingness to commit the same act again, in the playing out of a predetermined role again and again.

The Orestes in this play is the black mirror of the Orestes in the *Iphigenia in Tauris* where release from the guilt and pollution of matricide is made possible through the creative energies of myth and mythopoesis which, if restored to their proper paradigmatic function, can direct human action to redemption. In that play, Euripides resorts to the archaic value of myth as a 'template' for identity and for reintegration of self; he programs Orestes into a scenario of mythic adventure that had no place in his original myth.[47] This adventure not only recalls the earlier heroic voyage of the *Argo* past the Clashing Rocks to the same locale, but itself also conforms to the archetypal initiatory pattern of a journey outward into the beyond, into another world, with its ordeals, its quest both for a sacred talisman and for the release of a maiden.[48] The ancient model is particularly well-suited to Orestes' dilemma, for the rescue of the maiden who is his own sister is an exact compensatory act for the violence done to his own mother, another female of the family. At the same time, by his act, Orestes reverses his father's original outrage which was the sacrifice of that very same daughter.[49] Here, however, in the *Orestes*, the opposite holds true. The son aims to repeat both matricide *and* the sacrifice of the maiden. What is more, the private benefit in the *Iphigenia in Tauris* is accompanied by a positive public service, namely, the deliverance of the goddess and the bringing of her cult, now civilized, to Greece, an inverse parallel to Orestes' negative intentions in this

[47] A cult of Artemis/Iphigenia in Taurus can be attested, but it is generally accepted that the rescue plot was Euripides' own invention. For discussion see Burnett 1971, 73–5.

[48] See e.g. Neumann 1954, 195–219, on the pattern of the captive and the treasure. (Even the dragon combat motif which comprises the first act of this scenario is present in the *IT* through the choral ode on Apollo's slaying of the Pytho (*IT* 1235–82).) See also Guépin 1968, 120–46, on the specifically Greek material—the 'Kore Drama' and the 'Theft of the Palladium', especially in relation to the *Iphigenia in Tauris*.

[49] Oddly enough, no one seems to have noticed this crucial symmetry.

play—to settle private scores, and by further violence to another female, to do patriotic service to his country. That is, the first is an additive, incremental act, the second a subtractive, diminishing one.

Like the *Orestes*, the *Iphigenia in Tauris* also plays on the idea of a potential repetition of the violence of the members of the family towards each other,[50] but the situation is inverted. For Orestes, the inversion is only partial. To Iphigenia who is a double for the murderous Clytemnestra who slays males of her family, he is now the victim and not the slayer. To Iphigenia who is also an Erinys figure, his persecution by the outraged and vengeful female is a continuation and completion of the Furies' task. Iphigenia's situation is more truly an inversion. She is now the potential Clytemnestra, but she is also the sacrificer of the male of her family, an exact reversal of her original role at Aulis. But the repetition is arrested before its completion through recognition and reconciliation. Yet, by its near re-enactment, Iphigenia is able to discharge her own resentment, to come to terms with the traumatic events of the past, and to slough off the murderous role she has been forced by circumstances to play.[51] Orestes, for his part, has undergone a symbolic death, first, by his location in the land of the Taurians where Iphigenia is presumed dead and which itself, as Guépin points out, is a symbolic representation of an underworld,[52] and, secondly, by his willingness to submit himself to the sacrificial knife. Even more specifically, what proves redemptive there for all the parties—Iphigenia, Orestes, and Pylades who accompanies him—is the willingness of each of them at a given moment to renounce personal salvation in favor of the redemption of the other (*IT* 674–722, 1004 ff.), a secular act of sacrifice set within the frame of ritual sacrifice.[53]

[50] On the various correspondences in plot and themes between the *IT* and the siblings' earlier experiences, see Wolff 1965*b*, 90–107, Burnett 1971, 47–75, Caldwell 1974, 23–40, and Sansone 1975, 283–95.

[51] See especially Wolff 1965*b* 94, and Sansone 1975, 286, 287, who notes that 'what Orestes undergoes in the land of the Taurians is, in effect, a ritual reenactment of his sister's fate at Aulis'; it is 'not merely an *aition* but a paradigm'.

[52] Guépin 1968, 123–33.

[53] 'A purely human and spontaneous sacrifice is offered within the framework of the irrational and necessary ritual one . . . The ritual has been a test of human character, and once passed, it can be put to other use . . . It suggested the deception and limitation of human knowledge. It underlined, as it required, a capacity for sacrifice. Having shown themselves capable of sacrifice, finally, the actors themselves, as though having understood the ritual, make of it an instrument of deception and their salvation.' Wolff 1965*b*, 101–2.

Here, in the *Orestes*, when the news comes from the court that they are to die, even as the sacrifice of the two Greek strangers among the Taurians was decreed, the trio looks to re-enact that same redemptive action by the offer of self-sacrifice and expressions of solidarity (1045–99). But in the closed world of the city, the adoption of these other roles proves a theatrical gesture and explodes into absurdity and dissonance. When Electra begs Orestes to kill her, he peevishly gives the reply from the other play that killing one woman in the family is enough (1039; cf. *IT* 1007–8), and when Orestes and Pylades go through their routine, there is outright contradiction. For how can Orestes generously offer to spare Pylades their common fate and to send him home as he did in the other drama, when Pylades has expressly come to Argos because he has been banished from home by his outraged father? (cf. 765, 1076–7).[54]

Self-sacrifice offered and refused in the *Iphigenia in Tauris* was a prelude to beneficent intrigue that was to secure their release; self-sacrifice here takes place in a vacuum of despair, is made futile, and is immediately abandoned in favor of an intrigue that is repetitively destructive. The original motive for heroic and ennobling self-sacrifice is a role which is given to characters who are in a terminal situation, such as Polyxena in the *Hecuba* or Makaria in the *Heracleidae*. Polyxena would die with honor since life with honor is no longer possible. Makaria would sacrifice her life for the safety of the group. She sounds the patriotic motif which will be fully developed in Euripides' next play, the *Iphigenia in Aulis* (cf. *IA* 1369 ff.). Here, in the *Orestes*, the patriotic call is heard, but in an inverted way. There the noble characters were in a position to fulfill themselves by voluntarily undergoing self-sacrifice. Here, the characters suddenly seem to remember that they are males acting out female roles. They stop short, reverse the terms: they will display their patriotism by enforced sacrifice of a female.[55]

The repertory of tragedy and epic provides, as it were, a closet of masks for the actors to raid at will, characters in search of an

[54] Greenberg 1962, 183.

[55] It is tempting here to see a conflation of the two females in *Hecuba*: Polyxena and her voluntary sacrifice, Hecuba and her project of revenge (again directed in part towards the progeny of the offender who has betrayed his duty towards a child to whom, as *xenos*, he stands in the fictive relationship of kin). Only in the *Phoenissae* does Euripides give the sacrifical role to a young male in an act of the poet's own invention, but he is there clearly adapting the typical female gesture for the specific purposes of the play.

identity, of a part to play. In the frame of the psychological model, Orestes' compulsive addiction to role-playing is readily comprehensible. But the terms themselves, 'role-playing', 'persona', 'acting out', 'mask', are metaphoric terms borrowed from the theater, and it is, after all, a play that is being enacted, the most theatrical of all plays. It is the one play, is it not, in which the *deus ex machina* most specifically breaks the theatrical illusion of reality to inform us that this was only a play. What happened on stage (or rather just off-stage) did not really happen, and he, the director, has come forward to tell the audience that the play is over and done with, that it was a free exercise of the imagination, as insubstantial ultimately as the vaporized Helen.[56]

From the point of view of aesthetics, if tragedy is the mimesis of an action, this play is really the mimesis of a mimesis. And what we find in the *Orestes*, for the first time on an extended scale, is a truly self-reflective work of art, that is, like Hamlet's play within a play, art in the process of reflecting on art. David Kiremidjian in an essay on the aesthetics of parody observes that 'all examples of work of art in a . . . self-reflective state will have one thing in common. The form will no longer represent nature . . . The normal imitation of life will become the imitation of the artistic self, the object of the form having become the work itself, resulting in a kind of self-mimesis . . .' And the time in which 'parody itself becomes integral to the forms of primary art', transcends its normal functions of criticism and humor, is 'generally at the end of a tradition when established forms are exhausted', when pervasive original parody, like that in Joyce or Mann, is used to 'express modes of experience which are otherwise inaccessible aesthetically . . . Since [the contents] are, obviously, fixed by necessity, the artist instead requires that the adapted forms absorb modes of experience which they have never absorbed before, and hence effects an expansion of their potential.'[57]

[56] On the theatrical effects of the ambiguity surrounding Helen's supposed death, see Arnott 1973, 56–9 and Gredley 1968, 415–19, both of whom, in the interests of maintaining a consistent mystification as to Helen's fate, would excise 1503–36 as an interpolation, thereby losing the most significant moments of the encounter between Orestes and the Phrygian slave. Moreover, the juxtaposition and even alternation of two conflicting versions of Helen's end promotes a confusion that is equally essential to Euripidean dramaturgy (cf. e.g. the device of double fathers in the *Heracles* and the *Ion*).

[57] Kiremidjian 1969, 238–40. (I have slightly rearranged the order of the quotations.)

Or one might speak with Bert States of 'heavily ironic drama . . . [which] tends to show up late in a given dramatic tradition . . . All new drama . . . in its time may be viewed not only as the playwright-thinker's triumph over hitherto unreachable experience, . . . but as the audience's gradual triumph over the *old* drama . . . When the audience becomes relatively immune to the tensions through which the old dramatist has had sport with it, the new playwright, rising arrogantly from the audience once again challenges it "to play", to be re-engaged, . . . a new game at last.'[58] And I continue with another quote. 'The drama has, really, no choice but to go a progress through all the available possibilities in a continual struggle to retain its powers of fascination. The dramatist accomplishes this by becoming in turn more particular, more inward, more "free", more indifferent to moral questions, more paradoxical (a standard device for eluding discovery), by offering as much sensation as the traffic will bear, until he is finally performing with only a side glance at nature herself, reality observed being mainly the already formulated realities of the tradition to which he belongs. Fidelity to experience, moral qualm, truth—these are indeed perpetuated, but *in terms of the medium*. Decadent art [and this term is not used pejoratively] may even be great art, but it almost always requires a decadent audience to appreciate it.'[59]

Euripides has often been accused of destroying tragedy, and the loss of civic solidarity and fragmentation of cultural values blamed as the major social obstacles to its continued health. All this is true, no doubt. The form itself had also exhausted itself. From the mass of tragedies produced during a period of roughly a hundred years, we have only a few choice morsels of the best playwrights, none or little of the debris of the second-rate authors and second or third best tragedies, to say nothing of those which might have been rejected from competition altogether at the outset. How many times can one write about Orestes telling his story again and again and again? Euripides, in general, went further afield to work new mythological territory and to try new dramatic experiments, but Orestes, the proverbial cat, comes back. He can't stay away.[60]

---

[58] States 1971, 126–7.   [59] States 1971, 130.

[60] 'The fulfillment of form is, paradoxically, also its exhaustion and limit: an acknowledgment, namely, that it is these objects and these alone that form will accommodate. Ultimately, the objects victimize the form, stamp it, as it were, with fixed associations, and remove it from legitimate artistic circulation. This is another

From an aesthetic point of view, we can understand the exasperation of Orestes, having exhausted his entire repertory of mythic and
tragic stratagems in order to break out of his myth, but doomed
again to repetition or near-repetition in a mode that now threatens to
destroy him altogether, we can understand the exasperation of Orestes,
like that of Strepsiades in the *Clouds* of Aristophanes, that would lead
him to set fire to that brooding house of Atreus as the only way to get
that blasted Orestes and his infernal problems off the tragic stage
once and for all. Images of apocalypse belong to both social and
aesthetic domains.[61]

But he will go down in a blaze of glory. The scene on the roof is the
most complex palimpsest of all, telescoping the burning of Troy and
the sacrifice of Iphigenia, the coming about full circle to his own
childhood experience in another Euripidean play as a hostage at the
hands of Telephus, and the completing of a more local ring composition that begins in this play with the image of Tantalus suspended
between heaven and earth, a distorted and fugitive mutant of the
opening of the *Oresteia* with the watchman on the roof waiting for a
beacon fire, and finally above all, superimposed, Medea, triumphant,
broken loyalties avenged, the figure who is her own *dea ex machina*,
counterpointed to that poor Orestes, who, in the absence of the god,
the director of the play, has tried to take over and keep things moving,
but this was the best he could come up with (cf. 1179). This is the
point where Apollo appears in the space above him and seems to say:
'move over, you've had your chance. I'm taking back my *mythos*.
Your play is over.'[62] But Orestes is not to go totally unrewarded
for his efforts, his innovations, his creative amalgamations and
confusions. He is to be sentenced for one year to Parrhasia, the land

way in which art shows its relation to nature, in the same way that Aristotle
acknowledges it when he establishes the object of imitation as one of the distinctive
marks of the genres themselves', Kiremidjian 1969, 240.

[61] Cf. also Beye 1975, 296 who suggests that the house is 'the incarnation of the
myth of the House of Atreus, more still the symbol of the myth'.

[62] Hourmouziades 1965, 168 (echoed by Webster in Allen and Rowell 1968, 29, and
Arnott 1973, 60), remarks that at the end of the *Orestes* 'the arrangement of persons is
unique in that all the possible levels of performance are exploited to the full: the chorus
are in the orchestra, Menelaus on the logeion, Orestes, Pylades, and Hermione on the
roof, Apollo and Helen in the air'. Apollo's appearance above Orestes signals, of course,
the re-establishment of the hierarchical distinction between men and gods (as also
between author and actor), but the visual effect of the multi-level presentation might
also serve as the perfect spatial analogue to the palimpsestic text.

of free speech, to which he will give his name, Oresteion (1643–7; cf. 905).[63]

And, if the truth be told, Apollo does not really restore the *mythos* in all of its details. He, as director, reserves the right to alter the *mythos* or adapt it as he sees fit. The difference between him and the actor is that he has control of the proceedings, while the actor does not. So we note with interest that the trial is to take place at the Areopagus, as planned, although we note that any question of the judgment passed on Orestes being a founding act of justice is now out of the question. First, it is a redundancy of an existing court at Argos, and secondly, the god in a regressive nullification of the Eumenidean achievement has taken away from mortals the right and power to judge these difficult issues and has given it to the gods who have the freedom (or perhaps the license) to make their own choices at will. And we note too that there is no question even of the vendetta as a principle being superseded in any permanent way by a more advanced form of justice, for we are told, by the way, that Neoptolemus will go to Delphi to seek recompense from the god for the death of *his* father, Achilles, and will be killed there. Neither the god nor the mortal transcends the *lex talionis*. Yet divine justice of the traditional type is not always operative either. Men are not allowed to fight with gods, that is the rule, and Neoptolemus is to pay the usual price. In this play, however, Orestes, in an earlier fit of despair, had suggested idiotically that the matricide was Apollo's doing, and they should kill him instead (595), but the wrath of the god was not visited on him. Quite the contrary. In a similar vein, Tantalus' demotion from equal status with the gods at their banquet is countered by Helen's installation in the halls of Zeus as *paredros* ('one who sits at his side', 1683–8). On all levels, this is a truly arbitrary world.

The reference to Neoptolemus serves still another function, allied in another way to that same principle of arbitrariness, for by it clear allusion is made to the *Andromache*, a play which the poet himself has already written, a play whose plot we are told retroactively will never

---

[63] Smith 1967, 307. The *parrhēsia* might well be related to the *akolaston glōssan* of Tantalus, that most shameful disease (*aischistēn noson*, 10), and to the demagogue in the assembly who speaks with a brutish *parrhēsia* that is *athyroglōssos* (903–5; literally, possessed of a tongue without a door), and might well serve as an emblem of the general logorrhea which afflicts this play, one of the longest in Greek tragedy. Burnett 1971, 184, 185–6, points to the unusual length of the introductory material and to the 'monumental scene of confrontation and persuasion' which is 450 lines long, almost double those in the *Heracleidae* and the *Suppliants* (of Euripides).

take place. While this might, of course, be simply a device to inform the audience that the poet is exercising his prerogative to use a different version of the same myth, and is here taking the trouble to emphasize a truly 'happily ever after' conclusion, untainted by any negative resonance, it seems to me that more can be made of it. Certainly, it adds a new confusion, thus increasing the general epistemological doubt. Secondly, the Olympian god retains his authorial right to supersede the playwright-god in another act of arbitrary decision. The gesture is perhaps a self-conscious emphasis of the basic theatricality of the myth in both plays, no *hieros logos*, but just a play, no illusion of fidelity to a coherent tradition, but just another play.

There is special meaning, too, in the comparison I made between the firing of the house of Atreus and that of Socrates' Phrontisterion in the *Clouds*, which it may most resemble. Recent critics have noted the breakdown of genre regularity in Euripides, or rather the intrusion of elements appropriate to other genres and the emergence of new motifs, devices, tonalities that heralds genres not yet born.[64] There is, as Alastair Fowler says, a 'life and death in literary forms', and he rightly points to the last phase of this process where 'genre tends to mode . . . The equivalent mode, flexible, versatile, and susceptible to novel commixtures, may generate a compensating multitude of new generic forms.'[65] Like the mytheme of creation by the dismemberment of a primordial being, from Euripides' dismemberment of tragic integrity arises a proliferation of potential new forms, and, like that other mytheme of creation from chaos, that is, the evolution from undifferentiated or confused form to forms of greater definition and specialization, genre development will exhibit a parallel sequence. New literary forms will progressively detach themselves, formulate their own rules, find their own specific voices and claim their new entitlements to generic identity, and the whole process will begin again in a never-ending rhythm. *That* repetition is assured.[66]

---

[64] e.g. romance, pastoral, new comedy, mime, melodrama, and satyr play. See, for example, Burnett 1971 on satyr play elements in the *IT*, Knox in Cheuse and Koffier 1970, 68–96; and Arrowsmith 1964 on the mixture of genres.

[65] Fowler in Cohen 1974, 92.

[66] A preliminary version of this paper was presented at a conference, Directions in Euripidean Criticism, which took place at Duke University, March 1977. A later version served as the first Procope Costas Memorial Lecture at Brooklyn College, May 1977.

16

The Masque of Dionysus

HELENE P. FOLEY

From the earliest times Greeks worshipped Dionysus in a theatrical form—through masks, costumes, miracle plays, music and dance. Euripides wrote the *Bacchae* at a time when his contemporaries were becoming increasingly self-conscious about the nature of their theater god. In Aristophanes' *Frogs*, Dionysus, as spectator, actor and judge in his own festival, seeks to save the city by rejuvenating its dramatic art. Contemporary visual artists were just beginning to popularize the theatrical Dionysus, seated among actors who display the masks and costumes of plays performed in honor of a young and often effeminate god.[1] In this paper I argue that Euripides closed a career of increasingly manipulative and illusion-breaking treatment of dramatic conventions[2] by presenting us in the *Bacchae* with yet another *fin-de-siècle* 'theatrical' Dionysus.[3] Nevertheless, unlike many modern

This paper is drawn from my 1975 Harvard doctoral dissertation, *Ritual Irony in the Bacchae and Other Late Euripidean Plays*. A part of it was presented at the December 1978 APA convention. I wish to acknowledge here both the help of those who read and commented on the thesis, especially John Finley, Cedric Whitman, and Christian Wolff, and of readers of the present paper, Ann Bergren, Duncan Foley, Rick Griffiths, Piero Pucci, and the anonymous referees. I also thank Charles Segal for a copy of a paper presented at the Duke Euripides Conference in March 1977, which takes an approach complementary to my own, but reaches different conclusions.

[1] The controversy over the relation between the origins of Greek tragedy and the worship of Dionysus is irrelevant to my argument, since we know that Euripides' contemporaries thought of Dionysus as a theater god. See *Clouds* 518–19 for another reference to Dionysus as patron of comic poetry. The earliest known artistic treatments of Dionysus in a theatrical context are the Pronomos vase (*ARV*[2] 1336), the Peiraeus relief (fig. 51 in Pickard-Cambridge 1968), and possibly the fragments of a vase from Taranto now in Würzburg (*ARV*[2] 1338). These works date from the end of the fifth to the early fourth century.

[2] See, among others, Segal 1971, 610–12 and Winnington-Ingram 1969*a*, 129–42, and above, pp. 50–63 on Euripides' self-conscious treatment of dramatic conventions.

[3] My position here is meant to be complementary to and not exclusive of the standard—and I think, correct—interpretations of Dionysus in the *Bacchae* as a nature god or a god of religious ecstasy. The mysterious divinity of the *Bacchae* has

playwrights, he was less interested in a self-conscious exploration of his own drama than in the way art interprets human and divine experience for the city.

In the *Bacchae* Dionysus reveals himself to Thebes primarily through means which are common to theater and the larger Dionysiac tradition—voice, costume, music, dance, and song. It is precisely for this reason that the *Bacchae* is one of the few Greek plays in which we can make reliable inferences about the stage production from the text. We know the musical instruments that the chorus carried, and the major features of the costumes of all the principal characters with the exception of the messengers. We know that the mask of Dionysus was smiling (439, 1021). We can reconstruct much of the stage business concerning costume and musical instruments. The language of the play refers with remarkable frequency to the visual and musical experience on stage and emphasizes that both honoring and comprehending the god are essentially theatrical acts, an exploration of the nature of illusion, transformation and symbol. If the Thebans are to receive the god without disaster, they must, like Cadmus and Tiresias, accept a transformation of the ordinary self through costume and respond to the music, dance and emotional release that Dionysus offers. Compare, for example, the effect on Pentheus of Tiresias' speech about the god with Tiresias' and Cadmus' gesture of dressing and dancing as his followers. The physical transformation communicates to the king as the rationalizing speech does not. Sound, gesture and symbol express the god even more effectively than language. Pentheus, the ruler of Thebes, is destroyed through his inability to understand truth in the symbolic form that Dionysiac religion and theater offer to the adherent or spectator. Hence he finally cannot play a role, but surrenders to it. The *opsis* of the *Bacchae*, to use Aristotle's term for theatrical spectacle, is not simply a *hēdusma* or additional 'seasoning'. The plot or arrangement of events, the action or *praxis*, and the spectacle become for large parts of this play one and the same thing.[4]

multiple aspects; but I wish to stress, by emphasizing here the way in which Euripides presents Dionysus throughout the action, that the proto-theatrical form of his appearance is also a key to his dramatic meaning.

[4] See *Poetics* 1450[b]28 for Aristotle's discussion of *opsis*. I do not intend to imply here that the *Bacchae* abandons words as a mode of effective communication; this would be absurd in any drama. But both Dionysus in the prologue and the chorus in the parodos place extraordinary emphasis on presenting the god's divinity through

Up to the death of Pentheus, when the god withdraws from the
level of human action, Euripides has his Dionysus control the play
and make it a manifestation of his divinity (I). Dionysus makes the
death of Pentheus a kind of 'play within a play', which is characterized in the language and action of the text as a proto-dramatic festival. In his own 'drama' the god who fuses and blurs the antithetical
distinctions by which Greek culture defined itself—man and woman,
god and man—also blurs the distinction between the tragic and comic
genres. The terrible death of Pentheus is to the god, the mad Agave,
and the chorus of believers a cause for the kind of joyous celebration
which traditionally closed old comedy. Euripides, by contrast, offers
the audience in the final scenes an answer to Dionysus' play and a
tragic perspective on the same event (II). Finally, the way in which
Dionysus presents his mask to the audience precisely summarizes in
theatrical form the way in which Euripides uses the stage action to
illuminate the ambiguous nature of his patron divinity (III).

I. DIONYSUS' PLAY

Euripides has Dionysus begin the play by sending his followers into
Thebes to beat their drums about the palace of Pentheus 'so that the
city of Cadmus may *see*' (61):

> αἴρεσθε τἀπιχώρι᾽ ἐν πόλει Φρυγῶν
> τύμπανα, Ῥέας τε μητρὸς ἐμά θ᾽ εὑρήματα,
> βασίλειά τ᾽ ἀμφὶ δώματ᾽ ἐλθοῦσαι τάδε
> κτυπεῖτε Πενθέως, ὡς ὁρᾷ Κάδμου πόλις.

> Lift up the drums that are native in the land
> of the Phrygians, the invention of mother Rhea and myself,
> and surrounding these royal halls
> of Pentheus, strike them, that the City of Cadmus may see.[5]
>
> (58–61)

He will make himself manifest (*emphanēs*, 22) to Thebes through dance
(21). He will fasten on fawnskins and hand the *thyrsus* (Bacchic
wand) to the citizens (24–5). He has forced the female population of

---

voice, costume, music and symbolic actions—that is, non-verbal means of appre-
hending the god. After the stranger leaves the stage at 976, having completed his
plans for vengeance on Thebes, there is a gradual movement to a renewed emphasis
on effective verbal communication.

[5] The translations in the paper, unless otherwise noted, are from Kirk 1979. Greek
quotations throughout are from Oxford texts.

Thebes to adopt his costume (*skeuē*, 34). In short, Dionysus, himself in human disguise, will reveal his divinity to Thebes primarily through spectacle, costume and sound as he controls and stage directs the play.

The language and action of the play allow Dionysus, until the return of the second messenger, to make the play and the manifestation of his divinity part of one indivisible process. His role as stage director corresponds with his role in the plot—to demonstrate and then to avenge his divinity; his role as *chorodidaskalos* ('chorus leader', 58 ff.) is inseparable from his being leader and god of his worshippers; his role as producer of stage illusions matches his ability to inspire a change of mental state in his followers; and, as we shall see, his presentation of his smiling mask, his 'comic' performance in a tragic *agōn* ('contest'), communicates the meaning of his religious ambiguity for the audience. Dionysus makes the chorus his players and his destruction of Pentheus a 'play', replete with set, costume and spectators. Until the final messenger speech there is no action in the play that is not controlled by the god or voluntarily supportive of him (the chorus, Cadmus, Tiresias, the *therapōn* ('servant'), the first messenger) except, for a brief period, Pentheus' own. The play itself becomes the net in which the increasingly isolated Pentheus is trapped.[6] Euripides' characters, especially his gods, sometimes execute their own staging. Medea, for example, perhaps expresses her transformation to something more than human through her power to stage her final encounter with Jason from the chariot of the sun. But in this play the process becomes a pervasive expression of Dionysus' own nature, and of his control over theater as its patron. Yet Dionysus' 'play within a play' does not, like many modern 'plays within plays', or like the tragic parodies of ancient comedy, function primarily to distance the audience from the drama and call attention to and question its own reality as art; instead, it implicates the audience in the drama and calls attention to its own art as reality. That is, theatrical illusion demonstrates the reality of the god and illusion and symbol are our only mode of access to a god who can take whatever form he wishes (ὁποῖος ἤθελ', 478).

Dionysus begins the play by putting on stage (55 ff.) a chorus who are his followers, not the citizens of Thebes. They make his music and

---

[6] As has often been noted, Pentheus shifts from hunter to hunted in the play, but the preliminary stages of this confrontation involve music, dance, symbolic displays, and costuming.

use his instruments, sing imitations of his ritual songs to cult meters, dance his dances, tell his myths, and, in the palace scene, respond to a divinity that Pentheus can neither see nor control. They are, as I suggested, his players, for each ode reflects or anticipates the shifting demonstration of divinity promised in the prologue. In the parodos they display the god's costume, music and dance and invite Thebes to join in their worship (see especially 105–6). In the first stasimon, taking their cue from Tiresias' speech in defense of the god, the chorus shift to present in lyric form a similarly anachronistic view of the god as a fifth-century patron of symposia and festivals.[7] They endorse the opinion of the ordinary man (*plēthos*, 430), which is immediately voiced on stage by the *therapōn*.[8] The second stasimon marks the transition in Dionysus' position from 'powerless' to powerful as it moves from despair at the imprisonment of their leader to a recognition of Dionysus' divinity as it is manifest in the destruction of the palace and in the sound of the god's voice off-stage. Whatever we conclude occurs in the palace scene, whether nothing at all, or a major or minor change in the stage building, no stage business at this point could adequately imitate the apocalyptic destruction, including lightning and earthquake and a ruined palace, which the chorus see while Pentheus does not. The miracle must become for the audience more symbolic and prophetic than realistic. They see not a miracle, but a chorus enacting the experience of a miracle, or presenting a theatrical illusion.[9] The third stasimon (862–911) takes up the god's words in a previous scene—that he will avenge the god who is *deinotatos* ('most terrible') and *ēpiōtatos* ('kindest') to men—by moving from release to vengeance, using the same metrical patterns to express joy and anger; it is immediately followed by the scene in which Pentheus sees double, and sees for the first time the bestial

---

[7] For a more detailed treatment of the complex and multi-layered choral odes and their undermining of fifth-century ethics, see especially Arthur 1972, 145—81, and Diller 1955.

[8] See Dodds (1960) 117 and 131 on the relation between the first stasimon, the Tiresias scene, and the appearance of the *therapōn*. The movement noted by Dodds in the third and fourth stasimon from particular to universal which is contrary to Euripides' usual practice may arise from the exceptional responsiveness of the chorus to shifts in the fate of their cause in each preceding scene.

[9] For the most recent discussion of the palace scene with an up-to-date bibliography, see Castellani 1976, 61–84. I am still inclined to agree with Dodds (1960, xxxvii) that Euripides has put a 'psychological miracle at the center of the action'. Theatrical—or psychological—illusion are the only avenues by which the god can be worshipped and understood.

as well as the gentle aspect of the stranger. In the fourth stasimon the chorus prophetically imagine Pentheus' destruction on the mountain, soon to be reported by the messenger; the final ode celebrates the god's victory over Pentheus (1153–64).

In the *Bacchae*, then, the chorus replay or 'preplay' through partially ritualized song, dance, and music, what Dionysus and his converts enact with language and gesture only. At the same time they do not occupy the same position, emotionally, intellectually or perceptually, between the royal family and the audience as they do in other tragedies. They stand between us and the more extreme perspective of the maddened spectators to Pentheus' tragedy on the mountain, and their attitude, because of their exclusive allegiance to the god, comes to seem pitiless and inhumane. This creation of multiple audiences to the god's theatrical demonstration of his divinity makes the spectators conscious that they are viewing and interpreting the god's actions through a series of subjective perspectives and performances. Access to the god is indirect and symbolic; how we interpret what we see is a product of our own degree of involvement in and assent to the events before us.

In the struggle between Pentheus and Dionysus, god confronts man through music, costume, dance and stage illusion. Euripides represents Pentheus' inability to understand and control Dionysus not only through the king's failure to interpret his words, but through his failure to discern the god within the theatrical forms that express him. Just as Dionysus is god of wine and the wine itself (279, 284), so Dionysus is the god of theater and the theatrical forms that manifest him. His 'human' disguise and his divinity are, paradoxically, one and the same (see Section III). Every scene in the *Bacchae* up to the final messenger speech makes a major issue of Dionysiac costume and movement as a visible representation of the elusive god. Large sections of the two long messenger speeches, as well as the parodos, communicate his divinity through descriptions of the costumes, songs, and movement of the maenads. In the early scenes Pentheus' response to Dionysiac dress, a mixture of incomprehension, fear and attraction, precipitates his downfall; he rejects the god by rejecting the visible and aural signs of his worship. He reacts to his grandfather's offer of an ivy crown as if he were threatened with mental contamination (344). After a detailed examination of Dionysus' dress and appearance in their first meeting, Pentheus wishes to strip off parts of the stranger's costume on stage (495 ff.). His response to dance and music is equally violent. He tries to send the stranger to *dance* in the darkness of imprisonment in the stables (511). He also tries to stop the god's followers from making music, to suppress the insistent beating of their drums (513–14).

It is with theatrical weapons, also, that Dionysus destroys Pentheus. He entraps the king in a series of spectacles directed by himself. Twice, both in the stable scene, which the god reports as a kind of 'messenger' (616–37),[10] and in the final disaster on the mountain, Dionysus calmly sets the scene—in the second case replete with costume, actors and set—and then stands back or disappears into a position of heavenly observation, an unmoved spectator of human struggle. The stable scene, in which Dionysus teases Pentheus with a bull that Pentheus imagines is the stranger, and then with his own false image, is a sort of off-stage rehearsal for Pentheus' mad scene. Dionysus then lures Pentheus, in a manner unique in extant tragedy, to change his costume and become his own player/worshipper.[11] Through costume he separates Pentheus, by playing on his internal conflicts, from his chosen role as king and hoplite (see esp. 809 ff.). In the scene where Pentheus begins to succumb to the god's power, Dionysus clinches his victory through a detailed description of the costume he is to wear: long hair, a female

[10] The god's unusual 'messenger speech' teases the audience with its pretense of uncertainty about events that took place within the palace. See especially 629, κᾆθ' ὁ Βρόμιος, ὡς ἔμοιγε φαίνεται, δόξαν λέγω ('and then Bromius, as it appears to me at least—I am only giving my opinion . . .'), and 638. What we know to be true, since we know that the stranger is a god, is presented as speculation to the chorus on stage. The choice of the more 'primitive' (*Poetics* 4. 17–18) trochaic tetrameters rather than the normal iambic trimeters (although see Ox. Pap. 2, no. 221, for a fragment of a messenger speech in trochaic tetrameters from Phrynichus' *Phoenissae*) seems appropriate to the irony here—the mocking god appropriates the role of human messenger to his own inhuman ends. The chorus' belief in their god does not depend on full knowledge—for them the god's voice and the shaking of the palace are sufficient demonstrations of his presence.

Dionysus also predicts the content of the first messenger's speech before he speaks (657–8); the servant of the king does not merely report the events on the mountain, but advocates recognition of Dionysus' divinity (769–70). Hence Pentheus has no access to any perspectives that do not argue for the god.

[11] Pentheus' adoption of another costume/role has multiple implications. The psychological aspect has been much discussed. By becoming a maenad Pentheus moves into a space characteristic of the god, where the differences between male and female, human and divine, man and beast, spectator and participant, are lost. Pentheus' costume change makes him an ecstatic worshipper of the god, as well as his ritual double. For further discussion of these issues see especially Gallini 1963, 211–28, and Segal 1978, 185–202.

peplos (robe), a fawnskin, and a *thyrsus* (830 ff.). Pentheus, as he chooses how to act, wavers between donning the dress of the god's worshipper and putting on his armor and proceeding against the women with force (845–6). He believes he will gain through his disguise the enticing perspective of a mere spectator (945 ff., also 829). Instead, once he has dressed as a woman, he rehearses his part and adjusts his costume like an actor before a play (927 ff.); he relishes his resemblance to his mother or her sisters and imagines that his dress will endow him with the powers of a maenad (945), little realizing that his change of costume has committed him to becoming instead part of an 'unhappy spectacle' (1232, of Agave with the head of Pentheus) beyond his control. In the stable scene Pentheus contended with beast and stranger as separate images. Now he sees Dionysus as a beast, and in sensing that the stranger represents more than the man he has been playing on stage, he 'sees' the god and his inhumanness for the first time. Costume, costume change and acting thus become in this play a central dramatic image for understanding and worshipping the god.

The meaning of a scene in Greek tragedy rarely depends primarily on the role-playing and on the role changes that a character makes on stage. The reverse is true for old comedy. It is not surprising, then, that Euripides makes extraordinary use of what were primarily comic techniques in stage business to illuminate and help the audience to interpret the changes of costume and movement in the *Bacchae*.[12] Cadmus and Tiresias gracelessly but sensibly accept the worship of the god by donning his fawnskin and *thyrsus* and adopting a hobbling dance. The 'comedy' of this scene centers on their fussy concern to play their new roles correctly. As often in comedy the theatrical point lies in the lack of correspondence between inner and outer, the state

---

[12] Throughout Euripides' work there is a contrast between the comic and serious possibilities of role change. In the *Helen*, for example, Menelaus is restored from a ship-wrecked and almost comic nobody into an Homeric hero; simultaneously, Helen changes to mourning garb, a deception which leads to a symbolic remarriage between the two long-separated spouses. Control of costume change, or the use of role changes for deliberate deception, typically leads to a festive and rejuvenating outcome. In contrast, when Heracles' children put on mourning garments, the change of costume has serious implications, entrapping the characters in a larger pattern of action beyond their control and ironically anticipating the later sacrifice of the children by Heracles. Such costume change is relatively rare in Greek tragedy, however, and is generally reserved for climactic moments. In contrast, costume change becomes the basis for the entire dramatic action in the *Bacchae*, and 'comic' costume techniques are used for the first time in a play which has a disastrous outcome.

of mind and body and the costume and movement. The dramatic juxtaposition between the identical movements of the graceful and authentic chorus and the decrepit old men as worshippers of the god might be compared, from the point of view of theatrical effect, to a scene like that in the *Thesmophoriazusae* between Agathon, Euripides and Euripides' kinsman. The kinsman is too crude and masculine to adopt comfortably the female dress that the effeminate Agathon wears very naturally as an inspiration to his dramatic poetry. His inability to play the role is prophetic of his failure to maintain his disguise in the women's assembly and exposes Euripides' weakness as a dramatist; Aristophanes' own disguised heroes—like Dionysus in this play—have no trouble duping their victims. Cadmus, too, finally finds himself facing the tragic rather than the comic implications of his opportunistic (333–7) conversion to the god.

The same ludicrous fussing over Dionysiac costume is, of course, repeated in the terrible scene in which Pentheus tries awkwardly to rearrange his costume with the help of Dionysus. The king parodies the god. The visual effect is comparable to the confrontation between Heracles and Dionysus at the beginning of the *Frogs*. The fat and ludicrous god, dressed in an effeminate saffron robe, tragic buskins and a lionskin comes face to face with the original he is trying to impersonate, Heracles. Here we laugh as well at the inability of a divinity to carry off the kind of role change Aristophanes' comic heroes usually accomplish without difficulty. The Dionysus of the *Frogs* thinks that the costume gives him courage; instead it exposes his pretenses to true divinity and his cowardice. Pentheus' change of costume reveals his human limits; in imitating the god he does not acquire, as he expects, extraordinary powers over his environment, but the cerements of death (see 857–9 and 1156–7).[13] Only the smiling god of the *Bacchae* can change with sinister ease from divine to human and back, in all probability without even a change of costume (see Section III).

In the case of the comic hero, the voluntary transformation of self through costume is a form of temporary control over circumstances not subject in reality to the force of the individual's desires or actions. Cadmus and Tiresias try to make such a 'comic' accommodation to phenomena beyond rational control; by being willing to 'act' they can accept the god while retaining their identities. They are

---

[13] But see Dodds' commentary on πιστὸν Ἀιδαν in 1157.

simultaneously actors/worshippers and spectators. The mad
Pentheus retains no such comic distance from and perspective on
his role. To worship Dionysus—or to be a comic hero—is to adopt a
temporary change of role, and to receive in exchange participation
in a boundary-transcending experience. Euripides, by adopting stage
techniques from old comedy, can evoke in the minds of the audience
expectations it has about comic role playing—the ways in which
costume change can be used to expose the ignorance or the pretension of the hero's enemies, or to express the power, however temporary, of the hero's imagination over reality. In comedy we laugh at this
exposure of ignorance or manipulation of reality because the characters are grotesque and the consequences are minimal, temporary,
and certainly not deadly. In the *Bacchae* the identical theatrical
techniques expose with accelerating horror the tragic inadequacy of
man to understand and control either himself or his environment.
Dionysiac madness becomes the dark double of comic befuddlement.

II. DIONYSUS' FESTIVAL

Euripides marks the events leading up to and following the death of
Pentheus, beginning from Dionysus' transformation of Pentheus into
a maenad, and ending with the return of Agave with the head of her
son, with three stages suggestive of a ritual pattern, *pompē*, *agōn*,
kōmos (escorting procession, contest, festive revelry). As we shall see,
this pattern of events was used by contemporary Athenians to
describe the stages of a festival, very probably including the dramatic
festival at which the *Bacchae* was presented as part of the worship of
Dionysus. Thus, the ritual language of the play urges us, I will argue,
to think of Dionysus as presenting to Thebes a final demonstration of
his divinity which is a primitive equivalent of the sophisticated
mixture of tragedy and comedy through which he was worshipped in
the theatrical festivals of Athens.

In lines 964–5, after Pentheus has been costumed as a maenad
and is fully mad, Dionysus offers to be Pentheus' escort, or *pompos*, to
the contests, *agōnes*, ahead:

> τοιγάρ σ᾽ ἀγῶνες ἀναμένουσιν οὓς ἐχρῆν.
> ἕπου δέ· πομπὸς [δ᾽] εἶμ᾽ ἐγὼ σωτήριος,

> therefore, the necessary contests await you.
> Follow, and I shall go as your escort and protector.

This same vocabulary is used several times in the following scene. In 1047 the messenger says of Dionysus: ξένος θ᾽ ὃς ἡμῖν πομπὸς ἦν θεωρίας ('and the stranger who was escort in our mission'). Pentheus is being led by the god to a *theōria*, a word which can mean embassy, the experience of being a spectator, or spectacle, such as those presented at the theater or the games. The same is true in 829: οὐκέτι θεατὴς μαινάδων πρόθυμος εἶ ('you are no longer eager to be a spectator of the maenads').[14] In 974–6 Dionysus again speaks of the contest into which he is leading Pentheus:

> τὸν νεανίαν ἄγω
> τόνδ᾽ εἰς ἀγῶνα μέγαν, ὁ νικήσων δ᾽ ἐγὼ
> καὶ Βρόμιος ἔσται. τἄλλα δ᾽ αὐτὸ σημανεῖ.

> I am leading the youth
> to his great contest—and the winner shall be I
> and Bromios! The rest, the event itself will show.

In 1163–4 the chorus say of the 'contest' in which Agave killed her son:

> καλὸς ἀγών, χέρ᾽ αἵματι στάζουσαν
> περιβαλεῖν τέκνου.

> A fine contest, to embrace your child
> with a hand dripping with blood!

The *agōn* is followed by the triumphant return of Agave. She congratulates Dionysus for being *kallinikos* ('victorious', 1147; see also the chorus on the Cadmeian bacchants in 1161). The chorus reply with an invitation to a triumphal celebration—δέχεσθε κῶμον εὐίου θεοῦ ('so prepare to welcome the revel of the god of ecstasy', 1167)—and greet Agave as a fellow reveller: ὁρῶ καί σε δέξομαι σύγκωμον ('I see it, and shall accept you as a fellow reveller', 1172). Agave pronounces herself *makaira* and *eudaimōn* ('happy' and 'blessed', 1180 and 1258) for her victories over the 'beast'. Yet the play ends with Agave beginning a new *pompē* (1381, ὦ πομποί, 'O escorts'—if the lines are not interpolated), as she proceeds, lamenting, into lonely exile.

When they appear in conjunction, the three terms *pompē, agōn, kōmos* mean respectively a procession prior to a religious festival, the

---

[14] The translations of 829 and 1167 in this paragraph are mine, not Kirk's (see above, n. 5).

contest(s) celebrated at such a festival, and the festive revelry which follows such contests.[15] George Thomson has called attention to the similarities between this pattern and the official language used to describe the first day of the City Dionysia, where the statue of Dionysus is brought from Eleutherae to rest, for the remainder of the festival, in the theater.[16] The same suggestion could be made for the theatrical festival as a whole, with its day of procession, followed by the poetic contests, and concluding with celebrations in honor of the victorious poet.[17] Finally, this pattern is inherent as well, as Francis

---

[15] Winnington-Ingram (1948, 24 n. 3, and 128 n. 2) suggests that the pattern *pompē, agōn, kōmos (kallinikos)* is meant to refer to the Olympic games. The pattern does fit what we know of the games from ancient sources, both in the sequence and in the naming of the proceedings, and provides an apt conclusion for the contest of power, sometimes pictured in athletic terms (491, 800), between Dionysus and Pentheus. God and man, as Tiresias points out, share a desire for *timē* ('honor'; 319–21). At the same time the specifically *poetic* inspiration behind the costuming of Pentheus which inaugurates these contests is emphasized in the use of the verb *ekmousoō* in 825: Διόνυσος ἡμᾶς ἐξεμούσωσεν τάδε, 'Dionysus inspired these things in us'.

[16] Thomson 1940, 156–62. In the myth the Athenians at first resisted the god, but were smitten by a disease from which they freed themselves by manufacturing *phalloi* in honor of the god (Schol. Ar. Ach. 243). If Thomson were correct, both the festival pattern and the play would refer to the introduction of the god's worship into a city, but with varying results. Thomson finds the pattern *pompē, agōn, kōmos* in the Bacchae, in the Spartan initiation ritual, and in tragedy (131–2, 180), although he does not try to explore the implications of his theory for a study of the play. The major difficulty with Thomson's theory is our ignorance about the order of events at the City Dionysia. On the general problem see Pickard-Cambridge 1968, 63–6, and Deubner 1932, 138–42. The law of Euegoros, quoted by Demosthenes, refers to a *pompē*, and a *kōmos* which may well have occurred on the first day of the festival before the dramatic *agōnes*, but after a series of performances in honor of various gods at their shrines and a sacrifice to Dionysus. Nevertheless, I am arguing here that Dionysus is introducing to Thebes a 'primitive' or proto-theatrical festival, and that the pattern *pompē, agōn, kōmos* is clearly the standard and most easily recognizable structural form for most Greek festivals. Thus Dionysus in the Bacchae could conflate the initial day of the Athenian City Dionysia with its introduction of the god, the larger festival, with its dramatic *agōnes* followed by a celebration of the victorious poet, and comedy, with its comparable structural pattern, in a manner which could easily be recognized by the audience as an emerging version of the more complex and extended City Dionysia known to Athens. As I will also argue, Dionysus *introduces* his worship to Thebes through directing a 'play' that could be interpreted as either a 'comedy' or a 'tragedy'. For a more detailed treatment of the implications of treating the pattern *pompē, agōn, kōmos* as festal, and of possible allusions to festivals other than the theatrical festivals, see my Harvard dissertation (noted above) and Girard 1972, especially 170–200.

[17] See Aristophanes, Ach. 504 for *agōn* used of the theatrical contests at the Lenaia. For *kallinikos* used to describe the victorious poet and his hero see Ach. 1227, 1228, 1231, 1233, and Av. 1764.

Cornford has argued, in the language and structure of old comedy.[18]
In the *Bacchae* Dionysus uses this 'festival' or 'comedy' in order to make
the city of Thebes 'see' his divinity. He costumes Pentheus, and brings
him to a pre-arranged setting on the mountain as both spectator of and
participant in an *agōn*. Both the maenads on the mountain (the
doubles of their sisters in the chorus) and Pentheus begin as spectators
dressed by the god, and then, at the god's command, become
unwitting participants in a drama in which Pentheus is both mocked
and 'sacrificed' (934, 1114, 1127, 1135) by the god.[19] At the heart of the
agōn lies Pentheus' vain and momentary recognition of his situation
and his own disastrous errors of perception (*hamartiai*, 1120–1).[20] The
episode closes with a *kōmos* or celebration of the god's victorious
creation shared by an 'audience' (Agave and the chorus) whose minds
are under the control of or dedicated to the god. Dionysus' revenge
thus takes the form of a crude and terrifying 'theater' or proto-theater
in which Pentheus' death is—to the god—a divine joke, in which his
anagnōrisis ('recognition') is fruitless, and in which the spectator has
become an actor in a spectacle he cannot control.

The plots of myths about Dionysus' introduction of his worship to
new cities can end happily or disastrously.[21] Those who accept the
god are blessed with *eudaimonia*; those who reject him are punished

[18] Cornford 1934. Regardless of the truth of Cornford's theory about the origins of
comedy, this vocabulary was actually used in old comedy, and an analysis of the
regularities of comic structure along these lines is both more productive and more
convincing than it is in tragedy. See Pickard-Cambridge 1962, 194–229.

[19] See Dodds (1960) on 963 for a possible hint of Pentheus' role as a scapegoat. A
sacrifice to Dionysus took place on the first day of the theatrical festival (a bull) and
perhaps originally a goat was also sacrificed on the altar in the theater. See Burkert
1966, 87–121, for an interesting argument about the relation between the original
sacrifice in the theater and the dramatic sacrifices in Greek tragedy.

[20] Dionysus insists that Pentheus and Thebes must *learn* of his divinity (39, 657,
1345; on *amathia*, or ignorance, see 480 and 490). It is unclear precisely *what* Pentheus
recognizes in his final moments, or what he means by his *hamartiai* (1121), a failure to
recognize Dionysus' divinity, a failure to know who he was (506), or simply a failure
to know what he was getting himself into due to his madness. See Dodds' commentary
on this passage.

[21] Burnett 1970, 26 ff., gives examples of Dionysiac myths where the god is accepted
immediately and with happy results. In the longer *Homeric Hymn to Dionysus*, for
example, the sailors who fail to recognize the god suffer metamorphosis, while the
steersman, who does, receives *eudaimonia*, happiness. Burnett argues that Dionysus,
up to line 810, gives Pentheus a fair chance—unique in tragedies of divine revenge—
to recognize the god's divinity and receive his blessings. For a more extensive treatment
of Dionysiac myths, see Massenzio 1969, 27–113. As his analysis shows, even
immediate acceptance of the god usually leads to the sacrifice of the figure who
introduces his viticulture.

with madness and a deadly metamorphosis. Euripides retains this possibility of a 'comic' or 'tragic' outcome in the early scenes of the *Bacchae*. Dionysus will punish Pentheus only if he insists on resisting the god (50 ff.); he and his adherents argue that accepting the god means wine, festival and release from care. The similarities in the language of the early choral odes of the *Bacchae* and the comic chorus of Eleusinian initiates in the *Frogs* are for this reason not surprising.[22] As in comedy the god offers to Thebes the possibility of temporary regeneration through a reversal of normal social and political categories. An apparently powerless outsider, he confronts an opponent who is in some sense his 'powerful' double, and destroys the enemy of festive pleasure with mockery. By being granted temporary control over reality the comic or 'trickster' hero—like the god in this play— uses his ability to transform his and others' identity, and his ability to manipulate language, costume and theatrical illusion to bring the world into harmony with his aspirations.[23] The chorus welcome the return of the mad Agave, now a successful hunter rather than a mere woman (1167). In comedy the same gesture might well have resulted in a shared celebration between the city and the rejuvenated protagonist. But in the *Bacchae* the smiling god alone successfully completes a 'comic' action, as he celebrates through the returning Agave a triumphant *kōmos* (1167). Cadmus and Tiresias also make what at first appears to be the 'comic' adjustment to Dionysiac festival, and shrug off old age in dance. But Pentheus, by resisting the god, inverts a potentially comic outcome. He is destroyed while enacting what might be termed a parody of a comic plot. The comic hero transforms himself to succeed in his desires and to save his city heroically. Pentheus abandons his plans to don armor and fight for his city in favor of satisfying his personal curiosity; at the same time he interprets his dressing as a woman as heroic (961–2) and

---

[22] See *Frogs* 326–9 and *Bacchae* 80 and 106–7; *Frogs* 345–7 and the Cadmus/ Tiresias scene; *Frogs* 333–4, 376, 394, and 410 and *Bacchae* 160–1; *Frogs* 346 and *Bacchae* 380–1. In Thucydides 2. 38 Pericles describes the function of Athens' festivals as 'Further, we provide plenty of means for the mind to refresh itself from business. We celebrate games and sacrifices all year round . . . a daily source of pleasure that drives out grief' (Crawley trans., adapted). Burnett 1970, 27 stresses that Dionysus offers to Thebes a civilized public cult, which reverts to a dangerous and primitive form on the mountain only when the women are attacked.

[23] For discussions of the comic or trickster hero in old comedy and elsewhere see Whitman 1964, and Salingar 1974. Dionysus also shares the *ponēria* and deceptiveness of the trickster hero. Even those who join in the hero's fantasies, like Cadmus, do not always end by sharing his festive victory.

deserving of honor and celebration on his return (see 963–70). Pentheus becomes not a hero, but, as he feared when sane, an object of divine *gelōs* or mockery.[24]

Yet in the *Bacchae* precisely the same pattern of events is to the smiling god and his chorus a 'comic' celebration of Pentheus' exposure and defeat as an enemy to festival, and to the appalled second messenger and to Pentheus' family an occasion for tragic pity and lament. Once the god has left the field of human action, Pentheus' fruitless *anagnōrisis* (1113; 1120–1) and the inability of the maddened participants to pity their victim can be read as an abortive tragic action. Agave reaches and survives the full tragic *anagnōrisis* of her error denied to Pentheus (ἄρτι μανθάνω, 'I now understand', 1296) and accepts her fate, although she wishes never to see a *thyrsus* again (1381 ff.). She now sees the mask of Pentheus as human—the representation of her son and a cause for *penthos* ('grief'), not bestial and a cause for triumph. Cadmus creates sympathy for Pentheus by recalling the past kindnesses of the overzealous youth to his grandfather (1381 ff.). The second messenger is Pentheus' first sympathetic defender in the play and the first besides Pentheus to champion the men of the city (1036, if the text is correct), who have hitherto been silent or converted to the god. He laments the literal fall (1111–13) of his king (see esp. 1024 ff.). The adjective *perissos*, 'excessive', formerly used of Pentheus (429), is now applied to Agave's revenge (1197). The implication of these final scenes seems to be that gods may impose patterns of action of man, but tragic meaning—the reading and experience of these events as fearful and pitiful—is created by a strictly human perspective.

In the *Bacchae*, then, Dionysus borrows from the language, plot structure and stage business of comedy to make his theatrical demonstration of his divinity. As a god who presided over both parts of the dramatic festivals, comedy and tragedy, he dissolves and transcends the boundaries between the comic and tragic genres and

---

[24] Pentheus plans to mock the smiling god or his converts (286, 322, 1081, 1293), but ends up being mocked (250 (through Cadmus), 503, 842, 854). The same word, *gelōs*, suggests both laughter and scorn. Sacrificial and tragic victims may also be mocked, but here the combination of vocabulary (*gelōs* and *kōmos*), the god's smiling mask, and the god's dramatic strategies suggest the tone, if not the tone of comedy, as well as the traditional disgrace of being ridiculed by one's enemies. I share a sense of the tone of these comic scenes with Seidensticker 1978, 303–20. See also Dodds 1960, especially 192.

shows them as parts of the same experience—that is, parts of a divinity whose nature is expressed primarily by his ability to collapse or fuse oppositions and limits. Dionysus makes his victims see with pleasure what the sane mind would experience as painful. Pentheus 'would enjoy seeing what causes' him 'distress' (815); the mad Agave will think herself free from misfortune when she is actually supremely unfortunate (1259–62; see also 1232 as opposed to 1258). In a similar way the audience, trapped through comic/tragic irony and a partial identification with the god's cause (for we know that Pentheus is wrong), is torn between fear and horrified laughter at the king's delusions. Until the final scenes the god thus denies us clear access either to the comic laughter or to the tragic pity by which we control our theatrical experience.

Pentheus' terrifying transformation from spectator to spectacle shows in an extraordinarily theatrical form what it means to act or imitate—like all humans—without full knowledge. The god, like the comic hero, never confuses presentation with reality; instead he controls reality through presentation. By using language on multiple levels and exploiting the physical accoutrements of theater and/or Dionysiac cult, he can manipulate and transform the world to create an upside-down festival world that does not operate by normal standards. The tragic hero, or, from the divine perspective, the 'comic victim', is destroyed through his confinement to one level of language and sight. His imagination is limited by his own lack of self-knowledge, and the frame of the cultural order in which he exists. Pentheus insists that to believe in Dionysus he must see the god directly and at first hand, not indirectly and symbolically (the god shows himself to Pentheus in disguised form): τὸν θεὸν ὁρᾶν γὰρ φῂς σαφῶς, ποῖός τις ἦν; ('You say you actually *saw* the god? What was he like?'), he asks in 477. Or, in lines 501–2:

καὶ ποῦ 'στιν; οὐ γὰρ φανερὸς ὄμμασίν γ᾽ ἐμοῖς.
παρ᾽ ἐμοί· σὺ δ᾽ ἀσεβὴς αὐτὸς ὢν οὐκ εἰσορᾷς.

P. Well, where is he? He is not visible to my eyes.
D. Here with me; but you, because of your impiety, do not behold him.

Pentheus repeatedly seems unable to see—or hear—the implications of the speeches, sounds or images presented to him.[25] At the same

---

[25] For excellent treatment of the language of sight in the play see Massenzio 1969, 82–91. Among other points, he contrasts Dionysiac sight with Pentheus' narrower and more superficial desire to *spy*.

time he unconsciously responds to the god's message as he is finally
lured to the mountain by a desire to see or spy upon the god's forbidden rites (811–15, 829, 838, 912, 916, 956, 1060–2); in fact he is never
allowed, despite his wishes, to see the sacred activities of the maenads
on the mountain (1060, 1075) until the moment of his death.

When Pentheus is finally costumed and maddened by Dionysus he
comes on stage with a new and double vision. He sees two Thebes,
two suns; he sees, as the god says, what he ought to see (924):

> καὶ ταῦρος ἡμῖν πρόσθεν ἡγεῖσθαι δοκεῖς
> καὶ σῷ κέρατα κρατὶ προσπεφυκέναι.

> You appear to lead on ahead of me as a bull
> and on your head horns seem to grow!   (920–1)

Pentheus' ability to see only one level of reality continues in his state
of madness; he simply substitutes the beast for the smiling mask.[26]
His sight changes, and he has access to a vision of divinity unavail-
able to him before, but it brings no insight. He is unaware of the
implications that this bestial image has for himself. He cannot, like
the god, Tiresias, or the comic hero, 'see' and control his transformation at the same time. By contrast, the chorus of believers cap this
scene by evoking a *double* image of the god, impossible to normal
human vision, as a beast with a smiling face or mask (*prosōpon*):

> φάνηθι ταῦρος ἢ πολύκρανος ἰδεῖν
> δράκων ἢ πυριφλέγων ὁρᾶσθαι λέων.
> ἴθ', ὦ Βάκχε, θηραγρευτᾷ βακχᾶν
> γελῶντι προσώπῳ περίβαλε βρόχον
> θανάσιμον ὑπ' ἀγέλαν πεσόν-
> τι τὰν μαινάδων.

> Appear as a bull or a many-headed
> Snake or a fire-blazing lion to behold!
> Go, O Bacchus—around the hunter of Bacchants
> with a smiling face cast your noose:
> Under the deadly herd
> of maenads let him fall!   (1018–23)

[26] It is unclear precisely what Pentheus sees here—the stranger and his double
with horns (Dodds 1960, 193), a stranger who is part man, part bull, or a bull whom
he realizes is also the stranger, just as Agave refers to the head of Pentheus as that of
an animal, but simultaneously shows her awareness of its humanity (1185–7; see
Dodds 1960, 224).

The language and action of the play demonstrate the god's divinity indirectly and symbolically and deny that we can adequately 'see' Dionysus with human vision. The god can take any shape he wants (478), but is not fully visible to the human eye. In fact, even the chorus and the maenads on the mountain only hear, but do not see their god directly. He is a being who can successively or simultaneously appear as divine, animal and human. Pentheus defines the world through mutually exclusive antitheses and hierarchical relations. Man and woman, for example, are rigidly separate categories (822); each sex has its own sphere (217); one is subordinate to the other (786). Dionysus can simultaneously invert and subvert cultural categories: language, the roles of the sexes, classes and political hierarchy. To understand Dionysus is to understand that the order imposed on the world by human culture is arbitrary, and the permanent potential for a reversal or collapse of this order exists. Hence in the *Bacchae* the same words or symbols can have apparently incompatible connotations in the minds of supporters or opponents of the god, or at two different dramatic moments. *Sophia, sophos* and *to sophon* (wisdom, wise or clever, cleverness), for example, mean something entirely different to Tiresias or the chorus as defenders of the god, and to Pentheus as a defender of the cultural order; the chorus uses these terms in so many seemingly incompatible contexts that we lose any certainty of what the term means to the god's worshippers (see especially 655–6, 480; 203, 825, 1190; 395, 877 = 897, 1005). A *thyrsus* may at one point be a magic wand providing food and sustenance, at another point a weapon; at a third point this symbol of Dionysus' power loses its force and must be regarlanded (1054–5). Pentheus fails not only to see and interpret symbols, but he remains unaware or fatally resistant to the fact that linguistic signs can refer to more than one valid level of meaning at once. Unlike Dionysus (or the audience) he has no sense of irony or metaphor.

Dionysus and the chorus present to Thebes the possibility that Dionysiac festivals can express this potential for a reversal of the cultural order in a controlled form; the play offers multiple demonstrations that the spectator who can understand reality (and especially divinity) through presentation retains distance and identity. The play or festival on the mountain is the 'black' double of the play we have seen up to that point. The benign (*ēpiōtatos*) god of theater can by implication present drama—and myths—as a part of the social and political life of the city; the terrible (*deinotatos*) god presides over comparable 'festive' reversals of normality and identity outside the limits of the city and civilized control.[27] Thus, while Pentheus merely *imagines* that he 'suffers terribly' (πέπονθα δεινά, 642) while dueling with the image created by the god, he is still safe; but on the mountain he is utterly destroyed. The first messenger speech gives Pentheus the precise scenario for his own death and a chance—by learning through presentation—to avoid it; here animals, not humans, are sacrificed.[28] The initial debates (*agōnes*) between man and god become Pentheus' hopeless struggles (*agōnes*) on the mountain. The maenads literally see the king as a beast and tear him apart; unlike the chorus they become with Pentheus actors in the play, not spectators of the action. By contrast, the chorus—as spectators—simply *imagine* Pentheus as a beast; in the fourth stasimon, where they envisage Pentheus' death—they participate, but indirectly, in the god's revenge on Pentheus. Finally, the chorus' single-minded and pitiless identification with the god's 'play' is not that of the audience of Euripides' play, for that audience has access in the final scenes to a double reading of the god's drama that encompasses both a divine ('comic') and human ('tragic') reading of the same events.

In Plato's *Symposium* (223d3–9) Socrates argues with Aristophanes and Agathon that tragedy and comedy could be written by the same man. Socrates is presumably championing an unlikely cause.[29] Yet Euripides, by allowing the god of theater to make his own theatrical demonstrations of divinity, reveals the common ground

[27] As Girard 1972, 181 says of the *Bacchae*, 'la tragédie . . . ramène la fête à ses origines violentes, à la violence reciproque' ('tragedy . . . returns festival to its violent origins, to reciprocal violence').

[28] Dodds (1960, 169) suggests that the traditional story of the herdsmen and the maenads would have been celebrated in ritual and dance. Dionysus' effect on the landscape is consistently presented in the play as comparable to that of a poet like Orpheus or Amphion, whose poetry is so powerful that it can move nature (see 561–4, 113–14, 726–7).

[29] Aristophanes in the *Frogs* suggests that the health and nature of one theatrical genre are inextricably linked with the other. A good comedy should contain, as the chorus of initiates say of their rites, a judicious mixture of seriousness and mockery (391 ff.). The poet was famous for making his own comedies out of parodies of Euripides (see especially Cratinus, fr. 307, where the poet mocks Aristophanes for his imitations of Euripides). Both poets use the figure of Dionysus to make implicit statements about the relation between genres, and to defend the value of dramatic poetry to the city (*Frogs* 1419, 1502).

between apparently opposing genres, the shared preoccupation with human ignorance, pretension and lack of self-knowledge, with the relief from suffering and the exposure of the gap between man's godlike desires and his ability to achieve them.[30] In the *Bacchae* Dionysus brings drama to birth in Thebes as an experience and a form where boundaries are transgressed and cultural categories and oppositions are temporarily reversed or collapsed. Comedy allows its heroes to break the boundaries separating man and god, the socially encumbered individual and his heroic desires; its audiences revel— though harmlessly—in mockery, revenge, a delight in exposure and a free identification with its initially underdog protagonist. The god's 'comedy' with its Dionysiac audience, the chorus, is in many ways a more terrifying form of the genre. Yet when the god has withdrawn from the level of human action to the machine, Euripides' tragedy frames and changes our perspective on the divine drama. The final scenes restore—or from the historical perspective create—the traditional boundaries between genres, and draw a sharp (and specifically tragic) line between man and god, the individual and his heroic aspirations, audience and protagonist, and between laughter and tragic pity.

III. DIONYSUS' MASK

In the prologue Dionysus announces that he will manifest himself to Thebes in human disguise and reveal himself as a god to the city. To do so he says he has put on a human *morphē* ('shape') or *physis* ('nature'). He redundantly emphasizes (lines 4–5 and 53–4) his donning of this human disguise.[31] Why, then, does Euripides make

---

[30] Plato in the *Philebus* (48c–49c5) suggests in a very complex passage that tragedy and comedy are united by a concern with self-knowledge. Comic delusion is accompanied by weakness; ignorance in those who have the ability to retaliate is hateful and ugly. Pentheus' situation, as he moves from 'strength' to weakness, falls uncomfortably between the hateful and the ridiculous; the god's apparent 'comic weakness' at first obscures a hateful strength.

[31] No scholar has in my view convincingly explained away this redundancy on textual grounds. Willink 1966, 30–1, follows Bernhardy, although he too admits there are no strong linguistic grounds for condemnation. 'To defend 53–4 is to believe that Euripides spoilt his own elaborate structure (of the prologue), and that, too, with a doubly tautologous couplet (repeating 4), introduced by a repetitive conjunction, following a clause which it could not logically follow.' My point is that the repetition is meant to be functional and emphatic.

Dionysus draw our attention to this point? Presumably some visual confusion about the god and his costume must be made clear to the audience. Using the aorist participle the god says he has 'put on' mortal shape (4). The use of the aorist followed by a main verb in the present tense (5) suggests that the actor appears on stage already 'disguised' as mortal, yet we are also required to accept this figure as a god, Dionysus:

I have come, the son of Zeus, to this land of the Thebans, I, Dionysus.   (1–2)

Yet does this figure with the smiling mask (smiling as we know from lines 439 and 1021) look mortal? While we know little of tragic masking conventions in the fifth century BC we can safely presume that most masks in tragedy were not smiling.[32] Moreover, gods, while they regularly appear in prologues and epiphanies, rarely dominate the *praxis* of tragedies. This is not true of tragedies about Dionysus, where the god is traditionally presenting his divinity to those who have not yet recognized him. Yet the continual presence of this divine smile on the level of human action was not so commonplace as to have lost its freshness as an image expressive of the gulf between god and man.[33] The smiling mask is unlikely to have been an Euripidean innovation, although the masks of other gods in Greek tragedies are never described in the text as smiling. The smiling mask was most probably a convention for deities—or for Dionysus alone—whose significance no playwright before Euripides—in so far as we know—took the opportunity to call our attention to and develop so explicitly.

Dodds explains the textual redundancy here as the playwright's means 'of making it quite clear to the audience that the speaker, whom they accept as a god, will be accepted as a man by the people on stage'.[34] Dionysus thus enters the play poorly disguised as human in the fashion of Homeric gods or the testing god of folk-tale.[35] His

[32] For the scanty evidence concerning fifth-century as opposed to later tragic masks see Pickard-Cambridge 1968, ch. 4. Even in the fourth century the more stylized masks of the principal tragic or even upper-class comic characters are never described or pictured in art as smiling. There are no other direct references to masks in classical tragedy, and even in comedy it is difficult to abstract precise information on the nature of masks from texts.

[33] For further helpful comments on the god's smiling mask see especially Rosenmeyer 1963, 106–10, Wasserman 1929, 274, and Dodds 1960, 439.

[34] Dodds in his note on 53–4 also includes the views of previous commentaries.

[35] See Rose 1956, 63 ff., on divine disguisings in Homer, and Burnett 1970, 24–5 on the theme in the *Bacchae*.

mask is not (and perhaps this is true of his costume as well), by the conventions of Greek tragedy, human. Therefore, simply by his costume he manifests his godhead, his unhumanness to the audience. The tragic irony for which the play is justly famous has a visual level. That is, the audience sees by his mask that the stranger is a god, but Pentheus has no such theatrical cues by which to recognize him. The audience is being asked to be self-conscious about a costume and a theatrical convention. To sum up then, for the audience Dionysus' mask represents smiling divinity in human disguise, for the characters, a man. One mask represents two meanings in a manner that captures the central irony of the dramatic action.

John Jones has eloquently argued in *On Aristotle and Greek Tragedy* that the ancient mask was meant to be a fully adequate means of representing character:[36] unlike the modern mask ancient tragic masks 'did not owe their interest to further realities lying behind them, because they declared the whole man'. In accordance with this convention, the Greek tragic audience should not be required to 'peer behind the mask and demand of the actor that he shall cease merely to support the action, and shall begin to exploit the mask in the service of inwardness'. When 'the mind's construction' cannot be found in the face, masking becomes pointless. Jones' argument concerning the identity between mask and character for the ancient playwright is confirmed not only by most of the tragic practice of Aeschylus and Sophocles (such characters as Aeschylus' Clytemnestra are possible exceptions), but by post-fifth-century visual representations of poets who are shown composing while looking at masks.[37] Jones argues that Euripides' career is uniquely marked by a whole range of 'mask-piercing' and 'mask-exploiting' effects which challenge the ancient masking convention. Euripides 'pierces' masks by creating conflicts between a character's internal state and his role in the action of the drama. Thus, Hippolytus' tongue swears, but his mind remains unsworn (*Hipp.* 612). The mad Pentheus' willingness to dress as a woman reveals an unkingly temperament. That is, 'the mind's construction' is no longer fully to be found in the face or mask that

---

[36] The following paragraph summarizes aspects of the argument made by Jones 1962, 45–6 and 270.

[37] For an excellent treatment of this issue with examples from art see Webster in Anderson 1965, 5–13. Quintilian (11. 3. 73) says that skilled speakers borrow their emotions from masks, and Aristophanes also suggests that costumes can be a comparable form of inspiration for poetic composition (*Ach.* 411–12 and *Thes.* 97 ff.).

the actor presents on stage. In the case of Dionysus in the *Bacchae*, however, the playwright moves away from such 'mask-piercing' effects characteristic of his earlier work—that is, the exploitation of the action in the 'service of inwardness' that comes close to undermining the tragic masking convention—to make the most original 'mask-exploiting' gesture of his career. As we have said, by convention a tragic mask represents one character and one meaning. Yet Euripides has called our attention to the fact that the smiling mask of the god represents different identities to characters and audience. In addition, as the action of the play continues, the precise nature of what the mask represents to the audience becomes increasingly ambiguous. Certainly it continues to 'represent' divinity to the audience. Yet the visual effect of the smiling mask has the same doubleness as the language of the play itself. The *eudaimonia* promised by the chorus to the adherents of Dionysiac religion is horribly ironic when the same term is applied to Agave on her return from the mountain after her destruction of her son (1258). Similarly, the god's mask remains smiling, but the visual effect of this smile does not remain consistent. The smile of the 'gentle' stranger seems, from the human vantage point, to turn by the end of the play to a divine sneer, a ghoulish expression of inappropriate glee at a vengeance too easily executed. In short, Dionysus' mask, by becoming ambiguous, comes to owe its interest not simply to what it formally represents in a way characteristic of the normal tragic masking convention, but to 'the further realities lying behind it', the invisible forces that unite the benign and destructive aspects represented by the single sign of the god's smiling mask. The mask, then, represents the god to the audience, misrepresents him to the characters and, as we will now see in more detail, in the final scene the mask must be interpreted as an artifact or symbol representing the god, or as much as we, or the characters, can ever visually and directly experience of him.

Pentheus in his final mad scene with Dionysus sees double, two suns and two Thebes. The audience also sees double in this scene, although in a different way. On stage are two figures wearing long robes, two wigs of long curls, two figures carrying the same Dionysiac paraphernalia.[38] The sacrificial victim of the god—here his

---

[38] The god and his victim are mythological doubles for each other; the victim dies in place of the god, and the god thus appears to escape death. (See Hubert and Mauss 1964, 144 ff.) For futher examples in Greek myth of such doubling see Guépin 1968, and for a discussion of its possible anthropological and tragic significance see Girard

contemporary and his cousin—has visually become almost the ritual double he often seems to have been in religious and literary tradition. The god wears his costume and his ambivalent sexuality with sinuous grace and authenticity. The human figure pathetically parodies the divine in costume and movement; as often in comedy, the feminine image is imperfectly imposed on the masculine. Pentheus finds it awkward to assimilate what he has so long resisted. It is the masks of the two figures that remain for the audience most markedly different—one smiling and hence inhuman, the other presumably unsmiling and by tragic convention, human. At this pivotal moment in the play we set the divine smile of the god Dionysus against the mask of Pentheus the man. The presentation of the two masks isolated side by side against the similarity of the costumes visually anticipates in its significance the staging of the final scene, the total split between man and god, which becomes so poignant when in typically Euripidean fashion (cf. the *Hippolytus*) the characters are left to mourn with newly clarified vision while the god looks down from above. The smiling mask of the god suddenly retains no aspect of benignity, if indeed it ever had any before, beside the mask of the doomed and mortal Pentheus. Euripides has brilliantly exploited a poetic device known from Homer onwards—Homer with his two worlds, one of inviolable and often comic gods, the other of struggling and mortal men. *Iliad* I, for example, puts the two gatherings of men and gods, one dissolving into anger and disaster, the other into laughter, into deliberate juxtaposition.[39] The visual juxtaposition of the masks here also becomes a precise theatrical expression of the division between divine and human nature that lies at the heart of the play.

The mortal Pentheus survives in the *Bacchae* solely as the mask the character represents in Greek theatrical convention. For the audience the mask remains Pentheus' own despite his transformation by

1972, chs 5 and 6. It is difficult to tell how similar the costumes of Dionysus and Pentheus would have been here. They both almost certainly wore long robes and fawnskins, and probably *kothurnoi*, soft-boots. Both have long hair, although Pentheus' is poorly confined in a *mitra*, headband. In Ar. *Frogs* (46) and Pollux (4. 116–17) Dionysus wears the *krokōtos*, a saffron garment emphasizing his feminine side, and to the audience, his divinity, but we cannot be certain of this in the *Bacchae*. If both Dionysus' and Pentheus' costume were saffron, the audience as well as Pentheus would see 'two suns', two brilliant yellow costumes moving side by side.

[39] There is a similar contrast in *Iliad* 21 between the comic battle of the gods and the battlefield of men.

Dionysus in other respects, and finally it returns unchanged to the stage impaled on Agave's *thyrsus*. Only to the mad Agave does Pentheus' mask temporarily appear that of a lion, the victim of the glorious god and herself. (The text emphasizes this issue of the temporary distortion of what the mask represents by the use of the word *prosōpon*, mask or face, 1277.)[40] The conventional identification between the tragic figure and his mask formally corresponds to his dramatic situation. He cannot completely step outside of or internally withdraw from and control his character or his fate; he is strictly human. As Euripides' staging brilliantly demonstrates, the tragic character *is* his mask, and is ultimately limited in the action to what his mask represents. By contrast, gods are not limited to representing one character, one role, one place in the family, society and universe. They manipulate roles with a freedom found only in comedy, where the character's mask may, as here, represent contradictory identities to the audience and the characters on stage. By reducing Pentheus to his tragic mask, and by allowing Dionysus to exploit his mask in an extraordinary way, Euripides demonstrates through theatrical convention the nature of the division between god and man.

Dionysus appears in his final epiphany no longer 'disguised' as the stranger. Given the rarity of costume change in Greek tragedy, I am assuming with the majority of commentators here that the god wears the same mask and costume throughout the play.[41] At this point the audience has lost the superior position it had—in the form we call tragic irony—over Pentheus. The smiling mask now

[40] Agave's envisioning of Pentheus' mask as a lion is what Jones would call a 'mask-piercing' effect, for she now apprehends, like the chorus, the bestial side of her son, the inner self that was at odds with his outer role. Yet her sane vision restores his humanity.

[41] It is always possible that Dionysus changed his mask and/or costume in the final scenes, to appear as, for example, the Zeus-like uneffeminate divinity of all but the most recent vase paintings. Others have made similar speculations on Dionysus' appearance in the scene where Pentheus sees the god as a bull or, for example, on the mask of Oedipus after his blinding in the *OT*. On the other hand, as we cannot prove that mask change ever occurred in Greek tragedy, and because mask change without a highly stylized system of masks would probably be confusing to an audience, it is safe, and probably safer, to assume that it did not occur here or elsewhere in fifth-century tragedy (even in comedy the disguised characters appear to change costume, not masks). [Certainly if the smiling mask was the (or a) conventional one for Dionysus, there would be no need for him to change masks when he appeared as a god.]

represents a divinity to both characters and audience. In the prologue
the god tells us that he has put on a mortal shape and will make him
manifest to Thebes in a disguised human—that is, indirect form. Yet
finally, when it has become clear to us that Dionysus can only be
'seen' or apprehended symbolically and indirectly by the theatrical
means common to Dionysiac religion and Greek theater, he simply
appears before us, and before a city which has returned to sanity, in
his divine form in the epiphany. By theatrical convention, we are
asked to accept the *deus ex machina* as an adequate and direct visual
representation of the god. And as an audience, at least, we have
never ceased to see the god's mask as divine. Yet the message of the
action of the play is in tension with this final representation of the
god. The action demonstrates the god's divinity indirectly and
symbolically and denies that we can adequately 'see' Dionysus with
human vision. We can thus accept Dionysus' appearance in the
epiphany as true to what we have come to understand about the god
only if we consciously see the god's face as a *mask*, that is a theatrical
or symbolic rather than a direct or 'real' manifestation of the many-
faceted divinity. As Jones suggests, Euripides here exploits to its limits
the tragic masking convention. Euripides heightens the inscrutable
effect of the god's epiphany by making his final appearance so
gratuitous—an unnecessary addition to an already finished plot—
and so puzzling in respect to the prophecies he makes to Thebes.[42]
While we may 'understand' that Dionysus is a god, and have come to
realize with the protagonists a good deal more as well about how he
must be grasped, we do not finally fully control this knowledge. The
house of Cadmus, although it now accepts the god's divinity, faces
yet further inhuman punishments. The play is for the audience also
in a sense unfinished. The god makes clear that the repercussions of
the events at Thebes will continue to be felt in Greece in the form of
further barbarian incursions, reaching, by extension perhaps (here

---

[42] On this point see Winnington-Ingram 1948, 144: the *deus ex machina* is
'spectacular but empty'. His appearance on the machine reserved for divinities, rather
than on stage, emphasizes the division between god and man already clear in the
death of Pentheus. From another perspective, of course, it allows the characters a few
moments free of the influence of the god to lament and come to terms with their fates,
and to question the excessive nature of the god's revenge (1346 and 1348). Perhaps
Cadmus' unenthusiastic reaction to Dionysus' promise of the land of the blessed
(μακάρων τ' ἐς αἶαν, 1339) for himself and Harmonia (1360-2), is a further ironic
comment on Dionysiac promises of bliss. See Dodds 1960, on 1330-9 for a discussion
of Dionysus' prophecies.

I rely primarily on the allusions to contemporary life in the choruses) even to fifth-century Athens.

By suggesting throughout the action of the play that we have access to the god by theatrical means—through mask, costume, voice and music, or through illusion, symbol, and transformation—Euripides seems to make a strong claim for art's ability to represent a reality inaccessible to ordinary human sight. Thus, by means of the theatrical convention of a smiling mask (which is not human) the audience 'sees' Dionysus' divinity as the characters at first cannot. Yet if one mask represents different identities to characters and audience, if the smile that marks the mask means both benignity and destruction, and finally, if the mask in the epiphany can only be understood as a sign that represents forces which are in fact not directly accessible to the eye, then the audience can only make sense of its theatrical experience if it becomes conscious of the god's mask as a mask in the modern rather than in the ancient tragic theatrical mode.[43] Dionysus' divinity in the *Bacchae* can be understood through this power to control representation. Euripides makes his anomalous 'untragic' mask become the central mocking image of what we as men can understand of a force that cannot be fully captured by human vision.

---

[43] Dionysus was worshipped in Greek cult as a mask (among many examples the *kalpis* signed by Hypsis, *c.*510 BC (ARV 30,2) is particularly appropriate for the *Bacchae*, in that it portrays the worship of the mask of Dionysus in both his benign and bestial incarnations). The final scenes of the *Bacchae* help to clarify precisely why the god was worshipped as a mask.

17
Three Off-Stage Characters in Euripides[1]

IRENE J. F. DE JONG

INTRODUCTION: DRAMATIC AND OFF-STAGE CHARACTERS

The average cast of a Euripidean tragedy consists of eight different *dramatic* characters (τά τοῦ δράματος πρόσωπα), without counting the chorus. This number of different characters or roles can be related to the three actors rule, current in Euripides' time. Apart from these dramatic characters, however, there are also characters which, though belonging to the story of the play, do not appear on the stage. These *off-stage* characters,[2] as they might be called, remain unseen and 'exist' for us, the audience, only by virtue of the fact that other characters speak *about* them. They miss, in Pfister's terminology,[3] the multimediality of the normal, dramatic characters, who are heard and seen. An example of an off-stage character is Hyllus in *Heracl.*: in the prologue we hear that he is away, looking for a new refuge in case the Athenians send the children of Heracles away (45–7); in the episode 630–747 one of his servants informs Iolaus and Alcmene that he has come back with a large army; and, finally, a Messenger

Research for this article has been made possible by a fellowship of the Royal Netherlands Academy of Arts and Sciences. This article forms, in fact, a pilot-study of my monograph (de Jong 1991). I wish to thank the members of the 'Hellenisten-club' for their critical remarks, Marietje van Erp Taalman Kip and Jan Maarten Bremer for their second reading.

[1] The following studies have been most useful for this article: Arnott 1981; Burnett 1971; Cropp 1988; Denniston 1939; Erdmann 1964; Fischl 1910; Friedrich 1953; Grube 1941 (2nd edn. 1961); Heath 1987; Henning 1910; Kitto 1961; Lesky 1964; Lloyd 1994; Page 1938; Pfister 1988; Pohlenz 1954; Rassow 1883; Stevens 1971. The text used is that of J. Diggle, Oxford ²1987 (vol. I) and ²1986 (vol. II).

[2] Pfister 1988, 164–5 speaks of 'backstage characters': 'figures who are referred to verbally in the speeches of others, but who never actually appear on stage'.

[3] See Pfister 1988, 6–11 on 'drama as a multimedial form of presentation'.

reports how he—bravely, but unsuccessfully—challenged Eurystheus to a duel (802–18). Though he is the eldest of the children of Heracles, Hyllus is a secondary figure in the play: he is eclipsed by his sister Macaria, who sacrifices herself in order to secure victory for Athens,[4] and by his uncle Iolaus, who takes the lead in capturing Eurystheus, a feature ascribed by other writers[5] to Hyllus alone.[6]

But off-stage characters can also play important roles, like Apollo in *Ion*, who is intimately linked to the events as Creusa's lover, Ion's father and master, and not least importantly, god of Delphi, where the play is situated: 'Apollo has been directing the return action [sc. of Ion], but he has been one of the players too, *albeit an invisible one*, in the actions of vengeance or release. Indeed, he seems always to be at the very heart of the play, . . ., and there is a sense in which we watch a tripartite consultation of the oracle, as Xuthus, Creusa and Ion receive his words and react in their different ways. Apollo, however, does not merely speak in this play, he acts. Once in the past he had appeared on earth . . . and made the child about whom now everything turns, and on this stage he moves to defend his creation. He acts by means of a dove and a priestess . . . And finally he sends Athena, who represents him in his prophetic capacity, but who also announces once and for all the fact that he has taken an active part in the adventures of the principals' (Burnett 1971, 126, my italics).[7] Another example is Odysseus in *IA*, who is constantly present in the background as 'der Inbegriff des Widerstandes, den Agamemnon zu

---

[4] Cf. Pohlenz 1954, 355–6: 'der Schwester zuliebe hält ihn (Hyllos) der Dichter von der Bühne fern. Daß der bereits wehrhafte Jüngling Hilfsvölker sammelt und Eurystheus—freilich vergeblich—zum Zweikampf für beide Heere herausfordert, ist einfache Mannesleistung, die nur im Bericht zu unserem Ohre dringt', 'The poet keeps him (Hyllos) away from the stage for the sake of his sister. That the youth, who is already capable of bearing arms, collects reinforcements and challenges Eurystheus—admittedly in vain—to single combat for both armies, is a straightforward masculine achievement which only reaches our ears in the (messenger's) report'. For a possible explanation of Hyllus' marginality, see Wilkins 1993, xxii.

[5] Apollod. *Bibl.* 2. 8 and Diod. Sic. 4. 57. 6.

[6] Another example is Neoptolemus in *Hec.*: 'Achilleus' Sohn ist der Vollstrecker des Opfers . . . wird aber aus dem Streit um Polyxena, der ihm vor allen anderen angeht, vom Dichter herausgehalten: es liegt hier eine jener Ausschaltungen der natürlichen Hauptrollen vor, die für das späte Drama ebenso charakteristisch sind wie der Aufstieg der Nebenrollen', 'Achilles' son is the one who carries out the sacrifice . . . but he is kept out of the argument about Polyxena by the poet, although it concerns him above all others: this is one of those suppressions of natural main roles, which are as characteristic of late drama as is the emergence of secondary roles'. (Friedrich 1953, 33).

[7] See also Sinos 1982, 129–34.

befürchten hat, wenn er Iphigenies Opferung verweigert' ('the embodiment of the resistance Agamemnon has to fear if he refuses to sacrifice Iphigeneia', Friedrich 1953, 91).[8]

In this paper I will discuss three off-stage characters who play a very special role, viz. that of deadly victim: Creon's daughter in *Med.*, Neoptolemus in *Andr.*, and Aegisthus in *El.* Attic dramatic convention forbade the act of killing[9] to be shown on stage and the death-scenes of these three characters—as those of dramatic characters, e.g. Pentheus in *Ba.*—are, therefore, related by messengers (*Med.* 1136–1230; *Andr.* 1085–1165, and *El.* 774–858). The importance of these three personages is beyond question: by virtue of their role as victims they are the 'protagonists' of the messengers' narratives. But it remains to be seen whether and if so, how, the poet manages to mobilize the interest of the spectators, indeed move them by the deaths of persons they have not seen on stage.

CREON'S DAUGHTER IN *MEDEA*

a. Before the messenger-speech

This off-stage character is introduced in line 19 as 'Creon's daughter' and throughout the play we never hear her name. Not surprisingly, her name is not even certain: the hypothesis has Γλαυκή (Glauce) but the scholion on 19 gives Κρέουσα (Creousa). Dramatic characters refer to her by the role she plays in the plot (and which will become fatal to her): 'daughter of the king', 'newly married girl/ bride', 'royal bride'.[10] Her namelessness is a first indication that her

---

[8] The view of Elam 1980, 142–3 in this respect is too restricted: ' "I" and "you" are the only genuinely active roles in the dramatic exchange . . . Others are defined negatively by means of the unmarked third person, which . . . is not strictly personal at all, indicating, as it does, an excluded and non-participant other presented *merely* as object of discourse' (my italics). Pfister 1988, 164 gives as an example of a backstage character influencing the plot 'the kitchen-girl' Nell in Shakespeare's *Comedy of Errors* (III. ii. 71–153). One could further think of Gogol's *The Revisor* and especially Edward Albee's *Who's afraid of Virginia Woolf*: in the first act we get piecemeal information about a son, who is dead at the end of the second act, and in the third act turns out to be the invention of his 'parents'. I thank Edwin Rabbie and Albert Rijksbaron for drawing my attention to these plays.

[9] See for this question Bremer in Bremer, Radt, and Ruijgh 1976, 29–48.

[10] 324: τῆς . . . νεογάμου κόρης ('the newly wedded girl'; Medea is speaking), 444: ἄλλα βασίλεια ('another woman, a princess'; chorus), 554: παῖδα . . . βασιλέως ('the king's daughter'; Jason), 623–4: τῆς νεοδμήτου κόρης ('the newly wedded girl'), 783: παῖδα βασιλέως ('the king's daughter'), 804–5: τῆς

individual being is of no great importance. This is confirmed if we
look at the way in which her new husband, Jason, and her rival,
Medea, talk about her. The point at stake is the question why Jason
has deserted Medea. According to Medea, Jason had wanted a new,
young, and, especially, Greek bride (591–2, 623–5, and cf. 244–5).
Jason maintains that it was not infatuation which motivated his step
but pragmatic reasoning: by aligning himself with the royal house of
Corinth he can secure his, Medea's and their children's position, who
until then had lived as exiles (551–65, 593–7).[11] Some commentators
believe Medea, others Jason,[12] but either way, Creon's daughter as an
individual seems to be of no great concern either to Medea, who is hurt
because she is deserted, regardless in favour of whom, or to Jason,
who considers her primarily a means to regain his former royal status.

But Creon's daughter is not so unimportant as to escape Medea's
revenge. The plan to kill her gradually takes shape: in 163–5 Medea
prays for the destruction one day of Jason and his bride. In 260–2 she
is already one step further, ensuring the silent complicity of the
chorus, in case she finds a way and scheme ($\pi\acute{o}\rho os$ $\tau\iota s$ $\mu\eta\chi\alpha\nu\acute{\eta}$ τ') to
make her husband[13] pay. In 385 she chooses her weapon (poison),
and in 774–810, when all external obstacles have been removed,
discloses to the chorus her final plan: she will pretend to Jason to
repent of her former hostility and then strike him in a more devastating way than by simply killing him (as she had announced in 374–5),

---

$\nu\epsilon o\zeta\acute{v}\gamma o\upsilon$ $\nu\acute{v}\mu\phi\eta s$ ('the newly yoked bride'), 957: $\tau\hat{\eta}$ $\tau\upsilon\rho\acute{a}\nu\nu\omega$ $\mu\alpha\kappa\alpha\rho\acute{\iota}\alpha$ $\nu\acute{v}\mu\phi\eta$
('the fortunate royal bride'), 970: $\pi\alpha\tau\rho\grave{o}s$ $\nu\acute{\epsilon}\alpha\nu$ $\gamma\upsilon\nu\alpha\hat{\iota}\kappa\alpha$, $\delta\epsilon\sigma\pi\acute{o}\tau\iota\nu$ δ'
$\dot{\epsilon}\mu\acute{\eta}\nu$ ('your father's new wife, my mistress'; Medea), 978: $\nu\acute{v}\mu\phi\alpha$ ('the bride';
chorus), 1003: $\nu\acute{v}\mu\phi\eta$ $\beta\alpha\sigma\iota\lambda\acute{\iota}s$ ('the royal bride'; Paedagogus), 1065–6: $\nu\acute{v}\mu\phi\eta$
$\tau\acute{v}\rho\alpha\nu\nu os$ ('the royal bride'; Medea), 1125: $\dot{\eta}$ $\tau\acute{v}\rho\alpha\nu\nu os$ ... $\kappa\acute{o}\rho\eta$ ('the royal girl'), 1144:
$\delta\acute{\epsilon}\sigma\pi o\iota\nu\alpha$ ('lady'), 1179: $\nu\acute{v}\mu\phi\eta s$ ('the bride'; Messenger), 1234: $\kappa\acute{o}\rho\eta$ $K\rho\acute{\epsilon}o\nu\tau os$
('Creon's daughter'; chorus, 1233–5 delevit Weil).

[11] Note that vis-à-vis Aegeus (698 and 700) Medea sarcastically adopts Jason's
reasoning and speaks of $\ddot{\epsilon}\rho\omega s$ ('love') as a desire to become acquainted with those in
power.

[12] Medea: Fischl 1910, 65 and Page 1938, xiv ('doubtless there sat among the
audience many a gentleman who was tired of the wife whom he brought back from
his travels when he was young'); Jason: Grube 1941, 153.

[13] Line 262 (containing the names of Creon and his daughter) is considered by
many (Murray, Page ad loc., Grube 1941, 153 n. 1) to be interpolated, to make this
passage consistent with 288. The argument that 'Medea would be foolish to disclose
such a wholesale plan before the chorus has promised silence' is not valid, since in
163–5 the chorus also had heard Medea speak about the death of both Jason and
Creon's daughter; I am more convinced by the argument that the chorus in 267 is
only referring to Jason.

viz. by killing his new wife and their own children, thus robbing him of his present and future offspring. The execution of the first part of this intrigue, the killing of the bride, will be related in the messenger-speech 1136–1230,[14] but we hear the kernel of the story beforehand from Medea herself: she will send Jason and the children to the princess to offer a poisoned robe and crown as gifts; when the girl puts these gifts on, she, and anybody who touches her, will die a horrible death (784–9). In 930–75 Medea explains to Jason her sudden generosity; he is to ask his wife to ask her father Creon to let their children remain in Corinth. Although Jason declares himself confident that his charm alone will be enough to persuade his wife (944–5), Medea gives him the gifts as an extra means to win her over.[15] Exeunt Jason and the children.

The crucial question now is of course whether the princess will accept these gifts, which come from her enemy. The chorus does not expect her to be able to resist the grace and glitter of the robe and golden crown (938–84), and indeed soon the Paedagogus, who had accompanied Jason and the children, comes back to tell Medea that the princess has 'gladly accepted the gifts with both hands' (1003–4). Medea envisions the girl's death: καὶ δὴ 'πι κρατὶ στέφανος, ἐν πέπλοισι δὲ νύμφη τύραννος ὄλλυται, σάφ' οἶδ' ἐγώ, 'the diadem is now upon her head, and the royal bride is dying in the dress, I know it for sure' (1065–6). Not long afterwards a Messenger brings the news: ὄλωλεν ἡ τύραννος ἀρτίως κόρη, 'the royal girl has just died' (1125). A detailed account follows.

b. The messenger-speech

The Messenger begins his account at the moment when he and the other servants see Jason and the children entering the palace and going to the bride's quarters. From this they gather joyfully that Jason and Medea have settled their quarrel (1136–40). In his enthusiasm the Messenger follows Jason and the children into the

---

[14] Messenger-speeches often describe the outcome of an intrigue or *mechanema*, see Solmsen 1932, 1–17 and Erdmann 1964, 131–66 ('Mechanemahandlung als Darstellung der Botenrede'). Note that Medea's killing of her children is not reported in a messenger-speech, but their screams are heard from within, just as in the *El.* the killing of Aegisthus is reported, the killing of Clytemnestra 'overheard' by the public.

[15] Note the irony in Medea's words εὐδαιμονήσει, 'she will be happy' (952), μακαρίᾳ, 'fortunate' (957) and οὔτοι δῶρα μεμπτά, 'gifts not to be thought little of' (958).

princess' room. On entering he immediately focuses on her, eager to
see how his new mistress reacts to the children. She only has eyes for
Jason, however, whom she spots first. When she sees the children,
the Messenger can gather from her outward reaction (she veils her
eyes and turns away her head) that she is disgusted with their arrival
(1144–9). According to Wecklein,[16] these lines serve to make Creon's
daughter appear in a bad light and, thus, to render her imminent
death acceptable to the audience. I do not agree: the incident further
(after πρόθυμον ... ὀφθαλμόν, 'an eager eye', in 1146) characterizes
her as very much in love. As Page (ad 1156) remarks: 'she cannot
bear to see the children who remind her that Jason has long been
married to another woman'. It also heightens the suspense, since it
seems unlikely that she will accept Medea's gifts. Now it is Jason's
turn, who, also noticing her anger, proceeds to take it away with
words. In his speech, quoted directly by the Messenger (1151–5) and
partly dictated earlier by Medea in indirect speech (1154–5 ≈ 942–3),
he makes use both of his authority as an older person and as a man
and of the girl's love for him ('do it for my sake', ἐμὴν χάριν: 1155).
What clinches the matter for her, however, is the sight of the
beautiful presents (1156),[17] just as had been foreseen by Medea (965)
and the chorus of Corinthian women (982–4). Creon's daughter
'agrees to everything' her husband had asked: ἤνεσ' ... πάντα
(1157). πάντα ('everything') suggests a brief, perfunctory answer,
which is indicative of her impatience: she can barely wait to put
on her newly acquired possessions and look at herself in a mirror
(1156–62). Jason and the children go away, their mission being
accomplished, but the Messenger remains behind and is able to
describe the dress parade Creon's daughter 'overjoyed' performs for
herself (1163–5; ὑπερχαίρουσα (1165) reminding us of the earlier
report of the Paedagogus: ἀσμένη, 'pleased': 1003).[18] Only through

---

[16] Wecklein 1909. Cf. also Lesky 1964, 308: 'dieses lieblos eitle Geschöpf', 'this
loveless, frivolous creature', and Rassow 1883, 37: eamque nuntius non talem
describit, cuius mors nos valde misereat, 'the Messenger does not describe her in such
a way that her death will greatly move us' (my translation, I.d.J.).

[17] Note the aorists ἐσεῖδε ... οὐκ ἠνέσχετο ('she saw ... she could not resist':
1156) vs. imperf. ἀφῄρει ('tried to allay': 1150).

[18] The Messenger nowhere refers to the presence of the Paedagogus. Of course, he
also does not know that the Paedagogus had reported to Medea that Creon's daughter
had accepted the gifts. This explains why he begins his story with the return into the
palace of the children; his ἐπεί ('when', 1136) refers back to 974 f. See Rijksbaron in
Bremer, Radt, and Ruijgh 1976, 295–6.

one small detail does the Messenger anticipate what is to come: when the princess looks in the mirror, she smiles at the 'lifeless image of herself' (1162); ἄψυχος ("lifeless") ist gewiß jedes Spiegelbild, hier aber reflektiert der Spiegel eine Person, die schon das Kleid und den Kranz des Todes trägt' ('Every reflection is certainly "lifeless", but here the mirror reflects a person who is already wearing the dress and the crown of death', Erdmann 1964, 132). In 1167 follows the reversal.

Let us halt for a moment and look back at the first half of the messenger-speech (1136–66). The detailed report of the Messenger evokes a lively picture of Creon's daughter,[19] not as an individual, but as a typical young girl (cf. νεάνιδος in 1150): she is very much in love, impatient and impulsive, and concerned with her own outward appearance. We get to know her, not by what she says (no speech is recorded, only once we have a bare speech-act mention: ἤνεσ᾽, 'agreed' in 1157), but by her movements (προυκαλύψατ᾽ ὄμματα, 'she covered up her eyes': 1147, ἀπέστρεψ᾽ . . . παρηίδα, 'she turned away her cheek': 1148, σχηματίζεται κόμην, 'she arranges her hair': 1161, ἁβρὸν βαίνουσα, 'stepping delicately': 1164, πολλὰ πολλάκις τένοντ᾽ ἐς ὀρθὸν . . . σκοπουμένη, 'often and often stretching her foot out straight and looking at it': 1165–6) and facial expressions (πρόθυμον ὀφθαλμόν, 'an eager eye': 1146, προσγελῶσα, 'smiling at': 1162). The Messenger dwells on the girl's exhilaration (προσγελῶσα: 1162, ὑπερχαίρουσα, and πολλὰ πολλάκις: 1165) and stresses her delicate femininity (ἁβρὸν βαίνουσα,[20] παλλεύκῳ ποδί, 'white foot': 1164) to make the contrast to what follows all the greater. Thus, though he nowhere openly shows any engagement, it transpires from his presentation.

When he comes to describing her agonizing death-struggle (1167–1203), his pity and compassion become explicit: to witness her death was 'a terrible sight': δεινὸν ἦν θέαμ᾽ ἰδεῖν (1167) and δεινὸν θέαμα (1202), and cf. δεινὸν στενάξασ᾽ ('groaning terribly', 1184); he refers to the girl as 'unlucky': ἡ τάλαιν᾽ (1184) and τῆς δυσδαίμονος (1189); what befalls the girl is 'a catastrophe'

---

[19] Fischl 1910, 65, Henning 1910, 35: quasi oculis puellam videmus, 'we actually seem to see the girl'; Pohlenz 1954, 256: 'ein lebensvolles Bild des puppenhaften Prinzeßchens', 'a lively picture of the doll-like princess'; Lesky 1964, 308: 'Kreusa betritt die Bühne nicht, aber wie kennen wir dieses lieblos eitle Geschöpf', 'Kreusa never comes on stage, but how well we know this loveless, frivolous creature'.

[20] Cf. the Messenger's description of that paradigm of femininity, Helen, in *Hel.* 1528: ἁβρὸν πόδα τιθεῖσ᾽, 'placing her delicate foot'.

(συμφορά: 1179, 1195, 1204, [1221: del. Reeve and West]). Besides these explicit signs of compassion, there are also implicit ones: the princess' λευκὴν ... σάρκα, 'white flesh' (1189),[21] is 'devoured' by the fine robe and her εὐφυὲς πρόσωπον, 'shapely face' (1198), is completely deformed;[22] finally, note the military metaphor ἐπεστρατεύετο ('was advancing upon', 1185), which underscores her position as object of (Medea's) hostilities.

I turn to the central question of this paper: does the death of this off-stage character move the spectators? We do not know what the Athenian public felt, but we do have modern reader-reactions, e.g. a 'no' from Rassow 1883, 37 and a 'yes' from Grube 1941, 163. Perhaps the question should be reformulated as 'does the poet *want us* to be moved?' (whether he succeeds, of course, is a different thing). I think the following indications suggest a positive answer. To begin with there is the Messenger's emotional filtering[23] of the event, which I have just discussed. In the second place, there is Creon's reaction to the death of his daughter, recorded by the Messenger in 1204-11: the old man throws himself upon her corpse, cries out, embraces and kisses her, and laments her.[24] In the third place, there are the reactions of the Messenger's addressees, his *internal* audience:[25] Medea and the chorus. For Medea, it is a delight to hear about the suffering of her rival: δὶς τόσον γὰρ ἂν τέρψειας ἡμᾶς, εἰ τεθνᾶσι παγκάκως, 'you would give me double pleasure, if they died utterly terribly' (1134-5). Her gloating over her defeated enemies may be supposed to have the opposite effect on the spectators, viz. to arouse their pity for those who died so 'utterly

---

[21] According to von Arnim 1886 and Wecklein 1909, λευκήν ('white') stresses 'das Mitleiderregende', the pitifulness. In principle λευκός is a fixed epithet of the female skin and in 1189 it is only the contrast with 1164 which creates the effect of 'arousing pity' here. As a matter of fact, I think that λευκός when used of a woman's *face* need not necessarily be a fixed epithet. Emotions show themselves primarily in the face and if a woman's face were always pale, then remarks such as *Med.* 1175 and *Alc.* 174 would be meaningless. Thus, I tend to take the word in *Med.* 1148 (λευκὴν ... παρηίδα, 'white cheek') as an indication of emotion (note also the hyperbaton).

[22] One is reminded here of certain pathetic passages in the *Iliad*: κάρη δ' ἅπαν ἐν κονίῃσι κεῖτο πάρος χαρίεν, 'the head which used to be so handsome was now completely lying in the dust' (22. 402-3), and cf. 16. 796-9, 17. 51-60, and 18. 23-4.

[23] His focalization, see de Jong 1987.

[24] Contrast Jason's egoistic reaction in 1293-1300 and 1348: he does not grieve over his bride, but only considers the consequences for himself: his plan to become a member of the royal family and to beget royal children has fallen to pieces.

[25] For the distinction between internal and external audience, see Pfister 1988, 3-4.

terribly'. The reaction of the chorus (1231–5) is in fact a matter of scholarly dispute: if one reads only 1231–2 (as Wilamowitz suggested, and Page and Diggle do), the chorus pay no attention at all to the princess, but merely conclude that Jason suffers 'deservedly' (ἐνδίκως: 1232). If one takes 1233–5 to be genuine rather than an interpolation by a sentimental actor (to which view I feel inclined), the chorus express their pity for the girl, as they had done earlier in 978–88.

I conclude that this off-stage character—no less than Creon, whom the audience has seen on stage in 271–356—can be qualified, in Heath's terminology,[26] as the focal character, i.e. the 'centre of [the public's] sympathetic attention', of the messenger-scene. We have seen how the poet directs the emotional response of the spectators, the *external* audience, through the reactions of characters and chorus, but above all through the presentation of the event through the eyes of a sympathetic messenger.[27]

NEOPTOLEMUS IN *ANDROMACHE*

a. Before the messenger-speech

In the *Andr.* Neoptolemus is not only off stage for the public, he is also 'away' in the play: he is in Delphi (to atone for a former insult against Apollo: 50–5), whereas the play is set at Phthia. Indeed, his absence is a crucial element in the plot (allowing Hermione to try and get rid of her rival Andromache) and is often mentioned: ἀπών (50), τοὺς ἀπόντας (378), ἀπόντων (633), τῶν ἐκδήμων φίλων (1051). But, despite his absence, Neoptolemus plays, or rather, is made to play (by characters referring to him), an important role, viz. that of avenger. First, Andromache warns Menelaus, who has come to assist his daughter, that Neoptolemus, heroic warrior as he is, will never leave the death of his son unavenged (339–43): ὥσει δὲ σὴν παῖδ' ἐκ

---

[26] Heath 1987, 90–8. He introduces the term as follows: 'We saw . . . that the tragic emotions are to a large extent sympathetic emotions; this implies that tragedy has a *personal* focus. The audience is required to concentrate its attention on key figures in the action, and to do so sympathetically, that is, in such a way that they are involved with and respond to the fortunes and feelings of those characters. I shall use the term "focus" henceforth in this technical sense, of any character who is serving as a centre of sympathetic attention' (90).

[27] Creon's daughter has to wait until Corneille before she is allowed her début on the European stage and is endowed with a more individual character.

δόμων, 'he will throw your daughter out of the house' (344). Then, Peleus, who saves Andromache in the nick of time, says the same, but couched in more powerful language: ἣν ὅγ᾽ ἐξ ἡμῶν γεγὼς ἐλᾷ δι᾽ οἴκων τῶνδ᾽ ἐπισπάσας κόμης, 'whom my grandson will drag by the hair through this house and drive out' (709–10). The climax in this series is reached when Hermione, her plan thwarted and her father gone away, is struck with panic: ὀλεῖ μ᾽ ὀλεῖ με δηλαδὴ πόσις, 'Obviously my husband will kill me, will kill me' (856–8 and cf. 920, 927–8).[28]

At this point our perspective on Neoptolemus changes and from a fearful avenger he becomes himself the object of revenge. For Orestes appears, declares himself only too willing to take the frightened Hermione with him, and announces to her that he has set a deadly trap for Neoptolemus in Delphi. They had been rivals over Hermione in the past and he now sees a chance to avenge himself for Neoptolemus' offensive behaviour to him at that time (993–1008). As in *Med.* (and cf. n. 14), the messenger-speech will describe the fulfilment of the μηχανή, 'plot', but unlike Medea, Orestes does not give a detailed description in advance: ἣν (sc. μηχανήν) πάρος μὲν οὐκ ἐρῶ ('which (sc. "plot") I will not tell beforehand', 997). We only hear that Apollo and the slanders of Orestes will have a part in Neoptolemus' downfall (1005–6).

Whereas usually a messenger-speech follows immediately after a choral song, here the entrance of the Messenger is preceded by the arrival of Peleus, who, on hearing about Orestes' plan, wants to send a messenger to warn Neoptolemus before it is too late. His reaction is the first genuine sympathy shown to Neoptolemus in the play. Neoptolemus' two wives show little affection for him. Andromache makes clear on more than one occasion that she does not—as Hermione insinuates in 170–3—voluntarily share the bed of Neoptolemus (36–8, 390–3), son of Achilles (21, 25), murderer of Hector (403).[29] She calls him her δεσπότης, 'master' (25, 30, 391), reserving the qualification πόσις, 'husband' for Hector (227, 456, 523–5).[30]

---

[28] There is only one figure who thinks that Neoptolemus might react less vehemently, viz. the Nurse (844, 866–73).

[29] Through the use of the plural φονεῦσιν, 'murderers', Andromache puts Neoptolemus in the same category as his father.

[30] If Andromache is present on stage after 1047 as a silent character (for discussion of this question see Stevens 1971 on 1047–1288), her silence fits in well with this picture.

Hermione trades in her πόσις Neoptolemus without much ado, and her silence and indifference when Orestes announces his murderous plot against Neoptolemus are, I think, significant (see Stevens 1971 ad 1005–6). The chorus, in their second stasimon (464–93, cf. also 122–5), disapprove of one man having two wives and thus obliquely criticize Neoptolemus. One of the functions of Peleus is, therefore, to provide the Messenger with a sympathetic, not to say pathetic, sounding-board.[31]

b. The messenger-speech

The Messenger is a servant of Neoptolemus (δεσπότου: 1071, δεσπότης ἐμός, 'my master': 1110, 1146), who is himself emotionally affected by the news he brings (ὤμοι μοι οἵας ὁ τλήμων ἀγγελῶν ἥκω τύχας, 'O woe, woe! It is bad news that I, unfortunate man, am bringing': 1070). Accordingly, his account of what happened in Delphi is coloured, Orestes and Apollo being the villains of the story, Neoptolemus its tragic hero. The tone is set right at the beginning: we (Neoptolemus and his servants, including the Messenger) were sightseeing in 'famous' Delphi, while Orestes stirred up the Delphians against Neoptolemus, saying that he had come to ransack Apollo's temple (1085–99). Although the Messenger must have learned about Orestes going through town only afterwards, he inserts this piece of *ex eventu* knowledge at this point to make clear aggressor (cf. 1116: ἁπάντων τῶνδε μηχανορράφος, 'the contriver of all these things') and unsuspecting victim (cf. οὐδὲν τῶνδέ πω πεπυσμένοι, 'we knew nothing of this yet': 1101; and cf. 1125–6). After three days Neoptolemus goes to Apollo's temple and the Messenger takes care to indicate that (this time) Neoptolemus behaves piously and follows the prescribed procedures: he brings sheep to be sacrificed and has procured the assistance of the *proxenoi* ('official hosts', 1100–8). It is to be understood that Neoptolemus is serious when he says that he repents his offensive behaviour of the past. The Messenger stresses no less than three times that Neoptolemus came with honourable intentions (τῆς πάροιθ' ἁμαρτίας δίκας παρασχεῖν, 'to make amends for my earlier fault': 1106–7, εὐσεβεῖς ὁδούς, 'on a pious journey': 1125, δίκας

---

[31] That the Messenger is very well aware of Peleus' presence as addressee appears from 1135: ἂν εἶδες, 'you would have seen'.

διδόντα, 'making amends': 1163) and the spectators know (from
Andromache in 50–5 and Orestes in 1003–4) that this is the truth.
The Delphians, however, under the influence of Orestes' slander,
think that he is lying (1109–11). When he has entered the shrine and
is praying to the god, they attack him with swords (1111–19). The
Messenger does not hide his indignation about this cowardly attack
against an unarmed man: ὀξυθήκτοις, 'sharp-edged' (1118, 'a
conventional epithet . . . Here it may be intended to add emphasis to
the contrast with the unsuspecting and unprotected victim': Stevens
1971 ad loc.) and ἀτευχῆ . . . λάθρα, 'unarmed . . . stealthily' (1119).
But Neoptolemus fights back and the Delphians are put to flight, until
an intervention by Apollo brings about his end (1129–55). The
Messenger is full of admiration for the courage of his master, who
lives up to the standards of his heroic father Achilles (1120–40):[32] cf.
γοργὸς ὁπλίτης ἰδεῖν, 'a terrible warrior to behold' (1123),[33] and
φαεννοῖς . . . στίλβων ὅπλοις, 'gleaming in his bright armour'
(1146). Conversely, he brands the Delphians as cowards through a
comparison with doves (1140). Throughout this fighting scene he
also puts his master into the limelight through his use of historical
presents. Historical presents are in themselves a common element in
messenger-speeches, but this Messenger uses them, with one
exception (προσφέρει, 'brings': 1153), exclusively to describe
Neoptolemus' movements: ἔρχεται ('he goes', 1111), τυγχάνει
('he arrives at', 1113), προσεύχεται ('he prays to', 1117), χωρεῖ ('he
goes', 1120, 1140), ἐξέλκει (he draws out', 1121), βοᾷ ('he cries out
to', 1124), πίτνει ('he falls', 1149, 1152). His pity is expressed by
δεινὰς . . . πυρρίχας, 'a terrible Pyrrhic dance' (1135)[34] and πᾶν
δ' ἀνήλωται δέμας τὸ καλλίμορφον, 'his handsome body was
completely destroyed' (1154–5, the same 'beauty brought low'
motif as in εὐφυὲς πρόσωπον, 'her shapely face': Med. 1188). The

---

[32] The Messenger three times refers to Neoptolemus as 'son of Achilles' (1119,
1149–50, 1163), for which denomination see Stevens 1971 ad 14: 'Though N. is
repeatedly mentioned in this play the name occurs only here, partly on metrical
grounds, but periphrases reminding us of his lineage are sometimes dramatically
effective.'

[33] Cf. Stevens 1971 ad loc.: 'it is more likely that it [γοργός] means "terrible" and
that Eur. now uses, to express the messenger's admiration of N., the same phrase that
had been used sarcastically of Menelaus in 458'.

[34] Cf. Stevens 1971 ad loc.: 'to indicate that this time it is in earnest'. I disagree
with Lloyd 1994 ad loc., who contends that δεινάς 'emphasizes the messenger's irony
in describing N.'s desperate self-defence as a dance'.

Messenger ends with a bitter complaint against Apollo, who did not give Neoptolemus a chance to show repentance. Earlier he had shown indignation at the Delphians' abuse of the holy shrine for a base murder: δεξίμηλον ἐσχάραν, 'sheep-receiving hearth' (1138, the epithet indicates what the altar should normally be used for, cf. 1100–2) and κραυγὴ . . . ἐν εὐφήμοισι δύσφημος δόμοις, 'an unholy uproar in a holy place' (1144–5, the juxtaposition underlines the desecration).[35]

After the messenger-speech Neoptolemus does appear on stage . . . as a corpse, and is lamented by his grandfather (1173–1225). This elaborate kommos indicates the importance of this off-stage character, whom some scholars (Friedländer,[36] Friedrich 1953, 47 and 56; Pohlenz 1954, 287; Erdmann 1964, 138) have even called the real hero of the play. Others reach exactly the opposite conclusion on account of his off-stage status: 'obviously, the play is not "tragic" with regard to any individual: we never even meet the man who dies' (Conacher);[37] 'perhaps the underlying cause of mediocrity is the fact that, in this play, we have never met Neoptolemus and cannot be very interested in him' (Lattimore),[38] and cf. Grube 1941, 213. I take a middle position and follow Heath 1987, 93 in considering him the focal character, not of the entire play but of the messenger-scene. As Heath remarks, most focal characters have focus only in a given scene and mobility of focus is a characteristic trait of Greek tragedy. The *Andr.* offers a good example, because in this play the focus shifts from Andromache to Hermione to Neoptolemus and finally to Peleus.

As in the case of Creon's daughter, we see that the emotional reaction of (one of) the Messenger's internal addressees (Peleus) and the Messenger's biased presentation (manifesting itself in part explicitly, in part implicitly, through the subtle use of repetition, comparison, historical presents, epithets, and direct speech) are the

---

[35] Thus I go further than Stevens 1971 ad loc. ('the juxtaposition brings out the special horror') and disagree with Burnett's analysis (1971: 152) of the fighting-scene in terms of 'Neoptolemus' new crime' (one detail: in 1138 he does not 'sweep the sacred objects from the altar', but abandons his position on top of the altar). Lloyd's comment (1994) ad loc. ('a temple is an inappropriate place for fighting, but Apollo evidently approves of the attack') annuls the effect of the Messenger's—critical—focalization.

[36] Friedländer 1926, 79–112: 'Denn als Abwesender bestimmt er alles, was auf der Bühne geschieht' ('Because in his absence he determines everything that happens on stage', 101).   [37] Conacher 1967, 172 and cf. 21, 179.

[38] Lattimore 1958, 115–16.

means by which the poet is able to turn even an off-stage character into a focal one and to trigger the pity of the external audience.[39]

AEGISTHUS IN *ELECTRA*

a. Before the messenger-speech

The third off-stage character to be discussed is, like the other two, the victim of a revenge-scheme. The main charge which the avengers Electra and Orestes hold against Aegisthus is, of course, his complicity in the murder of Agamemnon (10, 86, 124, 164–5). As the moment he must pay for his crime comes closer, he is even called '*the* murderer of Agamemnon': for the first time in 599, when Orestes launches the revenge-project (λέξον, τί δρῶν ἂν φονέα τεισαίμην πατρὸς . . .; 'tell me what we should do to repay my father's murderer?'), and cf. 763 (Messenger), 769, 869, 885 (Electra) and 849 (Orestes).[40] But Orestes and in particular Electra have another reason to hate Aegisthus, viz. his behaviour *after* the murder, about which the Farmer tells us in the prologue (1–53, notice that Aegisthus' name turns up no less than seven times: 10, 12, 17, 24, 28, 32, 42): Aegisthus has taken over Agamemnon's sceptre and wife, tried to kill the boy Orestes, prevented the adolescent Electra from marrying somebody of her own station, tried to kill her, and, finally, set a price on Orestes' head and married off Electra to a poor farmer.

The Farmer does not explicitly condemn Aegisthus' behaviour. For this we must turn to Electra, who considers Aegisthus' marrying her off to the Farmer an act of *hybris* (59, and cf. Orestes in 266). In 319–31 she gives more details, describing what she often must have

[39] Cf. also Rassow 1883, 36: 'If Euripides wanted to gain the effect that we will pity these men (Hippolytus, Orestes, Neoptolemus, etc.), he had to put them before our eyes in such a way as to make them worthy of our pity. Thus it was necessary to choose messengers, who not merely report the disaster, but who are convinced that these men do not deserve to suffer this disaster, and who are able to express their feelings eloquently. This art is all the more praiseworthy in *Andromache*, since Neoptolemus, whose death is reported, never enters the scene during the whole play' (my translation, I.d.J.). Kamerbeek, 1943, 46–67, seems to have overlooked the messenger-speech when he says: 'pendant toute la pièce le poète n'a rien fait pour éveiller de la sympathie à l'égard de Néoptolème' (64).

[40] Thus, I consider the gradual focusing on Aegisthus as 'the murderer' as more than 'not inconsistent' (Denniston 1939 ad 9–10).

seen herself[41] (how Aegisthus goes out driving Agamemnon's chariot and revels in holding his sceptre) and what she has heard from others (how Aegisthus jumps on Agamemnon's tomb, pelts his grave monument with stones and abuses the absent Orestes). Details like ἐς ταὐτά ... ἅρματ' ... πατρί, 'in my father's very chariot' (320) and ἐν οἷς "Ελλησιν ἐστρατηλάτει, 'with which he commanded the Greeks' (321) are expressive of her indignation at Aegisthus' touching objects so intimately linked to her father. There is also a hint that Aegisthus, who did not join the Trojan expedition (cf. 917), is strutting with borrowed feathers. Another revealing detail is his drunkenness (326). In the prologue the Farmer had stressed Aegisthus' fear (for reprisals from Orestes and Electra): 22–3, 25–6, 39 (and cf. the Old Man in 617). Drinking, apparently, helps 'the famous' Aegisthus[42] to forget his fear and even makes him defiant.[43] As we will see, Aegisthus' fear is also an important element in the messenger-speech.

Aegisthus' death is planned in 596–639 with the help of the Old Man. He informs Orestes that Aegisthus happens to be near by, in the country, preparing a sacrifice to the Nymphs with only some servants (not his usual bodyguard: 616) around him. All Orestes has to do is to let himself be seen by Aegisthus, who will certainly invite him to share in the festivities. The rest is up to Orestes to think of 'as the dice may fall' (639: πρὸς τὸ πίπτον). How they fell we hear from the Messenger in 774–858.

b. The messenger-speech

Aegisthus does indeed offer an invitation to Orestes, who pretends to be a Thessalian on his way to Olympia, and is then, at the height of

[41] In the comparable passage S. El. 254–309 Electra emphasizes how she has to bear the sight of Aegisthus in her father's house: ὁρῶ (260), ἴδω (267, 271), εἰσίδω (268), 'I see'; ὁρῶσα, 'seeing' (258, 282).

[42] I take ὁ κλεινός (327) not as an ironical reference to Aegisthus' sham royalty (so Denniston 1939), but to his lack of a real war-record (cf. S. El. 300–2; ὁ κλεινὸς ... ὁ σὺν γυναιξὶ τὰς μάχας ποιούμενος, 'the famous one ... who makes his wars on women'): he insults powerless women and men who are dead (Agamemnon) or absent (Orestes).

[43] Whoever thinks this interpretation of Aegisthus' drinking too modern, I refer to Iliad 20. 83–5, where we hear of alcohol (οἰνοποτάζων, 'drinking wine') making Aeneas boast that he will confront Achilles, a thing he shrinks from doing when sober.

the sacrificial ceremony, killed by him. At first sight, the chances of
Aegisthus' engaging the pity of the spectators seem low, since, as we
saw above, up to the messenger-speech they have not heard much
good about him. Also, the Messenger belongs to the Orestes-Electra
camp (ἀδελφοῦ . . . πρόσπολον, 'a servant of your brother': 766)
and he considers Aegisthus' death not a catastrophe, but a victory
(νικῶντ' Ὀρεστήν: 762). His internal audience (Electra and chorus)
cheers at his news (771–3, 860–79), and after the messenger-speech
Aegisthus' corpse is not lamented but taunted (907–56). However,
not a few modern readers sympathize with the victim Aegisthus: 'Der
Botenbericht zeigt Aegisth, das Opfer, als einen arglosen gastfreund-
lichen Mann, den siegreichen Orest dagegen als einen verschla-
genen, gefährlich geschickten und gänzlich skrupellosen Mörder . . .
Ohne Zweifel, scheint mir, will Euripides den Aegisth nicht als einen
Bösewicht zeichnen und als solchen enden lassen' (Erdmann 1964,
142–3, 'The messenger speech shows Aegisthus, the victim, as a
harmless, hospitable man; the victorious Orestes, on the other
hand, as a cunning, dangerously skilful and entirely unscrupulous
murderer . . . Without doubt, it seems to me, Euripides does not want
to depict Aegisthus as a villain and let him die as a villain'); cf. Kitto
1961, 336; Grube 1941, 308; Pohlenz 1954, 313; and Arnott 1981,
184. How to explain this sympathy for Aegisthus? Arnott 1981, 185
suggests: 'At one level this murder is described in objective narrative
as a vicious, cowardly assault. At a second level, however, the same
murder is imaged, mainly but not exclusively by Electra with the
chorus, as a feat of high heroism superior even to victory in the
Olympic games' (185). But it is even more complicated than this,
since the Messenger's narrative is not objective and does not present
the assault as 'vicious or cowardly'. On the contrary, the Messenger
is convinced of the righteousness of Orestes' deed and his report fully
savours the the irony of the situation, Aegisthus courteously
entertaining his own arch-enemy and prospective murderer.

Let us take a closer look at the events as they are seen by the
Messenger. The Old Man had told that Aegisthus finds himself on his
horse-pastures (623). These turn out to be an idyllic place ('a watered
place'), in which Aegisthus is busy 'cutting sprays of tender myrtle'
(774–8). The Messenger gleefully dwells on these details to show
how completely off guard Aegisthus is. For his external audience
they may, on the contrary, shed an ugly light on Orestes' deed to

come.[44] Upon seeing Orestes and his companions (Pylades and the Messenger), Aegisthus acts exactly as predicted by the Old Man (cf. 637: ὅθεν ⟨γ'⟩ ἰδών σε δαιτὶ κοινωνὸν καλεῖ, 'he will see you from there and invite you to share in the feast'): indeed, he literally drags Orestes into the house, not taking 'no' for an answer (779–89). On his part, Orestes adds intentional irony to Aegisthus' unintentional irony, for the first time in 795–6: εἰ δὲ ξένους ἀστοῖσι συνθύειν χρεών, Αἴγισθ', ἕτοιμοι κοὐκ ἀπαρνούμεσθ', ἄναξ, 'if strangers may join with citizens in sacrificing, Aegisthus, we are ready and do not refuse, lord'.[45] When the preparations for the sacrifice have been made (798–803), Aegisthus prays (for the good luck of Clytemnestra and himself, the bad luck of his enemies), a scene which triggers strong emotions in the Messenger (804–10): he sarcastically refers to Aegisthus as μητρὸς εὐνέτης σέθεν, 'your mother's bedfellow' (803; cf. Electra in 930: 'And this was what all the Argives said of you: "The man is his wife's, and not the wife her man's"') and adds his indignant[46] commentary on Aegisthus' use of ἐχθρούς 'enemies': 'meaning you and Orestes' (808). The identification of the Messenger with his master and the cause he is fighting for enables him even to read the latter's mind: δεσπότης δ' ἐμὸς τἀναντί' ηὔχετ', οὐ γεγωνίσκων λόγους, λαβεῖν πατρῷα δώματ', 'My master prayed the opposite, not voicing his words: to gain his ancestral house'. The ensuing scene of the sacrifice of the bull-calf is a masterful piece of suspense and irony (810–38): Aegisthus asks 'the Thessalian'/Orestes to display his Thessalian ability to flay a beast and thereby himself hands him a murder weapon (λαβὲ σίδηρον, ὦ ξένε, 'take a knife, stranger'),[47] which the latter uses . . . to do as he is asked. The Messenger's admiration for his master's butchering skills finds expression in a comparison

---

[44] Cropp's note (1988) ad 777–8 ('A charming setting for the horror to come') seems to mix up the focalization of the Messenger ('charming') and the evaluation by his external audience ('horror').

[45] Cf. Denniston 1939 ad 795: 'The rightful king speaks to the usurper with hidden irony'; Cropp 1988 ad 796: 'perhaps with irony in the use of Aeg.'s name . . . The separation of ἄναξ, "my lord", can also have ironic effect.'

[46] Not 'somewhat naïvely' (Grube 1941, 308).

[47] Cropp 1988 ad 815–17 tentatively suggests that Aegisthus asks this 'to test Or.'s claim to be a Thessalian'. This would spoil the irony of the whole scene: Aegisthus is mortally afraid of Orestes, but not for a second suspects that 'the Thessalian' is Orestes.

('the hide he skinned off quicker than a runner completes two horse-track laps'), which nicely ties in with the consistent imagery of Orestes as an athlete (cf. 614, 761–2, 751, 862–4, 872). The bad signs of the entrails lead to another ironical exchange: (Aegisthus) 'Stranger, I dread some alien guile. There is a son of Agamemnon, most at enmity with me, a foe to my house.' (Orestes) 'So you fear foul play from a fugitive, you, the lord of the city?' We have dramatic irony in θυραῖον (Aegisthus thinks Orestes is far away, whereas he is standing next to him)[48] and above all the existential ἔστι (Aegisthus telling Orestes that there is a certain Orestes),[49] and intentional irony (of the type employed by Orestes before in 795–6), when Orestes refers to himself as a mere φυγάδος, 'fugitive', to Aegisthus as πόλεως ἀνάσσων, 'the lord of the city'. Then Orestes asks for another knife and finally kills Aegisthus (835–43). As in the case of Creon's daughter, an internal reaction to the murder is reported by the Messenger: Aegisthus' servants at first prepare to avenge their master, but when Orestes reveals his true identity—which is confirmed by an old servant in 852–3—and declares that he has not come as a public enemy (οὐχι δυσμενὴς ἥκω πόλει τῆδ' οὐδ' ἐμοῖς ὀπάοσιν, 'I do not come as an enemy to the city or to my followers', redresses Aegisthus' πολέμιός . . . ἐμοῖς δόμος, 'an enemy to my house': 833) but to avenge his father's death, they crown his head 'rejoicing and hallooing' (844–55). Thus, even Aegisthus' retainers choose Orestes' side. Notice that last small scene also allows the Messenger to mention Orestes' and Pylades' courage (845): they are not merely secret schemers, but men prepared also to fight in the open. The Messenger concludes his report by saying that Aegisthus deserved this πικρὸς δανεισμός, 'bitter return' (858, cf. Orestes in 638 πικρόν . . . συνθοινάτορ', 'a bitter fellow-diner'). So much for the pitiless point of view of the Messenger, which, I hope to have shown, is not objective: he is biased, in favour of his master and against Aegisthus. One last detail may confirm this. The very first time he refers to Aegisthus, the Messenger uses ὁ κλεινός (MSS followed by Denniston and Donizetti in the new Teubner)/καινός (Diggle, followed by Cropp) ἄναξ, 'the famous/new lord'. If we

---

[48] This irony has been missed by Denniston 1939 ('But in a sense it is οἰκεῖος, it comes from his own cousin') and Cropp 1988 (who has no note).

[49] The existential force of ἔστι, which is suggested by its place at the beginning of the clause, is overlooked by Cropp 1988, who translates 'Agamemnon's son is the man most at enmity with me, a foe to the house'.

choose κλεινός, 'famous', the Messenger mirrors the irony of Electra in 327;[50] if we choose καινός, 'new', he anticipates the irony of Orestes in 796 and 835 and makes clear that, like his master, he considers Aegisthus an usurper (who deserves to be punished).[51] Either way, his reference is charged with emotion.

The Messenger's focalization is not shared, as we saw earlier, by most modern readers.[52] That Aegisthus deserved to be punished nobody will deny (his death is ordered by the gods: 87–9). But somehow the account of his death arouses the pity of the external audience. This is due (1) partly to the content of the Messenger's story, (2) partly to its graphic and realistic style. Ad 1: Orestes slaughters Aegisthus with a butcher's cleaver as if he were an animal; note the echo of ἀναρρῆξαι ('break', 837 of the bull-calf's breast-bone) in 842: ἔρρηξεν 'broke' (of Aegisthus' spine). How pitiful it is to be killed like an animal might be learned from . . . that victim of Aegisthus himself, Agamemnon: Αἴγισθος . . . ἔκτα . . ., ὥς τίς τε κατέκτανε βοῦν ἐπὶ φάτνῃ. ὣς θάνον οἰκτίστῳ θανάτῳ, 'Aegisthus killed me, like one kills a bull at the manger. Thus I died a most pitiable death' (Od. 11. 410–12).[53] Ad 2: the 'clinically exact detailing of the effect of the death blow' (Arnott 1981, 186) in 839–43, which the Messenger obviously revels in, may have the opposite effect on the external audience.

---

[50] I disagree with Denniston 1939 ad 776: 'κλεινός: simply a title of royalty, which the speaker can use of Aeg. though hostile to him. Irony would be somewhat out of place in this matter-of-fact passage.'

[51] Cf. Cropp 1988 ad loc.: 'it emphasizes Aeg.'s usurpation, now to be punished'.

[52] Exceptions are Rassow 1883, 35: 'For in Electra he aims in the narration to make the murder of Aegisthus by Orestes a most just case and therefore depicts Aegisthus as a most unworthy man, who fears even the tricks of fugitives' (my translation, I.d.J.); Denniston 1939, xxx: 'Euripides makes Aegisthus more repulsive [than Sophocles does]'; and Gellie 1981, 6: 'many critics find something repellent about the way in which Aegisthus is killed . . . He (sc. Orestes) is compared unfavourably with Hamlet who shrank from killing his uncle at prayers. But Electra is not the Hamlet kind of play. It does not expect from its players sophisticated principle but an emotional design and a story-line that will be acceptable to the sceptics in the theatre . . . what Euripides has given us is a pragmatic and efficient Orestes. He has been eager to satisfy not our sense of propriety but our sense of likelihood.' The position of Cropp 1988, 154 is not entirely clear to me: 'Aeg.'s present behaviour does nothing to lessen the enormity of his past crimes; the pleasant light in which he is now put is partly designed to show how the guilty one brings punishment on himself by his own blindness to danger' vs. '[the speech] sets problems in the enactment of justice through the gruesome murder of an unsuspecting victim, who in this portrayal never recognises Or. or the onset of justice'; which is it, 'blindness' or 'unsuspecting'?

[53] I owe this suggestion to Jan Maarten Bremer.

In my view, then, there are indications that Euripides wants to make Aegisthus the focal character of the messenger-scene, notwithstanding the overwhelming sympathy in the play (the Messenger included) for his murderer Orestes.

CONCLUSION

Before turning to concluding remarks of a more general nature, I would like to ask one final question: why are Creon's daughter, Neoptolemus, and Aegisthus off-stage characters in the first place and why are they, at the moment of their death, nevertheless turned into focal characters? Creon's daughter is kept off stage, because the conflict is primarily between Medea and Jason and her death is merely a means for Medea to hurt Jason. She is made a focal character, because her death is the prelude to that even more horrible murder, viz. of Medea's children: if we pity Creon's daughter, how much more will we pity the children. Neoptolemus is off stage, because the play is located in Phthia. His death, however, illustrates, perhaps in a more striking way than Andromache's plight in the first part of the play, the negative aftermath of the Trojan war—even for its victors: Neoptolemus dies through the hands of Apollo (whom he had insulted concerning the death of Achilles before Troy) and of Orestes (whom he had insulted by not giving Hermione, his reward for helping to destroy Troy, to him). Aegisthus is kept off stage because, within the double revenge exacted by Orestes and Electra, the more problematic murder of their mother is meant to receive most attention. At the same time, the death of Aegisthus sets the (emotional) tone for Clytemnestra's death, as in the case of Creon's daughter and Medea's children.

The aim of this paper has been to draw attention to the phenomenon of off-stage characters in Euripides by analyzing in detail three special cases, viz. off-stage characters who are killed in the course of the play. It has turned out that despite their invisibility these three figures can move the spectators at the moment of their death. Thus, narration, which lacks the immediacy of the action on stage, which the spectators see for themselves, can be effective all the same, exactly because of its indirectness of presentation. We see the events through the eyes (focalization) of the messenger, who shows his feelings (of pity, admiration, indignation) explicitly and implicitly (through his choice of epithets, comparisons, denomination, direct speech, repetition).

In comparison to drama, narrative also has a certain flexibility and amplitude, which, together with the emotional filtering of the messenger, account for the successful evocation of off-stage characters. The messenger takes his time (often at the explicit request of his addressee, cf. *Med.* 1133–4, *And.* 1083–4, *El.* 772–3) to tell his story detailedly and realistically (which is not the same as objectively or unemotionally). He introduces people in action,[54] not on a stage, but in carefully described surroundings; not wearing masks, but with their emotions clearly readable from their faces. The conclusion that off-stage characters can become focal characters demonstrates that, *pace* Horace,[55] 'telling' need not be less impressive than 'showing'.[56]

---

[54] Cf. Henning 1910, 34–6: Mores hominum nuntius plerumque non ipsis verbis depingit, sed eos ex rebus quas homines agunt cognoscimus, 'The messenger often does not depict the nature of people in his own words, but we get to know it on account of what they do' (my translation, I.d.J.). He gives as his 'optimum exemplum', his best example, Creon's daughter in *Med.*

[55] *Ars Poetica* 180–2: segnius irritant animos demissa per aurem | quam quae sunt oculis subiecta fidelibus et quae | ipse sibi tradit spectator, 'Less vividly is the mind stirred by what finds entrance through the ears than by what is brought before the trusty eyes, and what the spectator can see for himself.'

[56] Cf. Erdmann 1964, 88–9; Pathmanathan 1965, 6; de Romilly 1986, 91–2; Heath 1987, 153 ('If his descriptive and narrative rhetoric is powerful enough, the dramatist can overcome these technical limitations, extending his field of operation without loss of emotive and dramatic force').

REFERENCES

Abbreviations follow the conventions laid down in *L'Année Philologique*; note also:
RE=*Real-Encyclopädie der classischen Altertumswissenschaft*, ed. A. Pauly, G. Wissowa, and W. Kroll (Stuttgart, 1894–1980).

ABRAHAMSON, E. L. (1952), 'Euripides' Tragedy of *Hecuba*', *TAPA* 83, 120–9.

ADAMI, F. (1900), 'De poetis scaenicis graecorum hymnorum sacrorum imitatoribus', *N. Jahr. f. Klass. Philol.*, *Suppl.* 26, 215–47.

ADAMS, S. M. (1935), 'Two plays of Euripides', *CR* 49, 118–22.

ADKINS, A. W. H. (1966), 'Basic Greek Values in Euripides' *Hecuba* and *Hercules Furens*', *CQ* 16, 193–219.

ALLAN, W. (2000), *The* Andromache *and Euripidean Tragedy*, Oxford.

ALLEN, D. C., and ROWELL, H. T. (1968) (ed.), *The Poetic Tradition*, Baltimore.

ALLEN, JAMES T., and ITALIE, G. (1970), *A Concordance to Euripides*, Groningen.

AMANDRY, P. (1952), 'Observations sur les monuments de l'Héraion d'Argos', *Hesperia* 21, 270–4.

AMMON, C. F. (1789) (ed.), *Euripidis Hecuba*, Erlangen.

ANDERSON, M. J. (1965) (ed.), *Classical Drama and its Influence: Essays Presented to H. D. F. Kitto*, London.

ARNIM, H. F. A. VON (1886), *Ausgewählte Tragödien des Euripides: Medea*, 2nd edn., Berlin.

ARNOTT, J. F., and ROBINSON, J. W. (1970), *English Theatrical Literature 1559–1900*, London.

ARNOTT, P. (1962), *Greek Scenic Conventions in the Fifth Century BC*, Oxford.

ARNOTT, W. G. (1973), 'Euripides and the Unexpected', *G&R* 20, 49–64, repr. McAuslan and Walcot 1993, 138–52.

——(1981), 'Double the Vision: A Reading of Euripides' *Electra*', *G&R* 28, 179–92, repr. McAuslan and Walcot 1993, 204–17.

ARROWSMITH, W. (1959), Introduction to *Hecuba*, tr. D. Green and R. Lattimore, *Greek Tragedies*, vol. III, Chicago, 490–7.

——(1964), 'A Greek Theater of Ideas', in Gassner 1964, 1st pub. in *Arion* 2 (1963), 32–56, and see E. Segal 1968, 13–33.

——(1966), 'Luxury and Death in the *Satyricon*', *Arion* 5, 304–31, repr. Rudd 1972, 122–49.

ARTHUR, MARILYN B. (1972), 'The Choral Odes of the *Bacchae*', *YCS* 22, 145–81.

D'AUBIGNAC, F. (1715), *La Pratique du Théâtre*, Amsterdam.

AUSTIN, C. (1968), *Nova Fragmenta Euripidea in papyris reperta*, Kleine Texte für Vorlesungen und Übungen 187, Berlin.

BAIN, D. (1990), review of Yunis 1988, *CR* 40.2, 221–3.

BALLENTINE, F. G. (1904), 'Some Phases of the Cult of the Nymphs', *HSCP* 15, 77–119.

BARLOW, S. (1971), *The Imagery of Euripides*, London.

——— (1986) (ed.), *Euripides: Trojan Women*, Warminster.

BARNES, J. (1982), *The Presocratic Philosophers*, London.

BARNWELL, H. T. (1965) (ed.), *Writings on the Theatre*, Oxford.

——— (1982), *The Tragic Drama of Corneille and Racine*, Oxford.

BARRETT, W. S. (1964) (ed.), *Euripides: Hippolytos*, Oxford.

BECK, C. D. (1788), *Euripidis Tragoediae* III, Leipzig.

——— (1792), *Euripidis Tragoediae* I, Leipzig.

BENDER, L. (1934), 'Psychiatric Mechanisms in Child Murderers', *Journal of Nervous and Mental Disease* 80, 32–47.

BENVENISTE, E. (1973), *Indo-European Language and Society*, London.

BETTS, G. G. (1965), 'The Silence of Alcestis', *Mnemosyne* 18, 181–2.

BEYE, CHARLES (1975), *Ancient Greek Literature and Society*, New York.

BIEHL, W. (1957), 'Die Interpolationen in Euripides' *Hekabe* 59–215', *philologus* 101, 55–69.

——— (1965), *Euripides: Orestes*, Berlin.

BIERL, ANTON F. HARALD (1991), *Dionysos und die griechische Tragödie*, Tübingen.

BLAIR, HUGH (1783), *Lectures on Rhetoric and Belles-Lettres*, London.

BOARDMAN, J. (1952), 'Pottery from Eretria', *ABSA* 47, 1–48.

BOECKH, A. (1886), *Encyclopädie und Methodologie der philologischen Wissenschaften*, 2nd edn., Leipzig.

BOND, D. F. (1965) (ed.), *The Spectator*, Oxford.

BOND, G. W. (1981), *Euripides: Heracles*, Oxford.

BORGES, JORGE LUIS (1964), *Labyrinths*, New York.

BOS, J.-B. DU (1719), *Reflexions critiques sur la Poésie et sur la Peinture*, 6th edn., Paris, 1755.

BOTHMER, D. VON (1957), *Amazons in Greek Art*, Oxford.

BRADEN, G. (1985), *Renaissance Tragedy and the Senecan Tradition*, New Haven.

BRELICH, A. (1958), *Gli eroi greci*, Rome.

BREMER, J. M. (1971), 'Euripides' *Hecuba* 59–125: A Reconsideration', *Mnemosyne* 24, 232–50.

——— (1976), 'Why Messenger Speeches?', in Bremer, Radt, and Ruijgh 1976, 29–48.

BREMER, J. M. (1984), 'The Popularity of Euripides' *Phoinissae* in Later Antiquity', *Proceedings of the VIIth Congress of the International Federation of the Societies of Classical Studies*, Budapest.

——RADT, S., and RUIJGH, C. J. (1976), *Miscellanea tragica in honorem J. C. Kamerbeek*, Amsterdam.

BRETSCHNEIDER, C. (1834) (ed.), *Corpus Reformatorum*, Halle, 1834–60.

BRUMOY, P. (1785), *Théâtre des Grecs*, Paris, 1785–9.

BUDELMANN, FELIX (2000), *The Language of Sophocles*, Cambridge.

BURIAN, P. (1985) (ed.), *Directions in Euripidean Criticism*, Durham, N. C.

BURKERT, W. (1966), 'Greek Tragedy and Sacrificial Ritual', *GRBS* 7, 87–121.

——(1972), *Homo Necans*, Berlin/New York.

——(1974), 'Die Absurdität der Gewalt und das Ende der Tragödie: Euripides *Orestes*', *Antike und Abendland* 20, 97–109.

——(1983), *Homo Necans*, tr. P. Bing, Berkeley.

——(1985), *Greek Religion*, tr. J. Raffan, Cambridge, Mass.

BURNETT, A. P. (1962), 'Human Resistance and Divine Persuasion in Euripides' *Ion*', *CP* 57, 87–103.

——(1965), 'The Virtues of Admetus', *CP* 60, 240–55.

——(1970), 'Pentheus and Dionysus: Host and Guest', *CP* 65, 15–29.

——(1971), *Catastrophe Survived: Euripides' Plays of Mixed Reversal*, Oxford.

BUXTON, R. (1982), *Persuasion in Greek Tragedy: A Study of* Peitho, Cambridge.

CAILLOIS, R. (1959), *Man and the Sacred*, 2nd edn., tr. M. Barash, Glencoe, Ill.

CAIRNS, DOUGLAS (1992), *Aidos: The Psychology and Ethics of Honour and Shame in Greek Literature*, Oxford.

CALDWELL, RICHARD (1974), 'Tragedy Romanticized: The *Iphigenia Taurica*', *CJ* 70, 23–40.

——(1976), 'Primal Identity', *International Review of Psycho-Analysis* 3, 417–34.

CAMERARIUS, JOACHIM (1568), *Commentatio explicationum omnium tragoediarum Sophoclis*, in *Sophoclis tragoediae septem*, Geneva.

CARPENTER, THOMAS H., and FARAONE, CHRISTOPHER A. (1993) (ed.), *Masks of Dionysus*, Cornell.

CARR, MARINA (1998), *By the Bog of Cats*, Oldcastle, Co. Meath.

CASTELLANI, V. (1976), 'That Troubled House of Pentheus in Euripides' *Bacchae*', *TAPA* 106, 61–84.

CEADEL, E. B. (1941), 'Resolved Feet in the Trimeters of Euripides and the Chronology of his Plays', *CQ* 35, 66–89.

CHALK, H. H. O. (1962), 'APETH and BIA in Euripides' *Heracles*', *JHS* 82, 7–18.

CHAPOUTHIER, F. (1959), *Euripide: Oreste*, Paris (Budé vol. 6).

CHARLTON, H. B. (1946), *The Senecan Tradition in Elizabethan Tragedy*, Manchester.

CHEUSE, A., and KOFFIER, R. (1970) (ed.), *The Rarer Action: Essays in Honor of Francis Fergusson*, New Brunswick, NJ.

CLAUSS, J. J., and JOHNSTON, S. I. (1997) (ed.), *Medea*, Princeton.

CLEMEN, W. (1961), *English Tragedy before Shakespeare*, London (orig. pub. Heidelberg, 1955).

COHEN, R. (1974) (ed.), *New Directions in Literary History*, Baltimore.

COLLARD, CHRISTOPHER (1975a), 'Formal Debates in Euripidean Drama', *G&R* 22, 58–71 repr. McAuslan and Walcot 1993, 153–66.

—— (1975b) (ed.), *Euripides: Supplices*, Groningen.

—— (1981), *Euripides*, (Greece and Rome New Surveys in the Classics 14), Oxford.

—— (1991) (ed.), *Euripides: Hecuba*, Warminster.

—— CROPP, M. J., and LEE, K. H. (1995) (ed.), *Euripides: Selected Fragmentary Plays*, vol. I, Warminster.

CONACHER, D. J. (1967), *Euripidean Drama*, London.

—— (1972), 'Some Questions of Probability and Relevance in Euripidean Drama', *Maia* 24, 199–207.

—— (1981), 'Rhetoric and Relevance in Euripidean Drama', *AJP* 102, 3–25.

COOK, A. B. (1940), *Zeus: A Study in Ancient Religion*, Cambridge.

COPLEY, F. O. (1956), *Exclusus Amator*, American Philological Association Monographs 17.

CORNEILLE, P. (1660), 'Trois Discours du Poème Dramatique', in Barnwell 1965.

CORNFORD, F. (1934), *The Origin of Attic Comedy*, Cambridge.

COX, H. (1969), *The Feast of Fools: A Theological Essay on Festivity and Fantasy*, Cambridge, Mass.

CRAIK, E. (1988) (ed.), *Euripides: Phoenissae*, Warminster.

—— (1993), '$AI\varDelta\varOmega\varSigma$ in Euripides' *Hippolytus* 373–430: Review and Reinterpretation', *JHS* 113 (1993), 45–59.

CROALLY, N. T. (1994), *Euripidean Polemic: The Trojan Women and the Function of Tragedy*, Cambridge.

CROPP, M. J. (1988) (ed.), *Euripides: Electra*, Warminster.

DACIER, ANDRÉ (1692), *Aristotle's Art of Poetry*, ET London, 1705.

—— (1693), *Tragédies Grecques de Sophocle*, Paris.

DAEHNHARDT, O. (1896) (ed.), *Griechischen Dramen in deutschen Bearbeitungen*, Stuttgart, 1896–7.

DALE, A. M. (1954) (ed.), *Euripides: Alcestis*, Oxford.

—— (1967) (ed.), *Euripides: Helen*, Oxford.

—— (1969), *Collected Papers*, Cambridge.

DAWE, R. D. (1963), 'Inconsistency of Plot and Character in Aeschylus', *PCPS* 189, 21–62.

DENNIS, JOHN (1696), 'Remarks on Prince Arthur', in Hooker 1939.

DENNISTON, J. D. (1939) (ed.), *Euripides: Electra*, Oxford.

DERRIDA, J. (1967), *De la grammatologie*, Paris.

——(1972), 'La Pharmacie de Platon', in *Dissemination*, Paris.

DESCH, W. (1986), 'Der *Herakles* des Euripides und die Götter', *Philologus* 130, 8–23.

DEUBNER, L. (1900), '$E\Pi AYAIA$ (EPAULIA)', *JDAI* 15, 144–54.

——(1905), review of Eitrem 1905, *BPW* 25, 1401–5.

——(1932), *Attische Feste*, Berlin, repr. Hildesheim, 1966.

——(1952), 'Die Gebräuche der Griechen nach der Geburt', *RhM* 95, 374–7.

DEVEREUX, G. (1970), 'The Psychotherapy Scene in Euripides' *Bacchae*', *JHS* 90, 35–48.

DIANO, C. (1961), 'Euripide auteur de la catharsis tragique', *Numen* 8, 117–41.

DIGGLE, J. (1981) (ed.), *Euripidis Fabulae* II, Oxford.

——(1984) (ed.), *Euripidis Fabulae* I, Oxford.

——(1994) (ed.), *Euripidis Fabulae* III, Oxford.

——(1998) (ed.), *Tragicorum Graecorum Fragmenta Selecta*, Oxford.

DILLER, HANS (1955), 'Die *Bakchen* und ihrer Stellung im Spätwerk des Euripides', *Abh. Mainz*, 453–71, repr. and tr. in E. Segal 1983, 357–89.

——(1960), 'Umwelt und Masse als dramatische Faktoren bei Euripides', *Entretiens Hardt* 6, Vandœuvres and Geneva, 87–121.

DINGEL, J. (1967), *Das Requisit in der griechischen Tragödie*, diss. Tübingen.

DODDS, E. R. (1925), 'The $AI\Delta\Omega\Sigma$ of Phaedra and the Meaning of the *Hippolytus*', *CR* 39, 102–10.

——(1929), 'Euripides the Irrationalist', *CR* 43, 97–104, repr. *The Ancient Concept of Progress*, Oxford, 1973, 78–91.

——(1951), *The Greeks and the Irrational*, Berkeley.

——(1960), *Euripides: Bacchae*, 2nd edn., Oxford.

DOLLIMORE, JONATHAN (1990), 'Critical Developments', in Wells 1990, 405–28.

DOVER, K. J. (1968) (ed.), *Aristophanes: Clouds*, Oxford.

DREXLER, H. (1943), 'Zum *Herakles* des Euripides', *Nachr. Gött. Gel.*, Phil.-hist. Kl., 311–63.

DRYDEN, JOHN (1668), 'An Essay of Dramatick Criticism', in Ker 1900.

DUCHEMIN, J. (1945), $L'A\Gamma\Omega N$ *dans la Tragédie Grecque*, Paris.

——(1969), 'Les origines populaires et paysannes de l'agôn tragique', *Dioniso* 43, 247–76.

DUNN, F. (1996), *Tragedy's End*, New York.

DYK, J. G., and SCHAZ, G. (1792), *Charaktere der vornehmsten Dichter aller Nationen = Nachträge zu Sulzer's allgemeine Theorie der schönen Künste*, Leipzig, 1792–1808.

EASTERLING, P. E. (1973), 'The Presentation of Character in Aeschylus', *G&R* 20, 3–19.

——(1977), 'Character in Sophocles', *G&R* 24, 121–9.

——(1982), *Sophocles: Trachiniae*, Cambridge.

EASTERLING, P. E. (1997) (ed.), *The Cambridge Companion to Greek Tragedy*, Cambridge.

EBENER, D. (1961), 'Zum Motiv des Kindermordes in der *Medea*', *Rheinisches Museum* 104, 213–24.

EHRENBERG, V. (1946), 'Tragic Heracles', in *Aspects of the Ancient World*, Oxford, 144–66 (repr. from *Durham University Journal* 35 (1943)).

EITREM, S., *RE* s.v. Hera, 8. 369–403.

——(1905), *Kleobis und Biton*, Christiania.

ELAM, K. (1980), *The Semiotics of Theatre and Drama*, London/New York.

ELIADE, M. (1959), *The Sacred and the Profane*, tr. W. R. Trask, New York.

ELSE, G. F. (1957) (ed.), *Aristotle's Poetics*, Cambridge, Mass.

ERBSE, H. (1975), 'Zum *Orestes* des Euripides', *Hermes* 103, 434–59.

——(1984), *Studien zum Prolog der euripideischen Tragödie*, Berlin.

ERDMANN, G. (1964), *Der Botenbericht bei Euripides*, diss. Kiel.

ERFFA, C. E. VON (1937), *ΑΙΔΩΣ und verwandte Begriffe in ihrer Entwicklung von Homer bis Demokrit* (*Philologus Suppl.* 30.2), Leipzig.

EUBEN, J. PETER (1986) (ed.), *Greek Tragedy and Political Theory*, Berkeley and Los Angeles.

FAHR, W. (1969), *Theos nomizein: zum Problem der Anfaenge des Atheismus bei den Griechen*, Spudasmata 26, Hildesheim.

FARNELL, L. R. (1896), *The Cults of the Greek States*, Oxford.

FÉNELON, F. DE SALIGNAC DE LA MOTHE (1718), *Dialogues sur l'Eloquence*, Paris.

FESTUGIÈRE, A. J. (1960), *Personal Religion Among the Greeks*, Berkeley.

FINLEY, J. H. (1967), *Three Essays on Thucydides*, Cambridge, Mass.

FISCHL, J. (1910), *De nuntiis tragicis*, diss. Vienna.

FOLEY, HELENE P. (1985), *Ritual Irony: Poetry and Sacrifice in Euripides*, Ithaca, New York.

FÖRS, H. (1964), *Dionysos und die Stärke der Schwachen im Werk des Euripides*, Munich.

FOWLER, ALISTAIR (1974), 'The Life and Death of Literary Forms', in Cohen 1974, 77–94.

FRAENKEL, E. (1962) (ed.), *Aeschylus: Agamemnon*, Oxford.

——(1963), 'Zu den *Phoinissen* des Euripides', *Bayerische Akademie der Wissenschaften, Philosophisch-historische Klasse, Sitzungsberichte* 1.

FRANKLIN, D. (2000) (tr.), *Euripides, Bacchae*, Cambridge.

FRIEDLÄNDER, P. (1926), 'Die griechische Tragödie und das Tragische', *Die Antike* 2, 79–112.

FRIEDRICH, W.-H. (1953), *Euripides und Diphilos*, Zetemata 5, Munich.

——(1968), 'Medeas Rache', in Schwinge 1968*b*, repr. E. Segal 1983.

FRIIS JOHANSEN, H. (1959), *General Reflection in Tragic Rhesis*, Copenhagen.

FRITZ, K. VON (1962), *Antike und moderne Tragödie*, Berlin.

FURLEY, W. D. (1996), 'Phaedra's Pleasurable *Aidōs* (Eur. *Hipp.* 380–7)', *CQ* 46, 84–90.

GALINSKY, G. K. (1972), *The Herakles Theme*, Oxford.

GALLAVOTTI, C. (1974) (ed.), *Aristotele: Dell' Arte Poetica*, Milan.

GALLINI, CLARA (1963), 'Il travestismo rituale di Penteo', *SMSR* 34, 211–28.

GARLAND, R. (1985), *The Greek Way of Death*, London.

GARNER, R. (1990), *From Homer to Tragedy: The Art of Allusion in Greek Poetry*, London.

GARTON, CHARLES (1957), 'Characterization in Greek Tragedy', *JHS* 77, 247–54.

——(1972), 'The "Chameleon Trail" in the Criticism of Greek Tragedy', *Studies in Philology* 69, 389–413.

GASSNER, J. (1964) (ed.), *Ideas in the Drama*, New York.

GELLIE, G. H. (1980), '*Hecuba* and Tragedy', *Antichthon* 14, 30–44.

——(1981), 'Tragedy and Euripides' *Electra*', *BICS* 28, 1–12.

GENETTE, G. (1966), *Figures I*, Paris.

GIBSON, E., and KLEIN, S. (1969), *Murder 1957 to 1968*, Home Office Research Studies 3, London.

GILL, CHRISTOPHER (1996), *Personality in Greek Epic, Tragedy, and Philosophy*, Oxford.

GIRALDI CINTHIO, G. (1554), *Discorso . . . intorno al comporre delle comedie e delle tragedie*, Venice, in Guerrieri Crocetti 1973.

GIRARD, R. (1972), *La Violence et le sacré*, Paris.

GOFF, B. (1990), *The Noose of Words: Readings of Desire, Violence and Language in Euripides'* Hippolytus, Cambridge.

GOLDHILL, SIMON (1986a), *Reading Greek Tragedy*, Cambridge.

——(1986b), 'Rhetoric and Relevance: *Electra* 367–400', *GRBS* 27, 157–71.

——(1987), 'The Great Dionysia and Civic Ideology', *JHS* 107, 58–76.

——(1993), 'Reading Performance Criticism', in McAuslan and Walcot 1993, 1–11.

——and OSBORNE, R. (1993) (ed.), *Art and Text in Ancient Greek Culture*, Cambridge.

————(1999) (ed.), *Performance Culture and Athenian Democracy*, Cambridge.

GOULD, JOHN (1973), 'Hiketeia', *JHS* 93, 74–103.

——(1978), 'Dramatic Character and Human Intelligibility in Greek Tragedy', *PCPS* 204, 43–67.

——(1980), 'Law, Custom, and Myth: Aspects of the Social Position of Women in Classical Athens', *JHS* 100, 38–59.

GOWARD, BARBARA (1999), *Telling Tragedy: Narrative Technique in Aeschylus, Sophocles, and Euripides*, London.

GREDLEY, B. (1968), 'Is *Orestes* 1503–36 an interpolation?', *GRBS* 9, 409–19.

GREEN, C. C. (1941), *The Neo-Classical Theory of Tragedy in England during the Eighteenth Century*, Cambridge, Mass.

GREENBERG, N. (1962), 'Euripides' *Orestes*: An Interpretation', *HSCP* 66, 157–92.

GREGORIO, L. DI (1967), *Le Scene d'Annuncio nella Tragedia Greca*, Milan.

GREGORY, J. (1979), 'Euripides' *Alcestis*', *Hermes* 107, 259–70.

——(1991), *Euripides and the Instruction of the Athenians*, Ann Arbor.

——(1999) (ed.), *Euripides, Hecuba*, Atlanta.

GRIFFITH, M. (1983) (ed.), *Aeschylus: Prometheus Bound*, Cambridge.

——and MASTRONARDE, D. J. (1990) (ed.), *The Cabinet of the Muses: Essays on Classical and Comparative Literature in Honor of Thomas G. Rosenmeyer*, Atlanta.

GRUBE, G. M. A. (1941), *The Drama of Euripides*, London.

GUÉPIN, J.-P. (1968), *The Tragic Paradox*, Amsterdam.

GUERRIERI CROCETTI, C. (1973) (ed.), *Scritti Critici*, Milan.

GULICK, C. B. (1930) (tr.) *Athenaeus: The Deipnosophists*, Harvard.

GUTHRIE, W. K. C. (1968), 'The First Humanists', *Proceedings of the Classical Association* 65, 13–25.

HADLEY, W. S. (1894) (ed.), *Euripides: Hecuba*, Cambridge.

HAIGHT, E. H. (1950), *The Symbolism of the House Door in Classical Poetry*, New York.

HALLERAN, M. (1985), *Stagecraft in Euripides*, London.

——(1986), 'Rhetoric, Irony and the Ending of Euripides' *Heracles*', *CA* 5, 171–81.

HALLIWELL, S. (1986), *Aristotle's Poetics*, London.

HARDER, A. (1985), *Euripides: Kresphontes and Archelaos*, Leiden.

HARDER, T. (1967), 'The Psychopathology of Infanticide', *Acta Psychiatrica Scandinavica* 43, 196–245.

HARRISON, E. B. (1964), 'Hesperides and Heroes: A Note on the Three-Figure Reliefs', *Hesperia* 33, 76–82.

HARRISON, JOHN (2000) (tr.), *Euripides, Medea*, Cambridge.

HARTMAN, G. (1974), 'History Writing as an Answerable Style', in Cohen 1974, 95–105.

——(1976), 'Literary Criticism and its Discontents', *Critical Inquiry* 3, 203–20.

HARTUNG, J. A. (1843), *Euripides Restitutus*, Hamburg, 1843–4.

HASPELS, C. H. E. (1930), 'Deux fragments d'une coupe d'Euphronios', *BCH* 54, 422–51.

HAUPTMANN, J. G. (1741), *De Sophocle atque illius tragoediae*, Gera.

HAVELOCK, E. A. (1957), *The Liberal Temper in Greek Politics*, London.

HEATH, M. (1986), 'The Origins of Modern Pindaric Criticism', *JHS* 106, 85–98.

——(1987), *The Poetics of Greek Tragedy*, London.

HEATH, M. (1989), *Unity in Greek Poetics*, Oxford.

HEBERDEN, C. B. (1901) (ed.), *Euripides: Hecuba*, Oxford.

HEGEL, G. W. (1975), *Aesthetics*, tr. T. M. Knox, Oxford.

HEINEMANN, K. (1920), *Die tragische Gestalten der Griechen in der Weltliteratur*, Leipzig.

HEINIMANN, F. (1945), *Nomos und Physis*, Basel.

HEINSIUS, D. (1611), *De Tragoediae Constitutione Liber*, Leiden; *editio auctior multo* 1643.

HENNING, E. (1910), *De tragicorum Atticorum narrationibus*, Göttingen.

HENRICHS, A. (1975), 'Democritus and Prodicus on Religion', *HSCP* 79, 93–123.

——(1984), 'The Sophists and Hellenistic Religion: Prodicus as the Spiritual Father of the Isis Aretalogies', *HSCP* 88, 139–58.

HERMANN, G. (1831), *Euripidis Tragoediae* 1/1, Leipzig.

HESTER, D. A. (1971), 'Sophocles the Unphilosophical: A Study in the *Antigone*', *Mnemosyne* 24, 11–39.

HOGAN, J. C. (1972), 'Thucydides 3. 52–68 and Euripides' *Hecuba*', *Phoenix* 26, 241–57.

HOOKER, E. N. (1939) (ed.), *The Critical Works of John Dennis*, Baltimore.

HOURMOUZIADES, N. C. (1965), *Production and Imagination in Euripides*, Athens.

HUBERT, H., and MAUSS, M. (1964), *Sacrifice: Its Nature and Function*, tr. W. D. Halls, London.

IMHOF, M. (1966), *Euripides' Ion. Eine literarische Studie*, Bern and Munich.

IMMERWAHR, H. R. (1972), "Ἀθηναϊκὲς εἰκόνες στὸν "Ιωνα τοῦ Εὐριπίδη', 'Ελληνικά 25, 277–97.

JENKINS, IAN (1983), 'Is there Life after Marriage?', *BICS* 30, 137–45.

JONG, I. J. F. DE (1987), *Narrators and Focalizers: The Presentation of the Story in the Iliad*, Amsterdam.

——(1991), *Narrative in Drama: The Art of the Euripidean Messenger-Speech*, Leiden.

JONES, JOHN (1962), *On Aristotle and Greek Tragedy*, London.

JULLIEN, B. (1859) (ed.), *Les Paradoxes Littéraires de La Motte*, Paris.

KAMBITSIS, J. (1972) (ed.), *L'Antiope d' Euripide*, Athens.

KAMERBEEK, J. C. (1943), 'L'*Andromaque* d'Euripide', *Mnemosyne* 11, 46–67.

——(1948), 'On the Conception of $\Theta EOMAXO\Sigma$ in Relation to Greek Tragedy', *Mnemosyne* (ser. 4) 1, 271–83.

——(1966), 'The Unity and Meaning of Euripides' *Heracles*', *Mnemosyne* 19, 1–16.

——(1970) (ed.), *Sophocles: Trachiniae*, Leiden.

KANNICHT, R. (1969) (ed.), *Euripides: Helena*, Heidelberg.

KER, W. P. (1900) (ed.), *John Dryden: Essays*, Oxford.

KERÉNYI, K. (1949), 'Ziegenfell und Gorgoneion', in *ΠΑΓΚΑΡΠΕΙΑ*. Mélanges Henri Grégoire I, Université libre de Bruxelles, Annuaire de l'Institut de philologie et d'histoire orientales et slaves 9, Brussels.

—— (1950), 'Zeus und Hera', *Saeculum* 1, 228–57.

—— (1962), *The Religion of the Greeks and Romans*, tr. Christopher Holme, New York.

KERMODE, FRANK (1966), *The Sense of an Ending*, Oxford.

KEYSSNER, K. (1932), *Gottesvorstellung und Lebensauffassung im griechischen Hymnus*, Stuttgart.

KIREMIDJIAN, DAVID (1969), 'The Aesthetics of Parody', *Journal of Aesthetics and Art Criticism* 28, 231–42.

KIRK, G. S. (1979), *The Bacchae of Euripides*, Cambridge.

—— RAVEN, J. E., and SCHOFIELD, M. (1983), *The Presocratic Philosophers*, 2nd edn., Cambridge.

KIRKWOOD, G. M. (1947), 'Hecuba and *nomos*', *TAPA* 78, 61–8.

KITTO, H. D. F. (1961), *Greek Tragedy*, 3rd edn., London.

KLINZ, A. (1933), *Hieros Gamos*, diss. Halle.

KNOX, B. M. W. (1952), 'The *Hippolytus* of Euripides', *YCS* 13, 3–31, repr. in Knox 1979, 205–230, and in E. Segal 1983, 311–31.

—— (1970), 'Euripidean Comedy', in Cheuse and Koffier 1970, 68–96, repr. in Knox 1979, 250–74.

—— (1977), 'The *Medea* of Euripides', *YCS* 25, 193–225, repr. in Knox 1979, 295–322, and in E. Segal 1983, 272–93.

—— (1979), *Word and Action: Essays on the Ancient Theater*, Baltimore.

—— (1985), 'Euripides', in *The Cambridge History of Classical Literature*, i: *Greek Literature*, Cambridge.

KOVACS, D. (1987a), *The Heroic Muse*, AJP Monographs 3, Baltimore.

—— (1987b), 'Treading the Circle Warily: Literary Criticism and the Text of Euripides', *TAPA* 117, 257–70.

—— (1994) (ed. and tr.), *Euripides* I, Cambridge, Mass.

—— (1995) (ed. and tr.), *Euripides* II, Cambridge, Mass.

—— (1998) (ed. and tr.), *Euripides* III, Cambridge, Mass.

—— (1999) (ed. and tr.), *Euripides* IV, Cambridge, Mass.

KRAMER, S. N. (1969), *The Sacred Marriage Rite*, Bloomington, Ind.

KRAUSSE, O. (1905), *De Euripide Aeschyli Instauratore*, Jena.

KRAUSKOPF, I. (1977), 'Eine attische schwarzfigurige Hydria in Heidelberg', *Arch. Anz.*, 13–37.

KRIEG, V. (1934), *De Euripidis Oreste*, diss. Halle.

KROEKER, E. (1938), *Der Herakles des Euripides, Analyse des Dramas*, diss. Leipzig.

KUBO, M. (1966), 'The Norm of Myth: Euripides' *Electra*', *HSCP* 71, 15–31.

KÜHNER, R. and GERTH, B. (1898), *Ausführliche Grammatik der griechischen Sprache*, Hanover/Leipzig.

KURTZ, D. C., and BOARDMAN, J. (1971), *Greek Burial Customs*, London.

KÜSTER, E. (1913), *Die Schlange in der griechischen Kunst und Religion*, Religionsgeschichtliche Versuche und Vorarbeiten, 13:2, Giessen.

LADA, ISMENE (1993), ' "Empathetic Understanding": Emotion and Cognition in Classical Dramatic Audience-Response', *PCPS* 39, 94–140.

——(1996), 'Emotion and Meaning in Tragic Performance', in Silk 1996, 397–413.

LANCASTER, H. C. (1929), *A History of French Dramatic Literature in the Seventeenth Century*, Baltimore, 1929–42.

LANZA, D. (1963), 'NOMOΣ e IΣON in Euripide', *RFIL* 91, 416–39.

LARUE, J. (1964), 'Creusa's Monody: Ion 889–922', *tapa* 95, 126–36.

LATTE, K. (1968), *Kleine Schriften*, Munich.

LATTIMORE, R. (1958), *The Poetry of Greek Tragedy*, Baltimore.

LAUDUN DAIGALIERS, P. DE (1579), *Art Poétique François*, Paris.

LAWSON, J. (1758), *Lectures Concerning Oratory*, Dublin.

LAWTON, H. W. (1949), *Handbook of French Renaissance Dramatic Theory*, Manchester.

LEE, K. H. (1976), *Euripides: Troades*, London.

LEFKOWITZ, M. R. (1987), 'Was Euripides an Atheist?', *SIFC* (ser. iii) 5, 149–66.

LEMBACH, RÜDIGER (1971), *Euripides Ion. Eine Interpretation*, Frankfurt am Main.

LENNEP, D. F. W. VAN (1935), *Euripides: Poiētēs Sophos*, Amsterdam.

LESKY, A. (1972), *Die tragische Dichtung der Hellenen*, 3rd edn., Göttingen (2nd edn. 1964).

LICHTENSTEIN, H. (1961), 'Identity and Sexuality', *Journal of the American Psycho-Analytical Association* 9, 179–260.

LINFORTH, I. M. (1952), 'The Pyre on Mount Oeta in Sophocles' Trachiniae', *University of California Publications in Classical Philology*, 14, 255–67.

LLOYD, M. (1984), 'The Helen Scene in Euripides' Troades', *CQ* 34, 303–13.

——(1992), *The Agōn in Euripides*, Oxford.

——(1994), *Euripides: Andromache*, Warminster.

——(1999), 'The Tragic Aorist', *CQ* 49, 24–45.

LLOYD-JONES, H. (1961), 'Some Alleged Interpolations in Aeschylus' Choephoroi and Euripides' Electra', *CQ* 11, 177–81, repr. Lloyd-Jones 1990, 335–52.

——(1964), 'The Supplices of Aeschylus: The New Date and Old Problems', *L'Antiquité Classique* 33, 356–74, repr. Lloyd-Jones 1990, 262–77.

——(1969a), review of Vögler 1967, *CR* 19, 36–8.

——(1969b), review of di Gregorio 1967, *CR* 19, 38–9.

——(1979a) (tr.), *Aeschylus: Agamemnon*, Englewood Cliffs, NJ.

——(1979b), Introduction to Reinhardt 1979, xv–xxviii.

——(1983), *The Justice of Zeus*, 2nd edn., Berkeley.

—— (1990), *Greek Epic, Lyric and Tragedy: The Academic Papers of Sir Hugh Lloyd-Jones*, Oxford.

LOMBARDI, BARTOLOMEO (1550), *In Aristotelis librum De Poetica communes explicationes*, Venice.

LONG, A. A. (1968), *Language and Thought in Sophocles*, London.

LOOY, H. VAN (1992) (ed.), *Euripides, Medea*, Stuttgart.

LORAUX, N. (1984), *Les Enfants d'Athéna*, Paris.

—— (1993), *The Children of Athena: Athenian Ideas about Citizenship and the Division between the Sexes*, Princeton.

LUCAS, D. W. (1946), 'Hippolytus', *CQ* 40, 65–9.

—— (1959), *The Greek Tragic Poets*, 2nd edn., London.

—— (1968) (ed.), *Aristotle: Poetics*, Oxford.

LUDWIG, W. (1954), *Sapheneia*, Tübingen.

MCAUSLAN, I., and WALCOT, P. (1993) (ed.), *Greek Tragedy*, Oxford.

MCCLURE, LAURA (1999), *Spoken Like A Woman*, Princeton.

MCDONALD, MARIANNE (1983), *Euripides in Cinema: The Heart Made Visible*, Philadelphia.

—— (1992), *Ancient Sun, Modern Light: Greek Drama on the Modern Stage*, New York.

—— (1997), 'Medea as Politician and Diva', in Clauss and Johnston 1997, 297–323.

MACINTOSH, FIONA (1994), *Dying Acts: Death in Ancient Greek and Modern Irish Tragic Drama*, Cork.

MACKINNON, KENNETH (1986), *Greek Tragedy into Film*, Beckenham.

MACLEOD, C. W. (1982) (ed.), *Homer: Iliad Book xxiv*, Cambridge.

MANSO, J. C. F. (1792), 'Über einige Verschiedenheiten in dem griechischen und deutschen Trauerspiele', in Dyk and Schaz 1792.

MASENIUS, J. (1661), *Palaestra Eloquentiae Ligatae*, Cologne, 1661–4.

MASSENZIO, M. (1969), 'Cultura e crisi permanente: la "xenia" dionysiaca', *SMSR* 40, 27–113.

MASTRONARDE, D. J. (1974), *Studies in Euripides' Phoinissae*, diss. Toronto.

—— (1979), *Contact and Discontinuity: Some Conventions of Speech and Action on the Greek Tragic Stage*, Berkeley.

—— (1988) (ed.), *Euripides: Phoenissae*, Leipzig.

—— (1994) (ed.), *Euripides: Phoinissae*, Cambridge.

MATTHAEI, L. E. (1918), *Studies in Greek Tragedy*, Cambridge.

MATTHIESSEN, K. (1968), 'Zur Theonoeszene in der euripideischen *Helena*', *Hermes* 96, 685–704.

—— (1974), *Studien zur Textüberlieferung der Hekabe des Euripides*, Heidelberg.

MÉAUTIS, G. (1944), *Mythes inconnus de la Grèce antique*, Paris.

MELANCHTHON, P. (1545), *Epistola . . . de legendis Tragoediis et Comoediis*, in Bretschneider 1834.

MÉRIDIER, L. (1956), *Euripide* II, Paris.

MERIDOR, R. (1978), 'Hecuba's Revenge', *AJP* 99, 28–35.

——(2000), 'Creative Rhetoric in Euripides' *Troades*: Some Notes on Hecuba's Speech', *CQ* 50, 16–29.

MESNARDIERE, H. DE LA (1640), *La Poetique*, Paris.

MEYER, H. (1933), *Hymnische Stilelemente in der frühgriechischen Dichtung*, Würzburg.

MICHELINI, A. N. (1987), *Euripides and the Tragic Tradition*, Madison.

MILLER, H. W. (1940), 'Euripides and Eustathius', *AJP* 61, 422–8.

MITSCHERLICH, ALEXANDER (1970), *Society Without the Father*, New York.

MOLAND, L. (1877) (ed.), *Voltaire: Œuvres Complètes*, Paris, 1877–85.

MOLES, J. (1984), '*Philanthrōpia* in the *Poetics*', *Phoenix* 38, 325–35.

MORROW, G. R. (1960), *Plato's Cretan City*, Princeton.

MORVAN DE BELLEGARDE, J. B. (1702), *Lettres Curieuses de Littérature et de Morales*, La Haye.

MORWOOD, JAMES (1998) (tr.), *Medea and Other Plays*, Oxford.

——(1999) (tr.), *Bacchae and Other Plays*, Oxford.

——(2001) (tr.), *Trojan Women and Other Plays*, Oxford.

MOSSMAN, J. M. (1995), *Wild Justice: A Study of Euripides' Hecuba*, Oxford (repr. Bristol 1999).

——(1996), 'Waiting for Neoptolemus: The Unity of Euripides' *Andromache*', *G&R* 43, 143–56.

——(2001), 'Women's Speech in Greek Tragedy: The case of Clytemnestra and Electra in Euripides' *Electra*', *CQ* 51.2, 374–84.

MOULINIER, L. (1952), *Le Pur et l'impur dans la pensée des Grecs*, Paris.

MUELLER, M. (1980), *Children of Oedipus*, Toronto.

MURRAY, G. (1908), *Euripidis Fabulae ii*, 3rd edn., Oxford.

——(1910) (tr.), *Euripides: Medea*, London.

NEUMANN, ERICH (1954), *The Origins of Human Consciousness*, Princeton.

NEWIGER, H. J. (1961), 'Elektra in Aristophanes' *Wolken*', *Hermes* 89, 422–30.

NILSSON, M. P. (1906), *Griechische Feste*, Leipzig.

——(1955), *Geschichte der griechischen Religion*, 2nd edn., Munich.

NISETICH, F. (1980), *Pindar's Victory Songs*, Baltimore.

NORWOOD, G. (1948), *Greek Tragedy*, 4th edn., London.

——(1954), *Essays on Euripidean Drama*, Berkeley.

NUSSBAUM, M. (1986), *The Fragility of Goodness*, Cambridge.

OAKLEY, JOHN H. (1982), 'The Anakalupteria', *Arch. Anz.*, 113–18.

O'BRIEN, M. J. (1964), 'Orestes and the Gorgon: Euripides' *Electra*', *AJP* 85, 13–39.

——(1967), *The Socratic Paradoxes and the Greek Mind*, Chapel Hill.

——(1988), 'Tantalus in Euripides' *Orestes*', *RhM* 131, 30–45.

OGLE, M. B. (1911), 'The House-Door in Greek and Roman Religion and Folklore', *AJP* 32, 251–71.

OWEN, A. S. (1939) (ed.), *Euripides: Ion*, Oxford.

PADEL, R. (1974), 'Imagery of the Elsewhere: Two Choral Odes of Euripides', *CQ* 24, 227–41.

PAGE, D. L. (1938), *Euripides: Medea*, Oxford.

PARKER, R. (1983), *Miasma*, Oxford.

PARRY, H. (1963), *The Choral Odes of Euripides: Problems of Structure and Dramatic Relevance*, diss. Berkeley.

——(1969), 'Euripides' *Orestes*: The Quest for Salvation', *TAPA* 100, 337–53.

PATHMANATHAN, R. S. (1965), 'Death in Greek Tragedy', *G&R* 12, 2–14.

PELLING, C. B. R. (1990) (ed.), *Characterization and Individuality in Greek Literature*, Oxford.

PEROTTA, G. (1925), 'L'*Ecuba* e le *Troadi* di Euripide', *Atene e Roma* 6, 264–93.

——(1928), 'Studi Euripidei II', *SIFC* 6, 1–53.

PFISTER, M. (1988), *The Theory and Analysis of Drama*, Cambridge.

PFLUGK, A. J. E. (1829), *Euripidis Tragoediae* 1/2, Gotha and Erfurt.

PFUHL, E. (1923), *Malerei und Zeichnung der Griechen*, Munich.

PHILLIPPO, S. (1995), 'Family Ties: Significant Patronymics in Euripides' *Andromache*', *CQ* 45, 355–71.

——and SUPPLE, J. J. (1995) (ed.), *Sallebray: La Troade*, Exeter.

PICARD, R. (1950) (ed.), *Racine: Œuvres Complètes*, Paris.

PICKARD-CAMBRIDGE, A. W. (1962), *Dithyramb, Tragedy and Comedy*, 2nd edn., rev. T. B. L. Webster, Oxford.

——(1968), *The Dramatic Festivals of Athens*, 2nd edn., rev. J. Gould and D. Lewis, Oxford.

PLATNAUER, M. (1960) (ed.), *Euripides: Iphigenia*, Oxford.

POHLENZ, M. (1954), *Die griechische Tragödie*, 2nd edn., Göttingen.

POLLITT, J. J. (1972), *Art and Experience in Classical Greece*, Cambridge.

PONTANUS, J. (1597), *Poeticarum Institutionum Libri III, editio secunda emendatior*, Ingolstadt.

PORSON, RICHARD (1792), *Praelectio in Euripidem*, Cambridge.

——(1814), *Adversaria*, Leipzig.

PRELLER-ROBERT, PRELLER, L., and ROBERT, C. (1894), *Griechische Mythologie*, 4th edn., Berlin.

PRÉVOST, PIERRE (1785), 'Examen' of *Hecuba* in Brumoy 1785, IV. 480–504.

PUCCI, P. (1977), *Hesiod and the Language of Poetry*, Baltimore.

——(1980), *The Violence of Pity in Euripides' Medea*, Ithaca and London.

RACINE, L. (1808), 'Traité de la Poésie Dramatique', in *Œuvres*, Paris.

RADT, S. L. (1968), *Euripides Ioon. De Interpretatie van een Kunstwerk*, Amsterdam.

RAPIN, R. (1674), *Reflexions sur la Poétique d' Aristote*, Paris.

RASSOW, J. (1883), *Quaestiones selectae de Euripideorum nuntiorum narrationibus*, diss. Greifswald.

RAWSON, E. (1972), 'Aspects of Euripides' *Orestes*', *Arethusa* 5, 155–67.

RECKFORD, K. (1968), 'Medea's First Exit', *TAPA* 99, 329–59.

——(1985), 'Concepts of Demoralisation in Euripides' *Hecuba*', in Burian 1985.

——and LEMBKE, J. (1991) (tr.), *Euripides, Hecuba*, Oxford.

REINHARDT, K. (1960), 'Die Sinneskrise bei Euripides', in *Tradition und Geist*, Göttingen, 227–56.

——(1979), *Sophocles* (tr. Hazel and David Harvey), Oxford.

REISKE, J. J. (1743), review of P. Carmeli, *Tragedie di Euripide*, *Nova Acta Eruditorum* 12, 535–51.

——(1754), *Ad Euripidem et Aristophanem Animadversiones*, Leipzig.

RIEDWEG, C. (1990a), 'The "Atheistic" Fragment from Euripides' *Bellerophontes* (286N2)', *ICS* 15.1, 39–53.

——(1990b), '*TGrF* 2. 624—A Euripidean Fragment', *CQ* 40.1, 124–36.

RIJKSBARON, A. (1976), 'How does a Messenger begin his Speech? Some Observations on the Opening Lines of Euripidean Messenger-speeches', in Bremer, Radt, and Ruijgh 1976, 293–308.

RIVIER, A. (1944), *Essai sur le tragique d'Euripide*, Lausanne (2nd edn. Paris, 1975).

——(1972), 'En marge d'*Alceste* et de quelques interprétations récentes I', *MH* 29, 124–40.

——(1973), 'En marge d'*Alceste* et de quelques interprétations récentes II', *MH* 30, 130–43.

ROBERTS, D. (1987), 'Parting Words: Final Lines in Sophocles and Euripides', *CQ* 37, 51–64.

ROBORTELLO, F. (1548), *In librum Aristotelis De Arte Poetica Explicationes*, Florence.

ROMILLY, J. DE (1961), *L'évolution du pathétique d'Eschyle à Euripide*, Paris.

——(1986), *La Modernité d' Euripide*, Paris.

ROSCHER, W. H. (1886), *Ausführliches Lexikon der griechischen und römischen Mythologie*, Leipzig 1886–90.

ROSE, H. J. (1956), 'Divine Disguisings', *HTR* 49, 63–72.

——(1958), *A Handbook of Greek Mythology*, 6th edn., London.

ROSENMEYER, T. G. (1963), *The Masks of Tragedy*, Austin, Tex.

ROSIVACH, V. J. (1975), 'The First Stasimon of the *Hecuba*', *AJP* 96, 349–62.

ROUSE, W. D. (1902), *Greek Votive Offerings*, Cambridge.

ROUSSEL, P. (1950), 'La Famille athénienne', *Lettres d'humanité* 9, 5–59.

RUDD, N. (1972) (ed.), *Essays on Classical Literature*, Cambridge.

SAÏD, S. (1978), *La Faute tragique*, Paris.

SALINGAR, LEO (1974), *Shakespeare and the Traditions of Comedy*, Cambridge.

SAMTER, E. (1901), *Familienfeste der Griechen und Römer*, Berlin.

SANSONE, D. (1975), 'The Sacrifice Motif in Euripides' *Iphigenia in Tauris*', *TAPA* 105, 283–95.

SAXENHOUSE, A. W. (1986), 'Myths and Origins of Cities: Reflections on the Autochthony Theme in Euripides' *Ion*', in Euben 1986, 252–73.

SCALIGER, J. C. (1561), *Poetices Libri VII*, Lyons.

SCHEIN, SETH L. (1990), '*Philia* in Euripides' *Medea*', in Griffith and Mastronarde 1990, 57–73.

SCHLEGEL, A. W. (1808), *Lectures on Dramatic Art and Literature*, 1808; ET London, 1846.

SCHLESIER, R. (1983), 'Daimon und Daimones bei Euripides', *Saeculum* 34, 267–79.

——(1985), 'Héraclès et la critique des dieux chez Euripide', *Ann. Scuol. Normale di Pisa* (Cl. litt./filos.) 15, 7–40.

——(1986), 'Götterdämmerung bei Euripides?', in Zinser 1986, 35–50.

——(1988), 'Die Bakchen des Hades', *Métis* 3, 111–35.

——(1993), 'Mixtures of Masks: Maenads as Tragic Models' in Carpenter and Faraone 1993, 89–114.

SCHLESINGER, A. C. (1937), 'Two Notes on Euripides', *CP* 32, 67–70.

SCHLESINGER, E. (1966), 'Zu Euripides' *Medea*', *Hermes* 94, 26–53, tr. in E. Segal 1983, 294–310.

SCHMIDT, W. (1963), *Der Deus ex Machina bei Euripides*, diss. Tübingen.

SCHWINGE, E.-R. (1968a), *die verwendung der stichomythie in den dramen des euripides*, HEIDELBERG.

——(1968b), (ed.), *Euripides*, Darmstadt.

SCODEL, R. (1980), *The Trojan Trilogy of Euripides*, Hypomnemata 60, Göttingen.

SEAFORD, R. (1984) (ed.), *Euripides: Cyclops*, Oxford.

——(1993), 'Dionysus as Destroyer of the Household: Homer, Tragedy and the Polis', in Carpenter and Faraone 1993, 115–46.

SEGAL, C. P. (1971), 'The Two Worlds of Euripides' *Helen*', *TAPA* 102, 553–614.

——(1978), 'The Menace of Dionysus: Sex Roles and Reversals in Euripides' *Bacchae*, *Arethusa* 11, 185–202.

——(1982), *Dionysiac Poetics and Euripides' Bacchae*, Princeton (repr. 1997).

SEGAL, E. (1968) (ed.), *Euripides: A Collection of Critical Essays*, Englewood Cliffs, NJ.

——(1983) (ed.), *Oxford Readings in Greek Tragedy*, Oxford.

SEIDENSTICKER, B. (1978), 'Comic Elements in Euripides' *Bacchae*', *AJP* 99, 303–20.

SHEPPARD, J. T. (1918), 'The *Electra* of Euripides', *CR* 32, 137–41.

——(1949), *Euripides: Hecuba*, Oxford.

SILK, M. S. (1985), 'Herakles and Greek Tragedy', *G&R* 32, 1–22.

——(1996), *Tragedy and the Tragic: Greek Theatre and Beyond*, Oxford.

SINOS, D. S. (1982), 'Characterization in the *Ion*: Apollo and the Dynamics of the Plot', *Eranos* 80, 129–34.

SMITH, W. D. (1960), 'The Ironic Structure in *Alcestis*', *Phoenix* 14, 127–45.

SMITH, W. D. (1967), 'Disease in Euripides' Orestes', Hermes 95, 291–307.

SMYTH, H. W. (1956), Greek Grammar, Cambridge, Mass.

SNELL, B. (1948), 'Das frühste Zeugnis über Sokrates', Philologus 97, 125–34.

SOLMSEN, F. (1932), 'Zur Gestaltung des Intriguenmotivs in den Tragödien des Sophokles und Euripides', Philologus 87, 1–17.

——(1968), Kleine Schriften, Hildesheim.

SOURVINOU-INWOOD, C. (1997), 'Medea at a Shifting Distance', in Clauss and Johnston 1997, 253–96.

SPEARS, MONROE K. (1970), Dionysus and the City: Modernism in Twentieth-Century Poetry, Oxford.

SPIRA, A. (1960), Untersuchungen zum Deus ex Machina bei Sophokles und Euripides, diss. Frankfurt; Kallmünz.

STATES, BERT (1971), Irony and Drama: A Poetics, Ithaca and London.

STEIDLE, W. (1968), Studien zum antiken Drama, Munich.

STEIGER, H. (1898), 'Wie entstand der Orestes der Euripides?', Progr. Augsburg, Augsburg.

STEINER, G. (1984), Antigones, Oxford.

STEVENS, P. T. (1956), 'Euripides and the Athenians', JHS 86, 87–94.

——(1971) (ed.), Euripides: Andromache, Oxford.

STIBLINUS, C. (1562), Euripides Poeta Tragicorum Princeps, Basel.

STINTON, T. C. W. (1965), Euripides and the Judgement of Paris, London.

——(1975), 'Hamartia in Aristotle and Greek Tragedy', CQ 25, 221–54, repr. Stinton 1990, 143–85.

——(1976), 'Si Credere Dignum Est', PCPS 22, 60–89, repr. Stinton 1990, 236–64.

——(1990), Collected Papers on Greek Tragedy, Oxford.

STOESSEL, F. (1956), 'Die Elektra des Euripides', RhM 99, 47–92.

STOLLIUS, G. (1728), Introductio in Historiam Litterariam, Jena.

STONE, D. (1974), French Humanist Tragedy, Manchester.

STROHM, HANS (1957), Euripides, Interpretationen zur dramatischen Form, Zetemata 15, Munich.

SUTTON, DANA F. (1980), The Greek Satyr Play, Meisenheim am Glan.

TAPLIN, O. P. (1972), 'Aeschylean Silences and Silences in Aeschylus', HSCP 76, 57–97.

——(1977), The Stagecraft of Aeschylus, Oxford.

——(1978), Greek Tragedy in Action, London.

THOMSON, GEORGE (1940), Aeschylus and Athens, London.

THOMPSON, H. A. (1952), 'The Altar of Pity in the Athenian Agora', Hesperia 21, 45–82.

TIERNEY, M. (1946) (ed.), Euripides: Hecuba, Dublin.

TIETZE, F. (1933), Die euripideischen Reden und ihre Bedeutung, Breslau.

VELLACOTT, P. (1975), Ironic Drama: A Study of Euripides' Method and Meaning, Cambridge.

VERNANT, J.-P. (1966), *Mythe et pensée chez les Grecs*, Paris.

VERRALL, A. W. (1881), *Euripides: Medea*, London.

VIAN, F. (1951), *Répertoire des Gigantomachies figurées dans l'art grec and roman*, Paris.

—— (1952), *La Guerre des Géants: Le Mythe avant l'époque hellénistique*, Études et Commentaires 11, Paris.

VICTORIUS, P. (1545), *Euripidis Electra nunc primum in luce edita*, Rome.

VIPERANUS, J. ANTONIUS (1579), *De Poetica Libri III*, Antwerp.

VÖGLER, A. (1967), *Vergleichende Studien zur sophokleischen und euripideischen Elektra*, Heidelberg.

VOSSIUS, G. J. (1647a), *Poeticarum Institutionum Libri IIII*, Amsterdam.

—— (1647b), *De Artis Poeticae Natura ac Constitutione Liber*, Amsterdam.

WALDSTEIN, C. (1902), *The Argive Heraeum*, Boston and New York.

WASSERMANN, F. M. (1929), 'Die Bakchantinnen des Euripides', *NJW* 5, 272–86.

—— (1940), 'Divine Violence and Providence in Euripides' *Ion*', *TAPA* 71, 587–604.

WASZINK, J. H. (1969), Introduction, *Erasmi Opera Omnia* 1/1, Amsterdam.

WEBSTER, T. B. L. (1965), 'The Poet and the Mask', in Anderson 1965, 5–13.

—— (1967), *The Tragedies of Euripides*, London.

—— (1968), 'Euripides: Traditionalist and Innovator' in Allen and Rowell 1968, 27–45.

—— (1969), *An Introduction to Sophocles*, 2nd edn., London.

WECKLEIN, N. (1909), *Ausgewählte Tragödien des Euripides: Medea*, 4th edn., Leipzig.

WEDD, N. (1895) (ed.), *The Orestes of Euripides*, Cambridge.

WELLS, STANLEY (1990) (ed.), *Shakespeare: A Bibliographical Guide*, Oxford.

WEST, M. L. (1983), *The Orphic Poems*, Oxford.

—— (1987) (ed.), *Euripides: Orestes*, Warminster.

WHITLOCK BLUNDELL, M. (1989), *Helping Friends and Harming Enemies: A Study in Sophocles and Greek Ethics*, Cambridge.

WHITMAN, CEDRIC (1964), *Aristophanes and the Comic Hero*, Cambridge, Mass.

WILAMOWITZ-MOELLENDORFF, T. VON (1917), *Die dramatische Technik des Sophokles*, Philologische Untersuchungen 22, Berlin.

WILAMOWITZ-MOELLENDORFF, U. VON (1880), 'Exkurse zu Euripides' *Medeia*', *Hermes* 15, 481–523, repr. *Kl. Schr.* i., 17–59 (Berlin, 1935).

—— (1891) (ed.), *Euripides: Hippolytos*, Berlin.

—— (1895) (ed.), *Euripides: Herakles*, 2nd edn. 2 vols., Berlin, repr. 3 vols, Darmstadt, 1959.

—— (1896) (ed.), *Aischylos: Orestie*, Berlin.

—— (1923), *Griechische Tragödien*, Berlin.

—— (1926) (ed.), *Euripides: Ion*, Berlin.

WILES, D. (1997), *Tragedy in Athens: Performance Space and Theatrical Meaning*, Cambridge.

WILKINS, J. (1993) (ed.), *Euripides: Heraclidae*, Oxford.

WILLETTS, R. F. (1973), 'Action and Character in Euripides' *Ion*', *JHS* 93, 201–9.

WILLINK, C. W. (1966), 'Some Problems of Text and Interpretation in the *Bacchae* I', *CQ* 16, 27–50.

——(1986) (ed.), *Euripides: Orestes*, Oxford.

WILSON, J. R. (1968), 'The Etymology in Euripides' *Troiades*', *AJP* 89, 66–71.

WILSON, N. G. (1973), 'Erasmus as a Translator of Euripides: Supplementary Notes', *A&A* 18, 87–8.

WILSON, PETER (2000), *The Athenian Institution of the Khoregia*, Cambridge.

WINIARCZYK, M. (1984), 'Wer galt im Altertum als Atheist?', *Philol.* 128, 157–83.

——(1987), 'Nochmals das Satyrspiel *Sisyphos*', *WS* 100, 35–45.

WINKLER, J. J., and ZEITLIN, F. I. (1990) (eds.), *Nothing to Do With Dionysos?, Athenian Drama in its Social Context*, Princeton.

WINNINGTON-INGRAM, R. P. (1948), *Euripides and Dionysus*, Cambridge, repr. Bristol, 1997.

——(1954), 'Aeschylus, *Agamemnon* 1343–71', *cq* 4, 23–30.

——(1966), 'Euripides, *Bacchae* 877–81=897–901', *bics* 13, 34–7.

——(1969a), 'Euripides, *Poiētēs Sophos*', *Arethusa* 2, 127–42.

——(1969b), 'Tragica', *BICS* 16, 44–54.

——(1983), *Studies in Aeschylus*, Cambridge.

WOELCKE, K. (1911), *Beiträge zur Geschichte des Tropaions*, diss. Bonn.

WOLFF, C. (1965a), 'The Design and Myth in Euripides' *Ion*', *HSCP* 69, 169–94.

——(1965b), *Aspects of the Later Plays of Euripides*, diss. Harvard.

——(1968), 'Orestes', in E. Segal 1968, 132–49, repr. E. Segal 1983, 340–56.

YUNIS, H. (1988), *A New Creed: Fundamental Religious Beliefs in the Athenian Polis and Euripidean Drama*, Hypomnemata 91, Göttingen.

ZANKER, P. (1995), *Die Maske des Sokrates: Das Bild der Intellektuellen in der antiken Kunst*, Munich, ET A. Shapiro, Berkeley, 1995.

ZEITLIN, FROMA I. (1965), 'The Motif of the Corrupted Sacrifice in Aeschylus' *Oresteia*', *TAPA* 96, 463–508.

——(1966), 'Postscript to Sacrificial Imagery in the *Oresteia* (*Ag.* 1235–37)', *TAPA* 97, 645–53.

——(1970), 'The Argive Festival of Hera and Euripides' *Electra*', *TAPA* 101, 645–69.

——(1971), 'Petronius as Paradox: Anarchy and Artistic Integrity', *TAPA* 102, 631–84.

——(1990), 'Playing the Other: Theater, Theatricality and the Feminine in Greek Drama', in Winkler and Zeitlin 1990, 63–96.

——(1993), 'The Artful Eye: Vision, Ecphrasis and Spectacle in Euripidean Theatre', in Goldhill and Osborne 1993, 138–96.

ZIMANSKY, C. A. (1956) (ed.), *The Critical Works of Thomas Rymer*, New Haven.

ZINSER, H. (1986) (ed.), *Der Untergang von Religionen*, Berlin.

ZUNTZ, G. (1947), 'Is the *Heraclidae* Mutilated?', *CQ* 41, 46–52.

——(1960), 'On Euripides' *Helena*: Theology and Irony', *Entretiens Hardt* 6, 201–41.

——(1963), *The Political Plays of Euripides*, 2nd edn., Manchester.

ZÜRCHER, W. (1947), *Die Darstellung des Menschen im Drama des Euripides*, Basel.

ACKNOWLEDGEMENTS

1. Karl Reinhardt, 'The Intellectual Crisis in Euripides', English translation of 'Die Sinneskrise bei Euripides', in *Tradition und Geist* (Göttingen, 1960), 223–56, reprinted by kind permission of Vandenhoek and Ruprecht, translated by J. Mossman and J. M. Mossman.

2. R. P. Winnington-Ingram, 'Euripides: *Poiētēs Sophos*', *Arethusa* 2 (1969), 127–42, reprinted by kind permission of Johns Hopkins University Press.

3. C. Collard, 'Formal Debates in Euripides' Drama', *G&R* 22 (1975), 58–71, revised by the author, reprinted from I. McAuslan and P. Walcot (eds.), *Greek Tragedy* (Oxford, 1993), 153–66, by kind permission of Oxford University Press.

4. D. J. Conacher, 'Rhetoric and Relevance in Euripidean Drama', *AJP* 102 (1981), 3–25, revised by the author, reprinted by kind permission of Johns Hopkins University Press.

5. Mary R. Lefkowitz, ' "Impiety" and "Atheism" in Euripides' Dramas', *CQ* 39 (1989), 70–82, revised by the author, reprinted by kind permission of Oxford University Press.

6. H. P. Stahl, 'On "Extra-Dramatic" Communication of Characters in Euripides', *YCS* 25 (1977), 159–76, reprinted by kind permission of the author and the Yale Classical Studies committee.

7. Pietro Pucci, 'Euripides: The Monument and the Sacrifice', *Arethusa* 10 (1977), 165–95, revised by the author, reprinted by kind permission of Johns Hopkins University Press.

8. R. G. A. Buxton, 'Euripides' *Alkestis*: Five Aspects of an Interpretation', *Dodone*, 14 (1985), 75–89, revised by the author, reprinted from Lyn Rodley (ed.), *Papers given at a Colloquium on Greek Drama in honour of R. P. Winnington-Ingram*, Suppl. Paper 15 of the Society for the Promotion of Hellenic Studies, 1987, 17–31, by kind permission of the Council of the Hellenic Society and the editor of *Dodone*.

9. P. E. Easterling, 'The Infanticide in Euripides' *Medea*', *YCS* 25 (1977), 177–91, revised by the author, reprinted by kind permission of the author and the Yale Classical Studies committee.

10. R. P. Winnington-Ingram, 'Hippolytus: A Study in Causation', *Entretiens Hardt* 6 (1960), 169–91, reprinted by kind permission of the Council of the Fondation Hardt.

11. Malcolm Heath, 'Iure principem locum tenet: Euripides' *Hecuba*', *BICS* 34 (1987), 40–68, revised by the author, reprinted by kind permission of the Institute of Classical Studies, University of London.

12. Froma I. Zeitlin, 'The Argive Festival of Hera and Euripides' *Electra*', *TAPA* 101 (1970), 645–69, revised by the author, reprinted by kind permission of the American Philological Association.

13. Jacqueline de Romilly, 'The Rejection of Suicide in the *Heracles* of Euripides', English translation of 'Le Refus du suicide dans l'*Héraclès* d'Euripide', *Archaiognosia* 1 (1980), 1–10, reprinted by kind permission of the author and the editorial Committee of *Archaiognosia*, translated by D. Mossman and J. M. Mossman.

14. Donald J. Mastronarde, 'Iconography and Imagery in Euripides' *Ion*', *CSCA* 8 (1975), 163–76, revised by the author, reprinted by kind permission of the author, *Classical Antiquity* and the Regents of the University of California.

15. Froma I. Zeitlin, 'The Closet of Masks: Role-Playing and Myth-Making in the *Orestes* of Euripides', *Ramus* 9 (1980), 51–77, revised by the author, reprinted here by kind permission of Aureal publications.

16. Helene P. Foley, 'The Masque of Dionysus', *TAPA* 110 (1980), 107–33, revised by the author, reprinted by kind permission of the American Philological Association.

17. Irene J. F. de Jong, 'Three Off-Stage Characters in Euripides', *Mnemosyne* 43 (1990), 1–21, revised by the author, reprinted by kind permission of Brill.